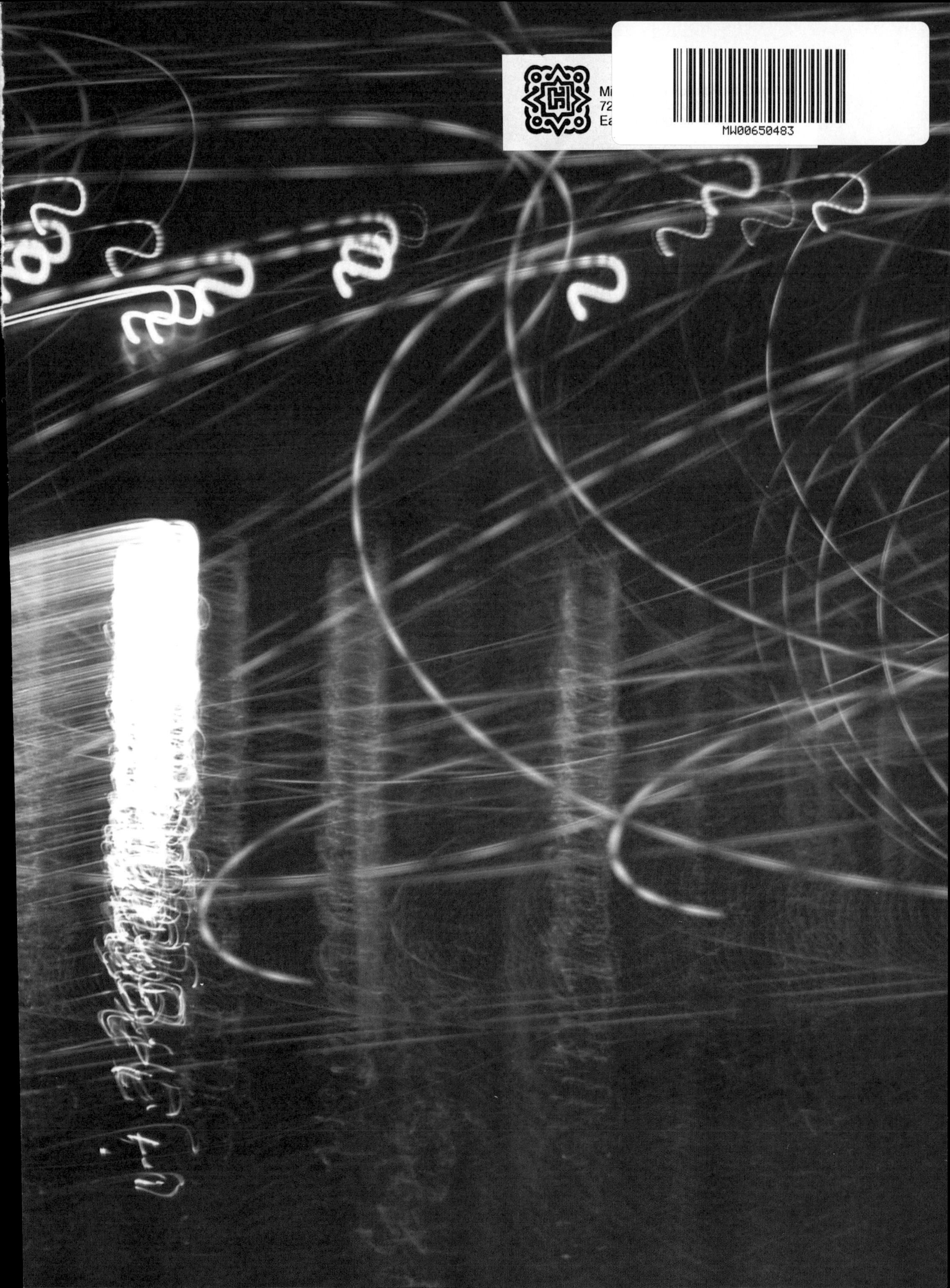

GO! THE ART OF CHANGE

GO!

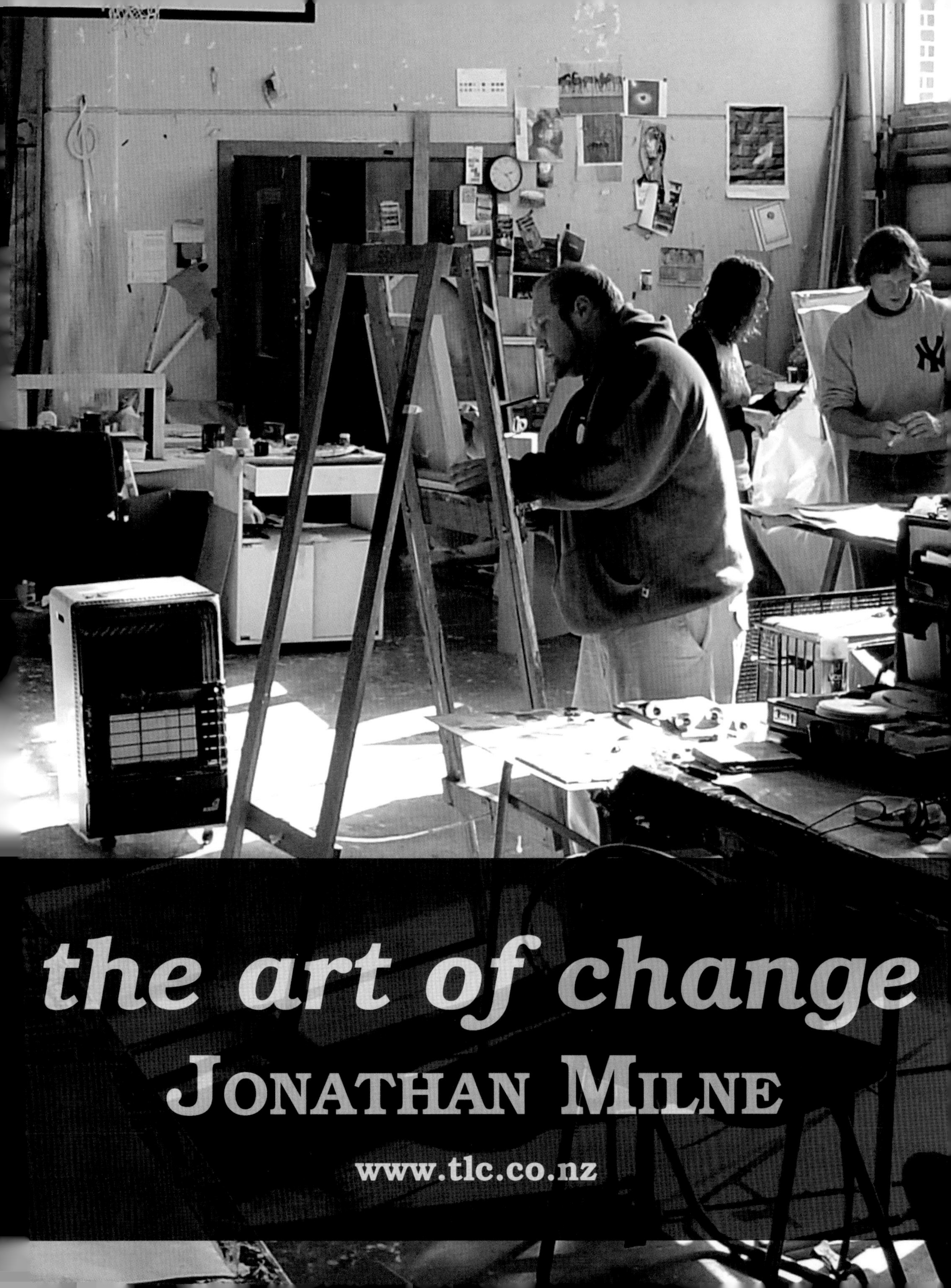

the art of change

JONATHAN MILNE

www.tlc.co.nz

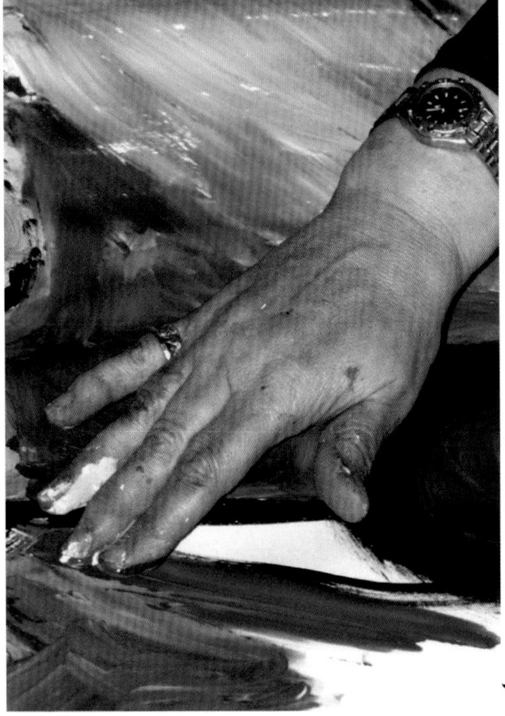

Thanks to TLC staff and students, Katharine White, Alice Wilson Milne, Erin King, Sarah Bolland, Matthew Bartlett.

Artworks, cartoons, photos of artworks and photos of artworks in progress are by Jonathan Milne or from his collection unless otherwise specified. Photos of historical figures are in the public domain unless otherwise specified. If you notice any incorrectly credited images, please notify the publisher so that correct credits can appear in future editions.

Printed in China by Everbest.

National Library of New Zealand Cataloguing-in-Publication Data

Milne, Jonathan, 1945-
Go! : the art of change / Jonathan Milne.
Includes bibliographical references and index.
ISBN 978-1-877448-30-0 (hbk.)
1. Learning Connexion. 2. Arts. 3. Creation (Literary, artistic, etc.) 4. Art—Technique. 5. Art—History.
6. Art—Marketing. I. Title.
700—dc 22

Steele Roberts Publishers
Box 9321, Wellington
info@steeleroberts.co.nz - www.steeleroberts.co.nz

go! the art of change

Items marked are action suggestions which invite you to respond.

Artist: George Cardno.

FOREWORD

This is more than a book – it is a journey through which we may discover a new basis for understanding the creative process in our own personal experience. Creativity is made clear, accessible and immensely entertaining. *GO!* offers bursts of insight and amazing realisations about the inter-connectedness of creative expression, visual perception and the cognitive process itself. It is written in a deeply human and playful style that constantly reminds us that creativity is the crucial element for living life to its fullest. *GO!* is an essential experience for art students, teachers and for anyone interested in the delight of self-discovery through creativity. Simply stated, *GO!* is really fun!

it is a journey through which we may discover a new basis for understanding the creative process in our own personal experience

There is a long history here – a prelude to the creation of *GO!* that has been witnessed by Jonathan Milne's friends, family, colleagues and his many students over past decades. It is the story of his own creative journey and the results of serious play, vision, hard work and courage applied to a deep sense of connection to the world. The details of the journey are not the important part – it is the journey itself that matters. It matters that he *made the trip and paid attention!* It is important that he really showed up, and changed the conversation about creativity, art, nature and getting things done. It matters, now, that his journey has led him to this offering of his discoveries from a long, ongoing inquiry into the nature of change, the foundations of knowledge and the mystery of creation.

Jonathan's characteristic intensity and *laissez-faire* good-naturedness are everywhere in *GO!* Those who know him will immediately recognise his brilliance and irreverent playfulness in these words and images. Jonathan has followed his own creative path for many years, as an artist, writer, government worker, and most significantly as an educator. *GO!* reflects Jonathan's unique position as an independent thinker – un-affiliated with the mainstream of the art world, higher education or academe. He has, at the same time, been closely involved with these institutions and the cultural structures they influence. Milne, like the creative explorers whom he most admires, is a consummate outsider who is paradoxically both defying and re-defining the mainstream. As an artist, educator,

he made the trip and paid attention!

and entrepreneur, Jonathan has, in a real sense, been writing this book for many years. He has written it as a gift to us all – from beginner to big league, *GO!* has something important to offer.

This is a definitive statement about Jonathan Milne's investigations and innovations in the field of arts education and the facilitation of creativity among the public. It's not just for artists anymore. He has produced his *magnum opus*, written in many layers, like an esoteric text to be understood concentrically depending on your level of initiation into the deepest realms of the creative process. *GO!* is written with multiple audiences in mind. It serves the needs of the uninitiated, people searching for deeper meaning and fun in their lives through creative self-expression. It offers a specific entry point into the visual arts, with well established but unique studio exercises introducing us to the formal foundations of visual expression, *à la* Milne.

GO! is also addressing arts educators – specifically the tutors at The Learning Connexion in Wellington, New Zealand, a hugely innovative art school which Jonathan Milne founded twenty odd years ago and now directs. He still regards TLC as a collaborative artwork in progress. *GO!* is at least partially intended to provide a philosophical and practical foundation through which the innovations and unique educational approaches of TLC can be extended and sustained. It is a great contribution to that particular collaboration. For them, and for all of us who are involved in arts education, Milne offers insights into how creative thinking can be nurtured and developed – encouraged to appear in our lives in myriad forms. Milne's ideas, as exemplified by the images, writings and studio exercises in this book, have already begun to receive acknowledgement and acclaim in the arts education community as well as the emerging psychological field of creativity theory. I sincerely hope that this publication will have a far-reaching effect on future generations of artists, teachers, psychologists and other creative problem-solvers. It's a 'must-read' for any 'cultural creatives' looking for a really good time.

GO! approaches the topic of creativity from a wide variety of perspectives, offering stunning insights into a variety of issues surrounding creativity. It seems important that the reader understand the multivalent structure of this book. It can be used as a 'how-to' book for artists and a primer for arts educators, an inspiring treatise on the links between art, health and science, as well as a wonderfully entertaining volume filled with Milne's dry and sometimes acerbic sense of play and wit. For artists and non-artists alike, *GO!* offers profound insights into what creativity is about and how art can be seen as a direct extension of our ways of seeing the world. It encourages us to respond with bold and innovative images and activities that offer new insights and meaning to those around us.

Milne speaks from his own direct experience of creativity and the wide variety of related subjects such as science, organizational development and planning,

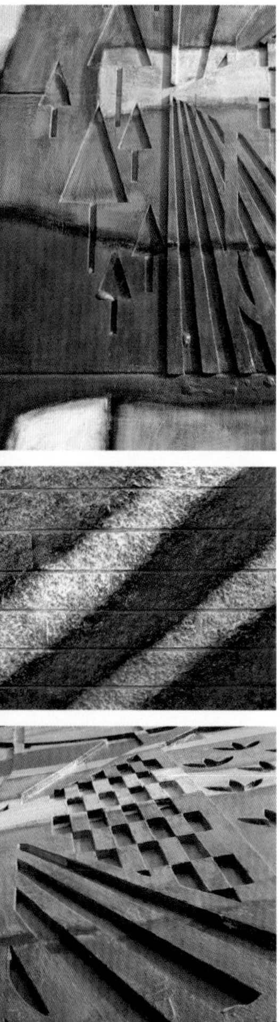

Details from the outside of The Learning Connexion's new premises in Upper Hutt, Wellington.

beauty and spirituality. Throughout the book we become aware of the author's deep sincerity and benevolence. There is passion and play that inspires a sense of adventure as we progress through the book's successively deep and engaging stages.

GO! is clearly written from the artist's perspective. To be fully appreciated, it must be understood as a work of art in itself. Like other successful works of art, *GO!* is both subtle and engaging. It speaks, as great art often does, to the deep sense of curiosity and exploration that may be humanity's greatest motivator. It offers us beauty and delight. It has such a vast array of visual images that we quickly find ourselves in a new pictorial universe; sometimes entirely new and jarring sights that lead us into surprising realms of possibility. The reader must move from the visual, to the practical, to the intellectual, to the dream state, sometimes in quick succession and occasionally all at once.

The integration of body and mind is key to Jonathan Milne's notion of how creativity actually works. It is both a strategy for the creation of innovative and effective images and ideas, as well as a state of mind in which we become more fully functioning beings. Creativity, Milne seems to suggest, is just a matter of being human at the highest possible level.

The cumulative effect of all this is slightly overwhelming. *GO!* offers us what many artworks try to achieve but relatively few actually deliver – *inspiration*. Now seen, perhaps, as a romantic and outmoded notion, inspiration was once equated with creativity. The 'inspired mind' is a vaguely antiquated term that once described the primary pre-condition for the creative act. Milne offers us inspiration at many levels – aesthetic, emotional and intellectual.

At first encounter, the ambition and size of *GO!* suggest that such a broad and multifaceted undertaking would have been better advised to have been an entire *series* of books – as it may well one day be. Further reflection, however, takes us to a deeper level of understanding Jonathan's intention. Each aspect of the book – the visual, the philosophical, the personal, the artistic and the scientific have a holistic effect. The sheer beauty of the book's visual elements actually *informs* the other dimensions. The philosophical aspects of the book relate inevitably to the scientific and the artistic. No single dimension of *GO!* can be separated from the others. Like creativity itself, *GO!* is about coming together – not pulling apart.

This is a deeply personal book. Milne has offered his deepest insights and the techniques for success and creative problem solving along with an engaging sense of humor that subtly urges us not to take this stuff too seriously. But as we laugh along with him, we realise that play is serious stuff. We find the paradox of something that is deeply personal and universal at the same instant. Milne has woven in stories and images of friends and family that give depth and emotional weight to the theoretical and the technical elements of the book. His willingness to describe creativity on a personal basis makes *GO!* emotionally real

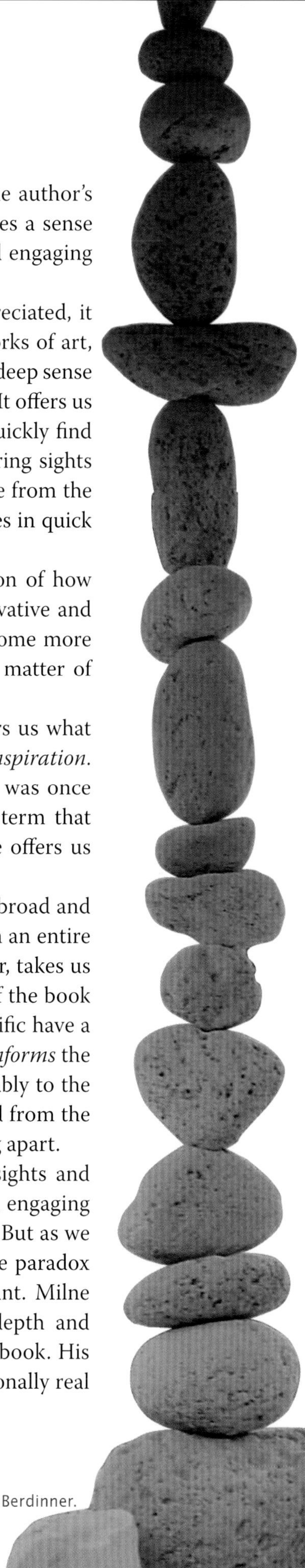

Artist: Dennis Berdinner.

creativity is the antidote to misery

and compelling. Anecdotes about those with whom he is closest illustrate the broad and transformative principles to which the book is dedicated. *GO!* offers us emotional doorways into states of awareness that seem to depart entirely from the mundane or merely practical implications of creativity.

Venturing forth into *GO!* is a creative experience in itself. The text and exercises which fill the book offer readers a direct experience of creativity. Simply moving through the text and beautiful illustrations leaves us with a holistic awareness that creativity is precisely what makes a group of experiences and activities greater than the sum of their parts. Milne teaches us that creativity is far more than a psychological phenomenon – it is an essential feature of being human. In writing *GO!*, Jonathan Milne fully tapped his own creative genius and humanity to lead us through many complicated principles into a direct realisation of our own creative potential. His book is more than an invitation for us to live more creative lives, it is a road map. It gives us the tools and insights to think outside the box – to speak outside the circle and to dance outside the sphere.

His book is more than an invitation for us to live more creative lives, it is a road map

GO! might be seen, from a certain perspective, as an *entirely* visual artwork. Its spectacular images include illustrations, but are also a personal portfolio of Jonathan Milne's artistic oeuvre. It's easy to think that many of the creative principles Milne discusses would be entirely clear without any text at all – just by looking at the pictures. It is entirely appropriate, though typically eccentric, for this visual presence to be intertwined with the writings and teachings of the artist. It suggests a new paradigm for artists to see themselves, not just as image-makers and not just as teachers – not even a combination of the two, but a full integration of the two social identities. When Jonathan is teaching he's still completely an artist. When he makes art, he is entirely involved in teaching. The new paradigm put forward here is of the complete integration of the artist-teacher-philosopher and social activist. Milne is pioneering a new way for artists to find relevance in a world which seems confused about the role of art and artists. He offers a new model of the artist as a social and spiritual explorer.

The implications of *rampant creativity*, set loose in contemporary culture are startling. From the creative journey – by *GO-ing* – we enter uncharted territory. That's the whole idea! Milne's subtext is that creativity is far more than self-expression. He implies clearly that creativity, when fully embraced, leads to greater humanity in the entire society. Compassion, connection and personal satisfaction are the inevitable consequences of creative activity. Its casualties are fear, suspicion, and mindlessness. Everything in *GO!* reminds us that creativity is the antidote to misery.

Michael Grady
Chair, Department of Arts and Consciousness
JFK University, Berkeley California

PREFACE

How to make your own miracles

There is a story, which may or may not be true, about a boy who feels compassion for a butterfly as it struggles to emerge from its chrysalis. He tries to help it by gently blowing his warm breath on it and is thrilled when the butterfly is able to flex its magnificent wings. But alas they are too frail for flight because the wings depended on the very struggle to gain strength. The boy is mortified to discover that his helpfulness produced a flightless butterfly.

There is another story, which I witnessed, of a doctor who provided antibiotic treatment for children in an isolated community who had a disfiguring skin problem. The parents had been sceptical about 'Doctor Steve' but after the cure they decided he must be some sort of magician. They took all their problems to him, believing that he would have a magic ointment for everything.

Art lives on constraint and dies of freedom.
—Michelangelo

Sometimes we are led astray by our quest for comfort. We buy books, hoping that they will do something magic. Books can indeed make a difference, provided we remember that we must build our own strength.

When you find an idea on a page and apply it in your own life, you make it your own. That's the deal. *GO! The Art of Change* offers ideas which you can test for yourself. If you don't get into action, nothing will happen.

I am used to people coming to me and asking for creativity 'ointment'. They hear that The Learning Connexion (TLC) offers a special kind of freedom which will solve their problems. Well, yes, TLC is in the business of miracles (along with all those teachers in the world who understand and love their craft). The catch is that the miracles don't happen unless you're committed to doing the work.

Michelangelo was talking about this when he said that art lives on constraint and dies of freedom.

Sculptor: Fiona Sole.

He wasn't the first person in the world to think this way. *Swatantra,* the Sanskrit word for freedom, is made up of two words, *swa* = self, and *tantra* = discipline.

Historically, discipline has often led education into trouble. Discipline is not about blind obedience to invented rules which serve no purpose. In the context of The Learning Connexion, discipline is about engaging with *what is.* Part of the challenge is to realise that 'what is' is constantly changing.

The discipline comes from the weather of their own lives

For those of us who live in Wellington, the weather provides a good example of constant change. Wellingtonians are used to the fact that they might get all four seasons in a single day, so part of our discipline is to be prepared for changeable weather. It's not a big deal, although it probably helps us to be adaptable in all sorts of other ways.

There are students who come to TLC thinking that it's a huge relief to be in a place where the usual rules don't apply. They're right in the sense that we avoid needless rules, and they're wrong if they think there's no discipline and no work. The discipline comes from the weather of their own lives.

We describe the process in a diagram called 'the creative spiral' (page 26). In effect we invite people to do something, pay attention to the response they get, and then do something again, this time taking on board what they've learned.

If you keep going through that cycle you'll discover education and you'll get into the habit of making miracles (which we call *creativity*).

Here is a personal example of how it can happen. When I was at teachers' college I was editor of the student magazine. The school funded a glossy front page which gave the thing quite a boost and subsidised production costs, but they decided they couldn't afford to keep paying for it. Suddenly we had hit the financial equivalent of a drought. Our response was to put a price on the magazine and sell it to the students. Much to the dismay of the skeptics, we sold enough copies to pay for the printing and make a small surplus. Perhaps this single event gave me the confidence which eventually helped to establish TLC. Certainly it taught me a great deal about feedback.

If students hadn't been willing to pay for the magazine we would have had to think differently. The challenge was to do something which connected with them. And that's the heart of what TLC means by discipline. It's full-on engagement with *what is* and the goal is to get the best possible result.

In the case of the magazine, part of the discipline was entirely conventional. We worked on proofreading and presentation in much the same way that could have been taught in the curriculum at journalism school. The more complex part of the discipline was to relate with our particular circumstances. We had to find ways to be free in the context of the school and within our role as trainee teachers. We had to be interesting enough to have a product worth buying and we had to deal with the complexity of people's feelings, prejudices and ambitions.

What we're saying at TLC is that learning has to bring all the factors together. Everything is happening at once, all the time. Everything we do results in feedback and the only way to grow is to respond creatively. It's the dance of life.

When a student exhibits a painting, for example, they're not just showing what they know about paint and colour, they're discovering whether their work connects with 'what is'. They're learning about their particular relevance.

The paradox is that students can make their first move to discipline by doing whatever they please. It doesn't matter, provided they pay attention to the results and make the next move. In the process they not only learn how to connect with the world, master all the necessary details of technique, and manage whatever weather the world presents. They also learn the best kind of discipline in the world. By an accident of language we call it *self*-discipline. I think a better name is *selfless* discipline. That's why we're here.

If you use *GO!* in the spirit of selfless discipline, you will find the magic.

Emily Jellyman.

The paradox is that students can make their first move to discipline by doing whatever they please. It doesn't matter, provided they pay attention to the results and make the next move

LET'S START HERE!

Creativity is about energy

Creativity can transform lives and change the world. In the context of nature it is called evolution. It is the process of effective change. It is about the beauty of shifting to more elegant forms of action.

Creativity starts early. The impetus to make sounds, to stand up, walk, make marks, to sing – these are features of the creative process which are part of who we are. This impetus can lead to symphonies, space travel and to a style of leadership that helps people to live creatively together.

When we go to school we sacrifice some of this early magic to the requirements of words and numbers.

When we've grown up it may look as though creativity is dead and buried but it is still there, waiting for nurture and always ready for a new awakening.

Many of us have a vague sense that we are separated from something important. We yearn to reconnect with whatever we have lost – even if we don't understand what it is or why we want it.

Part of my own four-year-old vision was to make marks on paper illustrating my wife 'Bertie' and our twenty kids. It's not the sort of thing that my first teacher was looking for – she had different priorities. I have since seen hundreds upon hundreds of kids drawing to communicate the mysteries and concerns of their lives. I'm sure that children use drawing to grapple with meaning and purpose. The marks I made to indicate my four-year-old vision of family were serious explorations.

The purpose of *GO!* is to help you reconnect with your creativity and refresh your sense of wonder. Art is our starting point and it may take you into any field at all – creativity knows no bounds.

GO! will also help you to explore why you're on the planet. If you want to learn only about art, it should be great for that too (and beware, art has a knack of luring you to all the places of the mind).

Art is our starting point and it may take you into any field at all – creativity knows no bounds

Success

There are other things. We are concerned about success. Every human being is extraordinary and we can all find a way to be successful.

"Before enlightenment, hew wood and carry water. After enlightenment, hew wood and carry water." —Buddha

It's unfortunate that sport, exams and other contests (including wars) give the impression that winners and losers are what life is all about. Really, the biggest part of life is co-operation. If you create something exciting which inspires people to live their lives with greater joy and optimism, you're contributing to co-operation.

Perhaps the hardest thing about success is to realise how close it is when we don't have it. I've had the privilege of moving from zero through to a multi-million dollar school and I learned something about patience during the several perilous years on the edge of failure. It could be that the biggest thing you do in the early stages is to keep your dream alive long enough for 'luck' to arrive.

keep your dream alive long enough for 'luck' to arrive

If you get rejected by a gallery, go to ten other galleries. If your advertisement gets no replies, figure out a different approach. If no one wants to hire you, hire yourself. Keep experimenting. Keep doing slightly different things until your actions give clues about what works. It takes patience and persistence to get to a place where something lights up and you reach a new level of understanding. The faint-hearted stay at home and watch television.

While success can be fickle (you never know when it's going to arrive, how big it will be, or how long it will last) you can still control aspects of your work. Before success and after success it's the work that matters – the rest is ego (that sense of self-importance which takes energy away from where it is needed). If you don't find some compelling joy in the work itself, keep searching until you find a creative path. Money is not a goal in itself, it's a by-product which enables you to do more of what you're good at.

Many little bonuses sneak up on us while we're being creative. We learn a special kind of awareness which makes a difference with friends, family, neighbours and perhaps, in the end, humanity. When we surrender ego to the trials and joys of creativity we discover who we are and learn how to make our contribution to the world.

In the context of our school, The Learning Connexion, creativity connects with values. The values have grown from three assumptions:

- *Everything is connected* – the planet Earth is an ecosystem (including us), and it is part of the gigantic, infinitely complex ecosystem called the universe.
- For humanity (and our planet) to be sustainable *we have to find ways to work in harmony* with each other and with our environment. It is about survival of the 'fitting-est' rather than survival of the fittest (although fitness counts).

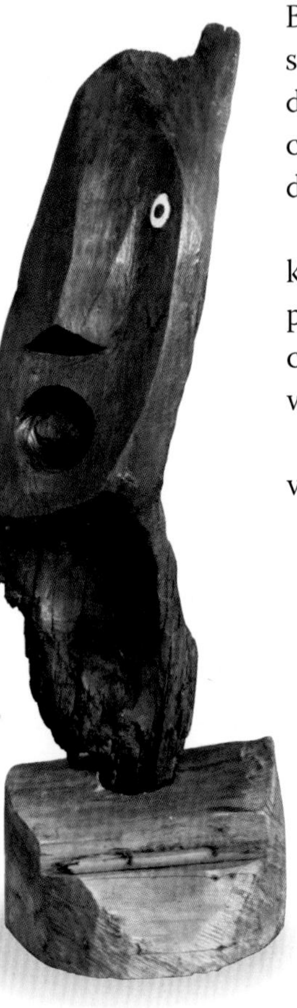

Sculpture by Richard Cowan.

Really, the biggest part of life is co-operation

- *There are broad patterns of behaviour* which are materially and spiritually beneficial and they happen to coincide with the requirements of sustainable creativity.

Although humans do hideous things to each other, we can move to a far more peaceful, dynamic and creative level of interaction. There is a connection between this daunting global goal and the highly personal process of learning about creativity through art.

RISKS When artists face the mystery of a blank sheet of paper they're forced to be creative because they can't make a mark without taking a risk. The ability to *take risks* is at the heart of creativity and can only be developed through practice. Art provides all the psychological 'reality' to learn about risks without (most of the time) any danger to life and limb.

The ability to take risks is at the heart of creativity and can only be developed through practice

INVENTION Art demands inventiveness and problem-solving, or it is stuck with copying. Artists have to learn how to be assertive and tenacious with their undeveloped ideas. They require an endless hunger for exploration and openness to new patterns and chance connections. They have to cope with indifference, negativity and lack of resources.

INTUITION Typically creativity involves *pattern thinking*, sometimes labeled *intuition*. It's a way of being able to make sense of things without being able to explain why. Like risk-taking, it is an internal process which requires endless practice. The practice isn't always easy because Western education tends to discount intuition.

Education has treated facts as sacred and now we're buried in them. Computer technology has flooded us with so much information that the only practical starting point is to step back and look for patterns in the mass of detail. Chaos Theory and other branches of mathematics have drawn attention to big-picture patterns; they're doing something parallel to the intuition of artists, who seek to make some sense of the seething detail of their worlds. Maybe it's business-as-usual in art, but 'facts' and 'patterns' have a distinctively new relationship in science. The shift acknowledges that we can no longer pin down all the facts and maybe we should accept that human intuition – with all its fickleness – is an amazingly useful instrument.

Creative people have to cope with indifference, negativity and lack of resources – that's all part of the territory

PERSISTENCE isn't mere staying-power – it can be about keeping a possibility alive after you've given up. 'Giving up' can turn into a creative act if it allows the ego to step aside and our deeper intelligence to find a result.

TESTING Science is about the study of repeatable patterns. This doesn't work for everything, but there are many aspects of intuition which can be examined on the basis of evidence. Much of Leonardo's rendering of 'The Last Supper' fell off the wall because the base-coat was unsound. Great painting: bad gluing, poor intuition.

TEAMWORK Infrastructure is important. Leonardo's helicopter concept didn't materialise for hundreds of years because the engineering capabilities weren't available to make it possible. Creativity is almost always a *team effort.* The sometimes glamorous role of the artist, inventor or innovative researcher is meaningless without a network of inputs.

Ehara taku toa i te toa takitahi, engari, he toa takitini

Mine is not the strength of one alone, it is the strength of many

COMMUNITY *Social context* is a dimension of creativity which is often ignored. Staid, conservative communities tend to be less creative than those which are well-resourced and more edgy. A moderate level of instability is a stimulus, whereas comfort is more likely to produce inertia. War (or the perceived threat of war) often launches important inventions. For example, the internet was incubated in the military. In the business world, competition and the wooing of customers makes for a dynamic and partly chaotic climate which can, on a good day, stimulate creativity.

Perhaps art has just as much survival value as great inventions. At its best, art holds communities together and establishes the platform from which other enterprises can grow. More importantly, it resonates with the deepest workings of the universe. Art confronts questions of meaning which can't be translated into logical explanations but which can inspire us with a sense of purpose and a joy for living.

THEORY & PRACTICE My fascination for creativity began in the 1960s when I was at university. I came upon the writings of Paul Torrance* and my interest/obsession has grown ever since. At that time it seemed that school and university had suffered a lobotomy and the creative dimension had been removed. Students were expected to learn what they were told, then regurgitate it in assignments and exams. Original thinking was inhibited until post-graduate study, by which time creative habits were in limbo. Students competed with each other to inflict dull essays and research on their tutors – all for the sake of graduating.

Here's what education looked like to me →

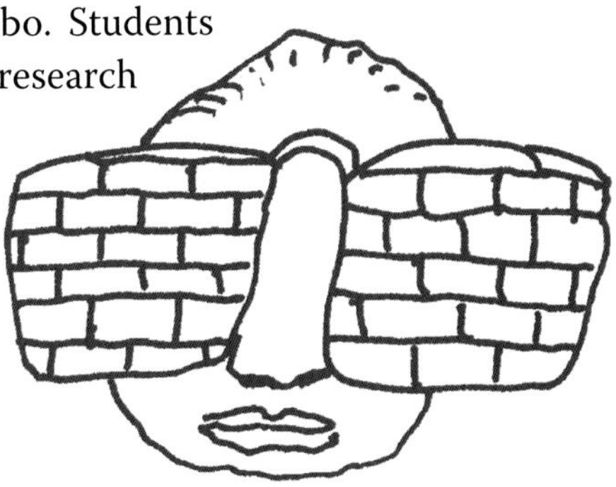

On the other side of youthful exaggeration I've learned more about what makes creativity work.

*American psychologist and author, described as "the father of creativity."

Artists connect with the breathing of the sea

Everyone has something to contribute to the creative process. Some are compelled to follow their creative itch; others, intentionally or not, provide support and some provide a useful resistance (which serves to test whether creative ideas are for real).

Creativity is not just about the arts. The creative process is echoed in every field of human endeavour where new ideas make a difference. The conceptual thinking required in art is readily transferable to other areas like science, maths, business, communication, and so on.

Creative people are conservative and radical at the same time. The conservative side is important because they need some inner stability to enable them to take the sustained risks demanded by creative work. They also have to operate in the real world and communicate with people who may be antagonistic to change. Creatives challenge rules; conflict goes with the territory.

Creativity needs big energy and incubation. Part of the process happens while you're asleep or doing relaxed, low-key things like having a shower, walking in the park or idly sniffing the flowers. When the ideas emerge they need energy and persistence to turn them into reality.

Naïveté (or innocence) features in creativity. It's as if an innocent mind can somehow see outside the box. At the same time this childlike quality has to be accompanied by mature discipline (seeing *inside* the box) to get results.

Creative people have the ability to float between an imagined world and the world as it is. They can link the possible with the actual and then take action to change the way things are. They have a high tolerance of ambiguity as they try to bring imagined ideas into reality.

When they are cruising in their imagination, creative people may seem remote, introspective and disconnected. Yet when they're bringing their vision back to the 'real' world they can be outgoing and extroverted. Others may find this pattern difficult!

Their satisfaction is fuelled by the work itself rather than by external rewards

Creative people seem to defy stereotyping. For example, they may think across the conventional male/female boundaries; be generous and mean; and politically 'left' and 'right' at the same time. Their strong questioning approach to life gives them a natural urge to challenge stereotypes, so they are unpredictable. They may even like certain stereotypes.

Creative people are typically passionate and critical. They will be driven by passion but can stand back and assess their work in a detached, rational way. Usually they are their own toughest critics.

Creative people have the ability to ride through negative responses to their work (even though they may feel deeply hurt). Their satisfaction is fuelled by the work itself rather than by external rewards.

11 A strong value base helps creativity. It provides stability in the face of criticism. Likewise a strong sense of purpose is a major asset.

12 Creative people can experience a high degree of emotional friction, yet they may be more stable than they seem. Conditions such as depression, anxiety, addictive behaviour and so on may primarily be a response to the pressure to conform. When people find a way to make their creativity flow, the dysfunctions usually diminish or disappear. Dysfunction may also provide a different kind of sensitivity which contributes favourably to creativity.

Then it's a question of boldness – having the courage to act on your decisions

13 Creative people learn to trust their intuition. They can think in patterns rather than step-by-step logic (although they have to do that too). The 'pattern thinking' usually combines intellect, senses and experience.

14 Creative people are *willing to make mistakes*. They are the ultimate experimenters and will come back to ideas again and again – sometimes over a period of decades – until they find a way forward.

15 Creative people have an unusual relationship with society as a whole. They may be seen as fools or heroes, depending on the results of their work. They require enormous faith in themselves to cope with the erratic nature of public opinion.

16 Creative people cause heaps of trouble (they invent bombs as well as sublime art and life-enhancing ideas), yet without them humanity would cease to evolve.

17 Positive creativity tends to endure; negative creativity tends to burn itself out.

There isn't any single pathway – each of us has to figure out the landscape for ourselves. An understanding of the general principles helps, and each person's story will contain relevant clues. It's a matter of listening carefully and adapting clues to suit your own situation. Then it's a question of boldness – having the courage to act on your decisions.

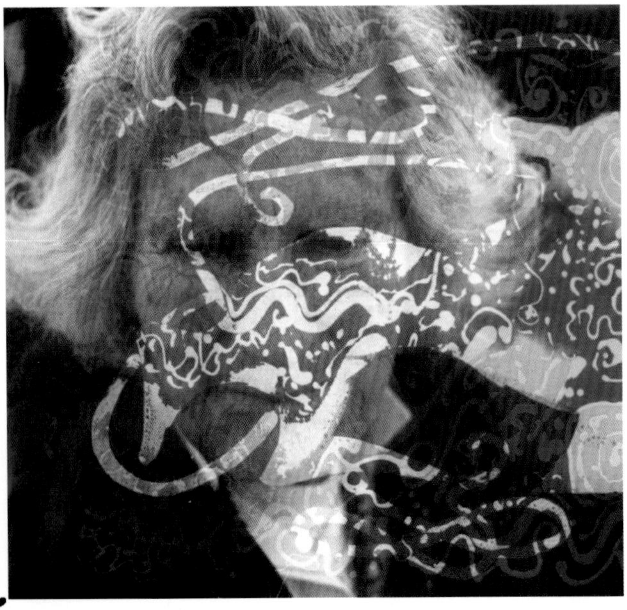

Complexity, connectedness and creativity

The photograph contains the essence of creativity. It was a mistake. The technicalities don't matter but I ended up taking a double exposure of a dearly loved aunt and a piece of artwork. Not long afterwards Aunt Cynthia died and we were left with the image of her merging with the universe. The photo was like her own mischief – things seldom went as planned with Aunt Cynthia. The

Accidental double exposure of Aunt Cynthia and a painting on fabric.

face and the painting combine well but it's the mistake that interests me more than the aesthetic result.

The strangeness of the double exposure runs parallel to the strangeness of science. Around the end of the 19th century physicists thought they were getting close to a clear picture of how the world worked. Then quantum physics arrived with a double exposure, showing that reality was not what it seemed. Most likely it will keep changing, much as Lao Tzu observed 2500 years earlier: "The way that can be told is not the eternal way," he said. "The nameless is the beginning of heaven and earth. The named is the mother of the ten thousand things."

Lao Tzu (6th-century BC).

We humans keep discovering more things about the nature of the world, and periodically we turn our ideas inside out. When Columbus crossed the Atlantic in 1492 he helped change the view of planet Earth. Modern science is another incredible journey which has changed our understanding of ourselves and the universe. Likewise art is part of the same journey – not just as a form of description but as a way of delivery into zones of truth which science can't reach.

Christopher Columbus (1451–1506).

Feedback and creativity

A 1994 documentary *The Colours of Infinity* vividly demonstrates a new way of seeing the world. Its theme is a fractal called the Mandelbrot Set (MSet), a stunningly beautiful mathematical creation which someone described as the "thumbprint of God". The MSet is infinitely complex and goes on forever (you can keep magnifying it and the details never end). It is built from a simple recipe:

$$Z \rightleftharpoons Z^2 + c$$

The numbers in the MSet feed back on themselves (hence the double arrow in the middle). Thus Z is a moving target. At first this may feel disconcerting if you expect that numbers always stay the same, but really it is a reflection of real life. These 'complex numbers' constantly change – just like ourselves and our friends – while at the same time maintaining some attributes which give them an identity.

The process of feedback is at the heart of creativity. You take something, do something to it and then respond to the result. This can go on forever, frequently generating junk and occasionally delivering treasure. It's how we learn, how we grow and how things evolve.

Feedback appears in many areas of the new science, especially in Chaos Theory. The beginnings of Chaos Theory are often traced to Edward Lorenz and

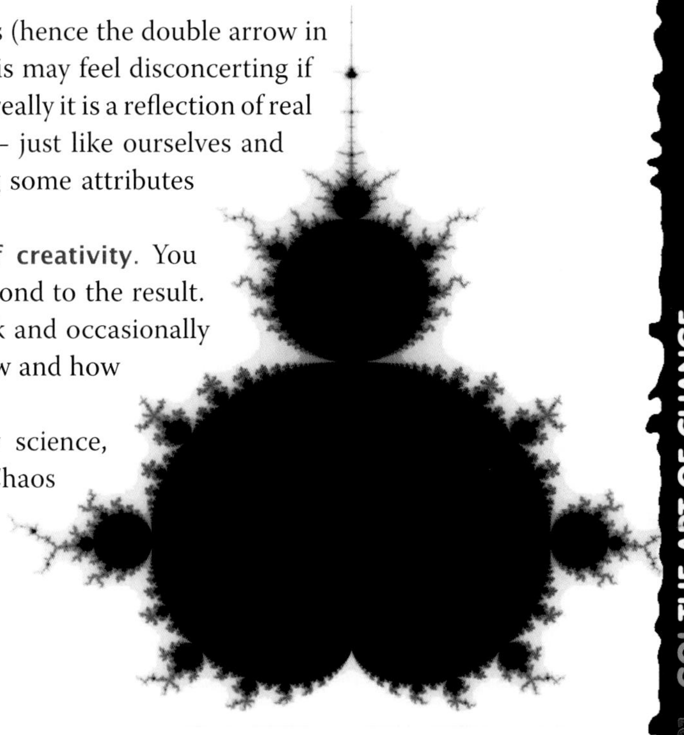

his studies of weather in the 1960s. Weather is a feedback system that we all experience and most of us have an interest in predicting it, even if it's only to plan a holiday or a picnic.

Isaac Newton (1643-1727).

Scientists have tried to create reliable models for the weather but have never quite succeeded. As I write this I'm sitting in the sun on what was predicted to be a rainy day. Nevertheless the weather behaves within certain patterns and the broad sweep is predictable even if the details are fickle. And that's what Chaos Theory is about. It isn't chaos at all – it's concerned with the underlying order of events which appear disordered on the surface.

A particular feature of weather patterns is one of the most intriguing aspects of chaos – sensitivity to initial conditions. In theory a butterfly could flap its wings in Africa and the cumulative effects could ripple around the world and increase to the size of a tornado in Florida. The butterfly effect is part of the new science of 'chaos' and although it doesn't prove that Newton was wrong, it indicates that complex and unpredictable events are part of a deterministic world.

You can study an aspect of the butterfly effect by exploring the 'lucky breaks' of successful people. You can also look back at the way you met your friends. There's often a fragile time when a friend might not have connected with you. Alice, now my wife, nearly went to an art school in a different city but decided (in slightly mysterious circumstances) to have a look at TLC. Later she came in to be interviewed and there was a staff muddle which left her stranded. I was the only person available and we had a lengthy talk.

You never know when you're in the middle of one of these life-changing coincidences. Although they make life look like a lottery, we play a big role in making our own luck. Education is about improving your 'luck'. Like the weather, 'luck' is not a matter of chance.

None of this is new. Benjamin Franklin was in effect talking about the butterfly effect when he wrote in *Poor Richard's Almanac* (1758):

Benjamin Franklin (1706-1790).

> For want of a Nail the Shoe was lost;
> for want of a Shoe the Horse was lost;
> and for want of a Horse the Rider was lost;
> being overtaken and slain by the Enemy,
> all for want of Care about the Horse-shoe Nail.

The combination of feedback and Chaos Theory illustrates how life itself is infinitely subtle and unpredictable. Religious imagery may be a way of talking about this same subtlety. W Chalmers Smith (1825–1908) was talking about it in his famous hymn:

> Immortal, invisible, God only wise,
> In light inaccessible hid from our eyes.

Is 'God' a label for the infinite complexity of the world we live in? The Gospel of Thomas hints at the possibility:

> Jesus said: If those who lead you say to you,
> See, the kingdom is in heaven,
> then the birds of heaven will go before you.
> If they say to you,
> It is in the sea,
> then the fish will go before you.
> But the kingdom is within you, and it is outside of you.

In the 'Age of Reason' religion and science looked more and more like combatants. Today they look as though they could re-converge (despite the anti-religious zealotry of scientists like Richard Dawkins). Who knows, perhaps they are using different language in an attempt to understand the same things.

It makes little difference whether prevailing beliefs emerge from religion, science or politics – if they are sound they will contribute to life, if they are flawed we imperil our survival. Matters such as global warming demand a global response which wouldn't have made sense in Newton's time. The creative challenge is that

each of us, with little more than the power of a butterfly, has the potential to change our collective destiny.

It wasn't Newton's fault that his ideas were the impetus for a grand misconception. The fault, if there is one, lies with ourselves. If the universe is approximately like the new scientific understanding then it reverberates inside each one of us. The big workings connect with the little workings. Lao Tzu's intuition may have anticipated 21st century science.

The same intuition surfaces in art. A few years before Lorenz got on the trail of Chaos Theory, and more than thirty years before Benoît Mandelbrot took the veil off the MSet, Jackson Pollock was painting in a fractal style. Pollock's work caused outrage and he was labeled 'Jack the Dripper'. Pollock knew he was on to something and his discovery was twisted into the art language of the day. He articulated his position when someone suggested that he should work more from nature. His reply: "Ah am nature."

The fractal nature of Pollock's art exists in our own lives. There is 'self-similarity' between the details and the big sweep of the whole canvas. If you take the time to look at some of the special events in your life you may be able to make new sense of the bigger patterns.

For example, at age nine I enjoyed helping kids with arithmetic. At age twelve I created a little art lesson and found it enthralling. These were clues about something which energized me. At the time they passed unnoticed because there was nothing to help them grow. It took thirty years before I reconnected

fractal (Mathematics) *noun*: a curve or geometric figure, each part of which has the same statistical character as the whole. Fractals are useful in modeling structures (such as eroded coastlines or snowflakes) in which similar patterns recur at progressively smaller scales, and in describing partly random or chaotic phenomena such as crystal growth, fluid turbulence, and galaxy formation.

Origin: from French, from Latin *fract-* 'broken,' from the verb *frangere*.

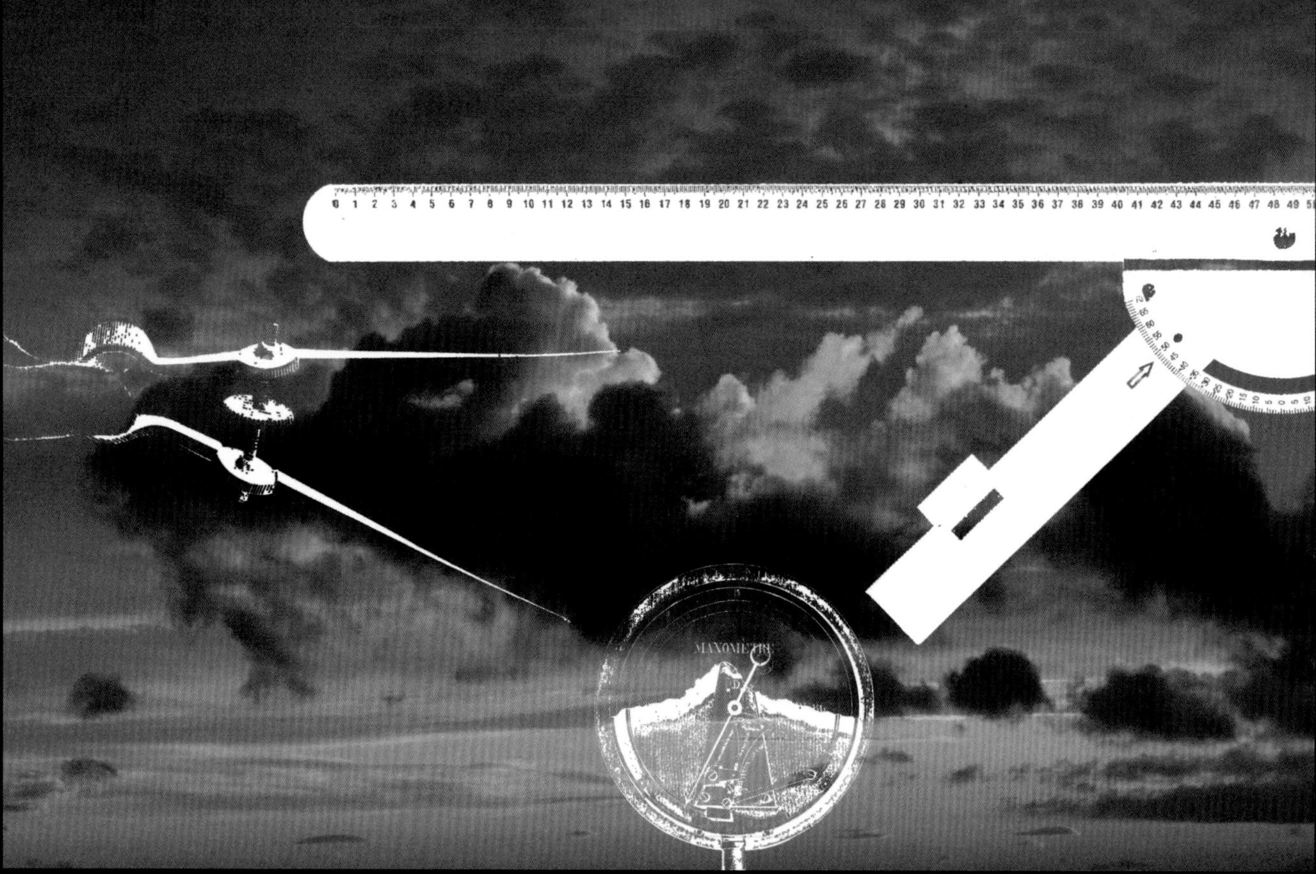

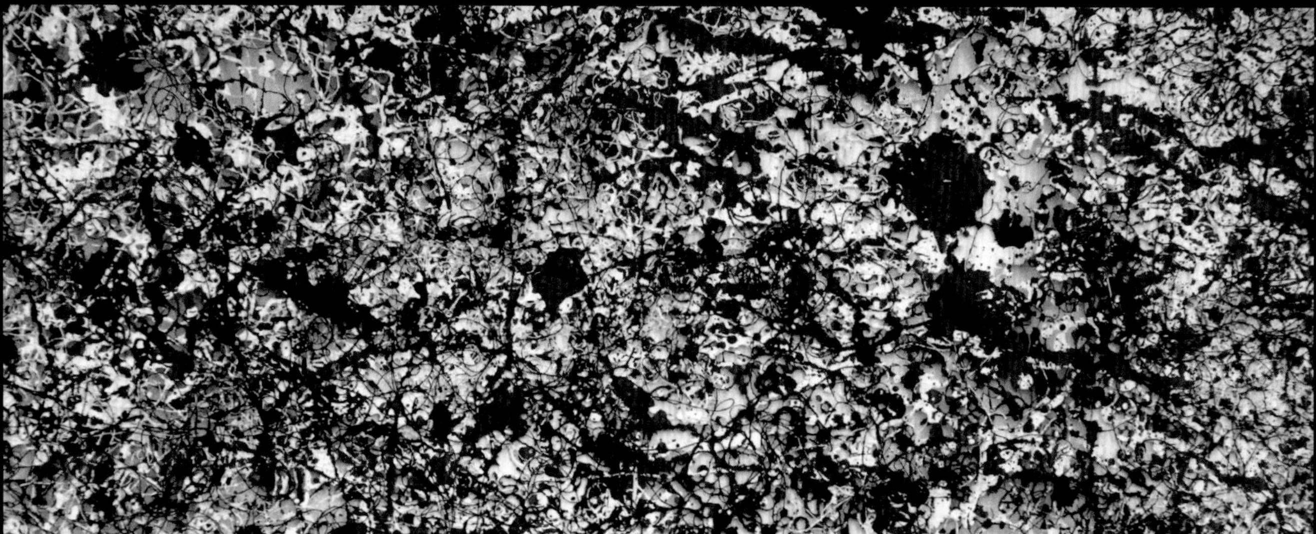

▲ Our tools have shaped (and often limited) our thinking. It's only recently that science has developed tools which come close to describing the structure of clouds. The tools of 'old science' don't do it. Likewise education can't work if it is driven by inadequate tools such as multiple choice questions and attendance records. If education is intended to maximize human potential then its tools will have to change.

▲ A Pollock-like detail from a work by Mal Edmonds.

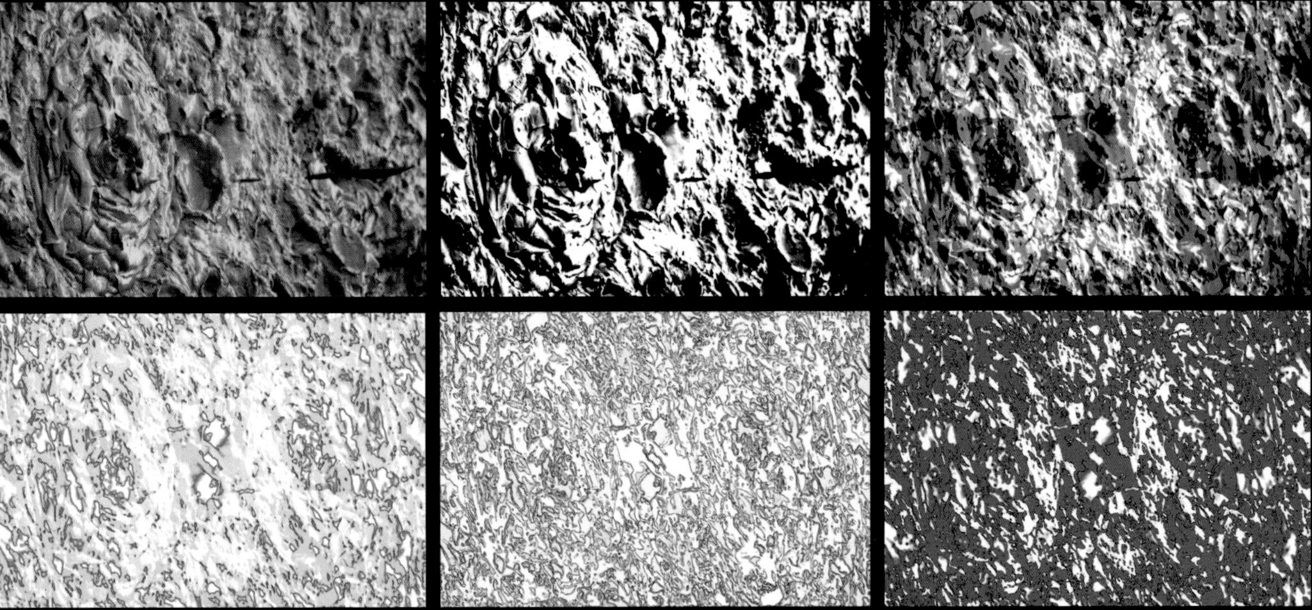

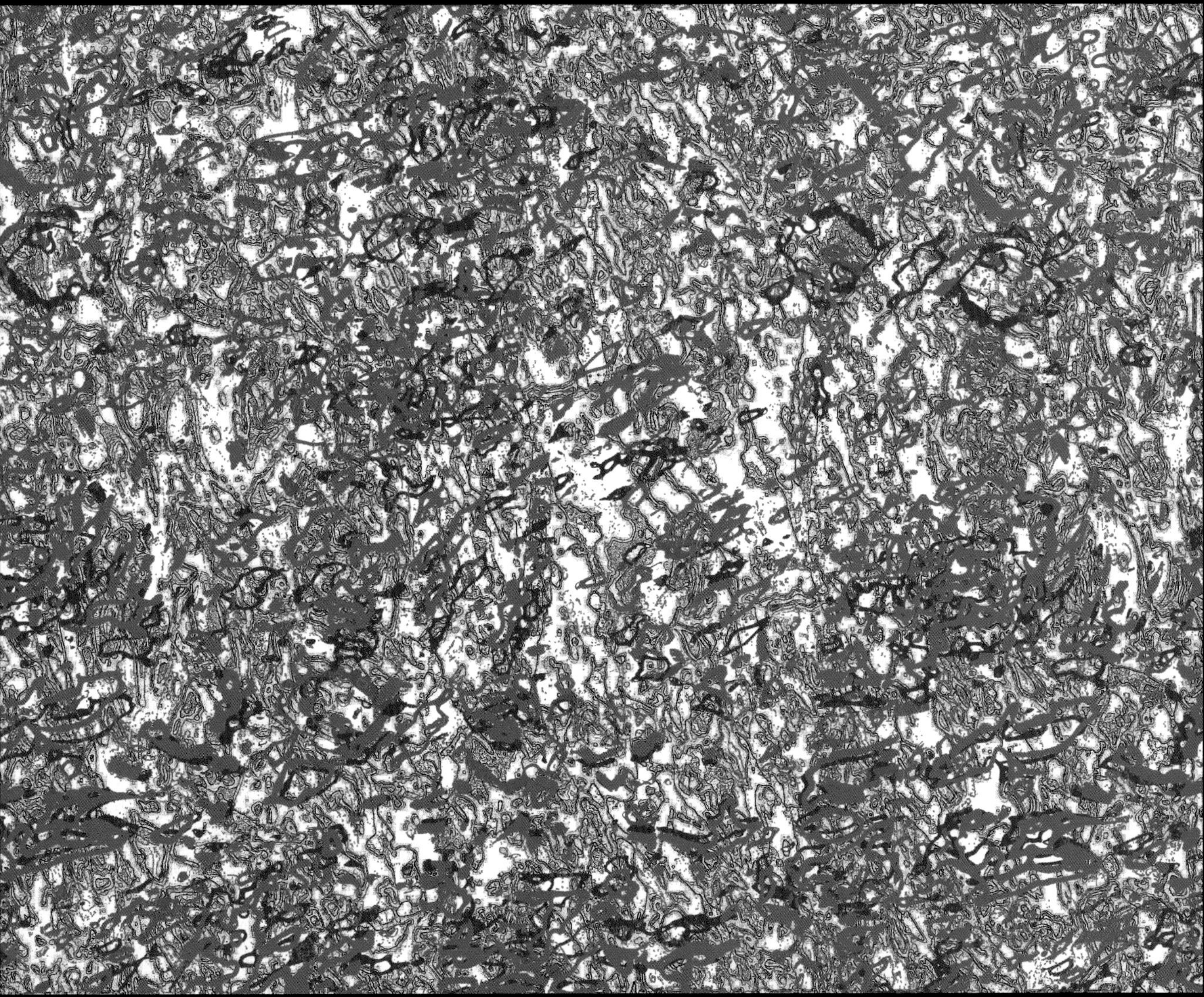

▲ If you play with photos of natural things you can generate images which illustrate the fractal nature of what Pollock was doing.

▲ It isn't a Pollock but it is built entirely from a real image.

with them and found that they were among the most vital patterns in my life. The resolution (through art, creativity and teaching) turned out to be extremely tough, but I was drawn to it like a mountaineer to the most difficult peak, or an astronaut to Mars.

Curiously the 'peak' is to some extent an illusion. What is happening is an interaction between yourself and the world. It's about finding something which is intensely relevant to yourself *and* to others. It may be totally selfish and totally generous at the same time.

Patterns in creativity

"Creativity begins with an affinity for something. It's like falling in love," says American researcher, Howard Gardner.

It was the artist Jasper Johns who said that you take something, do something to it, and pretty soon you end up with something. It may sound trite but it's one way to get the creative process started.

It was the artist Jasper Johns who said that you take something, do something to it, and pretty soon you end up with something. It may sound trite but it's one way to get the creative process started

Evolution is nature's creativity and among other things it has produced you and me. Nature sets the model for effective creativity.

THE CREATIVE SPIRAL Like the Mandelbrot Set, this is a feedback system. The idea could involve research and an assignment or project. In art it might be accompanied by warm-ups, sketches, photos and so on. The next step is action – do something in terms of the brief. Then get feedback to find out whether you've done something effective. Then review the results and shape a fresh input ('idea', 'brief' or whatever you prefer to call it). When TLC tutors give suggestions about how to evolve an idea they call it 'feed-forward'. With each circuit your creativity will spiral into something bigger and more complex.

The spiral can grow from any point. You might take a random action, receive some feedback and suddenly form an idea. For some it will be 'ready, aim, fire.' For others it will be 'ready, fire, aim', and sometimes it will be 'fire, ready, aim.' Depending on the circumstances, any of the options may be good.

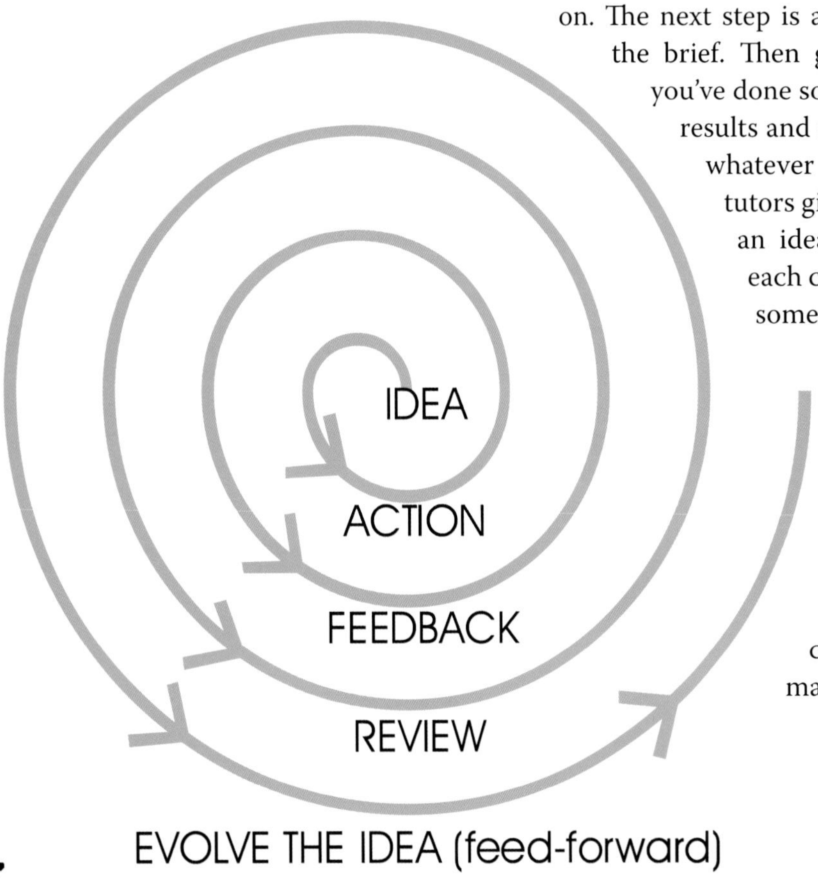

THE IDEA might start with *preparation.* Immerse yourself in a situation, explore, experiment and accumulate understanding.

Phase 2 is *incubation.* Allow your research to percolate in your mind. The old advice to 'sleep on it' is good. During this phase your mind makes connections and works subconsciously.

Then you might be fortunate and experience *illumination* – that moment when the idea takes what seems to be a viable form.

There are endless tactics to get started:

- Ask 'what if?'
- Copy nature
- Look at what others have done and create your own variations
- Visualise – imagine how an idea might be realised
- Meditate and pay attention to ideas that emerge

ACTION is the phase when you turn the illumination into something real. If the 'illumination' hasn't arrived, try the *take something and do something to it* approach. For example, take an item and squash it. Does the action take you to an idea?

- Play
- Experiment
- Explore
- 'Verb' the idea (perform an action on it)
- Follow through on your visualisation
- **Just do it**

FEEDBACK. Pay attention to responses

Read body language

Consider criticism objectively

Look at the results achieved by others and consider where you stand

Listen to the critics

Maintain a sense of humour

Let your ego have a rest

REVIEW is when you evaluate the result. Partly the review is your self-evaluation – are there changes you could make? Is the work finished?

Partly it will be for others. Did people like the work? Was someone prepared to pay for it? Did it attract critical acclaim?

What questions arose from the action? How can you take the idea further? Can you 'verb' your work in a new way? Do you need to build your skills to enable you to carry out your ideas? Would more homework help (researching new possibilities)?

Nature has had a few billion years to get used to the review stage of the cycle. Artists may have to come to terms with harsh reviews. The critics are beyond our control (especially if they're members of our family). If you get a negative response, think about it like the weather. If we have to go through a storm, we pay attention and look after ourselves. The weather itself is emotionally neutral. *Weather is weather and criticism is criticism.* It may be good to prepare yourself for possible nastiness by looking at cases where the critics themselves look silly:

Georgia O'Keeffe (1887–1987).

Clement Greenberg on Georgia O'Keeffe in 1946:

> ... the greatest part of her work adds up to little more than tinted photography. The lapidarian patience she has expended in trimming, breathing upon, and polishing these bits of opaque cellophane betrays a concern that has less to do with art than with private worship and embellishment of private fetishes with secret and arbitrary meanings. (Review, *The Nation*, 15/6/46)

O'Keeffe's art continues to prosper. JS MacDonald, director of the National Gallery of Victoria, wrote the following in 1939 about an exhibition of 240 Impressionist and other works on show in Australia, including artists such as Cezanne, Chagall, Gauguin, Matisse, Modigliani, Picasso, Van Gogh:

> They are extremely wretched paintings. We have seen the advertising efforts that have been made to urge us to swallow this putrid meat. There is no doubt that the great majority of the work called modern is the product of degenerates and perverts.

A famous piece of criticism came in Einstein's school report:

> Albert is a very poor student. He is mentally slow, unsociable, and is always daydreaming. He is spoiling it for the rest of the class. It would be in the best interests of all if he were removed from school at once.
>
> *Noted in The Power of Optimism by Alan Loy McGinnis*

Robert Kaupelis, in his excellent book *Experimental Drawing*, said:

> Almost all significant advances in art have looked strange, ugly and inaccessible, even to the artistic elite, when they were first experienced. (God! How I hated Pollock at one time!)

Criticism doesn't come only from critics. The *Dominion* newspaper in New Zealand reported in July 1993:

> An art student's exhibit of red jellies on plates was mistaken for leftovers from an exhibition party and dumped in a bin. Ceri Davies, 28, said her work, *Piece de Resistance*, involving 36 jellies and 17 plates on show in Birmingham, England, was meant to decay and give a visual metaphor for the mortality of all flesh. But on the fourth day of the exhibition, a duty officer in the arts centre saw the jellies were going off and scraped them into a bin.

Leonardo da Vinci (1452–1519).

Creative people find ways to cope. Andrea del Verrocchio said of his apprentice, Leonardo da Vinci:

> It seems to me that much of it boils down to his relative absence of fear. He always seemed less afraid of what other people may think, or demand or laugh at – more important perhaps is his lack of fear of his own 'inside', of his own impulses, emotions and thought. Not unlike a child, his mind has a window toward infinity; his toys are nature's elements; his discipline, the unknown; and his *bête noire*, the status quo. *(Quoted in Score, "The force that through the green fuse drives the flower" by Arnold Bonnet, vol.1, no.3, 1991.)*

Cicero (106–43BC).

The toughest test is life itself. We have to deal with external critics and we have to maintain the integrity of our own truth. Cicero (106–43BC) was talking about integrity and creativity when he identified six major mistakes:

1. The delusion that personal gain is made by crushing others.
2. The tendency to worry about things we cannot change or correct anyway.
3. Insisting that something is impossible because we can't see how it can be done.
4. Refusing to set aside trivial preferences.
5. Neglecting development and refining the spirit and mind, and not acquiring the habit of reflecting and reading.
6. Attempting to compel others to believe and live as we do.

Cicero's thoughts lead to the awareness that the creative spiral exists in a context. The external and internal 'weather' are intimately linked to our actions.

EVOLVE THE IDEA. Depending on the feedback and review, move into a new cycle and do it again, a little differently (or very differently if a big shift is indicated).

the toughest test is life itself

The inner climate for creativity

There is no such thing as the 'creative personality'

Creativity involves the wholeness of our selves and our world. Everyone can be creative (that is, they can come up with novel ideas that work). There is no such thing as *the* 'creative personality'. Rather, there are attributes present in all of us which we can nurture to improve our creativity. In principle it's another dimension of fitness and we can take steps to lift our performance. As with physical fitness, we can incorporate routines which will improve our creativity. It may sound paradoxical that 'routines' and 'creativity' are so closely connected, but that's the way it is. Indeed many of the core attributes of creativity look paradoxical.

Here's a list of personal patterns which make a difference (many more could be added):

- Flexible and open-minded, with some underlying obsessiveness and persistence
- Ability to get absorbed in activity
- Ability to be 'dreamy' and to visualise
- Trusting intuition and also being questioning/critical
- Comfortable with ambiguity and messiness, while having a strong sense of pattern and order
- Endlessly curious and observant
- Satisfied and dissatisfied
- Comfortable to be in and out of control at the same time
- Independent and willing to take risks
- Optimistic and healthy
- Driven from within – passionate
- Desire to accomplish (and a belief that the goal is achievable)
- Assertive – able to persist in the face of criticism and other adversities
- Arrogant and humble
- Willing to challenge convention while building on existing knowledge
- Willing to fire before you aim
- Able to spot gaps and inconsistencies in current practice
- Radical and conservative
- Creative habits (may include study, practice, effective routines for eating, exercising and resting)

TLC 'persona', one of several created as part of a staff development exercise. The idea was to make a sculpture (at high speed) which reflected each group's impression of the school's personality.

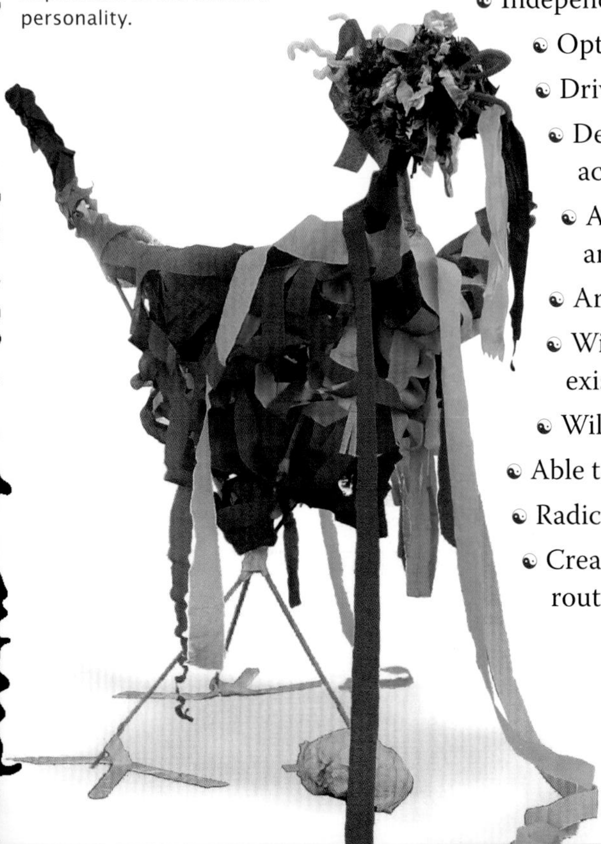

- Strong sense of purpose (which generates certain needs and a desire for change)
- Willingness to resolve things/experiences which get in the way of creativity

All these qualities can be cultivated, ignored or obstructed. It's like gardening – you can help the plants, neglect them, or be extremely obstructive and hit them with weed-killer.

The external climate for creativity

The environment for creativity is just as important as the activity of individuals. At The Learning Connexion we have steadily reshaped our organisation to make it more consistent with the creative needs of both our students and staff. If you're in a supportive environment it won't make creativity easy but it will help to make it possible.

The bigger climate is equally important, and it includes politics, decisions of government departments, the economy, acceptance by news media and attitudes of people in general.

Individuals and organisations have many opportunities to influence the creative climate. A small amount of pressure in the right place can bring about big changes. If the external climate is negative it is still possible for an institution to act like a raincoat and shelter its people from the weather.

Some of the major influences on the creative climate are:

- Supportiveness from local and national government
- A healthy economy
- Adequate infrastructure (for example, the relative cheapness of digital tools has been extremely important)
- Availability of skilled staff
- Suitable accommodation
- Suitable resources (both for making things and for studying the work of others)

At a one-to-one level there are additional factors:

- Supportive and tolerant setting
- Shared values (a sense of institutional meaning)
- Open communication
- Engagement with enthusiastic people who model effective creativity
- Engagement with (and relevance to) the wider community

- Celebration of individual and collective successes
- Effective structures to manage the tight and loose (open-ended) elements of creativity
- A climate of forgiveness; it doesn't help if people get caught up in blame and justification

Connecting

The starting point is to find patterns that energize you. Usually it takes only a short time (days rather than weeks) but everyone is different. The next stage is about connecting – finding how to engage with the world in a sustainable way. This is open-ended and lasts for the rest of your life.

When you let go of the myth of the lone genius you take the first step to designing your own future

The 'connecting' is complex. It involves more than a set of technical skills. An artist has to learn about promotion, business, customer relations, exhibitions and so on. With the things you can't do yourself, team up with others who can. It's the same for anyone who is willing to get out of the cocoon of a trade or profession and take it to a new creative level.

At TLC we support students as they explore the marketplace and meet the challenges that are specific to their own choices. The exploration is woven into the programme from Day One. We see creative learning as both personal and collective. When you let go of the myth of the lone genius you take the first step to designing your own future.

> The object isn't to make art, it's to be in that wonderful state which makes art inevitable. *Art educator Robert Henri*

1 What are your own responses to some core questions:

- What is creativity? (write it, draw it, paint it – find your own way to describe it and also check out the Web and delve into other people's views)
- Who has it?
- Among your acquaintances, who would you regard as especially creative?
- Are there any public figures you regard as highly creative – whatever their field of activity?
- Are there historical figures who seem to you to manifest a high level of creativity?
- How can you nurture creativity?
- What actions would make a difference to your own creativity?
- What community actions could make a difference?

The object isn't to make art, it's to be in that wonderful state which makes art inevitable

2 Ask a selection of people what they think creativity is. Or ask them for their views on a specific public issue which involves creativity. Approach people you wouldn't normally talk to and see what they have to say. Write down their comments (or take a voice recorder and transcribe later). From time to time we've tried this experiment using a video camera (as long as the participants are willing to be filmed).

One of the purposes is to get a sense of community attitudes to creativity. It might help you to know who your allies are. When people express negative views, try to figure out how they are being helpful to creativity. Is their negativity a call for better communication, improved effectiveness and less 'blah'? Pay attention!

Part 1
a human urge

Ella, 18 months, making art.
(Photo: Charlotte White.)

Creativity and the child within

▲ Ella, 26 months, face. From this point Ella's visual vocabulary grew fast without any 'teaching'. We showed interest in her work and provided her with materials.

Kids grapple with words at the same time they're exploring the feeling and appearance of mark-making. Ella's picture (at right) is already based on the symbolism of thoughts and the words for them – it consists of eyes, nose, mouth and hair. Adults often start with the same goal of making the picture 'look like' something.

There are seeds of creativity in every child, hungry for nourishment. You can see the whole story of creativity in children.

What happens at the beginning influences what follows. Everything is connected. Small causes can have big effects.

There are three reassuring points:

1. Patterns of behaviour can be adjusted.
2. Good early patterns can be retrieved, even if school and other influences damage them.
3. 'Bad' patterns often turn out to be part of a bigger, richer and better 'good' pattern (we can learn from mistakes). A 'bad' pattern is self-limiting. For example, spending on credit when you can't maintain the repayments is 'bad' (but it might be a step towards better money-management).

◀ At the same time Ella is equally excited about making marks for their own sake. It's hard to know what she's thinking but the placement and colour all seems to be purposeful.

The dynamics of creativity are the same for children as they are for adults.

Looking at children is a way to reflect on your own inner child. Ask yourself: Am I as spontaneous and adventurous as I was then? Have I got the same energy? Is life as exciting? How have I built creatively on my early life experience?

A few years ago I wrote this: "I watch kids in awe. To them, the entire world is magic. Yet it's just as magical for adults. Here I am, nearly 50, bursting out of my skin with excitement and energy because every day brings new magic. Yesterday I walked with my father (80 this year). He said he's never felt better. We just strolled around Wellington and looked. It's far better than going to a movie. I showed him a book on crop art, including the 160-acre portrait of Will Rogers. He was captivated. So the child in him is alive and well!"

It takes a long time to grow young.
—Picasso

The drawings illustrate some of the ordinary yet magical ways kids think through their art. It's almost as if five-year-olds can take you through the entire history of art without having any intellectual experience at all. Consider the images on the following pages.

Painting by Sarah, aged 4.

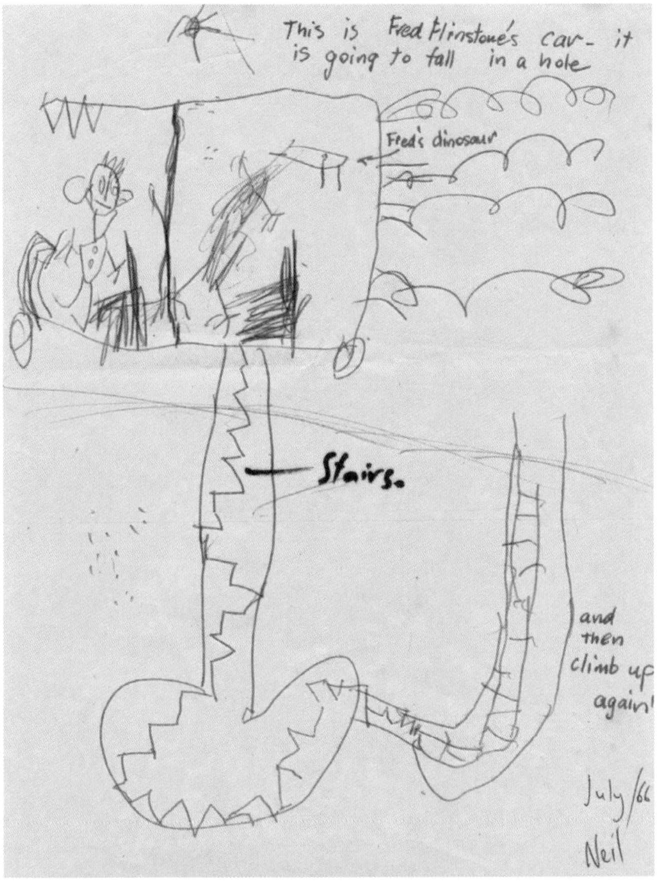

◂ Drawing by Neil (5) telling a story, showing movement and using 'cut away' graphics and narrative.

▾ Drawing by Sarah — the 'x's are words. Use of symbols to show that the person is talking (apart from comics it is rare to see 'noise' described in pictures).

⯯ Drawing by Sarah (age 4) … multiple legs indicate movement (with no knowledge of Duchamp).

▴ Sarah (3) feeding a horse. She went on to become a member of New Zealand's Olympic equestrian squad. This is about intuition rather than drawing. At age 3 Sarah seemed to know that her destiny was connected with horses. She was totally unafraid of them (even though the horse's head was as big as her). She went on to complete an MA in psychology but finally returned to horses — which have been the focus of her work ever since.

▶ Drawing by Neil (4). This drawing is with chalk on concrete and was about a metre high. Neil first drew in the 'innards' and then added skin. The hidden parts of the picture are at least as important as the finished result — the innards relate to the real-life fact that lots of what happens inside us is invisible from the outside. It's more like shamanism than a conventional drawing.

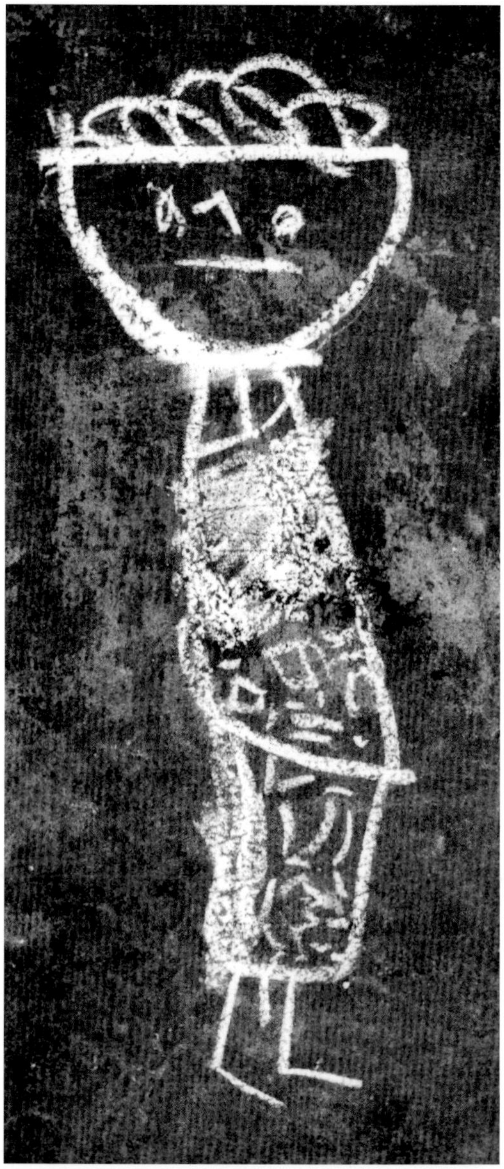

▶ Intuitive composition (and observation) by Sarah. Something about the balance of this drawing really appeals — and it's startling how the feeling and the appearance of the clothing is projected.

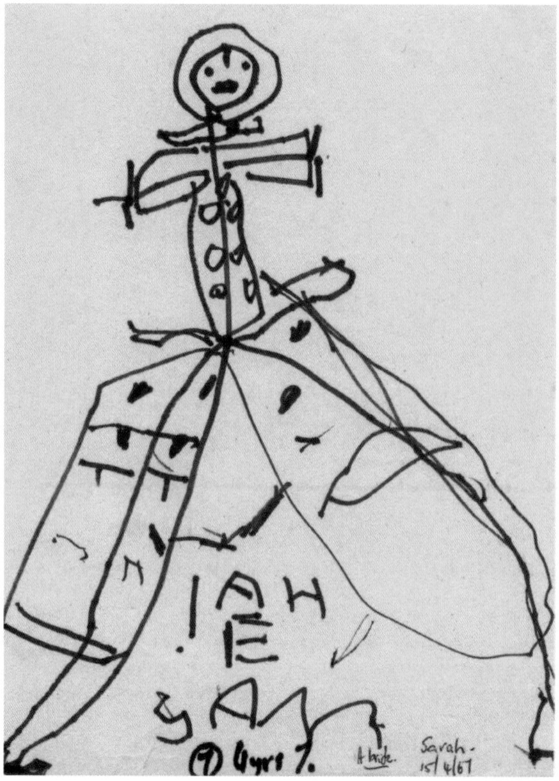

▼ Neil's cut-out image of a duck that hasn't got webbed feet and therefore has to use a boat. Science and humour meet here. The duck could still float if it didn't have webbed feet but Neil decided it would need a boat.

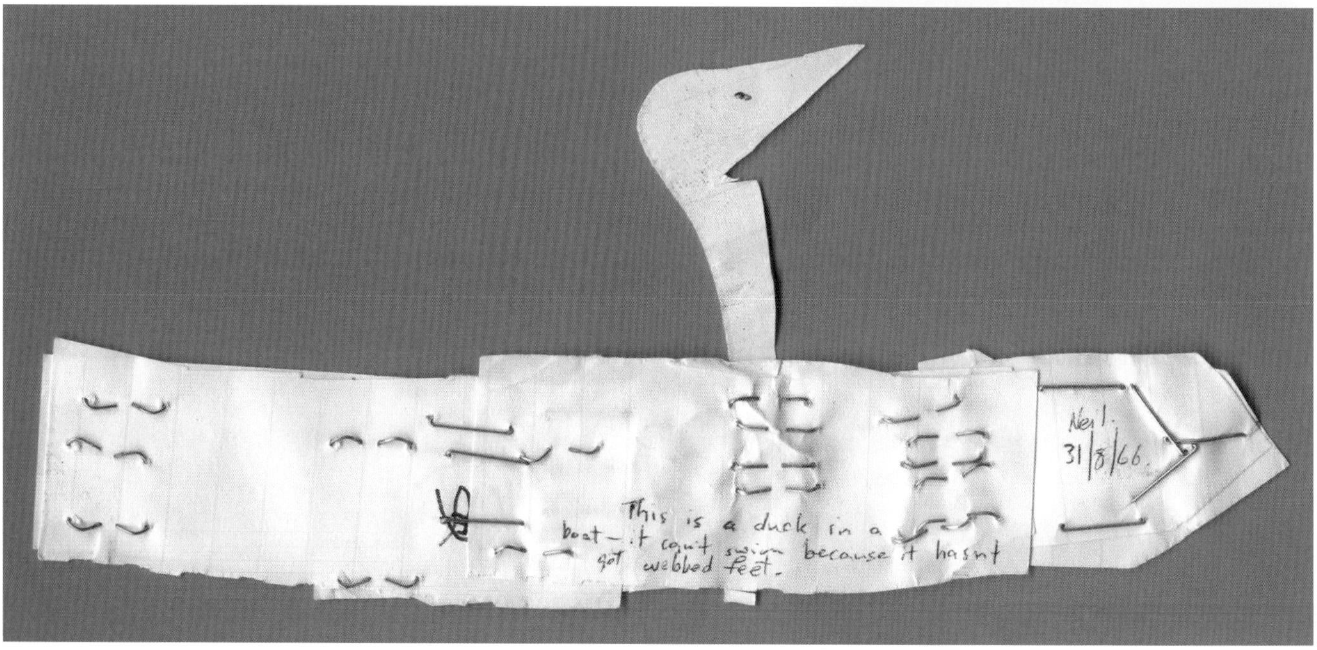

All these images have relevance to adult art. It's not just that they have boldness and energy, they have a conceptual depth which is breathtaking. How is it that schools take children like this and divert their energy into spelling and arithmetic? It's like taking Leonardo da Vinci and restricting him entirely to grocery shopping.

If you can access the child within, a lot of things will begin to flow. Kids are naturally intuitive (they use both 'pattern' and 'linear' thinking) and they can explore highly sophisticated ideas. They might not be able to explain what is happening but this doesn't mean that their thinking is somehow illegitimate. If we can *build* on this childlike approach (instead of diverting from it) and at the same time deal with the necessary grocery thinking, we can achieve awesome power!

If we can build on this childlike approach we can achieve awesome power

3 What does creativity mean to you? Create your own response (you can write, draw, paint, sculpt, sing ...). Browse what some of our students said – the list is a mere beginning.

Following through on intuitive ideas. (Keith)

Creativity is like living the life of Peter Pan and not growing up – keeping the creativity we are born with and using it, developing it, digging deeper.

Messing up the routine! Being spontaneous. Tuning into my feelings. Being inspired by art and reinterpreting it to produce my own pieces. (Alan T)

A change of paradigm

Developing unique ideas/thoughts into something real. Creativity is putting the real world on hold. Solving personal problems in a way that is whole. (Rhiannon)

Creativity is exploring the jungle of your mind.

Self-expression – looking at things from different angles. (Betty)

Unadulterated pleasure – looking, touching – feeling powerful. I love the impact the creativity of my children/grandchildren has on me. (Jude)

It's a life impulse – necessary! It's related to an enormous curiosity about the nature of things and of being! Excitement. A sense of integration and harmony. (Ralph)

Creativity is a mustard seed.

Thinking outside the square

Breaking free of established belief patterns and habitual conditioning

Creativity is my means of expressing the way I feel and think about what I feel and think.

4 What risks are needed to build your creativity? (Again, write your own response and look at the others).

Learn to loosen up (big risk for me!) (Rhiannon)

Risk dissatisfaction with the result. Risk isolation from others. Risk pushing boundaries. Everything worthwhile will always have risks. Risk always taking risks. (Keith)

Creativity is God's gift to us. Our gift back to God is using our creativity.

To physically move/leap for the initial steps. To put day-to-day living tasks on hold and just let creativity be. (Jude)

Creativity is seeking uniqueness.

Creativity is willingness to face the void.

To launch beyond my boundaries (how do I recognise my boundaries?)

To keep doing things – diversity – until I find resonance. (Ralph)

Keep at it. If something doesn't work, try it a different way. (Betty)

Be willing to fail/make mistakes. To hear the views and criticism of others without getting angry/defensive. Be able to commit to a task and let go of the feeling of 'missing out' on other things. (Alan)

Creativity is being yourself.

Creativity is my magic manifesting.

5 What skills are needed? They will vary according to your goal – again, write your own thoughts and look at a few examples below.

Mechanics of drawing, painting, colour, light/shade, artists' materials.

To keep tidy – my surroundings (home), diary (visual).

Painting big pictures.

Looking at people and things attentively.

Everything I haven't already learnt is a skill I need to develop. (Rhiannon)

Knowledge of art history and where to find information and examples of art. (Alan)

To move out of boxes/lines! (Jude)

Increase my intuitive understanding.

Understanding intimately the nature of materials and tools.

Computer skills – designing.

Skills already developed need to become instincts. (Betty)

Patience, communication.

Being more people-centred. (Ralph)

Observation skills.

To write down dreams a.s.a.p. after waking.

Setting out a main focus so as not to spread myself too thinly. (Keith)

Elements of creative success

Creativity is a labour of love

Many of the resources for creativity don't require money

Creativity can be relevant in any area of life

Inner (intrinsic) motivation provides the fire which cooks the creative 'soup'. Intrinsic motivation comes from within and shapes what you *want* to do.

interesting ▪ enjoyable ▪ passionate ▪ playful

Domain skills *(skills relating to your particular creative area). The skills require practice and may be highly complex.*

Creative thinking skills *(principles that apply generally to the creative process).*

6 Assess how you're placed in each of these areas. Write down your assessment of your own skills/attributes in each of these areas.

Creativity killers?

What do you think? Do these things have any merit? Can they (should they?) be part of the creative process?

Competition | Social pressure

Surveillance | Evaluation | Reward

Are there positive aspects of surveillance, evaluation, reward, competition and social pressure?

7 What are the ideal aspects of a creative environment?

In the flow

8 Think about a time when your creative responses worked really well. Here's an example from a student:

> When I was 13, I was playing cricket for Wanganui versus North Taranaki at a three-day tournament. North Taranaki had the strongest team in the competition. Strike bowler Regan, a fiery redhead who swung the ball both ways (and later played for Central Districts) had our team 40/9. I was always tenth batsman as the batting order was largely decided by who was best friends with the captain. The last batsman was the new boy. All the parents bar my own had given up hope and the cheering had ceased. Encouraged by my father's raucous hooting and my mother's shrieking we scored a hundred runs between us, knocking Regan for fours all over the park. There was no time to think, he bowled too fast, but we were sharing a flow and were unstoppable. I thought we had scored the winning runs with a glance for 3 down to fine leg and ran off the park with arms raised. Everyone was shouting and screaming for me to run back. We were one run short. The moment was gone and I was run out with the scores tied. (The good news is that one of the parents in the other team said one of our fours hadn't been signalled earlier, so we won anyway.)

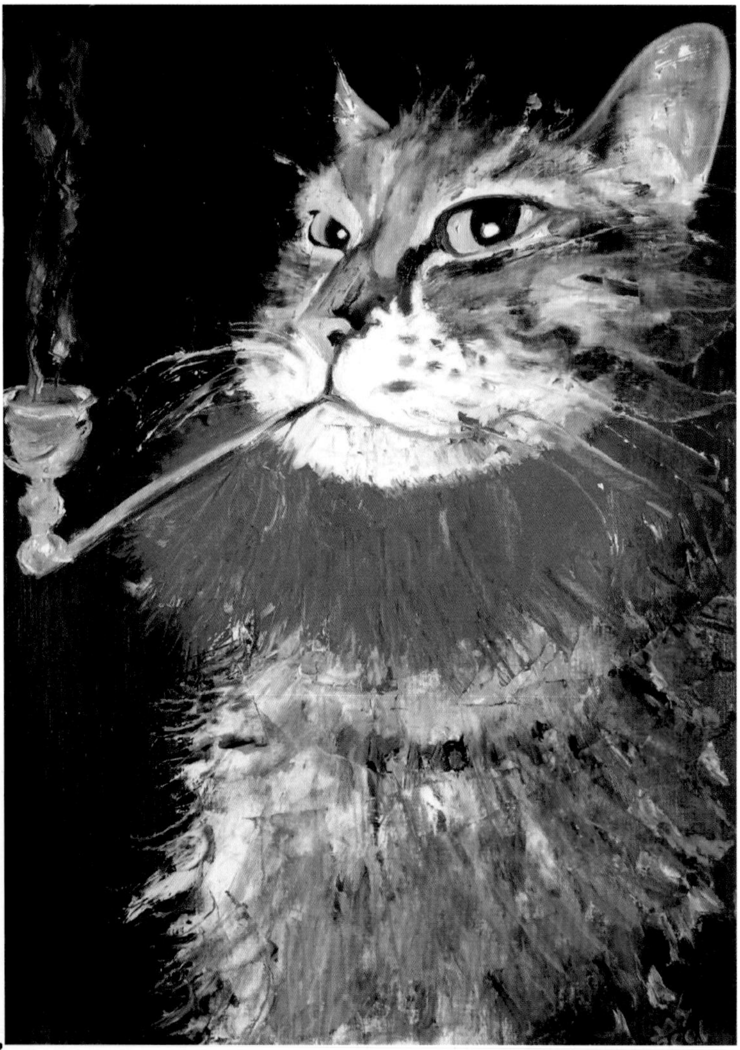

Artist: Katharine White.

Questions

9 Creativity is a dialogue. What are your own questions? Here are some to get started:

What are ways of holding on to your creative **being** and creative **energy**?

Where does creativity come from? **Where is it going?**

Can creativity be consciously **sought**?

If you're **addicted** to keeping your options open, how do you commit to an action?

What is **failure**?

When you have a creative block, how do you shift this to **regain your vision**?

How do you deal with **criticism**?

What is the **opposite** of creation?

Why did I believe my **blocks** over my feelings?

How is it that we are more creative when we are **relaxed**? How can creativity and those '**white moments**' be a part of all aspects of my life?

Are **thoughts** creative?

What is the **point** of creativity?

How do I **feed** my creativity?

Who are the **companions** of creativity?

Why can't I **think** of a question?

If you come up with something and find **it's been done**, is it still creative?

How can creativity be used to successfully obtain **world domination**?

Hitler created a theory … was this creative?

What is **success**?

What is **learning**?

Why is **experimentation** so important to learning and discovery?

What is it about taking risks that allows our mind to **work more freely**?

Creative writing

As a last touch on creativity and kids, here is a little piece of writing in which Charlotte (aged six) is working like a movie director – always focusing on action and immediacy. It's packed with drama and exquisite observation. Charlotte's spelling was 'creative' too, but we've amended that so as not to distract from the story.

THE STORY ABOUT CHARLOTTE IN FIJI

Mum and Dad have been planning for a long time. They are planning about our family going to Fiji and we have been saving our money by not buying many things. Finally Mum and Dad have discussed it out. We are allowed to go to Fiji. Now there is only three days until we will be going. We are packing for Dad and Kate because they are working on the farm. Tomorrow we will be going and we have packed all the things we can think of and we have found people to feed our dog and cat. Today we will be going and I have had my sick pill. First we will go to our grandmother's house for lunch.

Now we have had lunch we will be going to Auckland and it will take a long time. Now we have passed the half way mark. Now there is only one kilometre to get there. We are all half asleep except Dad – he's driving the car. There is an hour to go now and my brother has brought his electric train.

We will have about one flight to the main island of Fiji. We will stay in lots of motels before we'll get to the village.

We are there now. All the people in the village are crowding around the hut that we are staying in. We can all feel the heat and we have got lots of T-shirts. As the days went on we started to get used to the hotness. The people in the village swam in the sea. Near the village the sea was very dirty, it had bits of paper in it.

Going back – when we were at one of the hotels we went on a boat ride to an island. We were the only ones there. You could walk around it in half a day. After we had gone around the island we had lunch. After lunch Kate and I went around the island again. But we started on the other side. When we had gone a little way I saw a shell down in the rocks. It was beside two rocks. In the rocks lay a long black and yellow snake. Kate did not see it at first. … I asked her to pick it up. … She went to pick up the snake. I said, "Is that a snake?" and Kate said, "Oh my God I think it is!" We called Mum and Dad, Matthew came too. For quite a long time there was silence.

After they had come Matthew, Mum, Kate and I all watched Dad. We could tell he was examining it. Then Dad picked a stick up and touched the snake with the stick. The snake curled up in the rock. Then Dad said, "Let's get back – the boat will be here soon." When we were walking back I felt sick.

When we got back Mum had a look at her watch. She said it was nearly time to pack the lunch up. We all started packing up. After that Dad looked at his watch and said to Mum, "Your watch must be wrong because my watch says it is 2 o'clock." So Mum and I went around the island again.

The sea had gone up to the rocks. Mum and I had to swim around the rocks. We came to a cave going into the side of the island. Mum didn't want to go in the cave so I went in the cave. I found a shell like this [drawing]. After we went in there we went into lots of caves. I was scared going through the water because we had heard that the snake we had found was the most poisonous one on the island and if one came around the curve in front of us Mum and me would be dead. After that we walked on the rock.

When we got back it was time to go on the boat. So we quickly changed from our togs to our clothes. A few minutes later the boat came. When we got back we were all very tired so Mum and Dad ordered our dinner early so we could get to bed earlier.

Now we will go back to the village. When we got there – I will tell you about the hut. It was very small – it was as big as a bedroom. Kate, Matt and I all had to sleep on the floor and at night little frogs were seen with their glittering yellow eyes. One night at about midnight Matt woke up. He had been snoring, his mouth had been open and a frog's foot was in his mouth. He got up and said "Dad where's the torch? A frog's foot was in my mouth." And Dad gave it to him.

The End.

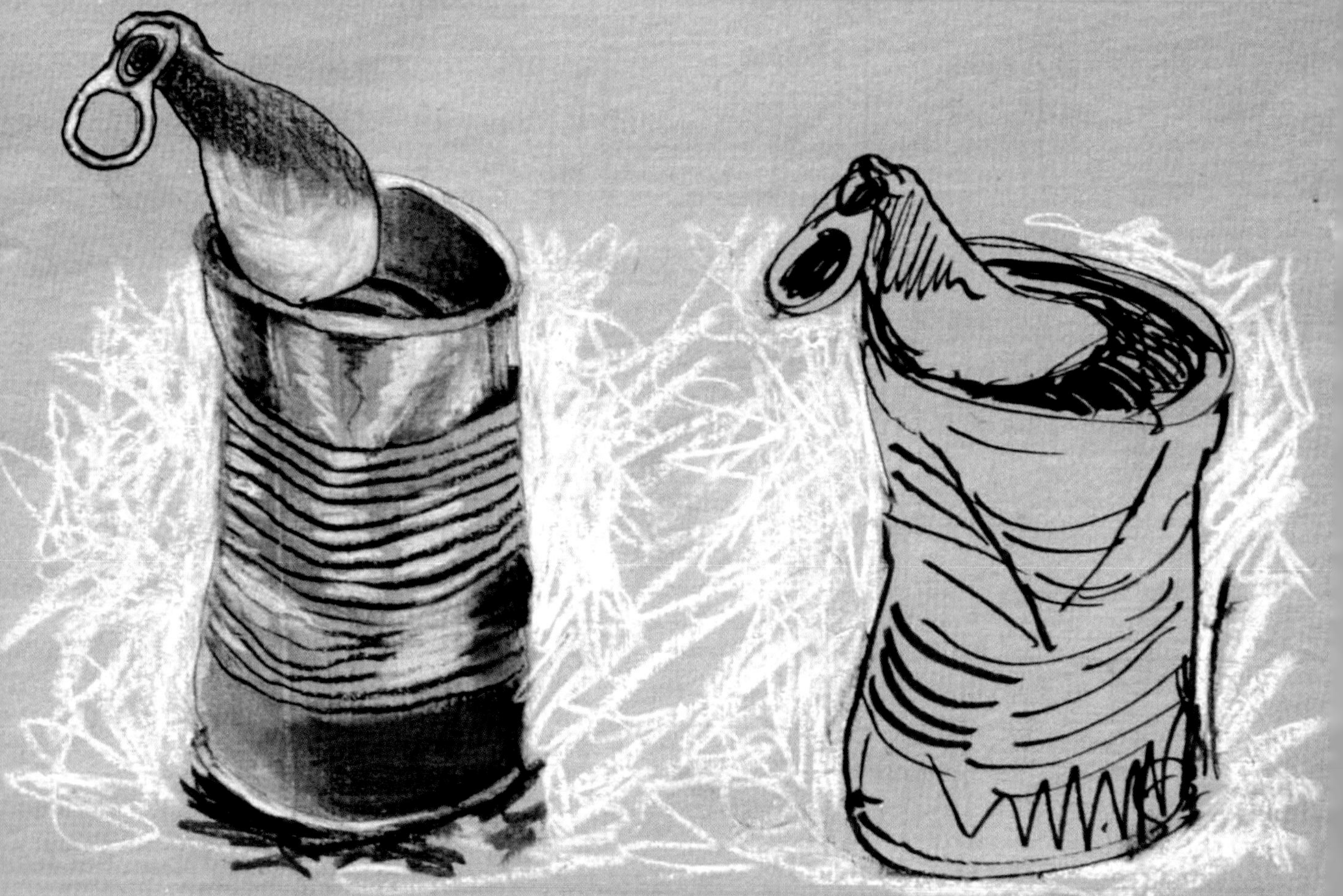

The magic of drawing

VISUAL DRAWING

Drawing is a door to discovering your own creativity. It produces quick results, prolific insights and useful riddles. This takes you into 'right mode' thinking (holistic, sense-based, as opposed to 'left mode' which is linear and 'intellectual'). The *doing* is essential. *GO!* is a catalyst but without your own action nothing will happen.

There are many different pathways to unleashing your creativity. Drawing happens to be easy and convenient. It lights up areas of thinking which are fundamental to a broader engagement with creativity. We're more concerned with the 'lighting up' than with drawing itself, but you may choose to make drawing a singular focus.

Visual drawing is drawing what you see. Initially the purpose is learning to observe – the drawings are by-products. Once you understand the process you'll be able to draw anything you can see. With a relatively modest effort, drawing can expand your mind and awaken new ways of communicating.

It's mostly a matter of paying attention and putting in the time

Drawing is as natural as walking and talking. Everyone can draw, including sceptics who firmly believe that it's impossible. Age is no barrier – old dogs learn new tricks with ease. The key is to discover how to use your perceptions so that your hand responds accurately to what you see. It takes a few hours to learn the basics and a lifetime if you really want to reach for the stars.

The best teacher of drawing is drawing itself. *GO!* can get you off to a flying start but after that it's mostly a matter of paying attention and putting in the time.

It's not mysterious or difficult – a little learning will take you a long way.

be patient – let it happen ▪ **persist** – keep at it ▪ **be playful** – enjoy

The only difference between success and failure is quitting. Practice the techniques until the drawing becomes part of you.

old dogs learn new tricks with ease

◄ Artist: Katharine White.

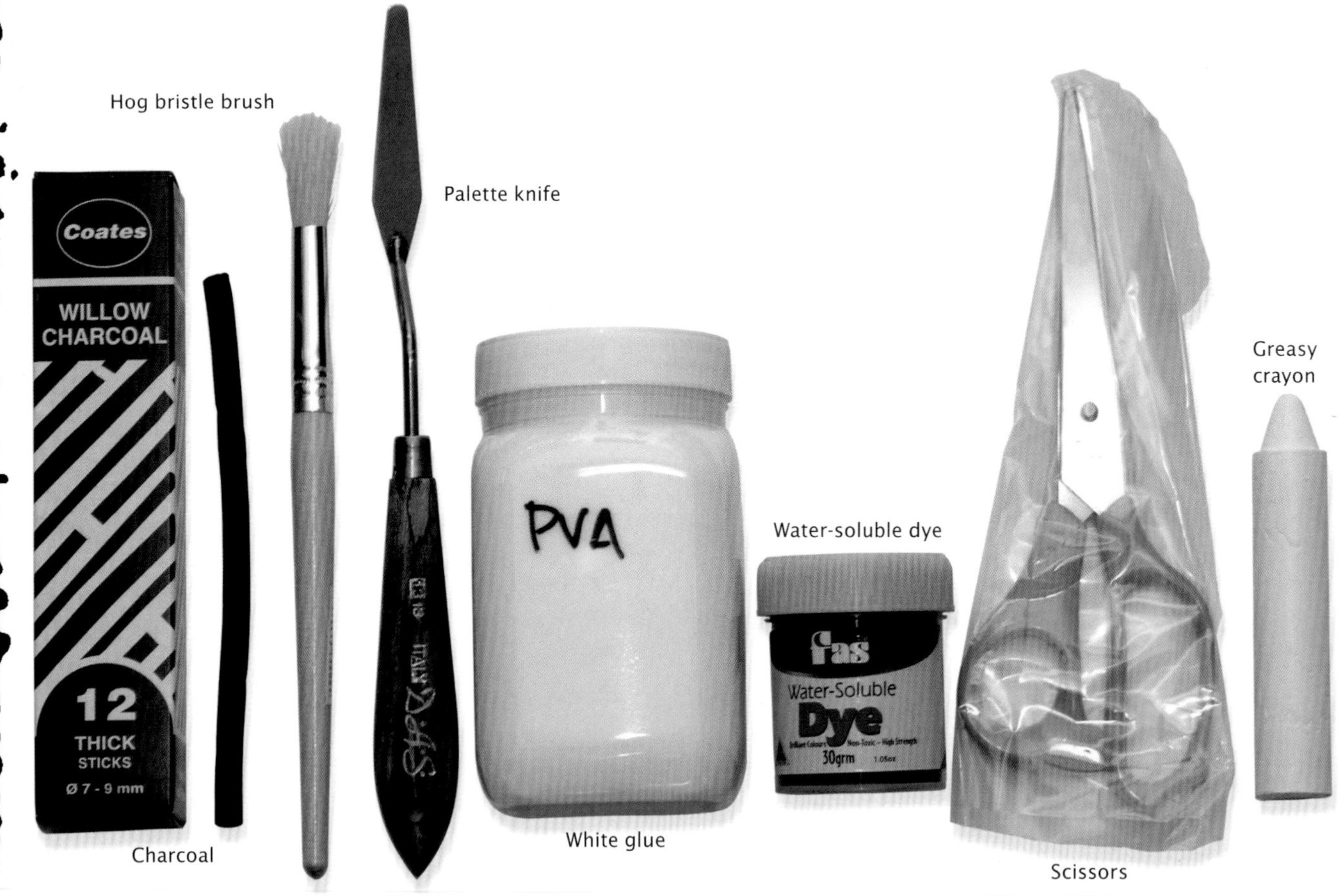

What follows are step-by-step exercises to lead you into drawing and 'mind power'. In a live class we'd allow two days to achieve a basic drawing/painting vocabulary and three days for 'Thinking for a change.' You may then choose to build on the basics for the rest of your life.

In addition to the materials pictured above, you might care to add:

- graphite pencil
- chalk pastels
- eraser
- craft knife
- additional brushes
- 50 sheets glopaque paper (or equivalent – a reasonably cheap paper that works with paint), any size from A3 to A2.

You will become familiar with:

- trusting your senses
- drawing with your 'other' hand
- drawing looking only at the subject, not the paper
- drawing the subject upside-down

- observing and drawing tones
- exaggerating what you see
- drawing at speed
- drawing only the negative spaces
- drawing how you feel about the subject, rather than what the subject looks like
- reading drawings

10 Take a piece of charcoal and draw a face – any way you like. The purpose is to show where you are NOW in terms of drawing. When you've finished, mark the date on the picture, sign it and keep it somewhere safe. Months (or years) later it may be interesting to look back and see how you've progressed.

11 Write your name in large block letters across the bottom of the page. Turn it upside-down and do a copy. Look at the shapes and repeat them as accurately as you can. If it works well you'll find two near-identical names when you turn the paper the right way up.

12 Write your signature large – so it goes right across the page. If you're working with someone else, have them do the same, and then swap pages. Turn the page upside-down and copy the signature. Look at the shapes and copy what you see (it's the same as action **10** with more wiggles).

When you sign your name you're making a kind of self-portrait

Put aside any thoughts of what the letters are – go with what you see. I'm told that forgers learn in the same way (is there a school for forgers somewhere?). When you really connect with what you're seeing, something special happens.

If you succeed in making a good copy of a signature, you've drawn a portrait. When you sign your name you're making a kind of self-portrait – it's your own distinctive mark expressing who you are (and that's another dimension of drawing).

The power of positive thinking

13 Here's an interlude to make the next steps even easier. It's about awareness and the power of positive thought.

Sit comfortably where you won't be interrupted. Have your drawing materials in front of you and ready for action. If you're working with someone else, have them sit facing you (on the other side of a table is ideal).

- Gently relax and listen to the sounds around you. Listen as carefully as you can. If you have a hearing impairment difficulty, pay attention to the air. Feel it touching you.
- Be aware of colours. Maybe focus on a particular colour and let it into your mind.
- Notice the weight of your body as you're sitting – the way you connect with the chair.
- Feel your chest move as you breathe.

We're like radar dishes taking in information all the time. Creativity flows from awareness. When you pay attention to your senses you'll find that much of what

We all have a history of successes

you need is already there. When you connect with your senses, it all becomes easier and miracles are there for the taking.

- Notice your feet; their warmth or coolness.
- Feel inside your mouth with your tongue.
- Notice how your eyelids blink from time to time.

The courage to trust ourselves is at the heart of creativity. All we have to do is to let our minds work in harmony with our senses. One of the by-products is that our own courage will inspire others. It's as if creativity is about sharing. It's a way to get beyond ego and worries to arrive at another space.

- Notice the warmth or the coolness of the air when you breathe in.
- Notice the more subtle feeling of the air when you breathe out.

The air is a reminder that we are connected. We share the same air and we also share the magic of creativity. It has been with us always and there will be times when it has worked so well that you can remember the details of what happened. Go to one of those times. Maybe you were playing sport and it all came together brilliantly. Or you were dancing, or doing something recreational. Or maybe you were learning a new language, or driving a car and suddenly it felt right. Think of any situation where you were fully 'in the flow'. Gently allow yourself to explore one of these memories (they may seem elusive at first but we all have them in abundance).

- While your mind is exploring, notice your heartbeat. There's no need to feel your pulse – just be still and aware. There it is – your heart looking after you, mostly without a thought.

While your heart is beating peacefully, go further into the memory of a time when everything worked beautifully. Recall how you felt. What could you hear and see?

When you want to be at your best, connect with the good time and take it with you into the new situation.

Put yourself back into this special time and allow it to be a place of power. Take these thoughts with you as we do some looking and drawing.

14 Look at the hand you don't normally draw with. Hold it comfortably in front of you and look at its edges. It's like caressing your hand with your eyes. Move lovingly around the edges and notice every tiny bump and every change of direction.

When you're ready, pick up a piece of charcoal and without looking at your paper draw the outline (it might help to clip or tape the paper so that it stays still). Focus entirely on the edges – it doesn't matter what the result looks like as long as you've responded faithfully to what you see.

You may find that 'drawing without looking' helps to put you in an effective state of mind. You can use it as a warm-up whenever you please. You can also use it to de-clutter your thinking and get focused.

It could be useful to label the drawings ('left-handed', 'without looking' etc) and keep them for reference.

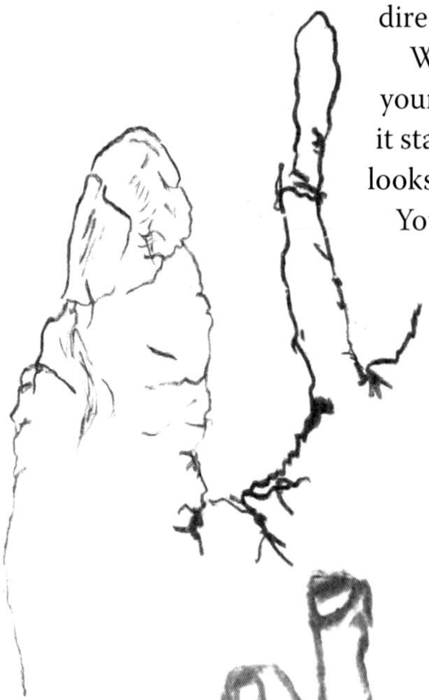

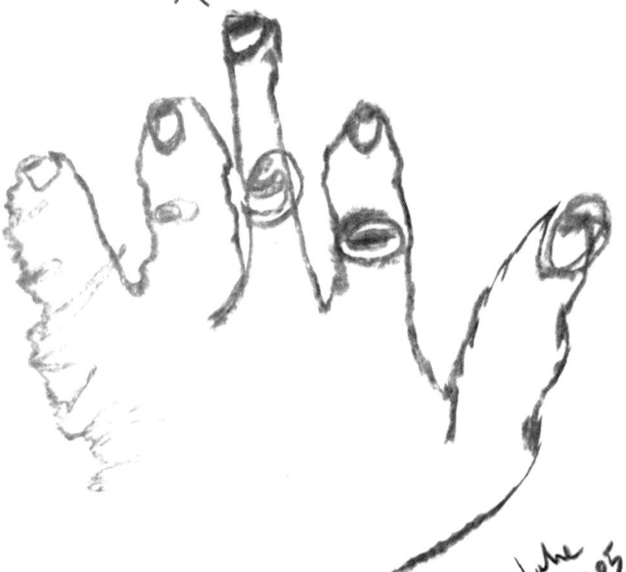

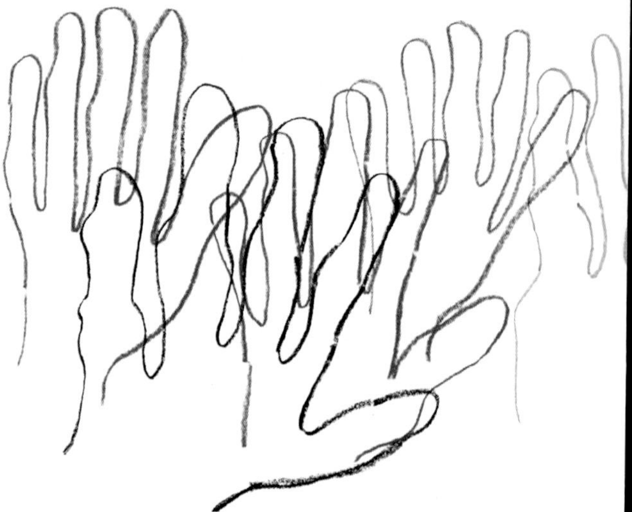

15 Take a fresh sheet of paper and pick up your white greasy crayon. Look at the face of someone sitting on the other side of the table (or if no one else is available, yourself in a mirror, or a photo from a book, or pause the TV/DVD). Do the same as you did with the hand – look carefully at the edges and notice all the 'wriggles'. Although a face may seem more complex than a hand, it's still a collection of edges (for the purposes of drawing).

Again do the drawing without looking at the paper (not that you'll see much – the white crayon is a demanding teacher). Press firmly because the crayon is a 'resist' for the dye that will be used later. If you see an edge, draw it. If you see nothing, draw nothing. If you forget where you are on the page, keep going. We're drawing edges and it's okay if things go abstract.

It's okay if things go abstract

Once you've completed the drawing, splosh on some rich, bright dye with a big brush. If your lines aren't heavy enough, press harder next time.

Look at the result. Even if it doesn't look like a normal portrait, does it have the feeling of what you've drawn? Put aside expectations of what a portrait is *supposed to be* and celebrate your work for what it is.

16 As before, but you can look at your paper to locate where you are on the page. Looking at white crayon on white paper isn't easy – you might have to pick up the paper from time to time and hold it so the light catches the lines.

If you've drawn an eye, you can pause, locate the starting point for the other eye, look back to the person you're drawing and then continue. Look lightly – the merest glance should be enough.

Build up the whole face (neck and shoulders too). Pay attention to everything. How does the hair go? Are there 'edges' to the nose? Are there 'edges' to shadows?

When you're done, splosh on the dye and see what's happened.

Sometimes the 'looking' drawing isn't as lively and exciting as the previous one. Maybe next time you'll choose to look less (or more). Each exercise is an experiment. It's as if you're teaching your body to draw (your ego can have a rest). If you do something that leads to a good result, do it again. If you do something that doesn't work, change your approach the next time.

Cheryl Hand.

I like to remind myself of the way babies learn to talk. They start with messy attempts and gradually get better and better. We applaud their successes and ignore the 'mistakes'. If you're a total beginner, be a patient and loving parent to yourself. It isn't a race and you'll get there in your own way.

Imagine if we looked at babies and decided whether or not they could learn to talk. It would be crazy, yet there are teachers who do it to their students in regard to drawing and then – worse still – some of us do it to ourselves.

No matter what others tell us, we can say *YES* to ourselves.

17 Repeat the same action as before (adjusting it to fit what you've learned) and do it with your non-drawing hand. If you're right-handed, draw with your left hand. If you're left-handed, draw with your right hand. If you have only one hand you can use a foot, or you can hold a pencil in your mouth –

think of possibilities rather than limitations!

If it feels strange, concentrate for all you're worth and let it happen.

You can look at the paper as much or as little as you like. The main thing is to pay attention to the face and let your 'other' hand put the marks on the page.

When I first tried this the results were boring but on another day it all clicked and I found myself drawing more accurately (and with more personality) using my other hand.

Artist: Katharine White.

I'm not sure what happens. Some reckon that it's to do with the wiring in our brains. Perhaps we relax because we don't impose heavy expectations on our 'other' hand. Maybe our dominant hand is so heavily used for writing that we suppress its ability to 'see'. There's scope for a doctoral thesis here but for the moment we're only interested in what works for *you*.

18 Same as before, using the hand of your choice, and exaggerate. Feel free to use charcoal or ink if you don't like the crayon. Think caricature. Observe carefully and make the features bigger or smaller as you please. Relax. Let's hope the pictures don't put too much of a strain on old friendships (mostly people will laugh). Draw pets or photographs if your friendships are frail.

Caricature might turn out to be a career move but here it's a way of exploring what happens when we loosen up a little. You might find that there's a sense of freedom in doing what you like with a face instead of being trapped by the restrictions of 'copying'.

19 Explore drawing what you feel. Betty Edwards uses the word 'analog' for these 'feeling pictures'. Her books *Drawing on the Artist Within* and *Drawing on the Right Side of the Brain* are superb for your art library.

Movie music is a kind of analog – the sounds convey much of what the director wants you to feel. You might like to think of analog drawings as visual music. Instead of using symbols or representation they use shapes and colours to convey feeling.

Divide an A3 sheet into eight. In the first frame, use coloured crayons

Artist: Katharine White.

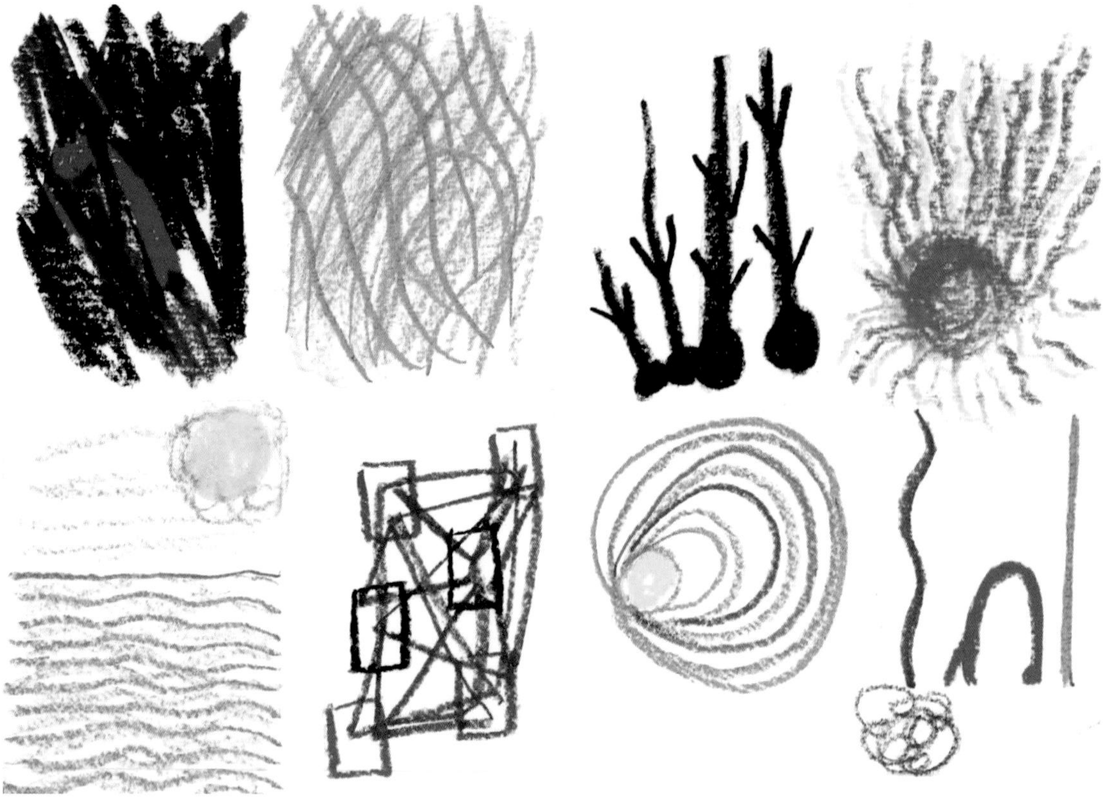

Example of the 'analog' set. Top row: anger, peacefulness, depression and energy. Lower row: pleasure, work now, ideal work and 'self-portrait'.

Another set: same themes as the first one but note the individual differences. Each person will have a unique result but there will also be things in common. For example, anger analogs tend to be red and black; often the marks are spiky and mostly there's big pressure on the crayon.

or pastels to make a scribble/doodle of *anger*. Let it happen – half a minute should be enough.

Continue in the next three frames with analogs of *peacefulness, depression, energy*.

For the fifth drawing, think of something really pleasurable and do a scribble/doodle of the feeling of that pleasure.

For number six we're getting more complex. Think of *work*. Work is different things to different people. It could be your job, if you have one, or it could be looking after your children, studying for a qualification, creating a book of poems ... it's your life and your choice.

Think about all the elements of work. Employment, for example, might have aspects which are exciting, boring, funny, stressful and so on. Include all the elements that are relevant to you (and keep to scribble/doodles – there's no need for symbols).

For the next frame, try a scribble/doodle of *work the way you would love it to be*. You're portraying the *feeling* of work. If you want everything to be different, then go for it! If your work suits you already, you might look towards a modest change – maybe the two pictures will be quite similar.

For the last of the eight frames, try a few marks which express the real you. If you're bold and stroppy, make a few bold and stroppy marks. If you're colourful, do something colourful. If you're whimsical, do lines which take the viewer through whimsical trails.

Anger	***Peacefulness***	***Depression***	***Energy***
Pleasure	***Work now***	***Ideal work***	***You***

To test whether the drawings say anything, work with a partner whose task is to read frames 6 and 7 and tell you how you feel about work. It's preferable to do this with someone who doesn't know you.

When taking the partner role I look at all the doodles (to get an idea of the person's visual language) and then use a mix of intuition and logic to make my guesses about work. Sometimes it's obvious (especially when the person intensely dislikes their work) but other times it can be remarkably subtle.

In effect we're doing analog readings whenever we respond to body language and the tone of someone's voice. It's so ingrained in our behaviour that we hardly notice.

It might feel novel to read scribbles as 'body language' but essentially it is the same – we're connecting with our innate skills of pattern recognition.

Keep in mind that our interpretations might be wrong. This isn't psychoanalysis or science. Play it lightly!

When you combine the analog approach and the earlier visual drawings, you've got a big window on the language of art.

It's by no means the whole story but it's a powerful start. It could help you understand why some of your less accurate portraits are still successful – if they convey strong feelings it might be unimportant whether they're visually 'correct'.

Do you ever wonder what makes a drawing or painting 'good'? Students often say it doesn't matter – beauty is in the eye of the beholder. But when I watch them doing their art, they can get quite agitated about whether it's good (and equally agitated about whether others will approve).

I've seen five-year-olds getting angry about drawings because they weren't turning out right. What's going on here?

In part it's a trick of language. 'Good' has different meanings. It is a word for moral approval, technical quality and it also means a thing (as in 'goods and services').

When you make art you've made a 'thing', but when people view it they're bringing with them their own understanding of the world. Their response is an interaction between the 'thing' and their own experience. 'Beauty' isn't in the eye of the beholder, it's in the alchemy *between* the art and the beholder.

20 Look at a photo upside-down and do a drawing with charcoal in the same way that you did the earlier crayon pictures. You can look at the paper as much as you like (you'll get a sense of what works best). Look at the edges and build the picture. The upside-down trick is to help free ourselves from preconceptions about the way a face looks. Instead of thinking about eyes, nose and mouth, draw the shapes and pay attention to relationships between them.

When you're finished, turn the drawing up the right way and make a decision whether it's good enough to continue. If it's too

Analogs can turn into fully developed art. You can do large works which concentrate entirely on feelings. Imagine the accompanying analogs increased to massive size.

wonky, treat it as practice, take a new sheet and try it again.

Once you've achieved an adequate outline, plunge into the tones ('shading'). Charcoal is wonderful stuff and you can get into it with your fingers and have a ball. Keep some tissues handy to deal with the grubbiness.

Think about tones the same way as you've been thinking about lines. If there's a shadow, draw it (and use fingers to smooth the edges). If there's a highlight, draw nothing (if you're using white paper) or draw in white (if you're using toned paper).

When it goes well you'll get a real sense of depth in the drawing – it will appear three-dimensional.

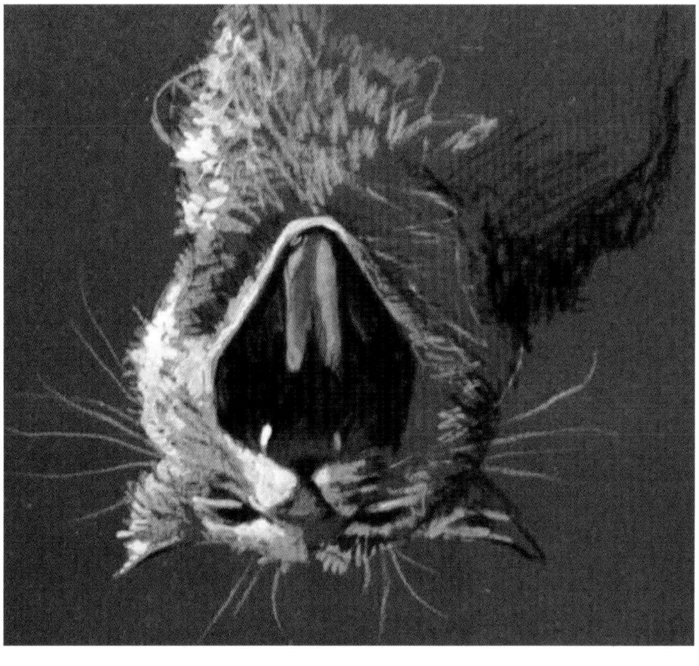

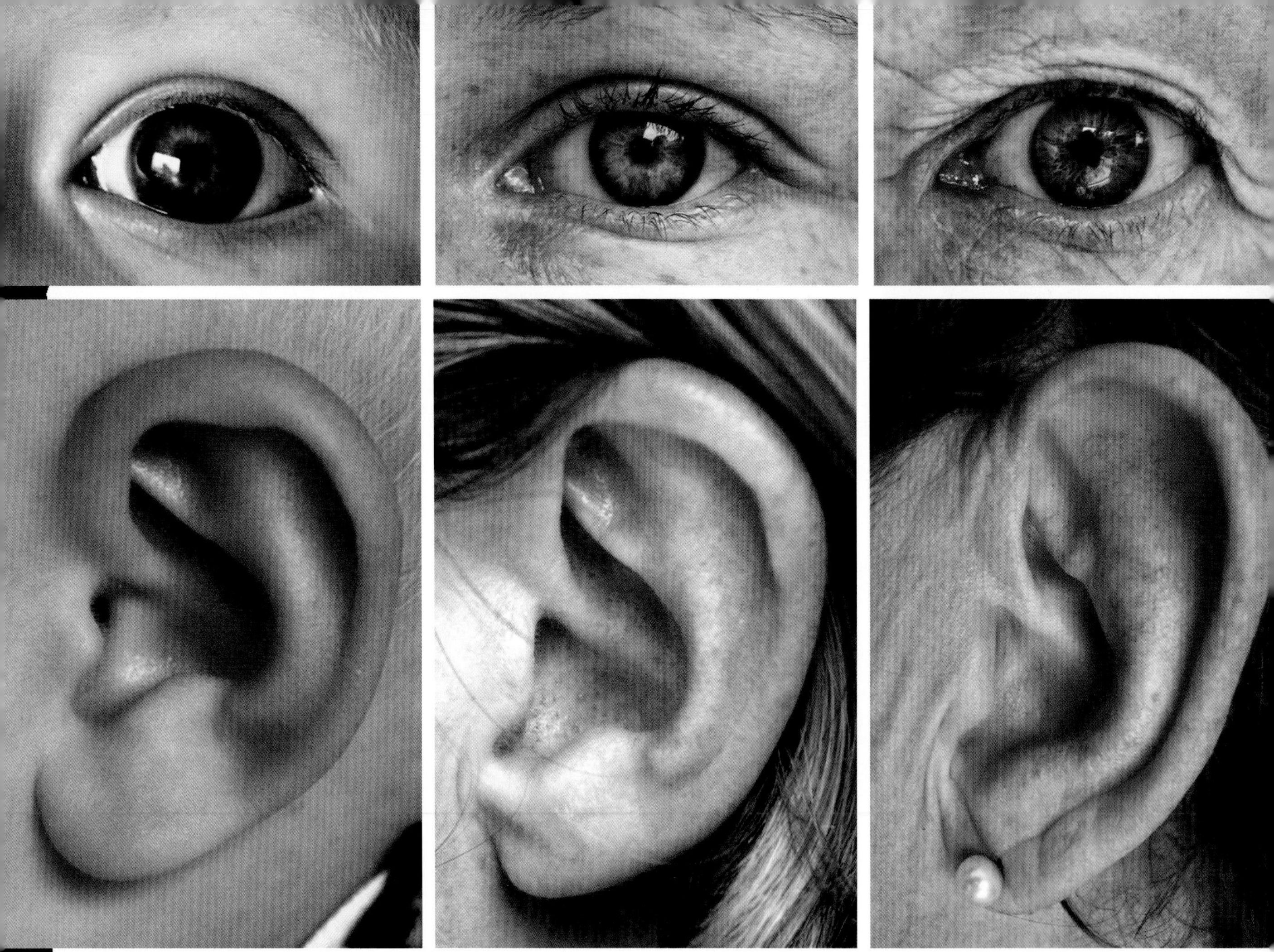

Eyes and ears of child, mother and grandmother.

21 Gather four different face photos (from magazines, your family album or whatever you can find). Choose a feature from each picture – eye, mouth, nose, ear – and draw it large (at least the size of an A4 sheet). Do all the tonal work (as in the earlier exercise) and pay attention to the attributes of each feature. How does the light fall? What are the shapes? Are there hard edges? How can you use tone to describe a shape?

Every eye is different and every eye has similarities with other eyes. Likewise all the other parts of facial architecture. Once you get to know the common features you can be freer to notice the differences which give each face its personality.

Friends, Romans, countrymen,
lend me your ears ...
—Mark Antony in Julius Caesar,
by William Shakespeare

Drawings from a beginners' class.

22 Draw faster than you can draw. A whole face in two minutes. You'll need a timer and some faces (friends are ideal – do it together – or use photos). Concentrate mostly on the outline (same as before). If you have time, smudge in the basic shadows.

The goal is to relate to wholeness as well as detail. See the whole face and let the detail follow. Try three drawings with your 'main' hand and three more with your 'other' hand.

If the first one doesn't work, try the next one differently.

Keep experimenting. Maybe draw without looking at the paper (or taking just a couple of quick glances). Take yourself lightly and be willing to let things incubate. You may find that your subconscious will do all the necessary thinking and within a few days everything will be flowing better than you ever dreamed possible. I enjoy seeing the looks of excitement and disbelief when it all comes together.

Success can be a distraction. It was the statesman Adlai Stevenson who said "Success is all very well as long as you don't inhale." It can spoil your concentration. If the next drawing goes wrong, it doesn't mean that the good one was a fluke.

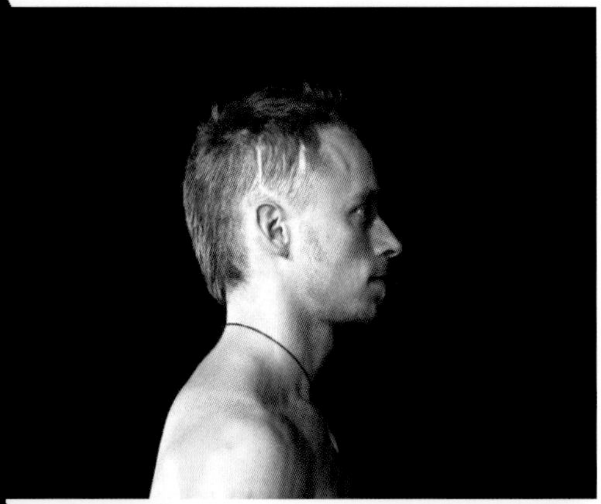

The 'not face' provides the exact profile of the 'face'.

23 Look at negative spaces. Here's another trick of language. We use labels like 'face' but we don't have a word for 'not face'. Yet if you look at the profile of a face and draw all the 'not face' you'll end up with the profile. When we talk of 'filling a cup' we mean 'filling part of the not-cup' (the cup stays the same whether filled or empty). So it is with drawing. The not-nose is as important as the nose.

The arrows in the picture below point out some negative spaces. The negative space for an eye is the space around the eye. If you look at the gap between the eye and the side of the face, it will help you to place the eye accurately. You might notice that we tend to bring the face to a symbolic square-on position and as soon as we observe negative spaces we are reminded of what is actually there (it's not a symbol).

Perhaps drawing includes a wrestling match between our 'left brain' (seeing symbols and concepts) and our 'right brain' (relating directly to what we see and our feelings about it). The goal of your practice is to get the left and right modes working in harmony.

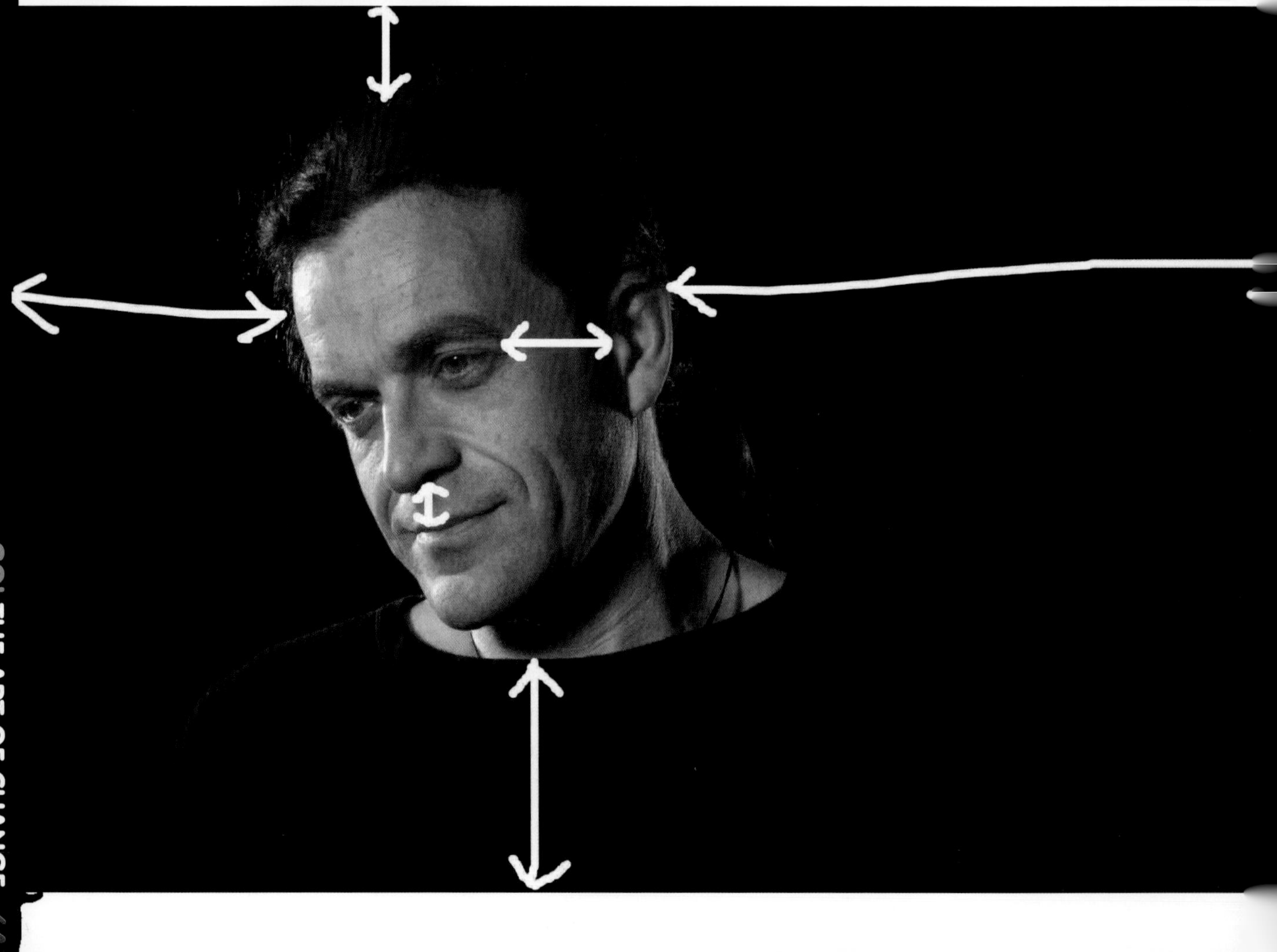

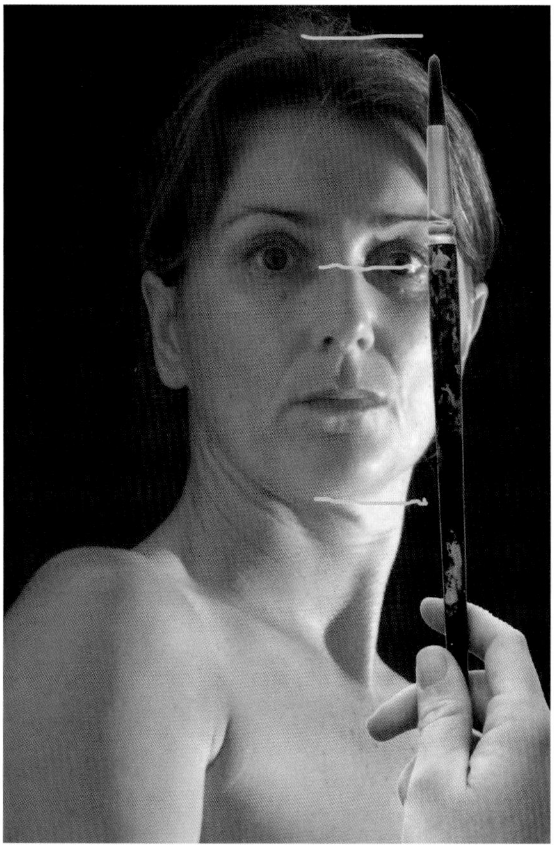

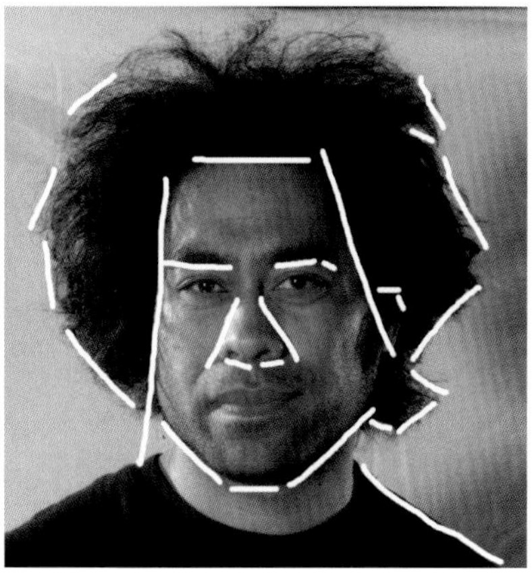

A methodical, submissive approach can provide the platform for imaginative drawing

Proportions are useful too. In this case the eyes are at the midpoint of the face (if you include the hair). You can check by holding a pencil or brush at arm's length and comparing the various distances within the face.

Another aid to 'seeing' is to look at the direction of lines. It may help to connect your left-brain expectations with what is actually there.

24 Return to a photo (or your mirror) and try a portrait incorporating all that you've learned so far. Draw at your own speed and think about what suits you best. Right-handed? Left-handed? Slow? Fast? Looking? Not looking? Negative spaces? Positive spaces? Noting directions of lines and proportions?

For the moment, concentrate on being *unimaginative*. All the information you need is in the photo (or mirror) and there's no need to invent anything. One of the paradoxes of drawing is that a methodical, submissive approach can provide the platform for imaginative drawing. It not only gives your mind a greater reservoir of information, it seems to put you into a mental state in which imagination flourishes.

Your drawing emerges from the negative (yin) to the positive (yang) as you add white

25 Try doing a picture (from a photo) with white pastel or conté crayon on dark paper. Suddenly all the tones are back to front – your drawing emerges from the negative (yin) to the positive (yang) as you add white. If you add too much white you can adjust with a black pastel (or compressed charcoal).

26 Use both black and white but work on paper that is either toned or coloured. The paper should be a mid-tone so that both the black and white show clearly. You're adding both the lights and the darks while the paper itself provides the mid-tones.

'Weezil' – pastel drawings by Katharine White.

Getting unstuck

What if your adventure in art isn't getting off the ground? Gradually you will find ways to get results. Maybe they are there already but you still don't feel confident about them. Remember to look after yourself as you would a child trying to take its first step. There's no hurry – just keep 'doing' and things will take shape in their own time.

I had a student who was convinced she was the first person in the world who couldn't draw. She came to classes for a few months and was highly critical of everything she produced. Eventually she decided to go back to a beginners' class. After a while a man sitting next to her said: 'I hope one day I'll be able to draw as well as you.' He innocently jolted her into awareness of her progress.

That's often the way it is.

One of the purposes of our teachers is to provide support and encouragement during those times when our self-belief falters. Later, when we are strong, we will be sustained by self-belief.

Sharpening your observation and being expressive

> Drawing is a passionate affair. *Tony Godfrey (Drawing Today)*

> Do not attempt to learn a formula, but to become sensitive, to feel more deeply. Do not try to master a particular technique … The rules of technique have been made by people who copied those who made the progress. You will paint well when you are able to forget that you are painting at all. When you are conscious of your medium, things become difficult, but when your interest is completely absorbed by the model – the idea – your materials become easier and easier to handle. Therefore, practice is the watchword.
>
> *Kimon Nicolaides (1891–1938)*

You will paint well when you are able to forget that you are painting at all

Eyewitnesses are notoriously unreliable because they are likely to 'see' what they think rather than what is actually happening. Observational drawing involves some gentle re-training, which enables us to be more objective.

One of the reasons for being a poor witness is imagination. It begins when we think in visual shorthand and then reconstruct our experience from the shorthand rather than from what we actually saw. Normally imagination is immensely useful. Spoken language depends on imagination because labels like *man*, *cold* and *lemon* are meaningless unless we're able to do some imagining. The book called *Don't*

Drawing is a passionate affair

▲ A real cave drawing showing intense observation side by side with the beginnings of symbolic drawing.
▲ Symbolic drawing by present day 'cave artist' under our house.

Think of an Elephant draws attention to the way we snap to an image.

At another extreme there are people, sometimes categorised as 'idiot savants', who can do astonishingly accurate drawings from memory but who appear otherwise retarded and lacking imagination. You might like to think of drawing as a means to awaken the idiot within. It's a win-win – you'll become considerably more accurate in observing the world, and instead of abandoning your imagination you will enhance it.

So why do we need to LEARN to draw? Why isn't it just 'there'? Probably because we're so clever at using our minds in a way that sidesteps drawing. The most ancient cave drawings reached marvellous levels of quality because drawing is a natural skill. The cave artists could SEE and it wasn't a giant leap to be able to DRAW.

As time went on, humans gradually made more use of their 'left mode' (logical/reasoning/symbolic) skills and their perceptual gifts got pushed into the background. The process of art became more difficult because of the shift of balance from SEEING and recording to THINKING and rationalising. At The Learning Connexion we're seeking to restore the balance and take that next step into CREATING.

Ella, 2½ years old, drawing of her 8-month-old sister Primrose. The symbolic elements (face, eyes, mouth etc) are linking with observation.

Ella the artist and Primrose the subject. Compare the drawing with the photo.

The following explorations build on skills of drawing what you see, feel and imagine. The goals are to:

- Become familiar with specific drawing skills such as line, tone, form, perspective, blending and proportion
- Improve spontaneity and risk-taking
- Explore some aspects of visualisation (creating pictures from your imagination)
- Try a variety of approaches to develop expression and power in your drawings
- Explore gesture drawing, life drawing, landscape, still life, animals, faces, flowers

The overall purpose is to produce pictures which have sparkle and personality, and to reinforce drawing skills so that it becomes second nature to use them.

The best teacher of drawing is drawing

Materials pantry

- **Charcoal**
- **Paper**: Sketch papers such as Bockingford and Glopaque are fine although it's good to experiment with different types of paper to discover how they work.
- **Pencils**: Softer pencils are generally better for drawing (6B is ideal). Pastel pencils provide a glorious range of colours.
- **Inks**: Indian ink plus some coloured inks if you want them. Be wary of colours that fade in the light.
- **Acrylic or water paint** are okay if you work with a brush rather than pens.
- **Pastels**: Chalk pastels such as Mungyo are fairly reliable and widely available (the colours are not guaranteed to last).
- **Erasers**: If you need 'em, by all means have 'em!
- **Brushes**: Smallish brushes (say a 3 and a 7) are worth having. Get nylon *or* sable *or* sable mixed with ox hair.

Depending on the size of your budget, you may consider:

- **Artist-quality crayons, oil pastels, oil sticks** etc: They are suitable to make saleable drawings that have the richness and colour of paintings.
- **Pens**: Dip pens are useful – get three or four different nibs. Reed, bamboo and quill pens are optional extras (you can make your own).

Nicki Ball in the TLC materials shop.

Observation in drawing

27 Draw one of your shoes without looking at the paper. The object of the drawing is to OBSERVE every detail carefully, gently, as if the pencil is caressing the form. It is unimportant whether the proportions turn out to be correct – this is purely about looking.

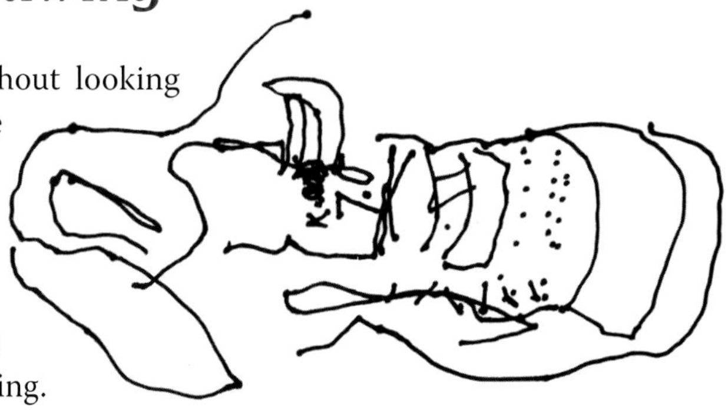

28 Following more or less the same approach, revisit action **22** (page 63) and draw a quick round of faces (real people if they're available, or from photos). You can glance at your paper to find out where you are but the aim is spontaneity – a fast response to what you see. Trust your senses and let them guide you through the drawing.

29 Draw a circle with your eyes shut. Have a look at the result. Draw a square with your eyes shut. Look. Draw a hand with your eyes shut.

Now, try drawing a hand with your eyes open (like the early exercise) and without looking at the paper. Try to include all the details of the hand's outline. Lastly …

Try the hand again with your eyes shut. Notice how observation reinforces imagination. As you observe you'll find that your drawing develops naturally.

30 Place any object in front of some crumpled paper or tinfoil. The goal is a special picture of something ordinary. The object and the paper will somehow complement each other. It doesn't matter what the object is, because the drawing will take on a life of its own. Spend about half an hour on this exercise (more if it needs it).

Compositional sketches.

31 Repeat the same thing but do it in one minute. What are the messages you get? What are the different 'values' of the two pictures? You could try a third in 30 seconds. You might find something special in the energy of working fast.

Zen archery has a lesson in terms of patience and spontaneity. Apparently in the old archery schools students would practise for a long time before being permitted to let the arrow go. They were taught to face away from the target, turn and instantly become at-one with it. The gap disappears. You can't miss.

32 Utilise quick drawings to explore composition (the arrangement of marks and shapes). If the quick marks don't look promising, discard them immediately. If you're going to commit hours, days or weeks to a picture, better that you feel okay about it from the start.

Fast compositional jottings.

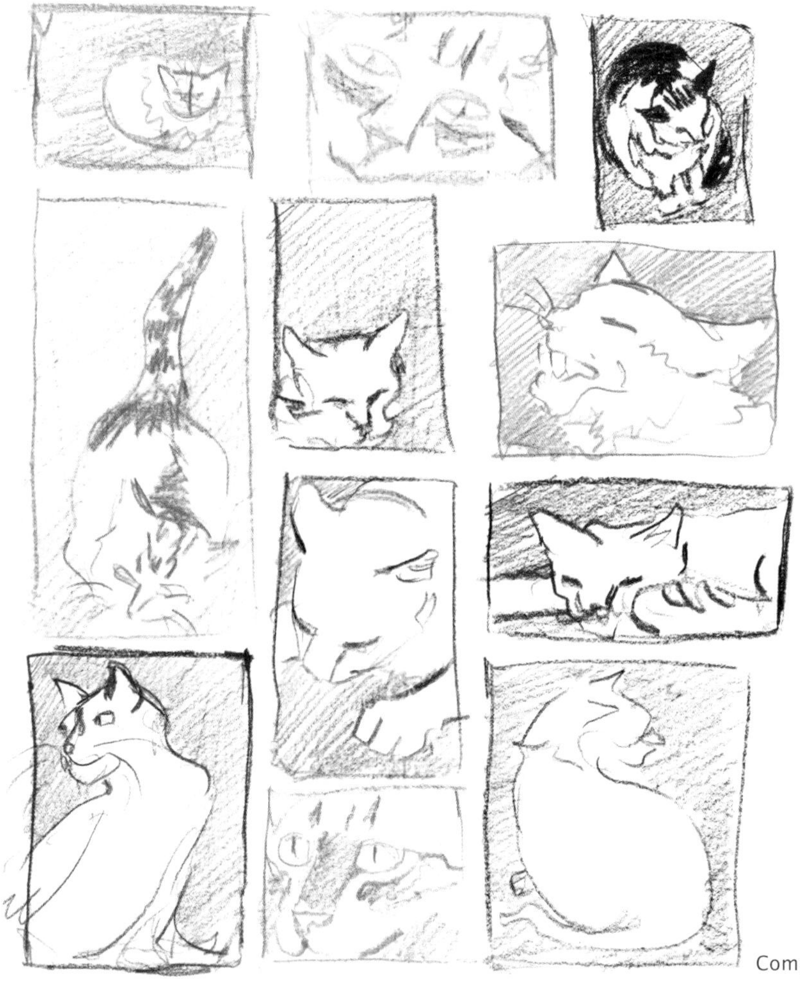

Compositional sketches.

Do a series of small sketches, about half the size of a postcard:

- of someone across the table
- yourself in the mirror
- from your photo album (whatever suits).

Think of different ways to place the image on the page. Be inventive! Composition is an active process. Decide where and how you are going to place the image. Composition not only makes a big difference to the impact of the picture; it puts you in charge.

33 Do a detailed drawing based on the composition you like best.

Patterns

Creativity is about seeing patterns and making new connections. Patterns are everywhere. Grass, trees, fabric, earth ... the type you are reading is a pattern. Search for patterns. What can you do with them? Draw? Paint? Photograph? Record in plaster? Dismantle? Reassemble? Repeat?

Here's the paragraph above repeated in Wingdings, a typeface which substitutes different symbols for our regular alphabet:

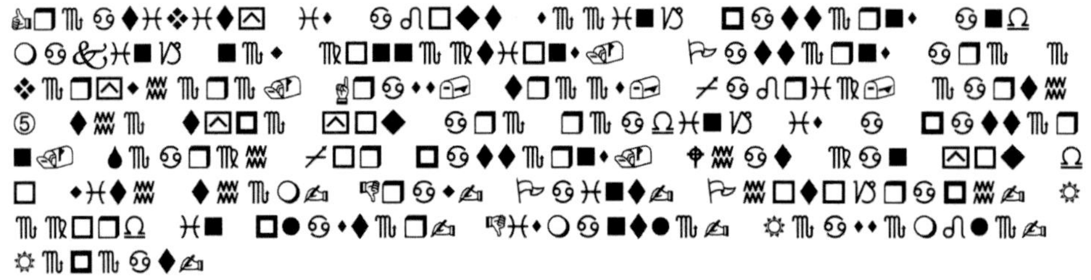

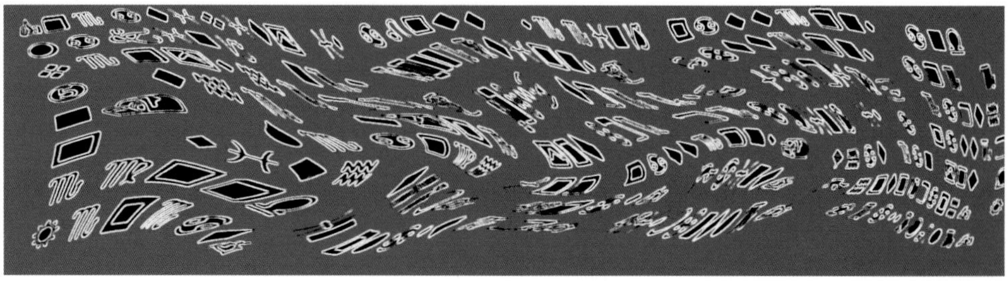

By taking the same process through distortions and overlays, something different emerges, but it's all connected to the original. Possibly 'mess' consists of enfolded and distorted 'order'.

Creativity is about seeing patterns and making new connections

Although it looks odd (like hieroglyphics) it's everyday language wearing masks. Artists and other explorers (scientists, researchers) are looking for the patterns behind the masks.

In our day-to-day world we find endless 'signature patterns'. Thus a piece of crinkled fabric may look similar to many other pieces of crinkled fabric. One flax bush may look like any number of other flax bushes.

it's everyday language wearing masks

Whereas visual drawing targets specifics, patterns are about generalisations. Patterns require elements in common. In terms of creativity, visual drawing takes us into the discipline of specifics which turn out to be the starting point for exploring patterns.

The pictures overleaf are of patterns, either 'natural' or a combination of natural and 'made'.

How can you generate patterns? Watercolour spatter, wet on wet, monoprints, dropping paint from a height, rubbings ...

34 Find a range of patterns, e.g. clouds, trees, or the lines on a plant. Record them in some way (draw, photograph, etc.) and play with them. Stretch, distort, dismantle, rearrange, combine with other materials, repeat, add colour, reproduce in black and white, etc. The purpose is to cultivate sensitivity to pattern and to routinely 'do things' to patterns (think 'how can I *verb* it?').

Each pattern has its own 'signature'. The flax could not be mistaken for the concrete or the water. The wide version of the flax consists of three copies of the same image roughly joined – but it looks fairly convincing because the 'signature' is consistent.

Stretch.

Duplicate and join.

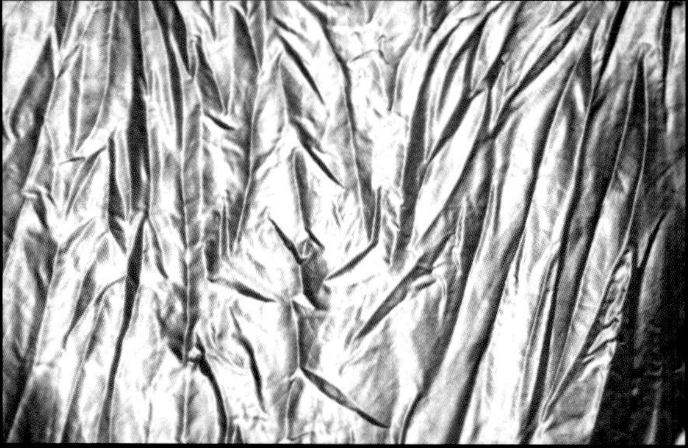
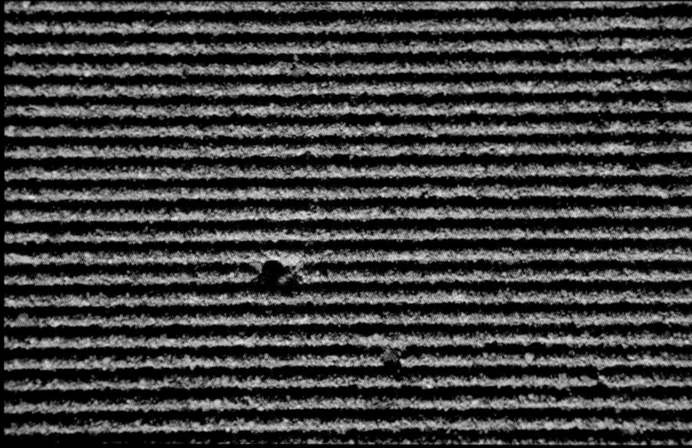
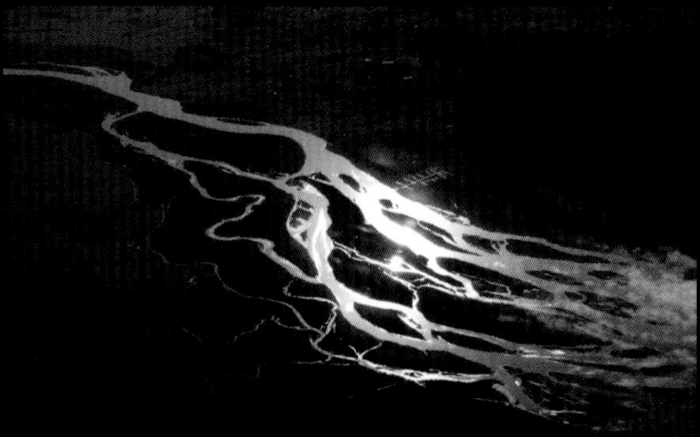

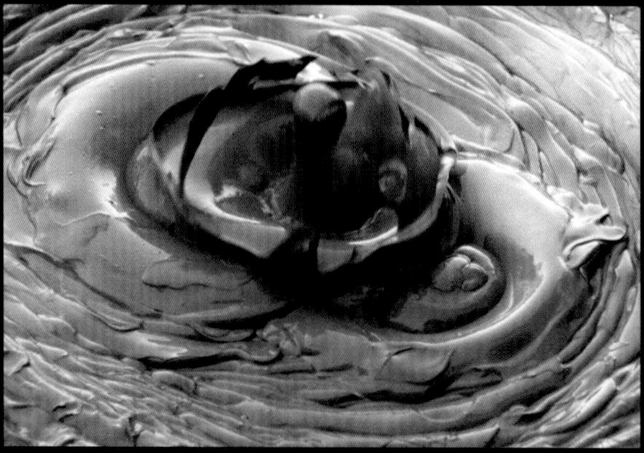

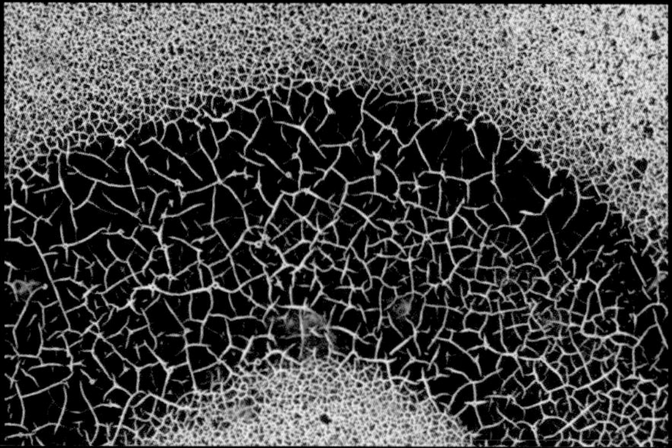

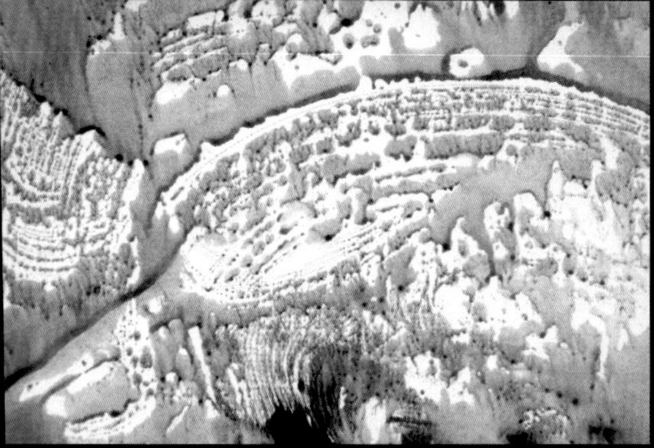

« Monoprint (paper squeezed against wet paint).

‹ Stencil (cut paper) spattered with paint flicked from the bristles of a toothbrush.

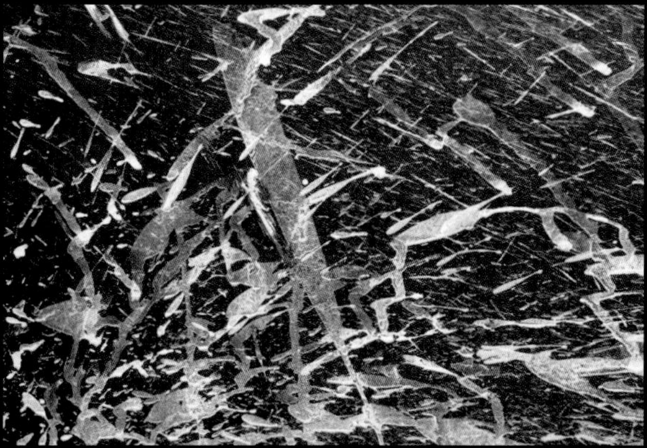

« Paint scraped back with a palette knife.

‹ Spatter.

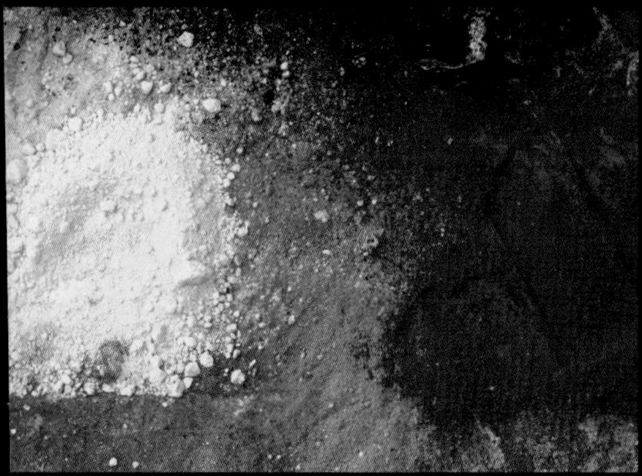
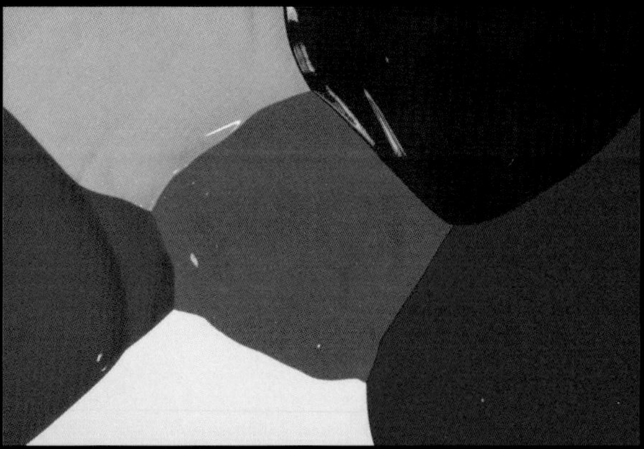

« Powder pigment.

‹ Paint poured into a dish.

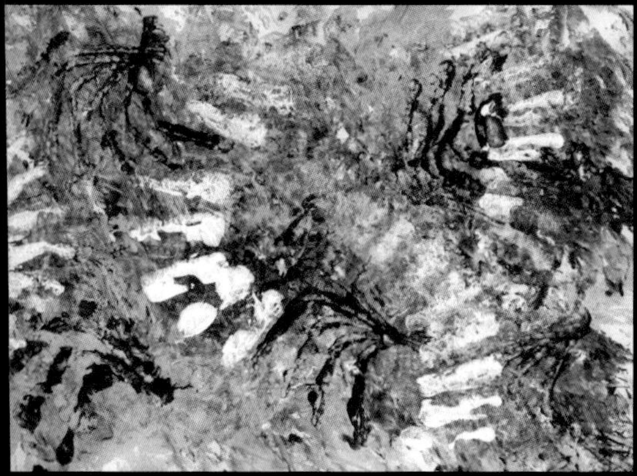

« Paint dabbed onto paper with a rectangular object.

‹ More dabbing, including the zigzag edges which are from a pattern cut into a potato.

« The foreground has been dabbed with a piece of carpet.

‹ Paint applied partly with crumpled paper and partly with the edges of paper.

Weezil transforming into 'pattern'.

Our response to pattern is so astute that we barely notice it happening. Attributes such as 'personality' and 'artistic style' are labels which relate to complex patterns but we can identify them with surprising ease. 'Body language' is a response to patterns which we learn through experience and utilise with great skill.

The Western tradition of education has had difficulty with fields such as 'art' and 'body language' because they don't fit comfortably with our convergent, linear approach to measurement. One of the consequences is that we sometimes trick ourselves through symbolic thinking. For example, I read of an experiment conducted with Aboriginal and European children in Australia. The task was to memorise the placement of 16 items on a grid of squares. The first items were things like keys, pocket knives and so on. Both groups did equally well. The second set of items were stones and the Aboriginal children had no difficulty but the Europeans floundered. To the Europeans, a stone was a stone. For the Aboriginals each stone had individuality – they could see beyond the name/label/symbol to the thing itself.

Take the patterns as far as they will go.

My interpretation of the experiment is that the Aboriginal children were better equipped to move between specifics and generalisations. They could choose whichever approach was more useful, whereas the Europeans were more limited. Art is a bridge which can integrate the two approaches.

Another bridge is mathematics – not a first choice for many artists, but mathematics is the study of all possible patterns. Art, from this point of view, is a branch of maths.

Computers, with their massive power to manage numbers, have built an elegant link between linear and pattern thinking. The link enables artists to use computer software to generate clouds, trees, oceans and synthetic planets. It also provides a means of bringing dead film stars back to play new roles, which is weird and shows how far mathematics has developed since Pythagoras and the square on the hypotenuse.

The exploration of pattern isn't only about images, it can take us all the way to the deeper workings of the universe.

35 Generate some of your own patterns, either drawing from objects you have collected or creating new patterns with paint. As you play with patterns you inevitably head toward the essence of things. I'm reminded of the Islamic approach to art, which has sought 'essence' rather than 'representation.' In particular no representation of God is allowed. The Hindu tradition sees our day-to-day reality as 'maya,' an illusion. It doesn't mean that you will win an argument with a fast-moving ten-tonne bus if you treat it as an illusion, but when you delve into the mystery it turns out that we are patterns of energy. Atoms consist mainly of nothing – they are as empty as outer space. A collision between a bus emptiness and a human emptiness tends to result in a funeral but art, science and religion share an interest in what happens beneath the obvious. Art may help you decorate your living room or take you to the essence of life. Perhaps it can do both at once.

As you play with patterns you inevitably head toward the essence of things

As you delve into pattern you might find that 'form' is an optional extra. Maybe paint – or whatever materials you use – will take on a life of their own.

36 Create a finished work in which pattern is a major feature. 'Finished' means that the pattern holds together in a way that has integrity. The American artist Paul Gardner said: "A painting is never finished – it simply stops in interesting places." A 'finish' is both arbitrary and real. It's a point of change, like crossroads or the point at which a stream merges into a river.

In the photograph the 'finish' of the water is the point at which the force of gravity and the force of the fountain are exactly equal. For an instant the water stops. In art we take an idea as far as it will go.

CHAPTER 3

Creativity: thinking for a change

Your greatest work of art might be yourself. The drawing is a beginning to finding out who you are. The purpose of this section is to learn more about yourself, your motivation, your deeper goals, and how to get into the pattern of creativity for the rest of your life.

Values and principles provide a formula for getting the best out of your energy. You're leaking energy if you'd rather be doing something else, or if you dislike yourself, or if you're blaming others for the way things are.

Here's the gist of the TLC 'class agreement':

1. Treat yourself with kindness and generosity. Take breaks as you need them. If you're getting stale, do something different.
2. Work with commitment and trust, even where things don't make sense, or feel uncomfortable. Be aware that frustration usually plays a part in good learning.
3. Be supportive.
4. If a problem arises, tell someone who can take action (and suggest a solution). If you don't communicate, it's your responsibility.
5. Focus on what works. Ask for what you *want*. Use your energy constructively.
6. Avoid blame and justification.
7. Recognise that if you stay safe, nothing will ever change (learning invites risks and mistakes – view each mistake as a gift that will teach you something if you choose to own it, and which will return if you reject it).
8. Work with patience, persistence and playfulness. Acknowledge that the only difference between success and failure is quitting. Difficulties often signal that something useful is brewing!
9. Participate! The more you give, the more you will receive.

If you don't communicate, it's your responsibility

◂ Artist: Fritha Burgin.

The agreement is a navigation tool for living effectively. There are many different ways to express the underlying ideas and you might like to weave it together with your own belief system.

If you're being a loving parent to yourself you'll be patient

Little changes may look like mountains

37 Try some writing with your 'other' hand. What does it feel like? Chances are that it's awkward, even though you know how to write. If you want to test yourself further, look at these letters in a mirror and draw a line between the outlines.

ART

38 Try writing with the computer mouse. Many of the skills we take for granted are 'body knowledge'. It's as if your writing hand knows the 'doing dimension' of writing.

When you learn a new skill, like drawing or painting, it takes time for the body knowledge to catch up with ideas that may seem simple to our cerebral brain.

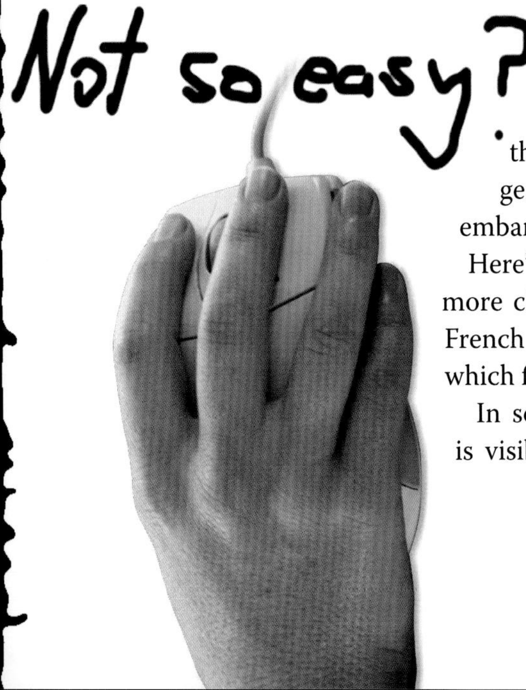

Children cope well with the slowness of learning but adults may find it frustrating. It throws us back into being a clumsy child. If you're being a loving parent to yourself you'll be patient! The skills of art and creativity are no harder than the skills needed to understand these words. Nurture them gently and they'll emerge over time. Have a chuckle at the embarrassments that occur along the way.

Here's a major difference between children and adults. Adults have more choices, even if we're not so pliable. We can choose to learn French or dentistry or algebra. We also have the tools to make choices which fit well with our own qualities.

In some areas (sports, music, maths, computing skills) aptitude is visible from an early age. Sports experts can test children and

estimate whether intense training is likely to produce a champion performer. So far there are no reliable tests to predict success in art and creativity, probably because the possibilities are so vast that they go beyond the limitations of conventional testing.

You can nevertheless make intuitive decisions which may be better than all of the tests in the world. The next exercise is a major exploration of intuition and the goal is to get clues about the direction of your creativity.

Ideally you'll work with three or four other people, but you will be able to get feedback in other ways even if you have to work by yourself. Feedback is important because it provides a mirror through which we get a different view of ourselves and our progress.

Who am I?

For thousands of years humans have found it worthwhile to use categories which indicate personality, patterns of thinking and body type. The ancient Greeks had the 'four humours' which persist in present-day language through the words *choleric, melancholic, phlegmatic* and *sanguine.* The Greeks were the ancestors of the Myers Briggs Type Indicator and the Keirsey Personality Sorter which are used extensively today.

If you're a mainstream personality the chances are that you'll fit into the world with relative ease because most of our dominant social institutions have been shaped by people like you. If you are a less common personality type these same institutions may feel as though they were designed by Martians.

Howard Gardner (Harvard professor of education) has added another dimension with his concept of *multiple intelligences.* Among other things, he is saying that individuals can have special qualities in areas which are not necessarily captured in regular intelligence tests or by grades at school.

Various profiling questionnaires can provide revelations about your learning style, interpersonal behaviour and career options. They can also make it easier to interact with people who have radically different styles.

I recommend that you explore questionnaires on the internet and try the one in this book. Check:

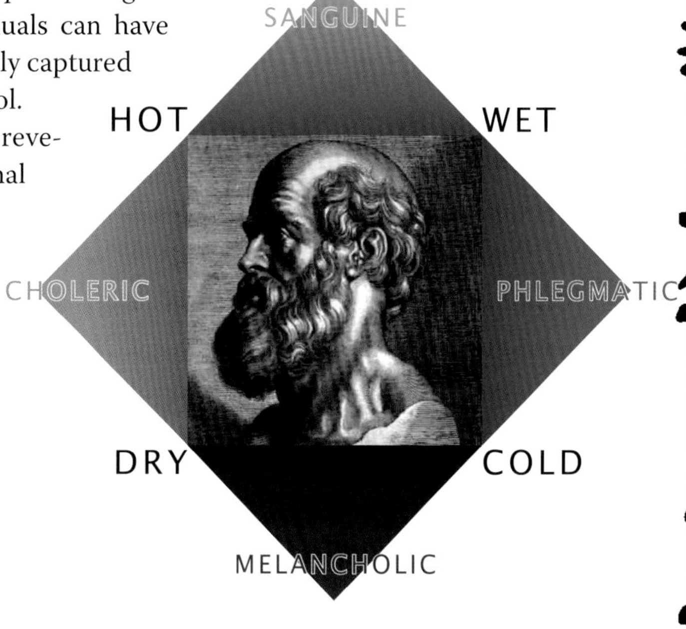

- www.keirsey.com
- www.humanmetrics.com/cgi-win/JTypes2.asp (Jung Typology Test)

Keep in mind that your answers don't place you in a pigeonhole – they're about insight rather than labels. For example, if you do the Keirsey Personality Sorter you might find that you have a big preference for keeping your options open (P). The opposite preference, for closure (J), could be the key to your sustainable creativity. In other words, by completing a few projects (achieving closure) you may arrive at the rewards that can flow from your openness and flexibility.

Personality is like 'handedness'. If you are strongly dominant with one hand you still have another one and you can use it if you choose. Regardless of your score in a personality report, you have *all* the attributes. The report should tell you which ones are dominant at this time.

As a kid I was very right-footed in soccer and I didn't understand that my best training option was to work on my left foot. So it is in personality. The under-used dimensions may be easier to improve than your natural strengths.

If you're a highly intuitive and imaginative artist I don't suggest that you spend a year working in a bank to strengthen your 'left-mode' attributes. If you want to learn more about money management, do it from your natural preference.

My own approach to money is 'big picture'. I enjoy creating beans for the bean-counters to count.

Artist: Mikisu Hall.

Thinking preferences

39 Each of the following words and statements relates to a particular element of thinking. Look through the list and mark × beside those that are most 'you'. Choose 34 descriptions that best fit the way you think.

1. 'big picture' thinker rather than a detail thinker
2. a feeling person
3. a place for everything and everything in its place
4. a thinking person
5. accurate feelings about what people are like
6. analytical
7. artistic
8. believe life should be a daring adventure
9. believe people come before money and rules
10. clear, rational judgment
11. communicator
12. compassionate
13. conservative
14. controlled
15. creative
16. critical
17. detailed
18. devoted
19. diplomatic
20. do it first and read the instructions afterwards
21. dominant (you tend to get your own way)
22. effective organiser
23. emotional
24. enjoy challenging authority
25. enjoy talking with people
26. expressive
27. factual
28. financially skilful
29. find it easy to relate to the feelings of others
30. good administrator
31. good at figuring out consequences in advance
32. good at making things happen
33. good at putting ideas together to come up with new possibilities
34. good at strong, clear and objective argument
35. good report writer
36. imaginative
37. impulsive
38. intuitive thinker
39. like things planned
40. like to test and prove ideas
41. logical
42. mathematical
43. musical
44. original
45. people-orientated
46. prefer clear rules
47. prefer safety first
48. prefer to do things your own way
49. prefer to follow the instructions rather than guessing how something works
50. problem solver
51. punctual
52. reliable
53. respect authority
54. risk-taker
55. scientific
56. sensitive
57. sequential
58. spiritual
59. technical
60. tend to think in metaphors and images rather than specific details
61. thinking, rational
62. unconventional
63. visionary
64. warm, friendly

Score

Circle each number that you ticked:

4	3	2	1
6	13	5	7
10	14	9	8
16	17	11	15
27	21	12	20
28	22	18	24
31	30	19	33
34	32	23	36
40	35	25	37
41	39	26	38
42	46	29	44
50	47	43	48
55	49	45	54
57	51	56	60
59	52	58	62
61	53	64	63
___	___	___	___
A	B	C	D

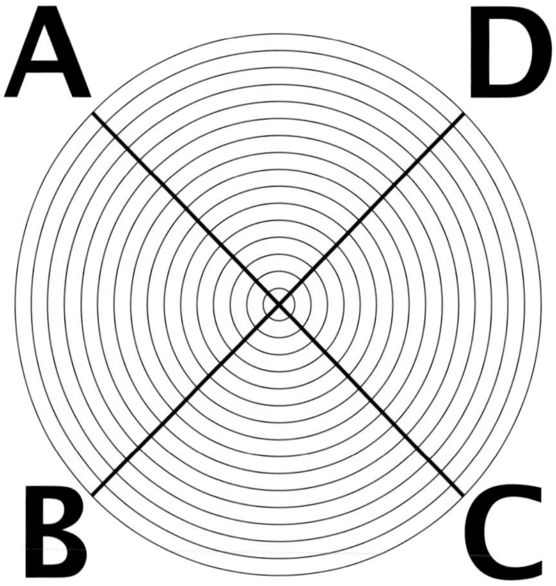

TOTALS
(1 point for each item)

Each of the circles counts for one point (starting from the middle). Mark your A total in the A quarter by making a dot on the diagonal line. Then mark your other scores in their respective quarters. Join the dots to make a kite shape. For example:

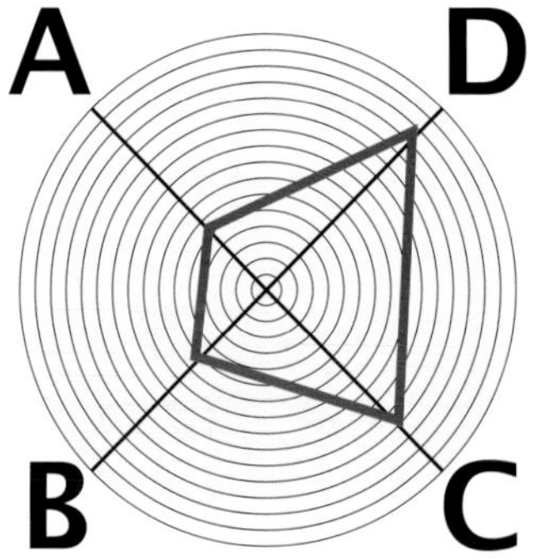

Note that it is an *approximation* and it may ebb and flow according to what you had for breakfast – but it's a useful guide to your preferences. It is ***not*** a guide to intelligence and doesn't tell you anything about the quality of your performance. Someone with a high preference for 'A' might be poor at arithmetic while someone with a low preference might be exceptionally good. On the other hand a high preference in a particular area suggests that you'll be drawn to this particular style and it might be the best starting place to build a wider set of strengths.

It may ebb and flow according to what you had for breakfast

The A/B attributes are 'left mode' and C/D are 'right mode'. In terms of creativity the knack is to achieve integration. If you're biased to C/D it's a matter of having enough competence in A/B to be effective (and sometimes that competence may be provided by your accountant, lawyer, plumber or computer whiz).

For further exploration check

- www.herrmann.com.au
- www.personalityresearch.org/intelligence/sternberg.html
- www.infed.org/thinkers/gardner.htm

Sequential, logical, rational, analytical, factual, theoretical, cerebral, calculated.

The big picture, synthesis, intuition, integrate ideas, anticipate change, problem solving, see patterns.

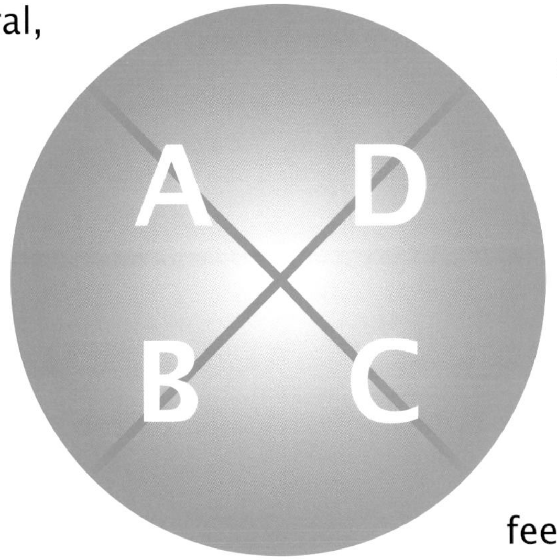

Orderly, consistent, stable, organised, on time, practical, meticulous, firm, clear, everything in the correct place, keeping to the rules.

Values, empathy, interpersonal, anticipate feelings, enthusiasm, persuasion, non-verbal cues, conciliation, warm-hearted.

A wish list

40 Think about what you would like to be able to do in a year's time. In five years? What would you really like to achieve in terms of learning and creativity? What skills would benefit you most? What would you love to do but have always thought you couldn't?

It's helpful to get a core list fairly quickly and refine it over a period of days or weeks. It may help to think in terms of the cues below (feel free to add other categories):

CONFIDENCE

Are there any areas in which confidence would make a big difference?

SKILLS/NEW LEARNING/NEW KNOWLEDGE

For example, if you'd like to be able to use a computer graphics program or fly a plane or speak a new language, this counts as new learning.

RELATIONSHIPS

Do you want/need any changes? What can you do to make the changes?

CAREER/WEALTH

What would you like? What can you do to help it happen?

ENJOYMENT/RELAXATION

Now and future

41 Let's return to the analog tool and this time work with paint. Each new 'doodle' will be about the size of this page. The themes are:

anger ▪ laughter ▪ boredom ▪ love

Move to a larger sheet (about A2) and on one half do an analog/doodle of what you feel about your life now. Include everything that is important – the good, the troublesome and so on. On the other half, do a doodle in paint of how you would like your life to feel.

Example of "life as it feels now" (left) and "life the way I would like it to feel."

It's goal-setting for feelings

There is no right or wrong way to make your analogs. The purpose is to reflect on your life and what it might become. It's *goal-setting for feelings.* Afterwards you can connect the feelings with the practicalities of any changes you decide to make.

Once you've done the analogs, put them aside for later.

An intuitive collage

42 Get a pile of magazines which have no further use. You might supplement the magazines with your photo collection and any other items which have strong personal value for you. Rather than risk precious items, take copies. Keep your eyes open for other things that appeal to you: shells, threads, nick-nacks, fabrics, pebbles, leaves ... anything at all.

Go through the collection and build a pile of images and things that cause a strong response. If you see a photo that excites (or repels), tear it out and add it to the pile. Feel free to be shameless. If you like the crown jewels or a naked body, include them in the collection. If you see something you 'should' like, ignore it unless it excites you.

Feel free to be shameless

When you feel you have an abundance of images/items, pause and ponder your future. Your collection includes messages from your subconscious about what is truly relevant in your life.

ASSEMBLING THE COLLAGE

You can assemble the collage in any way you like (having due respect for the property of others!). The theme is YOUR FUTURE. It will consist partly of the ingredients you've chosen and partly of the way you assemble them. If you want to act out a life of boldness and spontaneity you'll put the collage together in a different way from someone who is keen on order and control.

In our workshops students usually glue their materials onto paper, but some of them get into three dimensions and do some wonderfully unconventional things. Most of them take two or three hours; some get so engrossed that they work all night. The choices are yours.

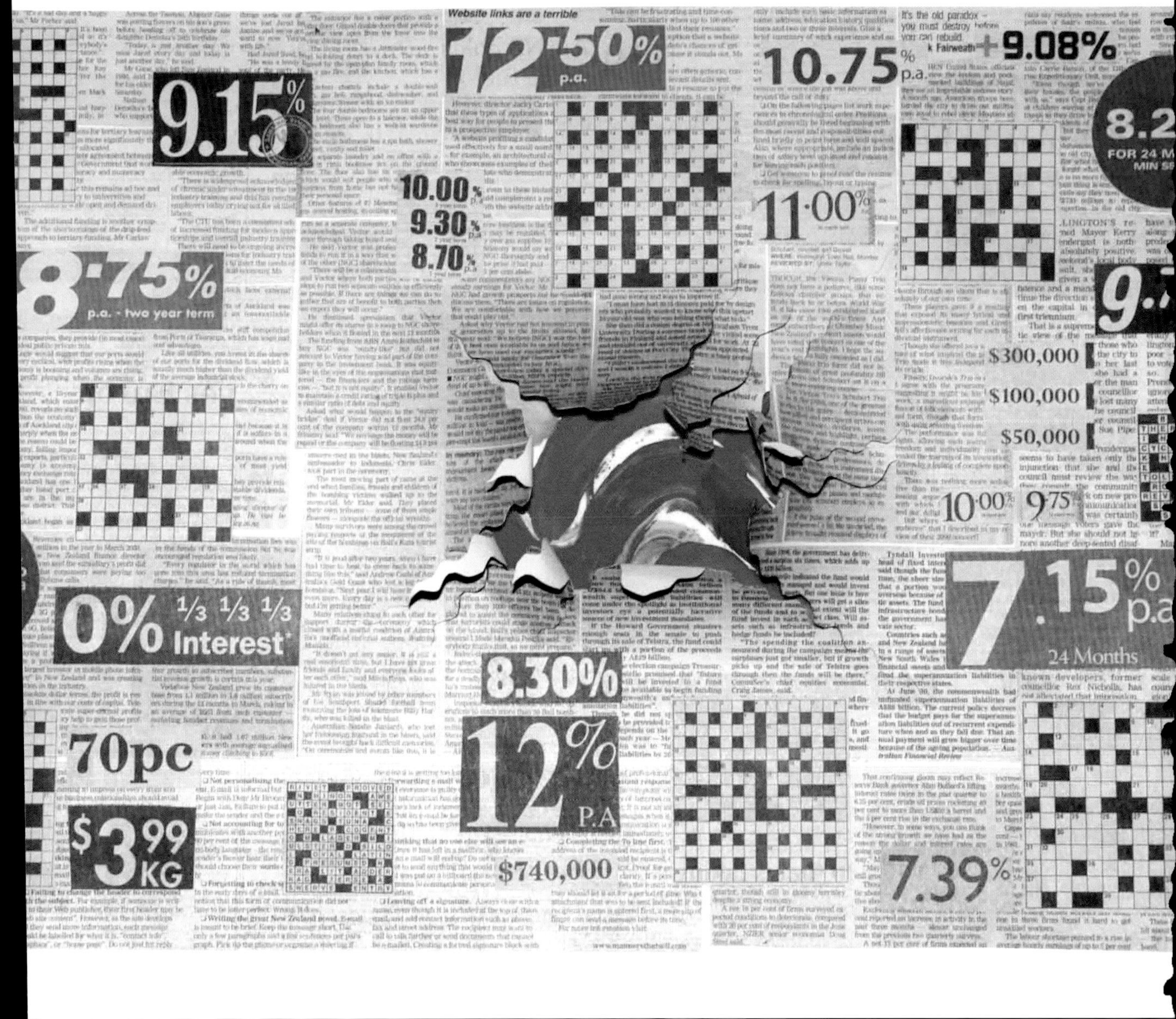

Don de Macedo

Details of collages by TLC students.

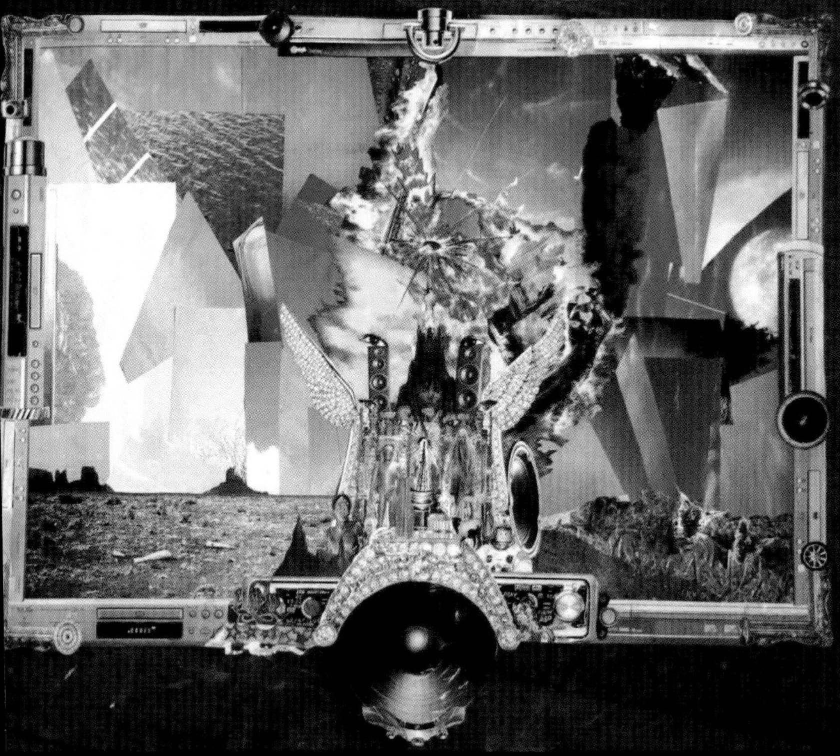

▼ Yen Comer-Hudson.

▲ Dan Mortimer.

◄ Sue Currie.

READING THE COLLAGE

Gather your analogs, personality questionnaire, wish list and collage. Each item provides clues about passion and purpose. The goal of the reading is to bring them all together and do some thinking about where you want to take your life and how to get there.

If you're working alone, the reading could be tough because you're seeking to look behind your rational shell. Try looking at it in a mirror – or upside-down – so that you get a different view.

If you're working with a group, make sure that everyone knows the rules.

1. Go gently and don't give advice.
2. If someone has a 'speed wobble', take it easy. What you're doing can sometimes bring up difficult stuff which tests our ability to have rapport and be supportive. If a person is suddenly distressed by an event from the past it's little different from the same event happening now. What would you do if a friend's mother had died? A parent had been accused of abuse? A person has been diagnosed with cancer? To a large extent our shared humanity gives the answers and enables people to navigate disturbing memories.
3. Have a supply of tissues available.
4. If someone needs more than the group can provide, encourage them to visit a professional and spend further time working on the issues. In a class we normally have an experienced counsellor on hand, although they are rarely needed. Effective listening often turns out to be the most beneficial response.
5. Relate throughout to the values statement (class agreement)
6. The group is no more hazardous than the life experiences the participants bring to it. Be conservative. If in doubt, stop. In a school situation we have facilitators but if you're working independently make sure that you have a Plan B if hazards emerge. TLC takes no responsibility for what you do outside the school!
7. Remember that it's only a conversation, although it goes beyond platitudes.

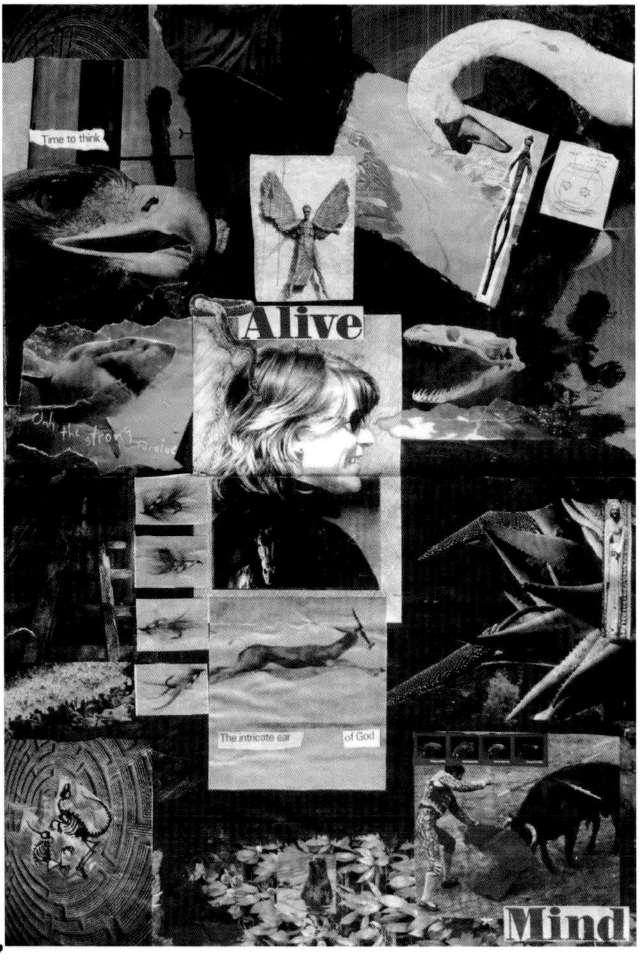

Katharine White.

I begin by asking a student to describe what's in their collage and the rest of us listen and think about possible questions. We also look for anything that stands out. During the conversation someone makes notes, which are finally given as a gift to the person who made the collage. If you're alone you will have to be your own detective and do it all without feedback.

We sometimes disguise our dreams

How has the collage been made? (loose, tight, wild, constrained ...)

Does it point to a particular yearning? (love, turmoil, nature, adventure, tranquillity ...)

How does it relate to people? (Are there many or few people in it? What sort of people? What sort of situations?)

Is there a leaning towards nature, science, humour, art etc?

When you're in a group, the interpretations might catch you by surprise. Other people have the advantage that they can experience your body language, which gives them extra clues. If you look or sound excited about a detail of the collage they can ask questions and perhaps find hidden treasure.

If you're doing the 'reading' by yourself, remember that we sometimes disguise our dreams. Families, friends and communities can play tricks which lure us away from who we are and they might be totally convincing. You see entire nations which maintain limiting beliefs and they sooner or later lead to the emergence of movements such as feminism, civil rights and gay rights to restore some balance.

Within your own family there may be hidden assumptions like "girls don't become engineers" or "boys don't teach kindergarten."

Awareness of self-limiting beliefs is a step towards change.

When you work with others they may help to bring your dreams into the light. Sometimes they are wrong – you are the only person who will know. It's *your* life and you make your own decisions.

Try to keep things on track during the discussion sessions. Initially it might not make sense and some participants may be very sceptical.

Part of your role when listening is to figure if people are being consistent. If someone says they really want to be a bank manager but they sound (and look) flat, then perhaps they don't feel passionate about it at all.

Martine Bairstow and her collage.

If someone gets stuck you might ask: "Could you tell us a little more about the image of ... [whatever it happens to be in the collage]?" You might also say: "What things did you really enjoy at school?" or "Can you recall situations when things really went well for you?"

Sometimes members of the group will have relevant experiences to share. It's a matter of telling the story without giving advice. "When I was in this situation I did ...... Is that relevant to you?" All the time you're leaving the choice to the individual.

It is no one's business to cast moral judgment on anything that is said. You might talk about possible *consequences* but that's different.

WHAT IS THE GOAL? HOW DO YOU KNOW WHEN YOU'VE FINISHED?

Ask: "Are you clear about your goal? Can you tell me what it is?" For example:

> "I'm going to explore the possibilities of teaching computer skills to beginners."
>
> "I'm going to art school to test whether an art career is right for me."
>
> "I'm going to work for a theatre company. If they can't afford to pay me, I can work six months without pay. I love theatre and I'm going to get a foothold somehow."

'Failures' are useful evidence and they may contain exactly the clues we need for our next move

In *Creating Affluence* Deepak Chopra says: *My purpose in life is to heal, to make everyone I come into contact with happy, and to create peace.* It's a good example of the passion we're looking for. It might sound a bit vague but it's sufficient to be a basis of action.

In a group session I'll ask the other participants if a person's goal is consistent with what they've learned during the discussion. If there's any doubt, explore further. Someone might say: "You looked more excited about surfing than you did about engineering." Would they be happy doing engineering on the Queensland coast where they can do plenty of surfing? Perhaps they could aim for the recreational side of the boat-building industry? It doesn't matter whether you end up with the 'right' answer – there may be hundreds of good options. What is important is to identify something that will get the best out of a person's energy because they're excited about it and brimming with optimism about where it might take them.

If you reach a place of indecision – no specific focus of excitement – it's okay to pretend. Try something, like you might try on a new outfit in a shop. If it turns out to be wrong, not much has been lost and you've at least learned something new.

Thomas Edison was an inspiration in this respect. Apparently he tried about 10,000 different ways to make a viable light bulb. When asked (after another failure) whether it was a hopeless quest, he said he now knew another way *not* to make a light bulb. The 'failures' are useful evidence and they may contain exactly the clues we need for our next move. Mostly we learn by doing; the passive genius is mythical, otherwise taxi drivers and hairdressers would rule the world.

A single creative step

Once you're clear on the big goal (even if you're 'acting as if') the next task is to decide on a single practical step that will take you closer to the goal. What do you need to do to make progress?

Some examples:

Big goal: *I'm going to explore the possibilities of teaching computer skills to beginners.* Little goal: Work with a beginner, identify their needs and figure out how you can make a difference.

Big goal: *I'm going to art school to test whether an art career is right for me.* Little goal: Ease my sense of perfectionism by letting rip with a huge 'bad' painting.

Big goal: *I'm going to work for a theatre company. If they can't afford to pay me, I can work six months without pay. I love theatre and I'm going to get a foothold somehow.* Little goal: Write down my credentials so I can show people what I can do, then get out there and start asking for what I want. Hold back on the 'no pay' option unless it turns out to be essential.

Chris Hodge's single creative step. Chris had been badly injured in a road accident and later had a difficult time with a government agency. Someone in the agency gave him a couch, which came to symbolise Chris's pain. His 'Thinking for a change' project was to incinerate the couch. It was a cathartic experience and he went on to develop new skills and a new career. (The project was approved by the Fire Department and people were on hand with extinguishers.)

Craig Miller got fully engaged with paint as a symbolic 'cutting loose'. (Photo by Tracey Grant.)

Rosie Solouota lovingly carved some stone.

Anton Booth invited the whole class to sign his arms as a means of getting to know people in a new environment.

◄ Alison Richardson decided that she'd lived too much of her life behind a mask and offered everyone the chance to have some fun and put colour into her life.

◣ Sarah Tohill (with lollypop) used scissors to move on from the limitations of her school uniform.

▼ Michael Groutsky moved into tactics extending the discipline of engineering into zones of greater freedom and spontaneity.

Do it!

Take action on the little goal and review what happens. If it feels right, plan the next little goal. If it exposes some missing steps, be patient and figure what you need to do to fill in the gaps. If the results leave you feeling nervous, embarrassed, incompetent or incapable, what do you need to do to go forward? These are all normal feelings and usually they are signalling that you're in unfamiliar territory. They diminish with time, and if the discomfort is too intense it's telling you to slow down and pay attention to things you have overlooked.

If you meet an obstacle that is beyond the reach of positive thinking (and positive action) you will probably have to adjust your aim (or wait for a miracle).

Once you get into the habit of pushing your boundaries you'll find that your creativity takes on a life of its own.

You begin to create opportunities which wouldn't have seemed possible.

My personal journey surged forward when I decided to commit my energy to teaching art and creativity. It took so long to get established (several years with no income) that I didn't dream we would produce New Zealand's largest art school or become an influence on global education. I still love teaching art and creativity and that's where my focus has remained. It's fun to be growing a school, employing lots of artists, travelling around the world doing workshops and running a bigger business, but these are all by-products. They feel like blessings from the universe and signs that something good is happening but they haven't changed my underlying purpose.

We've generated a sufficient body of research to show that 'Thinking for a change' is effective. It shouldn't be a surprise. All we do is:

1. Identify preferences and strengths.
2. Establish a goal.
3. Take a step towards the goal.
4. Repeat #3 as often as necessary.
5. Review progress and consider whether your goal should be adjusted.
6. Continue the pattern for the rest of your life.

It's nothing more or less than the creative spiral described earlier.

Artist: Kirsty Jones.

Part 2
drawing on experience

CHAPTER 4

Drawing from life

Life drawing is an old tradition which has become less popular in art schools. Yet it's an experience which can lift you to another level of creativity. Being confronted with a life model can feel even tougher than the problem of dealing with a blank sheet of paper. Life drawing has a built-in sense of urgency (the model can't hold the pose forever) and there is the psychological hurdle of showing that you're at least vaguely competent.

The model in turn is an example of miraculous engineering. When we draw each other we have the opportunity to contemplate our humanness and all that it means.

Students learn stronger drawing skills in life classes than anywhere else. You could achieve something comparable by working with fruit or furniture but it takes longer. Maybe it's the range and interaction of a typical life drawing 'workout' that makes it so much better than an intense engagement with an apple.

There are artists and critics who would say that the discipline of drawing is itself outmoded. They might be preoccupied with more conceptual aspects of art and in some cases they engage almost entirely with thinking and have assistants to deal with any craft requirements. Antony Gormley did a massive project in Western Australia, involving casts of 51 people. Although he had to do a lot of talking the casting itself was entirely computerized. Therefore it is true that there are alternative avenues for working from life, but the life drawing tradition is as valuable as ever. It offers a rich extension to the artist's vocabulary in terms of skills and ideas – and you are entirely at liberty to ignore it.

43 *(Use the images in the next few pages if you haven't got access to anything else.)* At the start of a session try the same exercises in the section on faces. Draw without looking, then with fleeting glances at the paper, then with your non-drawing hand. 'Looking' is important and 'correctness' doesn't matter.

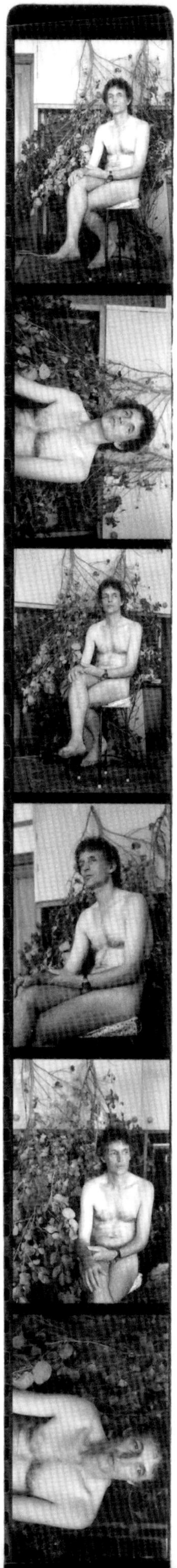

1986 — TLC's first class involved Jonathan as tutor, model and dish-washer. There's nothing like being a model to inform your understanding of what models can (and can't) do.

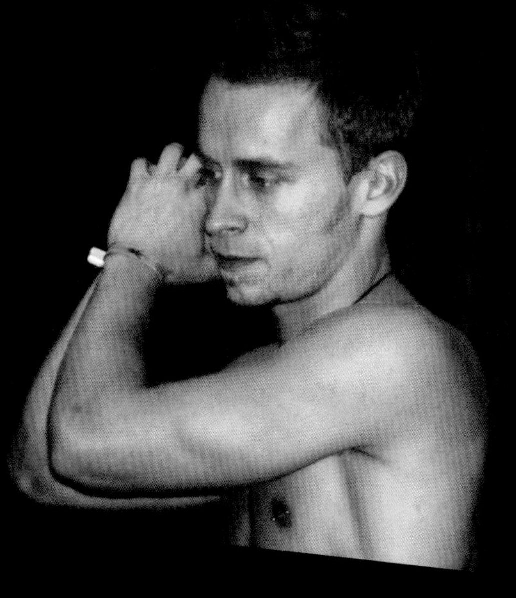
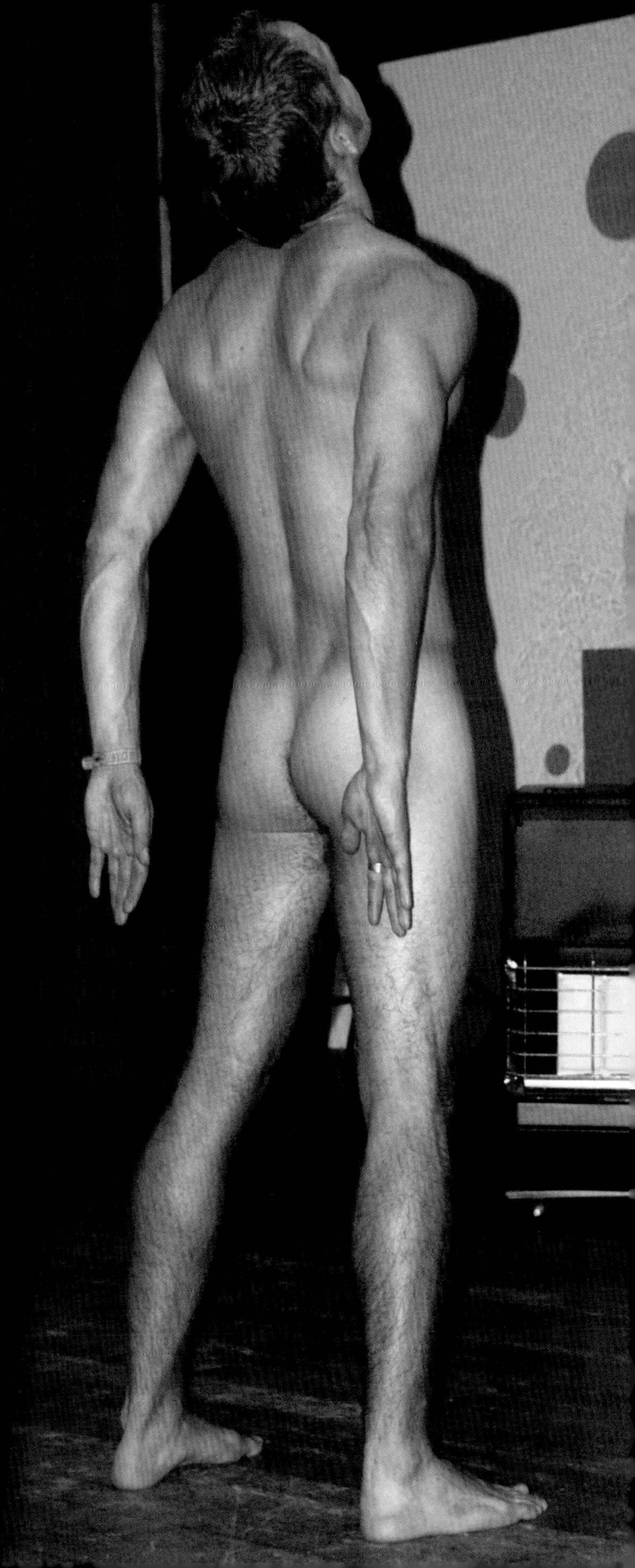

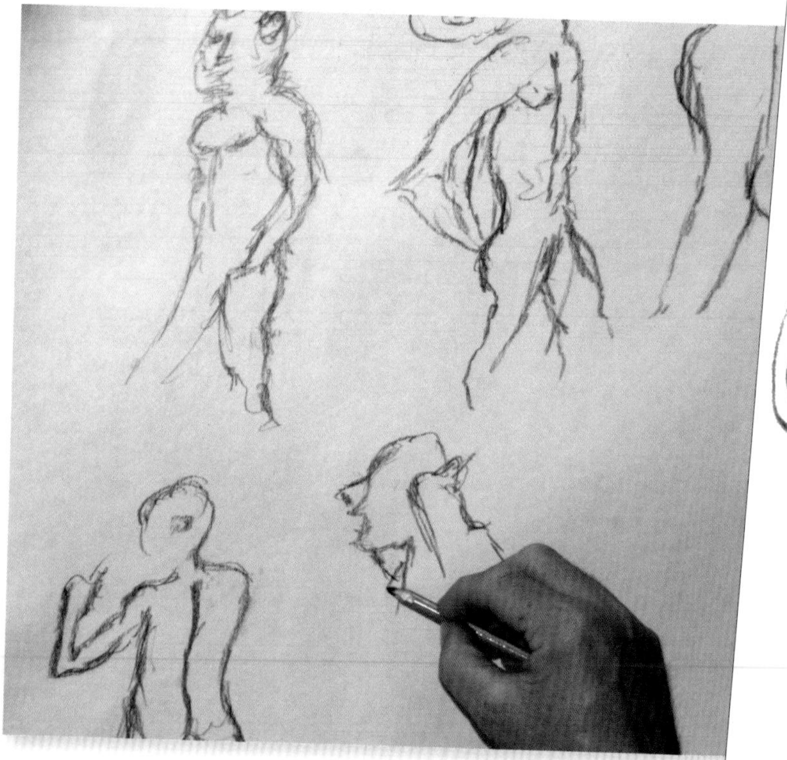

Katharine White — life drawings of Weezil.

A more developed (but fast) drawing using complex curved lines (wiggles if you prefer to sound less technical).

When you've done the drawing, think about it lightly. If you notice that the head is too big, just notice. It will improve next time. It's like learning a new language – concentration and practice get you started and it slowly becomes more fluent and relaxed with use. Criticism doesn't help because it tends to inhibit progress. You'll learn faster through a willingness to make mistakes and notice them without judgment.

Go ahead, be a heretic:

> It is absurd and a spiritual betrayal to copy directly from a model. We must also express the invisible, that which moves and has its being on the other side of a static object, that which is to the right and left of us and behind us. We cannot be content with a little square of life which is artificially enclosed like the stage of a theatre. – *From the catalogue of the Futurist Exhibition of 1912*

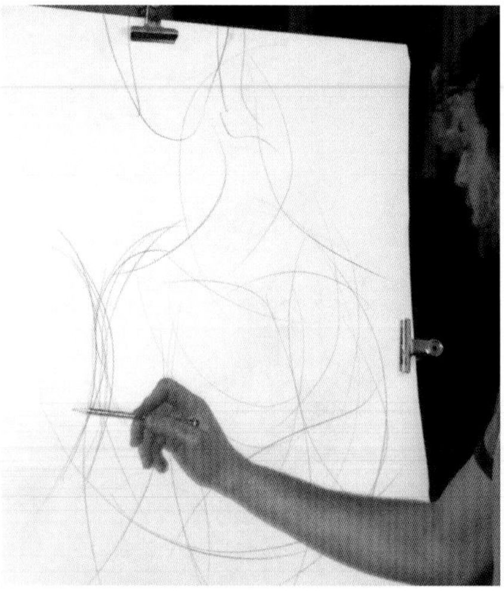

44 *Three lines*

a. Try a drawing using straight lines only. In his demonstration Sandro is working fast – about two minutes – and building form by overlaying lines and using different pressure on the pencil. To turn corners, overlay many straight lines until they give the impression of a curve.

b. Use only a simple curve. Same as before (and it's easier to turn corners).

c. Use a complex curve. The 'wiggle' enables you to build a rich, pulsating drawing.

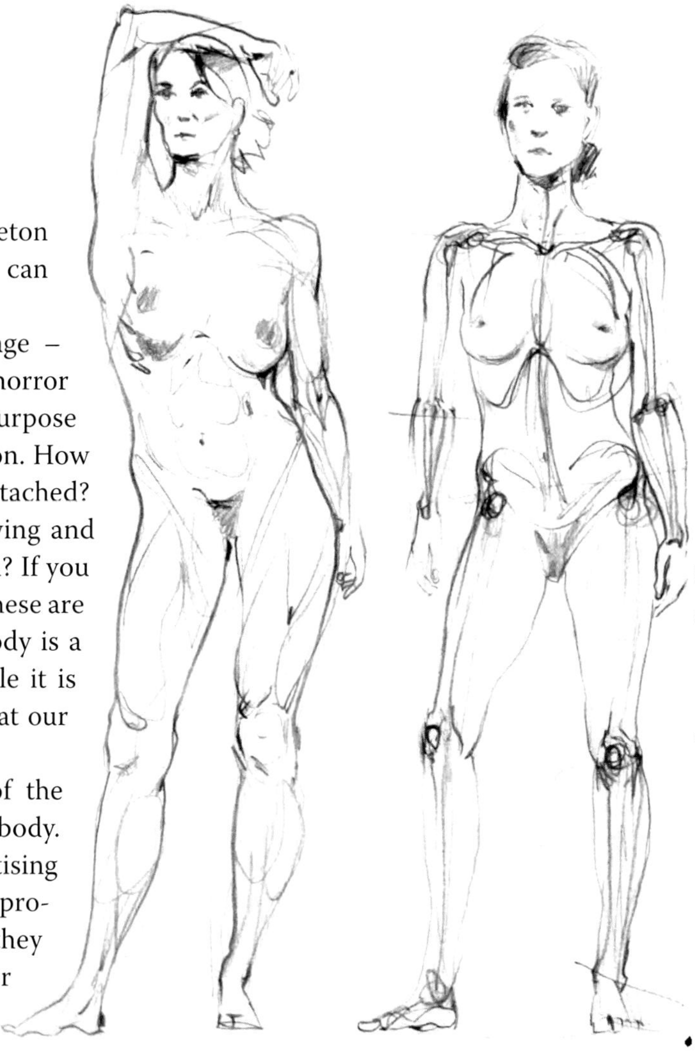

◄▲ Drawings by Christina Earle.

45 *Bones and muscles*

To increase your awareness of bodies, a skeleton and muscle diagrams (or medical models) can make a difference.

Skeletons carry some psychological baggage – they tend to feature as images of death and horror rather than as marvels of engineering. For our purpose it's the engineering that is the focus of attention. How do the bones work? How are the muscles attached? Can you imagine an x-ray view of a life drawing and figure out the muscles and bones of the model? If you want to delve into metaphysics or scary stuff, these are optional extras. I like the thought that our body is a gift and we should get the best out of it while it is ours. The classroom skeleton is a reminder that our 'ownership' is fleeting.

Add bones and muscles to get a sense of the underlying mechanics of the body. Keep in mind that it's like practising scales in music – the final production isn't the 'scales' but they may make it a great deal easier and more fluent. Your own judgment will make the final call and you may choose to depart from the 'rules' if you wish.

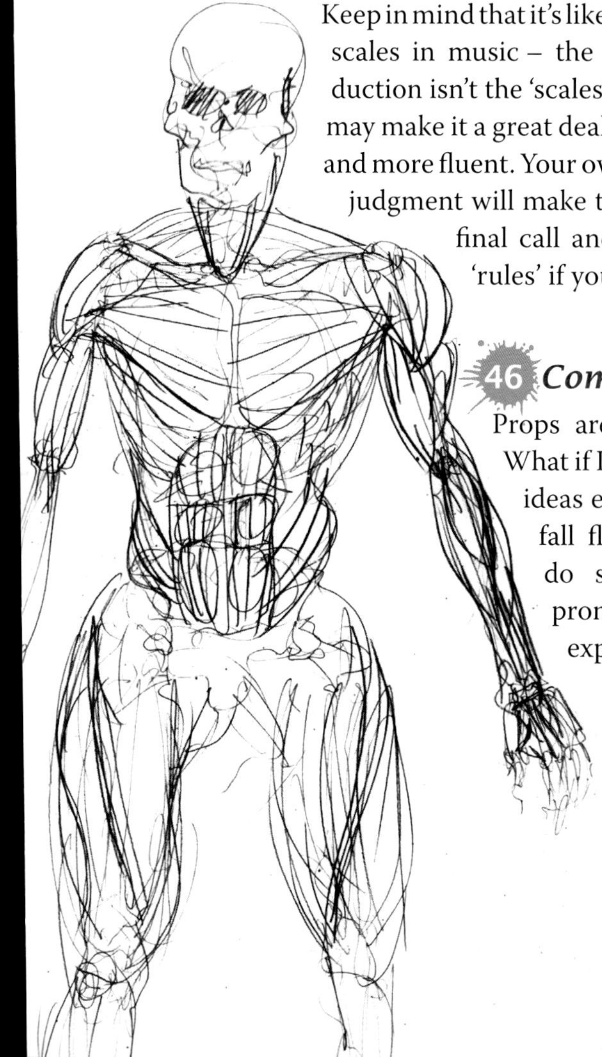

46 *Composition, props*

Props are an opportunity for free association. What if I put X with Y? As you start playing, fresh ideas emerge (and some of the preconceptions fall flat). It's a thinking process. You might do something similar while designing a promotional campaign for an organisation or exploring new ways to combine old ideas.

Play with props. Here the model and the skeleton are linked by a yellow sheet which provides a sort of skin for the bones. The lighting is warm and

Ruth Blair

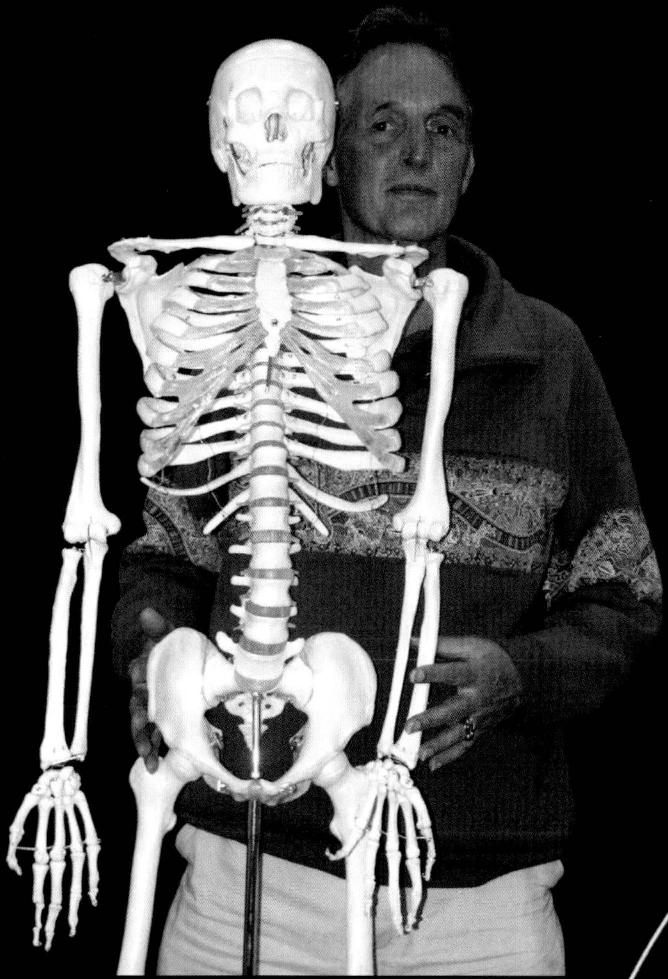

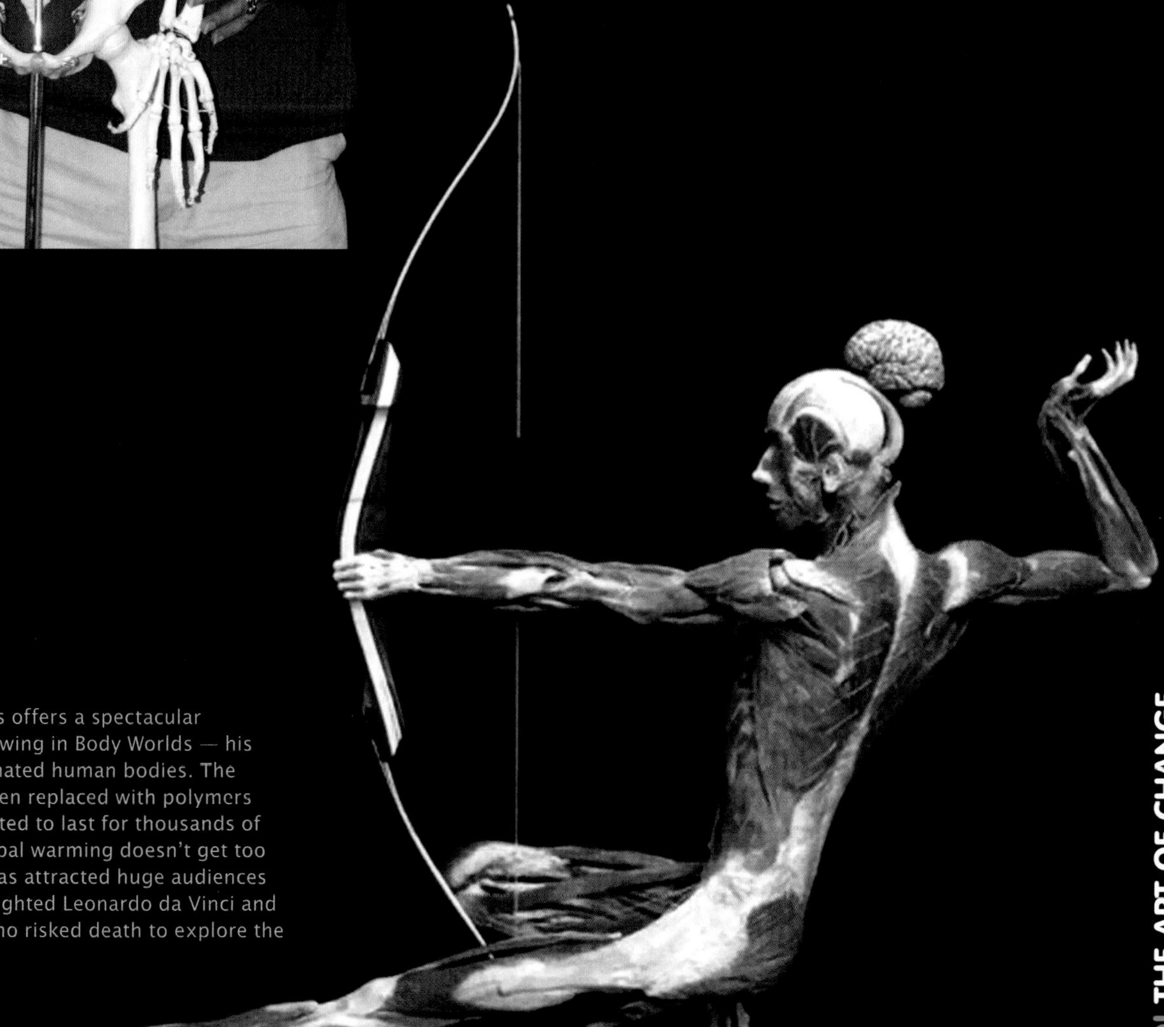

Gunther von Hagens offers a spectacular approach to life drawing in Body Worlds — his exhibition of plastinated human bodies. The body fluids have been replaced with polymers which can be expected to last for thousands of years (provided global warming doesn't get too hot). Body Worlds has attracted huge audiences and would have delighted Leonardo da Vinci and other anatomists who risked death to explore the workings of life.

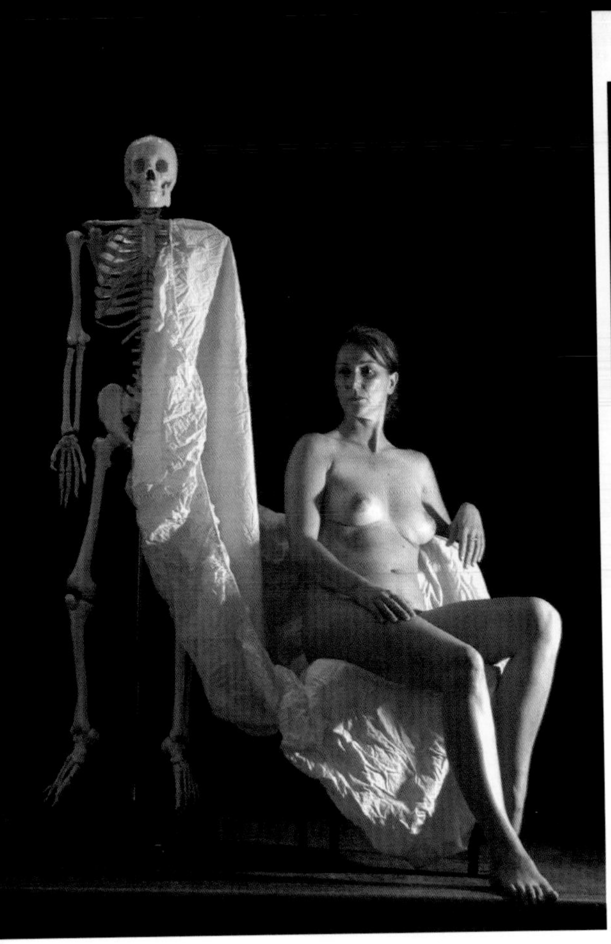

friendly. It's enigmatic – you can read things into it or see it as an opportunity to make abstract shapes. The photo could be an end in itself – life modeling doesn't lead only to paint.

The form of the dog looks fleshy and the nose could almost be a nipple. Dianne joined in with an engaging stare.

47 *Multiple figures*

Sandro has painted a number of couples 'live'. The figures are painted in a single session and further work is done later on the other elements. A project like this demands some advanced skills as well as willing models. Besides composing the people and the props, Sandro is recording the interaction between the models and his own response to them. Despite the artificial set-up (how often do you have an artist working with you as you cuddle your partner?) there is an intense realness that shines through. The pictures have something in common with the Andy Warhol movies in which the subject sat in front of a camera for several hours – the way in which people handle the strain of sitting is part of the result. Warhol sometimes managed to say a lot via movies which hardly moved.

While our life class was happening inside, these guys were mending the roof. If you want natural looking models, look around on warm days. From time to time themes like this have had a big presence in 'high' art.

▲ Sandro and Freeman White challenged each other to do a painting containing thirteen figures. It's as if they'd learned their craft in the Renaissance and put it to work in the 21st century. Sandro's painting (detail above, see also pages 476–7) is based on real people and is simultaneously old and new. Most of the 'sitters' were never together — they participated independently in photo sessions from which the final composition emerged. They are integrated by Sandro's connection with them. The gold leaf at the top adds an iconic feel to an artificial scene which could be bath-time at a commune, warm-up for a nude ballet or a glimpse of an unusual spiritual ritual. Alternatively you can skip any mystery and view it as a collage of life paintings with a few atmospheric effects.

▼ *The Wa's* by Sandro Kopp.

Michael Lobomodrov reflecting on Picasso.

48 *Wild and formal*

Start with wild paint and then include formal ingredients. This is one of Sandro's techniques. Along with the mystery of the razor blades in the out-size hands is the possibility that the smears of paint symbolize blood. The other picture is cherubic by comparison – an angelic child (actually a self-portrait from a childhood photograph) that might be on holiday from a Renaissance church. What is slightly disconcerting is the mix of free, gestural paint with classical representation. It's like visual time-travel and shows that traditional skills can extend the scope of the contemporary artist.

49 *Themes*

Try ideas of your own to create paintings which incorporate a model.

Kiri Saul added a Maori/Pacific stylisation to figures to express sacred sensuality. The arrangement is like a religious triptych or a stained glass window in a church.

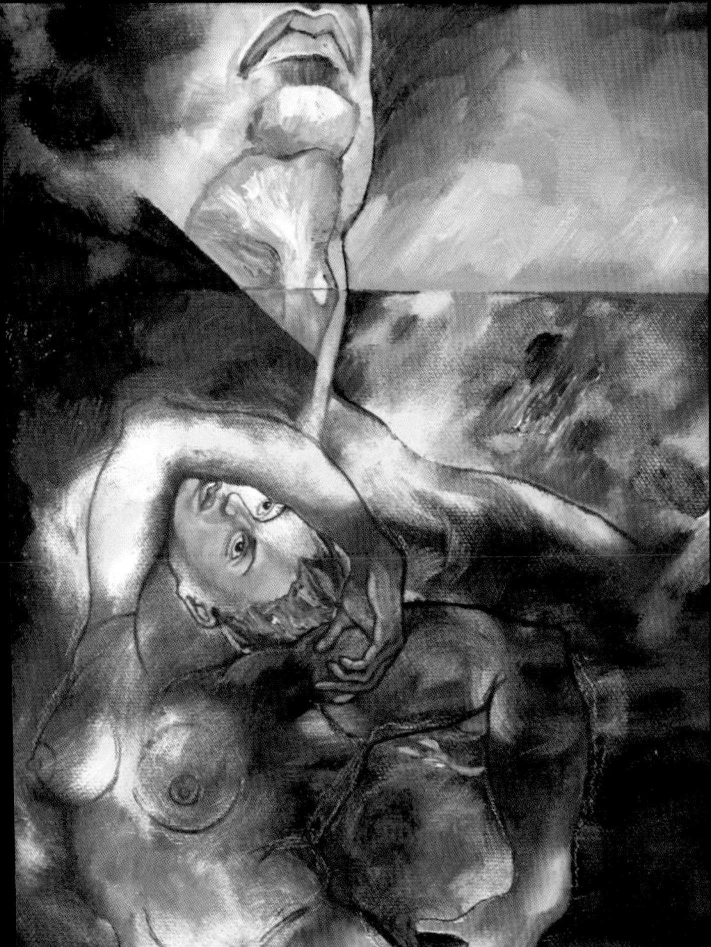

▲ Glen Snow's mix of male and female forms.

▶ A homage to Gustav Klimt (top) and Egon Schiele. Sandro immerses himself in the study of art history and the players — artists alive and dead — take on a presence in his life.

◄ The fetal pose of the model has become the centre of a spiral which links with the fabric. Whether it has a bigger meaning is over to the viewer. (Painting by Sandro Kopp.)

▼ A soft, broody seascape with an unreal shadow. The sea and sky are melancholic and the harsh rocks contrast with the soft, relaxed figure. (Painting by Sandro Kopp.)

50 *Exploring projections*

Projections offer another form of idea association. Slides and data images can be projected onto a model to take things into a different zone. The projection below left is a photograph of city lights and the one below right is from a painting by Natalie Keegan. How do we read the slashes of red and the spots? The model is both subject and canvas, camouflaged and clear at the same time.

From a painting point of view the down-side of projections is that they require subdued light. The upside is that they are a fast and easy way to play with ideas. You can scroll through your digital photo collection and then use a data projector to test the result. The resulting images might be useful for graphic applications (pictures in a book, billboards, advertisements) or they may be stepping stones towards new paintings.

The model is both subject and canvas, camouflaged and clear at the same time

For best results, use a colour transparency and set your camera on a tripod to photograph the projection. A data projector (used here) is relatively coarse and adds a pattern of its own.

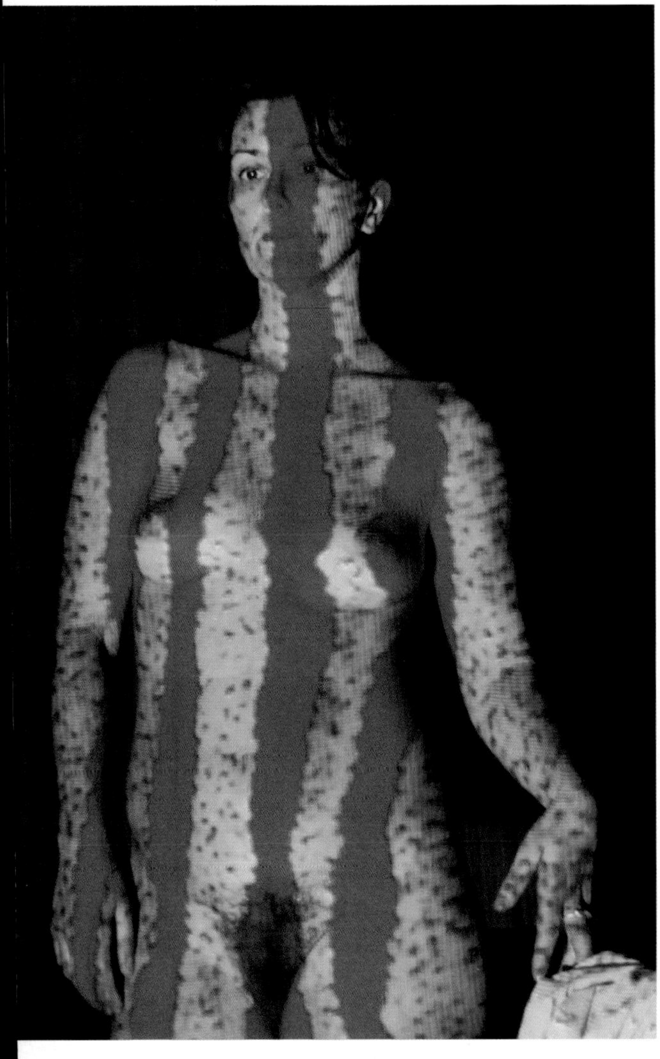

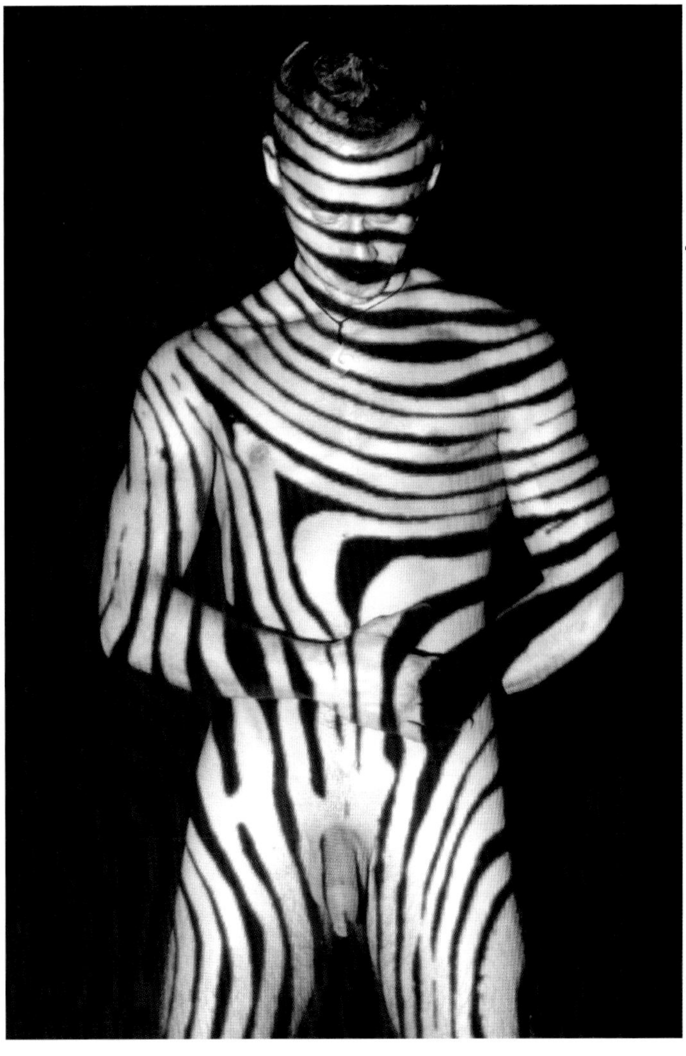

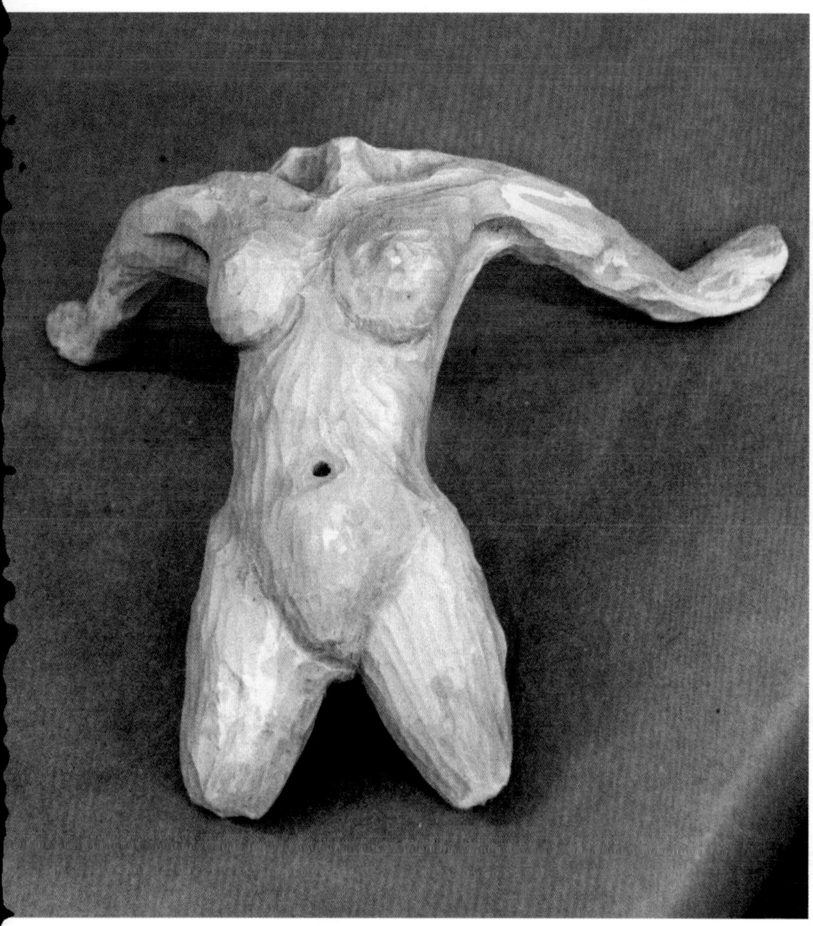

Sculptures by André Brayne.

51 *Life in the round*

Life 'drawing' can be extended into sculpture. The stylized figures at right, by André Brayne, are derived from the human figure but have a life of their own. TLC runs classes in which the students portray the model with clay, wax and other 3D media. It's similar and different from working in 2D – an outstanding option for sculptors who want to cultivate sharp observation and spontaneity. The work on the left, also by André, is a more literal interpretation in clay.

Try some 3D life work yourself. Initially it may be best to keep it quick (like a 3D sketch) but you may feel inspired to take it further.

The important thing is to infuse some urgency into your choices

52 The organic shapes of life drawing appear (albeit a little differently) in animals and landscapes. Edward Weston famously made capsicums look sensual and human. If you want to explore different paths, look around you and choose where to start. The important thing is to infuse some urgency into your choices – just as you have to do when drawing a model.

Life in landscape.

▲ Life in animals (with landscape and clouds as a bonus). ▲ Life in reflections on a car.

Life in clouds, driftwood, and
the billowing shapes of a flag.

TLC tutor Marc Hill with a work by Robyn Manning based on copying.
The technique transposes into design for backdrops in the theatre.

Your artworks are like

CHAPTER 5

Paint and creativity

In Firenze (in Italy), Alice and I stumbled upon an artist making a beautiful copy of a Raphael. It was a commission and he had found that copies earned more than his original art. He told us it was his 26th copy of the same picture but he learnt something new every time and each 'copy' was unique.

Copying has a long and noble tradition in Europe, especially via the monasteries in which literature was copied to enable works to be shared. An apprentice painter would learn by copying and later might do parts of a work, which was finally signed off by the master whose role was more like that of a film director than a solo artist. **The notion of the artist as an inspired loner is misleading** and the importance of copying is under-estimated. I think of it like the creativity of human reproduction. Our personal DNA arrives as a mix of copying and chance. Putting aside the issue of genetic engineering, we inherit DNA from both of our parents. There is a high level of accuracy in the copying and there are also surprises because we can't predict exactly which genes will make it into the cell which becomes who we are.

In art we inevitably receive information from history. Even a completely untutored artist is exposed to visual language, and this exposure produces a sort of copying. Historically the level of copying varies. With the artist we met in Firenze it was close to 100% but even he left a mark of his own personality in the work. With an artist like Jackson Pollock the personal imprint was much greater; nevertheless he was participating in a visual conversation which connected with the art that preceded him.

Self-portrait by Raphael (1483–1520).

Creativity emerges from the blend of copying and surprise. Your artworks (or your inventions in any field) are like new sentences in an amazing conversation. They come from the past and reach into the future.

At a technical level you can discover a great deal by directly mimicking the works of other artists. If you want to learn how Raphael painted, you'll get a lot of clues through copying his work. If you want to extend technical skills into creativity, you'll have to find ways to add some of your own 'DNA' to the mix.

in an amazing conversation

The black and white image consists of tide lines from waves on a beach. Combined with the Madonna and Child, maybe it's an image of 'Life Tide'. I could spend months playing with this single theme while maintaining the imprint of both the Raphael and the tide.

To get started, allow two images to 'fall in love' and then let them 'reproduce'. See where it takes you.

An alternative (and more difficult) approach is to allow yourself to 'fall in love' with the artist's IDEA.

Taking the Raphael again, supposing you decide that the idea is 'motherhood'. The next step is to look into your own world and ponder what this means to you.

The same Raphael might be open to many different themes. For example:

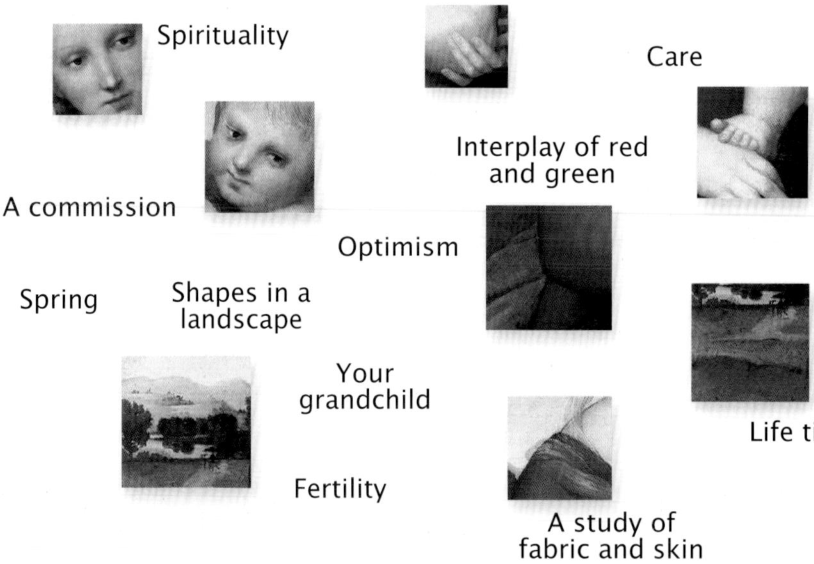

Raphael + X = something new.

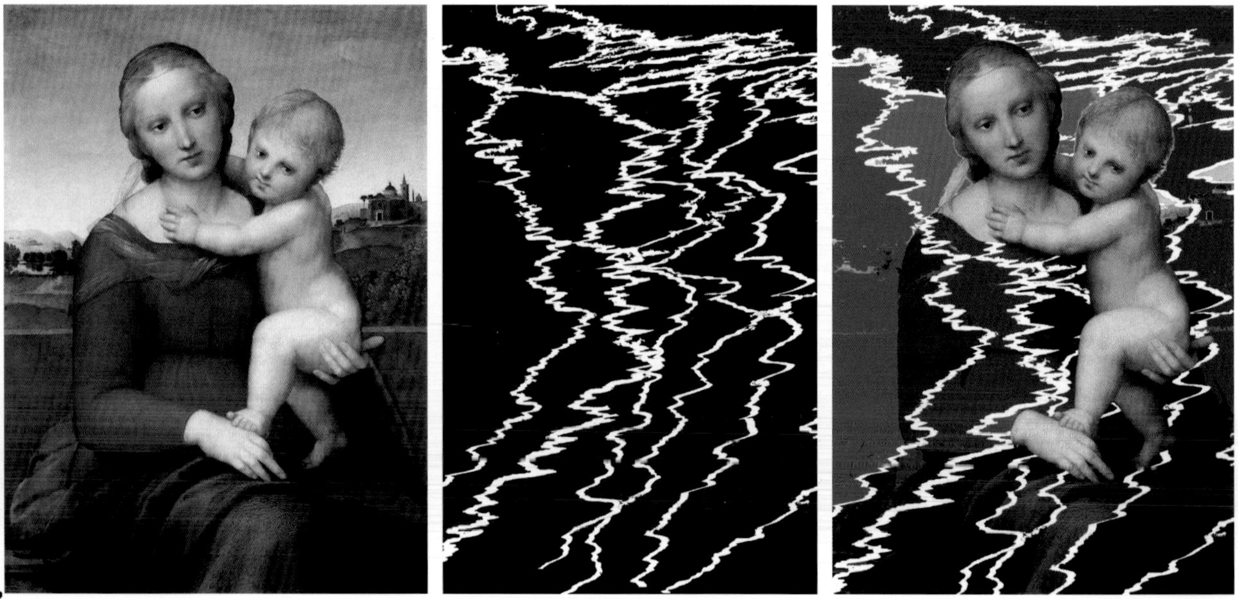

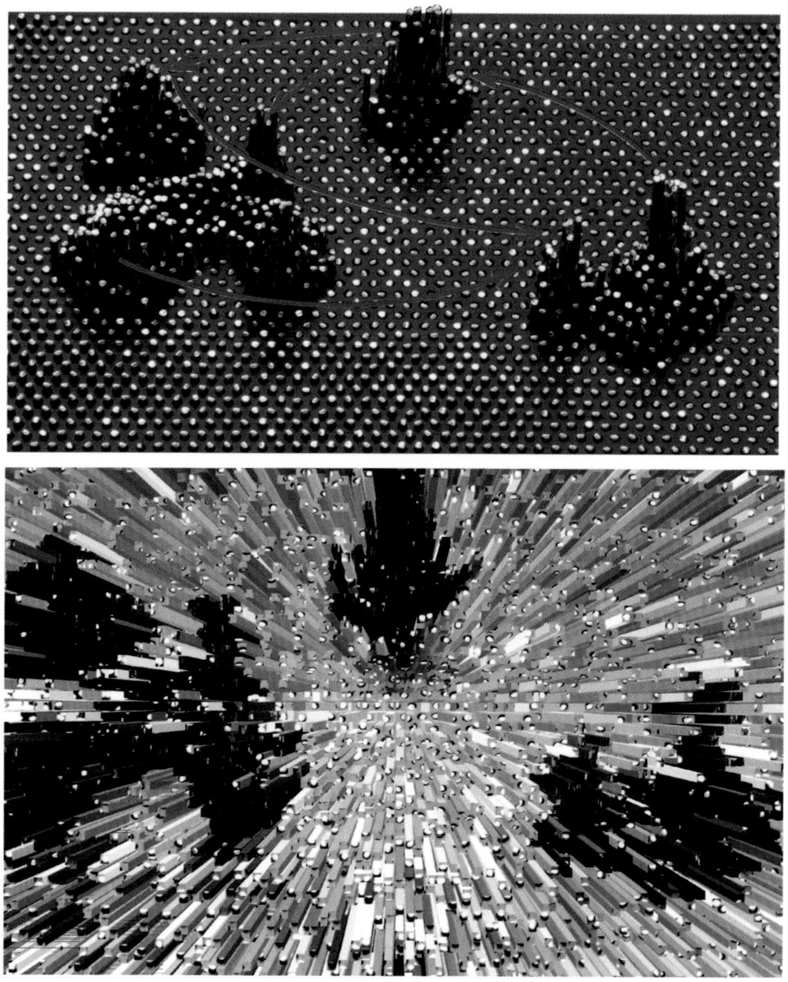

You can think of 'knowledge' as a development of each pin and 'creativity' as new linkages between the pins. The pins grow from learning what is already known (copying) and the creativity takes this knowledge into new combinations. And there can be an infinite number of pins.

And so on. There are no 'right' answers. The point is to choose an idea which interests you and then see what it generates when you combine it with your own thinking. It's likely that the technical elements of Raphael will diminish or disappear but the theme itself will enable you to explore something which may turn into art.

How should you deal with technical challenges? If you can't paint like Raphael, what do you do?

The copying component of creativity is often presented as art and there are huge resources which describe the various techniques. Schools, tutors, artists, books, movies and the internet are available for your questions.

The TLC approach is to encourage people to ask questions, and to support them in their search for resolution. Rather than prescribing a set of techniques, we offer some basics and then encourage students to be adventurous. We provide technical direction, if it's needed, when the process is under way. Tutors have to be enormously flexible and open, while at the same time having a wide grasp of practicalities.

From a learner's point of view you have to think for yourself at a time when your vocabulary of skills and experience is small. It's a matter of trusting yourself, as a child might, and just doing it. The doing, repeated and polished over the years, is the real response to the underlying questions. There are seldom any fast answers and the elusive quality called *technique* emerges over time.

Feel free to be ambitious. It's good to follow the example of young children who take on audacious projects undaunted by their technical limitations. If you can't yet draw and paint like Leonardo, try painting like yourself (that's what kids do – they've not heard of Leonardo and they get on with the job).

Here's an approach to use existing works of art as a launching pad for your own creativity. Take what you like and leave the rest.

It's good to follow the example of young children

Susan Knaap.

What is the idea behind Susan Knaap's work (at left)? My guess: It's a still life using bold colours and strong geometry to express the artist's feelings.

53 Set up your own arrangement(s) and try the same idea. It might start with flowers in a vase, items on a table, clothes draped over a chair ... anything you please. If you're feeling cheerful, work cheerful colours and movements into the painting. You can choose a mood or go with the way you feel. Possibly the still life itself will inspire a mood. Below are some examples

The key is exploration. Feelings and ideas emerge as you play with an image. I started playing with the messiest arrangement in the samples and felt attracted to the bits of orange. Then I sketched in some of the main flow lines in the picture and transferred them to a black background, adding back some of the non-orange bits.

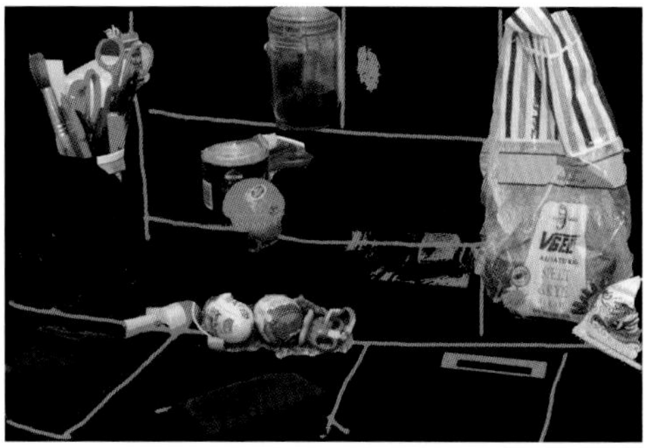

Something is beginning to happen. Is it better with the orange lines removed?

What about drawing?

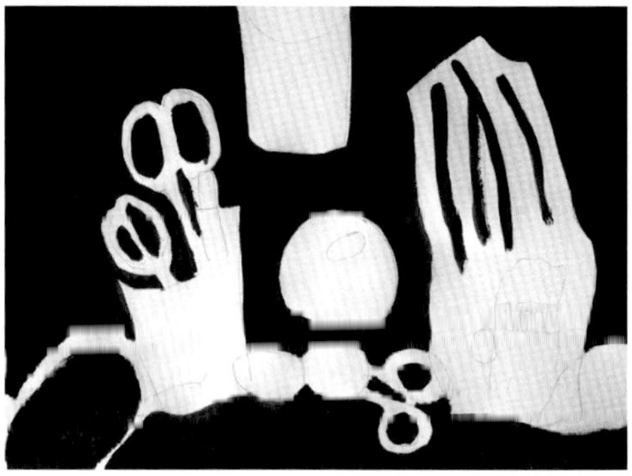

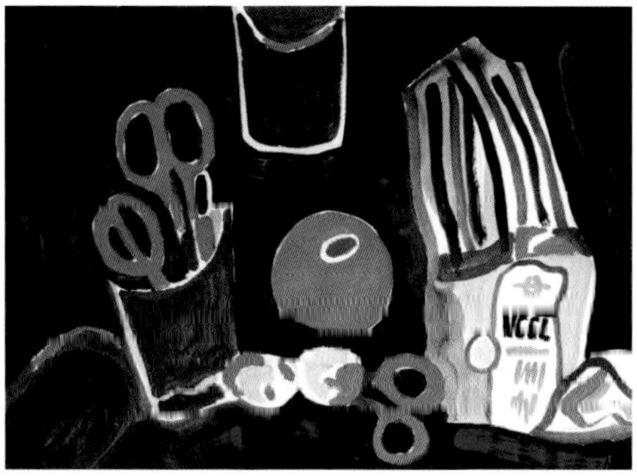

And painting? The last frame is getting close to the original goal: a still life using bold colours and strong geometry to express the artist's feelings.

All the explorations are research. You can keep going until something works. Your work is a conversation with materials and ideas. You may start with certain intentions but the *doing* can take you into new places. So the creative recipe is here again – you begin with a mix of copying and intention, and respond to the unexpected things that happen along the way.

If you sustain an exciting conversation for days or months, the chances are that your 'research' will be captivating. The emotional intensity can build in a crescendo and the endpoint is the possible birthplace of greatness.

Isobel Bird lured students and staff into creating a shared mandala during an Orientation Week.

Composition and tools

54 When you choose clothes for yourself, you're making a composition. When you decide on the layout of a new room (where to put things, what to put on the walls) you're into another sort of composition. Putting flowers in a vase also involves composition.

Why do we like things in one arrangement but not in another?

You can test the idea with photos. Find (or create) a series of five or more pictures of the same thing (a face, a scene ... anything which involves change so that each photo in the sequence is a little different). Which frame is the best?

Is 'composition' about getting rid of everything irrelevant until the picture contains nothing except what you want to say? In the picture on the right the wasp is on a window.

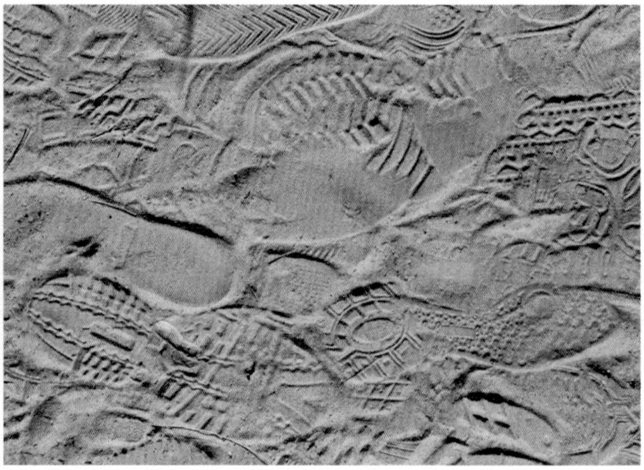

How about a more abstract approach – is one of the pictures of footprints a better composition than the other?

Here we're getting close to isolating composition, because most other factors are equal. Do you have any preference? There isn't a 'correct' answer at the end of the book – it's over to you.

The footprint photos are about choice (the images overlap but are different). I was able to choose from many different parts of the track and I could take the picture closer or further back. These choices are composition.

Use a base of sand (or something similar – flour will do the trick) and make patterns in the surface. Use anything to make the patterns – fingers, cutlery, things from your kitchen, toys, whatever suits. If you have a camera, take photos of various combinations and make choices as you go. Light from a low angle is best for showing the shadows (early morning, late afternoon).

Joan Miró (1893–1983). Photo by Carl van Vechten.

55 Use pastel or paint to make arrangements of lines and shapes – like a doodle. A4 is big enough. Try three or more variations and see how it goes. Check out artists like **Miró** and **Kandinsky** to see how they approached composition (the internet has massive amounts of information). Each 'arrangement' is like a little piece of music. There are many different tactics to get started. For example:

- Make a shape and then add another shape that relates to it. Keep going until it comes together as a composition.
- Look at natural shapes (landscapes, portraits, etc) and rearrange elements that you like.
- Choose a theme (e.g. geometrical shapes) and build a set.
- Using a computer, extract elements from other pictures and overlay them in ways that seem interesting.

Each 'arrangement' is like a little piece of music

And so on. Some will work better than others. With the ones that seem unsuccessful, think about what changes you can make. Sometimes the 'failures' morph into successes.

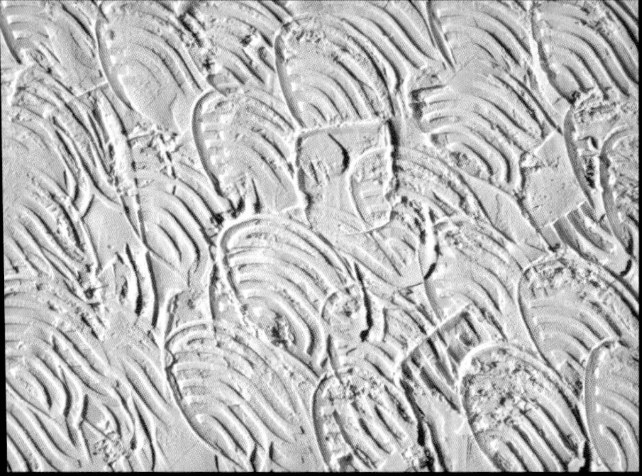

Using flour.

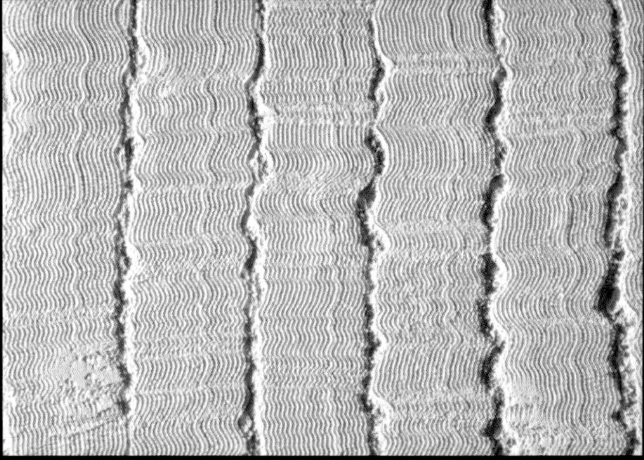

Old tangled rope (left) and pigment splattered on wet paper.

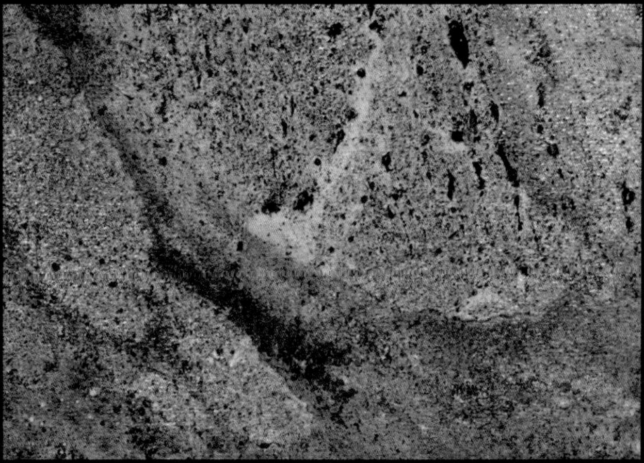

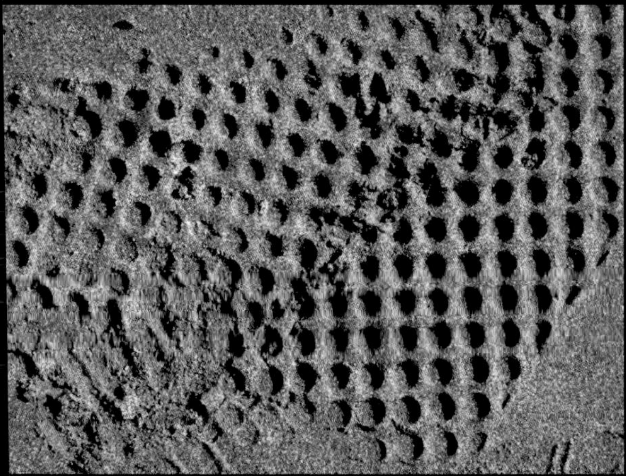

Sand.

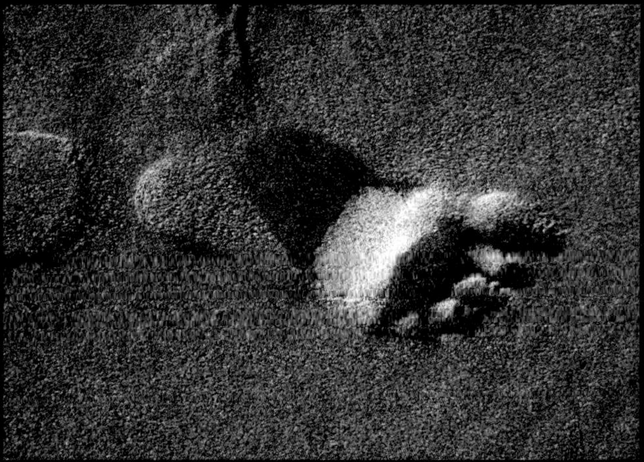

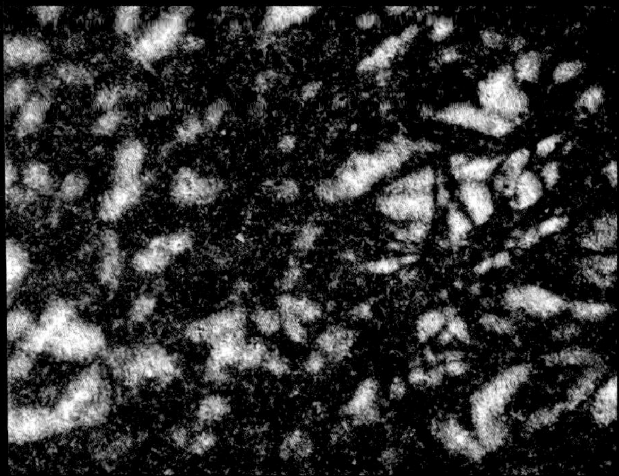

Shadows (left) and tyre tracks.

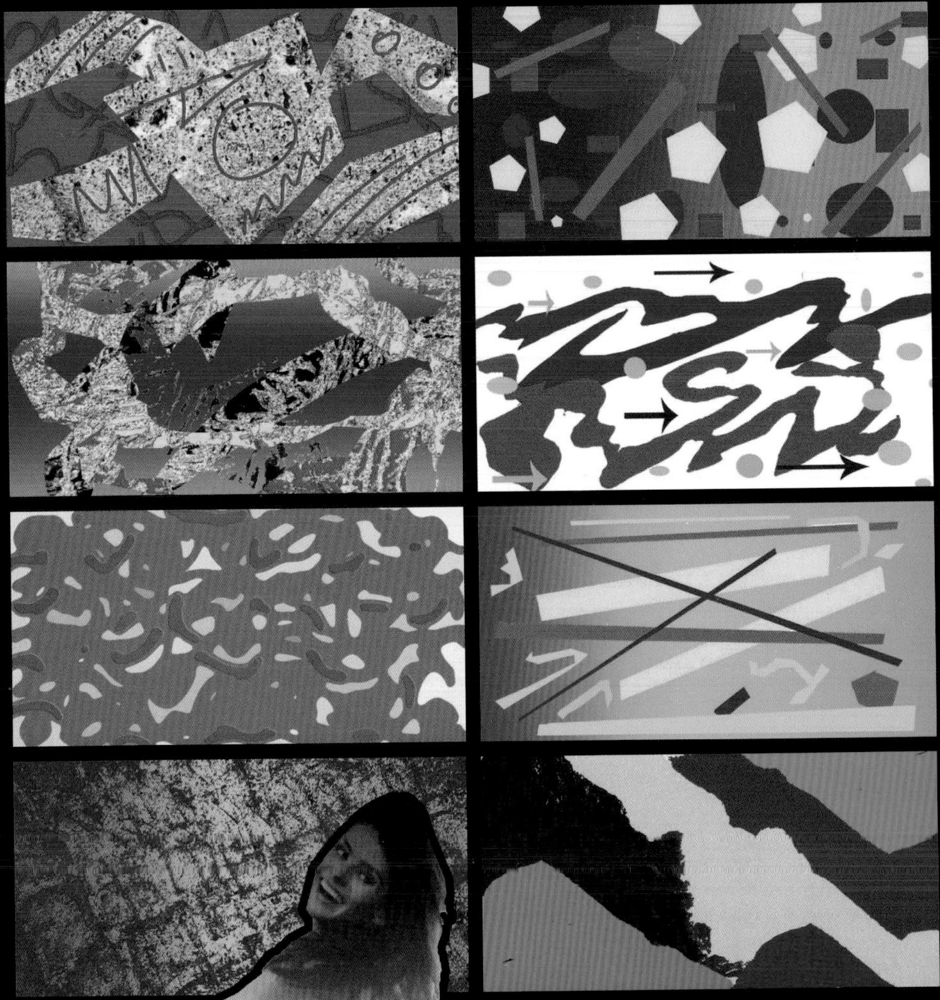

The same process applied to a collage.

56 Cut out a face from a magazine and place it in one of the doodles. What do you need to do to make it fit best? If you want to use the exercise as the basis of a fully developed picture, use the experiment as your guide and grow the work on a larger sheet of paper or board. You can also cut and paste with Photoshop or a similar program and mix painting with computer techniques. The creativity part of it remains similar – "take something, do something to it, get feedback, evaluate and decide what to do next." There's no right or wrong – the intention is to explore and find things that work. It may appear to be random but it isn't – at every stage your own sensibilities are shaping the results and drawing out patterns.

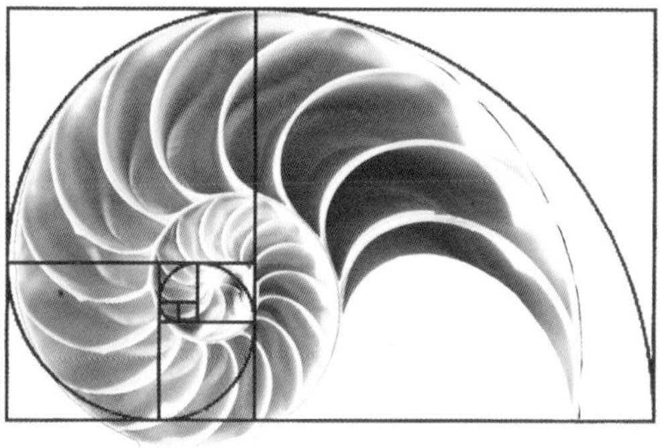

The spiral of the nautilus shell supposedly illustrates the 'golden ratio' (red lines). A real nautilus (photograph) probably didn't read Greek and has its own ratio.

We're making an organic exploration of composition. If it connects with theory, that's fine. If it doesn't connect (but still gives a result that you like) then it's time to review the theory. For example, there's a lot of compositional theory around the 'golden ratio' (approximately 1:1.62, the same ratio that appears in structures like the nautilus spiral – see diagram). The 'golden ratio' (see en.wikipedia.org/wiki/Golden_ratio) has a particular elegance but it's part of a very selective conversation. Mostly our visual conversations engage with things that don't fit the 'golden mean' and it would be a needless limitation. Likewise other theories may provide neat ways to systematise composition but they are inclined to stifle the complex experiential learning that takes you directly to things that work.

The face has been added via Photoshop rather than with cut paper but the principle is the same. Colours from the 'background' (painted paper ripped and arranged) have been 'stolen' into the face.

Again a mix of Photoshop and 'real' materials. The base is pigment thrown onto wet paper and glue. The fingerprint was initially real and the photo was placed behind it. Is there a 'background'? Is it aesthetic? Is the 'golden ratio' present? When I was making the image I wasn't responding to questions, I was making choices about how to present an idea. The questions came after the answer.

Tools

You don't need brushes to make paintings. You can use just about anything. Kitchens are full of painting gear and so are workshops.

57 Test at least ten different tools on a small scale (postcard-size is fine) to see how you can use them with paint. Possibilities:

- Cardboard (especially the edges)
- A dishcloth
- Pot scrubbers (there are several different kinds)
- Scrubbing brushes
- A sponge
- House painting knives
- A plasterer's trowel
- A 100mm house-painting brush
- A sliced section of potato or carrot
- Fabric (including coarse material such as sacking)
- Toothbrushes
- Combs
- Leaves
- Shoe soles
- Carpet scraps

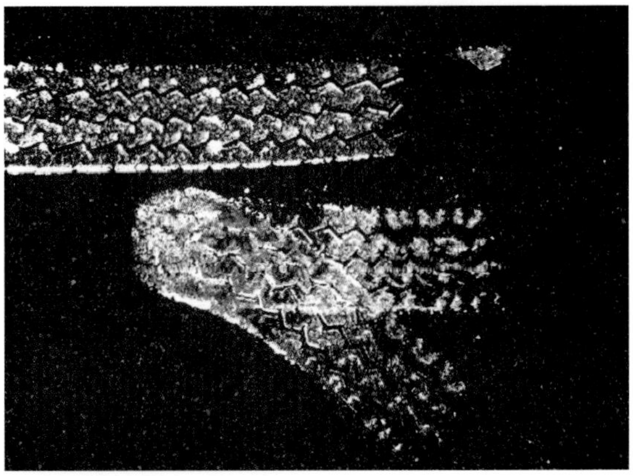

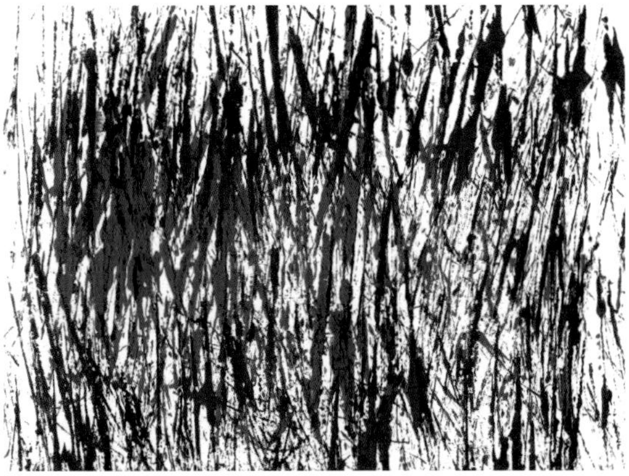

◂◂Car tyre and paint on pavement.

◂Grass dipped in paint and printed.

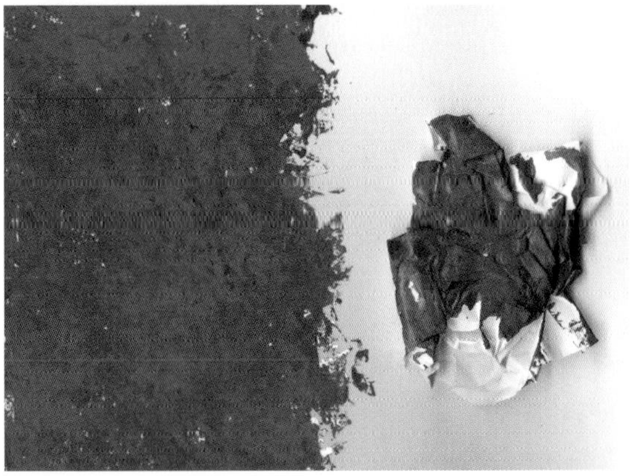

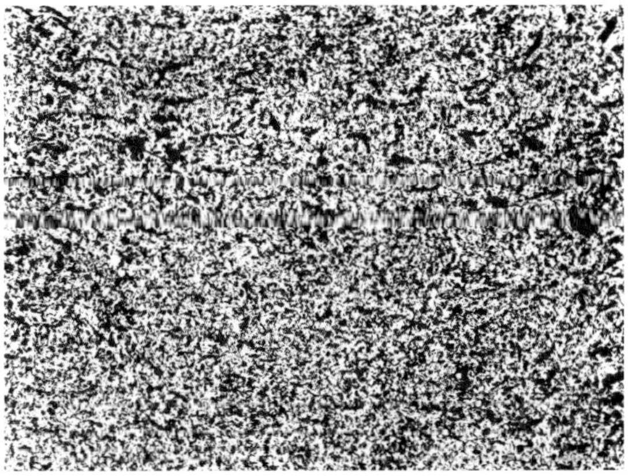

◂◂Paint applied with crumpled paper

◂Paint applied with a kitchen 'Goldilocks'.

◂◂Different results using paper.

◂Using a large trowel.

The creative tactic is to take something basic (paint) and explore what happens when you apply it with different tools. When you do your experiments have plenty of space available for drying them (and a rubbish bag to take the bits and pieces that you don't want to keep). Get right into it! Some of the tools will be surprising and the only way to find out what they do is to use them. Some of the works will give clues which could lead to more developed art.

58 Build an entire picture, abstract or representational (or a mix of both) without using any conventional artists' brushes. The goal is to apply some of your tools to get an intentional result.

Double textures partially blocked by a stencil.

A stencil (the inner piece can be used too).

Rosemary used for texturing.

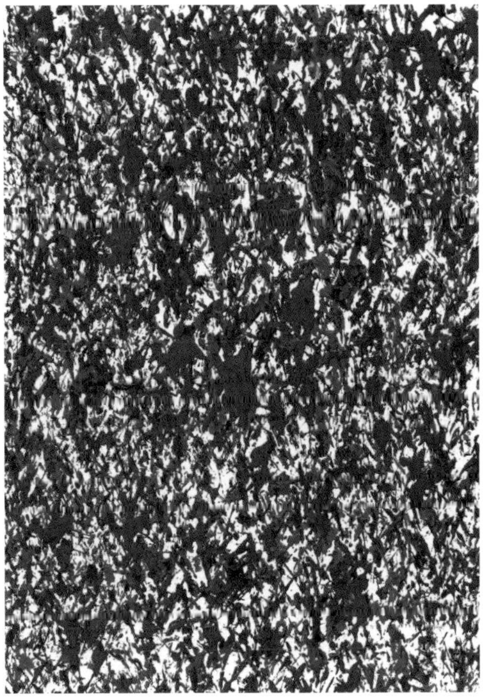

Rosemary texture.

Composite using the rosemary and crumpled paper images via the computer.

Maybe all patterns (by accident or intent) carry messages which go beyond the patterns themselves

Crocodiles and other patterns

In chapter 4 we began some work with 'analogs'. An analog is a pattern which connects with feelings/thinking through a visual expression. Maybe all patterns (by accident or intent) carry messages which go beyond the patterns themselves. Not everyone likes crocodiles but the ones in the picture are being grown for their patterns which are going to be transformed into expensive fashion accessories

Oyster catcher eggs.

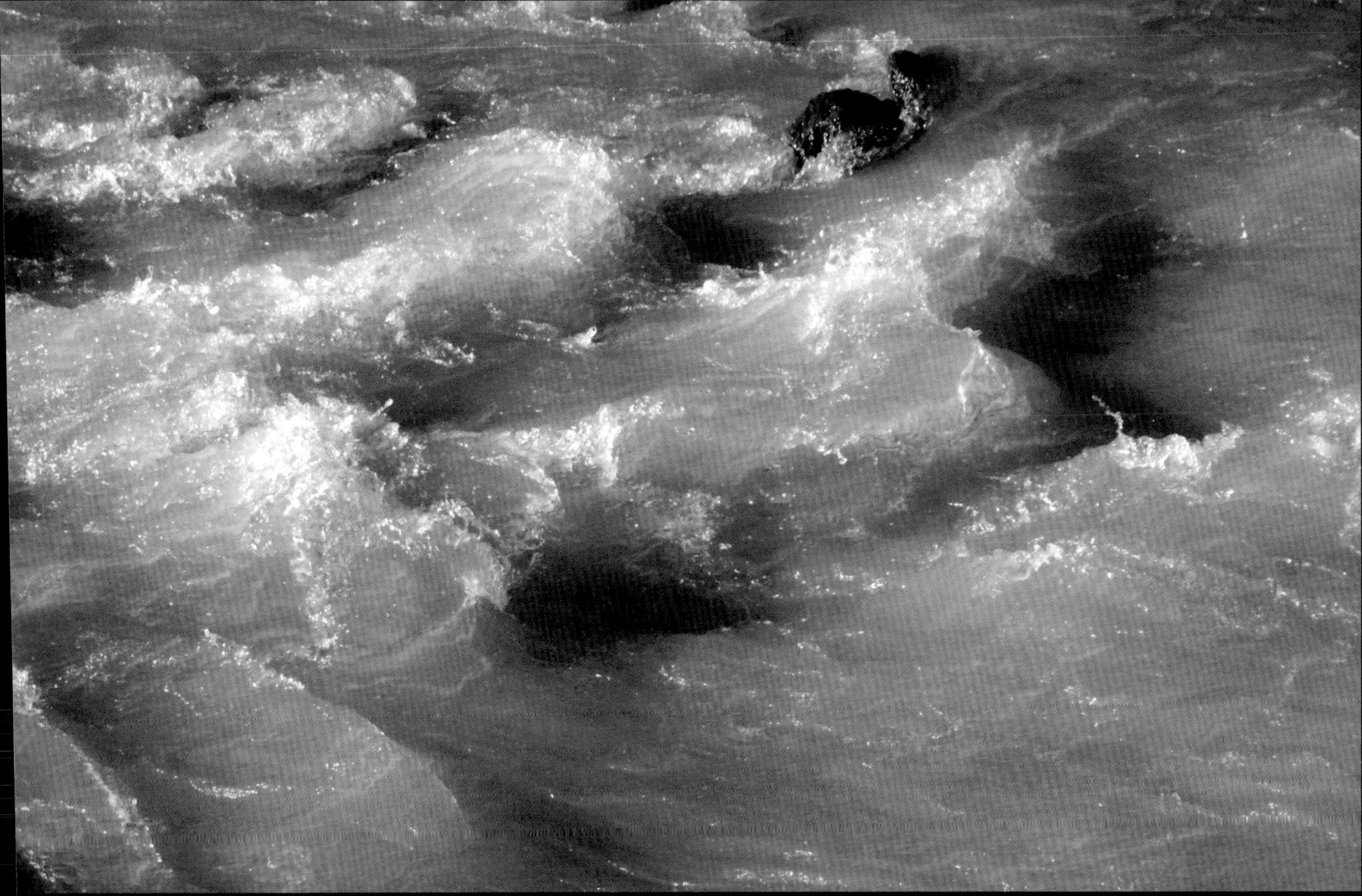

Glacier water, Fox River. Sludge in a pond, Otane.

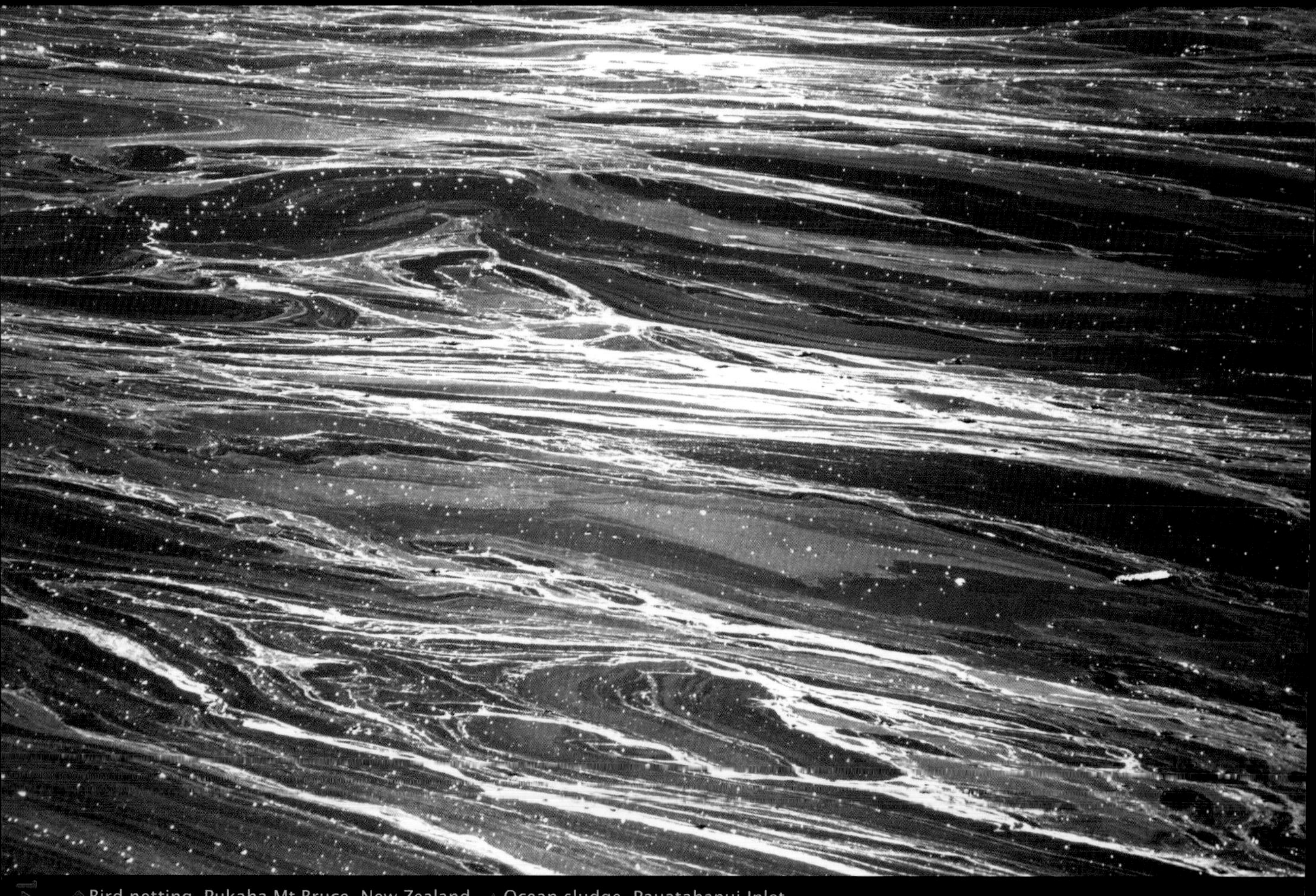

▲Bird netting, Pukaha Mt Bruce, New Zealand. ▲Ocean sludge, Pauatahanui Inlet.

▲ Mushrooms, Porirua. ▲ Egg shell, Pikarere Street, Titahi Bay.

Metal disks catching the light in the BART station at San Francisco Airport.

Spider web, Sebastopol. Buttercups, Titahi Bay.

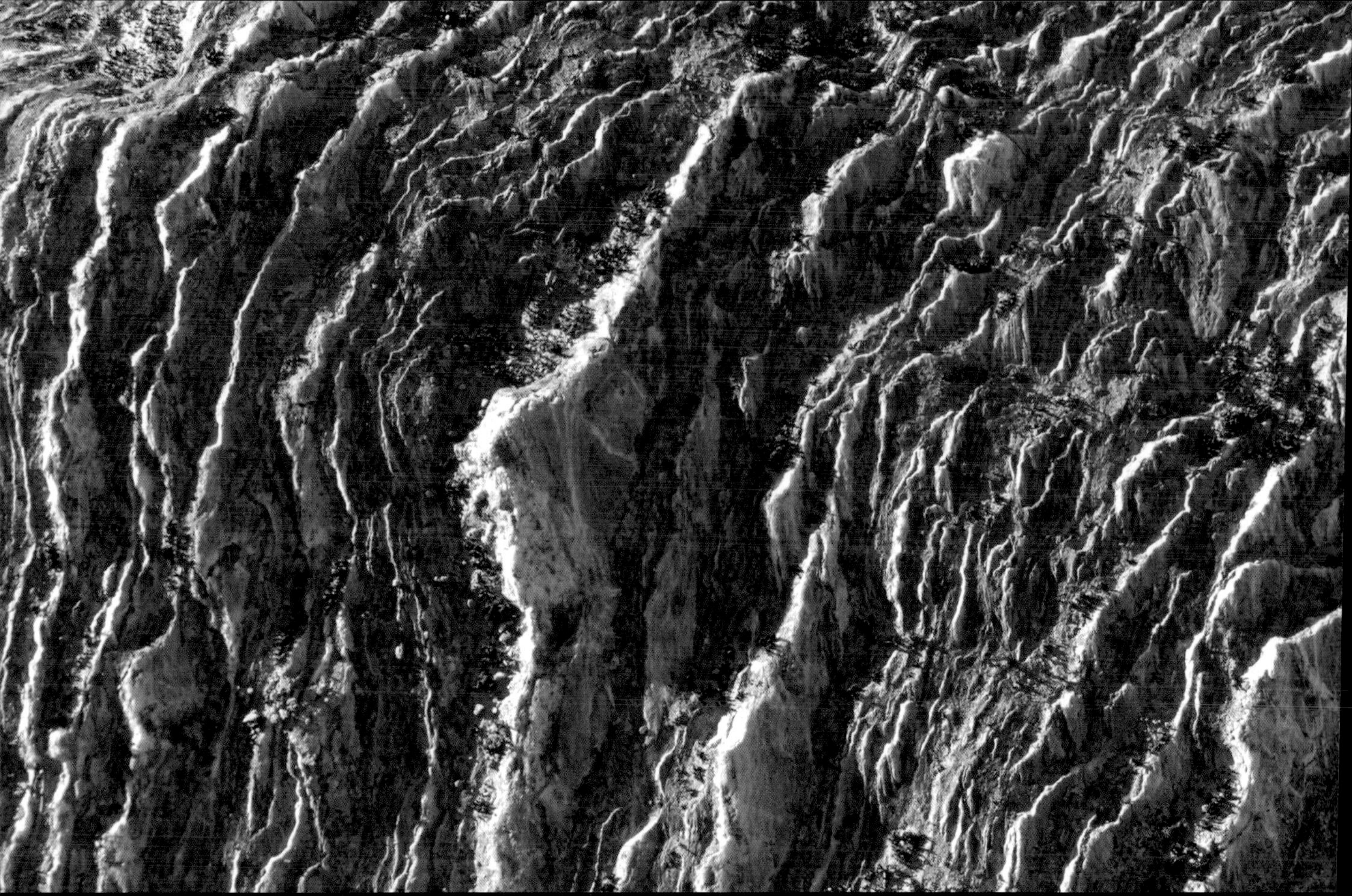

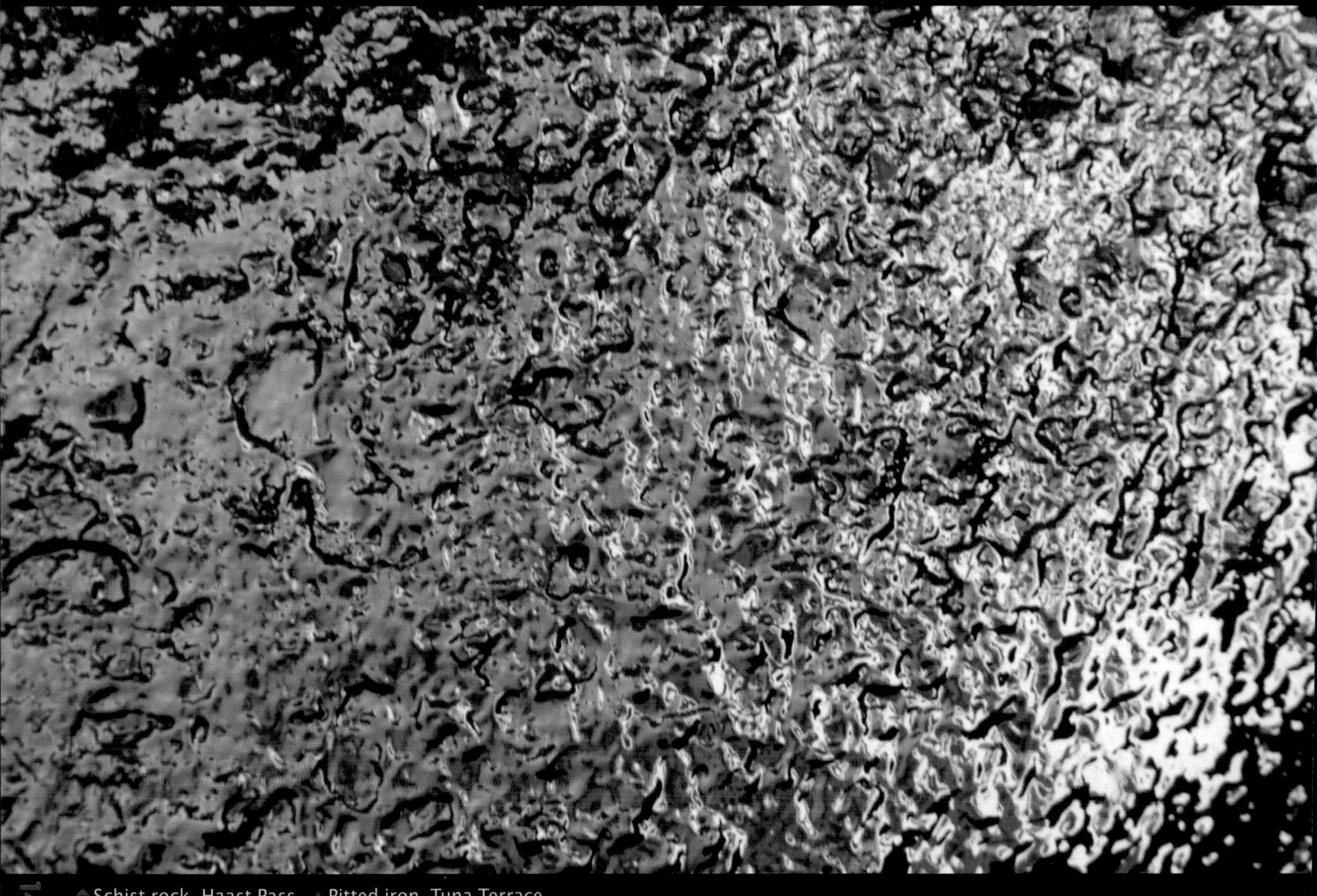

Schist rock, Haast Pass. Pitted iron, Tuna Terrace.

⌃Leaves, Inverness, California. ▲Gray heron in grass, Pauatahanui.

▸ Jenni Hutchinson.

▸▸ Charlotte White.

▾ Grand Canyon, Arizona.

(footwear, handbags, clothing). How is it that the pattern on a scary reptile becomes so desirable once its original owner has been turned into meat? The pattern 'says' something elegant. Bad news for individual crocs but maybe good news for crocs as a whole – the species is being farmed back from the brink of extinction.

Patterns enable us to see things and also to see the difference between things. When you recognise a friend you're responding to a pattern. Pattern recognition is high on the list of vital survival skills – if you can't distinguish friend from foe you might turn into snack food.

if you can't distinguish friend from foe you might turn into snack food

Patterns often come with a kind of paradox – they're similar but different. The pattern on the crocs is indisputably crocodilian but each skin is unique. One method of tracking crocodiles is to photocopy them when they're small (strange but true). The pattern is like a fingerprint and a grown croc can be identified from the pattern it had as a baby.

Science is about the search for patterns but it has limitations when it meets uniqueness. Your own subjective experience is unique and that is what shapes your 'creative fingerprint'

Part of TLC's research is to identify patterns that are favourable for creativity. *GO!* is inspired by evidence that suggests we can make a difference to our life patterns and become more effectively creative.

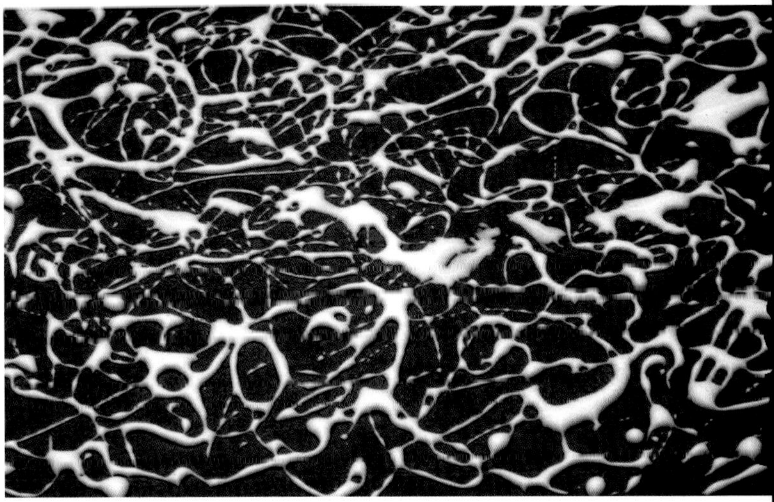

59 Look for patterns in nature. Take photos if you have a camera or make some sketches. Pay attention to 'self-similarity'. For example, the speckled eggs blend with their surroundings because they mimic the fractal edges of pebbles. All the silhouettes in the Grand Canyon picture are related even though they're each unique.

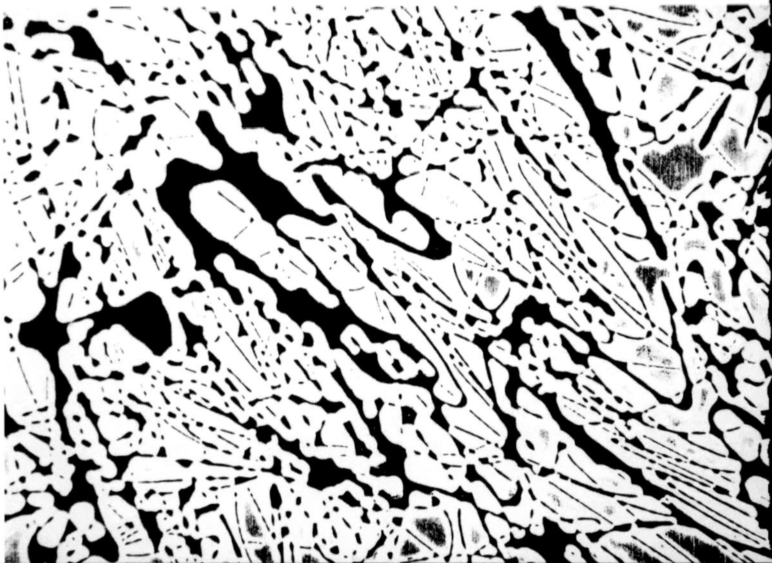

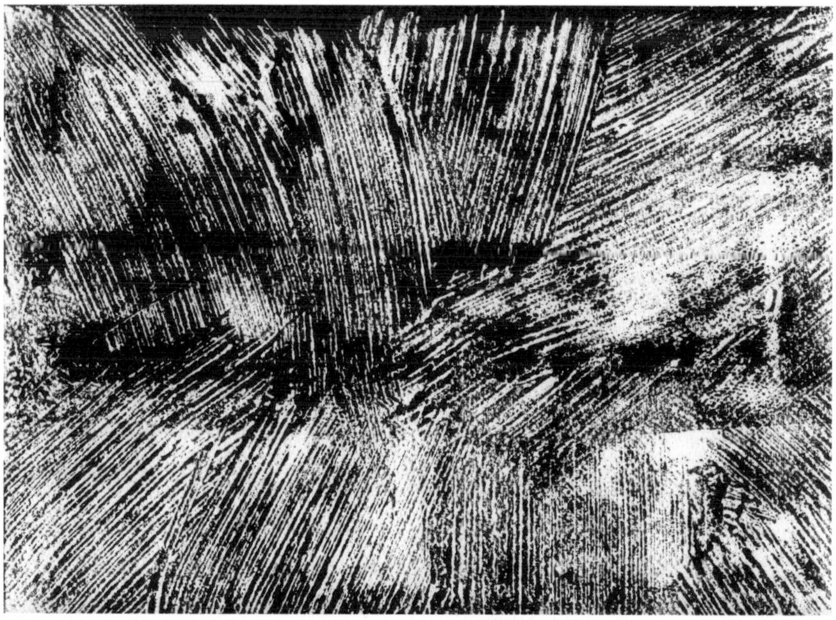

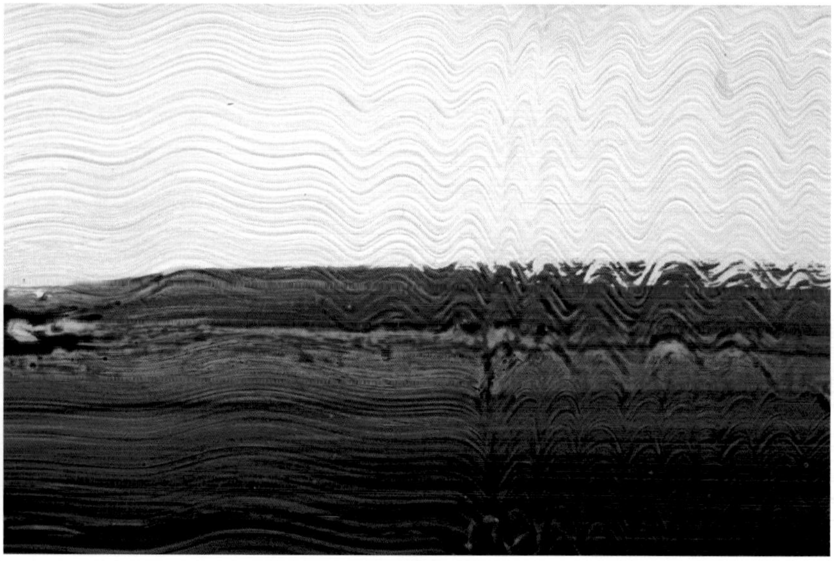

60 Make a portrait using fingerprints *or* torn pieces of paper only. If you want to see how this can be done on a large scale, check out the works of Chuck Close (go to Google and do a search and/or check your library). The goal is to explore ways in which one pattern can transpose into another and enable us to see things differently.

61 Take a few smallish pieces of particle board (A5 is about right) and dribble PVA glue onto them. Make each set of dribbles distinctive. Let the glue dry (it might take hours or days). Then use the boards to make a rubbing on a larger sheet of paper. Alternatively, use printing ink to create a print (as in the illustration). By rubbing or printing several boards you can create a composite picture. A small printing press makes the task easier.

62 Using some more boards, brush thick paint onto them, let them dry thoroughly and then try printing off the paint. Squeeze paper against the card so that the paint prints onto the paper. Continue as many times as you like and build a work from the multiple prints.

You'll get the best results with oil-based printing ink, a good roller and a press, although you can improvise with minimal equipment.

In addition to exploring pattern the purpose of these actions is to investigate how one medium (e.g. paint) can be translated into something else via a further action (printing) and then something else again by cutting and rearranging. You're doing something and then 'verbing' it.

Another option is to paint the textured surface with more paint and then rub it back with fine sandpaper. If you use fairly wet acrylic, gravity will take pigment into the deeper parts of the texture and give an interesting effect in its own right.

At right, texture made with a scraping blade and then painted and sanded. You can take it further by scanning the surface and playing with it on a computer.

The same basic techniques can be taken in many different directions. For example, you can add a different layer of wet colour, let it dry and then do further sanding or scrubbing. You can print the surface in different colours. You can print it on itself in reverse ... These are creativity explorations which may eventually be directed into a specific project – a poster, painting, wallpaper or whatever you choose.

You might see the patterns as an end in themselves or you can take them further.

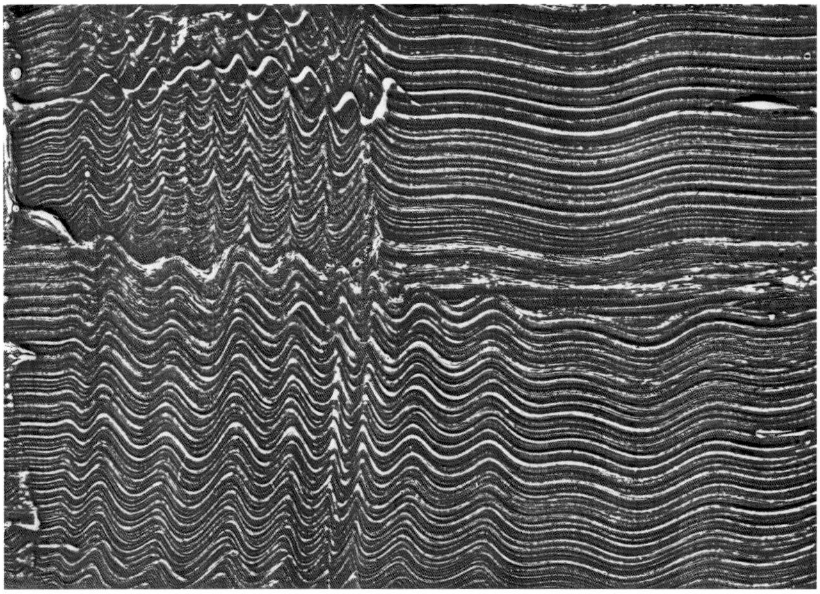

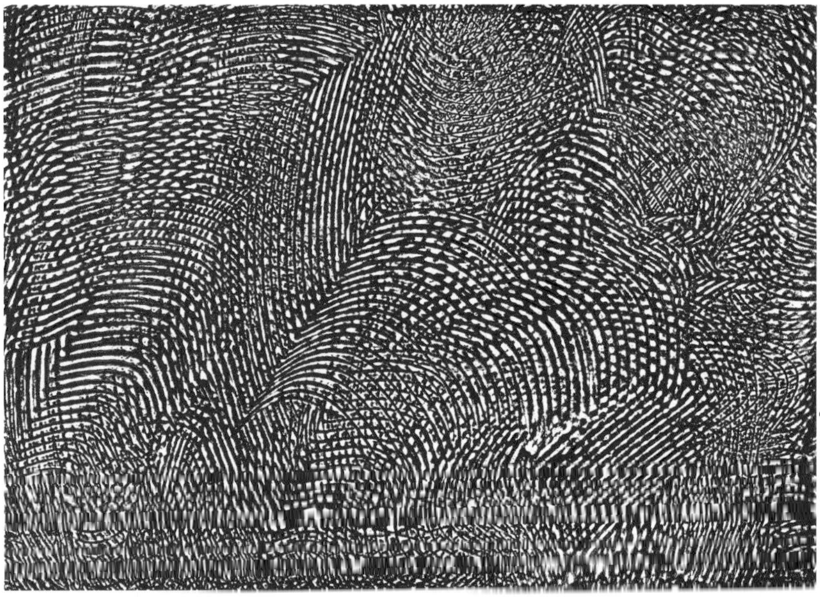

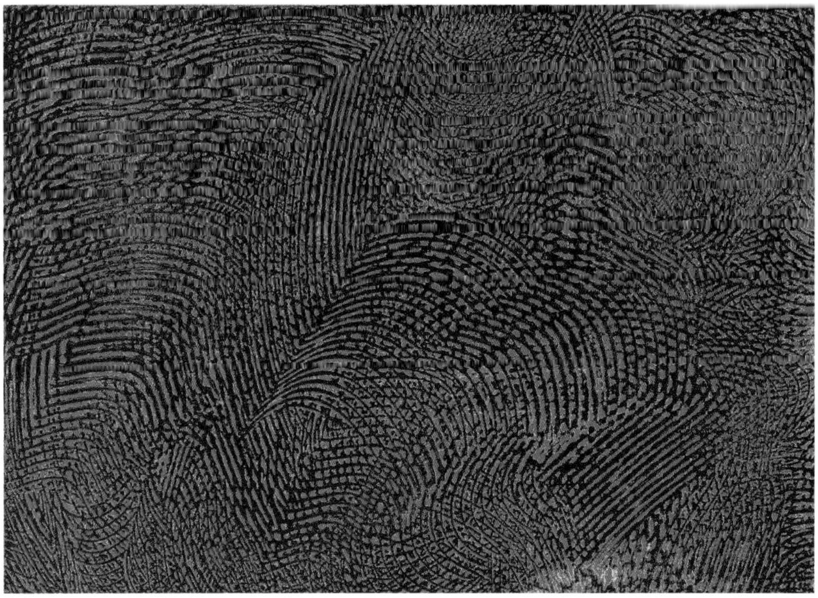

The drawing is based on a newspaper image. It felt to me that the people were burning civilisation. I scanned it into Photoshop and then turned it into a series of layers derived from one of the paint prints. In the final version some of the layers have a gradient (they change from lighter to darker). From the start I had a fairly clear idea of how I wanted it to look but there were a few false moves when I tried patterns that didn't work. It's a multimedia result which combines drawing, painting (to establish the texture), printing and computer graphics.

63 If you have the ingredients, try the process for yourself. If it seems too complex there are other ways. For example, take a texture of your choice, print it in different colour combinations (make the colours through Photoshop or with printing inks) and then cut the shapes you want and collage them together.

CHAPTER 7

Drawing for all you're worth

Form

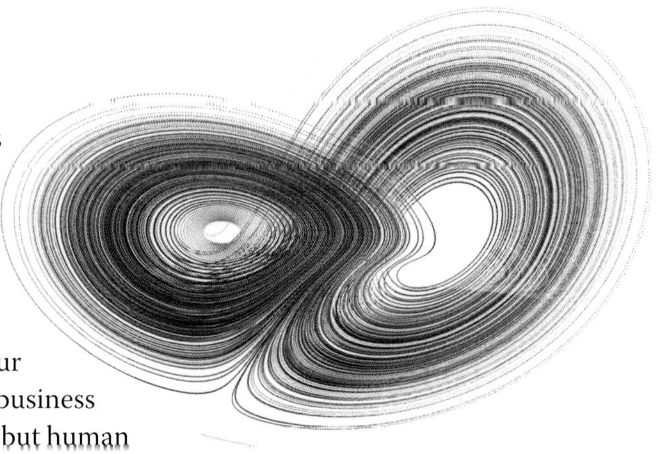

Form is a further investigation into seeing. It is the third dimension (after lines and shapes). In life our 3D experience is spatial and includes touch. In 2D representations the illusion of form is largely described by tone. Much of our communication is two-dimensional (books, television, movies, computers) and it skews our understanding of the world. For example, business organisation charts are usually two-dimensional but human interaction is multi-dimensional.

The Lorenz attractor, which relates to weather patterns.

The field of chaos maths has given new insights into form. The behaviour of a chaotic system may conform to a 'strange attractor' – which turns out to be as familiar as the weather. All the apparent chaos of weather is captured in the Lorenz attractor (shown in flat form above) which is highly ordered but not in the way that order is usually understood. Expect more of these new forms as people find better models to describe how the world works.

We owe a debt to the Cubists who came half a century before Lorenz's discovery. They started messing with form in ways that broke some of the shackles of conventional geometry. Whether they were 'right' doesn't matter – they took art into new places and helped to change the way we see the world.

Nevertheless the 'old geometry' remains useful and deserves some exploration. If you look at a Euclidean ball in various lights you can see how form is revealed. If the ball is on a lightly-toned surface it will receive reflected light which brightens the shadows. On a coloured surface it will reflect the colour.

◄ Amy Saunders in a TLC drawing workshop.

If there are other colours nearby, they will have an influence too. The pictures give clues about the complexity of shadows. Shadows usually show changes of tone — more subtle than the object itself and richly suggestive of the surrounding surfaces/lights.

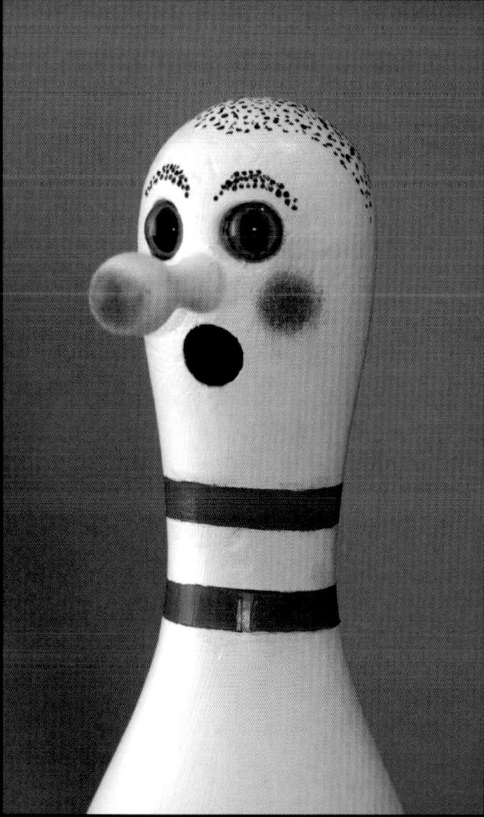

A head is more complex but similar tonal changes convey a sense of depth.

To some extent lines can help to define form. For example, the markings on the flower combine with the tone to create the three-dimensional feeling. Overlapping surfaces (the petals) and perspective (distant elements appear smaller) also indicate form.

You can isolate form by drawing or painting from white subjects. A piece of white cloth is a good way to get started. The face cast provides another option.

Form is as useful to the photographer as it is to the painter. All the same principles apply.

64 Drape a piece of white fabric over an object and draw the fabric as a way of investigating form.

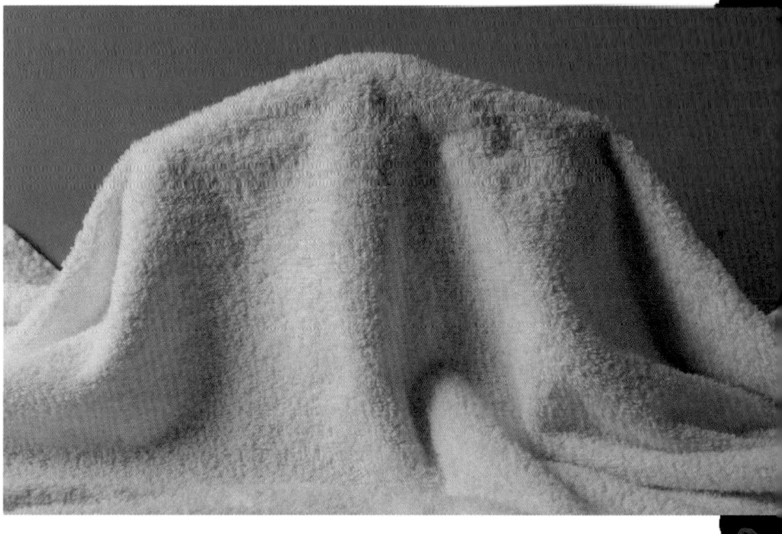

65 Set up a white still life arrangement. Think about the overall interplay of light and shade (you're making a composition) and then try a fast drawing in charcoal. Smudge the charcoal to establish shadows at high speed. If you're happy with the composition, try a slower and more detailed charcoal drawing (use the same principles as in the earlier portrait drawings). If a face cast is available, make it part of the picture.

66 Using a white jug (or similar object) as a centre piece in a colourful arrangement, create a drawing using pastel. Keep the white object neutral (white and grey) and make the other material as colourful as you like. The result should be a little surreal because normally white is full of colours reflected from other things.

focus on tones and be sensitive to where shadows change

67 Working from a photograph or real life, create a face that is black and white (no greys). The knack is to judge how much of the drawing should be black. It may not be flattering but it should help you to focus on tones and be sensitive to where shadows change. I've taken some artistic licence and used grey for the background.

68 Draw a self-portrait, this time with three or four tones (dark, mid, light). You may find it useful to work in colour or on black or toned paper and you can smooth the edges to build a rounded form.

Ruth Korver's sculpture shows a way of setting up a white arrangement (except for the 'blood').

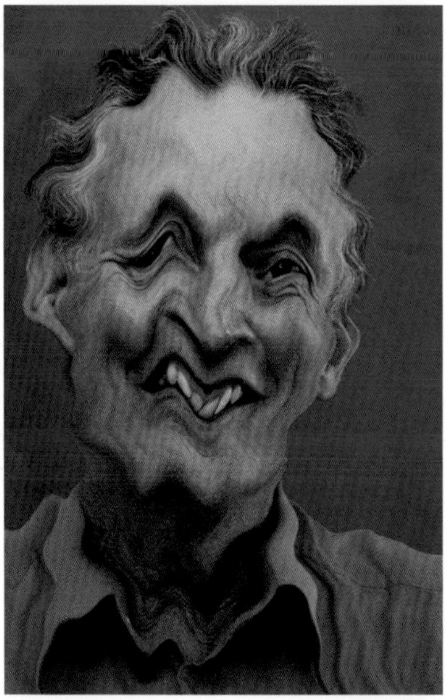

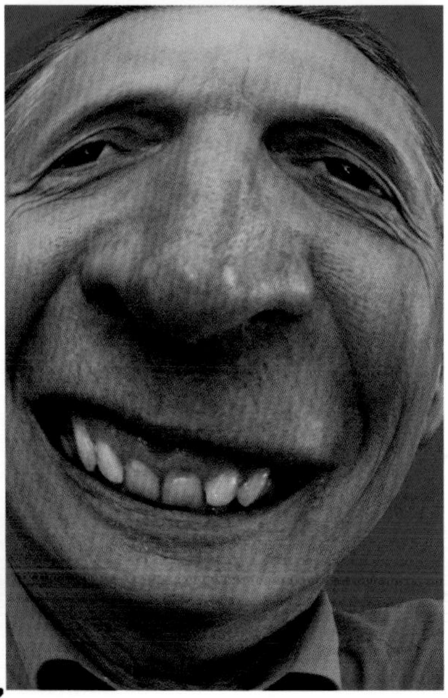

69 Just for fun, mark grid lines on a picture and then make a distorted grid by drawing freehand on your paper. The distorted version should have the same number of lines but the squares will no longer be square. Then translate the tones from the original onto the distorted grid. Behold, a warped form!

You can do similar things in Photoshop at the click of a button. For example, the face on the left (below) has been 'iterated' through the **Distort → Wave** filter. ('Iteration' is a mathematical label for 'verbing'.) Other than the initial shock value it probably does less than a cartoon drawn by an artist who can interpret both form and personality. Then again, an artist who can combine both approaches might take things even further.

I recommend that you apply yourself to some drawing so that you don't get snared by computer gimmicks which limit your growth. Your personal touch is 'organic' and connects with a much more complex range of knowledge than the computer.

When you're drawing, remember the exploration cycle – start small and fast to explore an idea, then sketch boldly and with total concentration when you move into a more developed work. If you're unhappy with the initial outline, set it aside and try another. Once you're satisfied with the basic structure, steadily increase the detail.

Highly skilled artists sometimes opt to cut corners and complete everything as they go. It's fun to watch because the drawing seems to emerge fully formed from the paper, but demanding because you have to hold the image in your mind throughout the whole drawing. Others prefer to go from the outline and work the whole surface so that the detail increases fairly evenly – more like developing a photo.

One of the purposes of exploration is to find out what suits you best. If a particular approach appeals to you, stay with it and do several pictures. If an exercise looks irrelevant, skip it (or return later). When I'm doing these things in a live class I like to see everyone achieve at least one reasonably 'finished' picture in each session. The completions

Top to bottom: original picture, Photoshop **Ripple**, Photoshop **Lens Distortion**.

are a creative habit – a discipline to nudge a work as far as you can take it with the skills you have at the time. The skills are cumulative – eventually you may be able to do wonders with projects which were initially beyond your reach.

Explorations using two or three colours

You can take a restricted palette into landscape and other areas of painting. It is another way to explore form and learn about the behaviour of different pigments. If you use complementary colours you will find that they dull each other when mixed and also produce rich, dark tones that minimise the need for black. When you use closely related (analogous) colours a completely different dynamic emerges.

70 Sketch a fairly simple scene on a sheet of A4 paper. Choose two or three colours and then paint the sketch. Try at least three different combinations – you can use the same theme each time (either trace or photocopy the sketch to save time). Note the way the colours behave when they're mixed and when they sit side-by-side.

On a larger sheet (A3 or A2) either sketch the same scene or a new one, choose a pair of colours and this time add black and white to the set.

Alice Wilson Milne.

Drawing by Katharine White.

Form and scale

Comic book artists are often adventurous with scale, perhaps because they are producing so many pictures that they search for variations to keep it interesting. For example, a close-up spoon might be as big as a middle distance figure.

Variations can be real or contrived. The surrealists played bizarre tricks with scale and the results were challenging and powerful. Scale can be a consequence of who and what you are. Children may see adults as giants – a statement of fact if you compare the sizes of adult and child. Imagine if you were an ant. A close-up cup would be colossal – as big as a skyscraper.

71 Draw a person or animal (from a magazine, yourself in a mirror etc.) with a kitchen item in the foreground. Make the object larger than the 'subject'.

72 Draw two faces on a different scale. You can be extreme (e.g. a face appearing in an eye) or you can use a more modest difference. Use no more than two colours, or, if you're desperate, you can use black and white as well.

73 Pretend you're a comic book artist and do five scenes of someone being chased. Use variations of scale which sit well in a series.

74 Try something surreal. For example a figure far smaller than a cup, a building far smaller than a car or a tree smaller than a cat. Play with ideas – be experimental.

⇑ Inverted scale by collage. ▲ A photo using the same principle of inverted scale. Alice Wilson Milne (left) and Robert Franken.

Part 3

being your own guru

Titahi Bay.

Tone and mood

I want to take a lateral approach to tone and mood by looking inwards and considering how we set the tone (or inner climate) of our creativity.

Good frustrations

How do you achieve the mysterious shift from a "technique" to a work of art? I suspect that it *always* involves an element of frustration. It surprised me because I thought creativity would be such an adventure that there would be no room for frustration.

If you think of very young children learning to walk and talk you can see it all happening. I'm told that kids can make 10,000 attempts to learn to walk and without actually doing the counting I've watched pre-toddlers and can believe the estimate. They work to make it happen and you can see huge tension and frustration combined with unlimited persistence and determination (often mixed with giggles and laughter).

The pattern is the same with all learning. When you extend your boundaries there may be some discomfort. In part it's the tension of risk-taking but mostly it is due to your mind trying to process the unfamiliar. Your mind can't know for sure if you're going to succeed and to some extent you have to work on faith.

'Positive thinking' is really a disguise for faith and it leads to better results than a belief in failure.

One way to turn things around is to look at negative situations as if they're teachers. That's what Edison did when he was discovering thousands of ways *not* to invent a light bulb. You can do it with your feelings too. For example:

FRUSTRATION *The mediocre turn frustration into an excuse; the great turn it into a motivator.* You might even get a sense of purpose by looking at your life and figuring what frustrates you most. The road toll? Lousy schools? Wars? Politics? Disease? Dreary television? Poverty? The choice is either to put it aside or

The mediocre turn frustration into an excuse; the great turn it into a motivator

to take action. If you take action, you may suddenly find that frustration energises your life. It's the same with art. If things aren't working out, pause to think how you can make a difference. If you keep doing the same stuff you'll keep getting the same results.

ANGER *is energy* (indeed every emotion is an energy state). Like money or fire, you can use anger positively or negatively. There's no point in denying it – if you're angry, you're angry. The dynamics are similar to frustration but anger is easier to work with because it provides instant momentum. Identify what triggers your anger and do something positive about it. Anger may be triggered by another person or an external event, but the cause is always inside you. To deal with it, go for the cause, not the trigger. If you're not sure what's going on, seek advice from a wise friend or a professional. Be assured that many of the greatest creative works in history have been driven by anger. It's also the fuel that powers many highly successful artists (consider Goya, Picasso and Frida Kahlo).

BOREDOM *If you're not having fun, you're not doing it right.* Boredom is a signal for change. Perhaps you're trying to please others instead of pleasing yourself. Perhaps you're slobbering around in victim mode. Maybe something inside you is telling you to stop being a wimp, to get up and take charge of your life. Maybe you've become immobilised by trying too hard. It may work better to "try softer" and go with the boredom. The English artist LS Lowry said it took three weeks before he got so bored that he had to paint. If you haven't got that much free time, try sitting still and concentrate on your breath for 20 minutes. Count each inward breath and after four breaths start counting from one. If you're extremely bored, try this twice a day for the rest of your life.

REJECTION *is information.* So you experience rejection. What's going on here? What messages are you giving? What messages are people receiving? What action can you take to achieve a better result? Try regarding rejection as an experiment. Each time you get rejected, change your behaviour. If you're an artist you won't necessarily change your art but you might change your gallery or your promotional methods. Eventually you'll find what works.

FAILURE is like rejection although you can fail without being rejected. Perhaps you put on an exhibition of your work and nobody bought anything. So what? It's all market research (and cheaper than hiring a consultant). Successful salespeople soon learn that the first rule of success is to *achieve more failures.* If you get only one success out of each ten attempts, ninety failures are required for ten successes. If you're making paintings, you may need to do ten times more.

Maybe something inside you is telling you to stop being a wimp

Failure invites you to review what you've been doing. Are you trying to reach the wrong people? Are you playing to your personal weaknesses rather than your strengths? What adjustments can you make? Are you trying to be successful instead of doing what satisfies you?

FEAR goes back to days when we had to respond to dangerous situations by turning on our adrenaline. Life has become more complex and there are endless situations which involve fear but which don't require the 'fight-or-flight' response. *The first step in dealing with fear is to take action.* This is why fear is such a good teacher – it invites you to do something about it. Without fear you'd have complacency and inertia.

Biologically fear developed to protect you – it pumps adrenaline to boost your body to maximum physical effectiveness. If you don't make use of fear (by taking action) the adrenaline has nowhere to go. It's likely to burn you from within instead of providing the massive surge of energy that it's designed for. The breath-counting exercise is good for fear, and so is physical exercise. You could pretend you were being chased by a lion even if your fear is about a boss who won't get out of his chair, let alone bite. It won't change your boss if you run a few miles but it can do wonders for your chemistry.

STRESS/ILLNESS They say that death is nature's way of telling you to slow down. Stress is like an early-warning light on the dashboard. It signals a need for some adjustment. Maybe more rest, more fun, different food, a visit to a health professional … Maybe it's about forming some new habits. Better fitness, changed affirmations, a fresh approach to life and work …

A sense of immortality breeds slothfulness

DEATH A sense of immortality breeds slothfulness. Perhaps it will turn out that we are immortal but it's good to give this life your best shot. Carlos Castaneda said: "When there is no way of knowing whether I have one more minute of life I must live as if this is my last moment. Each act is the warrior's last battle. So everything must be done impeccably. Nothing can be left pending … and there is no time for doubts or remorse. If I spend my time regretting what I did yesterday I avoid the decisions I need to make today." Hospice workers report the despair of those who die with the thought, "I wish I'd done that when I had the chance." People who experience big-time failure seem more serene than people who didn't dare. *If you've got a dream, take action now!*

75 Do a quick inventory of what your feelings are telling you. Check against each of the items above and note whether there are areas for adjustment. The awareness itself will take you towards effective change but there will probably be some additional work to be done.

Keep it simple and keep it attractive. The goal is to get the energy flowing more smoothly, not to create a new source of friction. Here are two personal examples. Many years ago my fitness was at a low ebb and I didn't know what to do about it. Then I inherited a dog who changed my life because I had to take him for walks. It was enough to establish a new habit which I have maintained ever since.

I gradually learned to focus on what works instead of being an entertaining critic

A more complex change occurred as TLC grew. Back in the eighties I felt highly critical of New Zealand's education system and wasted energy sniping at it. Several influences combined to help me change the pattern. I gradually learned to focus on what works instead of being an entertaining critic.

A by-product of positive thinking is that I've paid more attention to highly successful people. Many of their mind skills are identifiable and transferable.

That's a diversion into psychological tone. Let's return to the visual world.

Exploring tone

The goal is to understand how tone affects mood and to develop skills in managing tone. 'Tone' refers to lightness or darkness. A black and white photo of a painting will indicate the tones. A picture with mostly light tones is 'high-key' and a dark picture 'low-key'. Learning tonal control (using art media to accurately make tones) is almost equivalent to a musician practising scales.

Technical skill isn't an end in itself – it's a means of extending and refining creative language. One of the secrets of learning 'technique' is to find an enjoyable way to practise. My own tonal (and colour) skills improved when I was teaching large groups and did hundreds of one-to-one demonstrations in matching colours. I aimed to achieve a reasonable match within a minute and the pressure of the classroom forced me to practise much more than I would have done by myself. The pleasure of learning swept us all along.

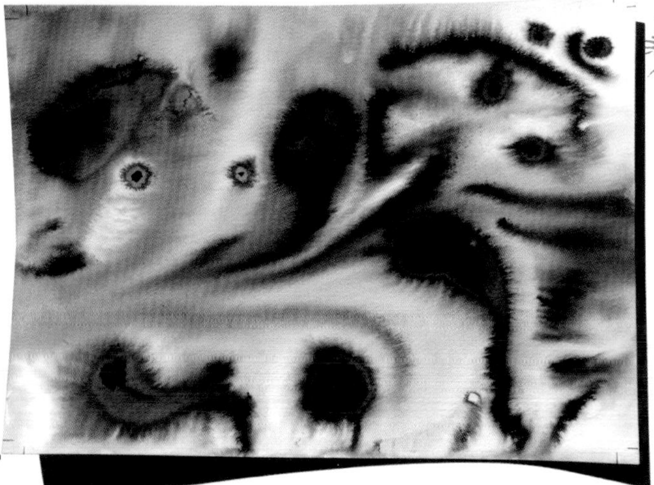

76 Dampen a sheet of drawing paper and dab Indian ink onto it. Depending on the wetness the ink can 'explode' into beguiling effects which give you abstract tonal pictures within seconds. If you like the way it works, try several – from very light tones through to dark and moody.

77 When the ink is dry, choose one of the sheets and incorporate a face which fits in with the shapes and tones. Look at the examples and you'll get the idea.

78 Starting with a simple scene, work at postcard-size to try different tonal combinations. Paint quickly and play with possibilities.

79 Do the same with a face. Try a high-key image, a dark image and a contrasty image (one with strong lights and darks).

80 A big drawing can be seen as a series of little drawings. When you look at fragments of a picture you may begin to see it in a different way. Fractal maths includes the notion that the whole is reflected in the parts – which leaves you with the possibility that a drawing of a fragment is very similar to a drawing of the whole.

it's a means of extending and refining creative language

Middle left is a copy from a book; the others are from photographs.

- Choose a picture and draw a grid on it (2.5 cm [one inch] squares are about right). Choose a frame within the grid and draw the little picture, taking care with the tones.
- Try some other fragments. Are there any frames that work well in their own right? You can cut a frame in a piece of paper and move it over the picture to find shapes that appeal to you. (A tonal exercise transposes into composition.)
- Try expanding a frame into a full-size painting. Instant abstraction?

Two possible details for further work — extracted from the larger photo.

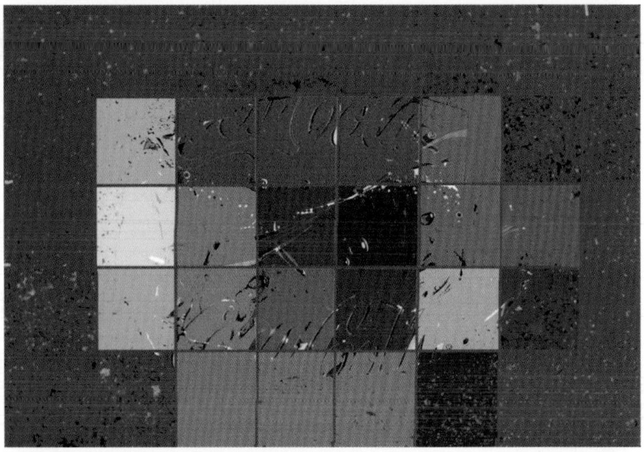

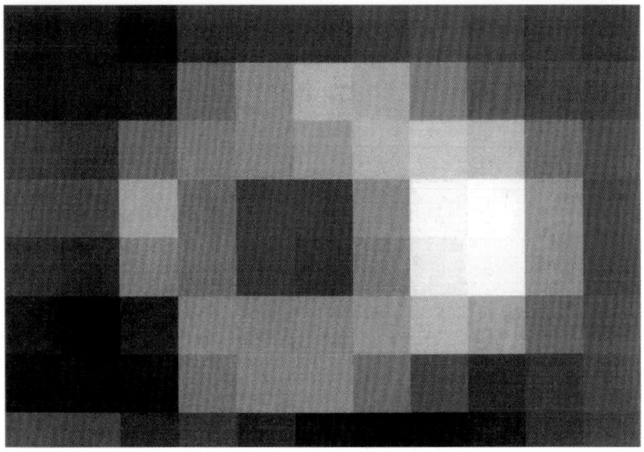

⮝ The squashed Coke can isn't exactly an 'old master' but…

⮝ here's the tonal idea applied via computer…

▲ and reduced to shades of grey. It feels odd to do it 'by eye' but it gives valuable insight into tonal structure and composition.

81 Work from a photograph or 'old master' drawing:

- Divide your drawing paper into a grid (say 8 lines across and 10 lines high)
- Do the same with the picture
- Use pencil or charcoal and tone each rectangle with a single flat tone that is equivalent to the *average* tone of that area in the picture.

It's like making huge pixels and of course the purpose is to make you suffer so that you will feel like an artist.

The other purpose is to understand the tonal spread of a picture. You may have to do some visual gymnastics figuring the tones of the colours – think of yourself as a black and white camera. It can be a puzzling task but rewarding once you figure out what's happening.

Abstraction

Abstraction is one of the most emotionally loaded terms in art. It provokes some sharp responses which sound as if they belong to a debate on religion rather than art.

In literature an 'abstract' is a summary – it encapsulates ideas in the most economic way possible. You could think of it as something highly concentrated which has meanings that extend beyond itself. In art the word 'abstract' is often used to mean 'non-figurative' (that is, art which isn't 'of' something). It also describes art which is concerned with the arrangement of non-representational elements.

My father expressed distaste for abstract art but when he walked along a beach he'd be captivated by interesting shapes. Was he connecting with abstraction?

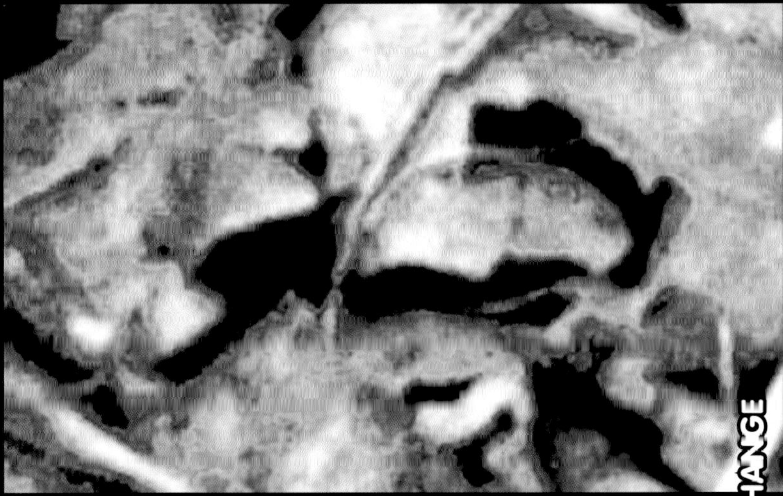

Consider this picture and look into the parts.

A view of the area towards the top left (with the colours exaggerated). Abstract?

Even more simplified, a detail within the detail. Abstract?

Another potential path towards abstraction is to draw without looking — and then keep playing.

The work will gradually take on a life of its own and you can move it in whatever direction you choose — including a step back to representational.

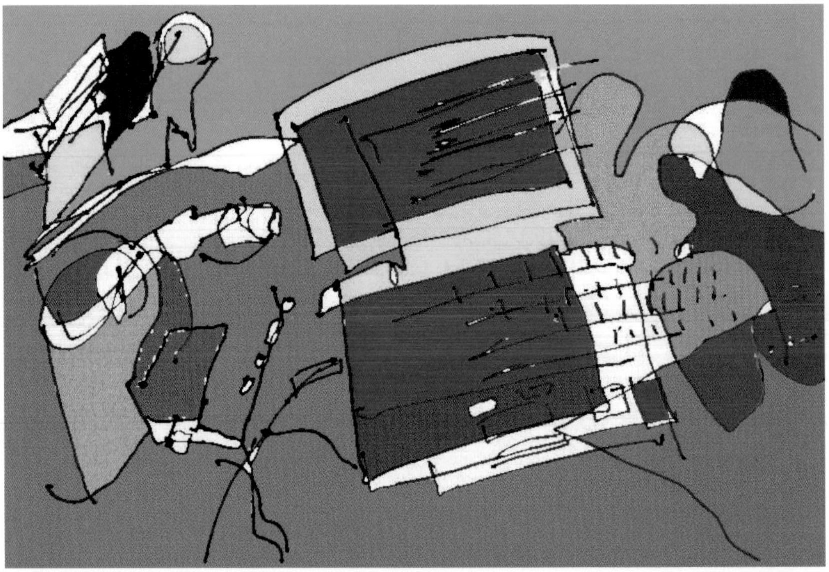

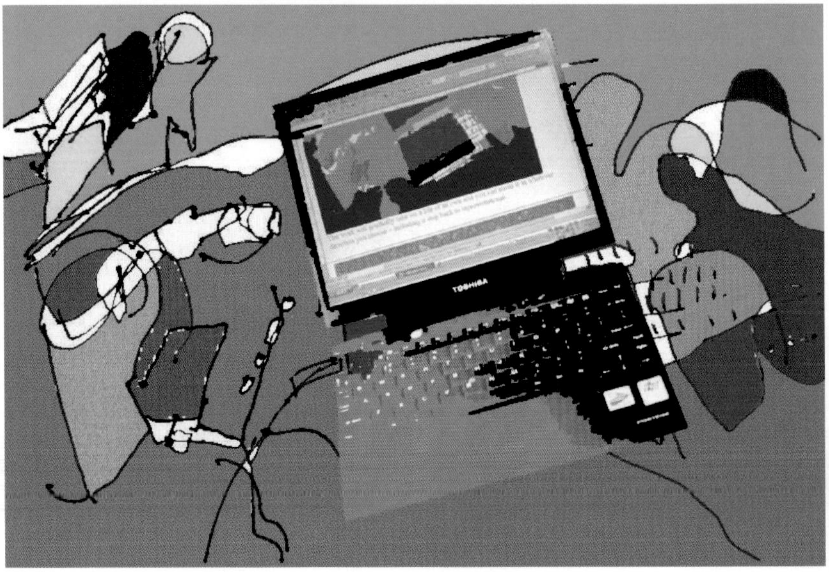

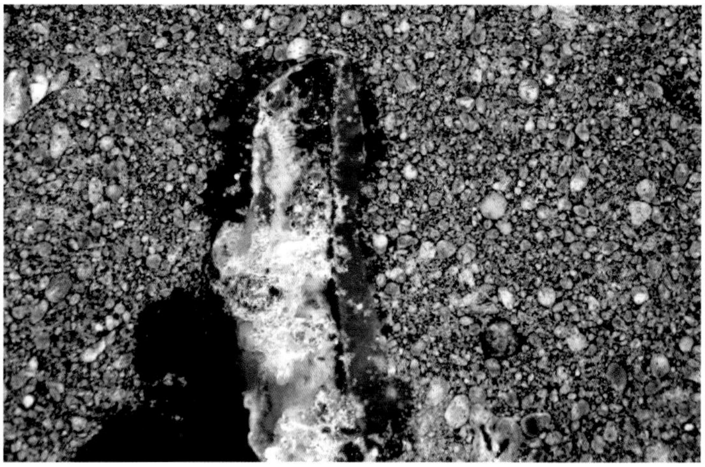

TLC's Masterclass works on 'materiality' and they go straight to the nature of materials rather than doing anything symbolic or representational. Are they doing abstraction or getting to the essence of the material? Or both?

Kasimir Malevich, 1878–1935 said: "Art no longer cares to serve the state and religion, it no longer wishes to illustrate the history of manners, it wants to have nothing further to do with the object, as such, and it believes it can exist, in and for itself, without 'things' ... feeling, after all, is always and everywhere the one and only source of every creation" (quoted in Vicky Perry's *Abstract Painting*). Was Malevich stating something profound or justifying his own position? Or both?

Abstract? (wax floating after being heated out of casts during 'lost wax' casting).

Our Masterclass students do work that *is*. But the 'is ness' can be 'read' in complex ways which are part of a shared visual language. At one level it is similar to my father 'reading' driftwood. At other levels it may be poetic, intellectual, spiritual, beautiful and so on. Music can explore similar territory through sound (and seems to be more easily accepted because that's what it has always done).

One of our multi-sense experiments is to have people paint music. The results are usually abstract and can be just as intense as the sounds themselves. Another entry point is analog drawing in which scribbles and shapes are used to describe feelings and situations. Are analogs abstractions?

Perhaps it's best if you keep all these possibilities in mind as we explore further.

Pigment emphasises the fractal structure of the crumpled paper. Arguably the fractal — the underlying 'recipe' of the crumples — is an abstraction in itself. Artist: Billy Wilson.

82 Recalling the exercises on 'analog' pictures (chapter 4), try a series of images in which the themes are:

- Flow
- Jazz
- Opposition

You can use paint, photography, a computer, cut-outs – whatever medium you prefer.

Your picture will focus on one of the many meanings that each word has. For example, 'flow' might relate to being 'in the flow' (when everything in a creative process is as near as can be to perfect). You might relate to the flow of water, air, time, life ... it's your choice.

83 Revisit the idea of looking into the details of a photo to find other elements. Make a frame by cutting a small rectangle in a piece of paper and then look for segments which express a feeling (anger, peacefulness, turbulence, energy, joy – you name it). Then think about what you might do to make a portrait or a landscape have the same emotional qualities. Try some quick sketches – and if you like any of them, take them through to more highly developed pictures.

Is this too literal for 'flow'? I like the idea that the tiny ripples connect with the ocean, the sun and the moon.

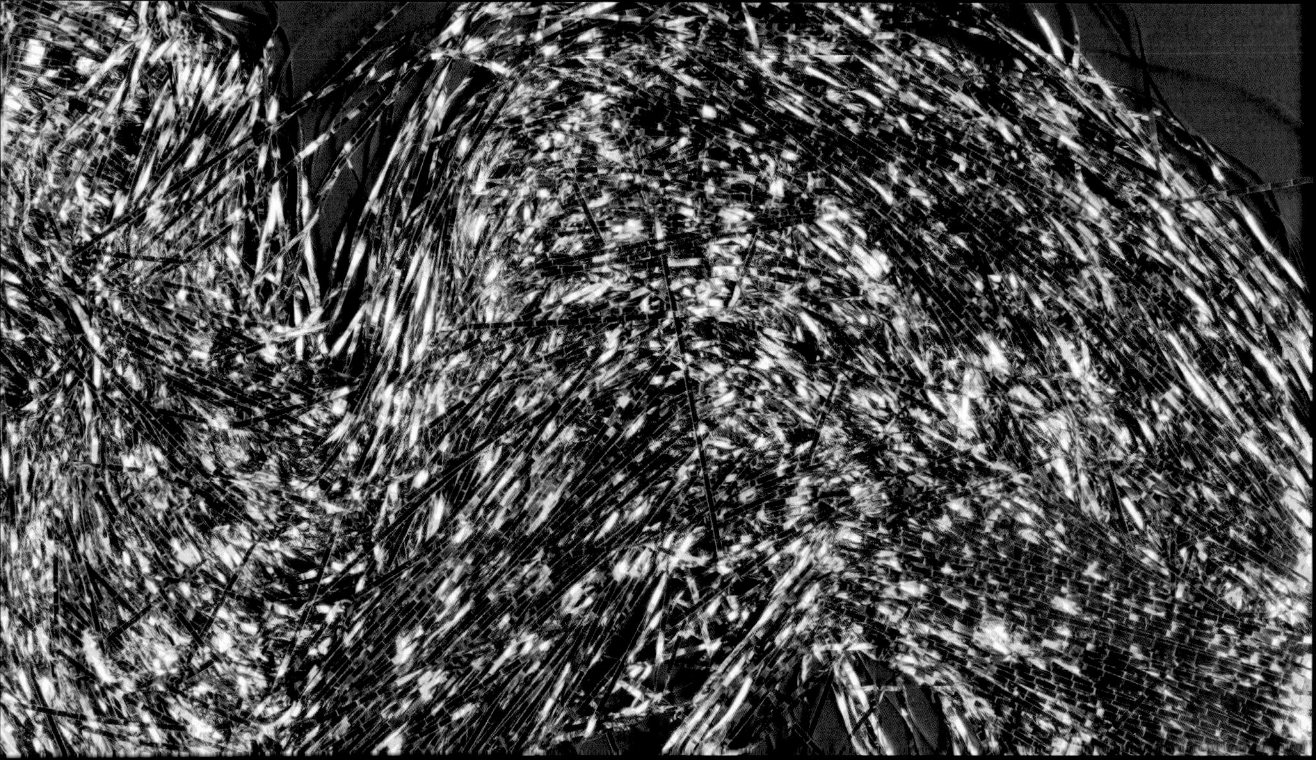

▲ Flow.

◀ Opposition.

▼ Jazz.

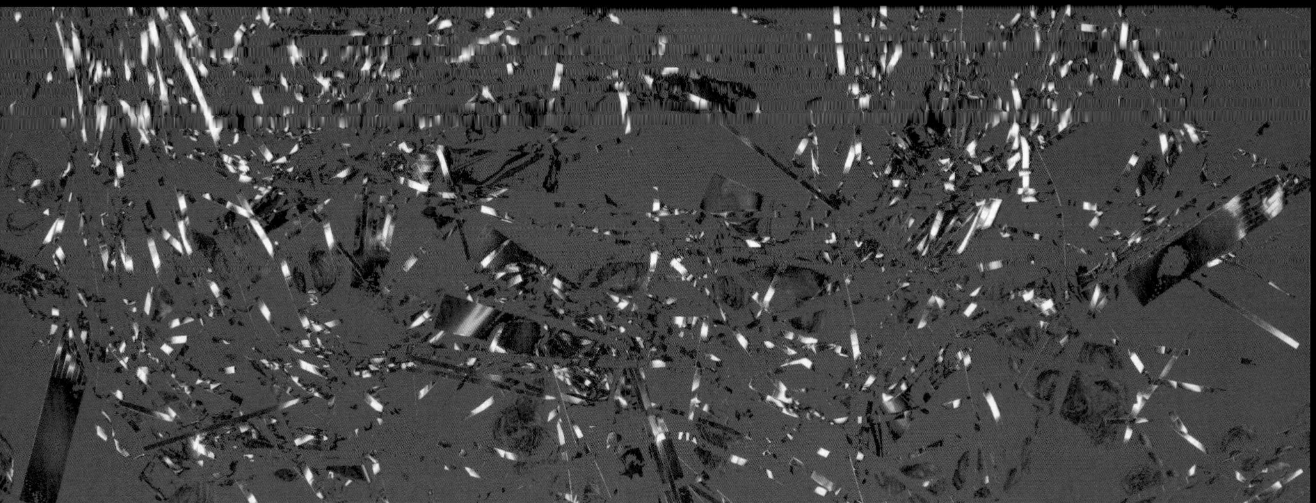

84 Create a portrait or landscape that has a specific emotional quality which is portrayed mostly by colours, shapes and lines rather than by direct representation.

85 Rip bright fragments from a series of magazine photos and compose them on an A4 sheet to express the feeling of *happiness*.

86 Do the same with more subdued colours and the theme of *balance*.

87 Use paper in a way which connects with the material qualities of paper. You can move into three dimensions. What does paper *do*? Think of verbs such as rip, curl, tear, fold, cut, crumple, stack and weave.

Play and see what you come up with. Is it abstraction? Certainly it's a way of viewing the elements of an image and reconstructing them.

Photo: Katharine White.

88 On whatever scale you please, make an assemblage with the theme 'rip, drop, spatter' and see whether any fractal patterns emerge. A fractal includes 'self-similarity' (small details have some similar attributes to large details even though they're different). A fractal can be expressed as a mathematical abstraction and you're doing maths (and abstract art) through these actions.

The photos below show how crumpled paper maintains a similar pattern as it is crumpled smaller and smaller (it's the same piece of paper – the images are successively enlarged).

A magnified detail from the third stage would have a lot in common with the first stage. You may find that the same fractal process occurs with dripped and dribbled paint – and you can have multi-fractals by including rippled and crumpled paper.

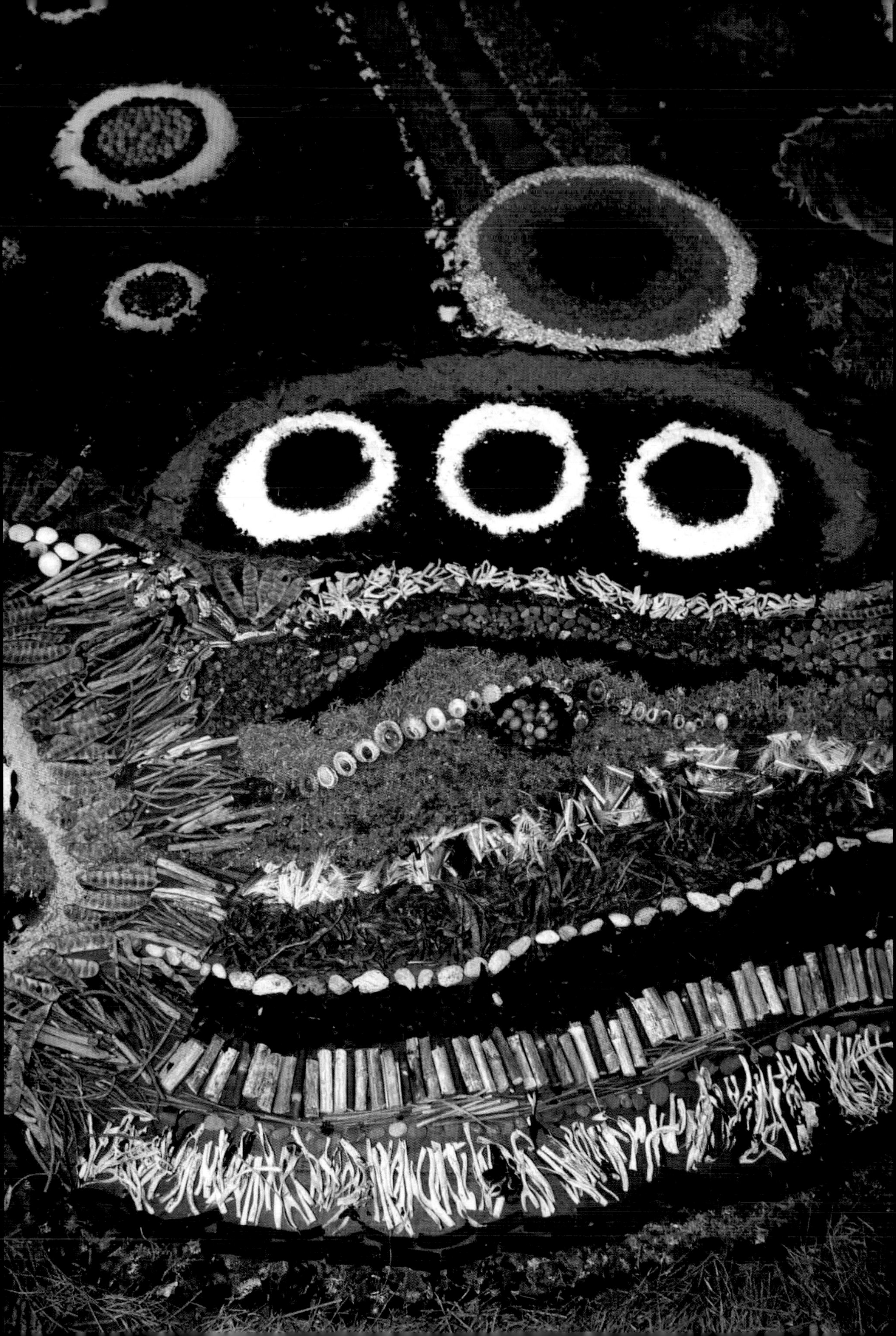

Colour basics

Colour is primal. Our perception of colour has developed through millions of years of evolution and is overlaid with all the reflexes that helped humans to survive. Our response to colour might be tangled with ancient courtship patterns, dominance behaviour, danger signals, security and so on.

There's nothing right or wrong about our personal preferences and there's no telling how these preferences originated. It's more relevant to explore our personal response to colour and (from an artist's perspective) learn how colour works.

There's nothing right or wrong about our personal preferences

The goal of this section is to help you to recognise your own sense of colour and learn how to make use of it in terms of creating art. It doesn't matter if you're the only person with your particular preferences. What does matter is to identify what you like – trust your own feelings without being distracted by any notion of what is 'right'. After that it's important to practise with colour – the more you use it, the easier it becomes.

89 Search magazines for at least three examples of colour usage which you like (strongly and enthusiastically!). If they're in disposable mags, cut them out and build a collection. Identify any features that your set has in common

◂ Closely related colours (e.g. reds and purples) are 'analogous' colour schemes. The photo is a detail of a work that covered a whole studio floor. It was assembled by a team of students who had gathered the materials mainly from the Wellington coast (the seaside smells were intense!).

Examples of monochrome colour schemes
(the pictures are made up of variations on a single colour).

◀▼ Examples of 'opposite' (complementary) colours. The kingfisher has a mix of blue and orange and so does the flower.

▼ Blue and orange in the late afternoon, Porirua Harbour.

▲ Red and green at full throttle.

▶ The reddish feathers of the kaka contrast with the greenness of the foliage. Subdued contrast can work well.

◀ Sometimes a colour set is hard to classify. This one is predominantly orange and dark greys but there are many other colours playing a part.

▶ The whole rainbow in action, O'Hare Airport, Chicago.

90 If you haven't worked with colour it's worth doing a few simple exercises to discover the basics in regard to your own particular paints.

Create a colour wheel in which the three primaries are blended as carefully as possible to make a sort of rainbow.

Do the same with the secondary colours (straight from your tubes).

Try mixing complementaries and then mix samples from the mixture with white.

The three sets are:

blue* ~ *orange
red* ~ *green
yellow* ~ *purple

Each combination makes a different 'neutral' and each pigment will have its own characteristics. For example, each 'blue' will make a different neutral in combination with each 'orange'.

The pigments in the tubes haven't read books on colour theory and they behave in their own unique way.

If you're working with other people it's useful to compare results. The more the better. With a team you can quickly create an encyclopaedia of colour combinations.

Everyday language can be confusing when we talk about colour. For that reason some technical labels may help.

'Hue' is the name of the colour.

'Value' is the lightness or darkness of the colour (also called 'tone').

'Chroma' or 'saturation' refer to the intensity of the colour. A very pure, intense yellow thus has high chroma while a muddy ochre yellow has comparatively low chroma.

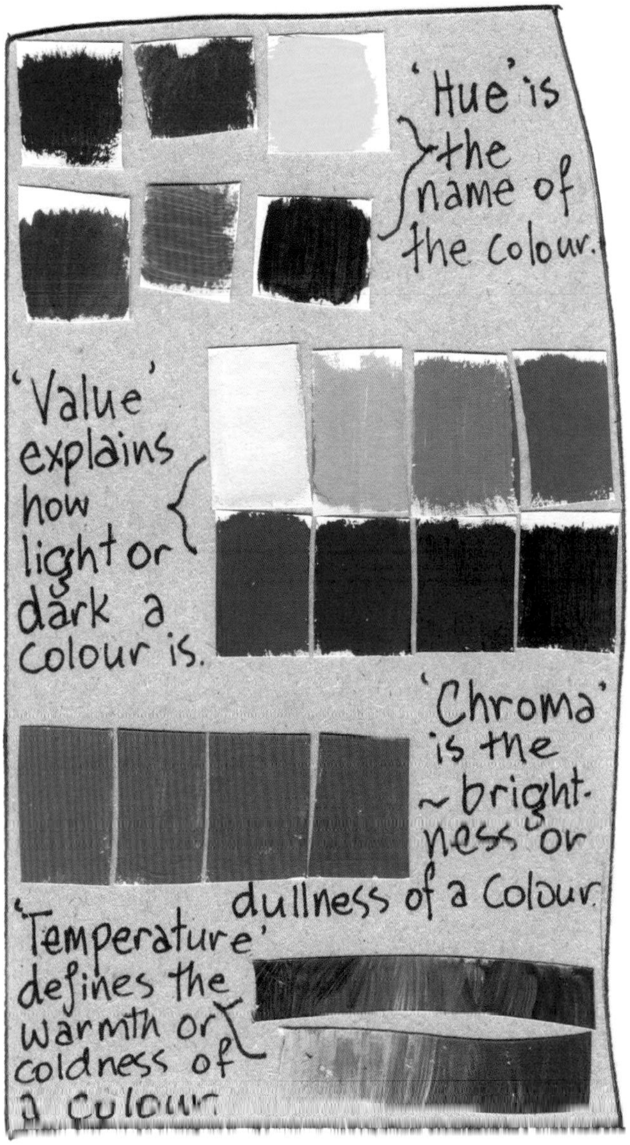

91 Choose a 'tertiary' colour (browns, greys etc) in a photo. Isolate the colour (see photo overleaf) and then use your knowledge from the earlier exercises to figure out what colours could be used to recreate it. Try to manufacture it for yourself using your own paints. The key steps are:

- Identify the dominant hue (what is the main colour?). Sometimes there's a choice. For example, with turquoise it can work equally well to say that the main colour is green or blue. A piece of paper with a small hole in it can help to isolate the colour you're working with. Our eyes are easily fooled.
- What other colours are involved? Sometimes this is counter-intuitive. For example, a slightly dull red may include green. You may be able

to get clues by looking at the original with a magnifier because this will show the dots of colour used in the printing process. It's quite rare to find pure colours. (Note: you may use both primaries and secondaries for matching).

- Once you've got the right colour mix it may be necessary to add black or white to adjust the tone (I prefer to do this last). It may take considerable practice until you can do it at speed.
- If you go wrong, the 'mistake' provides useful information because it tells you to try a different combination. Often mistakes can be adjusted to produce a successful result – after all, the whole process is essentially about juggling the balance of primary colours and it's impossible to stray very far!

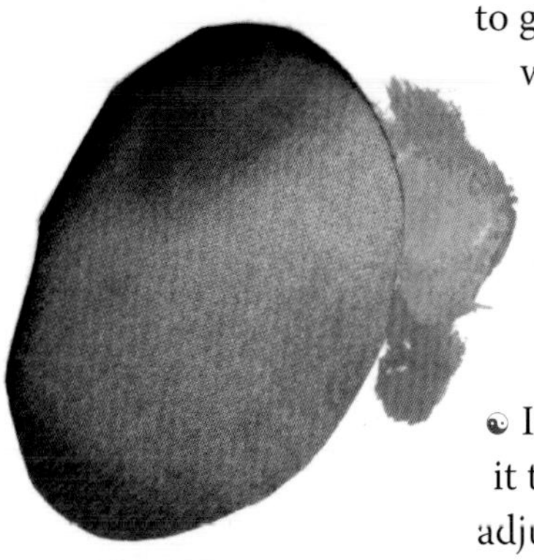

Close up of the 'isolator' showing a segment of the photo and the approximation of the colour in paint.

if you go wrong, the 'mistake' provides useful information

Repeat these steps for a variety of colours until you understand the principles and can achieve reasonably accurate results every time.

Experiment on the 'colour isolator' and work your way toward the most accurate match that your pigments will allow (sometimes you'll need extra colours to get it exactly right).

92 Once you've isolated the key colours, try using them in a different context to see if they still produce an exciting result. Possible tactics:

- sketch an entirely abstract or imaginative picture and then paint it with the same colours that appear in the original example (i.e. the colours that you strongly like).
- take an existing picture, make a drawing of it and then go back to the colours from your example.
- if you wish you can make a colour photocopy of an image and paint the copy in the same colours (it may help to glue the copy on a board before you start). Although this may not stretch your imagination it's a good way to practise colour management.

If you already have a good understanding of colour theory you can apply it to any project – representational or non-representational. Decide on a tactic (complementary colours, analogous colours, high-key, low-key etc) and then create a picture.

Before you get into the finished painting it's a good idea to make a little 'colour rough' – about the size of a postcard – as a quick check on whether you've got things right.

Katharine White chose this particular set of colours and applied them to a photocopy of a cat.

Hanne Erikson-Map (right) with TLC jewellery students.

CHAPTER 10

Techniques, practice, insight

> Drawing taught me not only to have trust in that which I could not see, but also to trust and have reverence for the fully visible world around me ... it can teach you to understand the difference between knowing about something, seeing something and really knowing something. *Adriana Diaz*

When you draw without looking at your paper you can get totally absorbed in 'seeing'. It's so easy that the benefits often go unnoticed, yet it can open the door to a lifetime of enjoyable drawing.

In itself observational drawing is a passive process – you go with what is already there and it's more like a devotional craft than a creative process. There's a place for craft within creativity, just as there is a need for a sense of surrender in life, but creativity goes beyond craft and there is more to life than surrender.

Creativity is like walking, which is the art of falling over and saving yourself by taking a step forward. It's a way of achieving balance through being off-balance.

Feeling, *composition* and *abstraction* are labels for open-ended techniques which take us beyond the given.

In the following exercises, the goal in each case is to move down a path of your own choosing. To get on the path you start with the drawing skills we've already explored and add new ingredients. Some possibilities:

- Focus on gesture.
- Add or exaggerate colour.
- Select a small area and draw it large.
- Use an unusual tool – for example a quill, a rag or a piece of potato.
- Use a distinctive style such as heavy outlines, dots, blends, lines drawn in the same direction.
- Ripping and rearranging images.

- Use an unexpected association in the picture. For example, the forms within crumpled paper might be incorporated with a mountain range.
- Explore the patterns of chance.
- Draw with total devotion to detail.
- Use a computer to manipulate images.
- Reverse tones.
- Deform objects to see them differently.
- Forgery.

93 Warm up with four or five quick drawings without looking at the paper. When you're ready, move into a series of very fast 'gesture drawings'. You're trying to portray weight and movement with the fewest marks possible. Use whatever is available for subject matter. Normally we'd do gesture drawings in a life-drawing class but you can take the same approach with images in photos (or on television), pets, trees in the wind, people in a park, clothes draped over a chair, different finger shapes with your own hands ...

94 Use your own face (and your expressive skills) to portray feelings. Observe your looks in a mirror. Make an angry face and have a go at conveying the core gesture through a drawing.

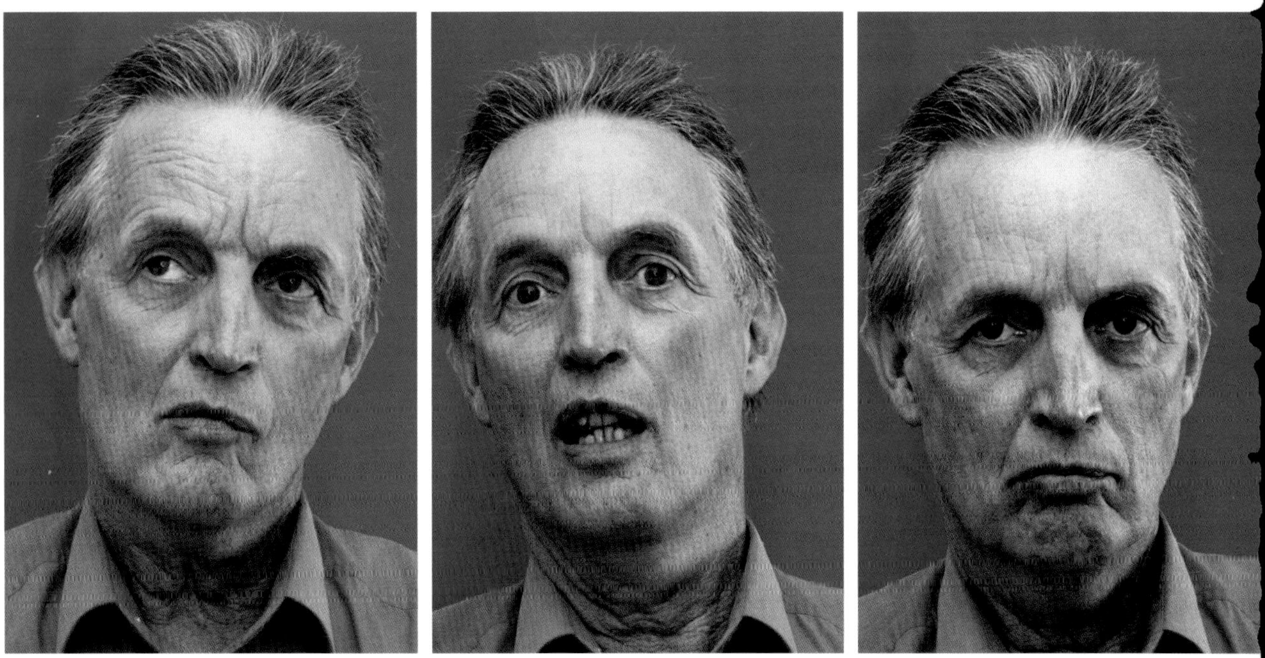

You might try:

frightened ▪ puzzled ▪ happy ▪ laughing ▪ sad ▪ making a point

Find a photo of a face portraying a clear gesture and create a more fully developed drawing that captures gesture and form. Here we're building on the skills you've been practising earlier. Use whatever techniques you like. You could draw right-handed, left-handed, without looking at the paper, from an upside-down picture, fast, slow ... whatever works best. Use charcoal or, if you wish, plunge into colour with pastels.

95 Take a picture of a face and rip it into pieces. Arrange the torn pieces into a different composition on a page and draw the result in charcoal or pastel. Again you're drawing what you see but the shapes force us away from preconceived ideas about how a subject should look. Even though it could be somewhat surreal, treat it with the same care you would use in a portrait.

96 Choose another picture of a face and rip a piece out. Draw the photo at high speed (about one minute). Now add a realistic, slow drawing of the missing piece. The fast/slow combo is a way of learning more about the different qualities of your own drawing. It can also produce something intriguing for the viewer. If you like the technique it's an option for making a series of works (and there are many variations – you can use paint, colour, actual photos or whatever combination takes your fancy).

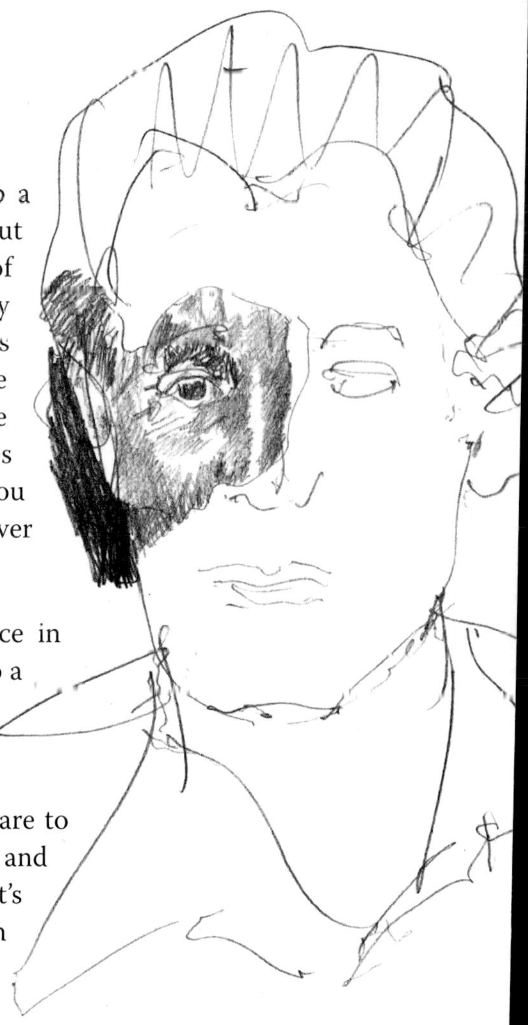

97 Play with forgery. Rip a photocopied face in two and carefully glue one side of the face onto a sheet of heavy paper or cardboard. Moisten the back of the photocopy for a couple of minutes, apply the glue and then roll it onto the backing like a piece of wallpaper, taking care to remove wrinkles and bubbles. When it's dry, do a fast sketch of the missing part of the face and then, directly on the glued-down part of the photocopy, do a careful pastel or paint rendering. If it works, you can use it as a technique to make finished pictures. The distinctly 'unfinished' element adds tension.

▶ A variation on ripping (Katharine White).

The dance of line

98 Exploring edges

Lines are edges which divide one thing from another. The edge of the wetness in the photo divides wet from not-wet. Or you could see the water as a line in itself, dividing one part of the road from the other. By using Photoshop you can explore the edges in other ways.

Edges often contain wonderful mathematics and physics. Why did the water flow as it did? How did it generate a distinctive roughness? Many of the answers, should you wish to pursue them, are in chaos and fractal theory. Unlike Euclidean geometry these are branches of maths which connect with the real world instead of the abstraction of straight lines, circles and so on. Wriggly edges of this type crop up repeatedly in nature. They also appear in graphs showing prices on the stock market. They are rough edges which are giving clues about some of the most fundamental processes of the universe.

Here it is again (above) with the different personality of the edge of a cloud.

In mathematics a line has length but not width. Hence the edge of the water mark is a 'line' and the wetness itself is an 'area'. With the clouds, consider the edge rather than the clouds themselves. Similarly with the trees in the picture below (rendered in black to draw attention to their fractal edge).

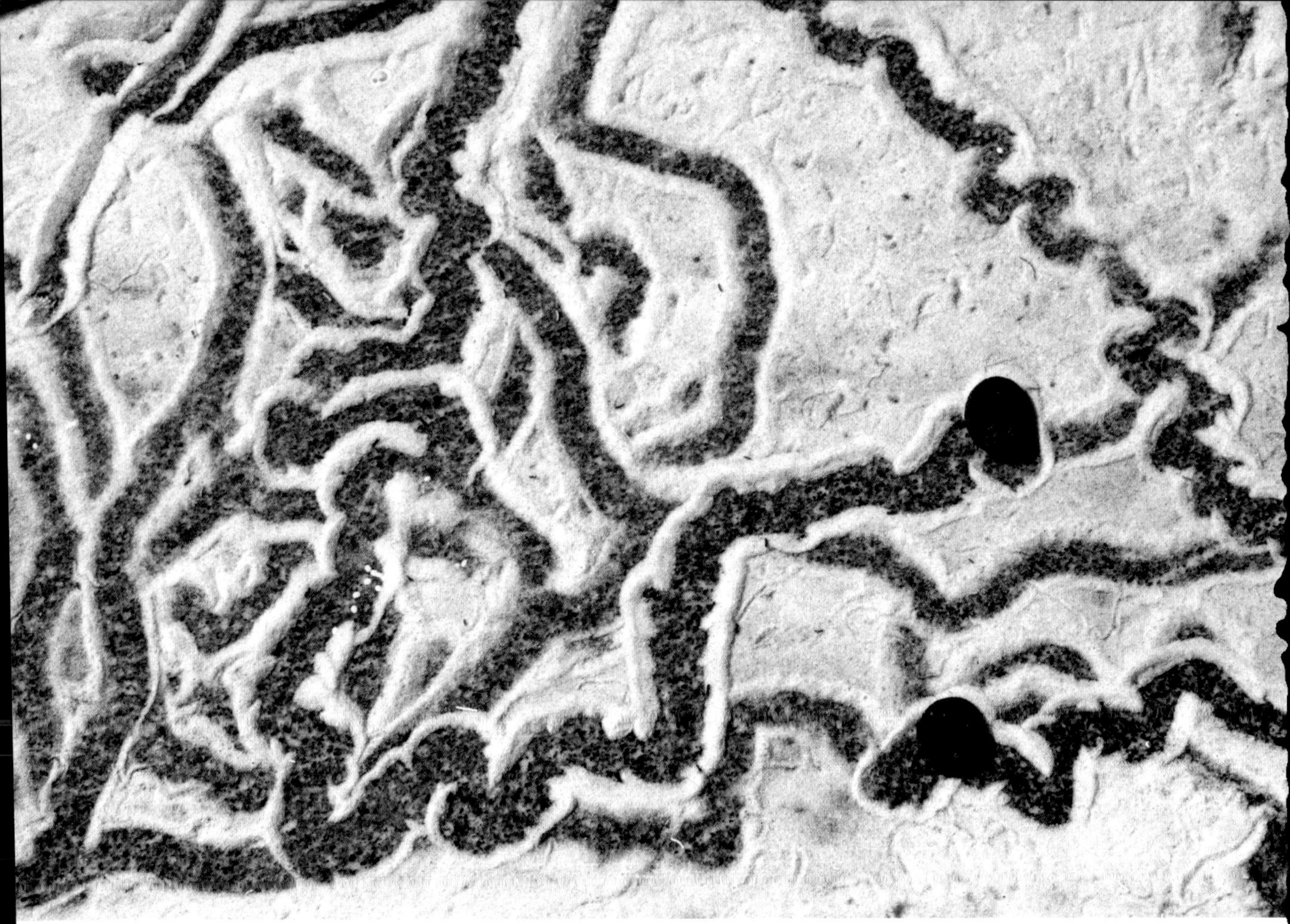

In both art and maths a line can create an area, not only by making a boundary (as in the edge of a shape) but in filling the area. I found two Queensland shell fish doing some inspired maths.

If you have access to a computer and a drawing program you can play with lines in ways which might have thrilled Leonardo.

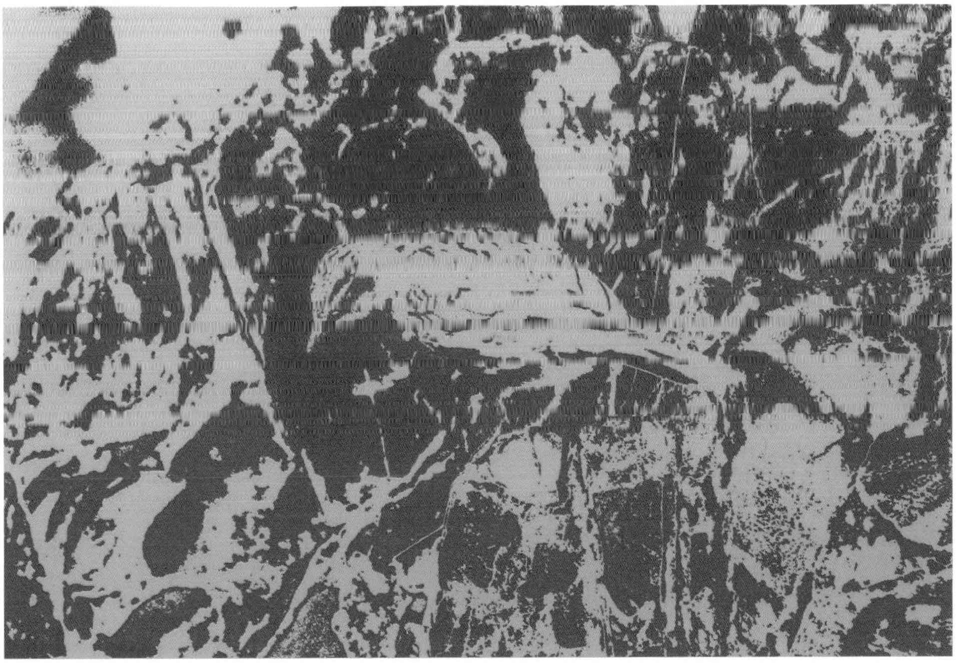

Everywhere that colours meet is a line that isn't there. The picture is a reminder that many lines are inventions. Rocks and faces, for example, don't have lines around them until we invent them.

Philosophically edges are useful and dangerous. Nations have lines around themselves but astronauts who view the Earth from space don't see them because they're imaginary. The yin/yang icon symbolises the awareness that divisions are not quite what they seem:

The dark side of the symbol contains a touch of light and the light side contains a spot of darkness. They are part of the same thing. A person who has always been totally blind cannot know darkness because dark can't be separated from light.

In the world, edges blur. It's convenient to say that our skin is our edge but really it isn't. We share air and thoughts in ways that can't be fully defined. We are like the yin/yang symbol, and so is art.

Art and language use lies to explore the truth. The yin/yang symbol is a lie (it uses the illusion of black and white to tell us that black and white don't exist).

Artists, forever searching for more direct means to connect with truth, often use real things to sidestep the problem of symbolism.

Here's a 'real' work by Sarah Bullied. It's no longer real – it became a photo in a book. But the original was real and the lines were made by real mesh. The saw was under tension from a real line of rubber (seconds later it broke).

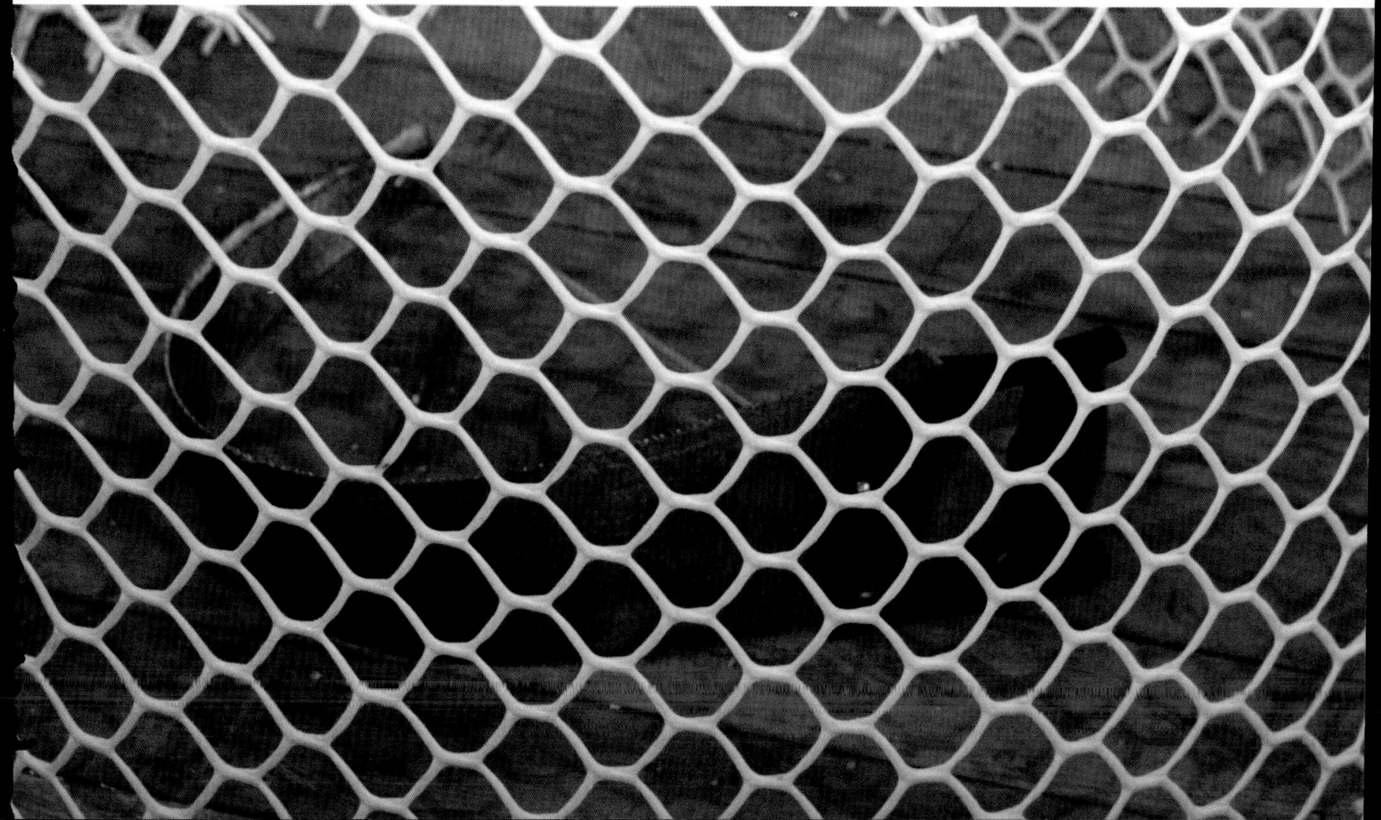

Lines in a glass brick.

▶ Wriggly lines created by emperor moth larvae on a squiggly gum, Queensland.

▼ Detail from a painting by Sarah Bullied using a big brush to create lines.

⯯ A grass line family.

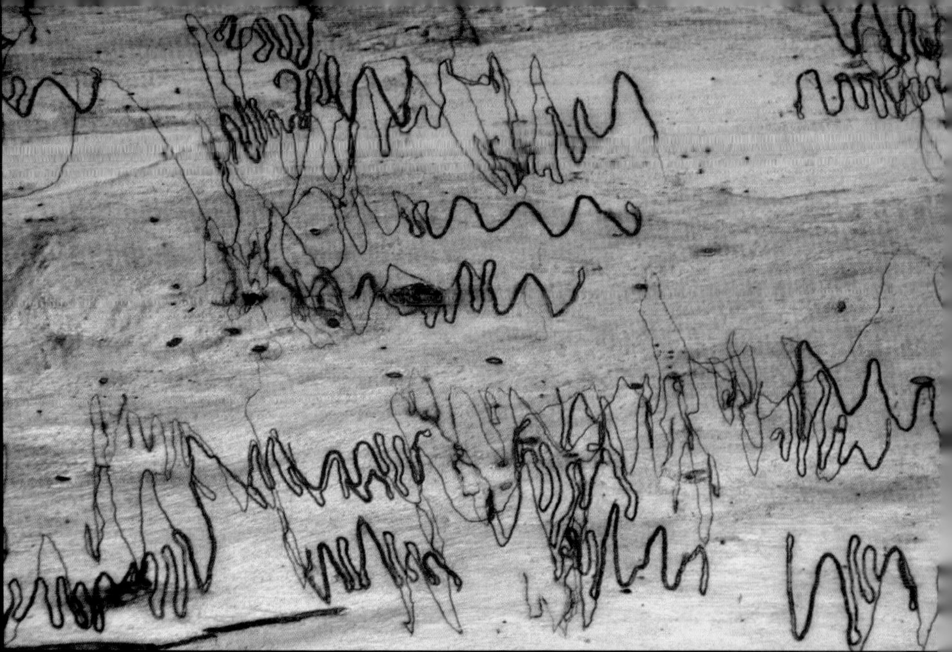

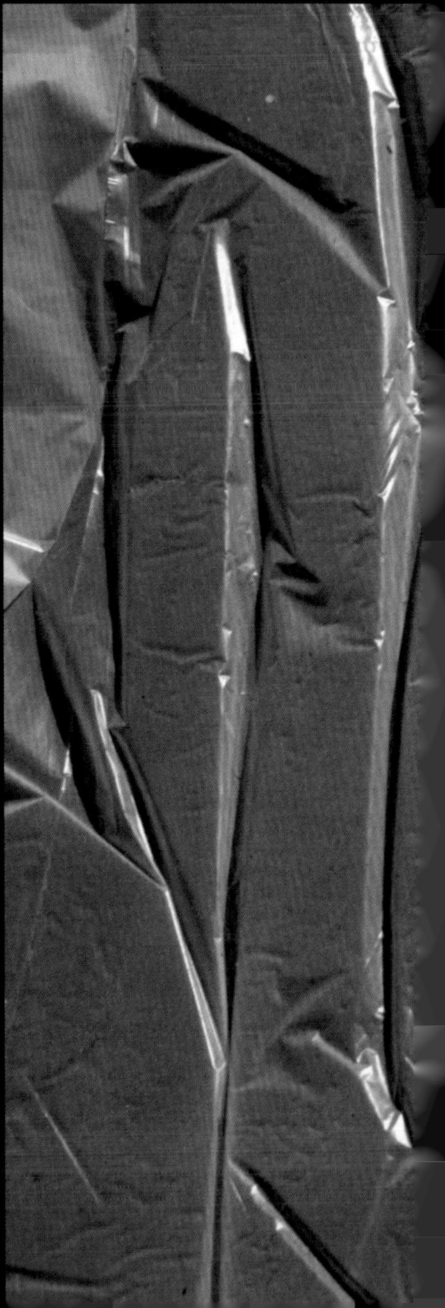

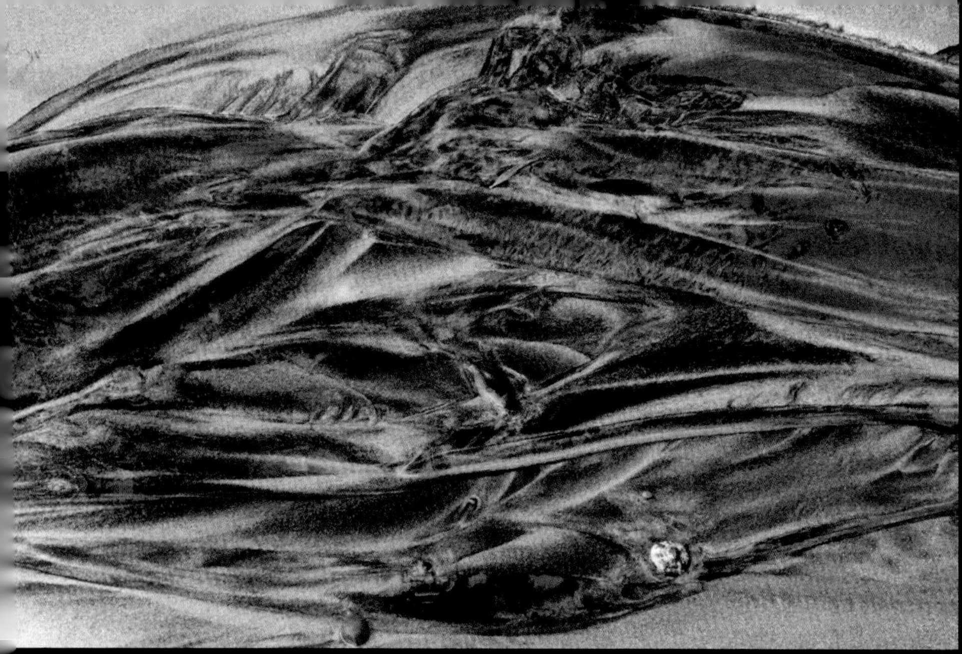

◂ Flow lines in sand.

◣ Lines created by plastic squeezed against a window.

▾ Bubble lines (froth on a beach).

▿ Cracked concrete lines.

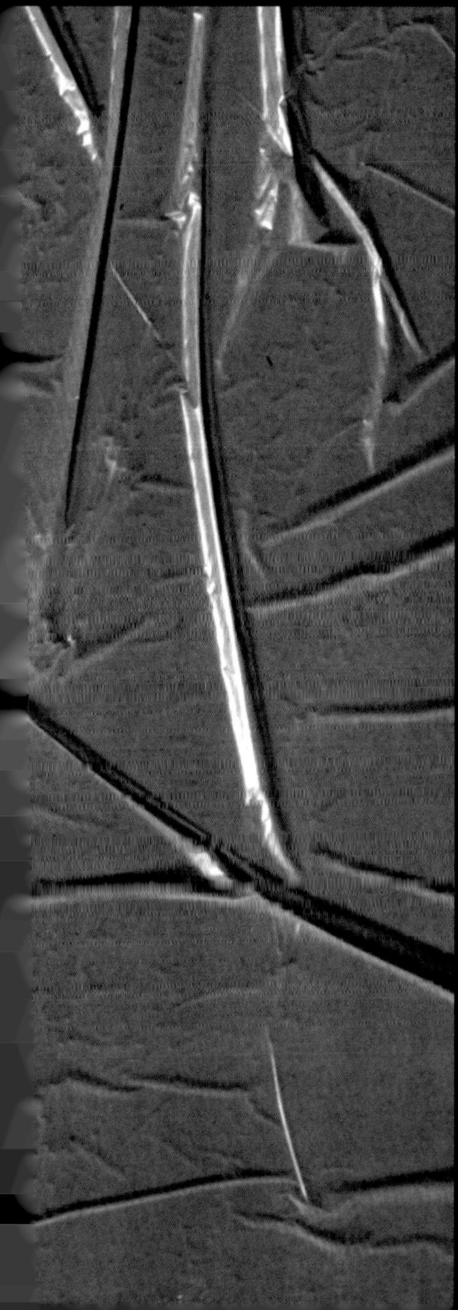

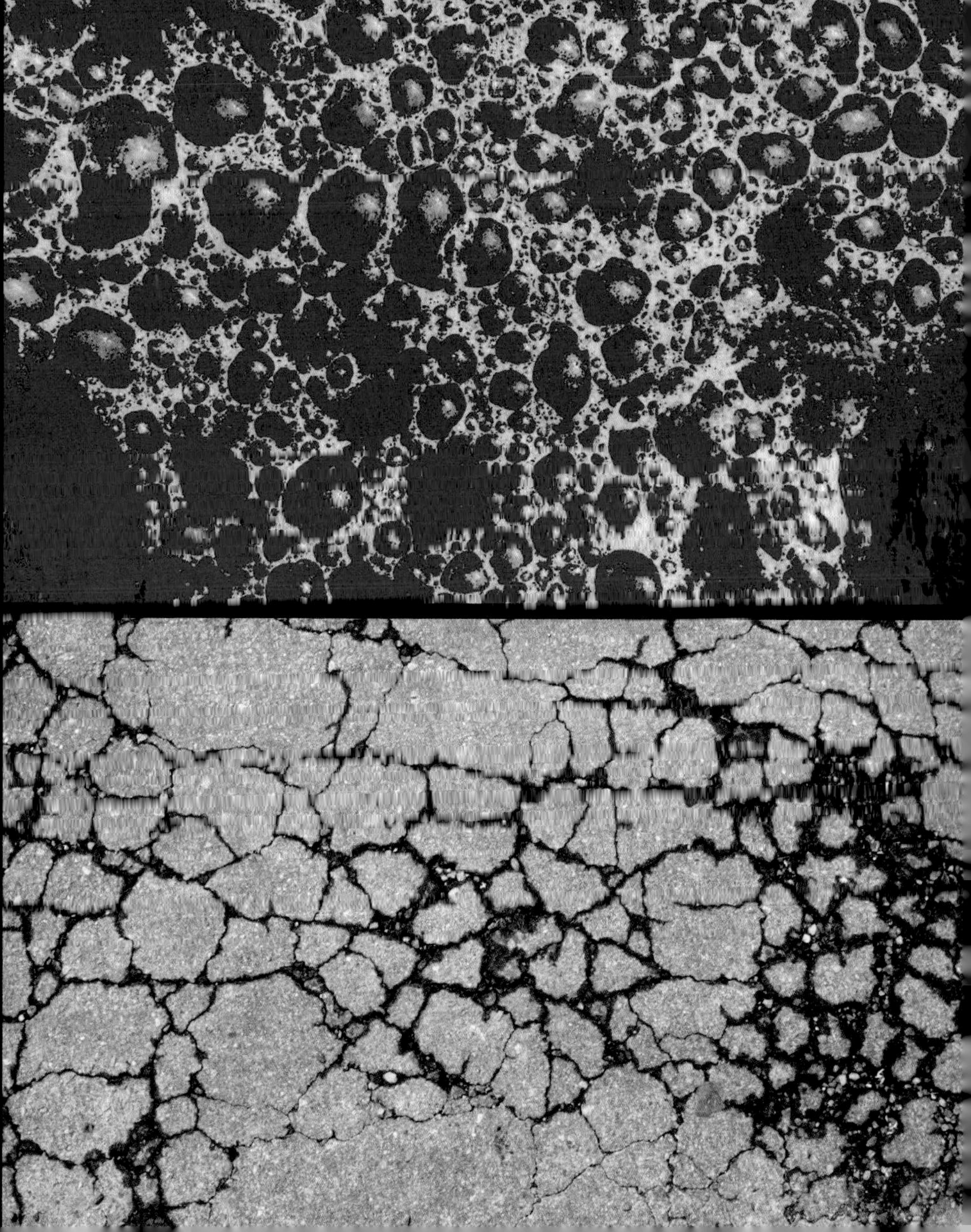

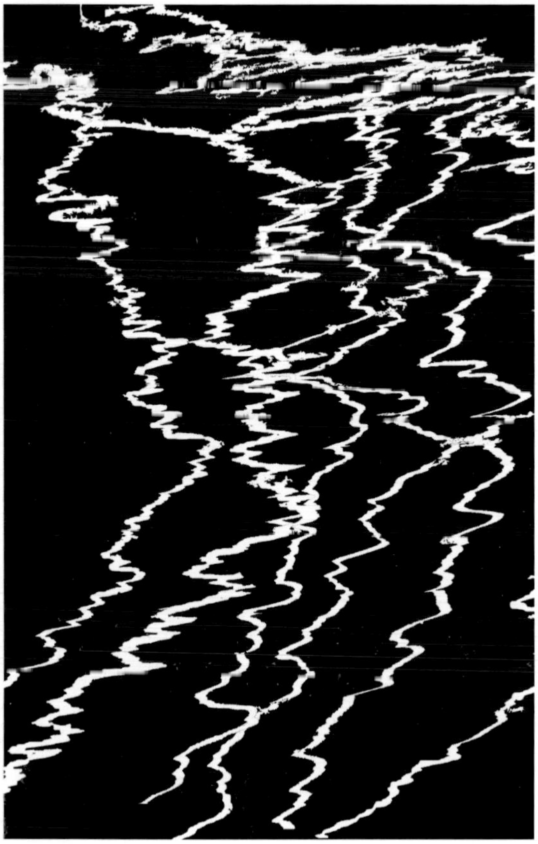

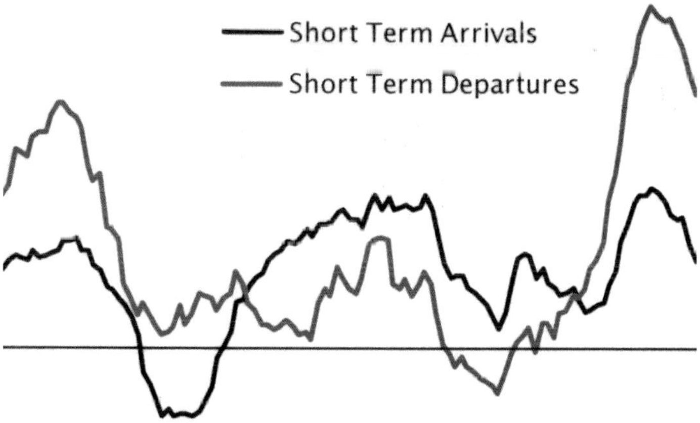

Tide lines (the edges of waves on the shore) and the waves of a typical graph relating to the behaviour of people.

Think beyond the limitations of 'drawing' and connect with the world in new ways, both through your observation and your imagination. Something as innocent as 'line' can open a door into a new and wonderful realm.

99 *Discover and invent families of lines*

Explore families of lines. Thin, fat, wiggly, zigzag, broken, curvy – these are a start. Look around you. What other sorts of lines can you see? What lines can you invent?

100 Make an arrangement of similar items on a page. Use nails, buttons, leaves, pieces of ripped paper – anything that you can find. I tried it with plastic spoons and let them arrange themselves by dropping them from a metre above the paper. I prefer the 'accidental' patterns to the shapes that would develop if I deliberately placed each spoon.

Then draw or photograph the spaces around and between the objects. It's a back-to-front picture in which you can put all your attention into the 'negative shapes'. You can assume some poetic licence if you feel you can make the shapes

Something as innocent as 'line' can open a door into a new and wonderful realm

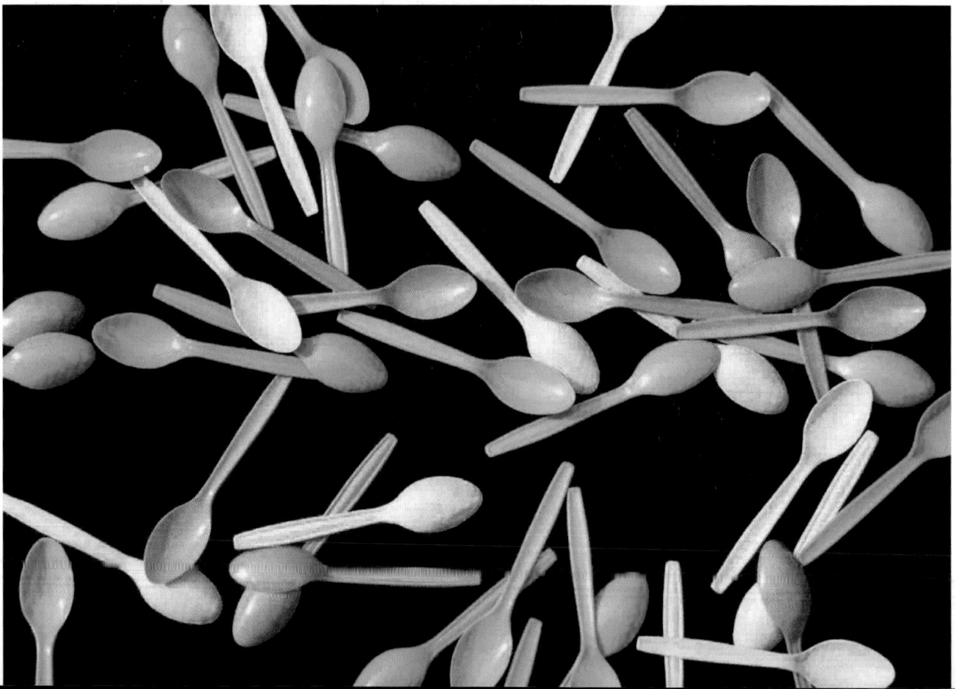

more interesting by adjusting them – there's no need to do a slavish copy. If you wish, draw some of the positive items in careful detail. (It's a variation on the previous exercise.) You can take the same approach to patterns within nature (paying attention to the ways in which things arrange themselves naturally.

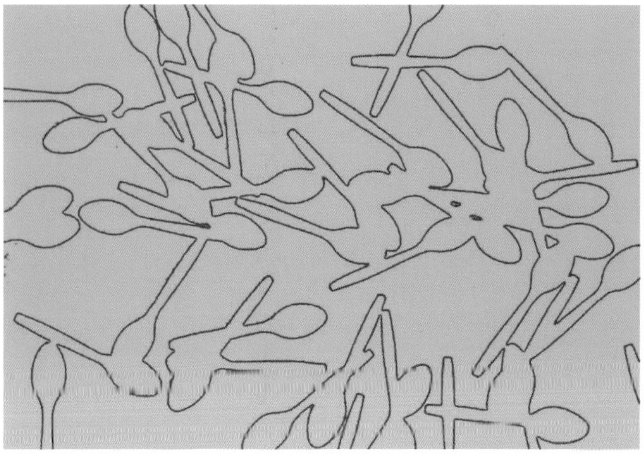

If you're drawing, rather than using photos, the shapes will take on a life of their own. In the beginning it's usually mundane (the spoons didn't feel promising but I bought them anyway). I tried several different things in Photoshop and some – like the outline – looked promising. **Polar Co-ordinates** produced this:

It's a whole lot faster doing it on a computer and that brings us to the question of technology. Is Kate's cat more authentic than my photos? 'Hand art' (drawing, painting, etc) has different qualities from 'digital art' but they can be equally authentic and can be combined. The art is in the experimenting – and the imagining.

101 *Exaggerations and reversals*

The ingredients are simple but the relationships are immensely complex.

Ice forming on the window of a plane has something in common with the 'accidental' pattern of the spoons. Next, the same ice, exaggerating the positive and negative attributes.

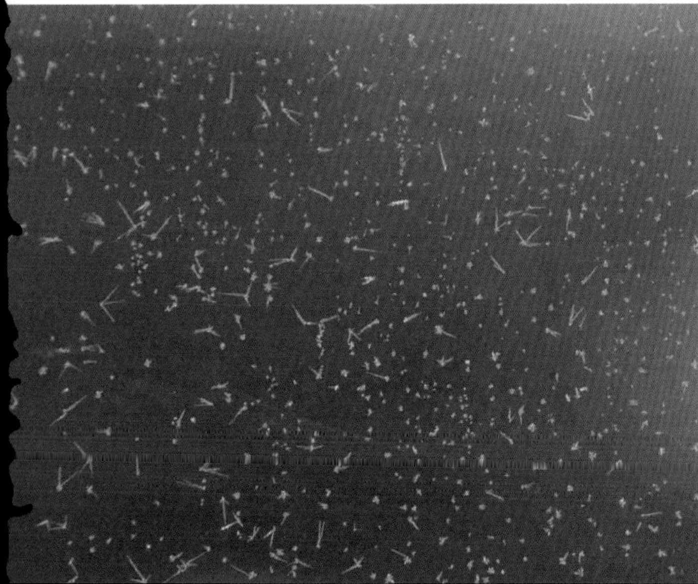

Cracks on the surface of a rock. The same pattern turns into a strange net when reversed.

'Natural' shapes may seem different from manufactured shapes but humans conform to similar laws of shaping. When you stand back (or fly above one) you can imagine a city as a crystalline structure which is as organic as rocks and hills.

Reverse the colours and you could almost be looking at a chemical structure.

And when you play some more the abstraction increases.

Another way to see things differently is to squash them. I liked the twisty lines and uneven reflections on the deformed Coke can. Unlike Andy Warhol's Coke images this was the real thing, complete with sugary stickiness.

102 Deform an object or photograph and either draw it or turn it into a new photo.

Besides taking you into drawing and photography these ideas invite you to think about the world in different ways. There isn't any 'correct' way to make art – you can explore and invent for all you're worth. Find what works for your own skills and style.

If all else fails, think laterally. Some of the Renaissance masters used camera-like devices as a drawing aid – they had no qualms about using technology to get a desired result, and you can do the same. If you find you can make use of a scanner, projector or any other tool, try it out.

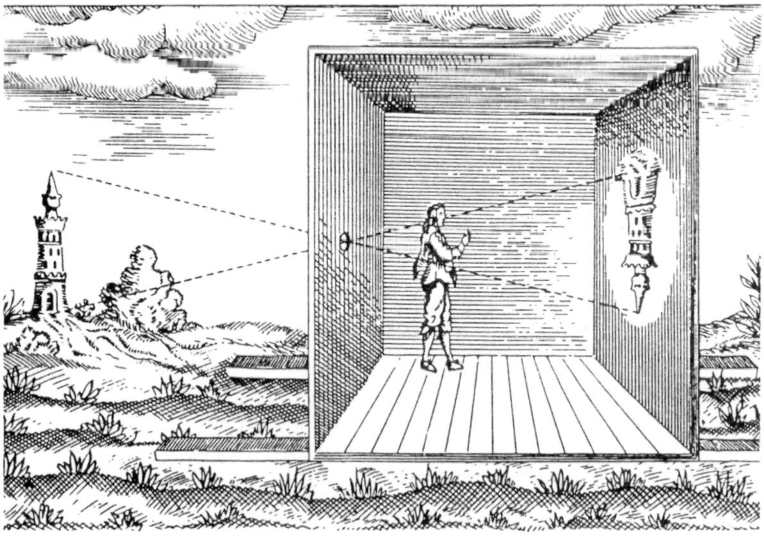

Part of your research is to find out whether the personality of your painting/drawing is helped by technology. You might be surprised to find that your 'faults' are more appealing than slick technical skill. What you see as your faults may actually be your style – the very ingredient which makes your art special.

Early art technology — the camera obscura.

103 Draw a face using a pen, pencil or charcoal and make it out of a single line (as a snail would have to do). Experiment for a start (on a small scale) and then try using the line to build form as well as edges. This goes back to the snail 'drawing' – making lines to create a surface.

What you see as your faults may actually be your style – the very ingredient which makes your art special

104 Draw another face using pastel lines of whatever length and colours you choose. If you want to extend further you could try the same thing with paint and lead yourself into a new set of projects.

The evolution of art

There are big transition points in art and creativity. Decisions are required. You can think of this like branches on a tree or veins on a leaf.

In the picture the veins show a complex pattern of splitting, which would go into finer detail if we could look at it through a microscope. Metaphorically the tree is making decisions throughout its body (humans do too – it's especially clear in our veins, lungs and nervous system). Each split leads to a finer line and ultimately to the edge of the leaf. At every edge the tree connects with the universe and gathers the stuff of life which the veins share through the whole body. Each decision ends up flowing both ways and the most extreme smallness connects with cosmic bigness.

Creative decisions are like veins, seemingly taking us into smaller and smaller places but eventually, if you have the courage and tenacity to stay on the path, connecting with the great oneness. If we stay with the tree image, creativity takes us out on a limb, then a twig and a leaf – and then the universe.

The goal of teachers is to take you along the path to that interface. They can't make your decisions, but our underlying connectedness somehow makes a difference.

I wonder about the story of the Garden of Eden in which 'Man' is separated from 'God'. Could it be

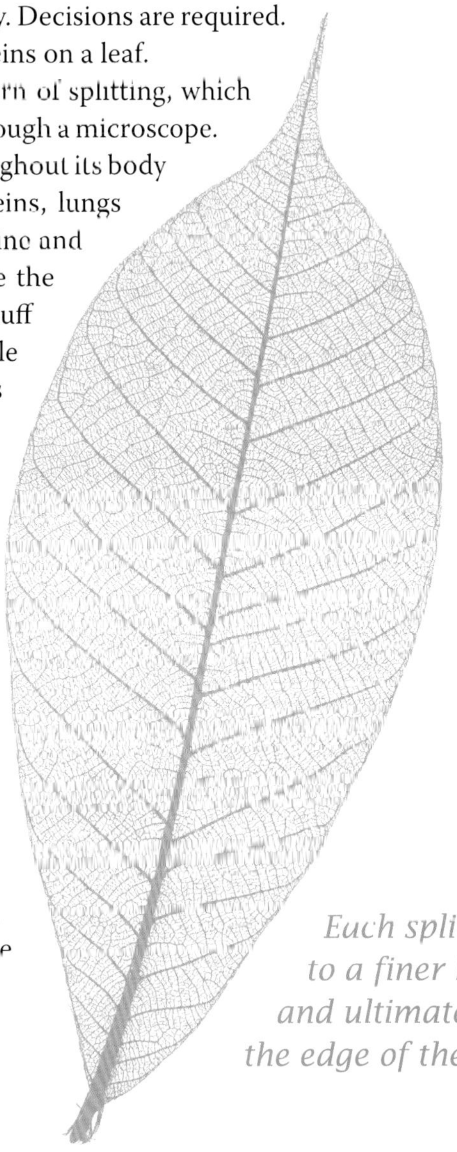

Each split leads to a finer line and ultimately to the edge of the leaf

◄ Sculpture by Gretchen Smith.

that the quest of art is re-integration? Is art one of many veins, all of which lead to the edge which is also the centre?

Teachers are at once helpful and deceptive. The American/Japanese sculptor Isamu Noguchi said: "You've got to become yourself, and the only way to become yourself is to deny your teachers … Any person that I have been influenced by I have been obliged to betray, in a sense. It's only from freeing ourselves from the obligation of being beholden to others that we are really free."

Once teachers let go of the notion that they are there to instil pre-ordained ideas they are free to get into the magic of teaching

His approach to art was *flow* rather than *force*. "You can find out how to do something and then do it, or you can do something and then find out what you did. I seem to be of the second disposition."

TLC uses the slogan 'Ready, *fire*, aim' which sounds like a severance recipe for teachers. Yet it is the opposite. Once teachers let go of the notion that they are there to instil pre-ordained ideas they are free to get into the magic of teaching. It is about sharing, dancing, participating.

A good teacher can help with the craft of art. A great teacher will go beyond ego and craft to the soul of art. Noguchi: "Eventually you are all alone and no one is going to help you much because you have denied them all. And you have to deny yourself too, because it's your own past that is going to then constrain you. How to become free of that is very important."

The world itself is a teacher. Noguchi said, "I like to think of my work as having some kind of relevance. No matter how abstract and no matter how small or how big, it has a kind of a voice which other people can hear."

"It is the accident that gives you the key to creation" —Isamu Noguchi

He paid attention to mistakes. "It is only your mistakes that force you beyond your own imagination into something new. It is the accident that gives you the key to creation."

Art itself subdivides like a leaf. But not like a leaf. No matter how you play with it the leaf structure doesn't illustrate what really happens because everything in art feeds back on everything – it's not a progression but a feedback process. It may look plausible but it's wrong.

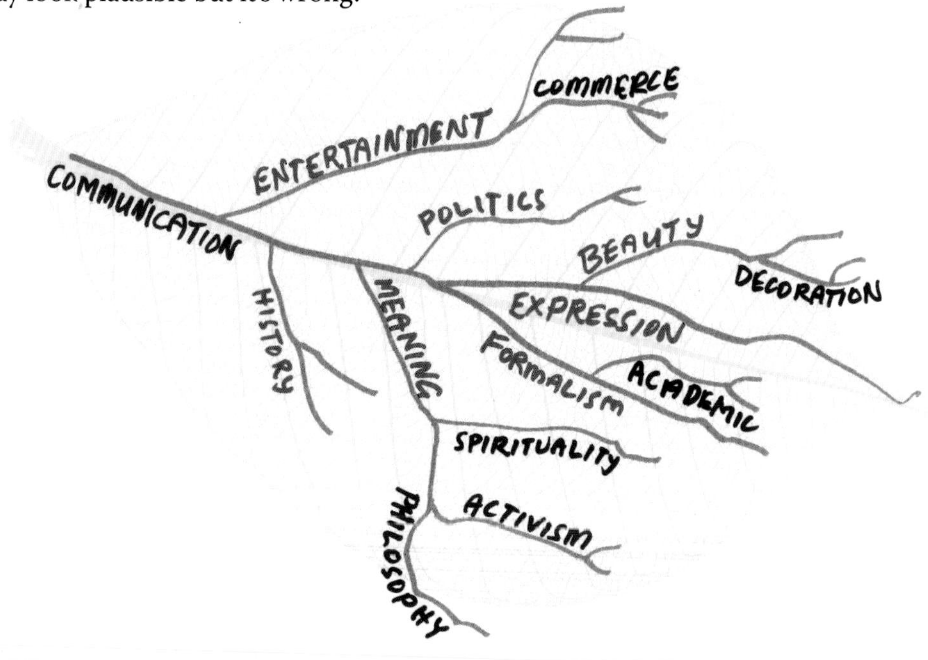

The real deal is so complex we can only guess at its structure. The ingredients are interacting within an infinitely complex fractal pattern which defies conventional labels. Maybe it looks like this:

Or this:

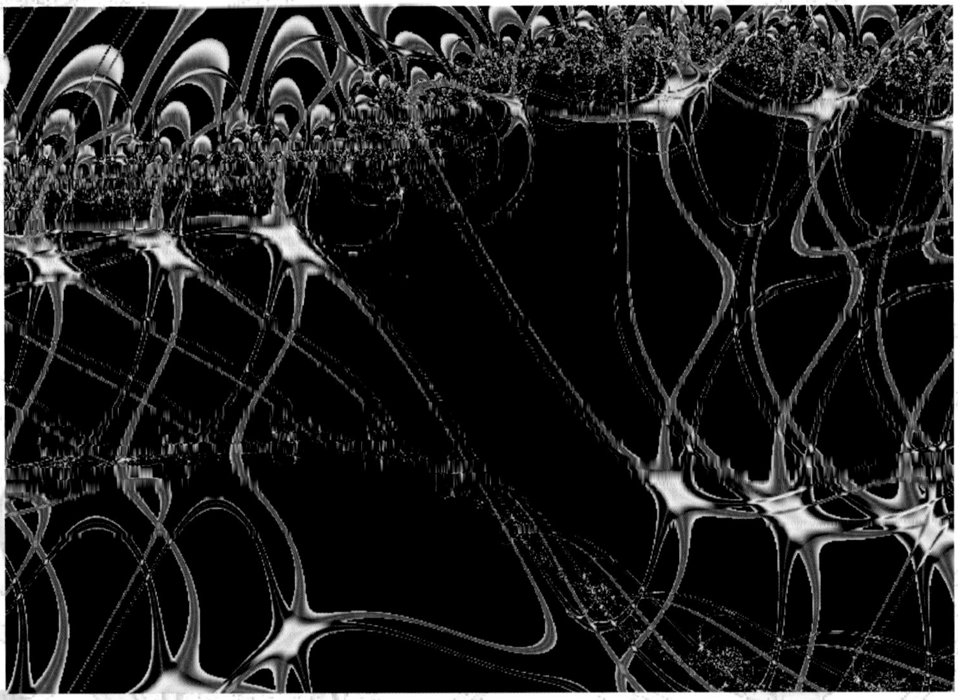

These two images are both fragments of the Mandelbrot Set which is a complex feedback system. The history of art, if it could be turned into a single graphical image, is certainly going to look more like the Mandelbrot Set than the usual linear portrayals.

Whichever way it goes, it's not like the neat A to Z transition. It's probably fractal, a 'strange attractor' which unfolds forever, has an elaborate pattern and infinite variety. It's a feedback system in which each outcome shapes every new result. When you look at the history of art you're looking at a creativity machine that produces the whole range from junk through to masterpieces.

The complexity of art gives endless scope to armchair critics. You'll hear talk of the latest absolute best thing in art and it's important to think of it as another event around the 'strange attractor' of art. Maybe it's junk, maybe it's brilliant. Maybe it's about people trying to sell something. Part of the creative process is to decide which critics are worth listening to.

The complexity of art gives endless scope to armchair critics

It was fashionable in the late 20th century to say that painting was dead. That fashion lingers. Bollocks. If you love paint, it's alive.

I've heard that computer-based art by indigenous people is the leading edge. Bollocks. Leading edges are inventions from the advertising industry.

Peter Adsett at TLC is dedicated to 'materiality' in art. His work challenges the idea that material in art stands for anything other than itself. Speaking of his work in *Two Laws*, a dialogue in painting with Aboriginal artist Rusty Peters, Adsett said: "Rusty's paintings are not representations of law, they are law. They carry an incredible amount of knowledge and power. They are the site, and that is the power of the work."

Walking Buddha, Nakhon Pathom, Thailand.

"In my case there is no representation, because I set out to destroy that concept ... I do it by attacking conventions such as verticality, composition, colour, line and aesthetics." (*Two Laws* catalogue.) Adsett's work combines busy surfaces and simple but elusive shapes. He provides nothing to hang on to and reminds me of Mark 15:34 – "My God, my God, why have you forsaken me?" In Zen there is a saying, "If you meet the Buddha on the road, kill him." The spiritual reference is that *thing-ness* can be an obstacle. Peter Adsett's art throws us into a space where the materiality is intense and the thing-ness is no longer present.

This art is tough and uncompromising, a new revolution. But revolutions have a habit of transposing into evolution. Between 1928 and 1929, René Magritte painted a picture of a pipe entitled *Ceci n'est pas une pipe.* He was drawing attention to the fact that the painting was paint. It didn't stop him taking care with the illusion of a pipe.

Magritte said, "My painting is visible images which conceal nothing; they evoke mystery and, indeed, when one sees one of my pictures, one asks oneself this simple question, "What does that mean?" It does not mean anything, because mystery means nothing either, it is unknowable."

The illusionary side of art is partly about observation. To make paint into an illusion of a pipe, Magritte had to observe a pipe. A side effect of observation

Discarded sculptures recycled as part of a conceptual artwork by Tony Labat, di Rosa Preserve, California.

is that it can take you into a different place. It can be a meditation during which everything else in your life is suspended while you connect with your subject.

Should you go further down the path of figurative art? The choice is yours. When I was at art school figurative art was going out of favour and there was a whole room of abandoned casts of statues. It would be fun to have them back – an instant installation and great props.

Does life drawing have any value in today's world? It certainly can be relevant but it's a demanding discipline. Buying into drawing is like training for the Olympics, but there isn't a retirement age. In bygone days drawing was a given – an essential part of the artist's craft. Today it's an option. You can embrace it, ignore it, or use it as a stimulus to your visual thinking.

Leonardo was passionately interested in drawing and he had a scientist's curiosity about what happens under the skin. At considerable risk (it was a crime) he obtained dead bodies and dissected them to learn about muscles and bones. I doubt that he would have done that in the age of digital photography – a camera gets anatomy right every time without knowing anything. Your own eye – if you can merely see what is in front of you – will do the same, but needs a longer exposure.

"Mystery means nothing ... it is unknowable."
—Magritte

It makes it harder when you're confronted with the decision of making a long-term commitment. Everything in art is like that now – as it is in life. There are no givens except those passed on by people who believe in fairy stories.

The Eastern tradition took a different approach. You would sit before the teacher and nothing would happen until you asked a question. It has its advantages.

After Magritte (see en.wikipedia.org/wiki/Rene_Magritte).

Bernie Neville talks about the problem in *Educating Psyche*. "We learn very little by being told the answers to questions we have not asked. Learning originates in the actions of the learner, not those of the teacher. A great deal of what we learn we learn by a sort of absorption, or we just 'pick it up' through experience, as we go along, without the need for teaching. It is only in schools that we abandon this natural way of learning. We tell children (or adults) things and expect them to remember them. I believe we tell them largely in vain. The learning they do has little to do with our telling."

My first art teacher, Maurice Smith, a member of the Royal Academy, advised: "Learn anatomy and forget it." His view was that it improved your drawing but had to become a reflex so that it didn't get in the way. A similar argument was made for the virtues of learning Latin – it was supposed to improve your English. But why not go straight to English? Learn drawing by looking at things and drawing them.

"We learn very little by being told the answers to questions we have not asked"

Feedback is better than Latin or anatomy. If you're working with others, share your work and pay attention to the responses. As you get more skilled, share your work more widely. Learn how to use the visible to express the *in*visible. Beautiful skills in realism are only a starting point.

Contemporary art may look thoroughly fragmented – not like a tree splitting into many branches but like something too weird to be described as a tree at all. Instead of attempting to make sense of it in 'isms', it's worth thinking about the common factors.

- All art is communicating something (even art which says it isn't).
- All art involves something that can be described.
- All art is done for a purpose (even art which says it isn't).

Let's put aside the mysteries of art for a moment and consider the advertising industry. Advertising first has to gain attention. It doesn't matter how, although there are physical and financial restraints. Blowing yourself up on prime-time television would gain attention but you wouldn't be around to enjoy the results. Buying an entire issue of *The New York Times* would gain attention but you might not have the money to pay for it.

In the early days of TLC I stood in a $5 suit (appropriately it was a Rembrandt) on Wellington's main street and encouraged people to paint me. Tourists took photos, we achieved good newspaper coverage and a few enrolments. I

walked around town in the suit – one half untouched and the other half looking very colourful. I gained attention in all sorts of friendly and unexpected ways. It turned out to be a good piece of performance art. It communicated something whimsical about an icon (the suit); it symbolised the tensions between the 'right' and 'left' brains; it produced commercial results and satisfied my desire to be different – and note that this was done in the heart of the capital's commercial/government precinct.

All art is approximately parallel to advertising although it doesn't always have a commercial component. One way or another art is communicating ('selling') something about humanity.

Individuals can advertise without going through an agency (wearing a sandwich board in a busy street can gain considerable attention and you can do it entirely by yourself). Advertising agencies do their own thing and don't need the approval of the Royal Academy or any other organisation (although they are supposed to operate within national laws). There is still a power structure – organisations with money can go to the best agencies and command the biggest media exposure. In the art world the heavyweight galleries and big institutions have a disproportionate amount of power, but the patterns are changing. Increasingly artists are able to make independent choices and find alternative pathways to earn a living through their creativity.

Galleries earn their keep to the extent that they focus attention on their artists. Artists who don't gain attention can be like flowers that don't attract insects to pollinate them. They can disappear without trace. If you think of flowers – and advertising – there are endless tactics to gain attention. The same applies to art and it is hardly surprising that the variety is so daunting.

Increasingly artists are able to make independent choices and find alternative pathways to earn a living through their creativity

Up until the mid-20th century art seemed to slot neatly into defined 'movements' (mainly when we look back on it), but the neatness was partly due to limited vision. Mostly it involved Western museum art and either ignored the rest of the world or tucked it into a few footnotes. It also ignored a large part of the Western world (women were marginalised, most minorities barely existed and it was quite a narrow slice of the human condition that made it onto the gallery walls). A seething cauldron of pent-up artistic energy boiled over into what has been loosely labelled 'post-modernism'. Anything that gained attention was suddenly 'art'. Whether it has any enduring value depends on whether it 'speaks' to later generations. Elvis Presley looked like a passing fad in the 1950s but he's the best selling dead singer of all time. Artists that look faddish may endure and others who seem important may vanish.

Instead of trying to tuck things into historical boxes it can be more useful to explore the questions that artists were asking.

Sometimes (like my suit painting) aspects of the question don't get clearly articulated until after the event, but a non-verbal question is still a question.

In looking at art 'movements' we are looking at questions and creativity rather than a tightly defined story of art (there isn't one)

The Expressionists, for example, asked whether art could be pared back to expression rather than having to carry all the baggage of realism. The Surrealists asked if art could abandon ordinary reality and make its claim in the surreal world of dreams and chance. Pop artists asked if the low art of advertising and mass production could be embraced in a new way as high art.

In looking at art 'movements' we are therefore looking at questions and creativity rather than a tightly defined story of art (there isn't one). The history of art provides a cross-section view of part of human evolution. Let's take a diversion into some of the great questions, keeping in mind that they may still be highly relevant, with a twist or two of fresh thinking, to your own artwork. Much of your creative development is a mix of learning about the questions and skills of the past and formulating new questions and skills for the present.

IMPRESSIONISM Responding to the 'impression' of a subject rather than slavishly staying with academic conventions. *What are today's academic conventions? How are they getting in the way?*

CUBISM Thinking of subjects in terms of their underlying (Euclidean) geometry and then going with new shapes, rhythms and multiple viewpoints so that the work takes on its own 'thing-ness' rather than being purely a representation. *What are some new ways of looking which take us beyond Cubism?*

SURREALISM Delving into the realm of dreams and imagination and claiming this as the one area of freedom still available to art. *Are dreams relevant? How can you use them in your art?*

EXPRESSIONISM /FAUVISM Focusing on feeling rather than visual realism. *Question: Does feeling connect in any way with the current interest in materiality?*

ABSTRACTION Exploring relationships between colours and shapes. *Are such relationships arbitrary or is there a natural pattern underlying our preferences? Could a computer generate successful abstract art by itself?*

DADA Outright contempt for traditional art and academic values; acceptance of all things as art (art is what you choose it to be); acceptance of change and decay (rather than the illusion of permanence). *Were the Dadaists right? What challenges would they be putting to the art world today?*

POP Utilising mass-produced items of popular culture ('low' art) as gallery artefacts and events. Shifting attention to ideas rather than the craft of art. Providing a new sort of dialogue through the ephemera of commerce. *Is Pop art still happening? As we get more and more 'commodified', has the world of commerce hijacked the world of art?*

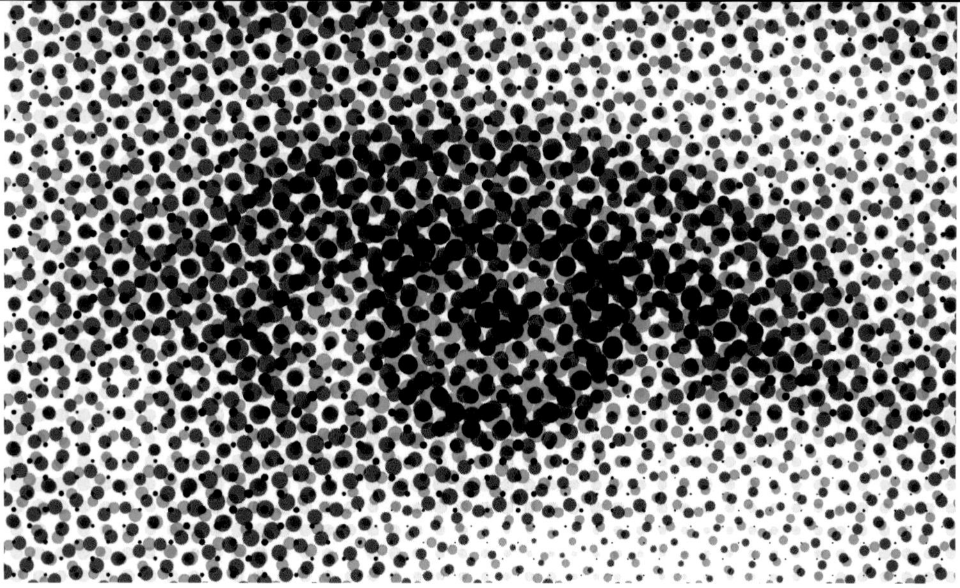

Impressionism

(About 1870–1895.) The Impressionist legacy centres on three major issues: *spontaneity, the science of colour and light, realism and nature.* The Impressionists were concerned with *real life.* They wanted to convey an accurate 'impression' of things as they are. This led, naturally enough, into an exploration of *colour and human perception.* The Pointillists (**Seurat** in particular) moved into a careful scientific analysis of colour that foreshadowed modern printing processes (which convey an impression of colour by using the three primary colours plus black, printed in the form of small dots).

Detail from George Seurat's A Sunday Afternoon on the Island of La Grande Jatte

Spontaneity remains important. The idea was to observe real things, especially landscape, and to paint boldly and directly. The dominant schools of the day emphasised studio painting – sketches were sometimes done to collect information but raw nature was regarded as too uncouth for the aesthetic sensibilities of the artist. In their context the Impressionists were revolutionaries. It's possible that they also understood that bypassing our calculating 'left brain' unleashed different aspects of intelligence and opened doors which were closed to the academics.

The concern with spontaneity led to insights about *perception* – in particular the fact that humans 'invent' much of what they perceive. A modest amount of accurate visual information is enough to enable the viewer to reconstruct the missing details.

Self portrait by Rembrandt (1606–1669).

This wasn't really a new thing – painters like **Hals** and **Rembrandt** had explored similar ground more than 250 years earlier. What happened in the late 19th century was that this approach to painting slowly became dominant whereas previously it had been regarded as a mere step along the way to producing serious work.

More recently there have been investigations into the threshold of human perception – what is the smallest amount of information required to trigger recognition? In an informal way the Impressionists explored the same theme but weren't awarded with doctorates.

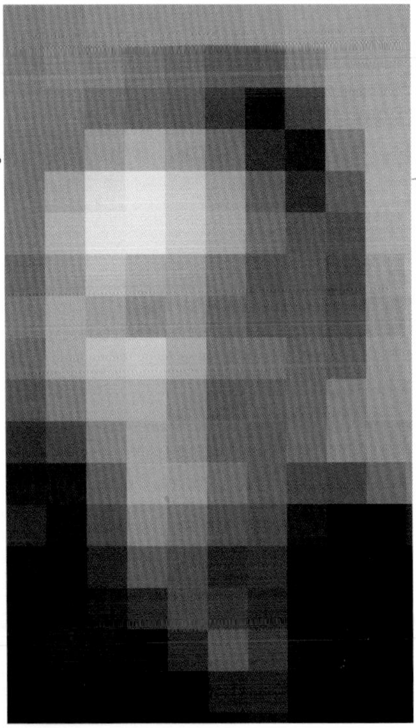

105 Look at examples of the work of Impressionist artists. **Manet**, **Monet**, **Pissarro**, **Sisley** and **Cassatt** are a good start (the internet has abundant information, as do most local libraries). Imagine, as best you can, living in their time. There are no automobiles, radios or televisions. Photography is black and white, expensive and rarer than flush toilets. Average life expectancy is less than 50 years.

The art establishment looks like the British Empire – large, overpowering and inflexible. The industrial revolution is in full swing and its mechanical effectiveness is strengthening the philosophical model of a clockwork universe.

In this environment artists are looking at the world and contemplating the failure of academic art to portray nature in an authentic way. Look at documentaries, explore history books and attempt the impossible feat of seeing through their eyes.

The purpose, besides learning about art and history, is to consider creativity in action. Impressionism wasn't just a change in style – it opened new possibilities of interpreting the world and the consequences were far-reaching.

Self-portrait by Mary Cassatt (1844–1926).

In art we sometimes muddy our progress by paying homage to the false idea that creativity is entirely about newness

106 'Forgery' is one way to explore different areas of art. Find an Impressionist work you like and either copy the whole picture or enough of it to get a feeling of what the artist was doing.

The copy is one of the oldest forms of learning, not only in art but in most of what we do. Our language skills come from copying and kids get big encouragement to mimic the sounds and actions of adults. In art we sometimes muddy our progress by paying homage to the false idea that creativity is entirely about newness.

Copying is not the enemy of creativity – it is part of it. Aim for balance – enough 'craft' skills (learned by copying) to provide the ingredients for effective novelty.

Larry Carr with his Van Gogh copy.

107 Do some experiments – about postcard-size – with dots of colour. Get the feeling of the way they merge to become different colours when you stand back from them.

What would Seurat have given to do Pointillism at the press of a button in Photoshop?

108 Find a photo of a suitable scene and paint an 'Impression'. If you want to free yourself of the need to draw, paint directly on a photocopy.

The mindset for copying is different from being in the open air, painting what you see – do your best to imagine you're outside.

109 Find a scene you like and be an Impressionist for a while. I think of the Impressionists as 'realists with feeling'. They wanted to break out of the limitations of academic painting and respond directly to the world as they saw it. They realised that the viewer does much of the work when looking at a painting – detail is less important than an accurate impression. They had a deep understanding of painting and it's hard to come close to their sophistication (it may be over-ambitious to expect your first attempt will be featured at Sotheby's). This won't stop you from role-playing an Impressionist and achieving insight into the things that challenged them.

Cubism

A central part of the theory of Cubism was an illusion – the natural world isn't made up of make-believe solids based on Euclidean geometry. Cubism developed between 1907 and 1914 and could be viewed as the clockwork universe going into spasms.

Its real value was in rethinking the nature of art rather than the structure of nature. In creative terms it was a 'provocation' and its value was less in the theory than in the exploration. It changed the artist's view from a 'point' to a complex 'god's eye' view that could see different angles of a subject in a single image. The Cubists used materials in a way that took art a big step towards being a thing in itself rather than a representation. Cubism spawned some enduring work because it demanded radical thinking and took art into a new space.

After Cubism the clockwork universe was forever changed.

Cubism was started by **Braque** and **Picasso**. Picasso said they sought "pure truth without pretension, tricks or malice". (p.97, *Picasso, Creator and Destroyer*, by Arianna Stassinopoulos Huffington). At this level Cubism had a vaguely scientific, analytical quality – it was about the representation of objects in terms of many-faceted solids ('cubes' and other forms), often incorporating multiple viewpoints. In practice it embodied:

- *stylisation/abstraction* (simplification of the appearance of things)
- use of *collage*
- *defiance of traditional methods*
- a *challenge* to the basic understanding of what 'art' is
- incorporation of *other influences* such as the African masks which appear in Picasso's *Les Demoiselles d'Avignon*
- *decorative qualities*
- *depersonalisation* (in some of its forms it was virtually the opposite of Expressionism – highly cerebral and unemotional)
- *social commentary* (Cubism sometimes defied its own gravity and became highly expressive – e.g. *Les Demoiselles*; and it also echoed the feeling of the times – the shift towards mechanisation and expanding mass production).

It's difficult at a distance to relate to the sense of outrage caused by Cubism. It was called "a return to barbarism and primitive savagery, a repudiation and an utter abasement of all the beauties in life and nature". (*Le Journal,* p.117)

The Cubists implied that it was unnecessary to be a slave to literal form. They fumbled towards the understanding that a picture didn't have to be 'of' something – a picture *is* something.

All of this began at about the same time that the nature of atoms was being uncovered; quantum physics was beginning to emerge; an obscure fellow called Albert Einstein was formulating theories that were to have great significance; and scientists generally were faced with a challenge about the fundamental nature of reality. The art of the 20th century is part of the process of coming to terms with deep uncertainty.

Albert Einstein (1879–1955).

Much that passed as Cubism was too ugly to gain the enduring public approval that finally came to the Impressionists. But 'ugly' had advantages – artists were able to extend their vocabulary without the burden of 'beauty'.

110 Look at examples of Cubist works. Picasso and Braque are central to the investigation but it's worth having a close look at **Cézanne** even though he died before 'official' Cubism began. Cézanne produced paintings that were made primarily with slabs of colour which were highly 'composed'. Although his work remained figurative (there was always a clear and recognisable subject) he made a jump into a new creative orbit. Cézanne related to paint like a musician – he was concerned with the 'arrangement' although he also maintained elements of realism.

Self-portrait by Paul Cézanne (1839–1906).

111 Find a Cubist work which interests you and try a 'forgery'.

112 Play with some experimental Cubism. For example, do a Cubist rendering of your face. What happens when you abandon the need to be literal?

113 Try a more fully developed work in the Cubist style. Keep in mind the sense of 'music' you're composing planes and shapes rather than being realistic. You may also be combining different views into a single frame – the back of the violin as well as the front.

Violin by Anne Johnstone.

114 Try some Cubist collage. Again the goal is composition.

▲ Katharine White.

▶ TLC student work.

Fauvism

Fauvism (about 1900–1906) embodies much of what was central to the Expressionists and can be broadly viewed as part of Expressionism. 'Fauve' means 'wild beast'. It is said that the critic Louis Vauxcelles entered an exhibition by **Vlaminck**, **Derain**, **Marquet**, **Puy**, **Rouault** and **Matisse**, and caught sight of a neo-Florentine sculpture of a child's head. He exclaimed: "Donatello among the wild beasts!" Another version of the story is that the term was inspired by Matisse's heavy hairy overcoat, which made him look like a bear. In any case, Vauxcelles used it in his review and the newly labelled Fauves were proud to own it.

Historians sometimes argue that Cubism was partly a response to Fauvism. In any case the Fauves shook the art traditions of the day and their influence is still alive and well. In particular they had a passion for intense, spontaneous colour and they believed that the inner, emotional world was more important than the literal, outer world or intellectual constructs.

Henri Matisse (1869–1954).

In creative terms the Fauves and the Expressionists explored the possibility that *expression* could be treated as an art zone in its own right. The later development of Abstract Expressionism went a step further and removed figurative content.

The Fauves were a loose-knit group who were bonded by their commitment to expression and the idea that painting is done for its own sake. They owed much to **Van Gogh** and **Gauguin**, and also relate a bit to **Delacroix**, **Daumier** and **Courbet**. They shared numerous intellectual contradictions (Matisse and Vlaminck differed on almost everything) but their goals were not intellectual and they seemed to be able to accommodate vast differences of opinion.

Fauvist style, TLC student.

Jean Paul Crespelle writes:

> Vlaminck, who represents instinct as opposed to reflection and research, is the complete antithesis of Matisse. He wanted to burn down the École des Beaux-Arts, whereas Matisse said he had never rejected its teaching and would enumerate the influences he had undergone. Vlaminck insisted that other people's painting had no interest for him and claimed that he had never been inside a museum. This was completely untrue, and he later admitted it. "I often stated that too much museum visiting corrupted the personality, just as a close acquaintance with the clergy leads to a loss of faith. But don't misunderstand me. I am not against the lessons that a museum can teach. I don't say it's a waste of time to look at a picture by Poussin or Courbet. I remember too clearly what a revelation Van Gogh and Douanier Rousseau were for me. But I do say that it is dangerous to look at other people's pictures, and even more dangerous to copy them."

it is dangerous to look at other people's pictures

The Fauves gave birth to the Abstract Expressionists. **Kandinsky** produced some of the most compelling abstractions ever painted – many of them still feel fresh.

115 Look at Fauvist works. Vlaminck, Derain, and Matisse are a good start. If you delve a little deeper you might find works in the Fauvist style by Braque which illustrate that historical categories are not always what they seem. Boundaries are blurred.

116 Find a Fauvist work which interests you and try a 'forgery'.

Wassily Kandinsky (1866–1944).

117 Play with some experimental Fauvism. For example, do a Fauvist rendering of your face.

118 Try a more fully developed work in the Fauvist style. Keep in mind the sense of exuberant colour (wild, over the top, straight from the tube) and passion. One possible tactic (which probably wouldn't have suited Vlaminck) is to use a Fauvist colour-set on top of a photocopy. This way you can achieve the emotional oomph while retaining some realistic structure.

Expressionism

Self-portrait by Goya (1746–1828).

The Fauves may have been more preoccupied with colour but they shared some of the emotional intensity of the Expressionists. Vlaminck, for example, said: "Instinct is the foundation of art. I try to paint with my heart and my loins."

'Expressionism' is commonly used to describe a style rather than a specific group of painters. Thus **El Greco**, **Grünewald** and **Goya** have Expressionist aspects.

Van Gogh and Munch might as well be called Expressionists although the conventional wisdom is that the movement didn't begin until about 1905.

The Expressionists valued feelings, honesty and intuition. They were 'primitive' or naïve in that technical finesse was not a central concern.

Suddenly art was within the reach of the untrained – or at least the less-trained – because it depended on sensitivity and passion rather than the skills of visual illusion.

Ernst Ludwig Kirchner, a member of the Expressionist group known as Die Blaue Reiter, said:

> We believe in development and in a generation of people who are both creative and appreciative ... We want to acquire freedom for our hands and our lives, against the well-established older forces. Everyone belongs to us who renders in an immediate and unfalsified way everything that compels him to be creative.

Expressionist portrait built into the paint on a discarded palette.

119 Look at examples of the work of Expressionist artists. **Kirchner**, **Nolde**, **Marc**, **Beckmann**, **Dix** and **Grosz** are a start (and keep in mind that the Fauvists can be viewed as part of the same show).

120 Relate to 'analog' painting as a connection with Expressionism. For example, do analog paintings of passion, excitement and anxiety.

121 Using the feelings and style that emerged through the analog paintings, take the same approach into a visual subject (it might be simple – an apple – or more complex – a face). Do the results have anything in common with the work of the Expressionists? If it feels in the zone, move to the next exercise. If not, try a forgery of an Expressionist work that takes your fancy.

With the Fauves and the Expressionists forgery is all the more challenging because the painting projects huge energy. A passive copy isn't going to capture the spirit! What can you do to make the forgery more effective?

122 Play with some experimental Expressionism. For example, try an Expressionist approach to a picture of a room at home or a scene that you feel strongly about.

Surrealism

> A movement in literature and art from about 1919, based on the expression of imagination uncontrolled by reason, and seeking to suggest the activities of the unconscious mind. – *Macquarie Dictionary*

The Surrealist movement began as a defined group of members and was founded by the writer **André Breton**, whose approval was required to gain membership. This touch of formality is curious considering that the group continued the rebellion against established authority in the arts.

André Breton (1896 1966).

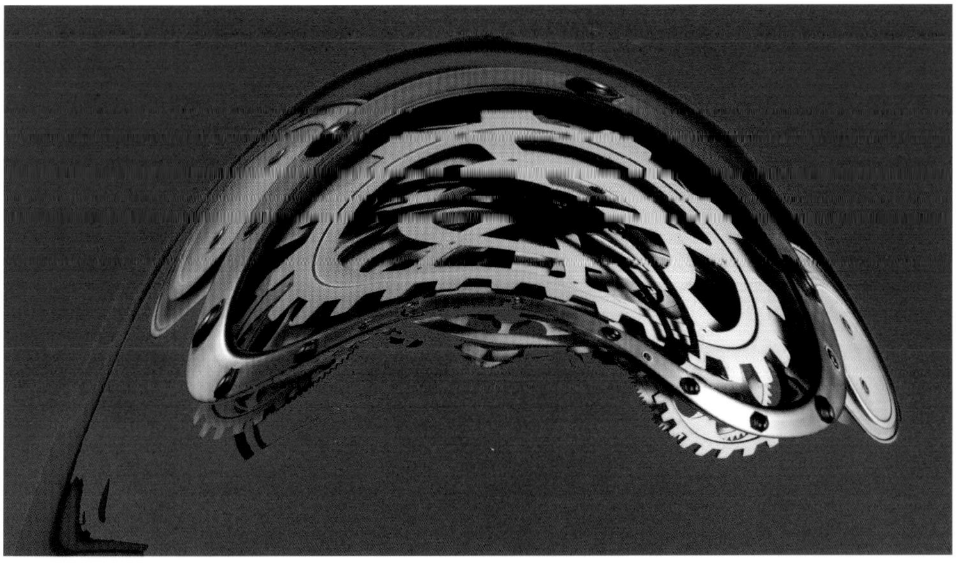

Surrealism played new tricks with the clockwork universe.

▲ Surreal life painting by Sandro Kopp, complete with dribbles that go in both directions and obscure words from Einstein. The eye reflects the figure and leaves the viewer (another eye) to grapple with a mystery that enmeshes *Alice in Wonderland*, Salvador Dalí and quantum physics. It's a particular type of visual poetry which invites you to construct your own interpretation.

▶ Artist: Katharine White.

Surrealism used the language of dreams and ambiguous images – as if nothing was ever what it seemed to be. People have been having dreams since the dawn of human life and many cultures have regarded them as seriously as our waking 'reality'. Around the beginning of the 20th century psychiatrists were exploring dreams as a means of getting deeper into the psyche of their patients. Just prior to the birth of Surrealism, Jung was developing the concept of the 'collective unconscious'. Once again, the thinking is that art and science seemed interactive even though the exact connections are elusive.

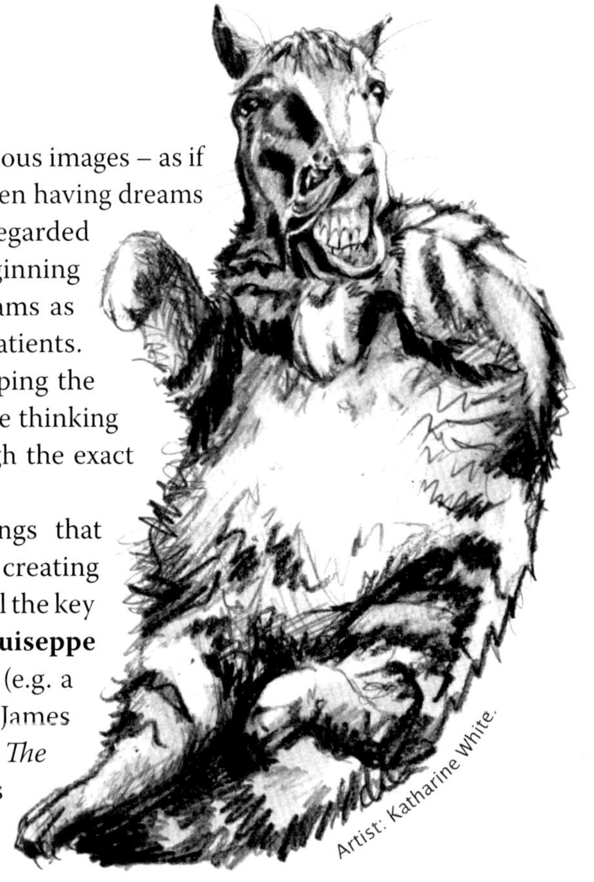

Artist: Katharine White.

There are many remarkable examples of paintings that anticipated the Surrealists. **Hieronymus Bosch** was creating his nightmarish images 400 years earlier and they use all the key devices of Surrealism. In rather more placid style, **Guiseppe Arcimboldo** was painting his double-image portraits (e.g. a face made up of vegetables). In 1782, six years after James Cook sailed to New Zealand, **Henry Fuseli** painted *The Nightmare* in which the images of the subconscious are brought to life. **Francisco Goya** also had some compelling adventures into the world of dreams (e.g. *Is there no one to untie us?* 1796–99). **Henri (le Douanier) Rousseau** painted many detailed, dreamlike pictures in the years immediately before Breton made Surrealism official.

Giorgio de Chirico (1888-1978).

123 Look at examples of the work of Surrealist artists such as **Magritte, Dalí, Ernst, Miró, Tanguy, de Chirico** and **Arp**. You might also investigate contemporary examples of work with a Surrealist influence – it's not only embedded in art, it shows up repeatedly in advertising, design, television and cinema. Choose one or two and make your own interpretation of what the artist was trying to do. Use that interpretation as the basis for a work of your own.

124 How could you come up with Surrealist ideas? Dreams? Fantasies? Playing with an imaginary world? Sketch out a few possible ideas.

125 Choose one of your explorations and create a more fully developed work in the Surrealist style.

Sculptor: Kelsey Connell.

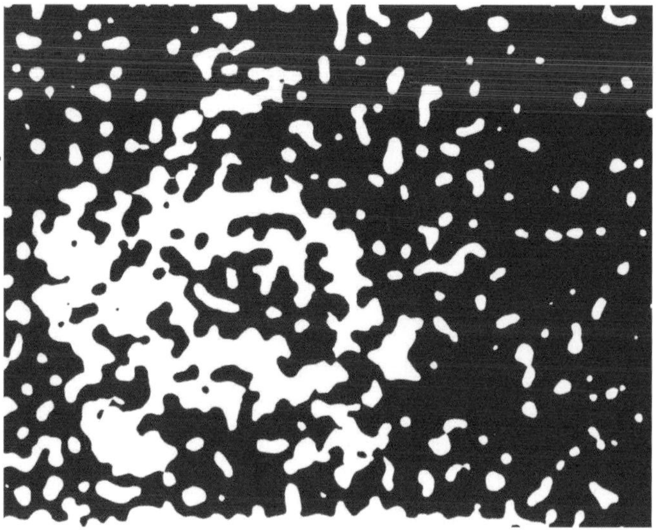

Like Schrödinger's cat, the abstract clock is both 'there' and 'not there'.

Abstraction

Abstraction finally cut the umbilical cord with figurative art. **Kandinsky** (1866–1944) is sometimes attributed as the father of Abstract Expressionism and he described his moment of illumination: "I was returning, immersed in thought, from my sketching, when on opening the studio door, I was suddenly confronted with a picture of indescribable and incandescent loveliness. Bewildered, I stopped, staring at it. The painting lacked all subject, depicted no identifiable object and was entirely composed of bright colour-patches. Finally I approached closer and only then saw it for what it really was – my own painting standing on its side on the easel ... One thing became clear to me: that objectiveness, the depiction of objects, needed no place in my paintings, and was indeed harmful to them." Kandinsky (at Murnau, 1908, quoted in *The Shock of the New* by Robert Hughes)

Jackson Pollock famously took abstraction further with his 'action painting' of the late 1940s and early 1950s. He worked on canvases which were on the floor and he dripped, dribbled and splashed paint in a totally intuitive way. He sometimes added ingredients such as bitumen, sand and glass to the paint. In the cautious American art world he was dynamite. *Life* magazine gave him its own splash with a large feature that exploited the controversy and catapulted Pollock into a troubled stardom.

Pollock made many succinct comments which conveyed what he was doing:

> It is only after a sort of 'get acquainted' period that I see what I have been about. I have no fears about making changes, destroying the image etc, because the painting has a life of its own. I try to let it come through.

every good artist paints what he is

> Painting is self-discovery. Every good artist paints what he is.

> "But, Mr Pollock, how do you know when you've finished?"
> "How do you know when you've finished making love?"
>
> *reply to a question about his work, quoted in Jackson Pollock, an Appreciation by Frank A Seixas, p.140*

> Modern art ... is nothing more than an expression of contemporary aims ... All cultures have had means and techniques of expressing their immediate aims – the Chinese, the Renaissance, all cultures. The thing that interests me is that today most painters do not have to go to a subject matter outside of themselves. Most modern painters work from a different source. They work from within.

"I *am* nature"

> New needs need new techniques. And the modern artists have found new ways and new means of making their statements ... Each age finds its own technique ... the strangeness will wear off and I think we will discover the deeper meanings in modern art.
>
> Art is coming face to face with yourself. That's what's wrong with Benton. He came face to face with Michelangelo – and he lost.
>
> My concern is with the rhythms of nature ... the way the ocean moves ... The ocean's what the expanse of the West was for me ... I work from the inside out, like nature.
>
> You can't learn techniques and then try to become a painter. Techniques are a result.
>
> You've got to deny, ignore, destroy a hell of a lot to get at truth.

One of Pollock's most telling quotes came when he was asked about working from nature. He said, "I *am* nature." Science has since given him some support. His dribble paintings have fractal and chaos patterns which are disarmingly 'natural' and they were created prior to the new quantum theories. I see something poetic in the fact that the art which is furthest from 'representation' turns out to be more directly realistic than the styles it rejected.

There's a rich assortment of Abstract Expressionists to explore and after Kandinksy and Pollock you could investigate **Willem de Kooning**, **Arshile Gorky**, **Mark Rothko** and **Franz Kline**.

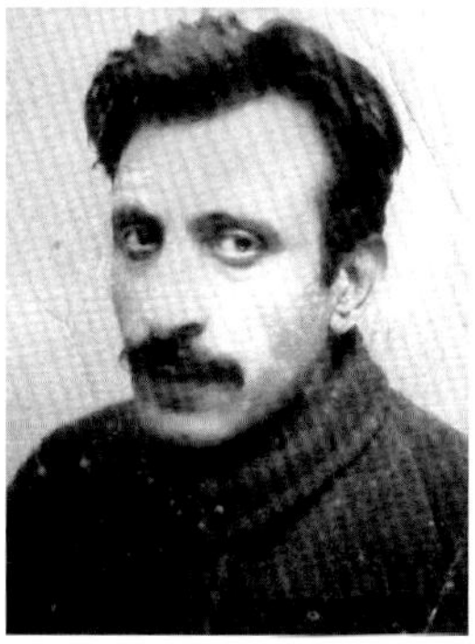

Arshile Gorky (1904–1948).

A 'not-Pollock' built of entirely natural shapes (kelp, water and rock).

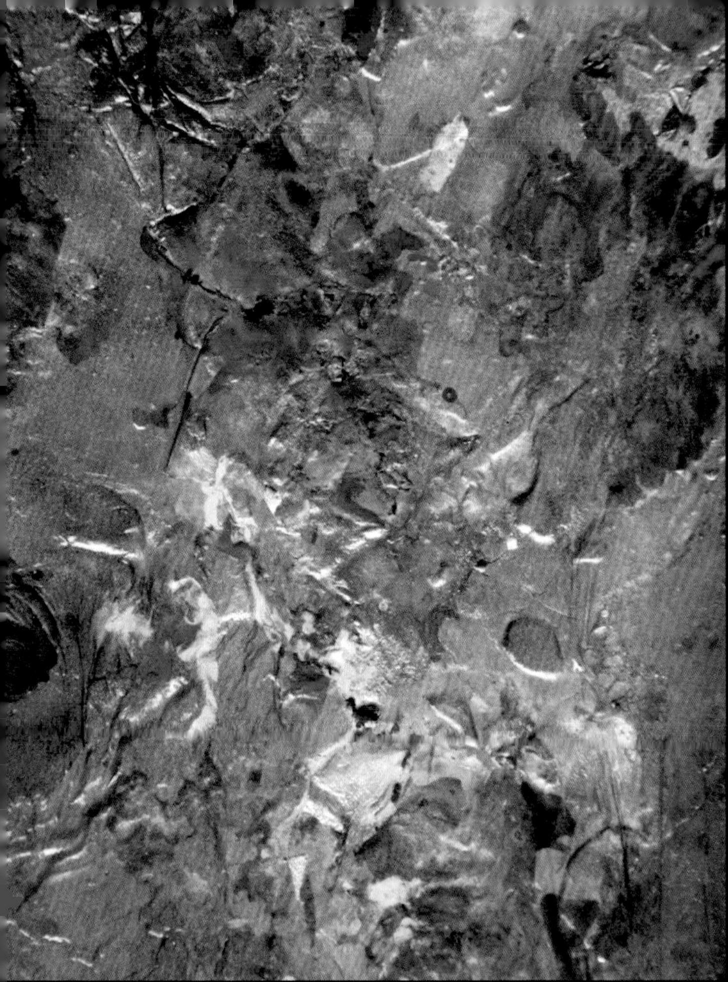

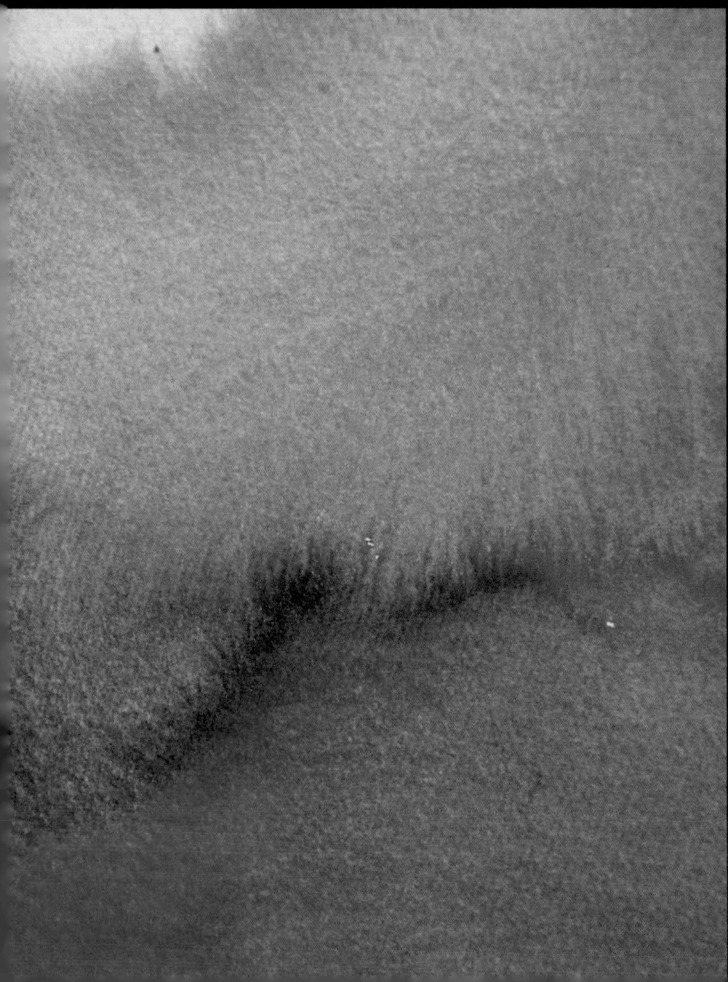
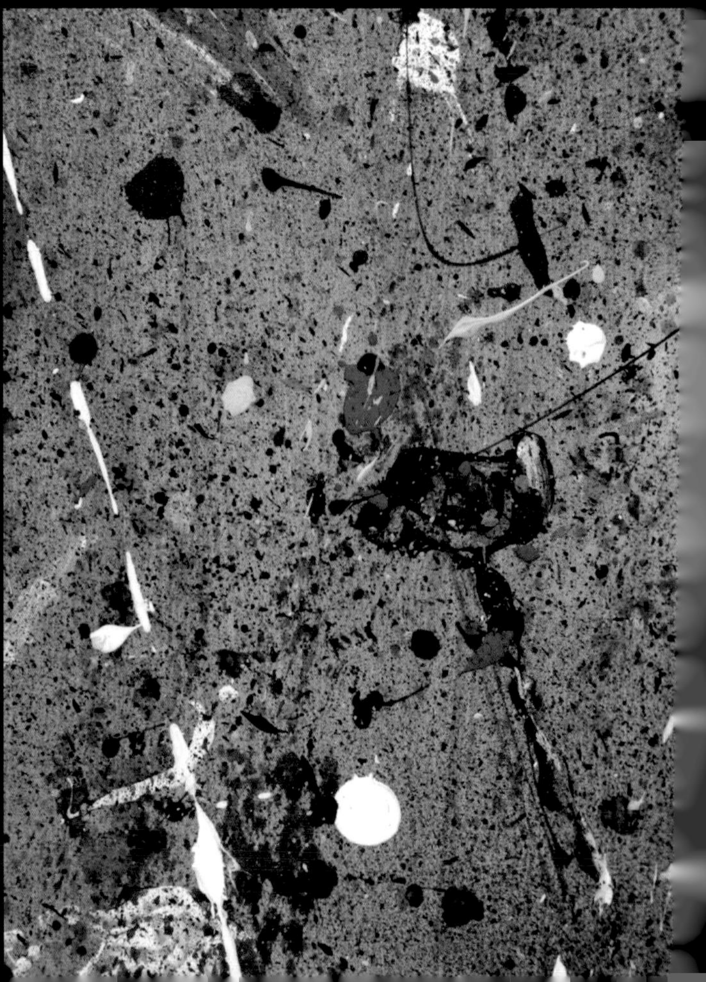

126 Select a few highly contrasting short pieces of music and freely paint your interpretation of the sound – quickly and intuitively. Compare the way each picture looks. Are they 'abstractions'?

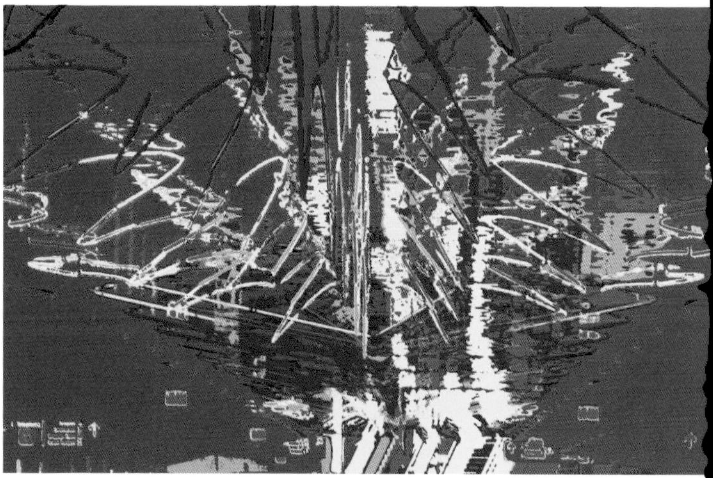

127 Play with photographs. Overlay, re-arrange, pay attention to colours and shapes rather than the subject.

128 Build an abstract (or mostly abstract) collage. You can do this with a mix of real materials (photographs, newspapers, magazines, found materials) or you can do it on a computer.

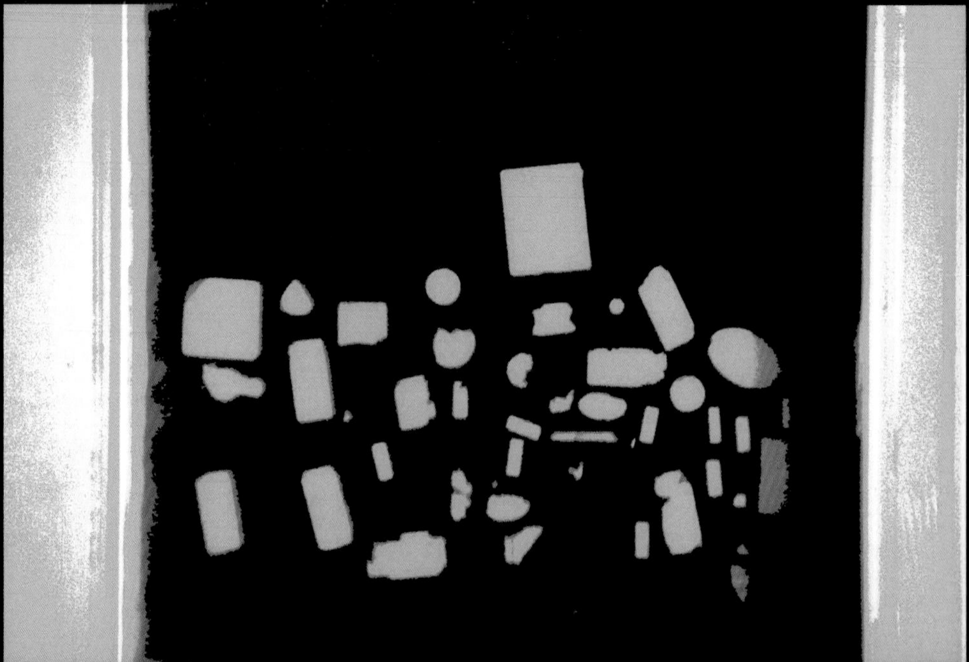

▲ The rough edges of Joy Snell's concrete figures seemed to work with the mixed turmoil of the 'abstract'.

▶ An abstract derived from stick-on notes. The placement isn't random although it didn't happen with any overall intent.

▲ 'Fun' by a TLC student. ▶ Chair painting by Sarah Milne.

129 Connect some colours. The first example is related to the theme 'Fun'. Colours were added and subtracted according to the way the work 'felt' at each step. Rather than the work being a response to an idea, it *is* the idea.

The colour idea played on a chair. Is it abstract or merely decorative? Is there a difference?

Paint on corrugated iron (detail, Bonnie McIntee).

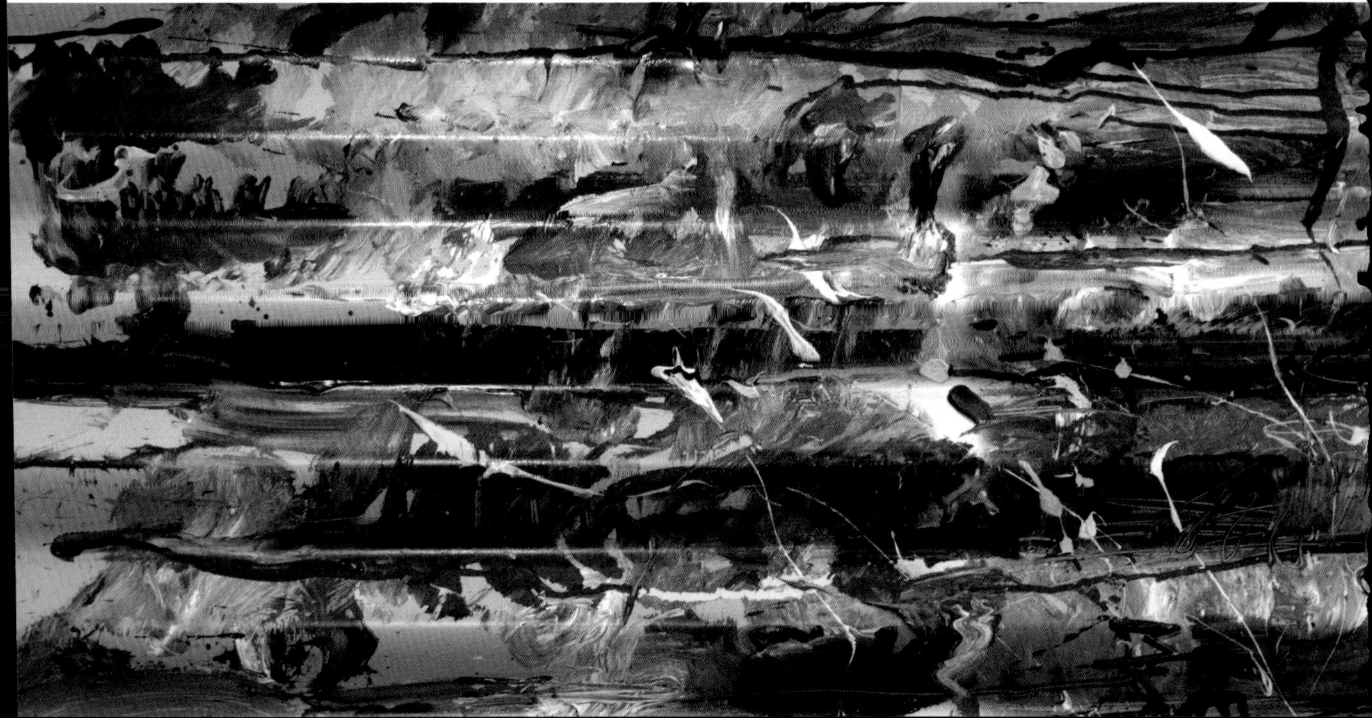

Dada

Dada is a relative of surrealism with a sharper social/political edge. It started in the turmoil around World War I and spawned a durable set of art ideas. The original Dadas felt that all traditional values were meaningless. They lived during a time when social institutions were wobbling and science was undermining some cherished beliefs about the place of humanity in the universe. One interpretation of the new world view was that the universe itself was meaningless. Artists were left to create their own meaning and to attack ideas and institutions which had reached their 'use-by' date. The result was a mix of intensely individual art and social activism.

The Dadas took delight in offending the establishment and part of their agenda was to do away with art itself. Tristan Tzara wrote that the true Dadas were against Dada.

Despite rejecting traditional values Dada art established an aesthetic of sorts. Duchamp's famous 1917 'ready-made', a urinal signed "R. Mutt," was both a parody and an item of mischievous beauty. Duchamp said:

> Whether Mr Mutt with his own hands made the fountain or not has no importance. He *chose* it. He took an ordinary article of life, placed it so that its usual significance disappeared under the new title and point of view – and created a new thought for that object.
>
> *Dada and Surrealism, Robert Short, p.25*

Through this statement Dada might be viewed as a parent of Pop art and a multitude of less-easily labelled material which currently features in art galleries and elsewhere. (Duchamp signed several urinals – another precursor of the Pop art love of mass production.)

Whereas Pop tended to pay homage to the products of mass production, Dada was inclined to sneer. While Futurist art took delight in things mechanical, Dada viewed 'the machine' with suspicion and hostility.

Part of the letting-go of tradition resulted in works created by 'chance'. Dada performances were unscripted and anarchic. Hans Arp described the scene at the Caberet Voltaire:

> Total pandemonium. The people around us are shouting, laughing and gesticulating. Our replies are sighs of love, volleys of hiccups, poems, moos, and miaowing of Medieval Bruitists. Tzara is wriggling his behind like the belly of an oriental dancer. Janco is playing an invisible violin and bowing and scraping. Madame Hennings, with a madonna face, is doing the splits. Huelsenbeck is banging away non-stop on a great drum, with Ball accompanying them on the piano, pale as a chalky ghost. We were given the honorary title of Nihilists.

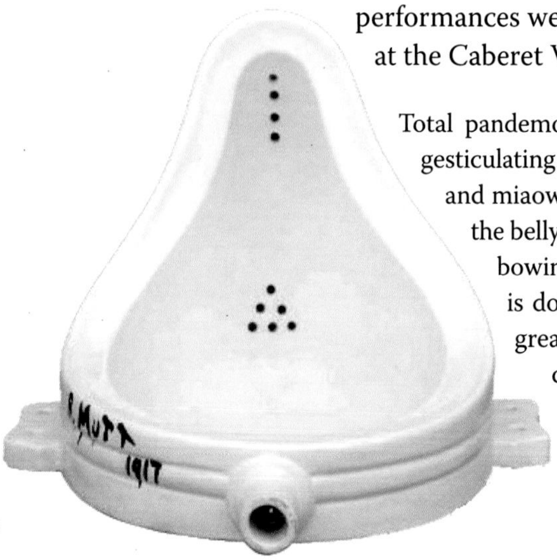

They had a paying audience but I haven't been able to find evidence of the box office receipts.

I think of the comedian Billy Connolly as a manifestation of the Dada spirit. Pamela Stephenson's books *Billy* and *Bravemouth* will put you in the picture. (If you can't handle swearing, avoid them.) Here's a typical Connolly line from *Billy*: "Before you judge a man, walk a mile in his shoes. After that, who cares? ... He's a mile away and you've got his shoes."

Connolly often sounds cynical and offensive but he also conveys a love and compassion which allows him to get away with things that others could hardly contemplate. Dada lives.

130 What use is it to attack convention? Can you see value in art which has a high level of negative content? What do you think about art as a vehicle for rudeness and irreverence? How might this sort of art make a valuable contribution to art as a whole? Try a version of your own. It involves some irreverence, like Duchamp adding a moustache to an image of the *Mona Lisa*. You could turn a picture or symbol upside down; combine it with something odd, use strange colours ...

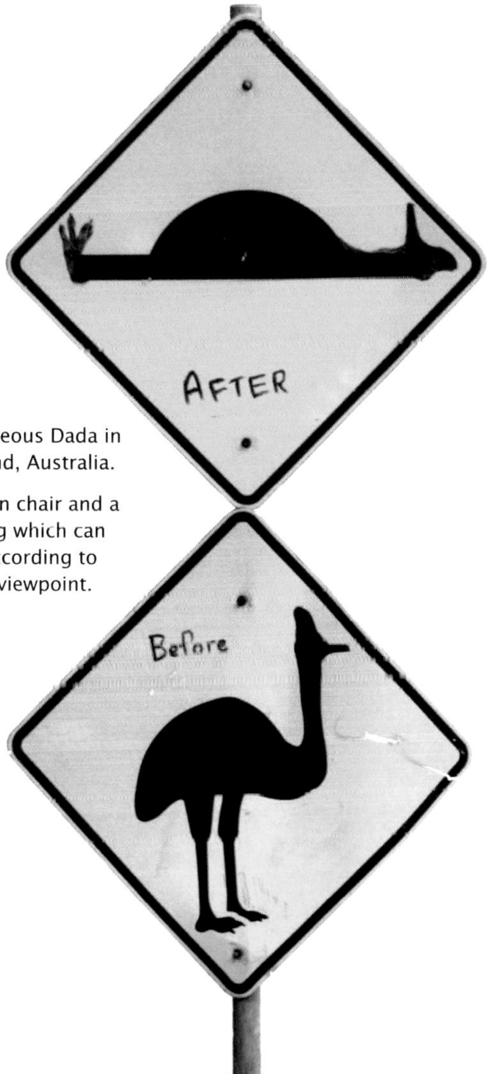

▸ Spontaneous Dada in Queensland, Australia.

▸▸ A broken chair and a tourist flag which can be read according to your own viewpoint.

◂ A cryptic combination of found materials (Julie Chamberlain).

▾ New Zealand is a land in which rugby football is a de facto religion. It's very macho and can be thrillingly creative if you can enjoy the poetry of battle. Perry Scott's pink rugby trophy is therefore sacrilegious. The frilliness and the colour give one message and the plinth and the shape of a ball say something entirely different. You're left with some riddles about communication, social values and the meanings we learn to attach to things.

131 Start a painting by throwing a cup of coffee at the paper. Black coffee is preferred (milk gets smelly, although smell can be part of art if you want it). Take care not to damage things (outside in the yard is ideal) and it's safer if the coffee is cold. When it's dry either throw more coffee or declare it to be finished. You can add other ingredients if you wish – there are no rules – this is Dada! What does it feel like – having to figure out the purpose of the work for yourself rather than following an established idea?

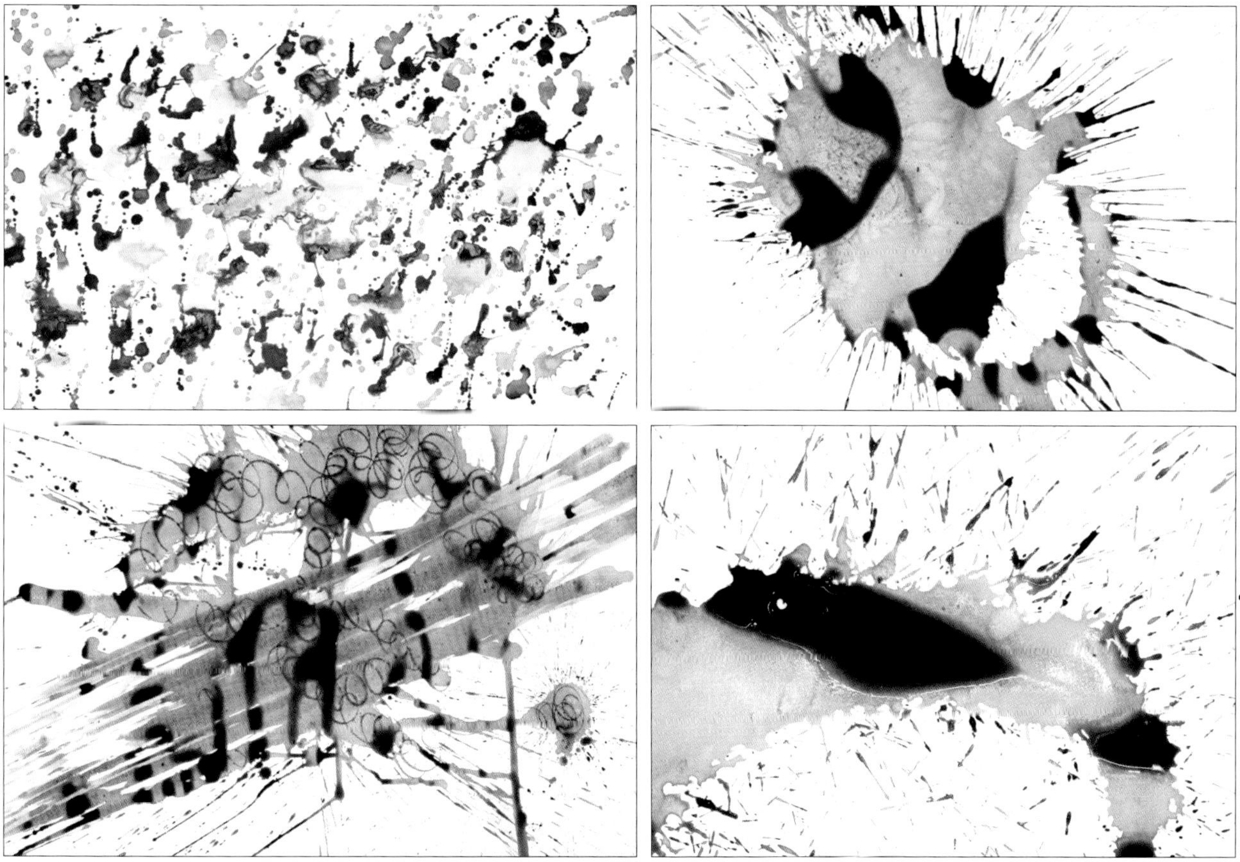

132 Work with a friend and do some anti portraits – pulling faces for example. The purpose is to defuse social pressures to look beautiful and take yourself seriously. After this, there isn't much to lose.

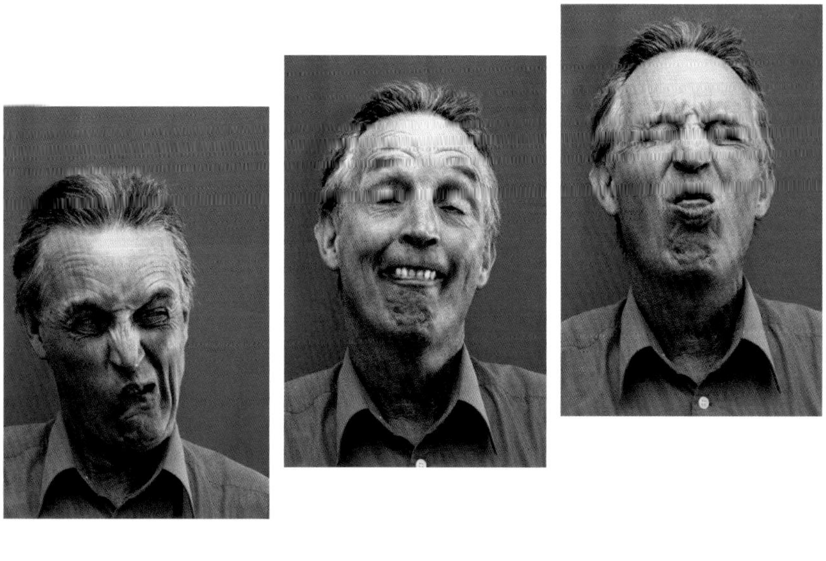

133 Do something downright weird with assemblage or collage. The illustration shows one that turned out to be an unfortunate sign of things to come. Coincidentally it's also an exercise in blending paint with the colours of a photograph.

▲ The 'cave painting on books' was done by an early TLC student and has a strong Dada point of view.

▶ A Dada-ish brief case.

A 'comment' on Pop art by New Zealand artist Dick Frizzell – an actual can of tuna with Frizzell's own label.

Pop

Pop was latent in Dada. Andy Warhol was almost an inevitable consequence. His Campbells soup can renderings have become an icon and his Brillo box show in 1964 caused a sensation.

Art dealer Ivan Karp said: "It was inconceivable that a gallery would turn over its space to these piles of boxes. We didn't have any idea what price to put on them because we didn't expect any sales. We came up with a price of $250 per unit and I think maybe two or three were sold ... The critical response to the show ... was essentially quite negative, even fierce and demonstrably unpleasant."

How is a Warhol box different from an ordinary Brillo box? It's like a Catholic relic (appropriately Warhol was Catholic) – the mundane item became invested with spiritual power through association with Saint Andy. Apparently they have risen in value to more than US$100,000.

the mundane item became invested with spiritual power

Before the Brillo boxes Karp had a big influence on Warhol's artistic direction. In the Melvyn Bragg documentary *Andy Warhol* (Phaidon) Karp says: "The artists working with imagery during that interval (late '50s, early '60s) were considered outsiders. The dominant force was Abstract Expressionism and the great heroes were Jackson Pollock, **de Kooning**, **Kline** and **Rothko**. You had to paint expressive style, out of your soul. The idea of doing blank, blunt, bleak, stark images like [Warhol's] was contrary to the whole prevailing mood of the arts. But it gave me a chill seeing it. In the vast intellectual perceptual abilities that I had, I said, "My word, this is an amazing idea, it's just the opposite of what we see these days." (It helps if you can imagine Karp's mischievous grin and New York accent.)

> [Warhol said] "Well, do you really like them?"
>
> "I said, Well, they are astonishing, but I like some better than others. Some of the paintings have all kinds of drip marks."
>
> He said, "Well you have to do that, you must do that, you must drip."
>
> I said, "Why must you drip?"
>
> He said, "Well, it means that you are an artist if you drip." Of course you pay homage to Pollock and all the great dripsters.
>
> I said, "Maybe you don't have to drip at all. Maybe if you're going to deal with these images, why not just deal with them?"
>
> He said, "That's just wonderful, I don't think I want to drip."

Stacked boxes, after Andy Warhol.

Warhol sounds simplistic and yet he was also complex and elusive. He sought fame, found it, and then his fame took on a life of his own. More than any Pop artist, Warhol became indistinguishable from Pop itself. The Dadas assaulted the notion of 'artist as genius' and Warhol moved into a zone of 'artist as phenomenon.'

Mathematicians have done a better job than art critics in showing how fame feeds on itself and the original cause becomes less and less relevant. Dead celebrities (including Warhol) have an uncanny way of increasing their celebrity. It isn't about art – it's about physics (and the Bible was onto it: "To he who has, more shall be given"). Sometimes (as with the 1927 stock market crash) giant bubbles burst, but they can also maintain stability. Sceptics might wonder whether art itself is a bubble mysteriously held aloft by believers.

A quirk of Chaos Theory (in mathematics) is that tiny beginnings can grow huge – so there is no predicting whether you're on the way to fame.

Julia Warhola by Andy Warhol.

The downside of fame is that it takes over from the reality of the person. In Warhol's case it was like a continuation of his art – he wanted to remove all sense of personal involvement and eventually he became myth. When he made an affectionate picture of his mother the critics were confused because it didn't fit the myth. Eric Shanes said: "... the thick paint simply swirls around or under the image of Julia Warhola without deepening our insight into her personality or even the painter's reaction to her." It's as if he's saying: "No more swirly expressive stuff Andy – it's not your brief."

The criticism shows again how orthodoxy emerges from revolution and conveniently overlooks complexities and contradictions. Pop began as heresy and not many years later Warhol's own deviations attracted stern glares from the 'art guardians.'

Every famous artist is, to some extent, a highly simplified icon and the simplification happens through an interplay of mass culture with itself. Warhol is not the first of the Pop artists but he demonstrates something quintessential about the *idea* of Pop. Keep in mind that the idea is the creation of others. It is a rough and ready map, much cruder than the coastlines recorded by early explorers.

In the case of Pop the 'edges' are something like this:

Every famous artist is, to some extent, a highly simplified icon

1. It uses elements of mass culture (symbols, pictures, mass-produced artefacts and so on).
2. It acknowledges, consciously or unconsciously, that mass-produced items have a profound effect on our lives.

Seriously large bow and arrow: *Cupid's Span* by Claes Oldenburg and Coosje van Bruggen, San Francisco. Recorded wolf noises waft from the grass and compete with traffic noise. It is a gift to the city from Doris and Donald Fisher (a new-fashioned image for old-fashioned social status). A sign says "Please Do Not Enter Native Grass Area or Touch the Sculpture."

As with all art you can read it (or ignore it) as you please. Maybe it's a tease — 'I left my heart in San Francisco' — with a literal variation of wolf whistles. Alternatively it's a trio of red, silver and brown which play handsomely against the blue sky. It offers a little duet with the steel cables of the bridge and a talking point for those who want to stroll in the park and be distracted from the routine cares of life.

Oldenburg has made many sculptures based on ordinary objects and it's an approach you can play with on Photoshop, even if no one is around to pay you more than $2 million for the real thing.

drawing attention to some-thing in a new and revealing way

3. The artist tends to be detached – somewhat like the artists who create advertising – although they are still concerned with real messages and may be highly passionate behind the façade.
4. Irony is a common feature.
5. Pop expresses something about its time. It is connected with the world and the apparent detachment may be an accurate observation of the way things are.
6. It is usually more concerned with an *idea* than with technique or aesthetic qualities. In many cases the artist adds little or nothing to what already exists – the 'art' is in drawing attention to something in a new and revealing way.
7. Pop challenged the boundaries of conventional art (although Dada was there first).
8. Pop initially focused on the elements of mass culture but artists have since grabbed these elements and used them in art which has a different agenda. It may be political, decorative, philosophical and so on.

The TLC exhibition team appropriated an appropriation (by McRay Magleby) of Andy Warhol's iconic soup can.

134 What is 'Pop' art to you?

What distinguishes Pop from Abstract Expressionism? (and what do they have in common?)

What do you think about ordinary mass-produced things (packaging, etc) being regarded as art?

How do mass-produced images shape our understanding of the world? (You might like to think about TV advertisements in particular.)

What are some of the hidden values of art in advertising – in other words, what beliefs are implied?

What are some aspects of Pop art which could be directly useful in your own work?

135 Check out some of the famous Pop artists (**Lichtenstein**, **Rauschenberg**, **Hamilton**, **Segal**, **Oldenburg** etc). Sketch a few ideas that use Pop imagery to say something relevant about your own world. Develop one of the ideas into a finished work.

ay something
elevant about
our own world

Artist: Anmea Winterburn.

Sue Lloyd.

CHAPTER 12

Building a painting

There are infinite ways to make paintings. It is an accident of history that painting was used primarily to portray the visual world and the craft of painting (in the West at least) was dominated by skills of representation. Music, which had no such burden to simulate reality, was free to be 'abstract' while painters had to be 'realistic'. Around the beginning of the 20th century a series of rebellions crashed through the barricades to embrace ideas that had long been forbidden.

While many artists thought they were in danger of being replaced by cameras, others felt liberated as they explored new territory

Part of the change came through photography. While many artists thought they were in danger of being replaced by cameras, others felt liberated as they explored new territory. For a while there was a big gap in understanding. During the 1950s when I went to school the revolutions were already old but they were largely ignored outside the art world. The public pinnacle of art in New Zealand was the Kelliher Prize which rewarded realistic landscape painting. Although artists still managed to infuse occasional touches of excitement they had to remain anchored in the 19th century. Not least among their problems was the uncommercial nature of the revolutionary art. When 'new art' becomes acceptable 'established art' it may also become extremely expensive, but at the time of the revolution it may be considered worthless.

In the midst of all the chaos, artists have managed, more or less, to redefine their role. We are now seen more as creative communicators and we are free to use a vast repertoire of styles.

Many species of realism are still thriving along with hybrids and some esoteric forms of conceptual art which have separated entirely from the physicality of paint.

Is there any point in learning old disciplines that may no longer be relevant? Well, yes. They're as relevant as you make them. There are schools which still proclaim that "painting is dead" and I fancy there are many fresh and entrancing paintings which would say (if they could) "rumours of our death have been exaggerated." Every glib cliché invites an equal and opposite cliché.

Don deMacedo.

Old-fashioned skills conveniently dampen the fires of criticism from people who are easily impressed by representational art. Maybe that's a cop-out but for some of us art is tough enough already – we don't need friends and family telling us we don't know what we're doing.

Exploration of representational painting is a means to understand the nature of paint itself. It's a way of taking your art language into places which might otherwise be unreachable.

The principles are the same as drawing but wetter.

Many books do a good job of showing the basics of painting but it's hard to show movement and time on a static page. What we can do here is provide some recipes and the rest is over to you. Keep in mind that practice is what takes you to new levels.

Drawing is the foundation of representational painting. If your drawing isn't as fluent as you want it to be, feel free to 'cheat.' Use a projector or do tracings. Find ways to concentrate entirely on the paint.

Go at it *fast and bold*. Get the big foundations in place, then move to increasing the detail. If it goes wrong you've merely lost a few minutes and you can either let the paint dry and work over the top or do a fresh drawing and start from zero.

Disasters are useful because they give you the opportunity to experiment. You can try things you might otherwise have avoided. Nothing is lost if it doesn't work.

When you're building a painting, keep relating to what comes next. Paint obeys the laws of physics and is more complex than charcoal or pencil. In the early stages you're having a crash course on the behaviour of paint. It can be frustrating but the good news is that the first fifty years are the hardest.

The sequence is:

UNDERPAINTING Big shapes, highly simplified but still fairly accurate and using colour that is going to be appropriate if some of it shows through to the final image.

the first fifty years are the hardest

Sue Currie.

Katharine White.

Katharine White.

MAIN VALUES Reasonably accurate colour and placement but little detail – good brush control helps because these are the marks that build most of the final picture.

Katharine White.

DETAIL The human eye obligingly invents detail and you need only give it a few clues – it's surprising how little you need.

136 *Plan a painting*

You might find it more convenient to work from a photo (or a combination of photos). Otherwise you can work from a still life or do a self-portrait from a mirror. The first step is to do a series of very fast charcoal roughs to get the 'feel' of the picture and make the first steps towards planning the composition. Follow the same drawing techniques that we've already explored – and take them in your own direction.

Goal: Partly it's a thinking process – as you work on the picture ideas will grow. Partly it's a matter of organisation and simplification – you're figuring out how to present the subject in the way that best expresses what you're trying to say.

137 Figure out the basic colour matching. You might decide that a blue/orange palette gives you most of what you need (combined with black and white this is often a good base for portraiture).

Goal: It's like organising some cooking – you're figuring out the ingredients. Sometimes it's hard to calculate the exact amount of colour needed for various parts of the picture and it helps if you have a clear idea of how you're going to produce the colours. This is also a vital preparation for the underpainting because some of the colour will show in the finished work.

▲ Lauren Platzer — painting at speed. ▼ Slower. Less zing?

taking

existing ideas into new places

CHAPTER 13

It isn't cheating

Creativity is not about reinventing the wheel – it's about taking existing ideas into new places. All ideas are connected to things that have gone before them. Indeed we do so much copying that it's easy to overlook the value of building on things that have already happened. There's much to be gained from direct copying and there's even more to be gained from 'analytical copying'. In other words, try to work out what an artist was trying to do, then convert the idea to your own use.

In the beginning it may feel difficult to read a painting – just as it can be difficult to ask for a taxi in a foreign language. It's possible that your interpretation will be wrong but it's your privilege to make your own choices. Art allows more freedom than taxis – and anyway, errors may lead you to places which are worth visiting.

Art allows more freedom than taxis – and anyway, errors may lead you to places which are worth visiting

To get started it makes sense to choose works you like. The goals are:

1. Learning how to read art.
2. Digging for a concept or 'recipe' that might have been a starting point for the work.
3. Applying that concept to works of your own.
4. Building your technical repertoire by applying both the techniques and the thinking that are necessary for the particular approach.
5. Increasing your awareness of what is relevant to you.

You could apply the same approach to discovering how anything works – it could be a shoe, a clock or a caterpillar. The advantage of art is that it's relatively easy to convert your creative insights into products of your own. You could do the same sort of thing with shoes but it would probably require a bigger investment to get started. Applying it to a caterpillar would be more complex although nature has been doing it for a very long time.

◄ Painting by Edmund Dickie.

138 Use geometric shapes, colours and symbols of your choice, and apply some of the paint without using a brush.

139 Recollect personal experiences which had dramatic intensity. Anything will do for a start – relationships, calamities, humour, adventures – whatever comes to mind. Draw the event freely – as if you were a child. If you wish, do the drawing directly with paint. Keep it simple and bold – let the paint itself engage with the meaning of the story (like an analog picture – see chapters 3 and 4).

What is the idea behind the work?

Take it back to an underlying concept

If you like the concept, use it to make works of your own

There are now infinite possibilities

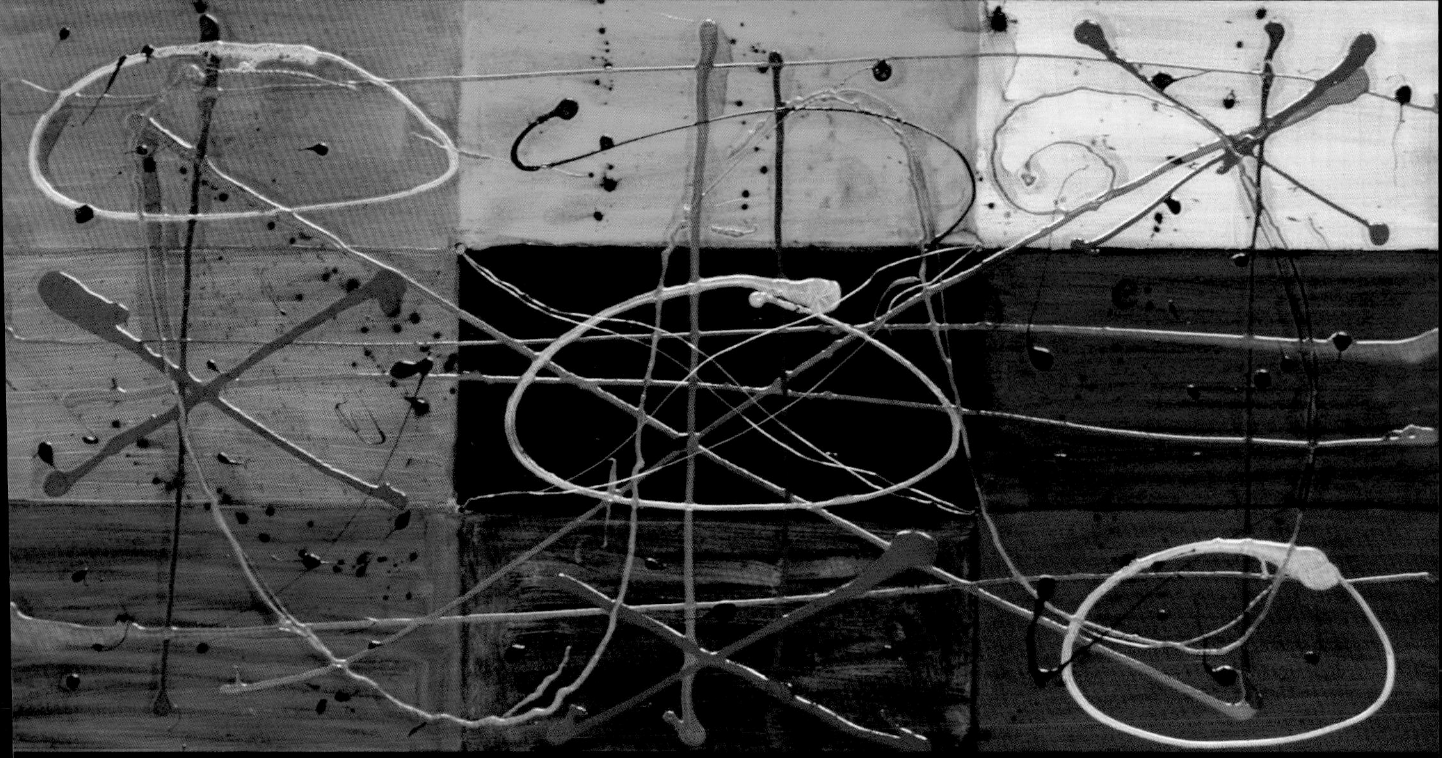

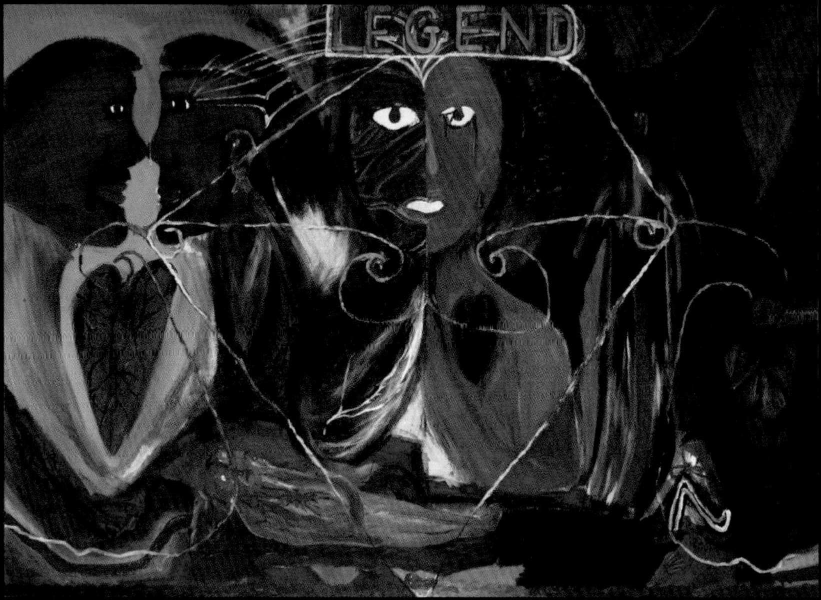

▲ A possibility: "Playing with colour, rectangles and paint squeezed direct from the tube while pretending that it's about noughts and crosses." (Christine Kernahan)

◀ Intensely remembered image/feeling of a domestic drama between a cat and a bird. Bold, childlike approach to the painting, more theatrical than realistic; strident colours and busy design add to the sense of edginess. (Eddie Budd)

▲ Rather than a single incident Robert Rangi used more or less the same approach to tell the story of his life.

Self-portrait superimposed (with a mischievous touch of humour) on a famous picture. (Vernon Waretini)

Catherine Hayes took a Vermeer painting as the starting point for this self-portrait.

140 In part it's copying and it's also a way of appropriating someone else's technique for your own purposes. Select a work that you like and figure out how to add your face. The earlier section on 'building a painting' is a guide but you may have to modify your approach to suit the task.

141 Paint a face using extremely aggressive brush strokes. Chances are you'll invent it from your imagination rather than from observation. Combine it with whatever words you choose. Aim to sustain the same high energy throughout the picture – the background, the words and the face itself.

142 Take a photocopy of a face (highly contrasty lighting is ideal) and cut away the shadow areas with a craft knife. Hold the result vertically against a board or background of your choice and use a spraycan to apply colour. Add some realistic ingredients (whatever is meaningful for you – Terence says he likes anything with an exoskeleton).

What i

◂ A self-portrait in which highly realistic painting (the flies) is combined with loose brush strokes and a stencilled face. The 'found' base (a scrap of laminated particle board) adds some randomness and mystery. Who am I? What is my place in the universe? (Terence Turner)

▾ A mix of Fauvism and comic book art used to make an enigmatic, Zen-like statement. What is "the vent where the sound leaks"? (Stephen Clover)

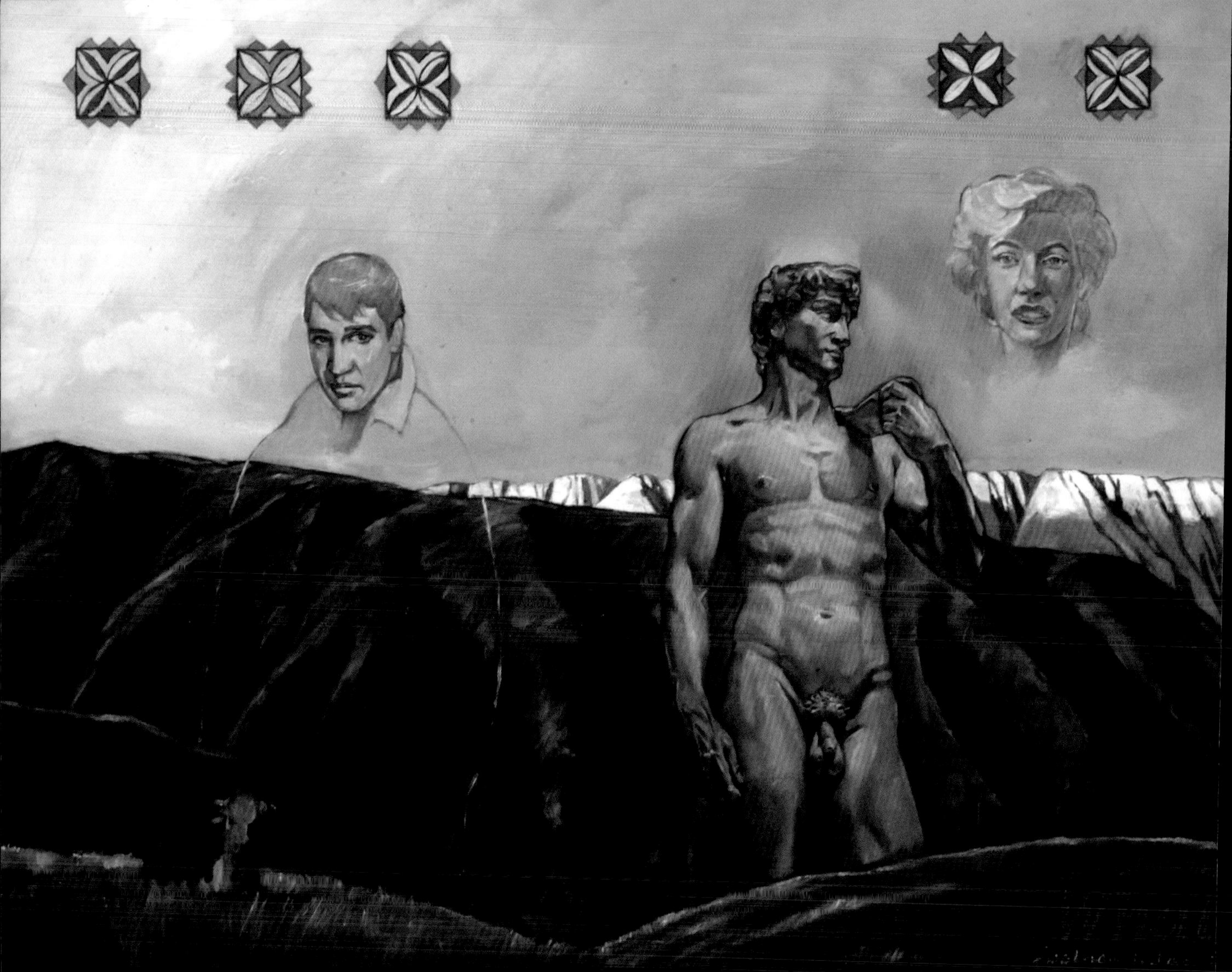

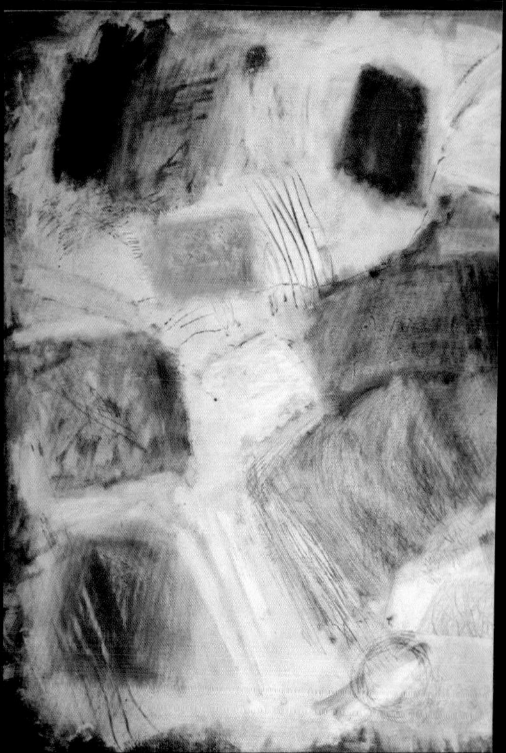

▲ Cliché images assembled in a realist landscape to provide a different way of looking at both the clichés and the environment. I chose the images and commissioned So'otage Tuifao to paint the picture. He totally changed the original landscape and added Samoan symbols to put his own stamp on the result.

▶+▶▶ Using intuitive choices to make visual music with colour. (Sue Lund)

▶▶▶ Careful observed character portrait with clothing to match. (Claudine Stace)

▶▶▶▶ Katharine White's self-portrait adds an imagined ingredient (the mask) and expressive brush work

143 Assemble some images which have become iconic. Mona Lisa, Einstein, Elvis, the Virgin Mary, John Lennon, Queen Elizabeth II, George Washington and Mickey Mouse are examples. So are inanimate objects (chair, camera, aircraft, bicycle etc). Make a selection and place them on a picture of a landscape of your choice. Paint a picture of the assemblage using a realistic style (and adjusting the tones and colours so that everything looks connected).

144 Make marks on a board with colour. Add a new colour that feels right. Keep adding. Where necessary, adjust (or totally change) any colour that didn't work out. When it all seems to work in a satisfying way, stop. If it doesn't initially come together, be willing to return to it as many times as necessary (it may take weeks).

145 Choose a character you know (the more expressive the better). If they're willing to model for you, do a portrait from life. Otherwise take a photo of them wearing suitably expressive clothing and a typical look. Relate to the 'building a painting' principles and take them to a more resolved stage. Keep the whole surface in mind.

▸ Thinking about family; observing personality and the ways in which people present themselves to the world. (Richard Simmonds)

▾ Nino Guzzo connected with someone else's family and made this large portrait (two metres wide). It's highly sustained and very rewarding if you have the stamina. Establishing the drawing with a projector will speed up the job.

What is the idea behind the work?

◂ Create a stylised picture of an event so that the shapes come together with a kind of visual poetry. (Katie Jurgens)

▾ Use a three-dimensional surface as the base for a figurative image. (Katharine White)

146 Find a photo in your family album which captures something special about your family. You can either use a projector or do a sketch to get the shapes onto the background. Then paint it in much the same manner as the portrait. It's a more complex task to integrate a number of people – keep it direct and bold.

147 Choose an image of an event and do a series of sketches to become familiar with it. Take whatever liberties you require to bring the shapes into an interesting combination. In the example above, nearly everything has been related to geometric units, particularly rectangles and triangles. You'll need a blend of realism and invention. It will require considerably more preparation than the portraits but the same underlying techniques should enable you to get it done.

148 Choose a theme and establish a base with thick paint. (There are many commercial varieties, especially for interior decorating, but white house paint is just as good if it's thick and gooey.)

If you want the picture to be representational it's vital to relate to your intended result from the start. Even though the texture medium is a neutral white you'll need to get an effective structure in place (in effect, a three-dimensional drawing). If it's more abstract (like the picture opposite) the structure is just as important but the figurative element isn't present.

A technical diversion

The tools for texture work are all simple (although you can add more sophisticated items if you have them).

- Serrated cardboard
- Kitchen cleanser (containing some abrasive)
- Dishwashing cloth
- Fine wire cleaning pad
- Scrubbing brush
- Plastic fork, combs etc
- Coarse house painting brushes
- Scrubbing brushes

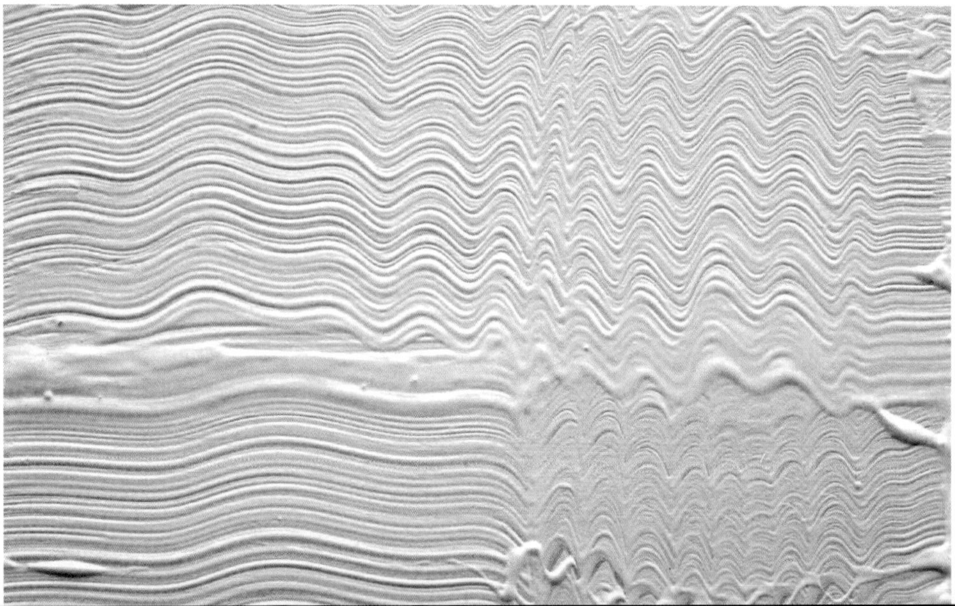

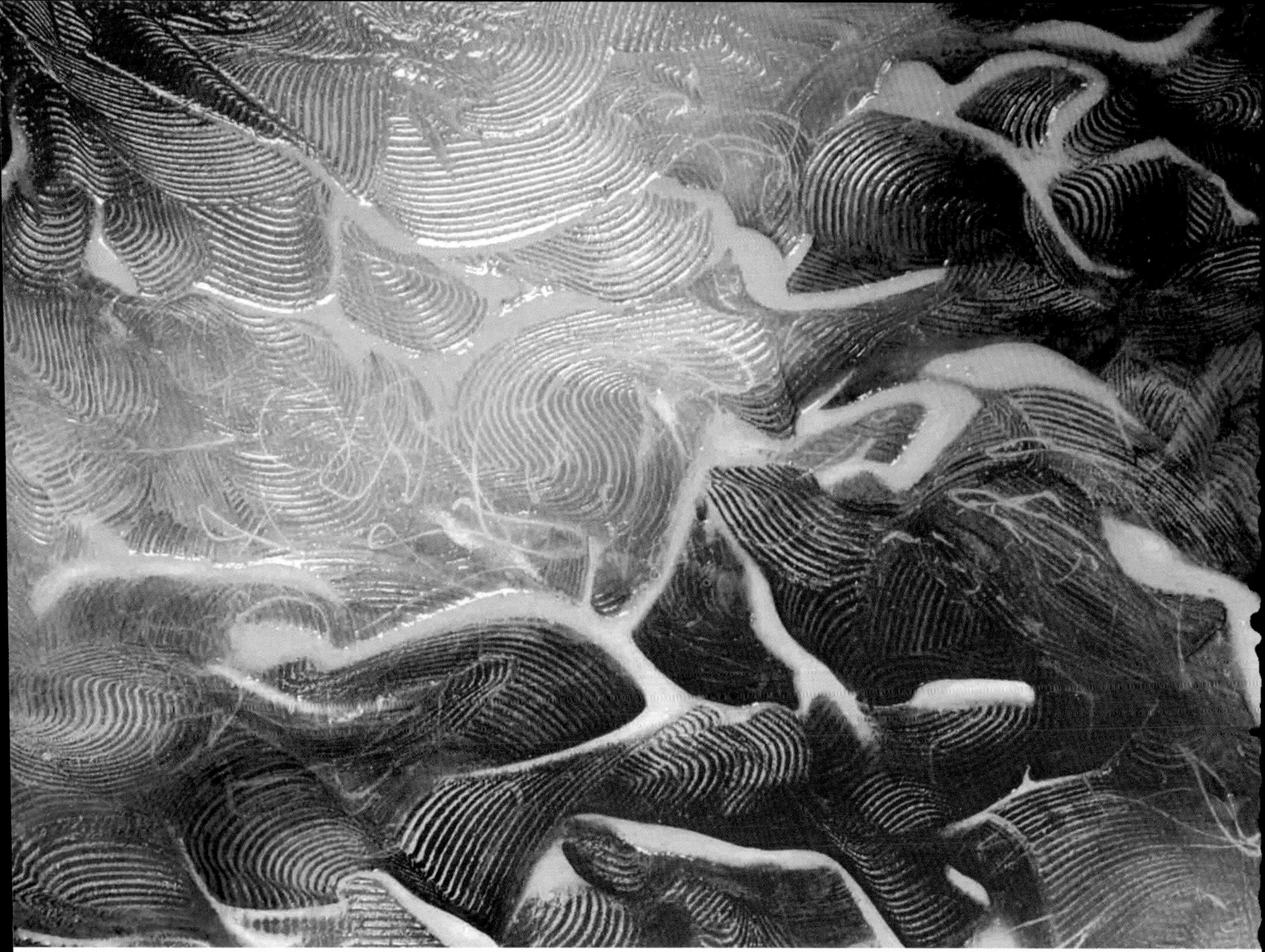

Let it dry (it may take days).

Apply fairly thin acrylic paint to the textured base. Again, let it dry.

Rub the dry paint with (say) a dishcloth and cleaning material. Wipe away any residue and add further paint.

Keep adding and subtracting colours until you're happy with the result.

A texture painting that started with a can of old paint and an idea to use only the primary colours. The texture was created with pieces of cardboard that had been cut with a zigzag edge. Once the textured layer was dry, thin acrylic was added. Each colour was dried separately — they are overlaid rather than mixed. Next the colours were partially rubbed off with a cloth and a powder abrasive. Paint was added and subtracted until it reached the intended balance. Patches of white were gently added with a sponge to bring out the pattern of the ribs. Lastly the work was heavily coated with acrylic gloss medium to give it a ceramic look.

Back to our main theme

149 Connect with any situation of suffering where you would like the world to be different (maybe war, disease, pollution, global warming – it's your choice). Create an idea which offers hope for change. Incorporate collage elements if you don't want to spend the time it takes to do realistic images.

150 Listen to music and paint what it feels like. Then incorporate a face in such a way that there is a conversation between background (the music) and the face. You can get the picture started in other ways – for example by painting a feeling (anger, ecstasy, laughter, etc) or by using a neutral technique such as rubbing colour on a surface.

◂ Thoughts about the suffering of animals; association with the suffering of people. (Katharine White)

▾ Using a painting of music as the base for a portrait and allow background and foreground to interact. (Heath Todd)

◣ A different version of the same idea. (Jonathan Milne)

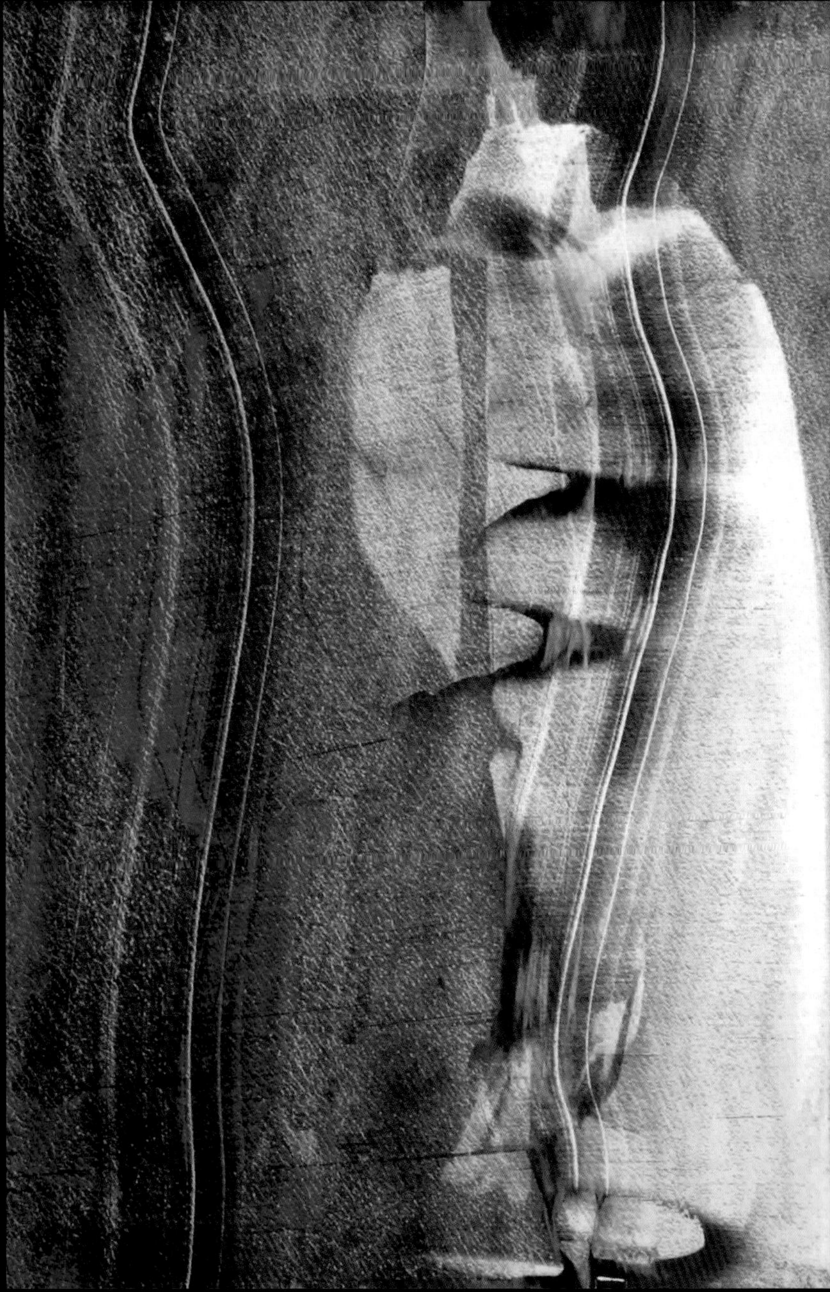

▲ A music image before incorporating the face.

◥ A different one with the face added.

▶ If you prefer to be emotionally neutral, take a big trowel, dob a few colours onto a board and sweep them quickly around so that they cover the board.

◂ Use paint to illustrate the way you would like an organisation or relationship to be. The end product is less important than the thinking process. Instead of using words ('friendly', 'supportive', 'enthusiastic', etc) you're using paint to describe what you want. It's a development of analog drawing (chapters 3 and 4) and draws attention to the fact that 'art thinking' can transpose into strategic thinking. The image communicates to the people participating in a discussion.

▾ Make a painting which is a conversation between lines and tones. (Kerrie-Ann Smith)

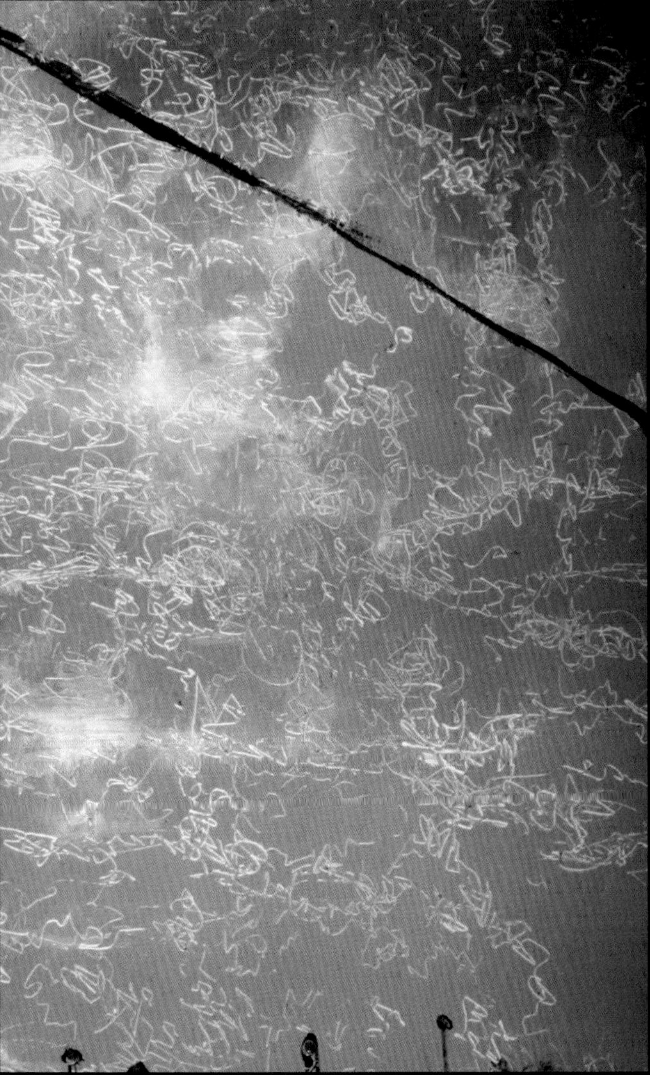

◂ An example of lines talking to each other within a larger work by Katharine White.

▾ Charcoal lines having a conversation and also describing faces, by Jennifer Bryant.

⩔ A painting by Katherine Ivory in which the lines create the tones.

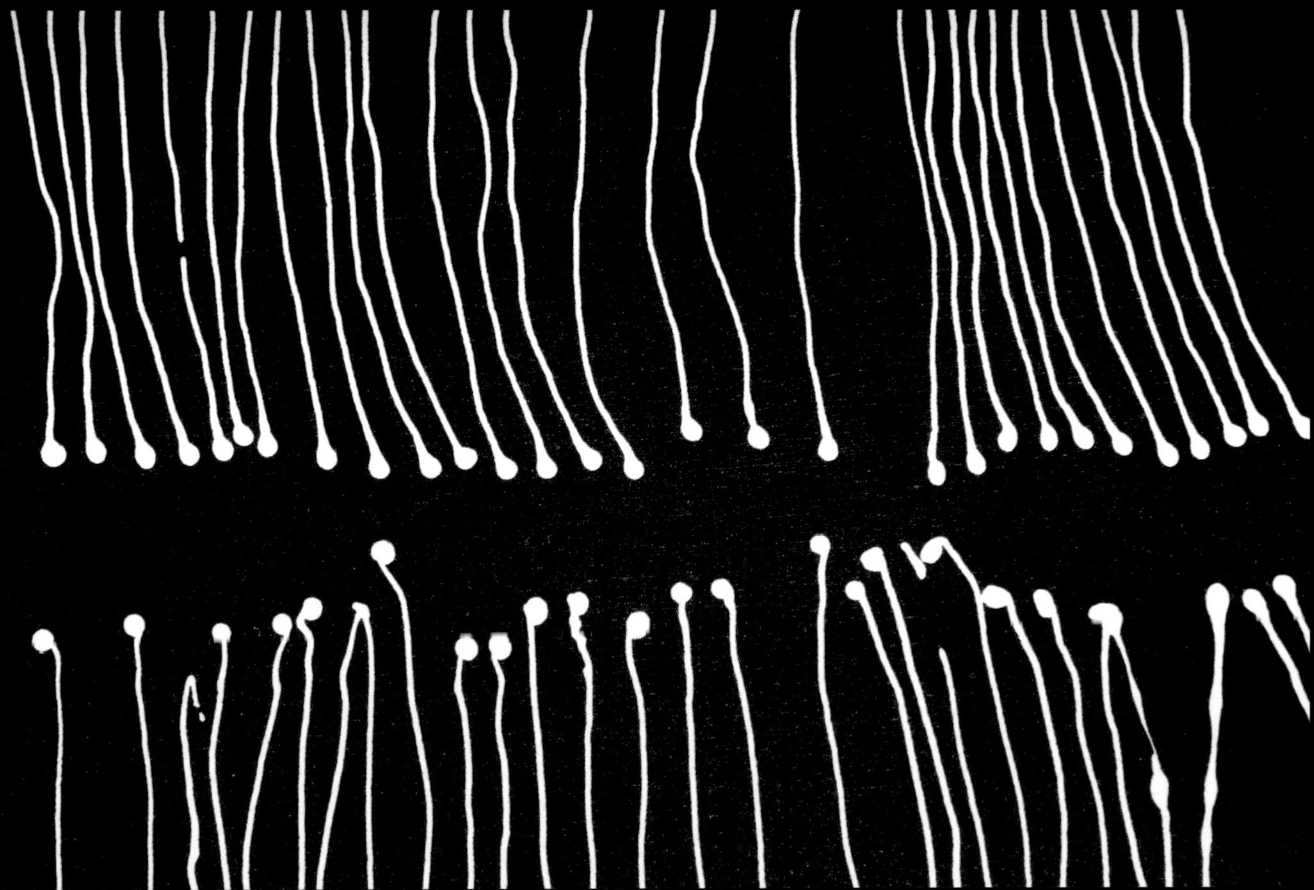

151 Start with a primed surface (white, black or any tone you prefer). Add colour and use a palette knife (or similar item) to scratch the paint while it's still wet. Allow the paint to dry if necessary. Add new colour, do more scratching. Let the layers creep over each other and keep playing. If you wish, create new lines by dribbling paint onto the surface. The goal is to create an interesting conversation between the lines and the tones. Go *with* the paint and be willing to follow it into unexpected places. It's like being a partner to the work rather than its 'master'. The painting is complete at whatever point you decide the 'conversation' is resolved.

The works as a whole are usually more eloquent than words and enable immensely complex ideas to be shared quickly, powerfully and without conflict

Within the context of TLC we periodically invite staff or students to do paintings that share their thinking about what they would like the school to be. The works as a whole are usually more eloquent than words and enable immensely complex ideas to be shared quickly, powerfully and without conflict. It's usually more effective than muddling along with 'vision' statements.

152 Preferably work with others (although you can do it by yourself if no one else is available). Test the idea with themes like "What I would like my community/country to feel like," "What I would like my school/workplace/family to feel like" and so on.

There wasn't one. This isn't a painting at all — it's mud spattered on the rear window of my car. The faint red lines are the demisting wires and the pyramid at the bottom could be one of New Zealand's volcanoes but is probably a piece of paper behind the window. But the mud suggests an idea. What can you do using random processes such as spatter to build a surface? What happens when you remove your own judgment so that the marks just happen? In the case of the mud I found the marks were richly varied and interesting. You might call it 'nature's art' — the outcome of allowing a natural process to take its course. The human ingredient is choice. I took the photo because the pattern appealed to me.

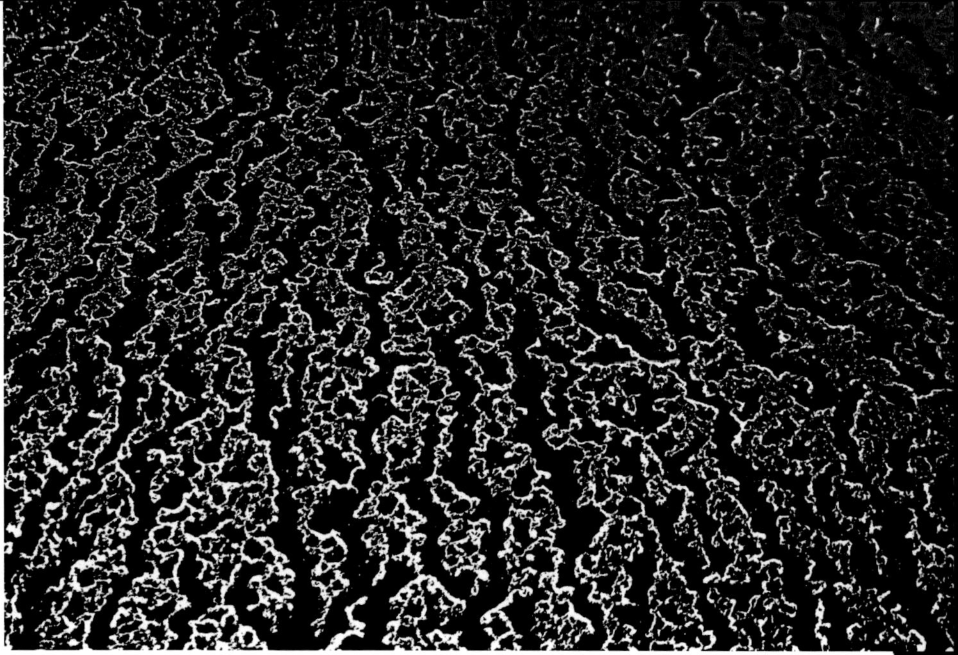

Another example of auto-art – this time dust which has flowed into streams.

A New Zealand artist attached a sticky surface to the front of his vehicle with the intention of making an artwork out of the bugs he hit while driving. Mud art is more compassionate than the bug art although the unpredictability has something in common.

153 Think of ways in which you can make art which shows a process. For example, a piece of paper taped to a sidewalk would gather footprints. In windy, dry conditions a sheet with wet glue (or paint) will collect the imprint of dust and other debris. If you place a glued board on a recently cut lawn, it will pick up pieces of grass. I've seen traps in bird sanctuaries which lure predators to a poisonous bait and record their footprints with the use of an ink pad. It would surely win the bird vote.

Poster boards (above left) are a sort of process art. Sometimes the encrusted layers of paper are so thick that they can easily be removed and recycled into art galleries.

Laurel Barr, a member of our faculty, has used things like old soap to convey process. She recently circulated a request for volunteers to wear pieces of sticking plaster until they finally fell off – then return them to her to be part of an artwork.

Laurel Barr's used plasters in a TLC staff exhibition.

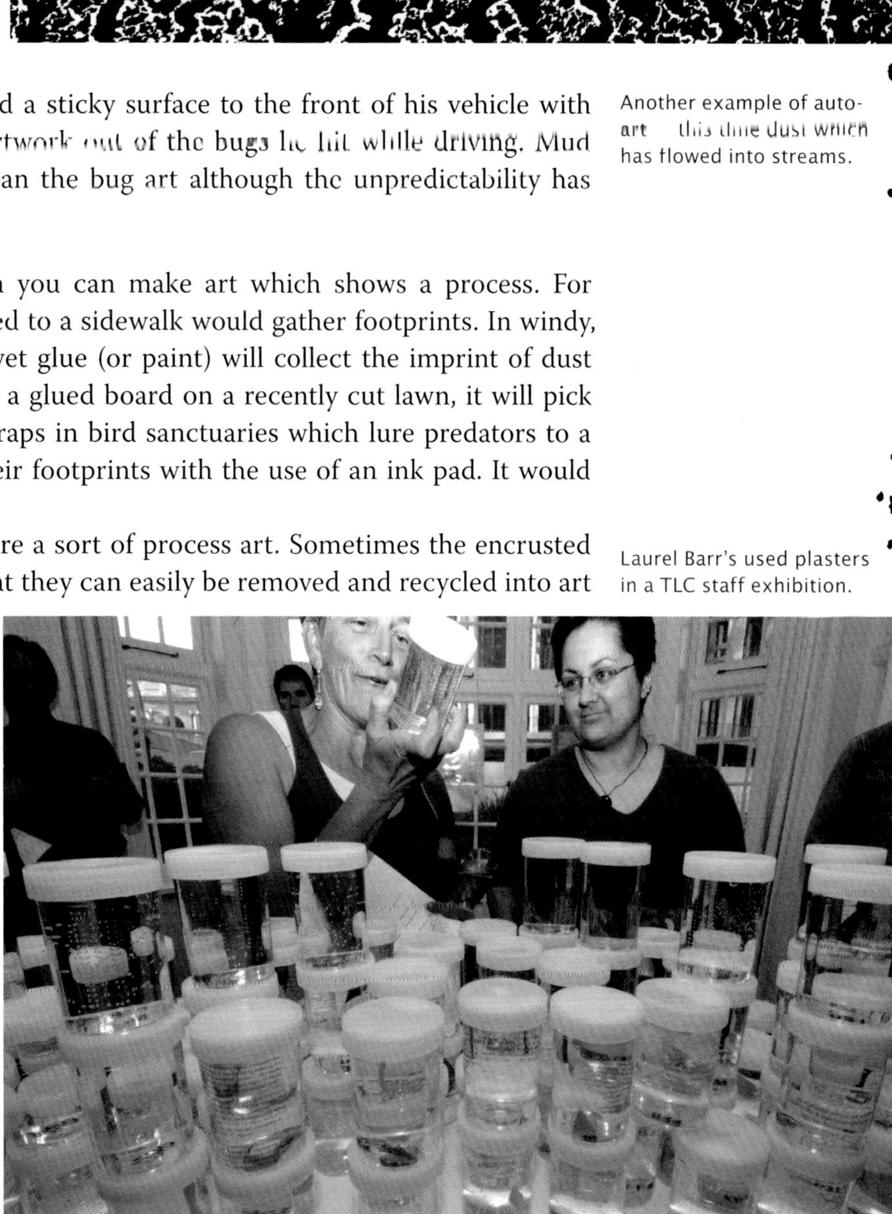

*Go **with** the paint and be willing to follow it into unexpected places*

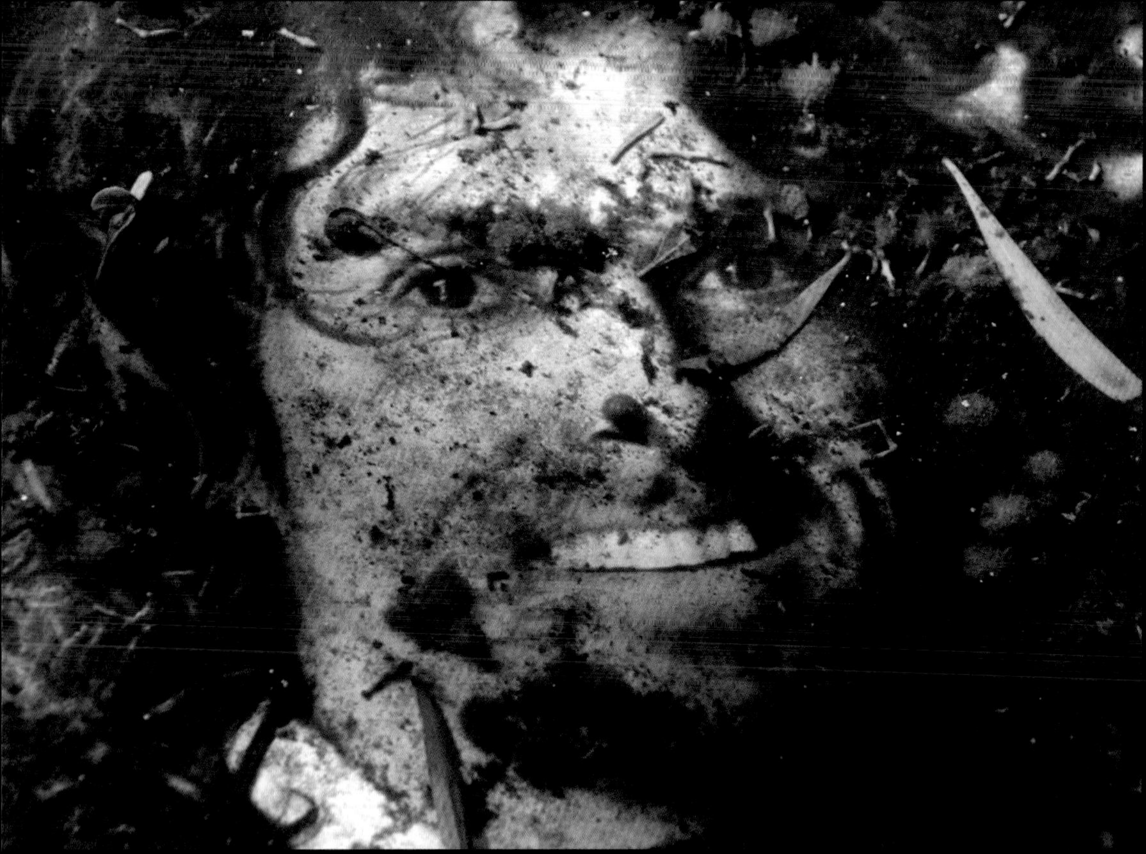

◂ Art itself decays (despite the best efforts of armies of conservators). You can approach the art like sticking plaster and expose it to deliberate change. The photo is my friend Dave on an abandoned election billboard. It's a little creepy but it says something about the passing of time.

▾ It's not a painting but it shows how weathering can draw out qualities which aren't present if we keep everything neatly controlled. The processes of nature can be the focus of our wonder.

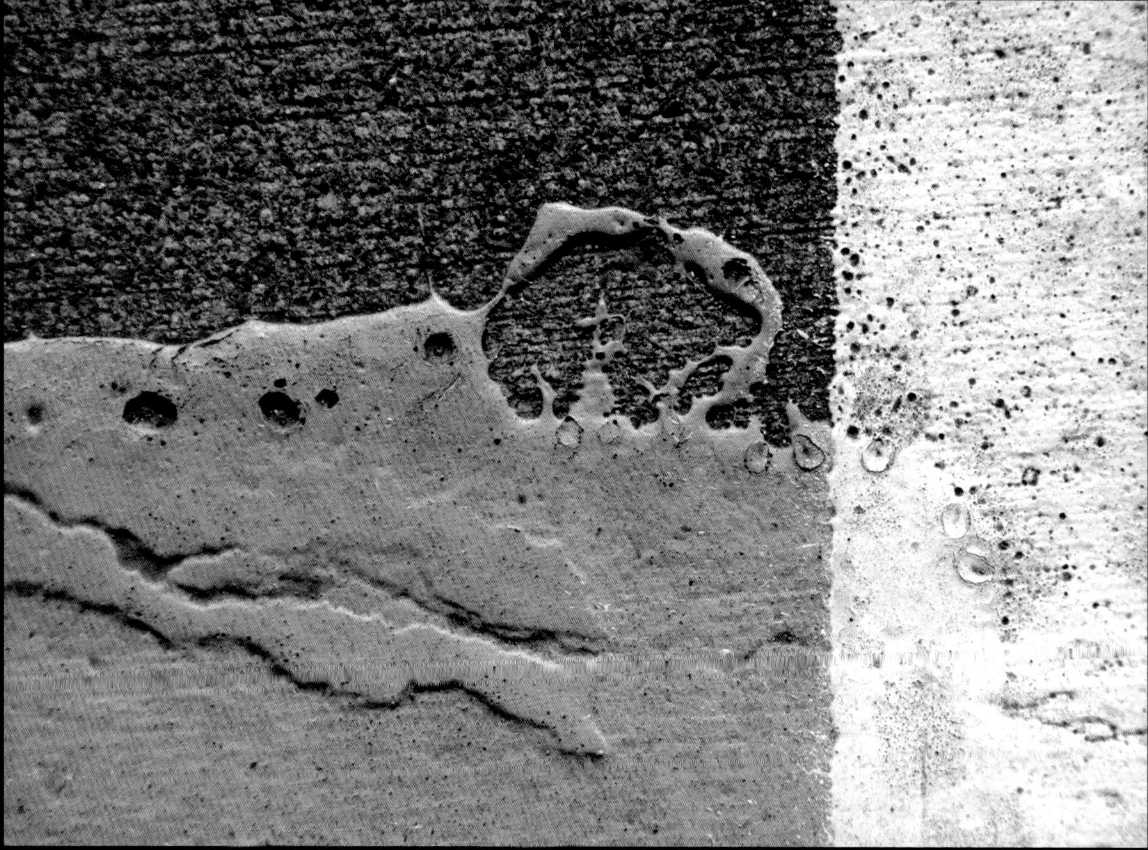

▶ It's paint but it isn't a painting. These road markings say something about wear and tear as well as the nature of the materials. Those edges are superb.

▼ Fire and rust.

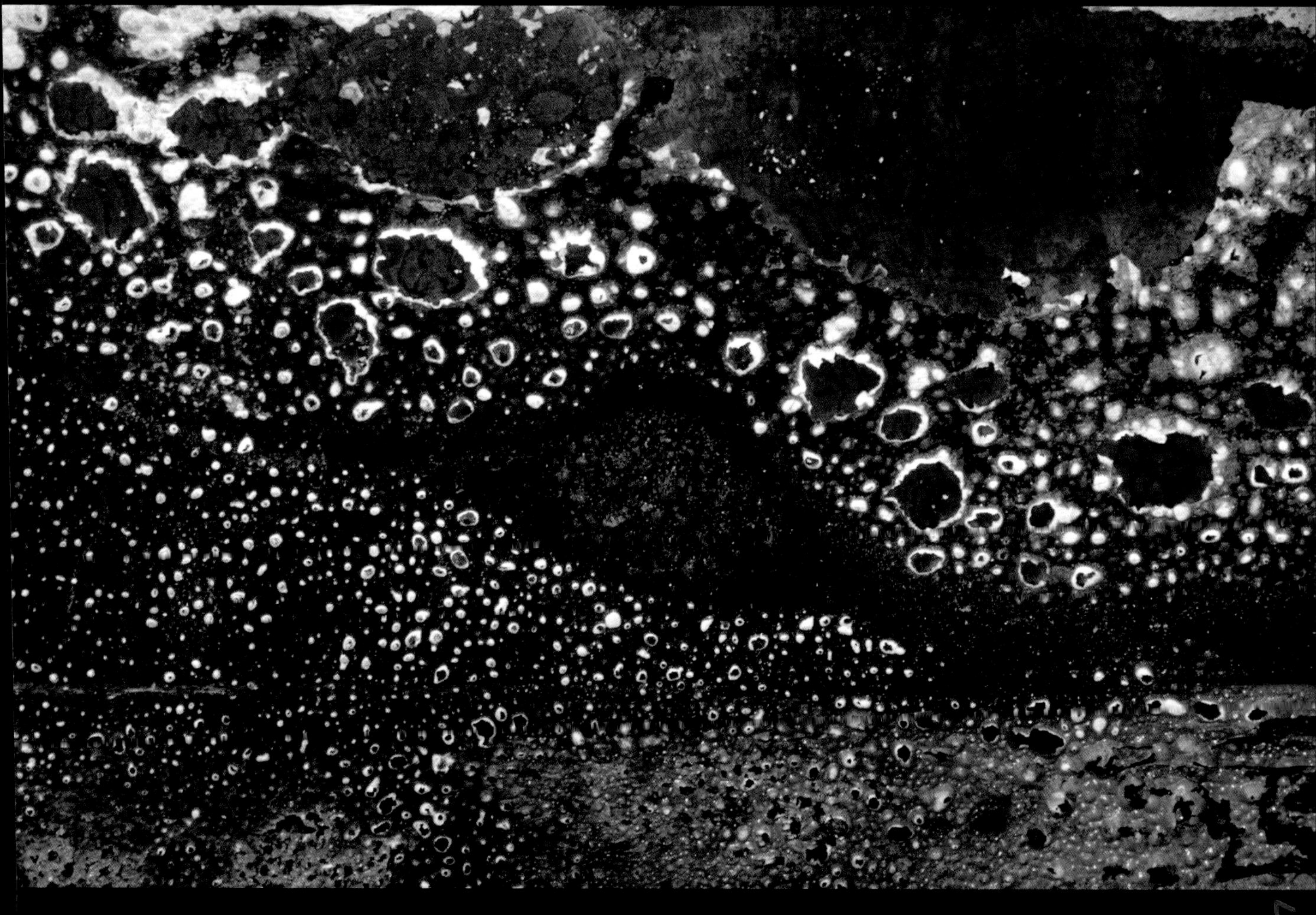

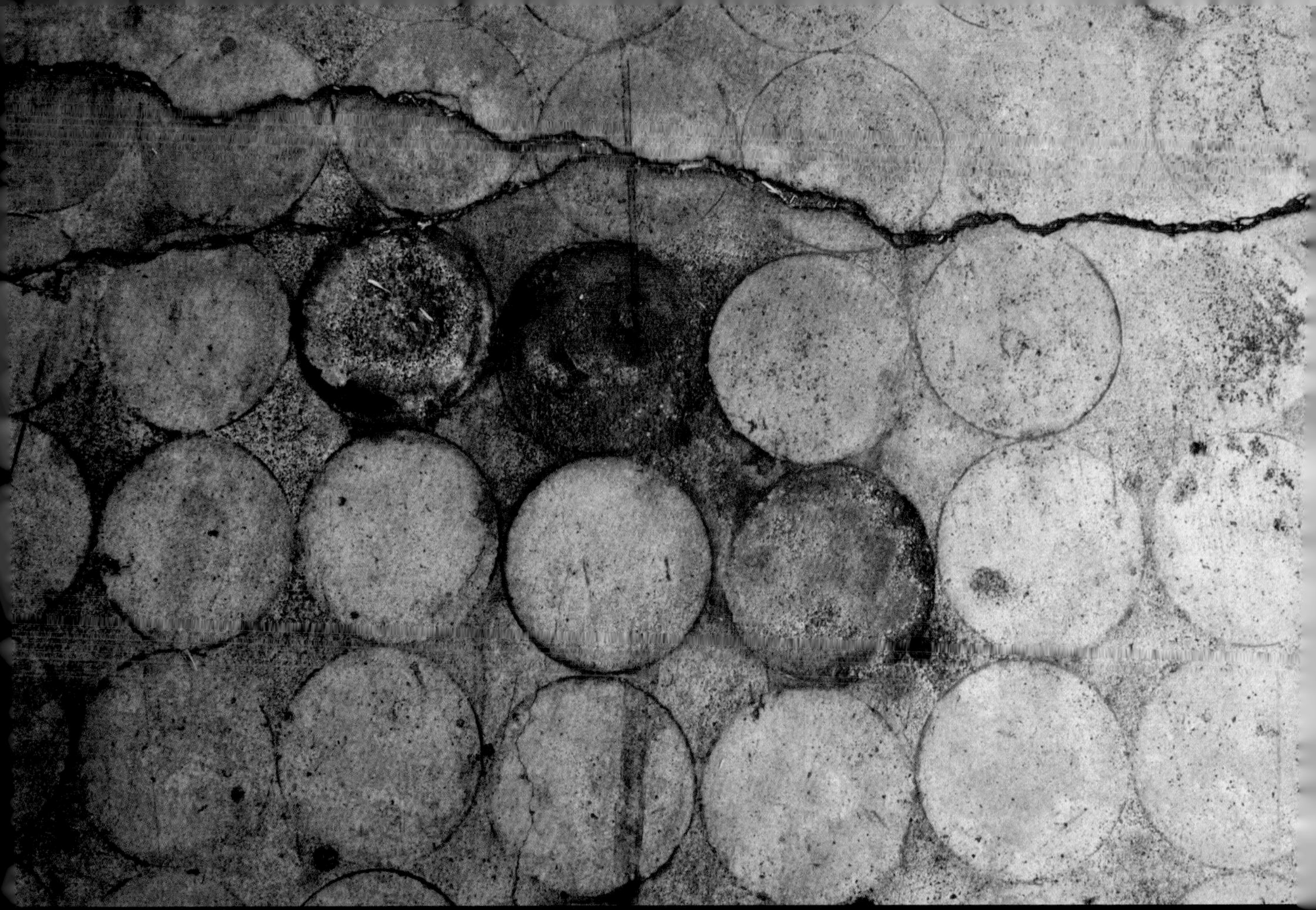

▲ The circles are from tins of tomatoes which were caught in a fire next to what is now the Arts Annex of JFK University in Berkeley.

▶ Discarded tar looking like octopus art by the side of a road — and gradually integrating with grass and other life forms.

The blob of wet plaster was placed on the floor by the door to the TLC Masterclass. The door was used to spread it across part of the floor. By the time visitors arrived for the student exhibition the plaster was dry. As people came and went it slowly broke up — and the 'art' was the mixture of human responses and the disintegration of the 'work'. Concept by Sarah Bullied.

like a

Photography

When I first saw a photograph being developed it was nothing less than a miracle. I was ten years old and a classmate showed me how it was done. I was agog. One minute I was looking at a white piece of paper and a few seconds later a picture emerged.

It was a few years before I got my first camera but that initial impression has stayed with me. I didn't develop a picture of my own until I was 18 and that was the beginning of many years in smelly darkrooms making prints. I became very slick at rolling film onto a developing reel in the dark. Then the world went digital.

I tentatively bought a digital camera, just to try it out (feeling guilty). Within a few days I was hooked. I haven't used film in years and I don't miss it.

Digital opened up new freedoms. I could take as many pictures as I liked and save a fortune.

Our photography tutors still love the mystique of the darkroom and to some extent 'chemical' photography is reinventing itself with new applications (photographs on wood, fabric etc, and crossovers with printmaking). As far as mainstream photography is concerned, it's good to be able to play with images on a computer instead of working in a dark, fume-laden room.

The low-middle range of the digital camera market is good enough to produce reasonable images and the prices continue to plummet. Access to a computer has to be factored into the cost. There's a counter-attraction in that excellent secondhand film cameras can sometimes be picked up for the proverbial song. My advice is to start digital if you can put a whole package together (camera, computer, software). Otherwise, a film camera will get you going. Alas, its resale value will be close to zip and you may grow out of it faster than you expect. If you have the opportunity, borrow a digital camera to get a practical experience of what it can do.

a camera is another way of processing ideas

In terms of creativity, a camera is another way of processing ideas. It requires some particular technical understanding but it's just an instrument, like a pencil or a brush but different.

Making photos

For technophobic photographers, cameras have never been easier. Most have an 'automatic' setting through which the camera estimates a correct exposure and takes care of the technical stuff. When you want results that don't fit the automatic settings it's time to learn to read the manual. There are hundreds of books (and free advice on the internet) which will take you through the technicalities. A tutor is even better because you can stay precisely with the questions that are important to you.

your whole personality manifests in the way you make pictures

The underlying principle of photography is that the effects of light can be recorded, either electronically or on light-sensitive film. There are endless subtleties which you can explore when you're ready. The best news is that you can make good pictures with minimal understanding of technicalities because you're already aware of things like colour, tone, composition and so on (unless you're reading the book backwards or taking a random dip).

Some principles:

Have your camera available. Murphy's Law says that the best photo opportunities will happen when you've left your camera at home. I deal with Murphy by carrying a little 10 megapixel Lumix on my belt at all times. I don't know if it's helped my photography but it has removed any need to make excuses. (It doesn't substitute for a more professional camera either – but it is light, unobtrusive and delivers pretty good results.)

Be daring. If you're looking at something which a million tourists have already photographed, think of another way of doing it. You'll find that your whole personality manifests in the way you make pictures. Enjoy it!

Find a strategy that suits you. If you want to compose and control your images you'll need a different sets of skills from an opportunist like me. Mostly I've worked for publications illustrating my own stories and I've gradually built up a collection running into tens of thousands of pictures. If I have a specific task (for example, "get a picture of the president") my first step is to get something 'in the can' even if it's boring. Then I get into higher-risk attempts. I rarely pose a photo but I'm happy to take 200 shots to get one that appeals to me. Other photographers do the opposite – they establish each shot with great care and don't wear out their shutter button. Some of us are like rabbits; others are like panda bears. You'll find most of the different styles in your local library and it's worth bringing home lots of books and immersing yourself in what others have done. Then return the books and be yourself.

stalk a possibility

Eventually read the manual. Get enough information to turn on the camera and make a picture. Later, when you're figuring out how to expose for shadows (or whatever the question is) search out the relevant bits and practise until you can do it without thinking.

I fancied getting a glider and a gull to symbolise something about humans and birds. The gull is an awesome flier! When I took the shot I was annoyed because the bird had come too close but when I saw the result I was delighted.

Share your pictures. As with paintings, you learn by the responses of others. Email images to friends and pay attention to what works.

Build themes. One of my most popular collections (among friends) consists of pictures of nature taken within two or three miles of home. It isn't *National Geographic* but it tells a story and has a sense of place. I keep in mind themes like sunsets, water, patterns and animals. Think about your own themes and get into the habit of connecting with them. Be patient. Something you do today might take twenty years to emerge in a collection.

Something you do today might take twenty years to emerge in a collection

151 Stalk a possibility. For example, if you watch at a pedestrian crossing, can you capture a close encounter between a vehicle and a pedestrian? If you're by the sea, can you catch someone being caught unexpectedly by a wave? If you're watching a game, can you capture the extremes (a play connecting with full force on the ball; the drama of a tackle)?

Cleanliness

Dirt and grime are interesting but unless you want them to be part of the picture they're a nuisance. A dirty lens usually diffuses the light and may not cause great mischief, but if the innards of the camera get grubby you may have nasty problems. Digital sensors are tiny and they show the effects of microscopic dust particles. Sometimes photography happens in really difficult environments – smoke, dust, rain, salt spray, pollen, mud – you name it. A little fanatical cleanliness helps to keep equipment free of unwanted invaders.

My subject was patterns — the way the chipmunk blends with its world — although the cute pose adds a little something.

I aimed for the whole circus of animals (they were entertaining tourists at a vista point on Highway 1 in California). These are images that are good for the photo album but they don't make it in their own right. The hardest part in scenes like this is that everything is happening so fast. It's why wildlife photographers spend days, weeks or months going for the best possible shot. A motor drive can be useful because it will deliver several frames a second (and I didn't have one when I needed it). Another challenge is to be awake to what you're seeing. I was so distracted by the cuteness of the animals that I didn't fully appreciate the way they were working like a troop of buskers. They were engaged in a dialogue with their environment and had learned how to use their energy to the best effect.

155 Stalk an event and be willing to take hundreds of images to get a result that most fully captures the drama.

I aimed for the horizontal bands of hills, ocean and rocks. It's a portrait of Wellington on a bright day with the wind blowing into the swell. Below left, a different wave and a fraction too bright. It's usually best to err towards under-exposure because it's easier to brighten a digital image than to darken it. Below right, a menacing dumper dominates the scene. In a short time I took 84 photos and wanted something better. People were waiting in the car ...

It's grainy and not technically
'correct' but the timing is right.

When taking photos I'm sometimes telling a story, sometimes having fun with shapes and colours, sometimes observing and exploring. Whether it's 'art' doesn't enter into it. But I do try to go to the max. I want the most evocative wave, the cheekiest chipmunk and the most compelling combination of bird and glider.

156 Create visual music by mixing patterns. It's fun to take photography beyond photographs. The earlier images of spoons and crumpled newspaper were visual play and this is how they grew:

Drop objects onto black paper and photograph them. In Photoshop on the computer use the magic wand tool and select any portion of black. (*NB: study books and tutorials and work with a tutor – these instructions don't give all the fine details!*) Go to the **Select** menu → **Similar** (all the black portions will be highlighted). Go to **Edit** → **Fill**. Select black from the fill options. This part of the work corrects the uneven lighting and makes the colours stand out better.

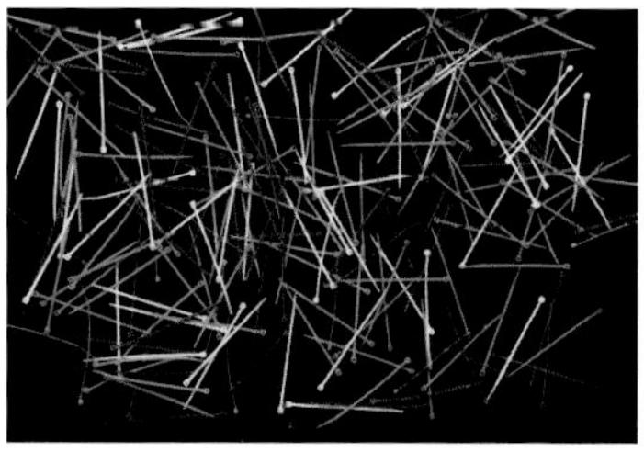

Choose (or create) an image that seems to go with the first picture. In this case I chose a hedge in which the twigs had a similar form to the ties. To resolve the hedge into two colours I went to **Filters** → **Sketch** → **Torn Edges**. 'Torn edges' divides the image into the background and foreground colours.

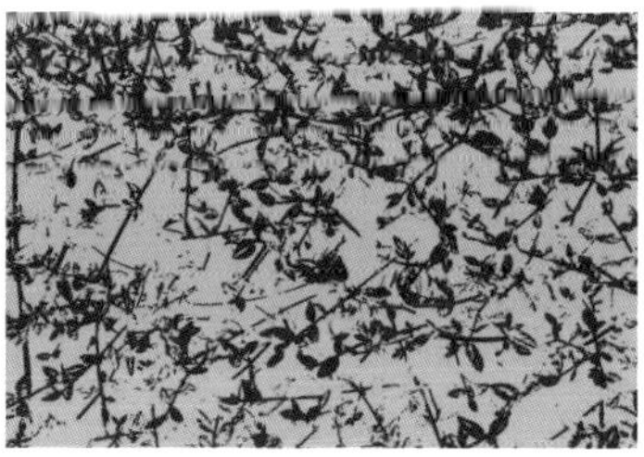

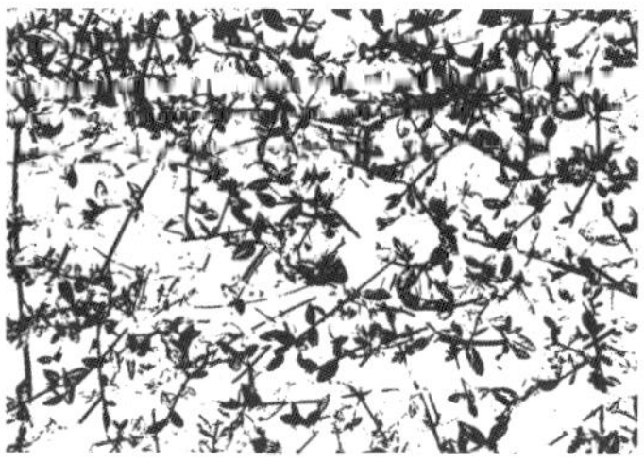

I extracted the purple (**magic wand** → **Select** → **Similar** → **Copy**) and dropped it onto the first image:

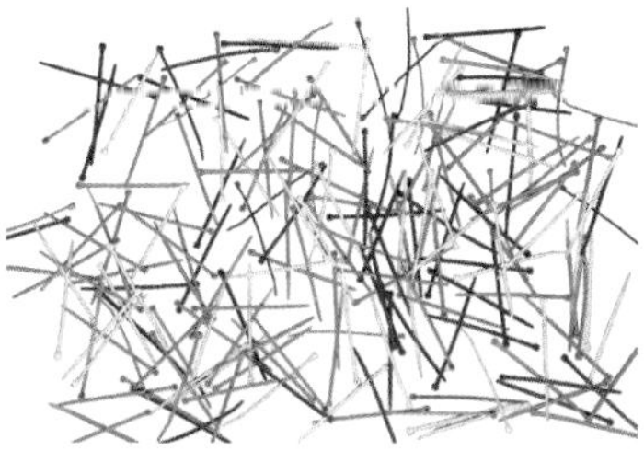

The purple looked overwhelming so I made it more transparent (**Layers** dialogue box → **Opacity** → **80%**). I then went back to the original and flipped it (**Image** → **Rotate Canvas** → **180°**). Then, to extract a copy of the coloured pieces, I used the magic wand to select a piece of black, then **Select** → **Similar** → **Inverse** → **Copy** and back to the composite with **Paste**:

When you get to this point (which could be regarded as a finished result) you may like to explore other filters (but save the file first so that you don't lose it). Here is what happened with **Bas Relief**. Although it wasn't an intended result it was a good accident.

157 Go slow and wobble. Defy the 'rule' to hold your camera steady. Set your camera on a fairly slow speed (8th or 15th of a second) and do 'wobbly' pictures of light at night.

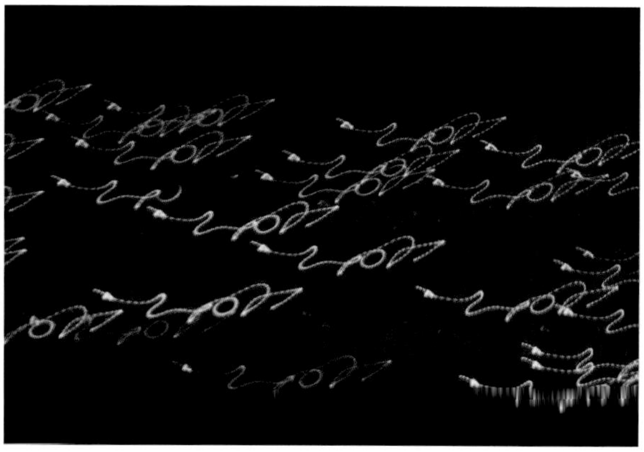

The 'writing' had potential so I played with it in Photoshop.

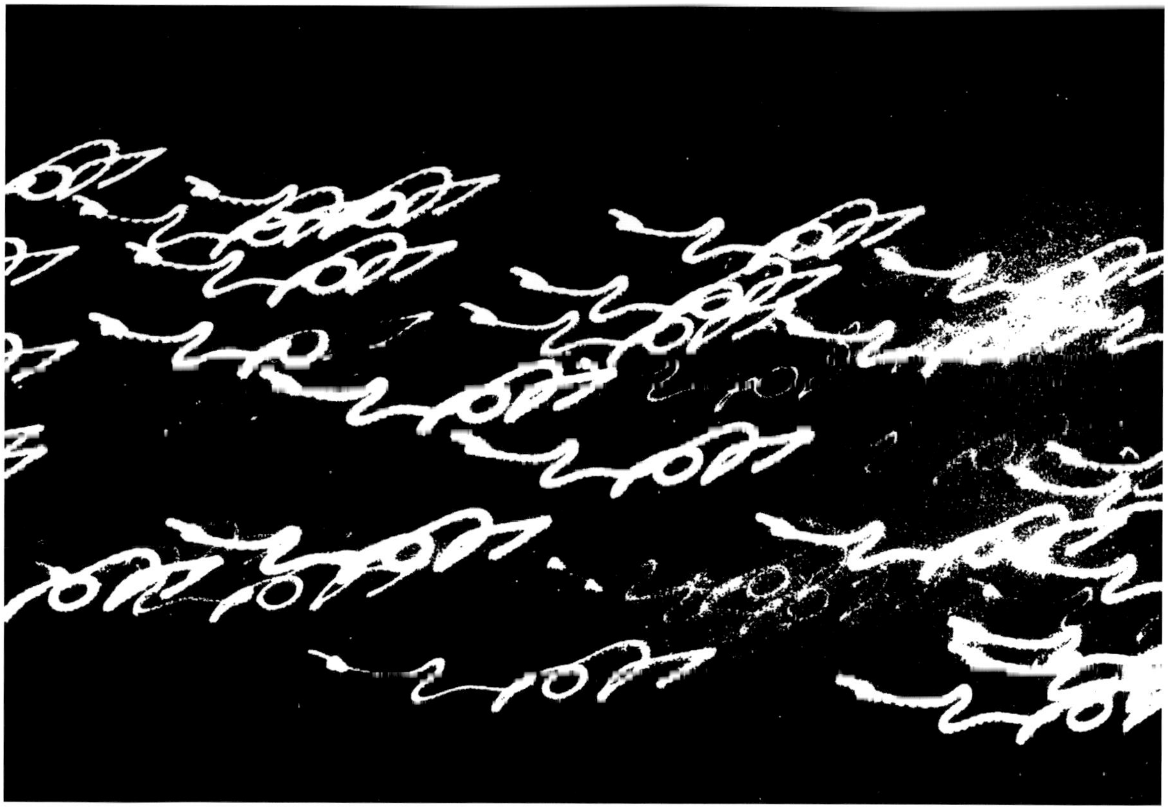

Again there's a touch of order and mystery. If it has no appeal for you, let it go by. If you like it, explore further.

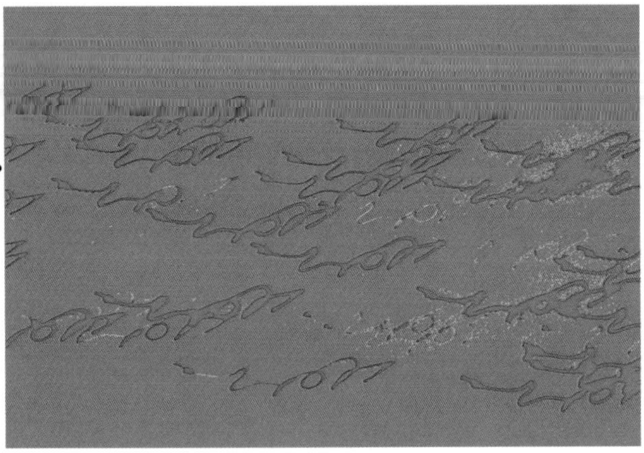
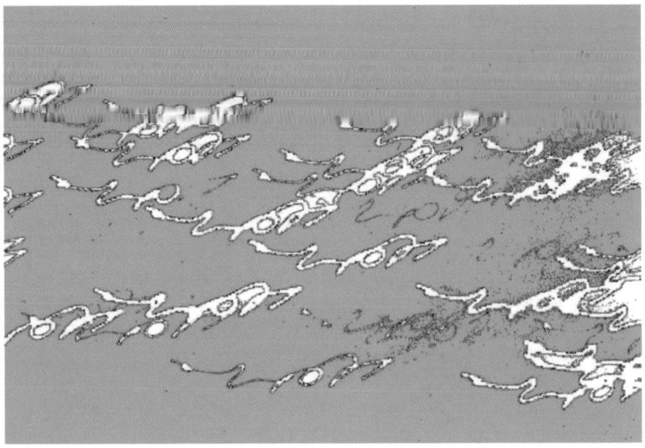

Left: **Neon Glow**. *Right:* **Trace Contour → Fill**

Each command on the Photoshop **Filter** menu works like a verb – in a few seconds the computer performs an action on your photograph and you produce something new.

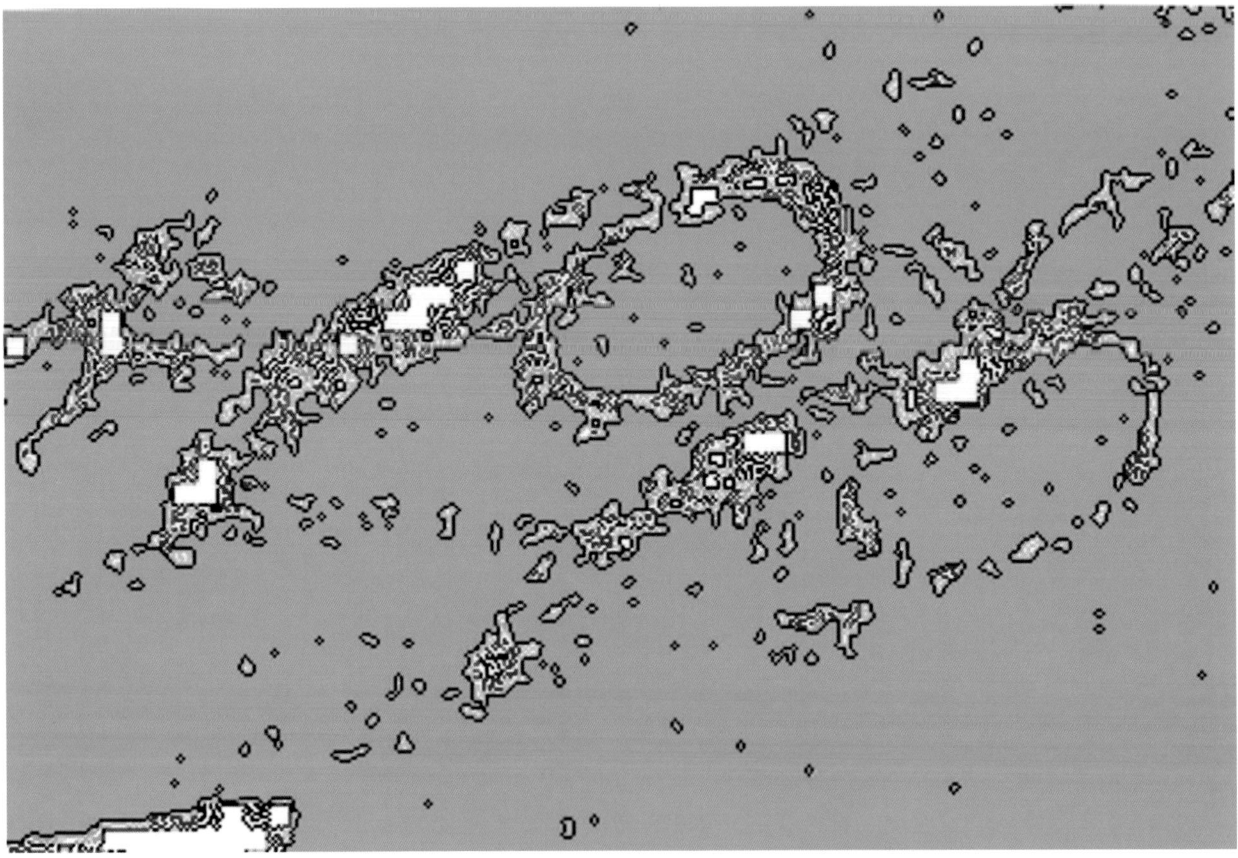

When I looked closely at a detail from the 'trace contour' result I thought it had a quality of its own – an expressionist nest of islands.

everything depends

158 *Using reflected light*

A lot of personal photography is about grabbing pictures of friends and family – often in difficult conditions and when people are in a hurry. If you make use of reflected light it can lift the quality. Ella, on the left, was a few weeks old and in the dim light of a bathroom. The towel is working as a reflector and lifting the light in the shadows. Mucha, on the right, is in a room with windows on both sides. When photographing adults you can use light reflected from a wall or have someone hold a white sheet or board to brighten the shadows.

Think about the background. Either make it simple (as for Ella) or so blurred that it doesn't intrude (Mucha). To achieve blurry backgrounds you need to have the widest possible aperture (the smaller the 'f number' the bigger the aperture).

Everything depends on your goal. I like spontaneous expressions and seldom do studio shots. The portrait at right was posed but in the natural light of an art workshop (the blemishes on the wall add some commentary). Same principle – light from both sides and enough to show detail in the shadows. Because the light is relatively dull it doesn't have the intense crispness of a studio shot but the mood is what I wanted. Even the off-balance position (leaning to the left) added to the intense stare.

It can be annoying when the right expression happens in poor or hopeless light but that's how it goes. You keep shooting.

on your goal

the mood is what I wanted

Ella established a perspective and Charlotte is looking at her, so the flow works even though they're not focused on the same thing.

If all else fails, get someone to attract attention (or yell "HEY").

A second later, the tension dropped

159 Achieving focus with two or more people in a picture. Each person in a picture establishes a kind of perspective with their line of sight. Although the children visiting TLC (opposite) are hamming it up, their attention (at least with those in front) is fairly focused.

160 Search for patterns. Look for things that really appeal to you. Think about close-up, distant and middle range. Patterns from the sky and flowers in the garden are two of the endless options.

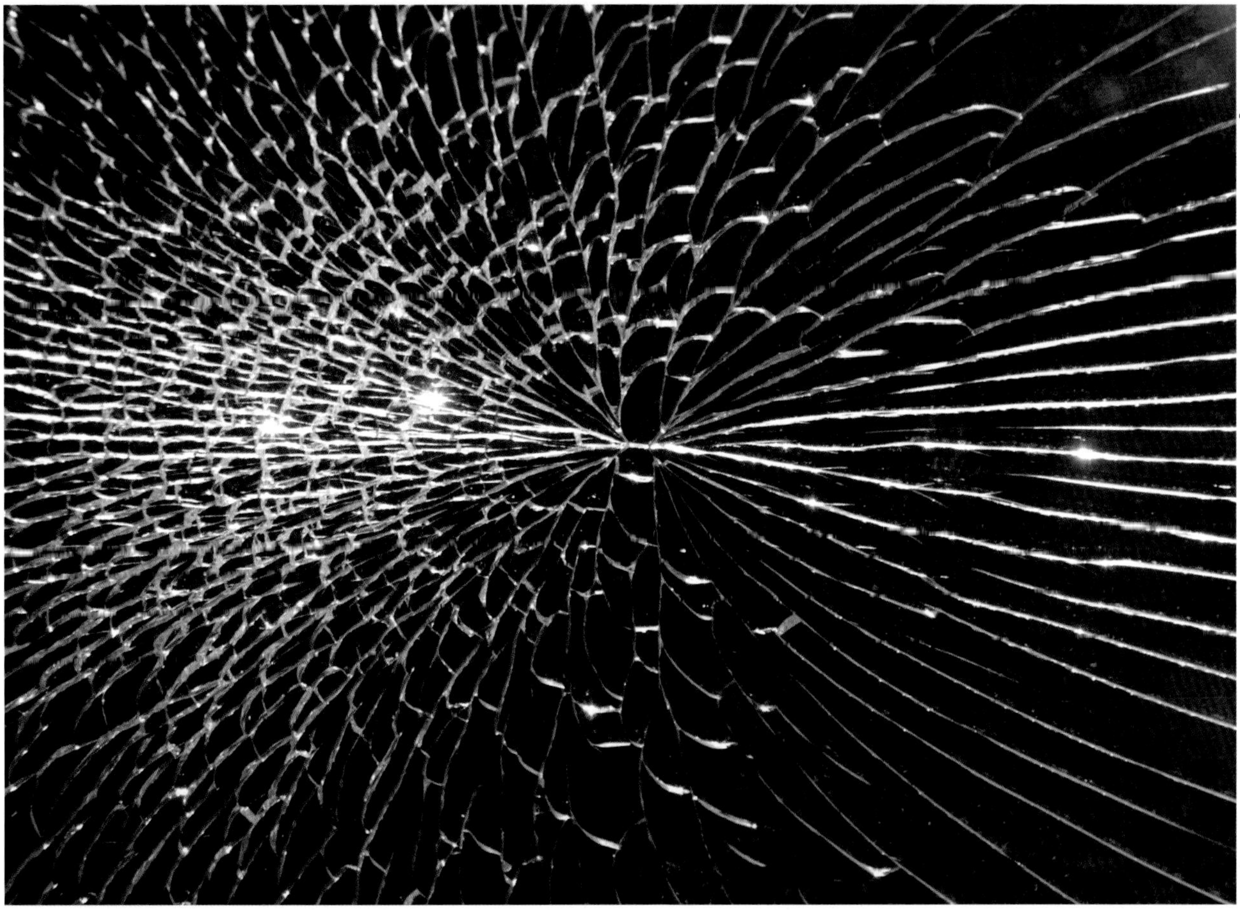

Fractured glass.

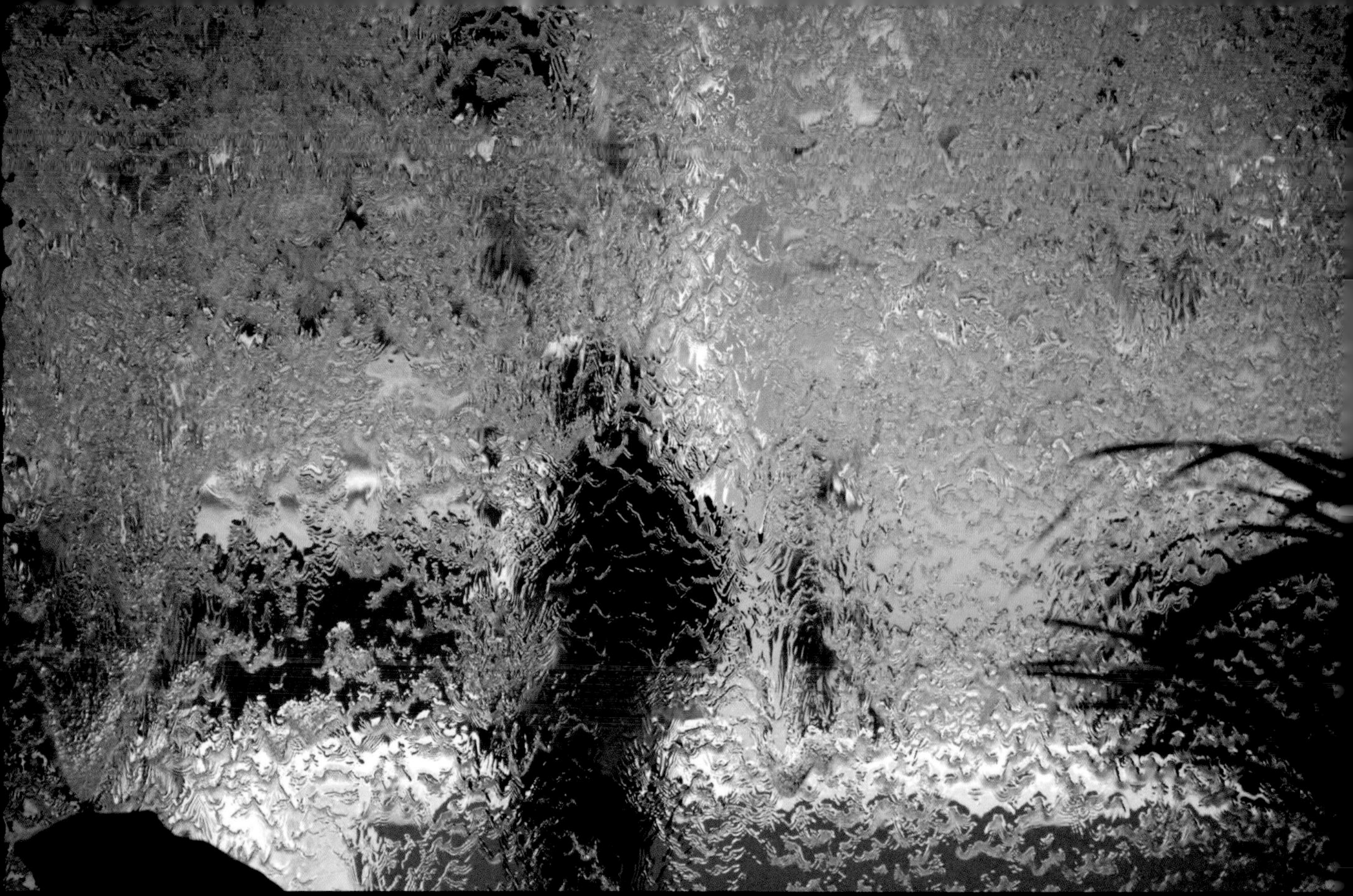

161 Photograph through net, water or glass that puts a layer between you and your subject.

▶ Lettering seen through net curtains which also carry the shadow. The greyness and the implied danger say something about hotels. The shadow warps the words into a different visual language, softer yet still sinister.

▲ The photo has an 'Op Art' effect arising from the screen itself (do you see illusory black dots?) and the slightly uneven background.

▲ The same screen with a person walking by. In the bright areas the light 'eats' the screen a little and creates a variety of effects different from what happens when you use Photoshop or a mechanical screen.

▲ A different sort of net — reflections in the façade of a Los Angeles building. A rigid, 'yang' environment has deformed to 'yin' curves in the dark glass.

▶ Landscape through mosquito netting. The barely decipherable horizon, sky and foreground provide unresolved clues and tension.

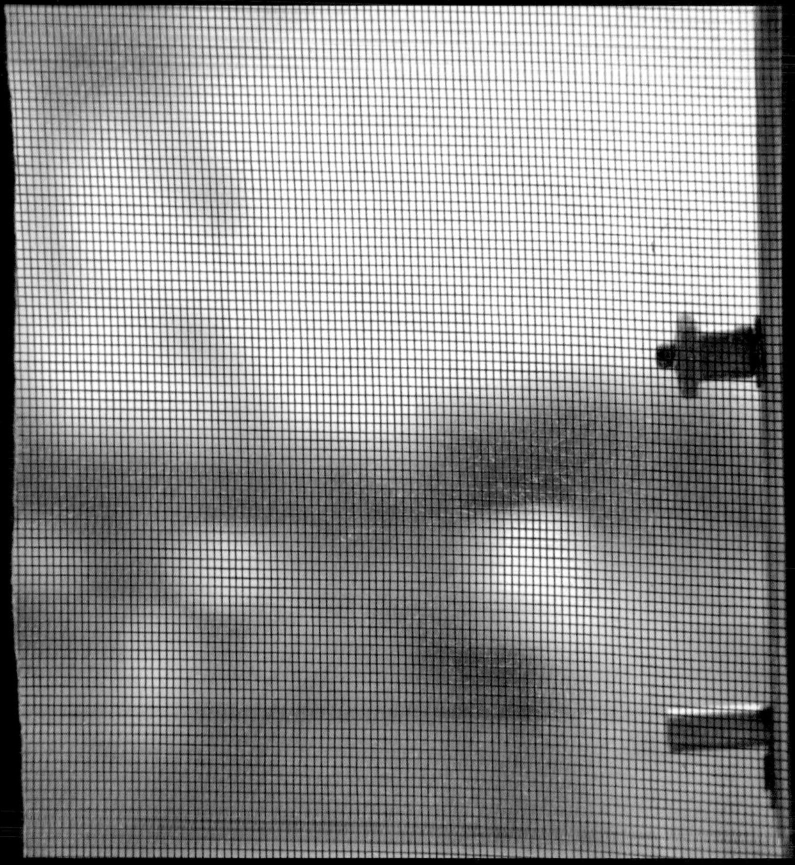

162 *Playing with tones*

In the days of black and white we 'dodged' and 'burned'. During an exposure in the darkroom this meant either blocking light (dodging) or letting more light onto the photographic paper (burning). Photoshop allows approximately the same techniques in colour images.

The original (*left*) needs a lift. The next version came by adjusting **Curves** in Photoshop.

Below left: tones selected with the magic wand tool. *Below right:* the original darkened (and the brighter spots in the background subdued via the clone tool). Then the original tones (*left*) were overlaid. This is only a rough demonstration – a more balanced (and plausible) result would require more time and finer adjustments.

163 *Reconstruct a picture*

Greyman, left, was busking in Wellington amidst the clutter of Cuba Street. The clearest possible background included an unfortunate line

I removed the background altogether and placed the figure on an artificial graded tone. Then I tried it on top of a picture of balloons in the sky. Your choice will depend on your goal.

164 *Faking it (again)*

An entertaining way to get into Photoshop is to take an old family picture and incorporate someone who wasn't born at the time. In the example I've patched my brother Mark into an image of my grandfather and great-grandfather.

Scan the images (if they're not in digital form). Clear-cut the image you want to shift (use the eraser, polygonal lasso tool and the magic wand to get rid of the background). Think about the way it's going to turn out. In this case the boots will be in grass so it isn't necessary to delete the grass – rather it's a matter of roughly cutting it with the eraser so that it blends with the grass in the second photo. Adjust the size of the first picture if it isn't right (in this case I increased it a little), then select the image and drop it onto the target picture. Move it into place, flatten the image (under **Layers**), then de-saturate to dispose of the colour. You can spend more time to make the fake more credible (fine adjustment of tones, removal of the watch, some gentle blurring and so on). And remember next time you're looking at a newspaper – that provocative picture may be a fake.

▲ Mike Grady and Alice Wilson Milne in Titahi Bay (where we live).

▸▸ Mike Grady at the Fox Glacier on the west coast of New Zealand's South Island. The image made me think of 9/11 and the wall of debris and dust in New York, but here the 'dust' is ice, gradually shrinking as the planet warms. (I tell a small lie — Fox is one of the rare glaciers which is in a growth phase.)

▸ Twilight fishing, Titahi Bay.

165 New Zealand's scenery is special and one of the treats is photographing family and friends in the landscape. Try it for yourself, perhaps making the people small and the land big. See what you can do with the sun and make it a kind of portrait in which the scenery is the real subject and the people give a sense of scale.

Contemporary 'cave art' in the sculpture area at TLC. Printing and 'stencilling' may be the oldest art forms.

CHAPTER 15

Printmaking

TOOLS

- Sheets of glass and/or plastic
- Oil-based printing inks (water-based is easier to manage but may not give such a good print)
- Rollers (a professional roller with at least 10cm diameter is much better than little craft rollers – but thirty times more expensive)
- A pencil
- A palette knife
- A3 or A4 printing press (highly desirable although you can work without it)
- A supply of suitable paper
- Imagination

The mental gymnastics of printmaking translate strongly into the use of computer graphics. Graphics programmes frequently make use of 'layers' which are similar to the blocks of an old-fashioned multicoloured woodcut. The two processes readily overlap. For example, you can dismantle a photograph into layers of colour and then print it. You can also 'Photoshop' a print and take it into places it couldn't have reached without the computer.

From a creativity point of view, printmaking is a workout for visualisation and reverse thinking. To some extent it depends on imagining a result, deconstructing the steps and then turning your thoughts into layers of ink. The mental gymnastics may grow some new connections in your brain!

▲ The yellowXpress manufactured by Homeprint, www.ur.co.nz/homeprint

▲ 40×10cm roller from Alma Products, www.almaproducts.co.nz — expensive but worth it.

My early art (and financial success) owed everything to printmaking. Screen prints and woodcuts were an accessible way to reproduce designs and sell the same idea many times. I've since moved full circle to the point of treating a print as a one-off process, either by hand-inking (so every print is different) or through monoprinting (making a single, unique item). My attention has shifted more towards the pleasure of ink and away from mass production.

Monoprinting

The name (sometimes 'monotype') refers to the 'one-off' attribute of the print (as opposed to other printing methods where the goal is to produce a series of almost identical works).

The excitement of the monoprint comes from the not-quite-predictable outcomes of putting pressure on an inked surface to make an impression on paper.

166 As a starter, roll ink onto your inking surface (glass, smooth board, plastic, etc), then press a sheet of paper against the ink. You can use a roller or printing press to apply pressure. After each print, re-ink in different ways. For example:

- partially roll different colours into the mix
- scrape ink from the inking surface (with a palette knife)
- partially wash the inking surface and take a print of the messy patterns

Retain all the prints and then move into a second round of printing when they're dry (it may take days). Keep going until you end up with something interesting.

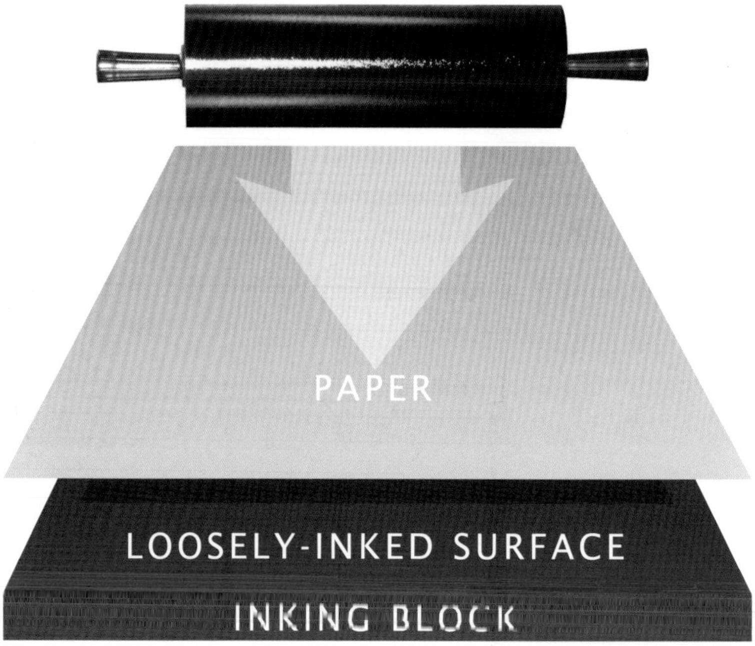

Use a roller to apply pressure if you don't have a press.

You can move to rich, Pollock-like multi-layers ...

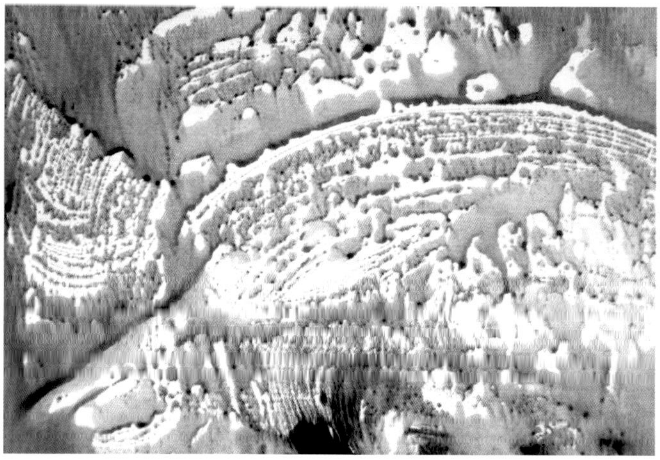

Or go for the highly unpredictable results of ink during the wash-up stage.

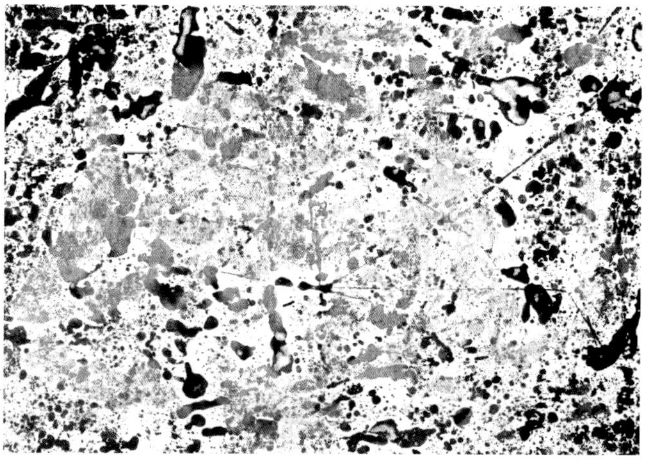

You can work with dribbled ink.

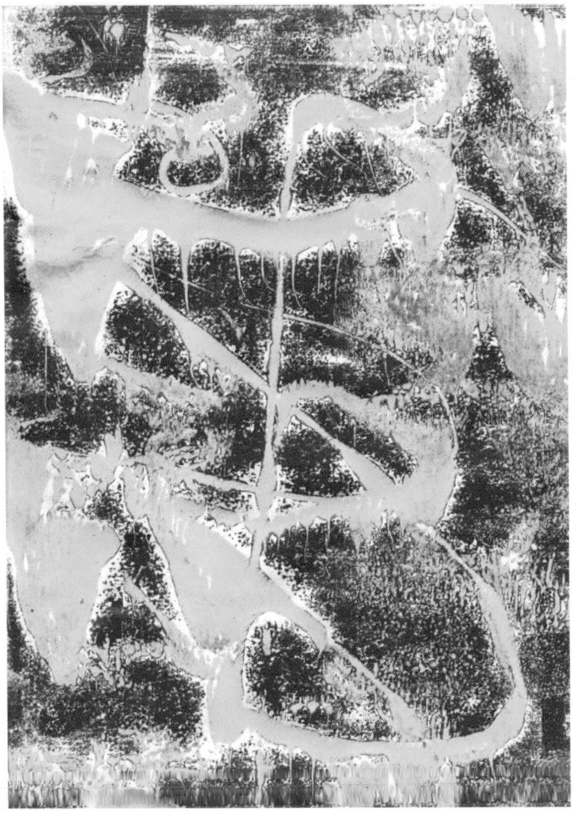

▲ Another variation is to introduce other design elements by using shapes of paper overlaid on the sheet you're printing. When you strip them off (or rearrange them) you're create a hybrid.

◄ When you get in close the textures are delicious.

167 Use a roller to ink a sheet of paper. Place the paper gently, ink facing down, onto the paper which will take the image. Draw marks on the back of the inked sheet and the pressure will transfer the ink. You can do more or less the same thing by putting your drawing paper on the top of the inking plate. In this case the monoprint will be on the back of the drawing sheet.

An alternative is to scrape ink off the plate with a palette knife (right) and squeeze the paper against the plate.

168 Using the same procedure, ink the back of a photocopy and draw to transfer the image.

Alternatively, ink the back of a blank sheet and then create your drawing, either from a model or a photo.

169 Place a sheet of clear plastic over a photo, paint the photo onto the plastic using printing ink then print the plastic on a sheet of clear paper.

When the ink is dry you can add additional layers of printing (this one was done as a single print and the paint was applied with fingers).

170 Beat patterns into wood and print the resulting surface.

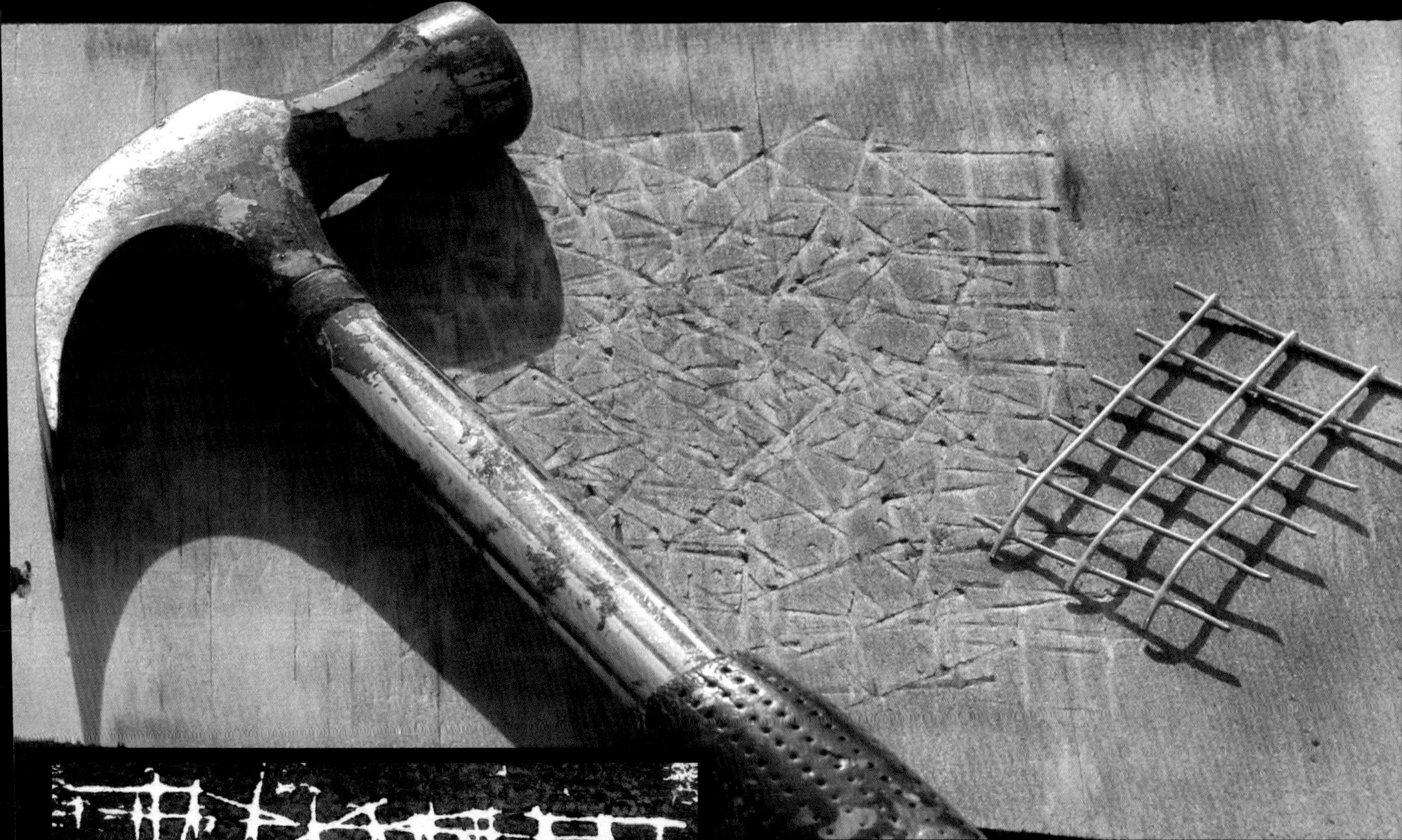

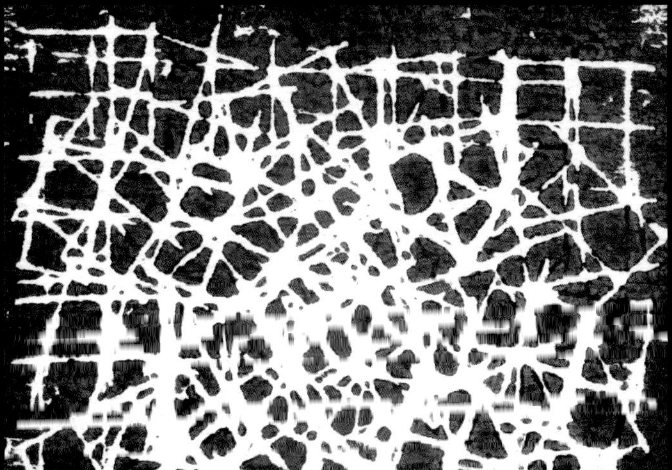

▲ The resulting print.

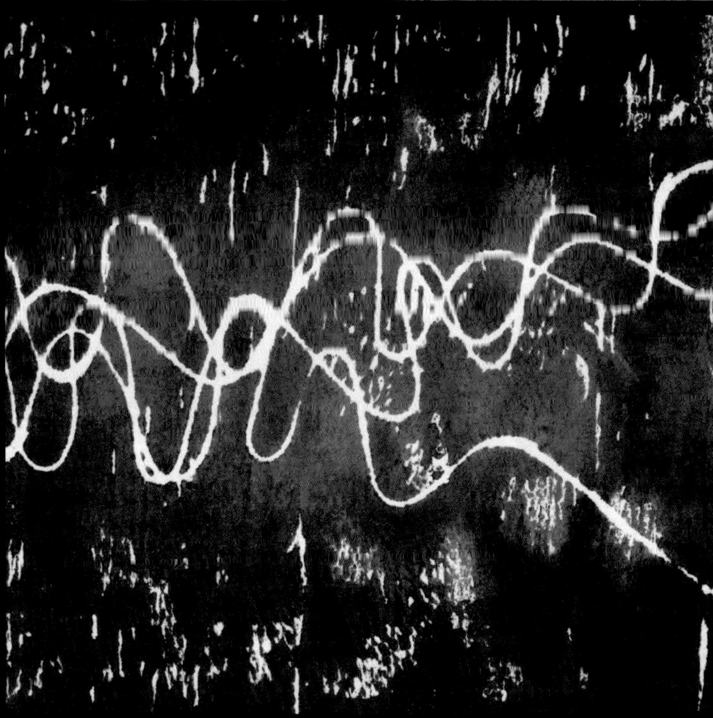

▶ The same process done with a piece of wriggly wire.

171 Print the unprintable. It started over dinner and the fish bones looked as though they might translate into a print. I used alkyd paint as ink but in the absence of a press the print was poor. I then tried a can of spray paint and the bones functioned as a stencil.

Finally I photographed the print and the skeleton and produced a Photoshop hybrid.

Printing ordinary items

By taking ordinary things like fabric, particle board, netting and so on, you can build a vocabulary of printmaking effects which may be useful in themselves or as an ingredient of further work.

172 Collect a variety of textured materials suitable for printing. The fabric on the left was carefully glued to a board, then inked and printed. The net on the right was inked directly – tricky because it moves – and then printed.

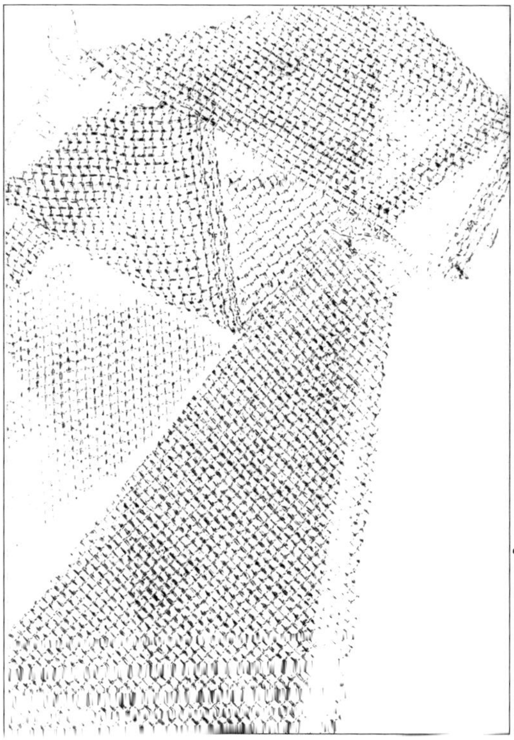

173 Glue prints can be intriguing. Dribble glue on a board, let it dry and then print. Depending on how you roll the surface it's possible to connect with the backing board and create a distinctive glowing effect (right). By playing with the same image in Photoshop and building layers and reversals you can make endless different patterns which take on a life of their own. They don't look too far removed from the blobby monoprints earlier in this chapter.

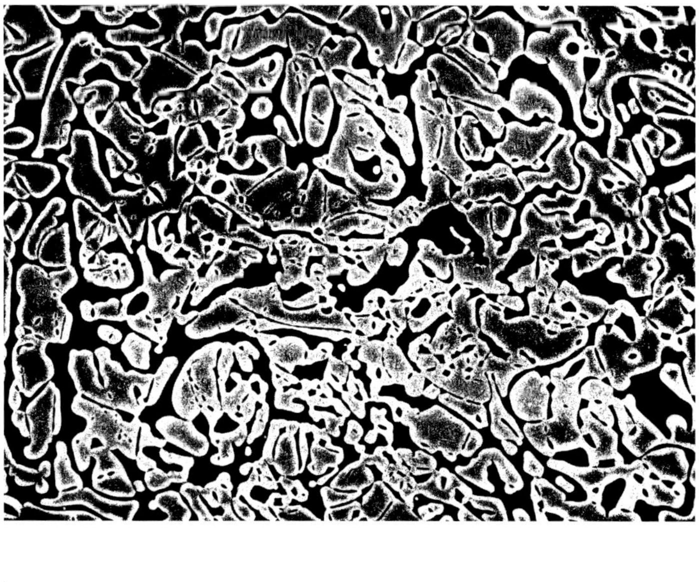

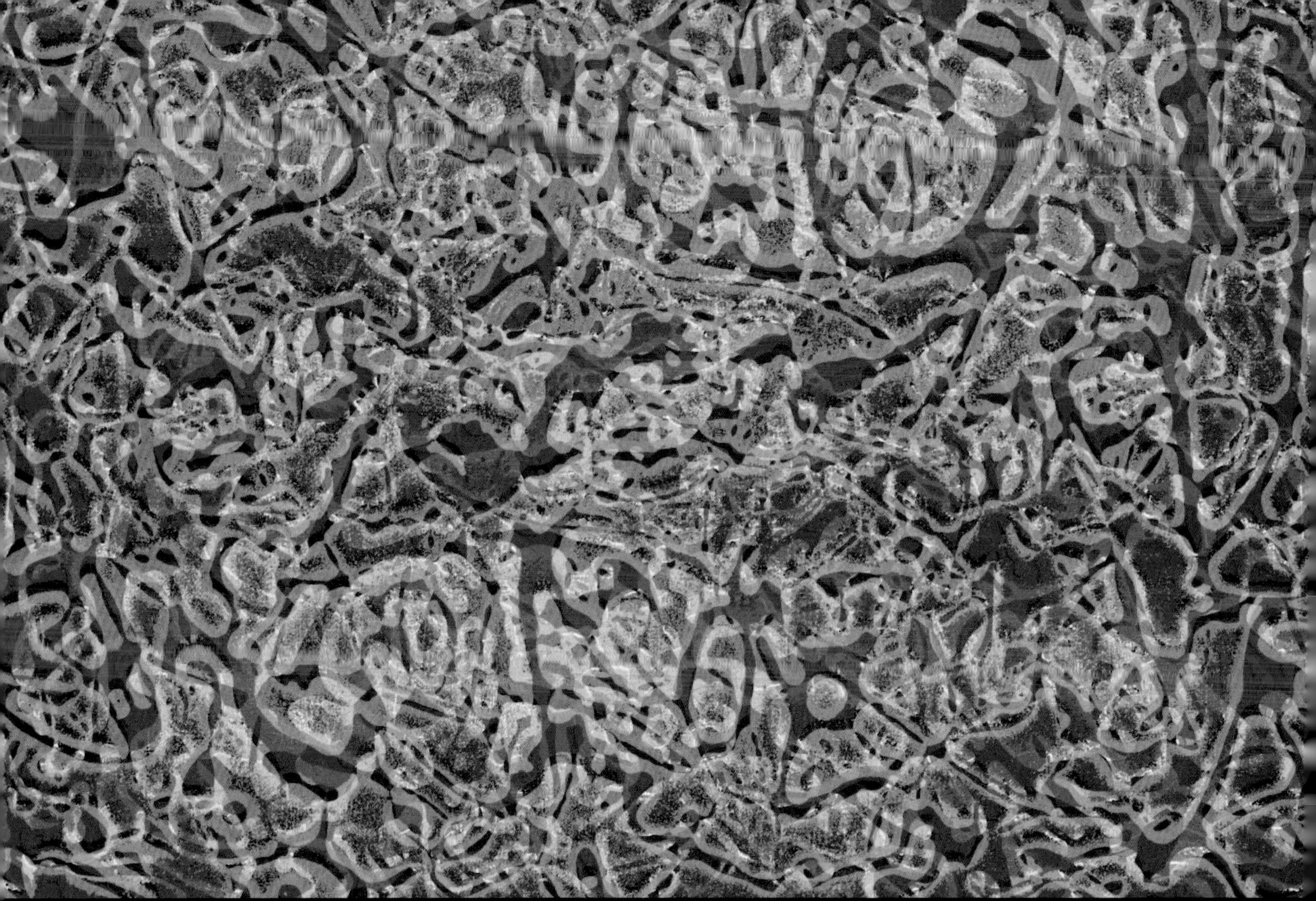

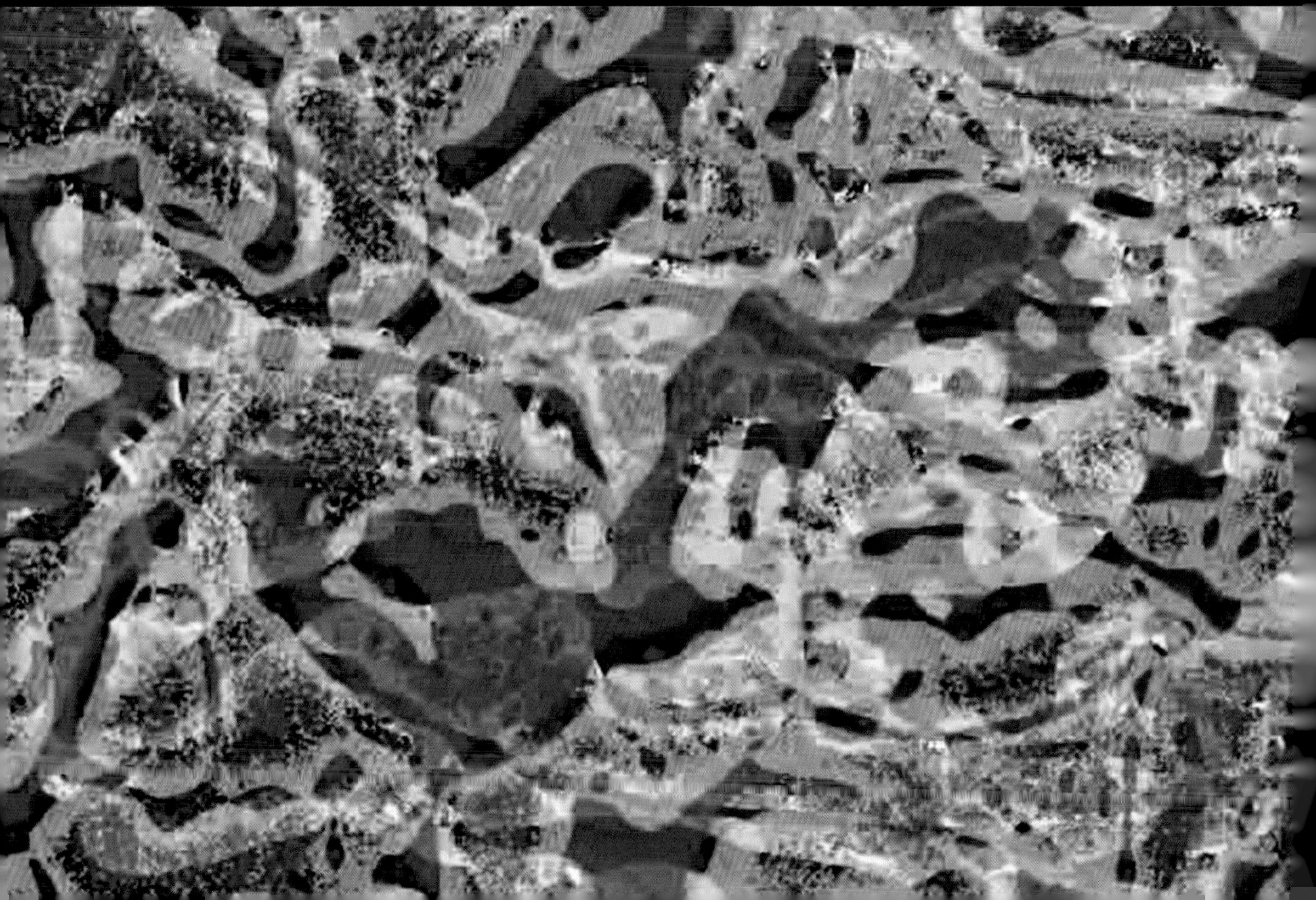

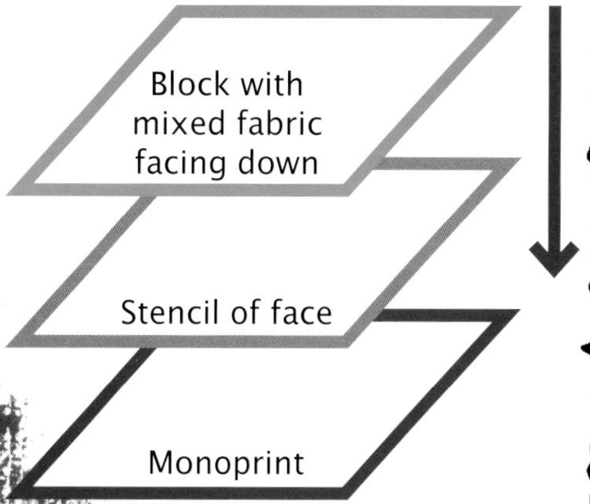

174 Combine techniques. The image below mixes a portrait with fabric printing and a monoprint.

Block printing

175 A linocut. The goal is to take a piece of lino and make your image by cutting away all the areas which are intended to be white. You'll need cutting tools and it makes things easier if you have a warmer to soften the lino. A flat-top stove on the lowest temperature setting is okay if you haven't got access to anything else. Move the lino off the heat when it gets too warm. Be extremely careful (a fire started by your art is not a good way to make new friends). And take major care that you don't lean on the hot element. Hot summer sun is a safer option if available.

▸ *Ladies in Waiting V*, M Dawson.

▾ Jude Shirley.

Lino print by one of my first students — a 12-year-old boy who had never cut a block before (circa 1964).

Stephen Clover.

By all means start with a cheap set of cutting tools. The cheapest have a handle with interchangeable blades.

Keep the cuts simple. A v-shape and a u-shape will do most of what you need.

Learn how to sharpen tools. You'll need a stone and preferably a mentor to show you how to do it.

Keep your hands behind the tool when you're cutting. If you want to ignore the rule, learn first aid. (You should have a good first aid kit available even if you work impeccably.)

Get used to cleaning. Turps-based inks require plenty of clean rags and lots of turps. Work in a well-ventilated space and use an appropriate respirator if you're upset by the smell or have safety concerns. Dispose of used rags with care (they're flammable and smelly).

Keep your work space free of dust and clutter.

Depending on the number of prints you may need drying racks, or wire lines to hang works on.

If you want to make prints of archival quality, obtain advice about the quality of paper and inks. Find out how to store and display your work.

176 *Reduction print*

The goal is to produce a run of prints in which many colours are printed from a single block. Normally the lightest colour is printed first and the block is cut some more (reduced) to prepare the way for the second-lightest colour. You continue until you've printed all the colours you want. At the last step the block usually has nothing left but the fine lines of the darkest colour.

The run is limited to the number of prints you take from the first cut. There are no second chances!

Preparation is important because you have to visualise how the stages will come together. The illustrations show two of Sue Currie's preparatory drawings and the final print, which involved three colours.

The lino block after the final round of cutting.

The finished print, by Sue Currie.

177 Mimic the reduction print with photography. Here the original photo was broken down into tones. **Posterise** in Photoshop or use the **Select Similar** command and separate the tones you want. When you're finished, commission a block maker to produce a set of blocks for each tone, then print them. If you ink each block unevenly all the prints will be different. There's no limit to the number you can print, although it may be hard to find a block maker who will do anything bigger than letter-size – beyond that it's a matter of getting into solar plates and doing it yourself. *Printmaking in the Sun* is the book to study! The plates, by the way, are relatively expensive.

Turn photographs into art prints. Subjects which break down into well-defined layers are ideal.

▲ Houses, Firenze. ▼ The solar plates have a beauty of their own. This is one of four used in the Firenze image.

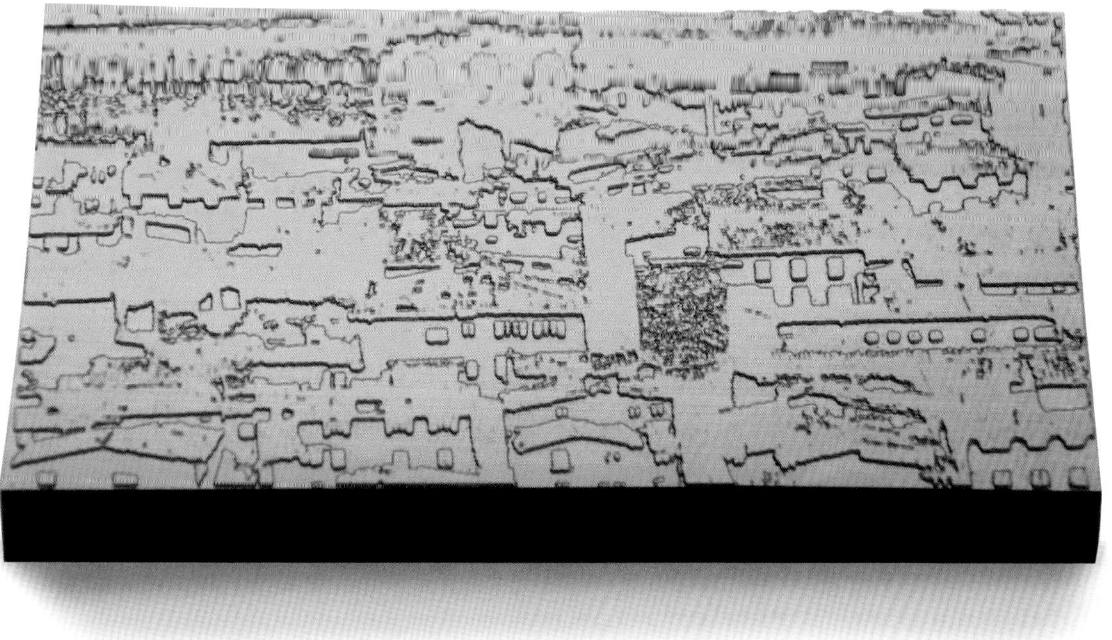

Part 4
navigating the 3rd dimension

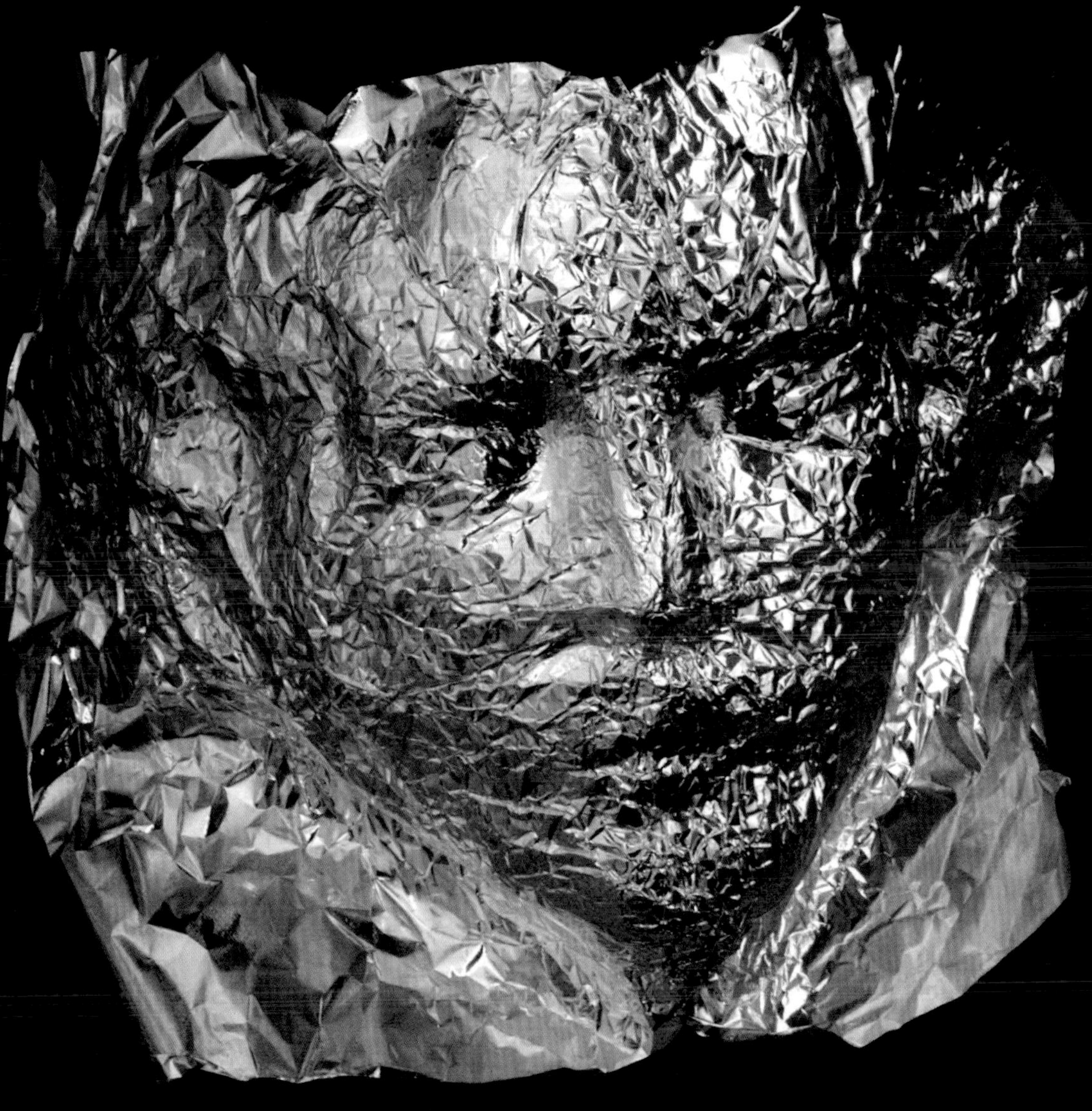

CHAPTER 16

3D

Artist: Ben Smith.

Take a sheet of aluminium foil, press it against your face and behold, a sculpture. Moulding a flat surface into a three-dimensional surface is a reminder that dimensions are related. The flat foil can turn into a four-dimensional work if a breeze picks it up and moves it around because time becomes an additional factor. (In other ways, time is already there – sculptures change with light, weather and decay – they are part of the natural world.)

Life itself is multi-dimensional – probably more than four – and sculpture connects with life in ways that are different from painting and drawing. Sculpture often escapes the sacred white box of the museum and joins the clutter of the 'outside' world. You can sometimes (but not always) touch it, walk around it, or under, over and through it. You can experience it in different lights and seasons, connect it with your environment and maybe see the world participating in it through corrosion, wear, bird droppings, lichen or whatever else is available to interact.

> *Sculpture has no fixed viewing point it is instead an experience of infinite different views and feelings*

Sculpture has no fixed viewing point – it is instead an experience of infinite different views and feelings. Not that 'flat' art doesn't have some similar properties. The scale and lighting of paintings turns into three dimensions when you add the viewer. With big paintings the viewer can move and experience the work from many different angles and distances, like a sculpture but different.

Many of our experiences of famous art are through books, computers or television, and something is lost in translation. A book image is something else. Not only has the physicality been diluted but someone else's decisions – and the requirements of publication – inevitably make something different from the original (unless the art *is* the book).

The blurring of boundaries between 2D, 3D and time-based art says something about the way we perceive. We *experience* art and it's not such a big deal whether

are different from painting and drawing

Melissa Wyman and Dion Burns making a body sculpture. Dance, if you think of it in these terms, is kinetic human sculpture. Our everyday lives are sculptural — we exist in a three-dimensional environment and our movements add the extra dimension of time.

the work is called a painting, sculpture, performance, concept, installation or whatever.

In the sections on 3D I'm going to concentrate on the nature of material and visualisation. The same factors apply to 2D art but space and time are more obvious with sculpture.

Part of the sculptor's art is to visualise the experience of the work. How will it look and feel in its context? How will it change our perception of the space/context? What will it add to our awareness and understanding?

The sculptor also has to deal with some engineering questions. How will the material behave in the conditions where it will be placed?

A starting point is to play with materials and discover what they do. The possibilities of sculpture emerge from this direct interaction with material.

An approach to 3D art

Sculpture is such a huge and diverse field that there aren't many how-to-do-it books on the subject. There's a bewildering range of techniques, many of which

unless we play and imagine

deserve several books. It is more commercially viable to publish books on famous sculptors than on sculptural methods.

Here I'm concerned with 3D as another avenue for experiencing creative processes.

It's like being at a free art gallery and the only entry requirement is a sense of wonder

Everyday experiences of buildings, gardens, furniture, food, tools, appliances and so on are sculptural. As I write I'm watching the steam from a cup of tea make three-dimensional shapes in the air. It's like being at a free art gallery and the only entry requirement is a sense of wonder.

I wonder whether the steam would be able to stand up if it was turned into clay or steel. Could you build a skyscraper based on the shapes of steam? If I arranged a dark background and lit the steam with intense light, what would it look like in a photo? Would it work in an art gallery, maybe with a big cauldron of water as the source for steam? Would it be possible to project a movie onto steam? Or scan it and download into a 3D computer progamme?

What if I invited staff at our school to think how the idea of steam might take us into creative change? How could a business be as flexible as steam? Are there advantages in being able to transfer (metaphorically) from liquid to air?

Are thoughts like steam? Where does the steam go? How many cups of tea are captured in the ocean outside my window?

At first it may feel indulgent to play with ideas. It doesn't put dinner on the table or pay the rent. But unless we play and imagine, we are stuck. Play opens doors to new ways of doing things, new ways of communicating, new ways of living.

"I start by getting students to visualize. They start from the inner space of their own mind which is pretty much how we perceive the external space. We see it as 'out there' but if we can think of it as a dreamscape it has its own reality. I invite them to imagine a very simple form like a sphere or a cube and to start by holding that object, maybe it's a tennis ball, and then doing exercises like expanding or shrinking it. They are then dealing with the notion of scale and you can get them to imagine that it is in their hand and half is black and half is white, then watch it rotate. That gets the object rotating, and they can put it down, expand it to as big as a house and walk around it themselves. In that exercise they're beginning to see dimensions of height, depth, scale, size, forms, movement, and that all happens before you get them to do anything with material." *Dennis Berdinner, [illegible] tutor*

Why bother about newness? We are part of the life tide. We can let life happen to us *and* we can exert our influence and *participate* in life.

I believe the life tide has direction. We evolve. The early structures of life have achieved greater complexity. The energy of the 'Big Bang', if that's where it started, has turned into you, me and everything else.

Sculpture, like life, is a story of energy. How does energy reach the highest level of efficiency? Conceivably the thing we label 'spirit' is high-level energy – 'steam' that reaches all dimensions.

All energy is connected to everything. The steam from a mug of tea is ordinary and sublime at the same time. Each action we take may be seen as part of a divine kinetic sculpture which can only be lived freely if we take it lightly. Think of

we're stuck

Low relief sculpture by Richard Cowan.

ourselves as steam seeking the best path through the air.

Sculpture is a mix of physics and expression. You may also choose (or not) to see these same processes as engagement with the sacred. Likewise industrial sculpture – designing shapes for vehicles, labour-saving devices and so on – can also be viewed as a step towards better use of energy.

A hidden feature of everyday objects is the involvement of other people. The chair I'm sitting on depended on the skills of a designer (sculptor), manufacturer, tradespeople, advertisers, retailers, bankers and others who were part of a large and mostly invisible team which helped to make affordable and practical comfort. The same people, who don't necessarily have any direct personal connections, are also part of a food chain, social systems, politics, education, economics ... and everything.

You may also choose (or not) to see these same processes as engagement with the sacred

A manufactured chair/sculpture has moved through a lot of interactions which tend to sift out the less effective designs and support the ones that work best. There will always be some new chairs which aren't an improvement – they are part of a turbulent zone of change in which creative humans look for better ways of doing things. The turbulence produces progress and rubbish. So it is in art. When you're doing art you're

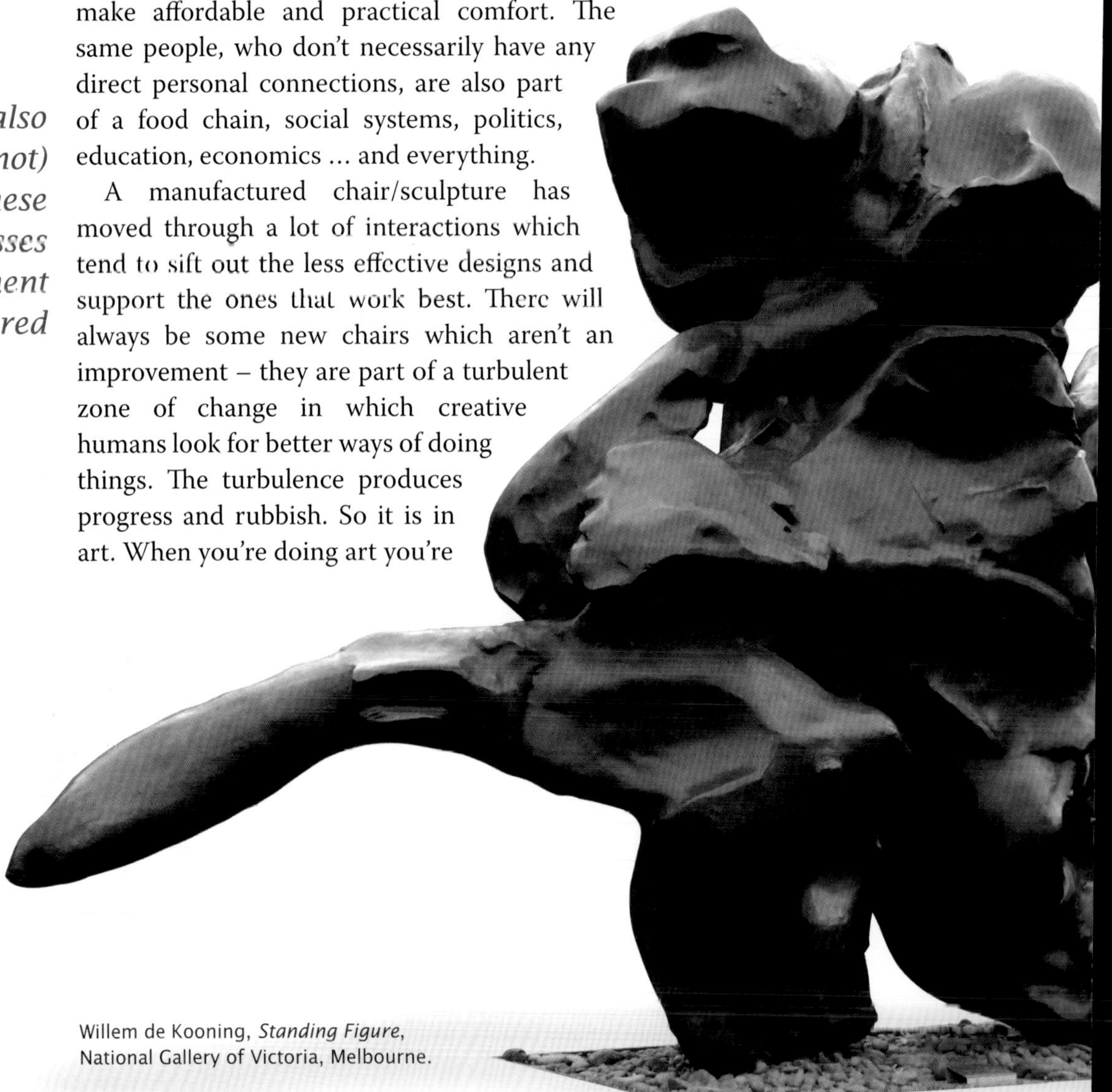

Willem de Kooning, *Standing Figure*, National Gallery of Victoria, Melbourne.

in the zone of turbulence and you're saying yes to the possibilities of greatness and rubbish. The history of creativity includes the history of mistakes but the net effect is successful evolution.

Art also involves the same connectedness as my chair. The business of sharing your art can be as simple as having a friend look at it, but further down the track it could involve promoters, gallery proprietors, curators, transport companies, financiers, valuers, conservators, photographers, critics, baristas and goodness knows who else. To earn a living as an artist you're setting in motion a considerable network and your personal skills and inspiration are only a tiny (though indispensable) part of it.

How does art achieve greatness? It works, just like a chair. It *does something.* It isn't only a thing, it is part of the alchemy of life. Paradoxically it can (and often does) start from the uselessness of play.

I am offering images and ideas with encouragement to play. Consider the images and ponder how you might transfer ideas into your own world and play with them. It doesn't matter whether you intend to be an artist – part of what we're doing is a creative workout which you can apply to make your life and career a work of art. *Sparks of Genius* (Robert and Michele Root-Bernstein) is a good book to explore if you're interested in greater detail on the connection between art processes and 'non-art' careers.

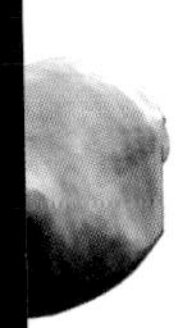

Initially an artificial idea for creativity is, well, artificial. If you can play through the awkward beginning period you'll discover ways to bring ideas to life and make them your own.

Each image could set you on the way to a lifetime of exploration. It's easy to offer a million ideas and not so easy to make a choice. That's why I prefer to trust my intuition to sift the ideas and draw me towards the ones that are important. You're not entirely on your own when you're moving through the mystery of purpose but the choices you make have to be yours.

In playing, certain things will take on meaning and you can choose to take them further.

your personal skills and inspiration are only a tiny (though indispensable) part of it.

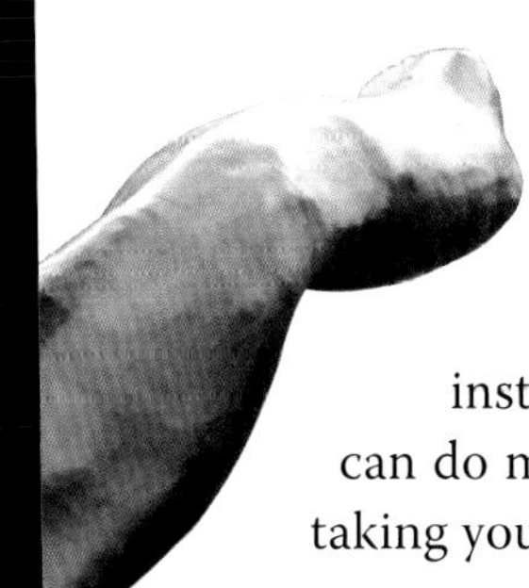

Naturally you'll come to technical hurdles and you'll have to figure whether you want to push forward or try something else. There are allies everywhere waiting to be your support team. Some of them are real people – tutors, friends and others who can supply assistance. Others are virtual – books, the internet, films and so on. A school is an intense concentration of allies who become an instant team and save a considerable amount of hassle. Not that a school can do much until you get into the habit of asking your own questions and taking your own risks.

CHAPTER 17

3D basics

Play and art meet engineering. How high will it go? How close together can structures be built? How long will it last? How do the shapes relate to each other? What are your feelings about it? You can give yourself an introduction to sculpture by asking the same questions of whatever materials take your fancy.

▲ Stacking your chips.

▼ Monumental stacking.

178 Rip lengths of light card, curl them by running them firmly over a hard edge, then drop them onto the floor so that they begin to build a structure. What happens? Can you make the structure taller by placing the pieces so that they support each other?

What happens if you apply two actions, such as 'stack and fasten'?

Glue gun used for the fastening.

The stacked and fastened version offers a radically different set of shapes when viewed from below.

The squashed version is a further option.

179 Using between one and three of the curled pieces, make a three-dimensional structure that might be placed in a house or in a garden or in a park. What would be the scale of the final object?

180 Using the additional element of glue (or adhesive tape), explore the same ideas again.

181 Obtain a few offcuts of plasterboard or particle board.

Take a length of plaster bandage and staple or nail the ends to the board so that you have a loop. If the ends are fixed at different angles you'll get a twist in the final result.

Wet the plaster with water (painting it on with a house-painting brush works well).

Invert the board so that the bandage hangs from it. Let it dry, then remove it from the board. Create different-sized loops using the same method.

Assemble the 'arches' in an arrangement of your choice and fix them to a base. This might be the finished maquette (the sculptural equivalent of a sketch) or it might be a starting point for further work. (Check the list of action words in the THINK←→ACTION chapter, page 351.)

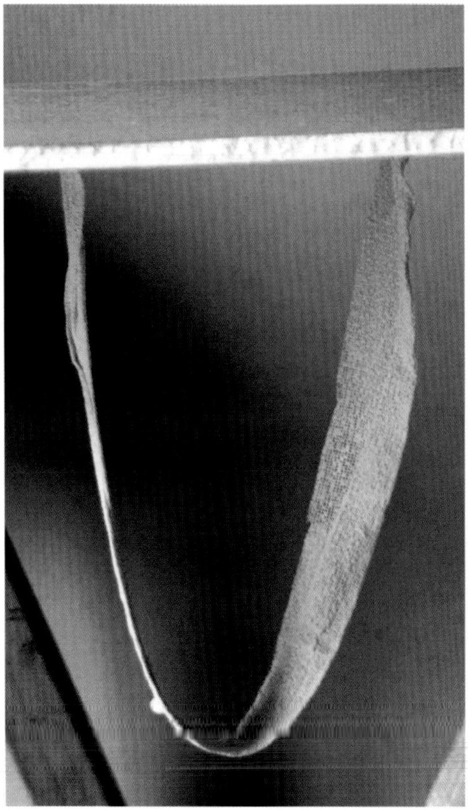

182 Choose an interesting surface which is okay to plaster. Rocks are usually okay because the plaster residue will be weathered away (be sensitive about your choices!).

Initially quite a small area will do for an experiment – a 20 cm (8 inch) square will do the job.

If you want the plaster to come off more easily when it's dry, a spray of cooking oil will help (again, be sensitive to the situation).

Cut a series of lengths of plaster. One at a time, dip them in warm water and gently press into shape on the surface you've chosen. Build up three layers, criss-crossing the bandages for extra strength.

When the plaster is dry, lift it from the surface. Depending on the nature of the surface it might bring a few bits and pieces with it – these will need to be removed as best you can (it doesn't matter if a few bits of debris stay with it).

Paint the underside of the mould and use it as the base for your loops. Imagine it in a landscape, maybe ten to twenty metres high and looking a million dollars when done in stainless steel.

The resulting mould might be regarded as a sculpture in its own right or the beginning of something else. It could, for example, be a base for the loops (and I would have had a photo to illustrate later developments but our builders didn't notice the artistic merits and sent all of the experiments to the rubbish dump).

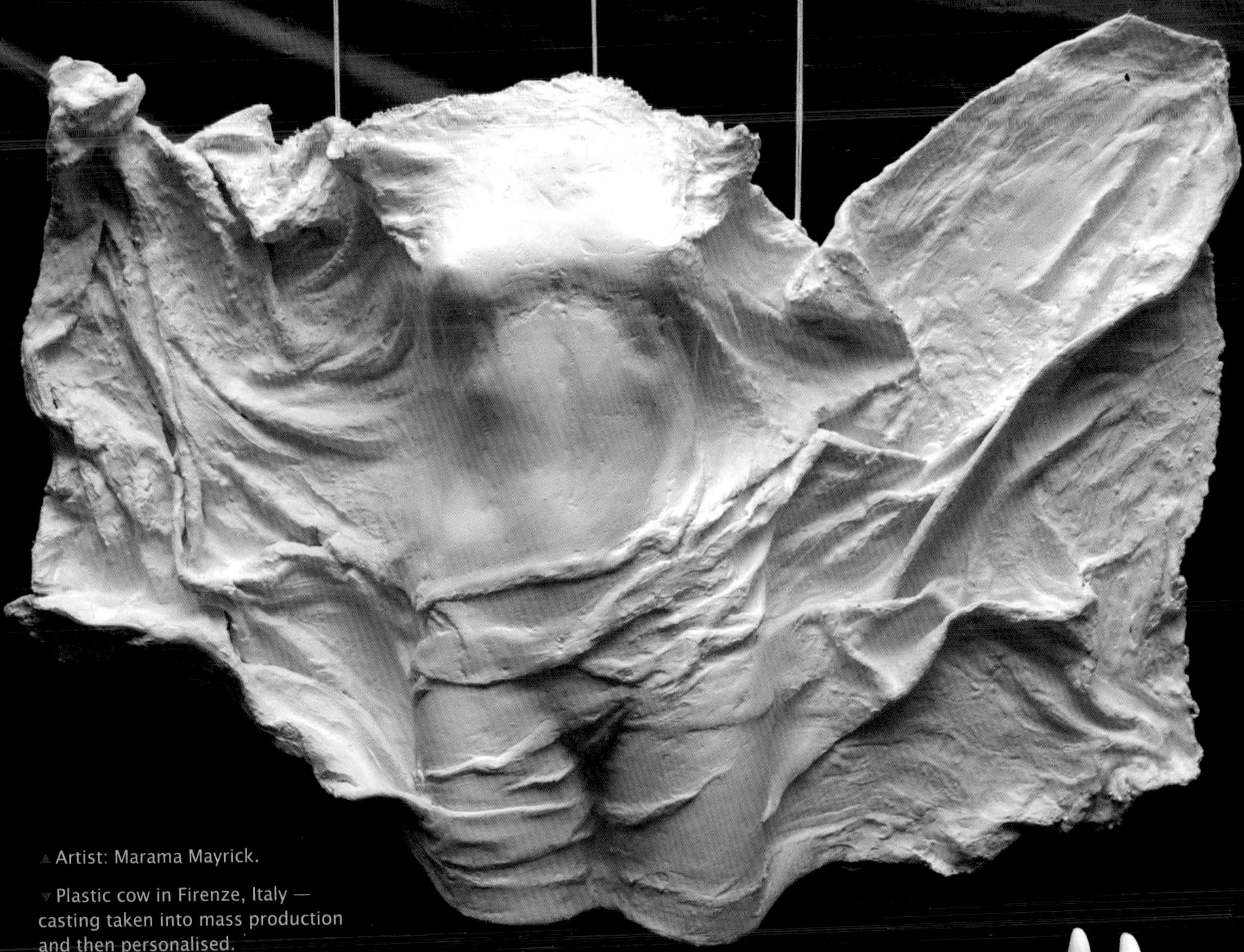

▲ Artist: Marama Mayrick.

▼ Plastic cow in Firenze, Italy — casting taken into mass production and then personalised.

183 A comparable technique can be used for a grander outcome. If you have an obliging model, a large container for mixing plaster, and a suitable piece of fabric, you can try something like the body cast illustrated.

Check out the section on 'Plaster as a Material' (page 359) and follow the instructions. Do a few small experiments to get an understanding of how it works. Depending on scale you may need an assistant to help you handle the materials.

- First prepare the plaster.
- Wear a dust mask.
- Gently pour the dry plaster of Paris onto the water in a large bucket. Allow about ⅓ water to ⅓ powder. The idea is to float a thin layer of powder on the surface of the water, waiting until it wets, then continue adding until the wetting gets slow. It's a matter of practice to get the right consistency – another reason why small experiments are part of the process.
- Vaseline the surface which will come in contact with the plaster (the model can be doing this while you mix the plaster).
- Use plenty of plastic sheeting as a backdrop (it's messy – first wet, then dusty).
- In effect the sheet replaces the plaster bandage used in the face cast.
- Once the plaster has reached a nice creamy texture, quickly dip the fabric into it and ensure it's well covered. Then lift the fabric over the model and arrange the folds in whatever way you wish. The drying happens fairly quickly and you have to work fast.
- When the plaster is dry, carefully ease it off the model.

Can you believe the toucans? Look at the shapes, balance, smoothness and colour. These two were behind mesh in a zoo. We are so clever at putting things in cages that we contrive to cage our own imagination.

CHAPTER 18

Observing

The achievements of nature are an encyclopaedia of sculptural knowledge. Nature is so brilliantly organised that it can lead you straight to an argument about the source of the organisation. What matters is that the products of nature have arisen in response to real needs. The beak of a toucan, for example, didn't develop to enchant visitors to zoos. It is a piece of engineering which works. It is part of an animal that can fly, play and look like a work of art. Scientists and artists can be incredibly smart but their cleverness barely reaches that of a single feather of a toucan.

We are so clever at putting things in cages that we contrive to cage our own imagination

184 How can you make sculpture which contains an equivalent sense of drama and is acceptably safe? The brief might be: "Make a sculpture in which one or more of the main ingredients is suspended and can move."

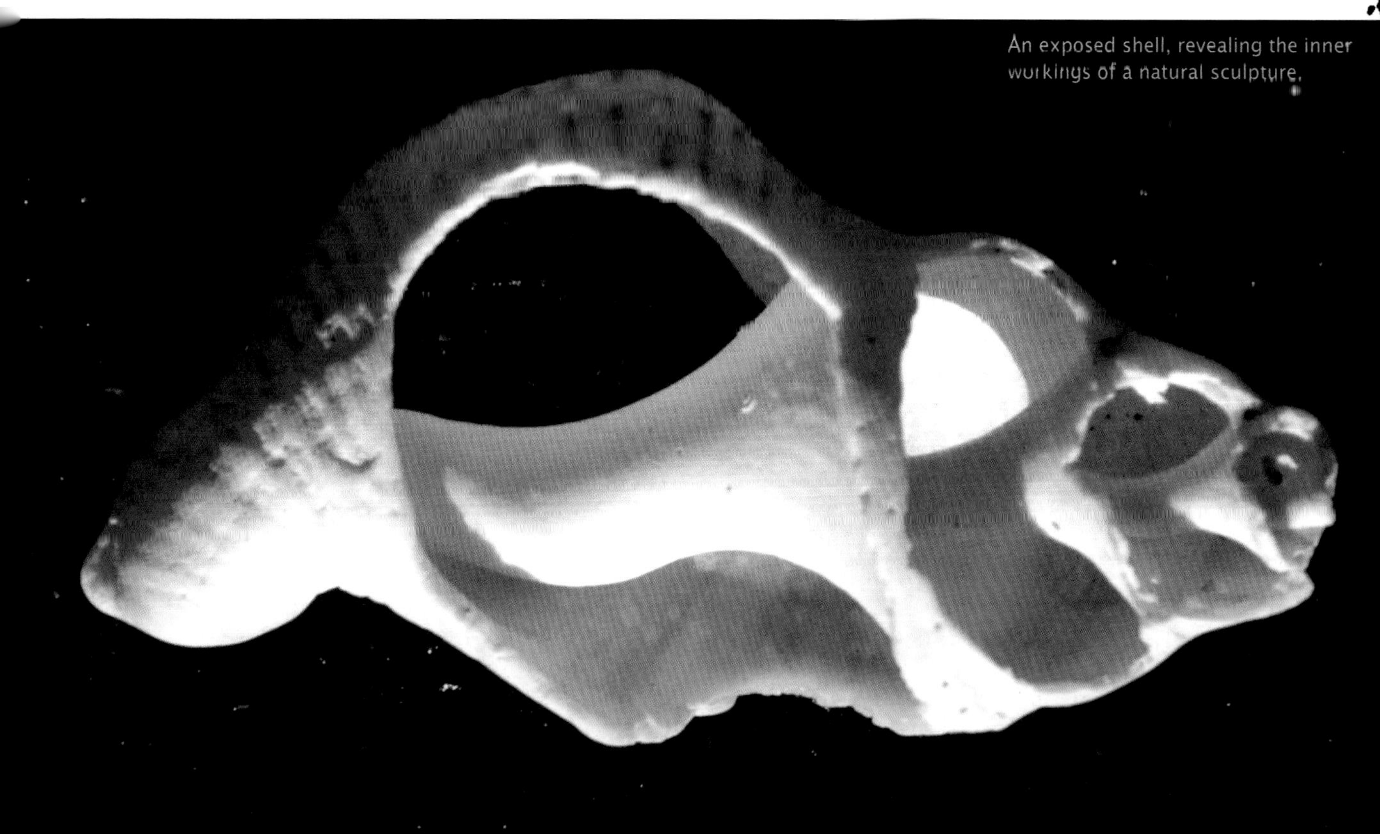

An exposed shell, revealing the inner workings of a natural sculpture.

▲ Look at the shadows which help to indicate the shape of the dog and the ornamental steel on the gate which says that those within are people of taste. It's another cage in the human zoo. Cages are a big sculptural possibility. What stories can you tell by putting ideas in cages?

▶ People live in here. Architecture is sculpture and the shapes in which we live have an effect on who we are. On the other side of these condominiums is an ocean view. I hope it moderates the cage. A question for sculptors, architects and engineers is, how can we make things which give people the best chance to be happy?

◄ Curved metal plates make a very organic surface at the Seattle Center. Building technology now enables architects to design much freer forms in which sculpture and architecture can merge in more playful ways.

▼ The San Francisco Museum of Modern Art isn't for living in but the architecture has a sculptural zing befitting the purpose of the building.

◄ Nature is the guide to what is possible in sculpture. Here's a flower which has its own impetus to grow and reproduce. It bends with the wind, repairs its injuries and attracts insects which distribute its pollen. It also knows the art of dying. The flower blooms, dazzles and withers away in a life cycle that generates new flowers.

▼ A regenerating potato. Maybe it wouldn't work as costume jewellery but the intense mass of spiky shoots is intriguing — a living sculpture. The outline coincidentally has a fractal pattern with a hint of the Mandelbrot Set.

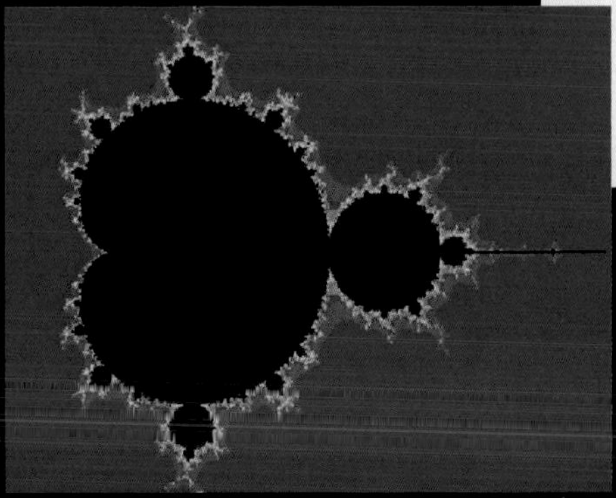

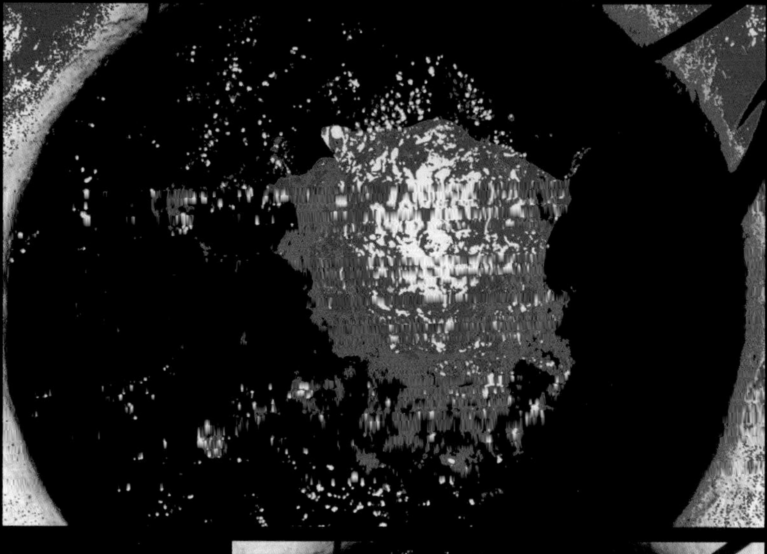

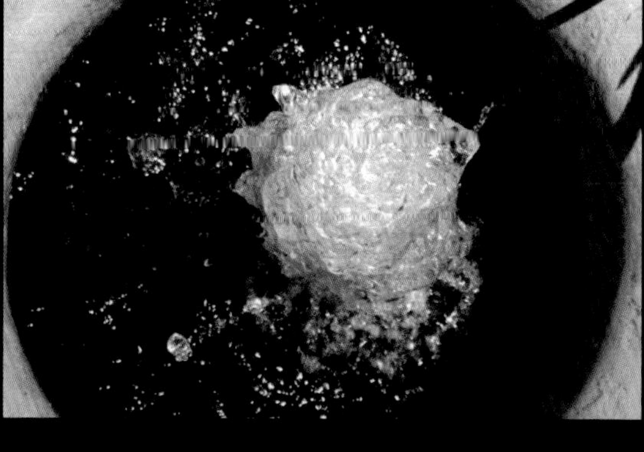

▲ Gardening often turns out to be a back-door approach to sculpture and painting. Gardeners have to figure out how to work with nature and be expressive at the same time. Their work transforms with the seasons and interfaces with insects, pests, pollution and the gaze of neighbours. Gardens are like the extravagant plumage of birds — and maybe they have a similar sexy role. Then again, they might be an expression of pure joy, pure art. (Bill and Carol Beavers' garden in Atlanta.)

◄ A fountain viewed from above. The modified colour is a reminder that what we see isn't necessarily what is 'there'. How does a fly see things? Or a bird? A camera can 'freeze' a column of water into a static sculpture which we can observe in a way that would normally be impossible. Water is fluid engineering. An upward thrust is having a battle with the pull of gravity. The turning point is chaotic and says something about the rhythms of life. These infinitely complex 'chaos patterns' are part of real-world geometry and yet we spend much effort in making false simplifications. Life, love, business, politics and war have more in common with the behaviour of water than with the neat diagrams of educators and strategists. Do the boiling water shapes have anything in common with their relatives, clouds?

◄ The water unmodified.

▲ Clouds, colour modified. Look for 'chaos' and 'fractal' structures in nature (often they go together). You'll find things which include 'self-similarity' (e.g. small parts of a cloud have similar shapes to the cloud as a whole). You'll find turbulence — the shapes are constantly on the move but still retain a particular identity. Static things like rocks may turn out to be turbulence in slow motion. You'll notice that fractals are everywhere. Fingerprints are fractal/chaos patterns. So are trees, clouds, mountains and the rhythm of traffic.

◄ Look for the mysteries in ordinary objects. The surface of the bucket has the property of disguising and describing itself through the things it reflects. The packet connects with the bucket via a reflection and has some interesting properties of its own. All of the items in the picture are end-products of highly sophisticated manufacturing processes which involve many different facets of human skill. When you think of all that goes into the making of a bucket it's more like the complexity of a tree than the rigid 'bucketness' of the object itself. You can regard the process itself as a sculpture which ends with the quirky individual choices of the people who finally take possession of manufactured products.

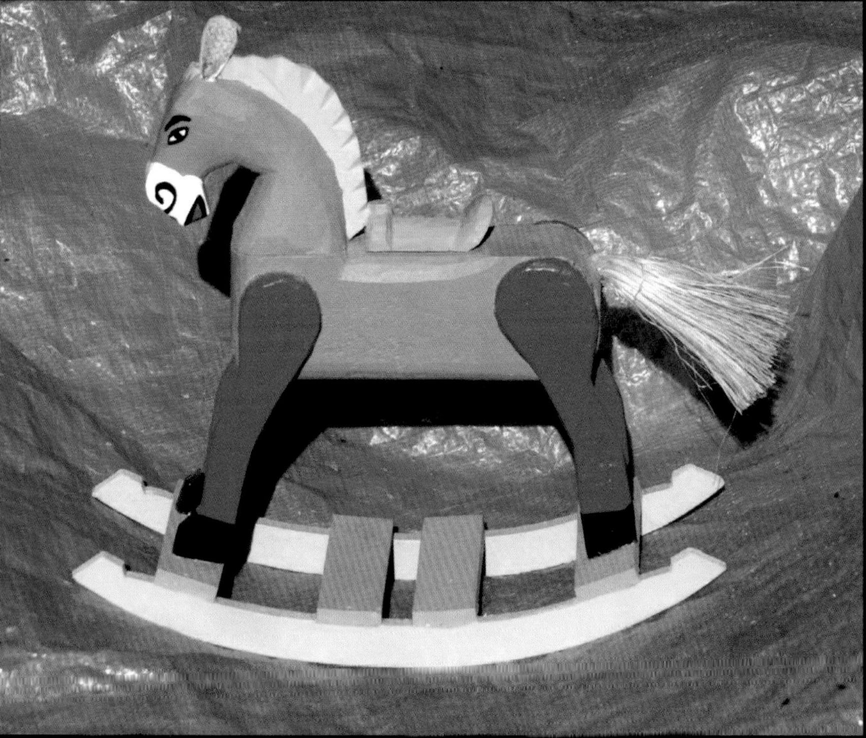

▲ It's a toy, a painted kinetic sculpture, a commercial, manufactured product, an icon, a focus of fantasy. How would sculpture change if we thought of it as toys? How might communities change if the playfulness of sculpture increased? Sculptors don't have to be toymakers but the lessons from toys might help them to think a little differently.

▶ A kinetic sculpture carrying the burden of nature and not much helped by the engineering of its stand. It's 'low art' — not intended for a gallery and yet connecting with nature in a way that often eludes 'high art'. Feel free to be as high or low as you please. Who decides what matters?

▼ The bag in a shop window display has taken on a heavy, metallic look which emphasises its form. Consider ordinary objects. Are they sculptures? Could you change the way they are perceived by retaining their form and presenting them in different contexts and different materials?

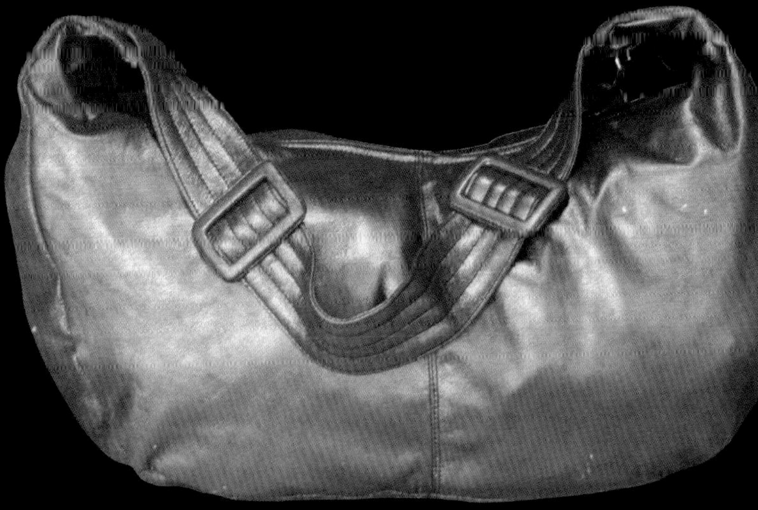

Workmen suspended in a cage, repairing Erskine plumbing. Shapes, colours, textures, geometry – and a gentle, non-industrial look on the face of the young man. Is it sculpture? Yes, if that's how you choose to see it. The ingredient of drama adds an extra dimension. What they're doing is dangerous and some of the gear is designed to protect them if things go wrong.

185 Drive yourself nuts and sculpt a stone in clay. The ordinariness of the stone is precisely the point of the exercise. How did the stone arrive at its shape? Where did it come from? How was it created? What are the different materials in it? Is it thousands or millions of years old? What clues does it hold about the history of the universe (not to mention physics and engineering)?

Francis Tunnicliffe entered the stone meditation and shaped the clay. In some of our creativity sessions we go further, inviting people to select a stone and think about the ways in which it reflects who they are. The stones rapidly shift from anonymity to highly personal elements in a group discussion.

At right is a rock on the beach, like a big crystal island in a sea of sand. Look at all the facets, from those catching the late sun through to those in deep shadow. And the sand, coarse and smooth, glowing on a cold day. If you were to have a conversation with the rock, what would you say? What is it saying about itself? The conversation is etched in everything you see. What is the sand saying? Where did it come from? Where is it going? If you look closely at the sand you'll see fractal shapes that are echoed in big boulders. Why is the world full of this magical geometry? As William Blake said in 'Auguries of Innocence':

To see a World in a Grain of Sand
And Heaven In a Wild Flower
Hold Infinity in the Palm of your hand
And Eternity in an Hour

William Blake (1757–1827).

Chaos patterns in the trash.

▲ It's gross, politically incorrect and fascinating. At first it may look like an ugly mess but it contains beautiful chaos patterns. Consider the distribution of the filter tips — poetry in an ash tray. You can seek out 'ready-mades' or create them for yourself by using random processes such as dropping or throwing.

▶ Berries and leaves with their own poetry of distribution. The elements in the picture have arrived by a mix of dropping (they fell from trees) and blowing (they are shifted by the wind). The framing of the shapes (I chose the image) is an intervention which might be considered 'unnatural' — but is there any real separation of art and nature?

◂ Art and nature cosy together in a tree trunk from which the artist has carved a seal and its baby. It's nonsense of course — a tree isn't a seal — but our minds are flexible enough to read meanings into things which previously meant something different. Part of art is to play with new meanings and share the occasional visual joke.

▾ Washing on a clothesline. At art school in the 1960s the job of replicating the forms with clay would have kept students occupied for ten weeks. Nobody mentioned that fabric under tension can give useful architectural and engineering information. If you invert the structure it can (with certain limitations) be used as a starting point to design buildings. What would our cities have looked like if we'd based our architecture on pliable fabric instead of straight lines?

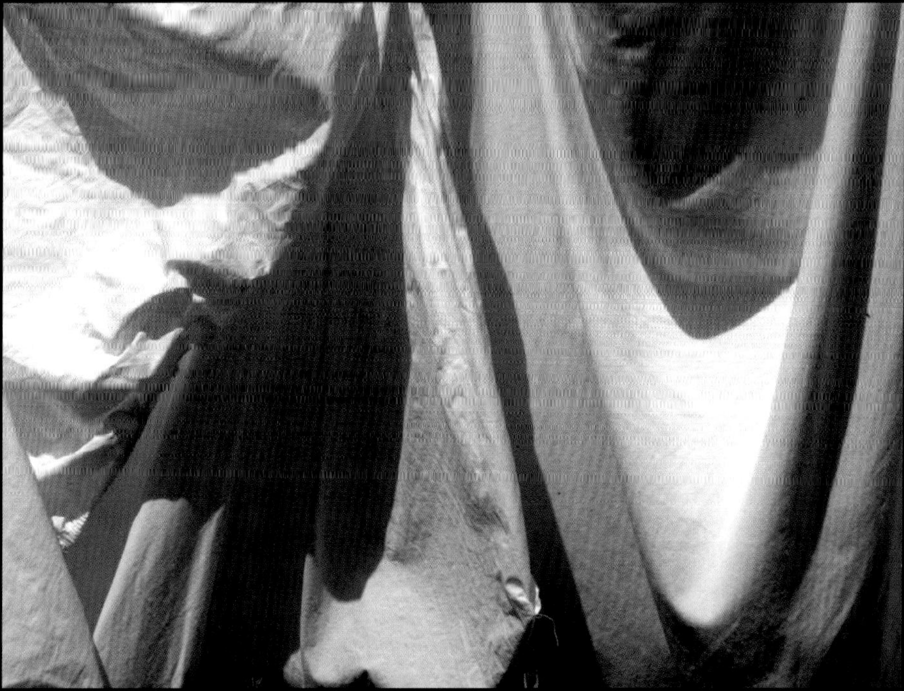

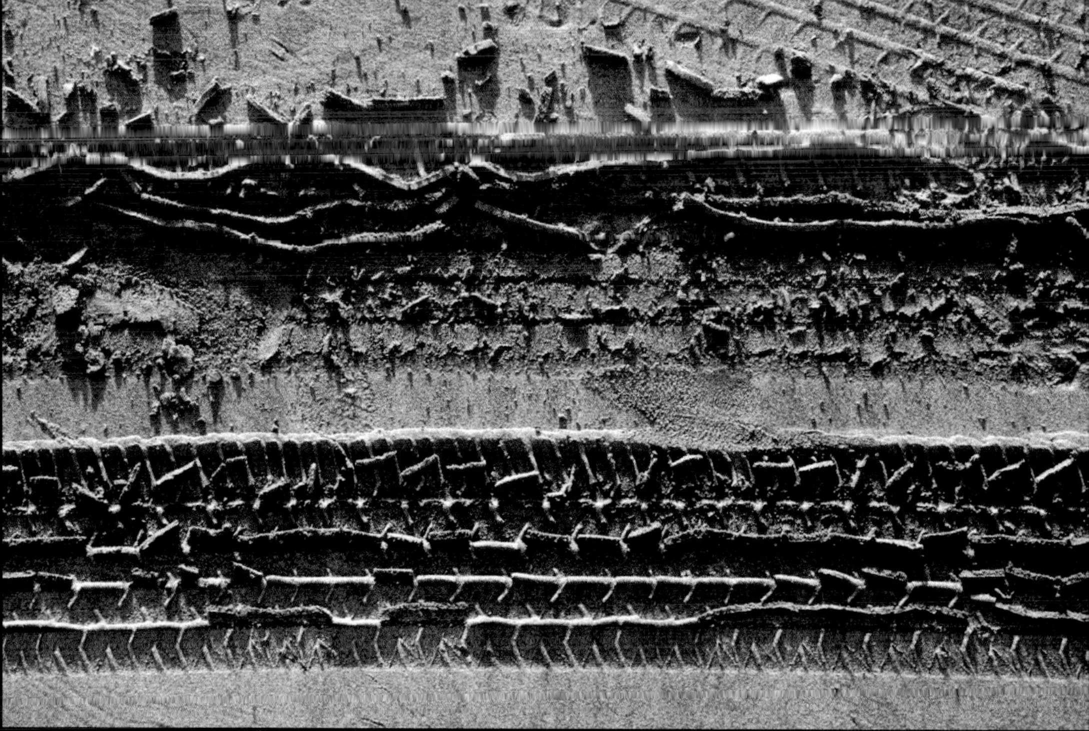

▲ Sand sculpture created by tyre tracks. Possibly you could make a cast by spraying fixative on the sand and using plaster to take an impression. Certainly there are electronic systems to translate the ephemeral into the more or less permanent. Could they be used to capture something so frail that a light breeze can destroy it? And wouldn't it be startling to see the horizontal tracks turned into the vertical tradition of displayed art. Alternatively, you might present an exhibition in which the art is the ever-changing set of footprints of the viewers.

▲ Seaweed smells. Not an especially attractive smell for humans. Our students once spent a five-day workshop using beach materials to make patterns on the floor of a studio. It looked great and smelt horrible. Why does art, other than the culinary varieties, make so little use of smell? The shapes of the seaweed are something else. Sometimes a tangle of cabling reaches this sort of complexity (or a major highway interchange). The neat cylindrical strands, the wriggly leaves and the seed pods sing of order and complexity. Is it potentially art? Soft cells of humans can be plasticised — could the same be done with seaweed?

▲ Driftwood on Otaki Beach, New Zealand, looking like an Andy Goldsworthy environmental sculpture but entirely created by the tide. The interplay of water, wood, stone and air sometimes generates attractive and orderly structures. When you're sculpting you might choose to relate to the same interplay and put yourself in accord with the processes of artless art. (Photo: Alice Wilson Milne)

▶ A shadow cast by the sun links us with the movement of earth and sun. If you know how to read it, a sculpture can tell you the time of day (and in any case will change its personality as shadows shift through the cycle of the sun).

CHAPTER 19

Think ←→ action

Creativity links action and imagination. Imagination is nourished when you do things and pay attention. Action is nourished when you imagine things and try them out in real life.

You can move in either direction. If you can't imagine anything, try some action and see what happens. If you look through this chapter you'll find words that require action – *press, mould, curl, rip, glue,* for example.

The actions (verbs) in the list (which is only a beginning – feel free to add) can serve as a stimulus, not just to sculpture but to other areas of art and to life in general.

add ▪ bend ▪ block ▪ break ▪ burst ▪ carve ▪ chip ▪ colour ▪ connect
copy ▪ curl ▪ cut ▪ desecrate ▪ discolour ▪ dismantle ▪ distort ▪ duplicate
enclose ▪ enlarge ▪ enmesh ▪ expand ▪ float ▪ fuse ▪ glue ▪ inflate ▪ melt
mimic ▪ mould ▪ move ▪ polish ▪ press ▪ pulverise ▪ reassemble
redefine ▪ repeat ▪ reveal ▪ rip ▪ sand ▪ shrink ▪ simplify ▪ squash
squirt ▪ stack ▪ straighten ▪ stretch ▪ subtract ▪ suspend ▪ transform
twist ▪ weather ▪ wet ▪ wrap

Move

We're surrounded by kinetic sculpture. Water, trees, clouds, fabrics, people and vehicles all share the factor of movement

André Brayne chain-sawing his way into a sculpture.

186 As a beginning experiment, take a toothpick and a piece of wire. Tie the wire low on the toothpick so that the length of wire on either side is equal. You can then balance the structure on anything that gives a stable base for the end of the toothpick. Depending on your ambition and resources you can take the notion of balance and movement into whatever forms take your fancy.

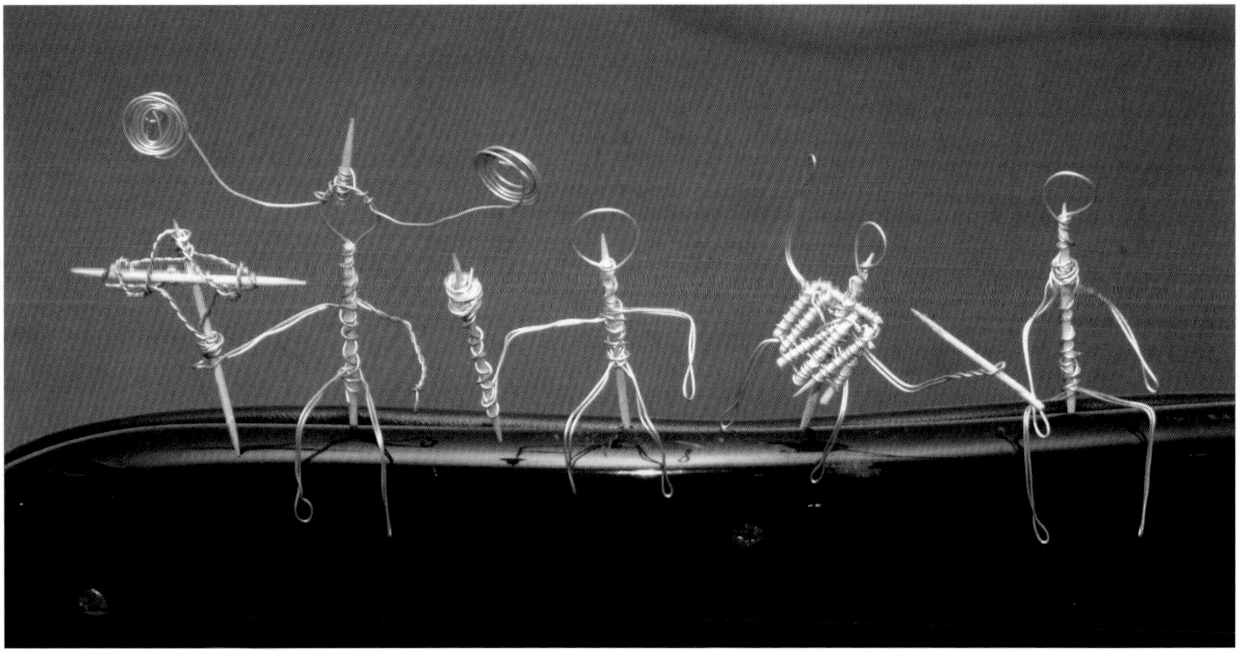

We used the toothpick-and-wire idea at a staff day and pretty soon a whole range of creative responses emerged. This little group was lined up on a chair like a mini-installation.

Sculpture on a point, Seattle. You can do this with any ingredients provided they balance each other and most of the weight is below the point.

▲ Multiple exposure of sculpture by Alan Tugwell. The elements may refer to Mondrian and de Stijl but the movement transforms something simple into gentle, colourful chaos.

▶ Alan Tugwell, figure on a gate. There is a marble at the base of the left leg and it achieves considerable stability in a small indentation on top of the gate. The shocked look on the face coincides with viewer expectations — when the arms are given a big shove the figure wobbles precariously but doesn't fall from its perch. The dilapidated gate complements the uncertainty.

▸ A tree is a moving, growing sculpture and is extremely difficult to duplicate. How can you make something which bends so easily in the wind, feeds itself and has strong roots to anchor itself in the earth? Within each leaf is a multi-celled food factory which takes energy from the sun and manages to be both tough and flexible. Gardeners, not aspiring to be artistic gods, plant seeds and let nature grow its own sculptures. They're onto something. If we can turn our art into a collaboration with nature we'll find ways to go beyond our human limits.

▸▸ The giant needle of Phil Price's *Zephyr* is engineered to move with the wind. It's like a big pointy leaf which achieves drama through size, colour and the controlled freedom of its movement. It also says something about the speedometer needle on Zephyr cars which were fast and desirable a few decades ago (at least in those countries which had been part of the British Empire).

▸▸▸ Sculptural installation, Emeryville, California. The mirrors move in the breeze, providing a reflection of the city and a direct view through the gaps. The columns are like animated skyscrapers flashing a garble of Morse Code as the mirrors randomly catch the sun.

▾ *Protoplasm*, by Phil Price, consists of a set of rigid forms mounted on bearings so that the sculpture as a whole makes surprising twists and swoops in the wind. Its shapes loosely relate to windows in the buildings and its movements almost make fun of the heavy, static city architecture.

TRANSPORT

◂ Maybe it wasn't intended as kinetic sculpture — a human-powered work of art pedalling through Napa Valley in California. Who needs a gallery? And how often do artists get this high on the Fun Scale?

▾ Sculptures outside the Christchurch Art Gallery. The elements at the top of the poles echo the curves of the building and move with the wind.

187 Try a few mini-sculptures that move. Consider the materials around you and think how they might be used with any of the following in mind:

connect ▪ enmesh ▪ glue ▪ inflate ▪ suspend ▪ twist

A mini-sculpture should take only a few minutes to create – it's the sculptural equivalent of a drawing. If you get sufficiently inspired to turn a sketch into a bigger work, seek whatever assistance you need and give it a go.

Kinetic sculpture on a large scale, Seattle Art Museum. The hand with the hammer moves and although it's totally predictable there's something about the size and starkness which makes it memorable. (*Hammering Man* by Jonathan Borofsky)

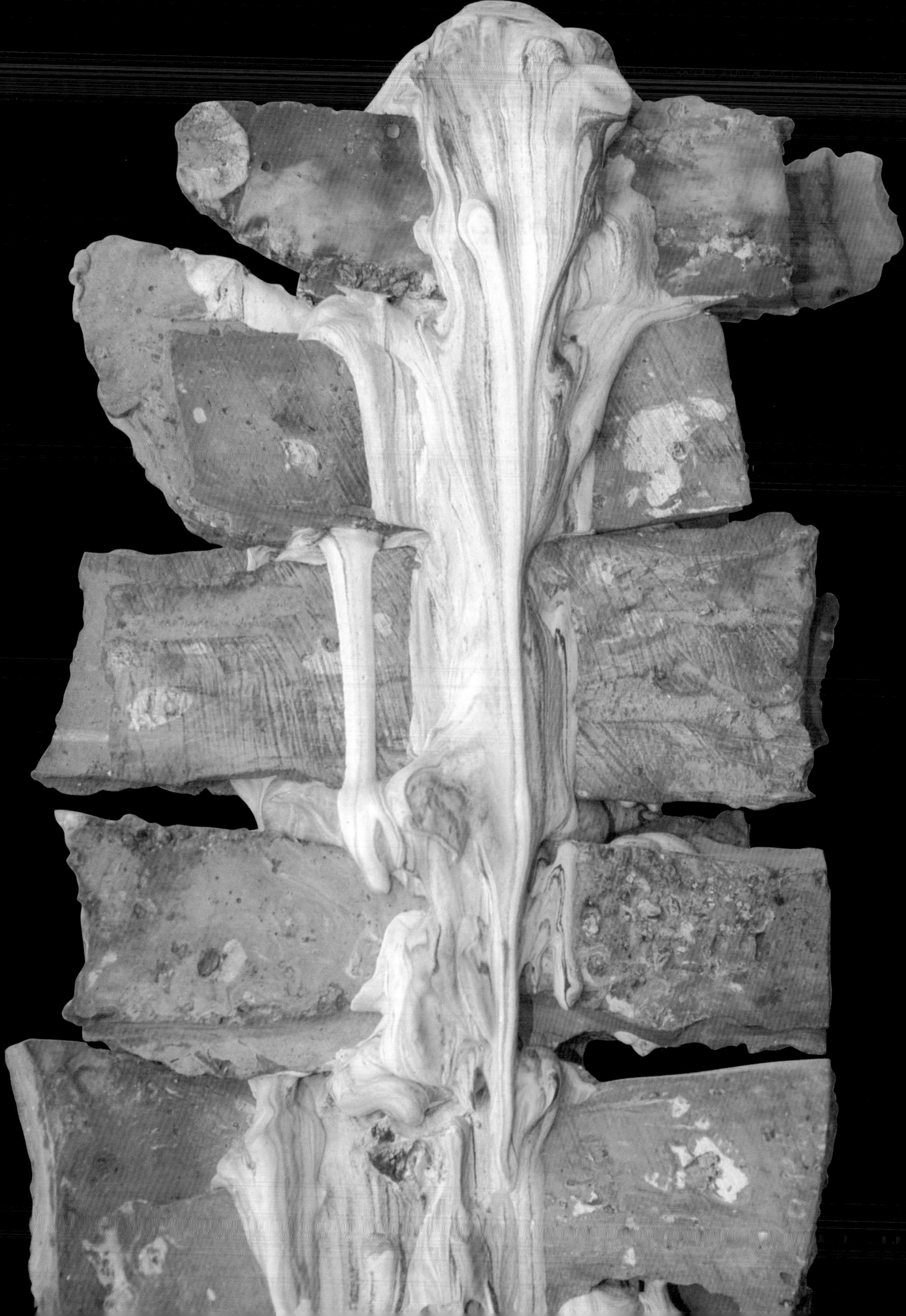

Chapter 20

Plaster as a material

188 What are the properties of a material? It's a fundamental question for creativity but often we skip it and assume things like 'paint is for painting,' 'plaster is for casting or carving' and so on. When you explore materials and processes you're always going to move beyond the obvious.

In this sense our exploration of plaster is a metaphor – it's an example of how you can intentionally search beyond ordinary ideas.

In principle we're doing something similar to the earlier section on 'Thinking for a change' which treats your life as a process. Here we're repeating the same sort of exploration with a material and some of the processes in which it can be used.

Wet plaster changes its characteristics as it sets. It can be runny, so it will pour and flow (the more runny, the weaker it will be on drying). Late in the drying it is crumbly. If you mix two batches of plaster with oxides and take them to the crumbly stage, you can add a sloppy mix to get a marbled effect.

When you explore materials and processes you're always going to move beyond the obvious

Put the mix on plastic (use strips of wood under the plastic to create a 'tray' about 15 cm long). Bend the plastic a bit to put a curve in the plaster. When you've made a series of slabs, stack them on each other and pour runny plaster on them to hold all the pieces together.

The purpose of the exercise is to extend your knowledge of the material. It should also produce some interesting 3D objects.

Casting a face

189 When I first had my face cast it was an amazing experience. It felt as though I was being turned into an egg. Fingers gently patted the material into place and I changed from a person to a sculpture. The plaster felt warm and as it hardened the people in the room began to talk as if I wasn't there. I could have sat for a long

It felt as though I was being turned into an egg

◄ Detail of work by Dennis Berdinner.

time under the mould but eventually it had to be lifted. It gave me some empathy for people who pay big money to have 'facials' and get pampered under a mud pack.

Later, holding the finished cast was like meeting myself for the first time.

CAUTION

There is a small element of danger in face casting – you do it at your own risk. If a person has difficulty breathing, remove the mask immediately (it's like removing a large piece of sticking plaster – it may take a few hairs but it's not a big deal).

It is okay for the model to keep his/her mouth open a little during casting. Cover the lips with plaster but leave a gap for breathing through the mouth (and keep the nostrils open).

Keep to a limit of three layers of bandage on areas that should be strong (forehead, around the edge of the face and along the top of the nose). For the rest, two layers should be sufficient.

People with sensitive skin should avoid the exercise (do a small test to check whether there's any reaction). Take special care around the eyes. It's important to cover the eyes with tissue. If you're worried about the risks, skip the exercise altogether (or be an observer rather than a participant).

Having said that, we've made thousands of masks at TLC with no side effects other than a few pulled hairs (although I've heard reports of the occasional bruise when too much plaster is applied around the bridge of the nose – the material shrinks as it dries and can squeeze the nose like a slow motion punch).

Materials needed:

- Gypsona (plaster bandage)
- Vaseline
- Toilet tissue
- Dust mask (use when mixing plaster)
- Plaster (fast-setting is preferred)
- Bucket
- Warm water
- PVA glue

If you're worried about the risks, skip the exercise altogether

Method

PART 1 : CREATE A MASK

If you have doubts about the process, try it first on a doll, a rock or some other object so that you gain a clear understanding of how it works.

Do the project with at least one other person (don't do it by yourself). Ensure that the model is okay to have their face covered with plaster.

COVER clothing with a towel or newspaper as the process is messy.

APPLY Vaseline to the face. Smooth it into the skin so that it doesn't interfere with the impression. It's best to 'sculpt' the Vaseline over facial hair rather than rubbing it in). Beards are a challenge because you have to fill them with Vaseline.

Model: Bruce Corson.

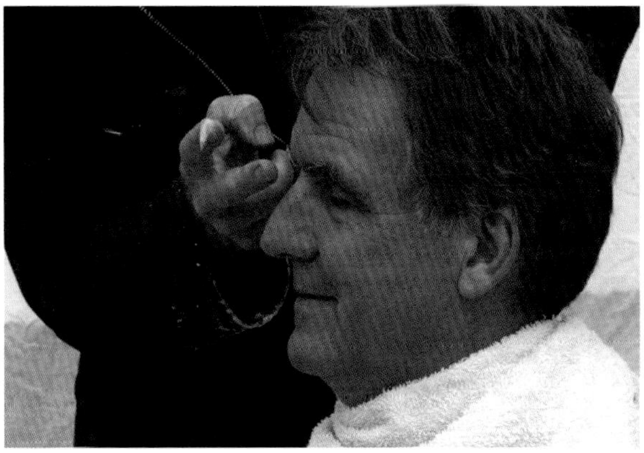

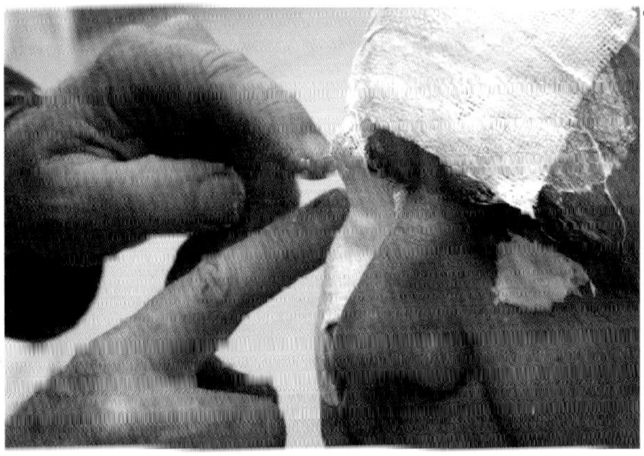

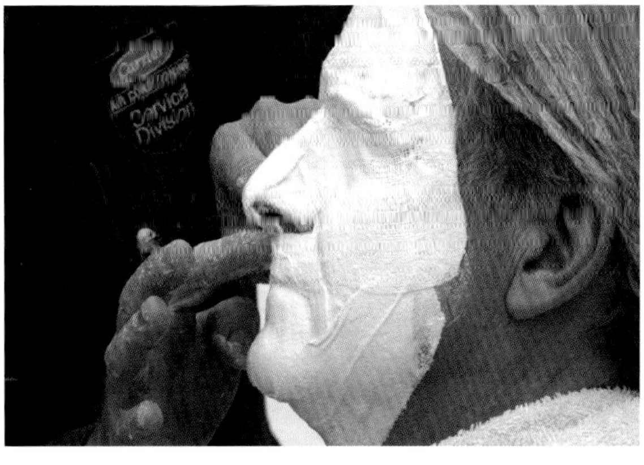

PLACE small strips of toilet tissue over the eyelids.

CUT your Gypsona bandage into 10–15 cm pieces. Smaller triangular shapes are good for the 'corners'.

DIP each piece into warm water before applying to the face. Warm water is more comfortable unless you're in a really hot place.

PAT each piece gently into place, making sure it gets into every crevice (except the nostrils – which must be left open!). It's an intimate process but if you're too cautious the cast won't be so good.

Keep chatting to the model (who should use 'thumbs up' to signal that all is well – or 'thumbs down' to indicate a problem).

OVERLAP your pieces and work your way over the face, beginning with a single layer.

USE big pieces for large areas like the forehead and smaller pieces for eyes and lips.

BUILD two layers over the face and a third layer around the edges and along the nose.

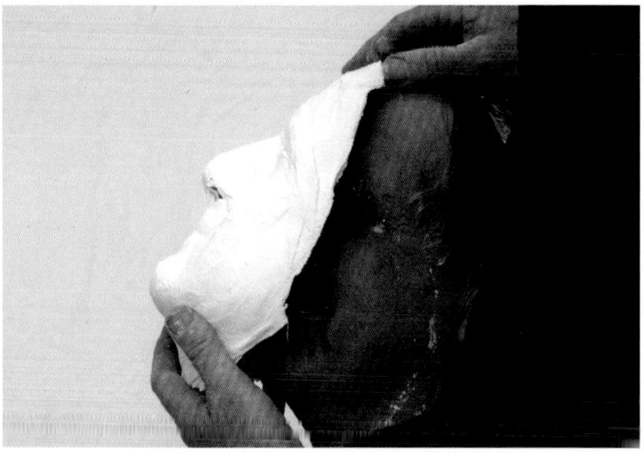

It takes about ten minutes to apply the plaster and three or four minutes for the final drying.

When the mask feels hard, invite the person to wriggle their face muscles to begin freeing the plaster from the skin. Then gently ease your fingers under the edges and apply enough pressure to encourage the mask to lift but not so much that you bend or break it. Usually you reach a point where it lifts off easily (you may have to gently trim some hairs if it won't budge).

Once the mask is off you can tidy up any details (and cover the nostril holes, either with clay or some more little strips of plaster). Then take a tea break or leave the mask to harden overnight (the plaster steadily gets harder).

Vaseline the inside of the mask as thinly as possible to preserve the detail.

PART 2: CREATE A PLASTER CAST

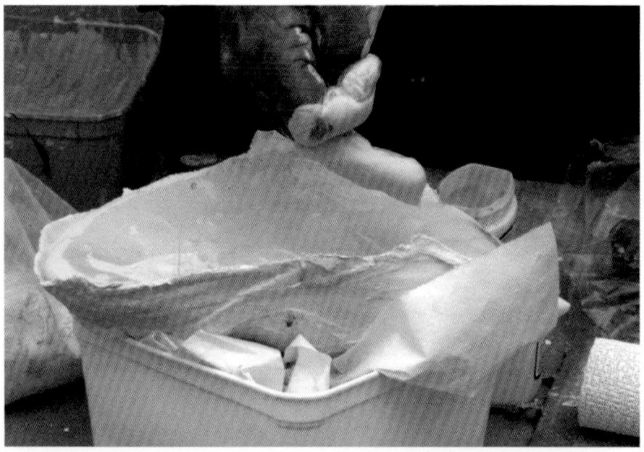

SET up the mould in a nest of newspaper in a container. The wet plaster is heavy and the mould needs good support or it will bend.

MIX your plaster of Paris by slowly shaking plaster onto 3 cm of water in a bucket. Shake more powder onto the surface until it stops getting wet.

ENSURE that there are no lumps by patting the side of the bucket for three minutes or so. Pour the plaster into your mask. Make sure the plaster gets into all the crevices (you can help it with your fingers).

ADD a loop of wire if you want to hang the cast on a wall. Ensure that the wire is well embedded (twist the ends so it will be secure).

LEAVE it supported in the nest overnight unless you're in a hurry. Although the plaster dries in a few minutes it will still be fragile and the extra drying time is a safety measure.

LOOSEN the edges of the mask and peel it away from the plaster. Depending on your luck (and your skills) it may come off neatly or be wrecked. It's the cast that matters.

REPAIR any blemishes to the cast – if there are bubbles, dampen the cast and fill them with fresh plaster.

190 *Making a mask*

This is a theatrical technique dating back hundreds of years. You can add to the cast using clay, wax or plastilina to make a fantasy face – just build on the cast and make whatever features you choose. When you've established the shape, apply Vaseline and add small pieces of paper that have been soaked in PVA glue (check thistothat.com/glue/pva.shtml for information). Build three or more layers of paper and take care to get a good clean finish. Use paste (or flour and water) rather than glue if you prefer.

Leave the mask for at least a day to dry (it may take longer – use your judgment). When it's dry, carefully lift it from the cast. You can then embellish it with paint, hair, glitter or whatever you please. Attach some hat elastic, cut little holes for the eyes and you're ready to go on stage or to a masked ball.

Remove the clay or plasticene if you want to keep the cast. Clean gently with a soft cloth and either soapy water or an appropriate solvent. Alternatively you can 'clean' it by applying a coat of paint. Then hang it on the wall or put it in the attic for posterity.

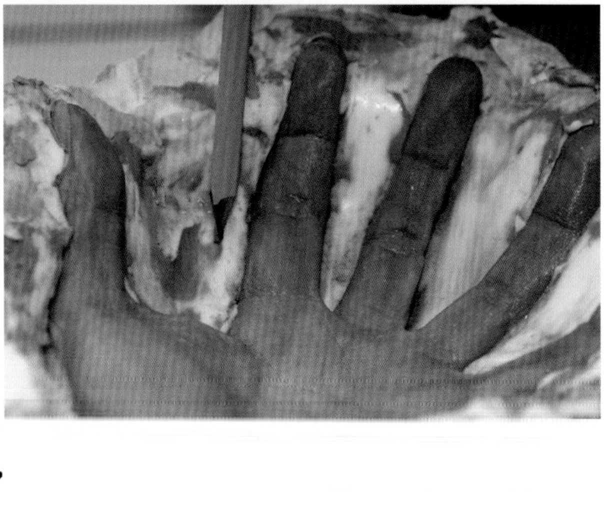

Casting with alginate

191 Alginate is a material derived from seaweed. One of its uses is to make moulds that give fine details. Many people experience this when they visit their dentist and have an impression made of a tooth. Sculptors use the same method but usually with less precision and with cheaper versions of alginate. (Check the internet for information on alginate – www.artmolds.com/category26.cfm is an interesting place to start).

You'll need someone to help.

STEP 1 Apply a thin coating of Vaseline to your hand and make a clay base to fit the shape you want. Snuggle it together as neatly as possible.

STEP 2 Mix the alginate according to the directions and apply it right across the hand and the clay as shown.

STEP 3 Apply a couple of layers of plaster bandages, then a layer of plaster to provide strength.

STEP 4 When the plaster is dry, ease it away from the clay and carefully remove any residue. A pencil or a sculpting tool is good for clearing the edges. The alginate side must remain undisturbed – resting on a bench is essential. When the skin is clean, add a fresh coating of Vaseline to the skin and the exposed plaster (keep it thin – every bump will be preserved).

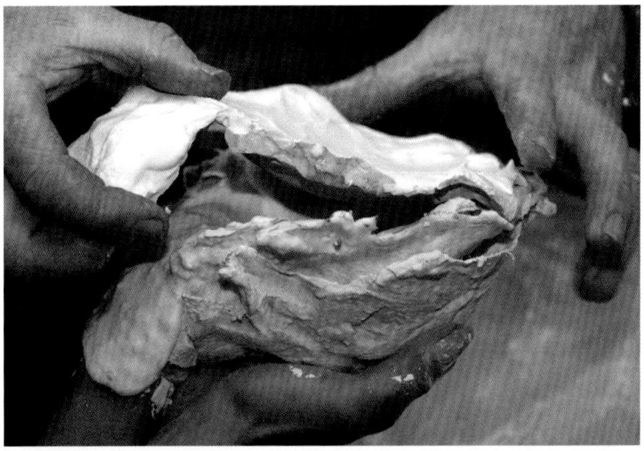

STEP 5 Repeat steps 1 to 3 on the underside of the hand. Allow the materials to dry. It can be boring waiting for plaster to set – you may be more comfortable if there's music playing, people chatting with you or some other suitable diversion.

STEP 6 Gently prise open the two sides of the mould, breathe a sigh of relief and carefully free your hand from the alginate.

STEP 7 Carefully put the two sides of the mould back together and tie them firmly in place.

STEP 8 Pour a creamy mix of plaster into the mould. To avoid air bubbles, vibrate the mix before pouring and do plenty of tapping on the outside of the mould to jiggle the plaster into all the spaces. Insufficient jiggling can lead to annoying things like missing fingers.

STEP 9 When the plaster is dry, undo the tie and remove the mould. If it's all gone well you've now got a wee bit of tidying up to do – smoothing the joins and repairing small blemishes. If you plan to do a bronze you'll move into a new series of steps which are broadly described below. You'll need expert help in a foundry (as they say on telly, do not try this at home).

The same system can be used to cast a face. In this case the cast was a one-off and the alginate is being torn away.

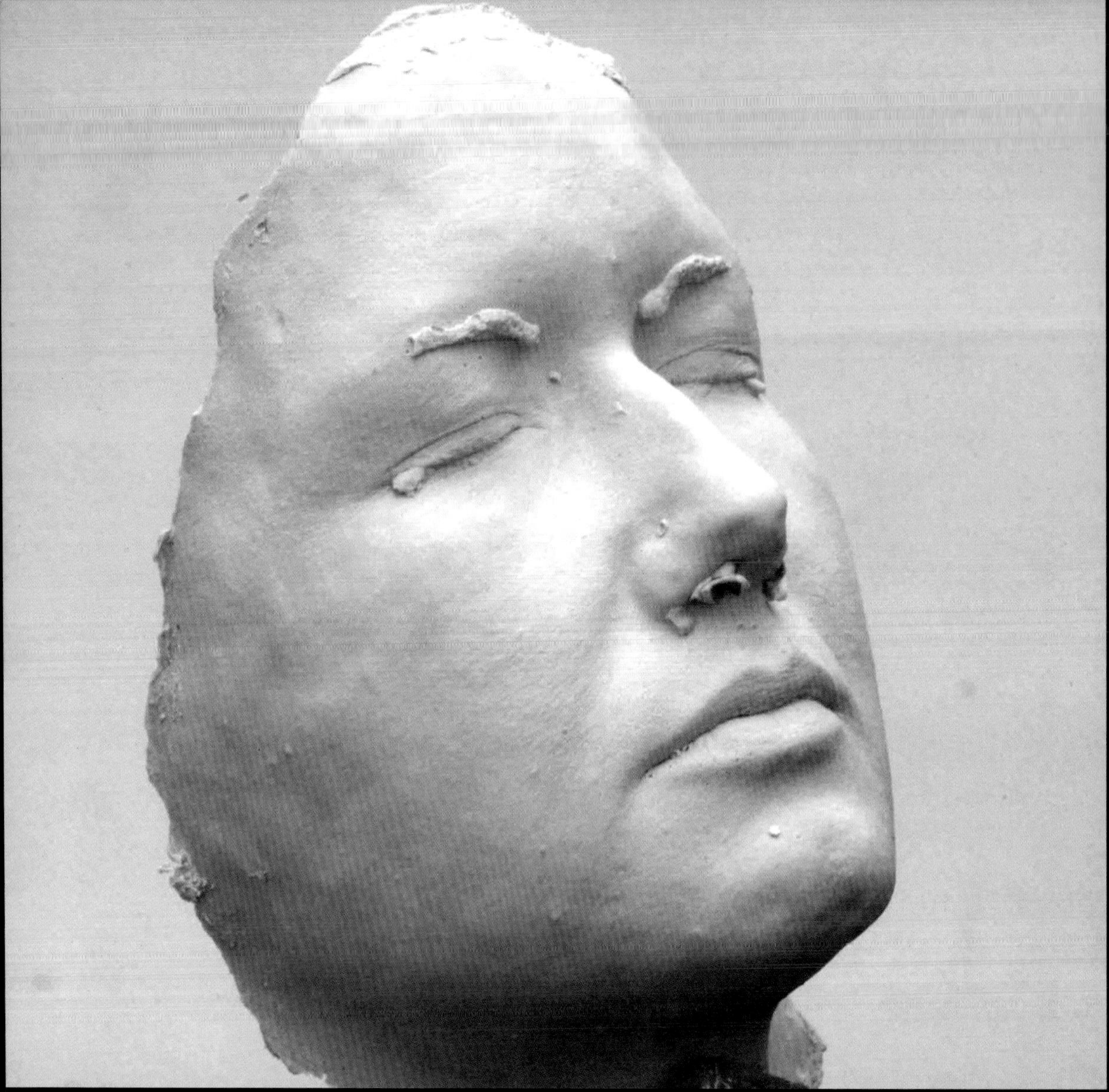

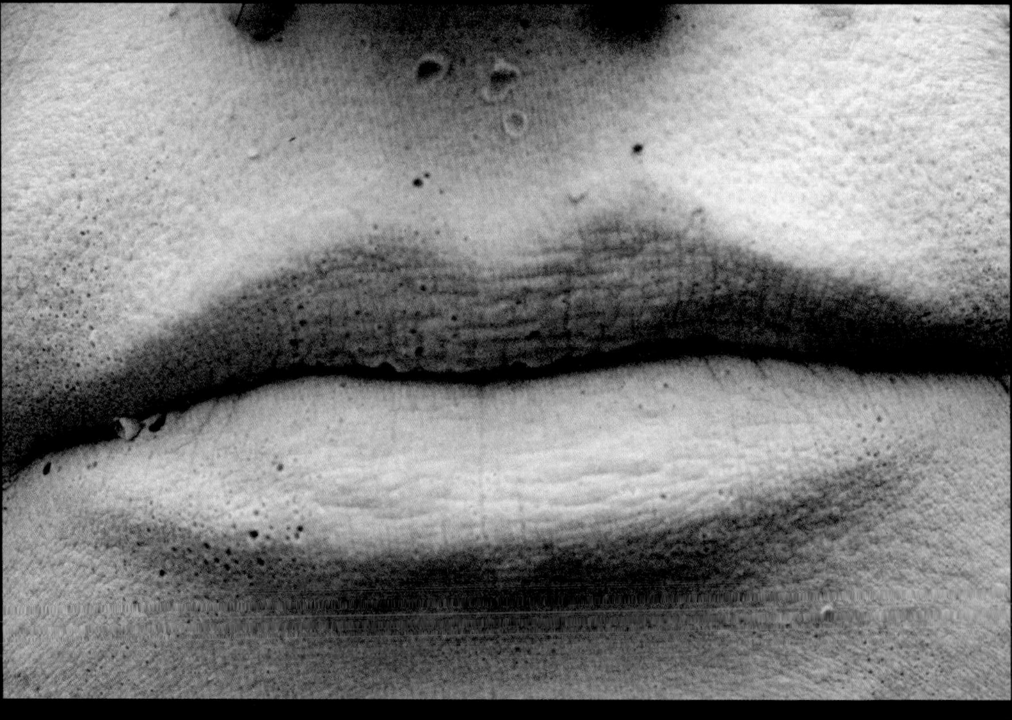

Alginate captures such fine details that one of the biggest challenges is to repair the blemishes.

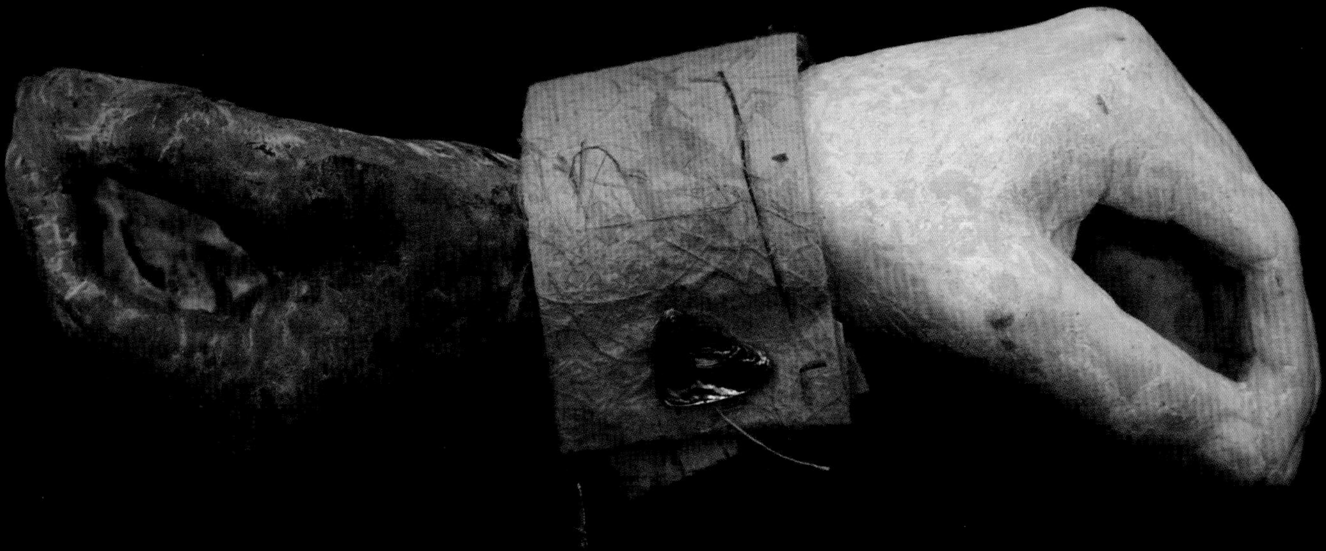

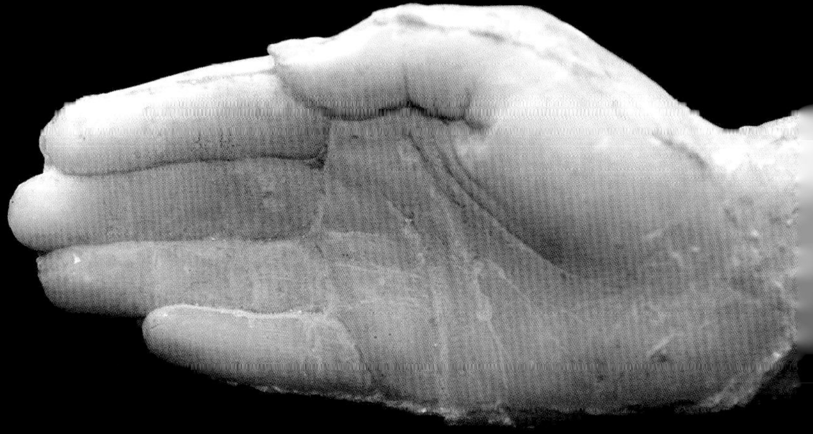

▲ Chocolate is an alternative to bronze (tastier but less robust).

▶ Or you can use wax. A hand cast in wax rather than bronze — more fragile but with (considerable) care it can be done in your kitchen.

▼ During one of our interviews, sculptor Dennis Berdinner combined a wax hand and a mummified bird. There's a moral there ... a bird in hand is not so good for the bird.

Bronze

Make a fresh mould from the cast, this time using silicone (check smoothon.com/liqrubr.htm for more information). The silicone is filled with molten wax and removed when the wax has hardened. After being tidied (same as for the earlier plaster) the wax is augmented with 'vents' (sprues) which are necessary to allow the bronze to get into all the required places. Initially the vents are lines of wax and they become pipes later in the cycle.

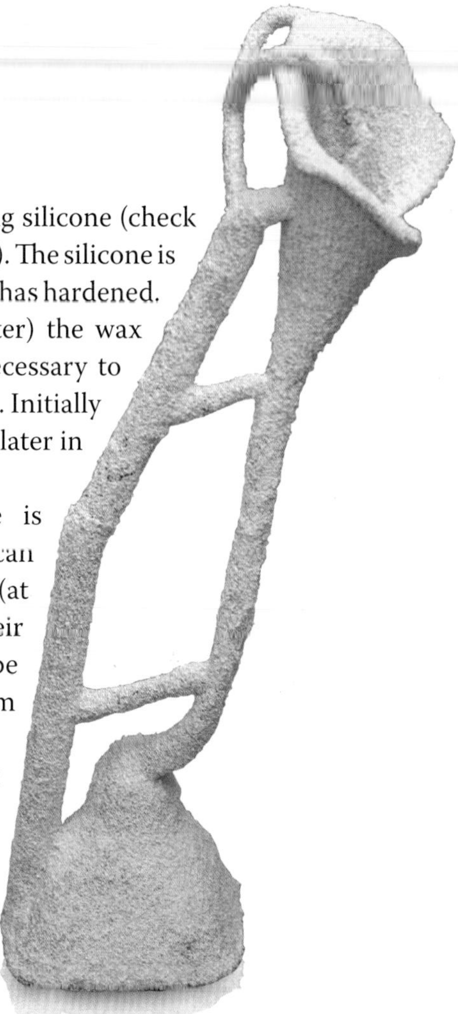

The slightly strange looking structure is then coated with ceramic material that can withstand the stress of molten bronze (at around 1150°C). The shells have their own persona and could even be the end product if you like them enough.

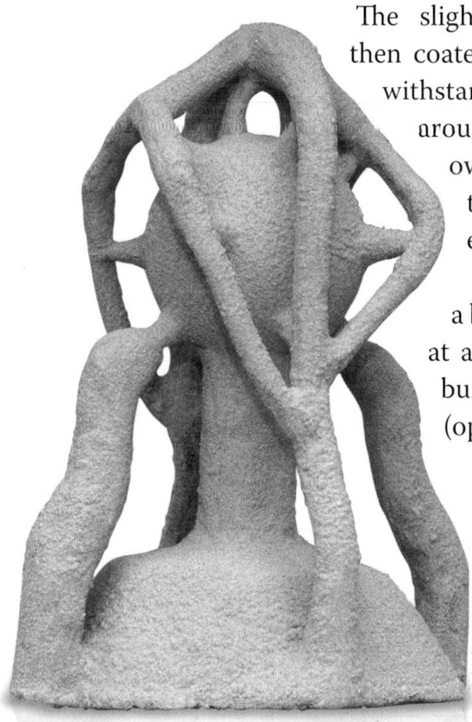

Normally a foundry would cast a batch of moulds rather than one at a time. The drama begins with burning the wax out of the shells (opposite).

▾ Once the artist has done yet another round of tidying (and on bronze it's hard work) the piece is complete except for the presentation details. This bronze was made from a hand sculpted directly in wax rather than using alginate — but the principles are the same once the wax is established.

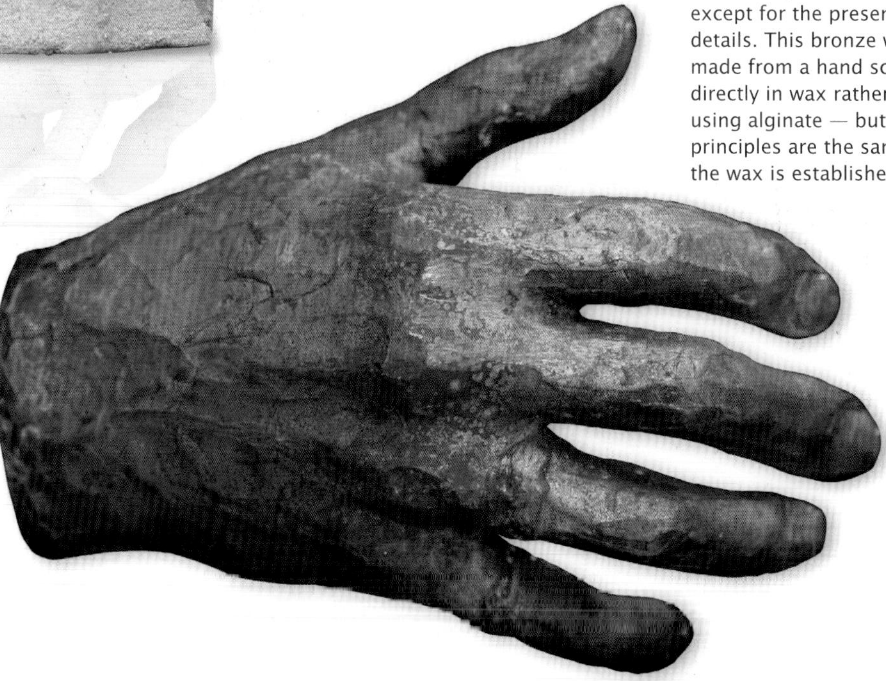

Dennis Berdinner melting wax from casts in the 'lost wax' process.

Then the bronze is poured.

▲ The same ideas can take you through to body casting. In this case the final cast was made with paper and shellac.

▼◀ Plastilina works by Josette Link (left) and Sue Currie.

Plastilina and wax

192 Plastilina, wax and clay are materials for three-dimensional drawing. The examples are 'sketches', about 14 cm high. There are many commercial products which serve the same purpose – they all have their own characteristics and it's a matter of personal choice.

If you prefer to make a stand for your sculpture, the first step is to do the carpentry. All you need is a solid base and a strong piece of pipe or dowelling of suitable thickness. Alternatively you can build your sculpture directly onto wire.

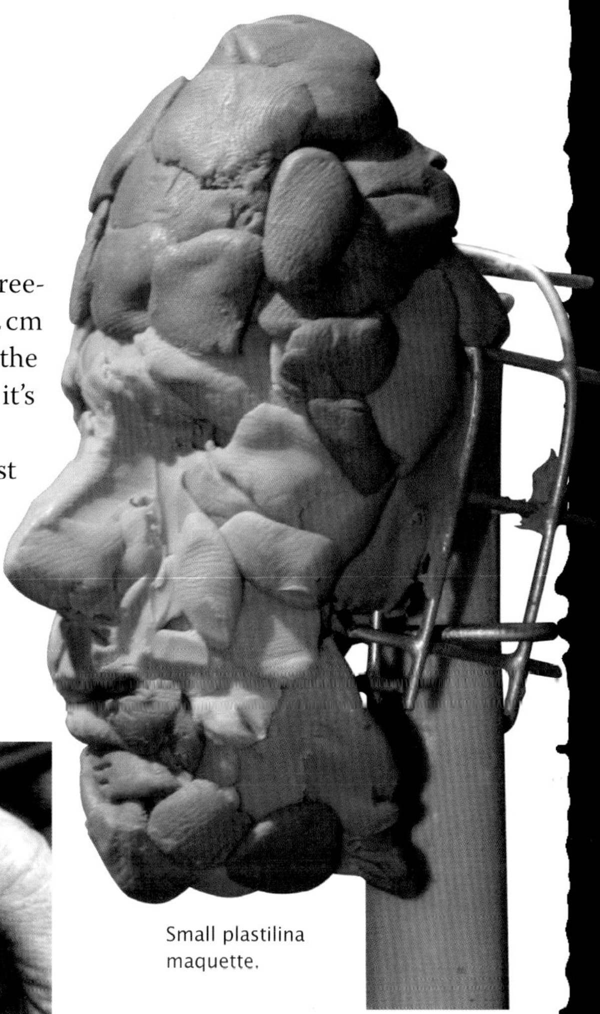

Small plastilina maquette.

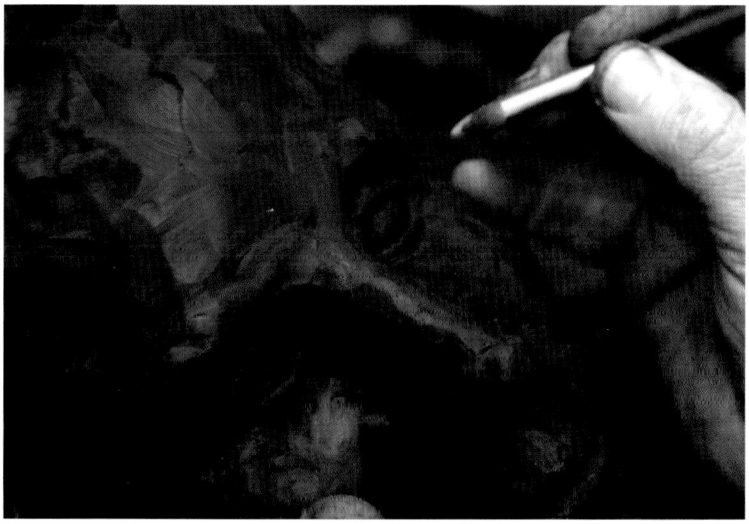

◂ Sculpting from life. The tool is an eraser — functioning as a shaper.

◂ The tool is a palette knife.

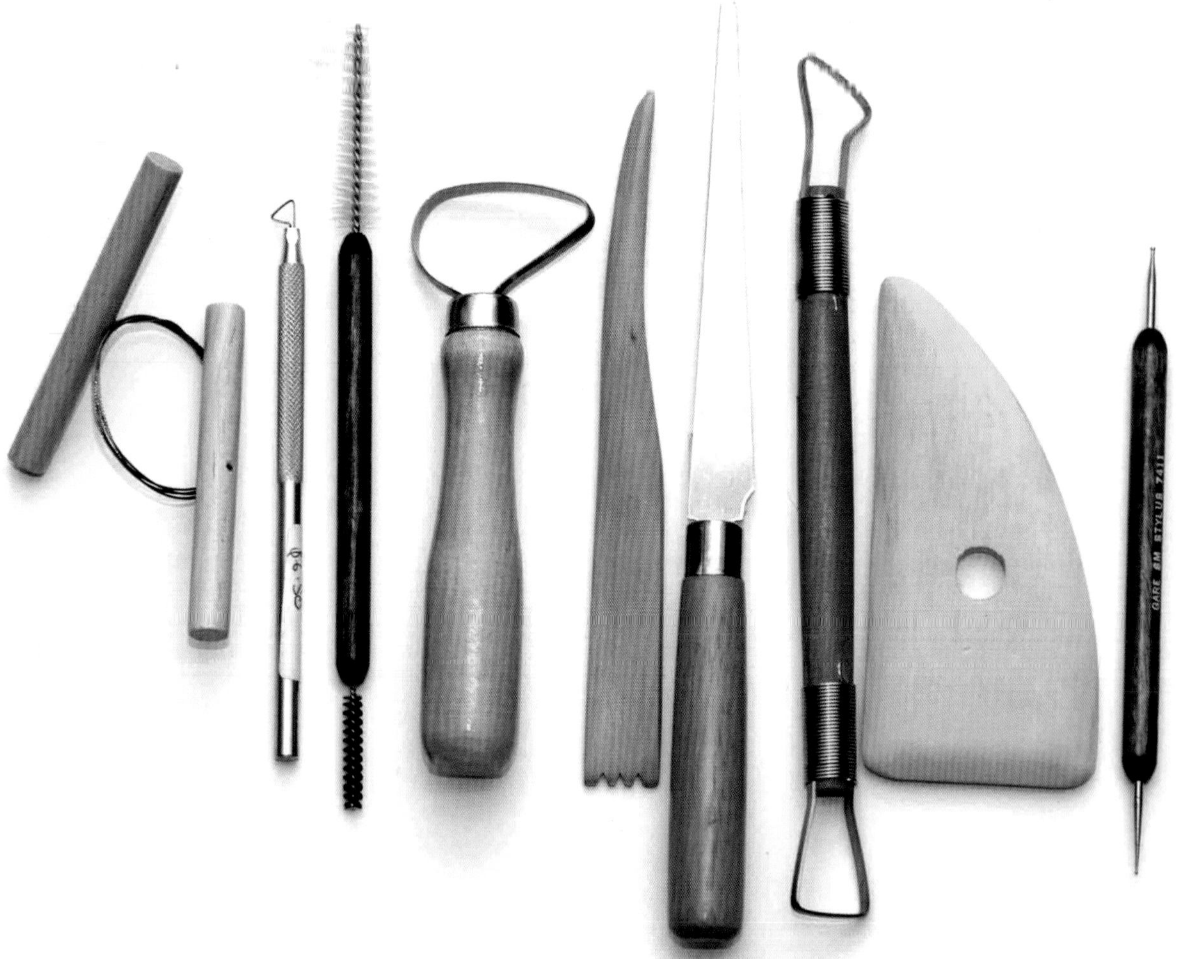

If you use clay, just add well kneaded pellets and build up the shape. Fingers are good tools although there are a few devices which might be worth making or buying (basically they are sticks, scrapers, brushes and wire loops – see the photograph above for examples).

Wax requires different tools and a gas ring is a big asset. You can use hot knives to add and subtract wax and you can warm extra wax in a wok or an old electric fry-pan so that it's more manageable.

Initially try a few abstract shapes to get the feel of the material. Think of:

pressing ▪ smoothing ▪ texturing
cutting ▪ adding ▪ subtracting

If you're ready to be adventurous, try shaping a head.

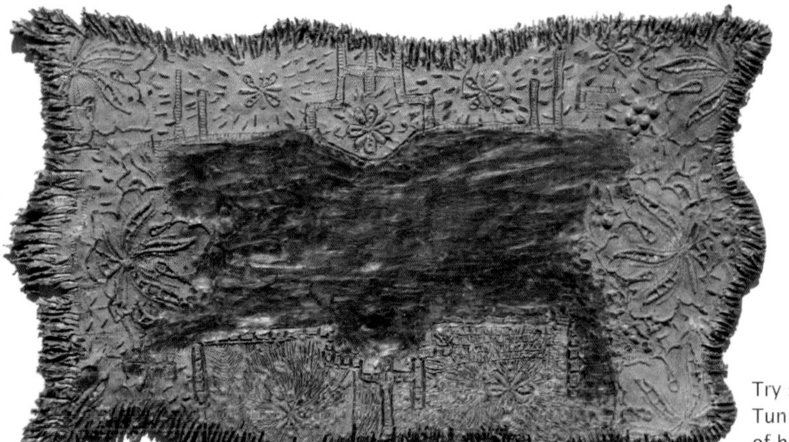

Try squeezing things against wax. Francis Tunnicliffe began with doilies, added some marks of his own and planned to cast the result in bronze.

▲ Wax trees in progress. Karla Vink was dribbling layers of wax onto a foundation, then shaping it as each layer was added.

▼ Bronze from a life study in plastilina.

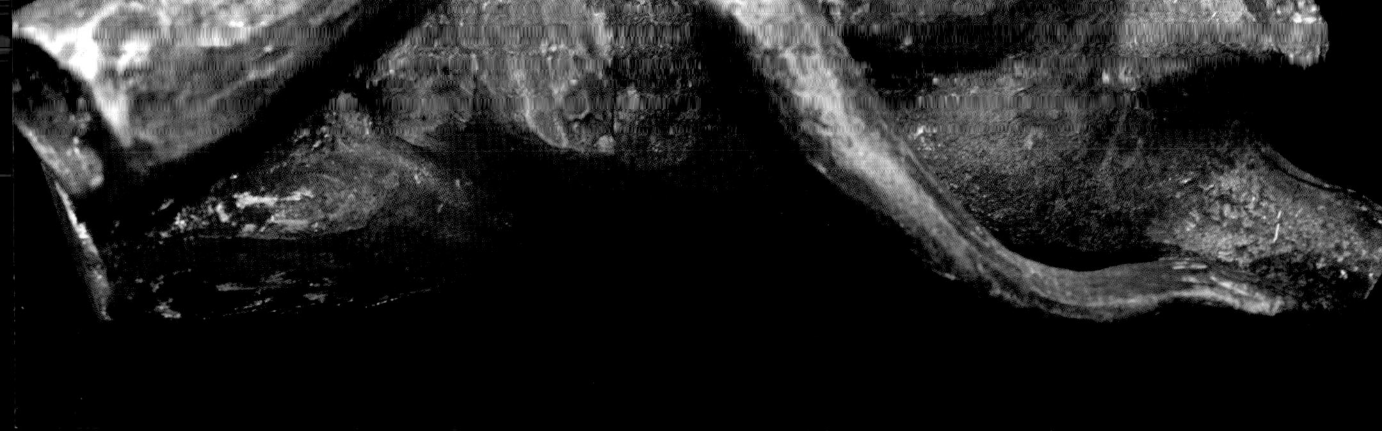

Plaster and mesh

193 Use mesh as a base structure ('reinforcing') for a sculpture made in plaster or concrete. As usual you might find it best to start small and test some simple shapes before you get ambitious. The mesh is a metaphor for the underlying organisation which serves as a platform for the visible elements of creativity. In other contexts you might say that practice is the 'mesh' – it's the hidden dimension of experience which enables an artwork to be performed. Within an organisation the 'mesh' consists of trust, routines and formal relationships.

▲▶ Joy Snell's figures are made with concrete trowelled onto a wire frame. When Joy's sculpture was knocked over the inner structure was revealed in the break (it has since been restored).

▶ Simple mesh forms given an anthropomorphic shape to which mysterious leaves have been added. (Susan MacDonald)

You might say that practice is the 'mesh' – it's the hidden dimension of experience which enables an artwork to be performed

194 Use mesh or linear materials as a major aspect of the finished work.

▲ Large figurative sculpture made of metallic strips, decorating a high-rise next to the San Francisco Museum of Modern Art. There is form and not-form (you can see through the 'solid').

▶ The same sculpture, showing the scale.

Creating briefs

195 Think about the intentions artists have when they begin a work. Intentions may operate at many different levels and the challenge is to dig down as far as you can go.

'Intention' is a philosophical challenge to 'laziness' and 'inertia'. Why do *anything*? There isn't a logical answer. Intention is like light to a leaf. We are drawn to it.

Unlike a leaf, humans have the choice to turn away from the light – to live an *un*intentional life. That's our privilege. Alternatively we can take the creative option and be intentional.

Consider the next picture. What was Alexander Liberman doing? What was the foundation idea behind the work? The answers will be creative formats for projects of your own. For example, you might guess he was taking simple geometric units and putting them together in a way which is sympathetic to a particular environment. As soon as you've reached this point you can recycle the idea into your own learning. Instead of copying Liberman you can use the same brief to produce a result which will be entirely your own.

Olympic Iliad by Alexander Liberman, 1984, Seattle Center.

Liberman himself may have had something else in mind – there are many different ways to make a start. It might be: "Clustering units of smooth, coloured steel in a park"; "Combining highly industrial forms with trees"; "Achieving maximum contrast between organic forms and manufactured forms." What is important is that each of these 'recipes' gives scope for individual interpretation – you are free to come up with your own creative response.

Liberman has used ingredients derived from a cylinder and constructed an overhanging lattice of steel which loosely mimics the shapes of the surrounding trees. The scale, colour and visual lightness (of heavy material) have a warm, engaging whimsy. The sloping column on the right doubles as a playground item because kids run at it and see how high they can climb before sliding to earth.

You are free to come up with your own creative response

Ideas like this typically start with a maquette – a small-scale three-dimensional 'sketch' through which the artist explores possibilities. You could play with the cores of toilet rolls and glue them together to investigate possible shapes. The second section of 'Sculpture 101' involves extending materials into maquettes and imagining different contexts.

If you set aside the fact that the finished work is ceramic, this piece by Rohana Weaver illustrates another approach to the repetitive use of similar elements. Is it relating to a sea anemone? Is it a ceramic descendant of Meret Oppenheim's famous fur-lined cup? Or a nightmare about boarding-school dinners? The tentacles are so basic and yet they pack quite a punch (and make rather pleasing sounds when you tap them).

What is your guess about a brief which could fit the work?

- "Create a sculpture based on a repetitive natural form."
- "Combine elements of a natural form with the shapes of a piece of crockery."
- "Translate a soft, fluid natural form into a piece of ceramic sculpture."

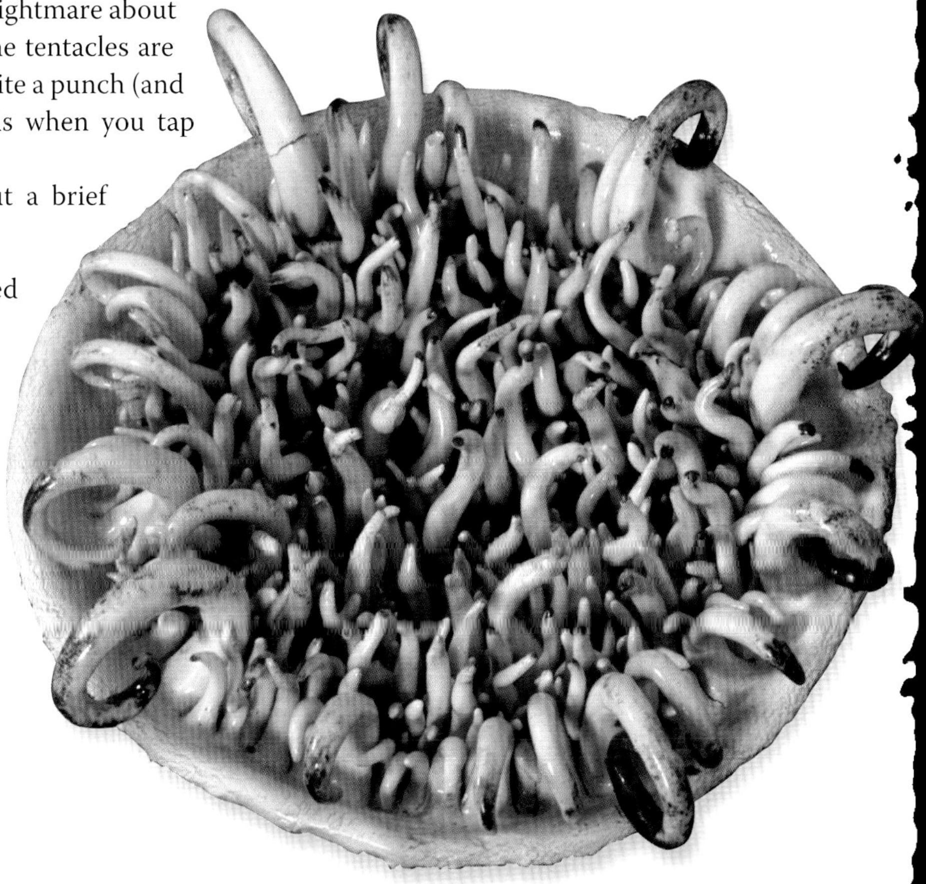

196 At the beginning of one of my classes I gave the participants pipe cleaners and pieces of rock (prepared with holes for the wire) to make maquettes. Within five minutes we had some ideas which I enjoyed and they're still on display in my office. The brief could be:

- "Take a hard natural object and combine it with something colourful and bendy."
- "Combine a cheap commercial item with something out of your environment."

▲ Sometimes sculpture is intended as illusion rather than a thing in itself. TLC students were among those who worked on the Lyall Bay set of *King Kong* (shown as it was dismantled). The rocks were sophisticated fakes and the incongruous suburban landscape was neatly avoided in the movie.

► Sculpture in which satire is a large part of the intention. Artist: Kate Cosgrove.

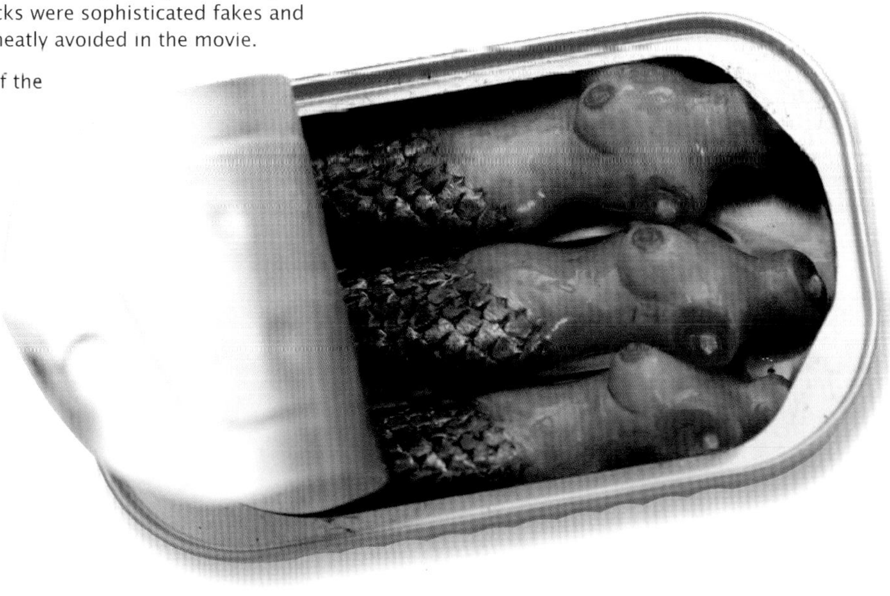

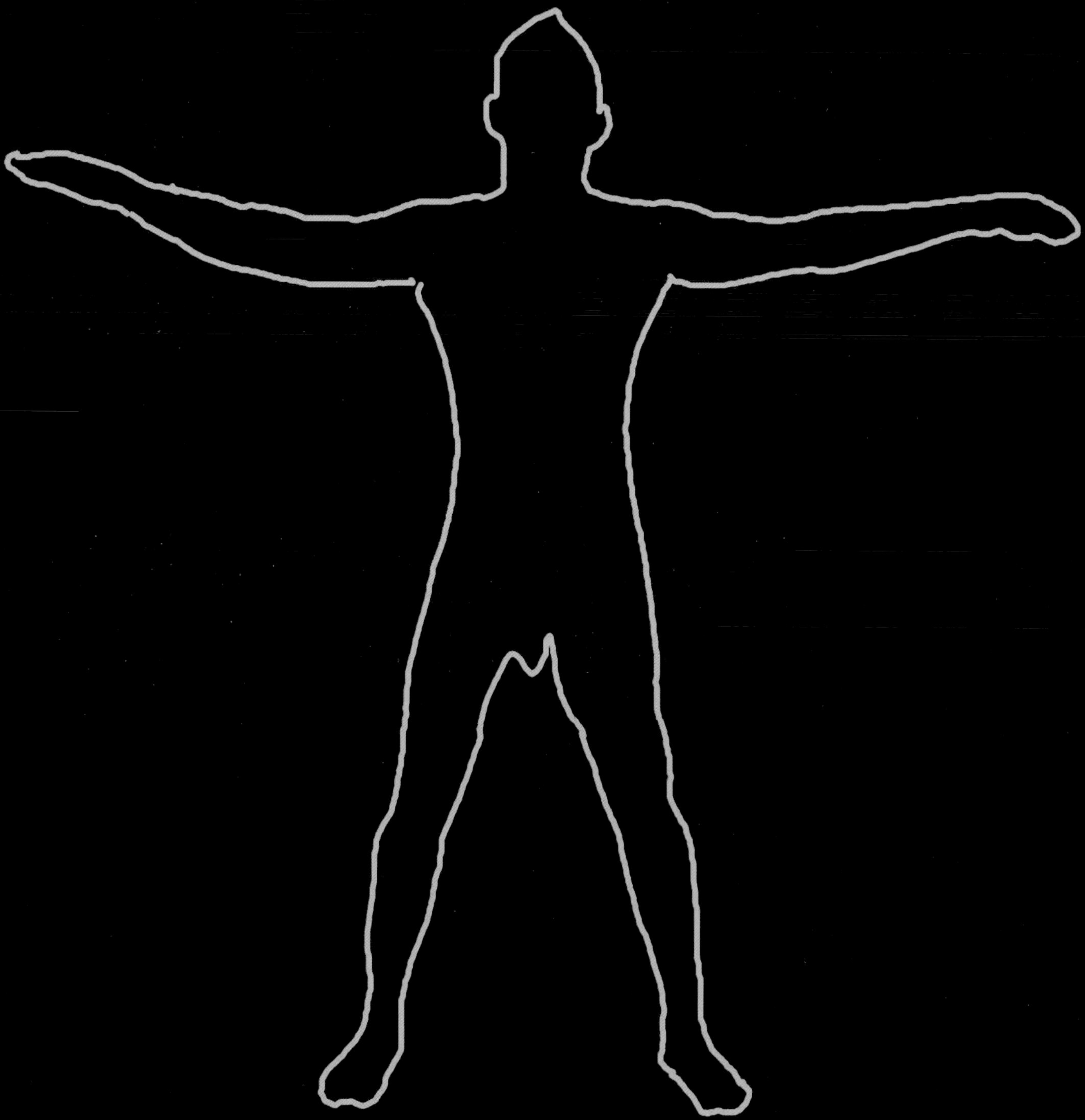

CHAPTER 21

Figurative sculpture

197 Lie down on paper (or concrete or anything that can be drawn on without inconveniencing others). Have a partner draw a line around your body – a little more carefully than they do in murder movies but the same sort of thing. Check out the proportions:

How does the width of your stretched-out arms compare with your height?

How many head-lengths is your height?

How many head-lengths is your torso?

Everyone varies but you soon notice that there are some general principles.

When I was at art school my tutor was keen on the discipline of representational sculpture and we had to work hard with measurements. It failed the fun test but it drew attention to the way in which forms work.

Now that I'm happily distanced from the horrors of art school I know that there was nothing wrong with this exercise, except that it was responding to a question I hadn't asked, and took so long that it put creativity to sleep. Today I would reframe those old assignments and treat them more like quick drawings than slow torture. They're equivalent to colour-matching and they lead to insights and the development of craft skills.

Dennis Berdinner's hand-made calipers in action. The tool was made from aluminium tubing and strips of rubber (and works well).

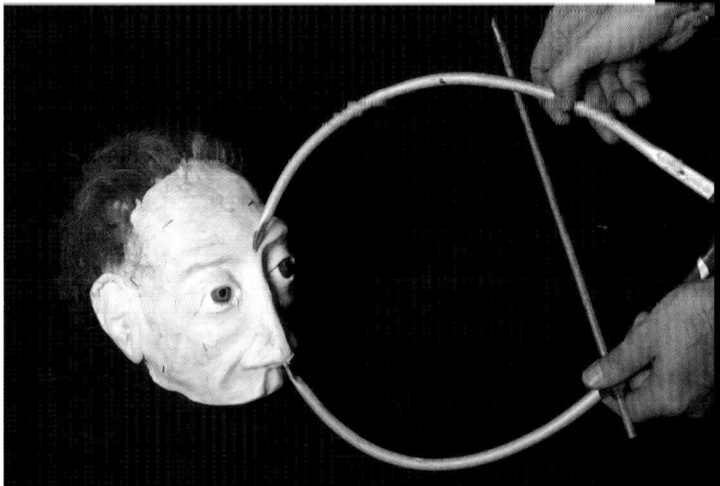

Representational sculpture is just as important as realistic painting. You're under no obligation to do it (or like it) but it offers rich possibilities.

198 Make a head out of clay (keep the scale small – a quarter life-size is okay). Measure the distances with calipers (if you have them) and divide by four if you're working to ¼ scale.

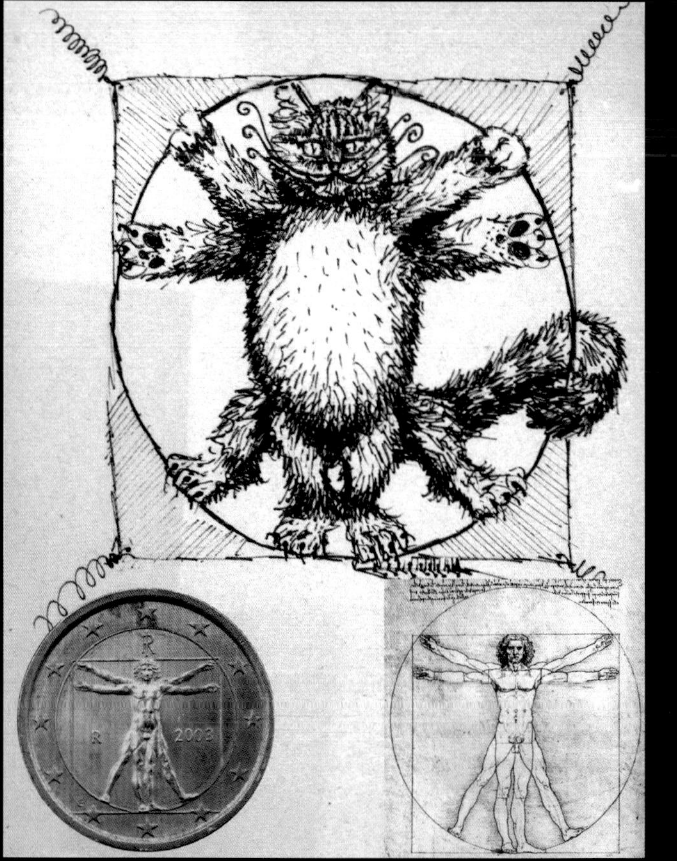

▸ Leonardo's famous illustration of human proportions, captured on a European coin and also by the inimitable Weezil.

▾ Europe contains a trove of figurative sculpture which is a sculptural instruction book for anyone who wants to study the techniques. This low-relief panel (*Cain and Abel*) by Lorenzo Ghiberti is on a set of doors at the Baptistery in Firenze, Italy, called *The Gates of Paradise*. As with many famous works it is a copy — the real thing was removed during World War II to protect it from looters and later cast in latex to make a duplicate. The original is held in a museum. Not that the copy diminishes the parable. The set of images served as a three-dimensional Old Testament for the Florentines. Ghiberti used the lost-wax technique to make the panels and spent 27 years (1425–1452) to complete the task.

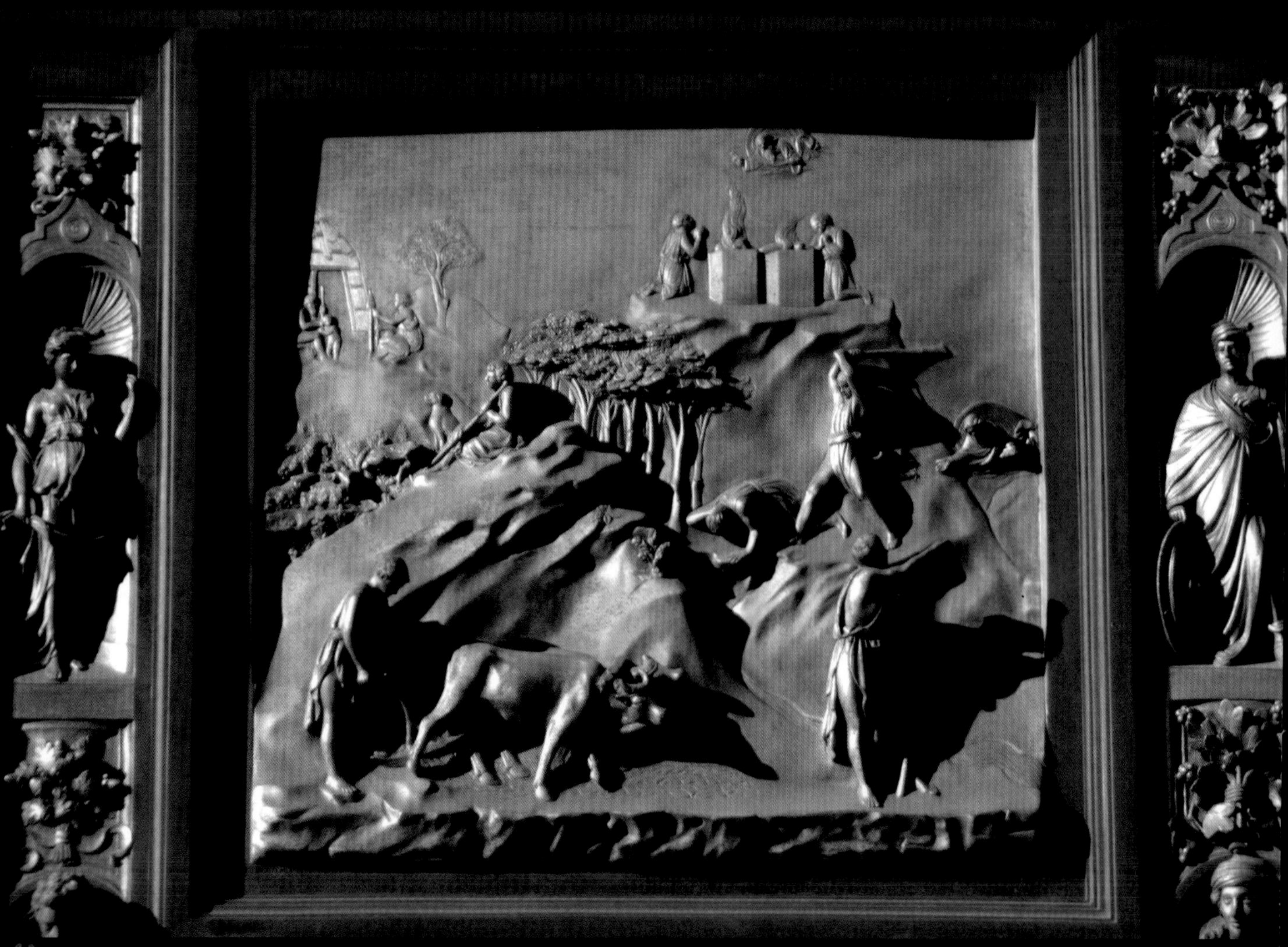

Balzac by Rodin. Part of Rodin's legacy is energy. He conveys an enduring excitement about human form and the bronze retains the freedom of clay. The work caused outrage when it was done — perhaps because it emphasised humanity rather than grandness. If you choose to work with clay you'll be doing well if you can use it to express a sense of flesh, bone and fabric as Rodin did. He used his eyes and responded sensitively to what he saw.

▲ Representational art has plenty of scope in advertising — corny or otherwise. Steel Pig BBQ, Seattle. Maybe there are many steel workers who are closet sculptors — in America you can buy steel dinosaurs, horses, cows and other animals, all crafted in a realistic style from a material that is heavy, industrial and far less friendly than the results suggest.

◄ New Zealand's Jeff Thomson does it all in corrugated iron. Here are some of Thomson's horses at the Gibbs sculpture farm, Northland, New Zealand.

► *Leg* by Alan Tugwell. Besides being a reasonably accurate version of a leg, it does a good job of connecting with the grain of the wood and performing a neat illusion of balance by being mounted on a steel rod through the toe.

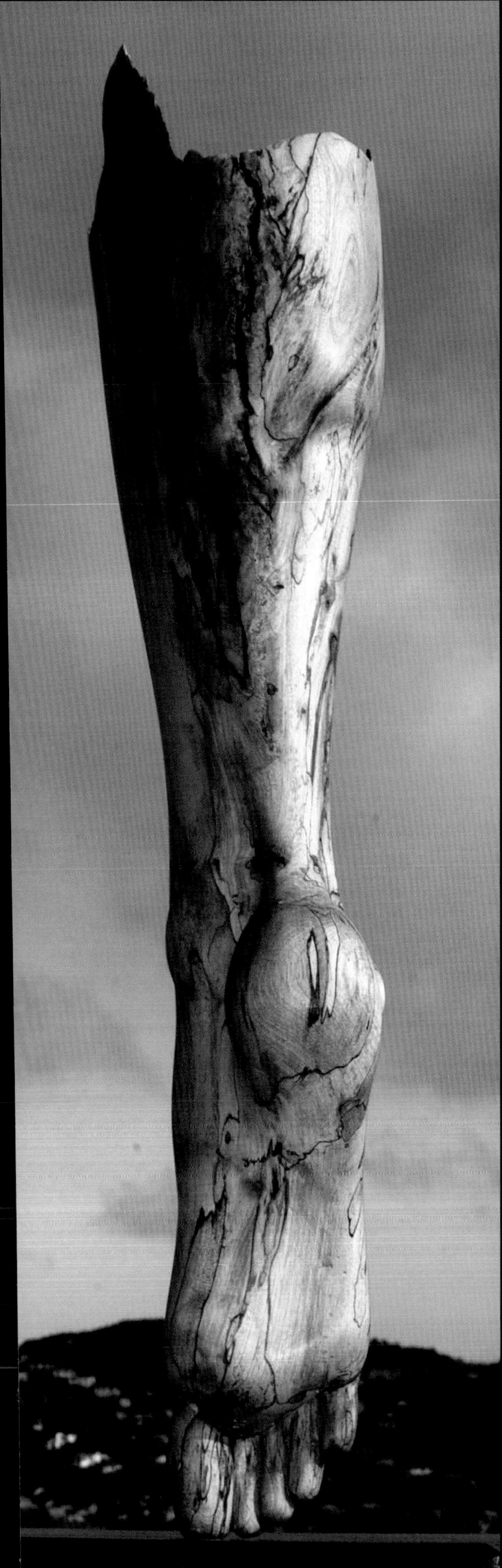

▲▼ A cheerful representational sculpture with a conceptual twist in Seattle. The figures use the same techniques as heroic sculpture and turn them into friendly, down-to-earth figures who radiate the joy of life. You can cast real people if you're willing to learn the appropriate skills. It's messy and exciting. If you want a high level of detail it can also be slow and expensive. On the plus side you may find wealthy people who are prepared to pay large sums for strong 3D images of themselves. For a relatively cheap version of the same process, check the section on face casting (page 361). The brief? Substitute a real form in a natural setting with a realistic sculpted form.

◄ ▼ Old-style heroic realism usually depicts famous men and reflects the tradition of dominant leadership. Sculptures like this speak of social relationships and, although the artist has to pay attention to form, the subtext says something about the approval of a particular role. You can almost hear the wind whispering 'God save the King' as Richard Seddon maintains his gesture outside Parliament in New Zealand. Not that Seddon was king — he merely represented a particular type of hierarchy. We have a statue of Queen Victoria too — definitely royal and with amazing biceps (imagine standing there all day with the bronze orb and the angel on your extended hand).

◀ Sometimes figurative sculpture provides a reminder of less regal things that not everyone wants to remember. In Savannah, Georgia, a figurative black family makes a statement through the melancholic ordinariness of what they represent — mum, dad and the kids. The caption, a quote from Maya Angelou, carries the sting: "We were stolen, sold and brought together from the African continent. We got on the slave ships together. We lay back to belly in the holds of the slave ships in each other's excrement and urine together, sometimes died together, and our lifeless bodies thrown overboard together. Today we are standing up together, with faith and even some joy."

▼ A Henry Moore sits in front of Fernand Léger at the National Gallery of Victoria in Melbourne. Moore isn't realistic but he is powerfully figurative and has a lot to say about humanity. It's one thing to cast a figure and another thing to get something with this intensity. Some of the power came during the blitz in London when Moore spent time drawing his fellow citizens in bomb shelters. Get yourself into such an extreme situation and the world will look different. Today it takes courage to stop and spend many hours observing. Then it takes a lifetime to translate observations into beautiful forms that make a new reality.

While the measuring may not be exciting it can build a much more objective awareness about what is actually there. It's equivalent to paying attention to the bank balance in a business or your sales results if you've put your art in a show.

3D and colour

Although we're used to seeing three-dimensional objects in colour (ourselves, for example) the colour can camouflage the form. Photographers sometimes prefer black and white photography as a means to describe form and escape the confusion of colour. Conversely, you might want to celebrate the confusion.

199 Consider the theme of painted objects and decide on a paint experiment of your own.

What material is available? A face cast? Found objects? A person?

Do you want to accentuate form? Camouflage? Dramatise?

Outdoor colour has a hard time. This Californian model goes inside when her restaurant isn't open. Her job is to attract attention — a low form of art befitting the shop dummy. Is she sexist and crass? She has personality and achieves one of the fundamental purposes of art — to be noticed. When looking at her I thought of Michelangelo, whose task with the Sistine Chapel was to draw attention to the Church. On that level the artists were kindred spirits.

◂ A bleak underpass in Emeryville turned into theatre with a painted bicycle cop (and several other sculptures). It has to rate as a brilliant use of a nasty space. The forms are made from cut steel (strong enough to handle the slings and arrows of whatever outrageous fortune happens in an underpass) and the paint glows under strong lighting at night. In a clever touch one of the works contains the cut-out letters of Emeryville which project onto the big wall in the background. (Vicki Jo Sowell, sculptor, with M Louise Stanley, painter, and Jeremy Hamm, lighting designer.)

▾ *Trompe l'oeil* painted figure by Karen Havican. The photographic lighting accentuates the model but in the context of the exhibition her feet were often in danger of being trodden on because people didn't realise there was someone in the chair. Karen does make-up for movies and special events. Her visual mischief is a sort of anti-form — she uses paint to make forms seem like something they aren't.

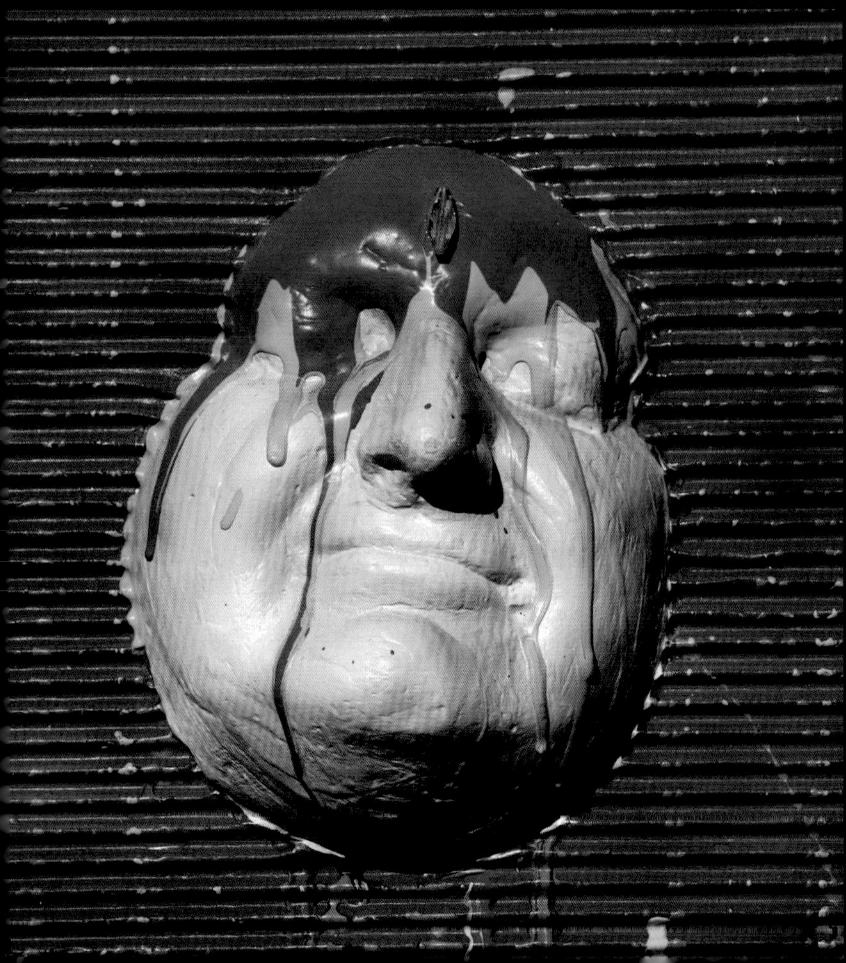

▲ Jeff Thomson offers some delicious colour as part of a big sea-shell sculpture in Lambton Quay, Wellington. He's using iridescent and other colours which give a special glow to the mundane shapes floating in a surreal, corrugated sea.

◄ Detail of a work by Ivan Bassett. The paint and corrugated cardboard add considerably to the Buddha-like self-portrait (done from a face cast).

► James Turrell has a different approach to colour. The photo is a detail of *Three Gems*, located at the De Young Museum in San Francisco. In part the work is intended to frame the sky and draw attention to whatever is happening. Turrell creates a contemplative environment like a cathedral. It's intense, contemplative and somehow consumes the viewer into an experience.

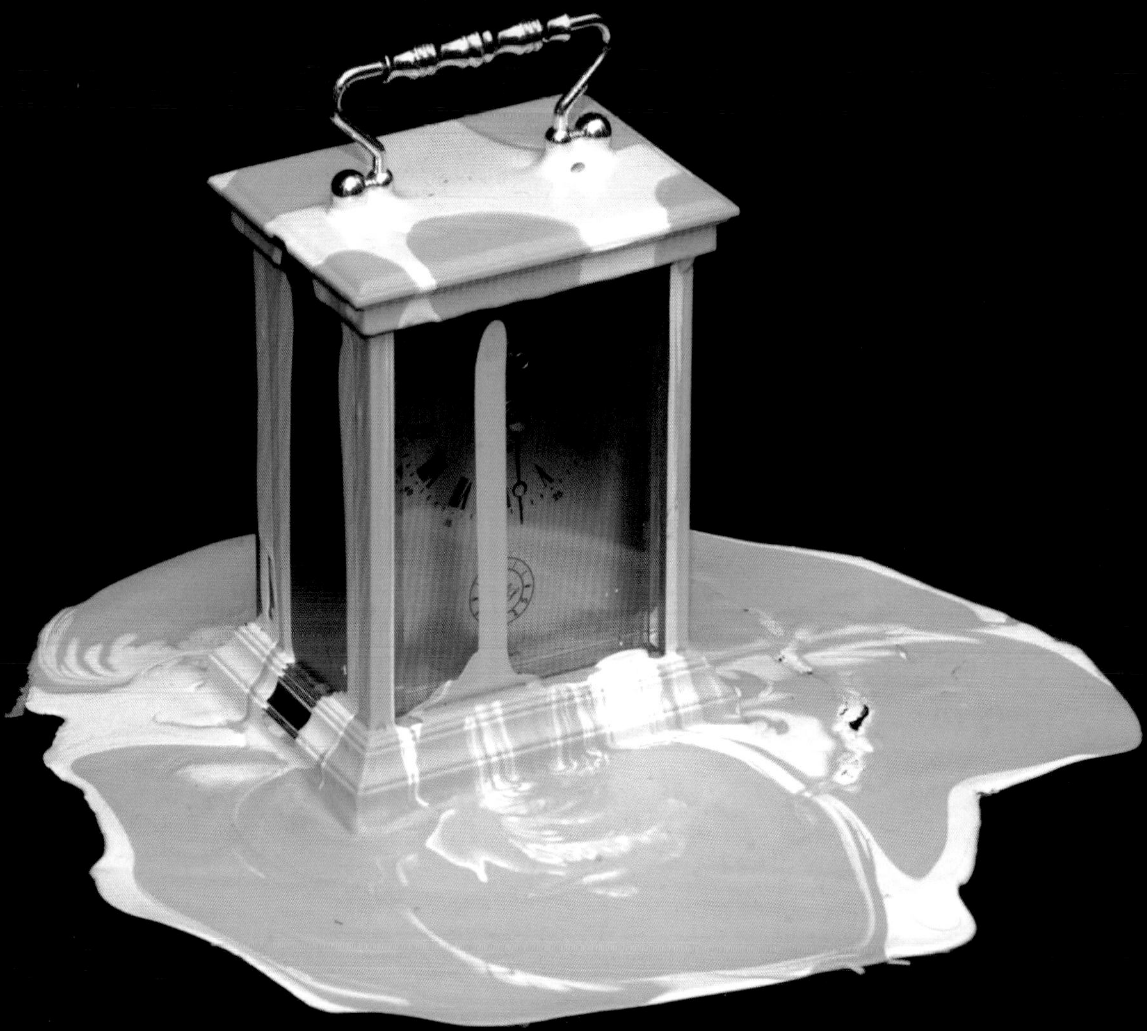

▲ Painted time? A reference to Dalí's melting clock? Here the paint helps to describe the form and distract from the function (the clock is there but the work is saying something more than the original object). Part of the attraction (or unease) is the combination of solid and liquid. Even though the paint is dry it looks wet and invites you to wonder how it was done. (Leonie Hall)

▶ The same paint technique applied to a plastic cup. The item was displayed on a wall so that the dribbles defied gravity and added to the mystery (along with the startling colours which say something fresh about the form). It's so easy that the technique soon loses its capacity to surprise — at which point you have to consider how to add a fresh dimension.

▶▶ Jeff Thomson's iconic 'gumboot', adopted symbol of the small New Zealand town of Taihape.

reconstitute

Patrick Amiot has gained a mix of fame and notoriety in Sebastopol, California, where his junk sculptures have achieved iconic status. Some love them, others don't. At their best the works have a manic, cartoon-like joy which distracts from the junk used to make them. The subjects have a cliché quality — like this surfer. The zany structural elements have forced the artist to be highly inventive. The combination, if you have a taste for it, is entertaining. Perhaps it's also philosophical — the notion that life is what you make of it, even if you're served a hand of rubbish.

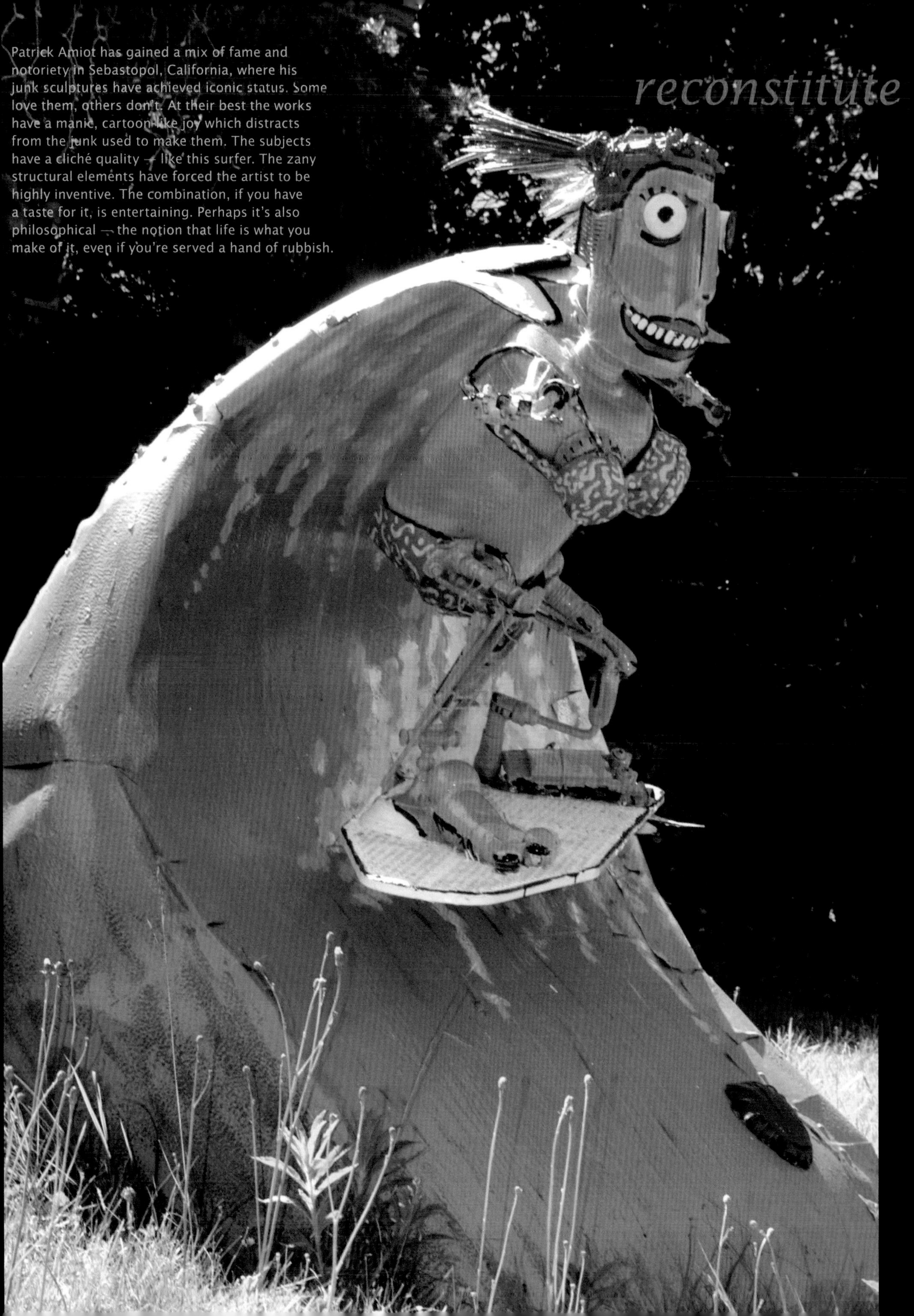

ordinariness into high art

CHAPTER 22

Junk sculpture

200 Play with junk and think about the ways in which different forms are transferable. It's a crossover with Cubism to the extent that it draws attention to the underlying nature of forms. Picasso was a master of junk and showed how to reconstitute ordinariness into high art. He was endlessly playful and offered fresh ways to see our world. The same tactic is available to anyone who takes the time to look and imagine. And it can pay. Picasso's bronze of junk, *Baboon and Young,* sold for US$6.7 million at Christie's in 2002 (see tinyurl.com/37ct4c for the image).

Getting down to the nuts and bolts of junk. The sense of fun makes the kayaker into an appealing item for the mantelpiece. In the photo he's on a glass table, which looks watery. The craftsmanship is relatively crude but could be taken further into the values of jewellery.

More junk by Patrick Amiot, featuring the VW cliché. Humour shines through and paint has been used to extend the story (and perhaps protect the art from decay — it's all headed back to rust). The biggest concentration of the sculptures is in Florence Street and one of the neighbours had a pile of unapologetic rubbish placed in her front yard and displayed under artistic lighting at night. She provided an example for all art critics — how much better the art world would be if they all made their points through their own art.

▲ The chandelier is an artefact of grandness and the bottles are at the other end of the status spectrum. Together, and with the right lighting, they make a feature in a restaurant in Tempe, Arizona.

▲ Detail of a mirror frame by Kath Cook. The junk is glued together, then spray painted to give it some visual coherence.

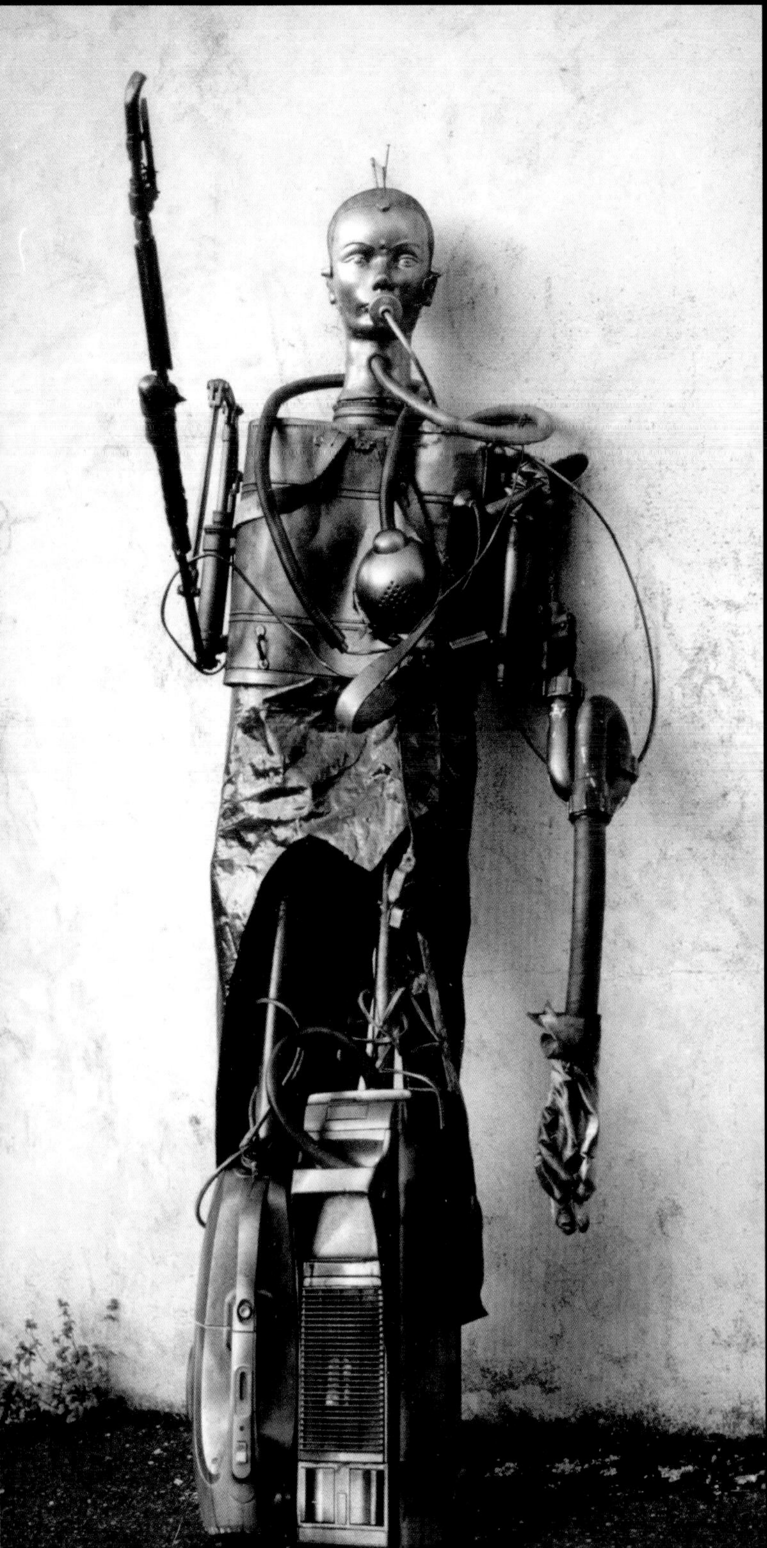

Detail of *Passage* by Dan Das Mann and Karen Cusolito on the San Francisco waterfront.

▲ Recycled timber and metal turned into a fish on the Wellington waterfront.

◄ Old car tyres transformed into art. (Artist: Amanda Kennett)

how little information

is needed to tell a story

CHAPTER 23

Sculpting water

Even the simplest water sculpture can be full of interest. The combination of thrust and gravity produces endlessly changing chaos patterns.

Water is sometimes unbelievable. You may have to freeze the motion with a camera, but isn't it surprising? Opposite is a friendly but otherwise mundane little fountain which could make a wonderful slow-motion movie. Imagine it enlarged to the size of a wall and playing so slowly that the turmoil is visible to our limited vision. Once you become aware of the behaviour of water you begin to know where to look for the most exciting action.

The ocean wearing a similar turbulence to the water in the fountain. It's a fractal pattern — something which is similar on different scales. There is order and uncertainty — the overall pattern is stable but each separate glint of sunshine is unpredictable. The waves on the right are from the wake of a boat and they add a different sort of geometry. Figure how little information is needed to tell a story. The sun, wind and boat are all invisible and yet they're present.

Are artists concerned to capture the maximum amount of information in the most economic way possible? Can a work of art be doing something equivalent to a mathematical formula? Is the photo, in its own small way, a relative of $E=mc^2$? Can the core elements of order be conveyed through art as well as through science?

Art and science have endured an unnecessary separation. They use different tools but share a lot of common ground.

Art is built around our ability to observe and to feel. We don't require numbers or formulas to experience sun on water – we can see it directly. We can even respond to a photo or painting of places and things we've never seen. Science is built around the notion of repeatable patterns and most commonly the patterns are expressed in relationships. $E=mc^2$ is a relationship – it says that matter and energy are interchangeable in a particular way. Science depends heavily on the tools of measurement, and until recently these tools weren't very good at describing wind-swept water on a sunny day. Now you can use a computer to render images of nature with an accuracy and ease that ancient artists could never have envisaged.

If we take the trouble to reconcile art and science we'll have something greater than will ever be achieved by their separation

The instruments of science have their limits. Science can attempt to describe love but it can't experience love. Art, on the other hand, can do things which intentionally trigger human feelings. That's why there is a painting rather than scientific formulas on the ceiling of the Sistine Chapel.

The artist's perception is different from scientific instruments but nevertheless we all perceive aspects of the real world. If the world is entirely connected, then each of our subjective experiences is connected with the entire universe. The connection might not immediately help us to construct a computer or a mouse-trap but it provides our intuition with some patterns to contemplate life, the universe and everything.

If we take the trouble to reconcile art and science we'll have something greater than will ever be achieved by their separation.

Here it is again (left) – this time a sheet of water falling in front of (and totally transforming) a busy street scene in Seattle. The water looks like ripped fabric letting through glimpses of vehicles,

Interactive water sculpture in Seattle. Jets of water squirt unpredictably from holes at ground level. Besides the visual connection with the city (echoing the trees and the poles) they are a challenge to anyone who dares to walk across. It can be damp but quite often people emerge dry from what seems to spectators to be a drenching. The girl in the centre below is not getting wet. It's a risk-taking game, a metaphor for creativity.

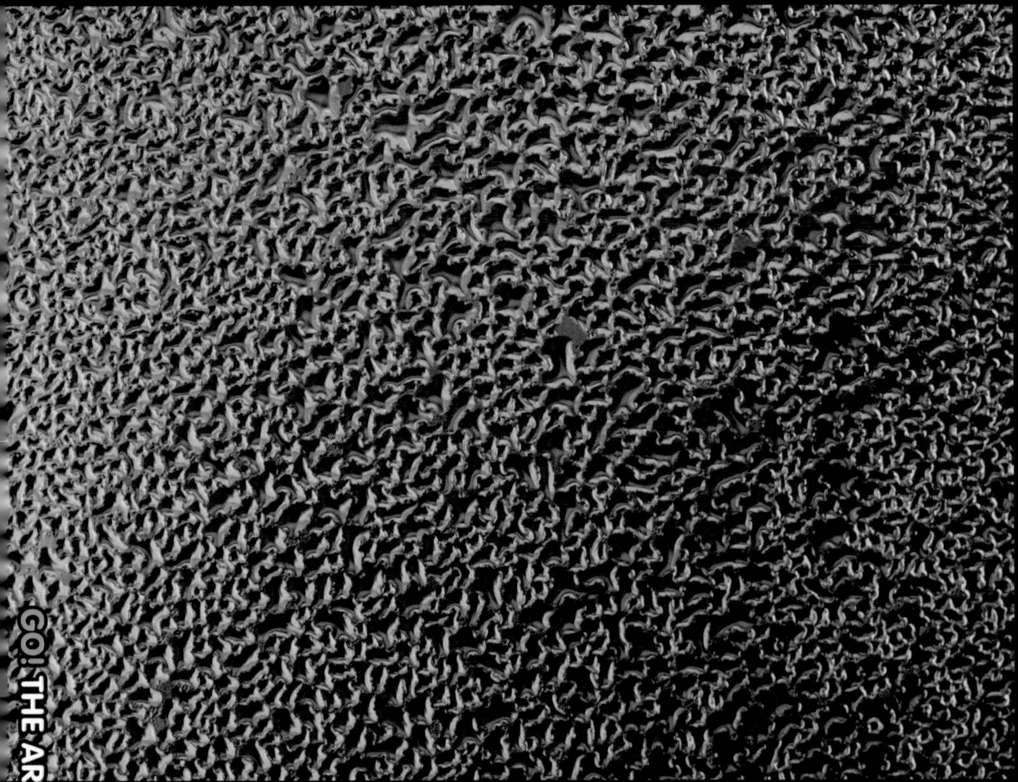

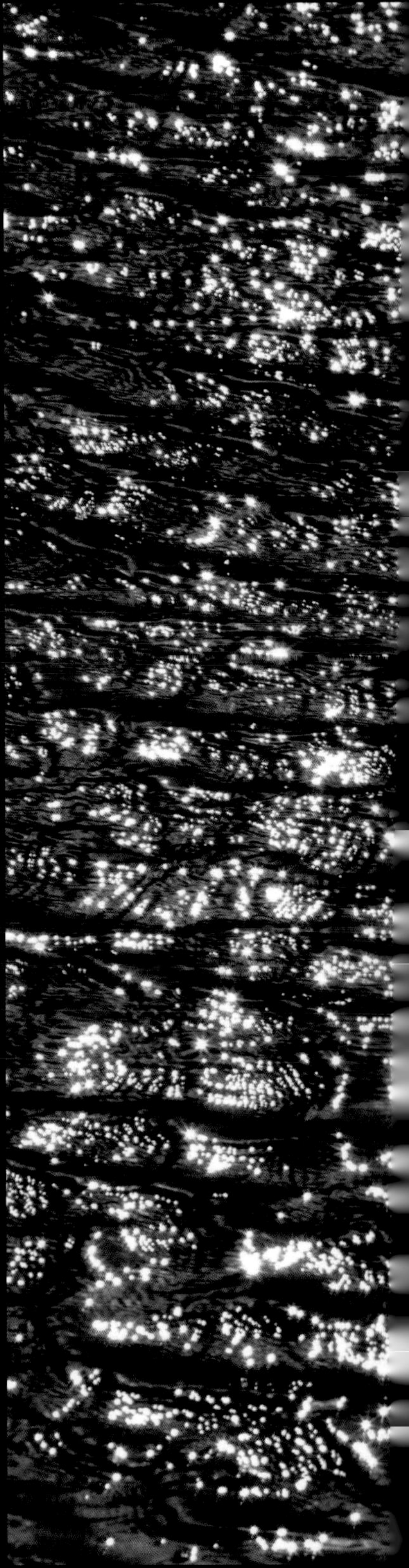

Ocean meets driftwood. A close-up of the 'Goldsworthy' from chapter 18 (page 349). The fragments of wood emhasize the explosive power of the sea, and the late afternoon sun accentuates the turmoil. At a price you could simulate it, but why not accept free admission to nature's gallery? (Photo: Alice Wilson Milne)

Water in the form of condensation on a window, Firenze.

Water in wind.

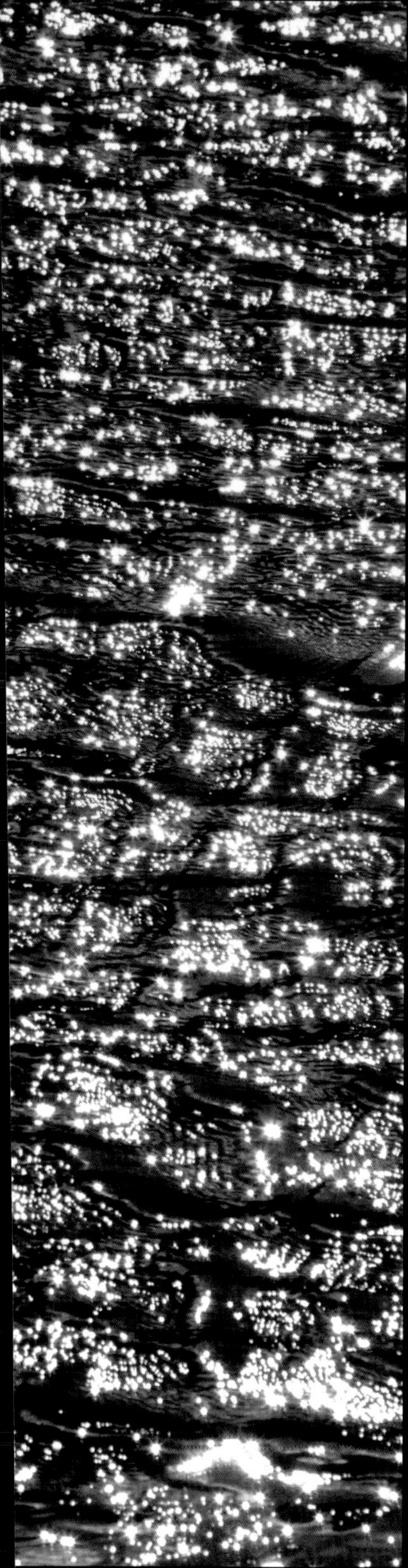

▲ Len Lye water sculpture, Wellington Harbour. The water is forced up a wriggling, slowly turning column and makes captivating patterns under the floodlights. Lye is a creativity study in his own right — one of his special gifts was to turn engineering into visual poetry (as with this example). He liked to combine simple elements and chaotic movement into a mesmerising kinetic dance. (See en.wikipedia.org/wiki/Len_Lye)

we're swimming in thoughts

buildings and people. I wonder if we have been taught to pull a veil, like the water, over our own perceptions so that we are barely aware of phenomena which are all around us and yet outside our learned range of seeing. At TLC we tried Rupert Sheldrake's experiment to test whether people can be aware that someone is staring at them. Our 840 trials showed a small margin which was 1.5% better than chance. Small but significant. My experience as a teacher is that thoughts are constantly jumping from person to person – not through words but by other means. The jumps can be as ragged as the rips in the water and they can lead to false conclusions, but I have no doubt that they are occurring all the time. It's as if we're swimming in thoughts. There are some challenging consequences. If we are sharing thoughts, should we build society around the belief that we are all separate? How can we determine intellectual property (and copyright) if thoughts are everywhere? Was it just coincidence that the Wright Brothers invented a plane at the same time as New Zealand's Richard Pearce, or was the idea 'in the air'?

Water attracts me as a medium because it's a reminder that our lives are fluid.

Water attracts me as a medium because it's a reminder that our lives are fluid. There can be shape and purpose to what we do but we are connected with the constantly changing energies of the universe. We're also transparent and our best qualities need the right light before they become visible.

201 Observe and photograph water. How can you sculpt with it?
A hose and some plastic?
Rearranging things on the edge of a river or the ocean?
The shower in your bathroom?
Using bright lights with water?
Oil on water? Bubbles? Anything that floats?
Water offers an opportunity for you to entirely rethink the nature of sculpture.

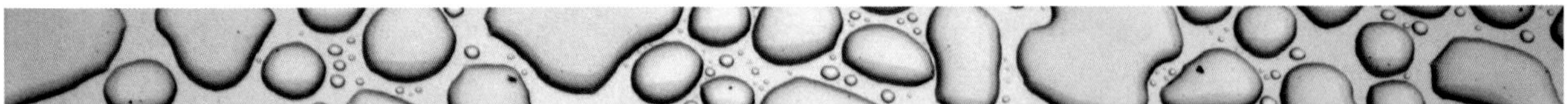

▲ ▶ Sometimes art does come down in the last shower, gently (above) or aggressively (in a downpour — right).

CHAPTER 24

Ready-made

Stacking, enmeshing, but is it art? Marcel Duchamp famously said a urinal signed "R Mutt" (a pseudonym for himself) was art because Mr Mutt chose it. As soon as you draw attention to something you've transformed it. If you're famous you might jolt much of humanity into a new way of seeing. If you're not famous you might inspire a couple of friends who in turn inspire a couple of other friends. If it spreads 30 times you may have reached more than 30,000,000 people, which suggests that a strong idea is just as effective as fame.

A strong idea is just as effective as fame

202 Notice the possibilities in familiar items. Sketch or photograph things that appeal to you and record them in your visual diary.

Think about their attributes and what might be done to place them in a different context. Duchamp's urinal on display in an art gallery demands a major conceptual shift.

Then go for it – assemble, collect, identify a series of ready-mades.

▲ Readymade assemblage of tyres and mesh.

◄ Curiously Mr Mutt is still active in Ithaca, New York. His toilet theme continues with the same sensitivity to manufactured shapes (and the subtle removal of gender bias).

▲ Columns of sunglasses in San Diego were like disembodied humanity staring back at itself. It involves stacking, repetition, variation and a complex design process taking into account the human face, the individuality of people and their circumstances. Some of them might work well to ease the glare of the sun. I recommend the yellow variety as a means of seeing the world more cheerfully.

▶ Months or years of posters created an artwork on a Santa Monica lamp post. It's the archaeology of fleeting communication. The rusting staples and the lost messages are a story of our constant efforts to be heard. Imagine all the time and collective effort to make it happen. Could you be that patient as an artist? And could you cope with the continuing disappearance of your ideas? Can you make your own work of art with an intentional and lengthy time dimension?

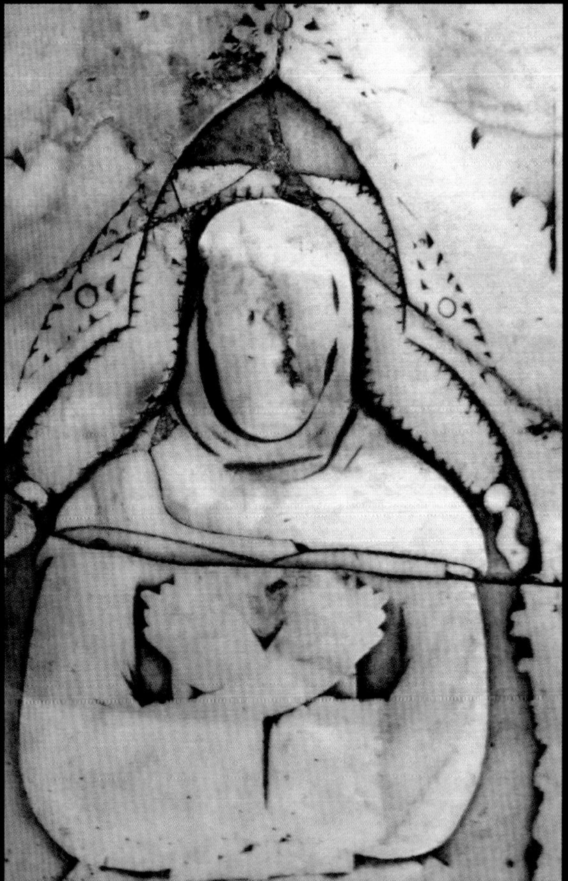

▲ Groucho Marx said that time wounds all heels. It wounds art too. This sculpture, hidden in a gloomy recess in the Duomo in Firenze, spent time within graffiti range and has turned into something different as a result of the weathering of vandals. If you can suspend judgment about graffiti it's worth thinking what the marks do, not only to the sculpture as a thing but also to the notion of art which is frozen in time.

▲ Telephone on a tree. The phone itself is a work of art, and in combination with a tree ('bush telegraph') it makes a sculptural pun.

▶ Marble figure on the floor of Santa Croce, Firenze, worn down by centuries of human feet.

▲An exploded balloon, Emeryville. Rubber transformed into the shape of a zany fish. So dynamic and accidentally meaningful. Can you find other 'accidents' that have sculptural qualities?

▲ A bag of rubbish with tension, form and mystery. That surface might seem boring but it provides an infinite number of reflective facets to bounce light to your eyes. Who needs computer games when we've got bags of trash to enthral us? And when we try to figure what is under the wrapping we're playing a sculptural game.

▲Different trolley and an alternative view of interesting decay. The rigid, industrial steel interacts with tide. I'm collecting images of trolley ready-mades — maybe I'll get a photo exhibition out of them.

▲Another study in entropy, this time contrasting an abandoned commercial symbol (the shopping cart) with the grass and weeds which are thriving in its presence (compare the drier, more stunted neighbours on the right).

▲ Be our guest, the entropy of a cheap motel in Seattle. You could do it as an installation but why not declare the real thing to be an artwork?

▲ An elaborate driftwood sculpture on the California coast. Not exactly a ready-made except for the materials. The delicate cross at the entrance acts like a glass barrier — you can't get through without wrecking it. How often do you find that people build structures when there is plenty of driftwood to play with?

▲ Boarded windows during a renovation. The light draws attention to the surfaces and the form. We lived with these boards for weeks and I almost miss the subtle tricks that were played by the sun.

Bring on the artist. The strong, iconic form of a fire hydrant suggests fresh themes for R. Mutt.

▲ Copies of Michelangelo's *David* as a ready-made, Firenze.

◄ Leaves on steps, another natural 'Goldsworthy', Firenze.

you bring your own wor
art and have a conve

CHAPTER 25

Conceptual

Roger Key's rubber gloves and pink rug (opposite) could allude to Barbie Dolls screaming to escape from the kitsch (or the kitchen). Or they could be a forest of big coral, reaching their polyps towards food. You can look at it as a collection of shapes and textures or you can add meaning. I find the bloated palms a little ominous – like dead hands expanding as they decay. But the pink and the fur are also friendly. Unlike art which delivers a clear message, Key is inviting participation. You bring your own world to his art and have a conversation.

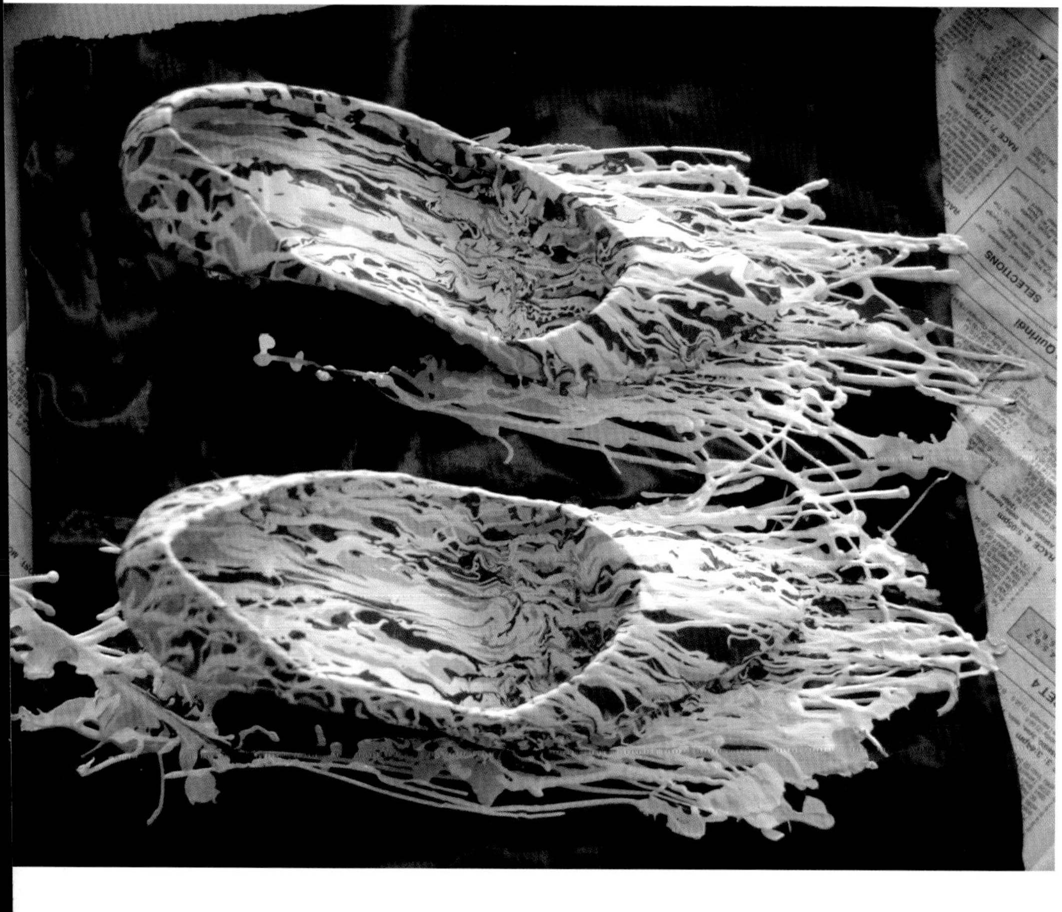

Katherine Ivory, work in progress. Are the ends of the shoes filled with paint? Is it all paint (and the shoes are ghosts)? Is it what happens when a painter implodes? Is there any point in turning a shoe statement into a paint statement? Would anyone want to buy dry paint dribbles? I find myself drawn to mysterious statements and I've bought a number of Katherine's works. Having a bunch of academic explanations might help me to place them in the context of history but it wouldn't change my fondness for them.

▵ Simon Perry's *The Public Purse* is also a public seat in Melbourne. Except for the rain it's as generous as a sculpture can be in inviting us to join it. The cutesy purse has turned into stone and steel and taken on a new sense of purpose which might appeal to art sceptics.

> Cones of paper, pink on the inside, glowing like flowers in the sun. The scale (this is a detail — the whole work was about 2.5 metres square) and the effect of light on the cones was so attractive that bees might have enjoyed the show. The moving light of the sun provided the same ephemeral beauty of a garden as it changes during the day. (Natalie Keegan)

> Maybe it isn't entirely conceptual to show a heart that looks like a heart. It's the metallic finish that makes the difference. Cold-hearted. Hard-hearted. The shiny, detached quality could belong to a photoshopped ice-queen selling the latest trendy sports car. (Sculpture by Stephanie Chung)

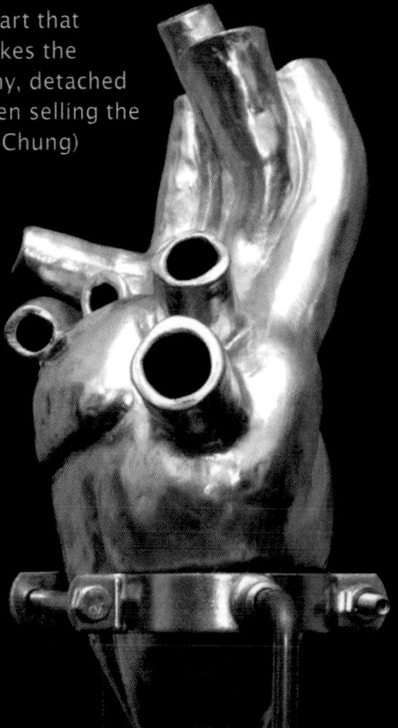

◂ Alice and a heart in San Francisco. The city provided the heart forms to a range of artists and celebrities who set to work with their personal take on the concept. The hearts were eventually auctioned in November 2004. Similar events have achieved success in many different places. Chicago did it with cows (which originated in Switzerland) and Los Angeles does it with angels. It's street art — out of the gallery and into the world. Improvisation sometimes stimulates powerful creativity but regardless of quality the streets are eventually cleared for fresh ideas. It's somehow reassuring that sculpture can move around.

▾ *Invisible City* by Anton Parsons, Lambton Quay, Wellington. The big Braille letters and steel slabs morph into high-rise buildings. For the sighted, the work is a link to the world of those who primarily hear and feel. The background clutter is the way cities are. The shrieking red advertisements offer flights to everywhere while the sculpture offers the world of imagination at no cost.

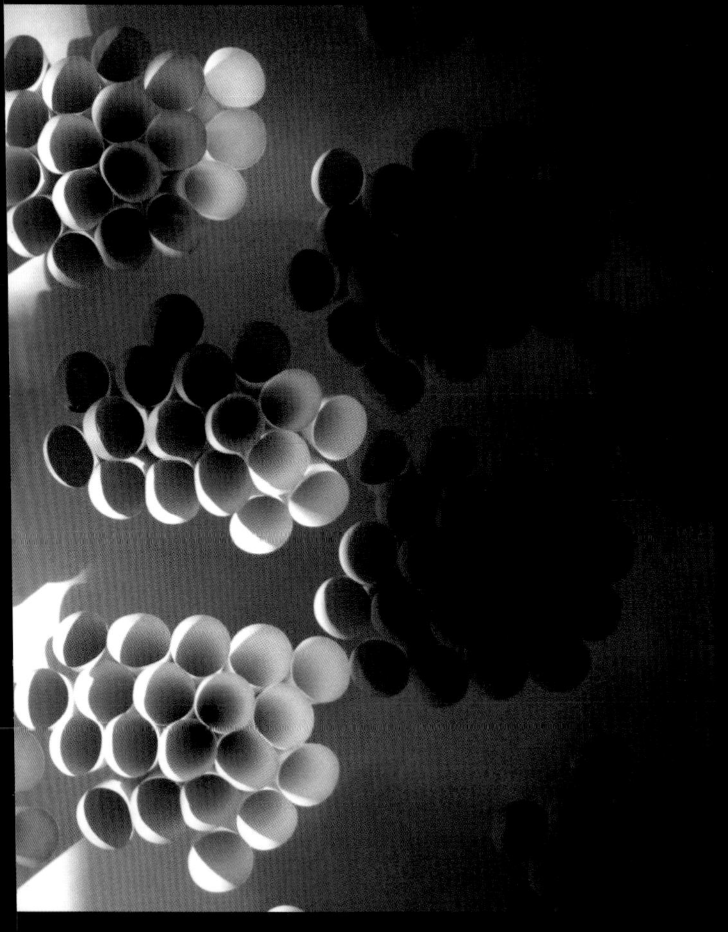

▶ When I was quite small one of the privileges of life was being allowed to iron handkerchiefs. Kids have different understandings of privilege but this iron covered with melted gunk is still disturbing. The streamlined shape is an example of beauty emerging from function (or in this case, dysfunction). (Rebekah Bell)

▶▶ Reconstituted white china leaves you to think about the label. Does it say 'White Lace'? And has it become lacier as a result of being smashed? Do the pieces join together? Is it a story about chips with everything? Can you view it like an arrangement of stones on a beach, free from human associations? (Amanda Kennett)

▼ Neil Dawson's fern sphere in Civic Square, Wellington, takes on the persona of a visiting planet at night. It's a work for which location and scale are everything. It is suspended over a busy part of the city and magnificently framed by the sky. Dawson's floating forms have graced many cities and despite their hard metal origin they somehow humanise public spaces.

▲ Natalie Keegan's dipped toys are both funny and sinister. They hang like executed symbols of innocence, while expressing outrageous mischief. They are revolting and fascinating. They also sold.

◥ Toilet rolls and paint. Playful and funny. Would you install it at home? Perhaps. The paper will discolour but it wouldn't be a big deal to periodically recycle the rolls and bring in new ones. (Kim Thompson)

▶ Why do rusty nails and white gloves look creepy? (Sue van Dalen)

How do you respond to 650 tons of steel, 5 cm thick, 257 metres long, 6 metres high and 9 metres submerged under Gibbs' Farm at Kaukapakapa? There it is in the photo. It's a work by Richard Serra and is regarded by some as the most important piece of art in New Zealand.

The first thing about the photo is that it only marginally makes sense. In real life you can get up close and personal and see something like this:

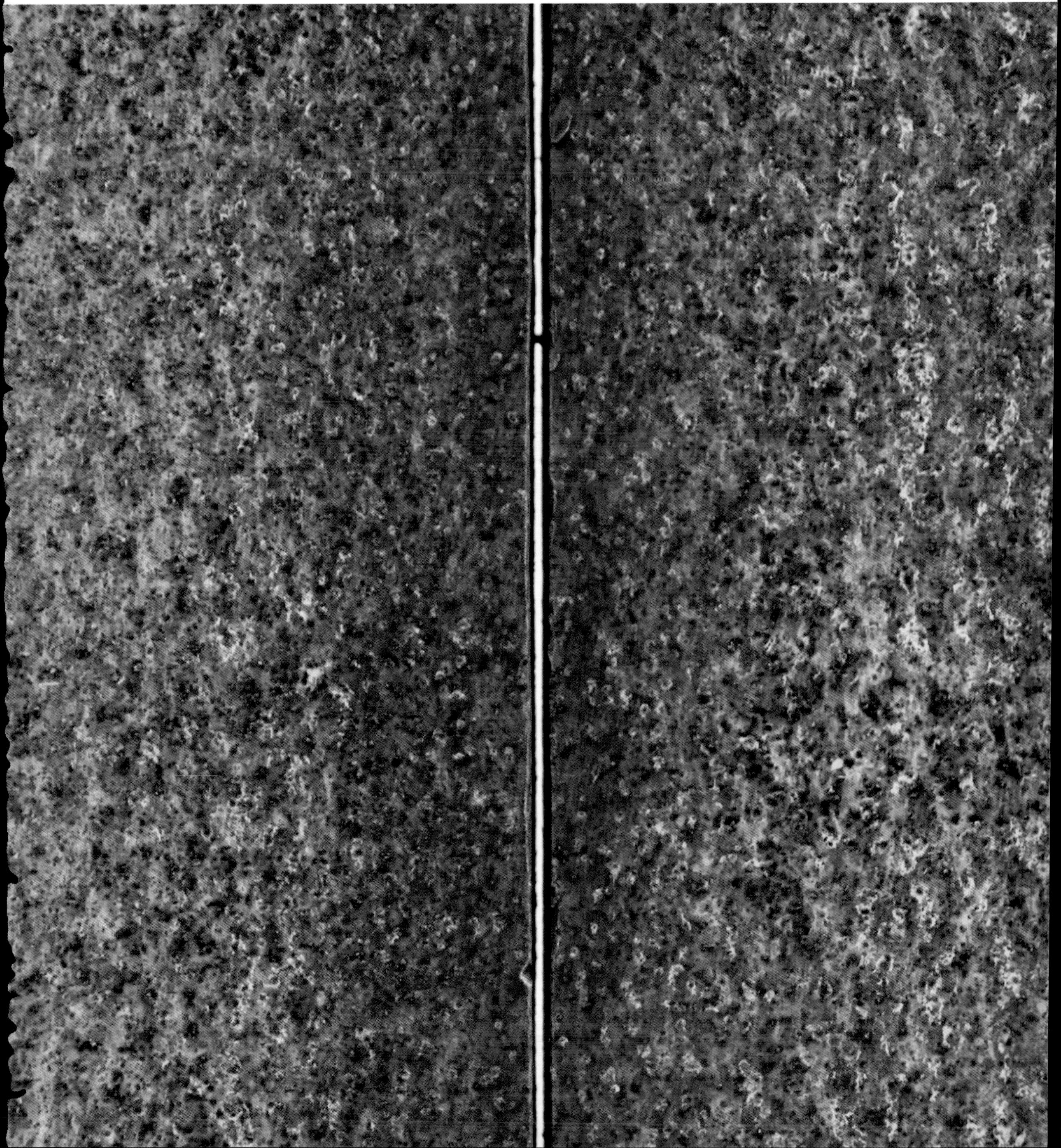

There's the gritty feeling of rusting steel and the uncanny precision of craftsmanship in the gap between the massive plates.

You can look at it end-on. That's me on the left and TLC stage 3 student Mal Edmonds on the right. I like the way Mal is navigating the mud. I also like the lanoline smudge-zone made by the sheep as they rub against the sculpture (these are details that don't usually happen in a gallery).

Or you can contemplate the scale from the middle distance (below).

There's something grand about this thing called *Tuhirangi Contour*. You can experience it from many different perspectives but there's no single view or experience that contains the work. It challenges the idea that beauty is in the eye of the beholder because its size is bigger than we can behold. And that's weird because the thing is so simple and yet infinitely variable.

It's highly technical (how did they install it and achieve such precision with the angles and seeming nonchalant

shape) while it's also sympathetic to the rolling hills and the lazy wiggles of west coast streams. I enjoyed it more than Michelangelo's *David* but it's hard to explain why. Partly it's because you can get so involved, whereas *David* (the original) is high on a pedestal and very untouchable. It's different to be with art that is so 'alive' that it is slowly being eaten by nature. I guess that's really happening to all art (and to ourselves) but in *Contour* the rust has a more obvious presence.

And the angles. The steel leans in ways that buildings generally don't. It has power and presence. It's Maximalist rather than Minimalist, as endlessly rich as nature itself.

Serra described his approach to sculpture in a PBS interview:

> When I first started, what was very, very important to me was dealing with the nature of process. So what I had done is I'd written a verb list: to roll, to fold, to cut, to dangle, to twist ... and I really just worked out pieces in relation to the verb list physically in a space. Now, what happens when you do that is you don't become involved with the psychology of what you're making, nor do you become involved with the after image of what it's going to look like. So, basically it gives you a way of proceeding with material in relation to body movement, in relation to making, that divorces from any notion of metaphor, any notion of easy imagery.
>
> As the work becomes more extensive and I had a need to walk into and through and around it, then you get involved with what effect the work has physically on your body as you walk. So, time and movement became really crucial to how I deal with what I deal with, not only sight and boundary, but how one walks through a piece and what one feels and registers in terms of one's own body in relation to another body. So, in that sense, as the pieces became bigger and you walked into and through and around them, they took on other concerns which were more psychological, even though implied and not specific in the early work, where process was the key to organizing the principle of how one would structure something.
>
> *(available at www.pbs.org/art21/artists/serra/clip1.html)*

This sounds as if it could be part of our TLC manifesto. It challenges us to think less about reading art and more about experiencing it.

203 The goal is to create something that commands attention and has something to say.

Go back to the action words to try some conceptual art. Choose any word or combination of words and get started. For example, you might decide to squash something – or enmesh or suspend ... or whatever action you choose.

Then contemplate. What further actions could you take? How can you move from action to meaning?

Ceramic sculpture by Gloria Young.

A performance piece directed by Katharine White (the model is Marlene Wallace). The underlying theme was genetic engineering and the action was like a gothic psychodrama. There's a frenzy of foam, flesh and symbolic blood. Next to the bath was a pile of commercial detritus and dead things which can be read as part of the bigger narrative.

▸ Zhan Wang, artificial rock, stainless steel, De Young Museum, San Francisco. The reflections change chaotically as you move from one view to another and the 'rock' almost disappears. You're left with an erie tension between solidity and illusion.

▸▸ A detail of the rock, giving a close-up view of its strange behaviour.

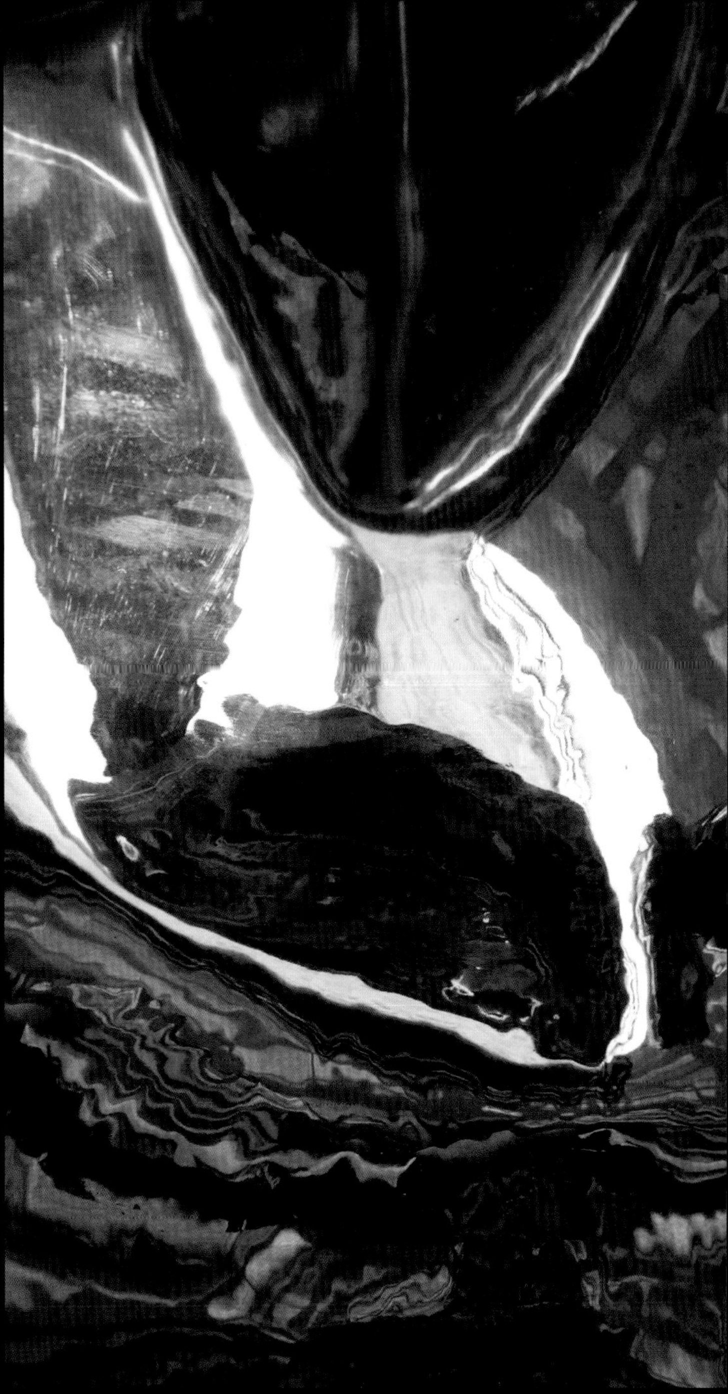

Part 5

beyond the 3rd dimension

QUAY GIFTS

Creativity and work

How might the experiences of creativity in art translate into creative work?

Work is partly about the processes of survival and even at this level it is creative. The invention of tools for farming, for example, enables humans to deal with the basics more effectively and thus generate spare time. We can use spare time to create weird things like art and books, which may be useless in terms of food and shelter, but which may be crucial to what we perceive as 'civilisation'. Or maybe our civilised pursuits are just a way of filling in time which other creatures (like lions) would use for sleeping. My assumption is that humans have found that the 'uselessness' of play complements the necessities. Thus a society which is good at play will probably have better plumbing.

A society which is good at play will probably have better plumbing

We live in a world in which deliberate creativity is an option. There is scope for art, poetry, tennis and football. Maybe there is also scope in 'necessary' jobs to incorporate more fun and to connect with a deeper sense of purpose.

Our immediate concern is with people who want to focus on art, and other creative activities which are unlikely to generate an immediate cash flow. Governments sometimes create opportunities via benefits or loans which enable people to step outside the regular work systems to do things which are generally important but non-urgent. Education is one such thing.

If you prefer to be independent of the government there are other ways to build resources. You can get the idea by walking through a supermarket and figuring which items are necessities and which are luxuries. The personal cost of the luxuries can be high. For example, the cost of ten cigarettes per day can add up to half a million dollars if the money was sensibly invested over 40 years. You might save the same (or more) by eating less often at restaurants, using public transport, disregarding fashion, and so on. It's the saving which gives you the opportunity to take some creative risks.

I realised things were difficult when I went to the rubbish bin in the kitchen to retrieve a stump of stale bread

My own starting point was not promising. I realised things were difficult when I went to the rubbish bin in the kitchen to retrieve a stump of stale bread – because it was the only food left in the house. I had a wife and baby and we survived by selling our car and buying a cheaper model.

Things were made harder (and easier) by the fact that I vowed never to work for a boss again. I thought that employment inevitably meant a sort of slave relationship in which creativity was impossible. Poverty seemed a better option.

The good thing about this attitude was that I had to think for myself. The tough part was to find a way to get some income for my thoughts.

I believed that business was about doing something I enjoyed and getting other people to pay for it. Thus an artist might have fun painting a picture and the buyer has fun enjoying it. Real life is a little more complex but the basic recipe worked so well that I eventually became a boss myself. Fairly quickly I was confronted by the fact that creativity is collective and it was my responsibility to foster a creative workplace.

At last count our school had nearly a hundred staff and a wage bill running into millions of dollars. Things have come a long way since I rescued the stump of stale bread. Yet the principles are the same – each person on the staff is seeking to do something they enjoy and it has to be relevant to others. My own role is to help connect needs with enjoyment. I encourage staff to think for themselves so that we're constantly reinventing the school. I also enjoy being an explorer, travelling around the world looking for new opportunities.

We've shifted away from the dominance model of employment. We operate as a non-profit organisation, even though we're constituted as a company. The collective views of staff shape what we can and can't do. Staff initiatives directly create our income. We can earn as much as we like if we can find the people who want to work with us.

Karl Marx (1818–1883).

If it sounds like paradise, it is and it isn't. Ultimately work is a state of mind and the structure of the workplace is only one factor. We'll never keep everyone happy all the time because that's not our business. The best we can do is to foster positive work relationships, respond to human needs and focus on work which is worth doing. And that is very different from companies in which directors and shareholders milk profits at the expense of employees and the wider community.

I still pay attention to the Marxist view which placed 'capitalists' and 'workers' on either side of an impossible divide. TLC offers a non-Marxist solution to the same problems of alienation which concerned Marx. In our own small, peaceful way we've brought work, community and money back into equilibrium. We're trying to shape something which is sustainable at all levels – providing excitement,

work is a state of mind

satisfaction and income while connecting to the needs of families, communities and the planet we call home.

The search for the right job may turn out to be an inner revolution. It's about the discovery of what really matters to you – and the willingness to abandon preconceptions. The creation of good work is a bigger process and we're favoured by being based in New Zealand in a social and political climate which is unusually open and positive.

One of the surprises (for me) is that most people have only a vague sense of the bigger picture. It takes time and experience to discover that personal creativity and collective creativity are intimately connected. Our whole organisation has had to learn how to do things a little differently, to be more patient, more assertive and more attentive to what's happening outside our own little world. It can be tough with passive people who expect others to solve their problems and make them happy

The best way to arrive at the big picture is to begin with the small picture. How can you personally achieve harmony between creativity, work, and the need to earn a living?

Work has a lot of negative connotations. Mark Twain said that something is work if you'd rather be somewhere else. At worst it is a means of paying the bills so that you can stagger through to retirement and die.

Samuel Langhorne Clemens, a.k.a. Mark Twain (1835-1910).

Large companies often require workers as a sort of human engine to move things around and make money for owners. Maybe the only reason people can survive this sort of work is that the companionship of others reduces the pain and may even infuse some joy.

From time to time I invite people to tell me about 'jobs from hell'. One student said that she was employed to suck the innards out of slaughtered chooks. That was the entire job. The only reason it existed was that the management hadn't been able to figure out how to do it economically with a machine (there was a sucking device but it needed a person to operate it).

That single job illustrates the problem of work in an industrialised society. If you don't go out and catch your own dinner there will be people who have to do it for you. All the dirty work becomes a 'job' and in some ways the goriness of the slaughterhouse is a symbol for a lot of less ugly but equally mindless tasks.

Imagine washing dishes until you die. Or moving things around in a warehouse. Or repairing mufflers. Or recording details of credit card transactions. Or being a check-out operator. Or painting the same white bridge all the way to eternity.

The search for the right job may turn out to be an inner revolution

The miracle is that people sometimes thrive in these situations, but for anyone with an urge to creativity the chances are grim.

So where did work come from? Over the page is a picture from my family album showing men clearing the land in 1899. For these guys, work meant timber for dwellings, grazing for animals and then food on the table. It was hideously hard.

1899 — colonists clearing land in Taranaki. John Milne is the one with the suit and the watch chain on the left (photos required serious dressing up!).

The winters were so harsh that it was typical for men to sleep with their dogs to stay warm. A 'three dog night' was as cold as it could get. My grandfather caught hydatids from his dogs – cysts which grew on the lungs and were nearly on a par with lung cancer.

Despite the hardship, the work had meaning – even if it was simply the basic connection with survival. As far as I know the family was remarkably resilient and many lived into their 90s at a time when the average life expectancy was 45. Even Len, the man with hydatids, survived into his 70s.

The picture on the opposite page, taken in 1888, shows the large workroom at Hallensteins clothing factory in Dunedin, New Zealand. The work done by these women was exchanged for money and the products were sold to other people. Here is alienation the way industrialisation shaped it – and it is still a prevalent pattern in the workplace today even though the raw edges may have been mellowed a little. Alienation doesn't mean that conditions are bad and people get no enjoyment – it means that the products are entirely or primarily being made for other people and the main purpose for the workers is to earn wages.

At the other extreme there are people who are exhilarated by work. My ancestors who felled the bush and tried to carve out an existence in a foreign land had endless adventures to share over a pint of ale (or a cup of tea if they were in the Temperance Union). They were taking big risks every day and there was a sense that each person was contributing to the family and the community. Maybe their situation – bleak as it was – contained many of the essentials of meaningful work:

- Each person can make a difference.
- The results of the work connect with everyday life.
- Risk-taking is an essential ingredient.
- Money is mainly a by-product rather than an end in itself.
- There is a strong sense of family and community.
- There's a psychological foundation through values/beliefs.

We can achieve much the same things in our lives today – minus some of the nastier risks.

- There is vast scope for creative people to sell their skills in a meaningful way.
- Risk-taking goes with the creative adventure. You can (mostly) choose your own risks and your creative life evolves from the way you respond to each new challenge.
- Through creativity you become yourself.
- The built-in satisfaction of creative work reduces (or removes) any preoccupation with money as an end in itself.
- The act of creation somehow engages us with a sense of deeper purpose – it's as if creativity and spirituality are part of the same picture.

Many highly creative people have an awkward relationship with work because they have an aversion to financial management. The New Zealand Arts Marketing Board says that this is one of the most sensitive areas they deal with in their seminars.

There's a lurking belief that 'work' (as in 'paid employment') may corrupt your art. The challenge is to keep the joy and also to get the advantages of money. Poverty is not an aid to creativity. On the other hand, if the need for money kills the joy, what have you gained? The notion of work as the opposite of play seems

After more than 20 years as a pro I still do my best work for the joy of it, whether or not I'm getting paid. —*Galen Rowell (Inner Game of Outdoor Photography and other books)*

The large workroom in Hallensteins' clothing factory in Dunedin 1888.

strange to me. Looking back over the experiences I have enjoyed most there is a common theme that work and play are integrated.

For each of us the task is to get work that fits our passion. This doesn't mean that it will be idyllic or completely free of boredom, hard slog, frustration and conflict. Far from it.

Does it matter if aspects of work are tedious? Think of kids at play. Sometimes they're able to deal with boring processes for long periods because they have a clear sense of purpose. I remember constructing tracks for bike racing and we'd work for hours clearing vegetation and digging the track. It was exciting. Prisoners on chain gangs doing similar work don't have much fun because they're separated from the purpose of their labour.

If your work connects with your life purpose it's going to be easier, no matter how tough things get. Purpose generates resilience. The same dynamics apply to learning. If you're purposeful and motivated, chances are you'll do well.

If your work connects with your life purpose it's going to be easier, no matter how tough things get

Anita Roddick (The Body Shop) takes a panoramic view of purpose. She says that people "want to work for a company that enhances the human spirit, creates friends and gives [them] a sense of being alive." Many companies have taken a narrower view but the pattern may be changing. Here's what Roddick sees as the new need:

> There's a better way of doing it, that ennobles the spirit, where a company can be run in a very moral way, make money, but enhance the spirituality of the workplace. Bringing spirituality into the workplace is very much saying, "Why should my workplace be any different from my home or how I interact with my family and friends?" How we do it in this company is by running it on feminine principles in which the major ethic is care.

Not that it stopped her from selling her shares.

The secret of finding the right work

It's like speed dating. Tom Peters uses the expression 'small starts'. That's it. Work small, succeed or fail and then take the next step. 'Failure' isn't a dead end, it's information. It's all to do with the creative spiral.

'Small starts' follow the pattern of nature. You don't see a giant tree emerge in a 'think big' puff of smoke. It starts with millions of seeds, most of which don't get far.

Work is different from a tree – you can have a job chopped from under you but your career may be undamaged because experience is cumulative and the failures aren't necessarily bad news.

TLC's orientation week follows the same principle. Everyone is invited to take a single step towards their creative goal. A small start. If the small start doesn't work, try another one. If it does work, build on it. TLC itself has grown into a multi-million dollar business and we're still doing small starts. We invite everyone who works with us to contribute small ideas which – if they seem to have any potential – we test. We intend to keep our creativity alive no matter how big we get – and that means we always have to think small *and* big.

There's nothing mysterious about business success. Here's a sample from one of our business development sessions with our whole staff:

TLC is based on attraction. Each student who enrols is somehow attracted to the school. Our salaries reflect our ability to stay attractive or, better still, to grow more attractive.

One of the by-products of the small changes is that they make life more fun for everyone. Energy flows more smoothly and people have a better chance to achieve creative results which in turn make everyone feel good and the flow continues to improve.

The first step in attraction is to help people be aware of who we are. The second step is to deliver the goods.

Sometimes a great idea arrives and causes a sudden, dramatic change. More often, a series of small ideas accumulate and when they reach what Malcolm Gladwell has called the 'tipping point' you achieve the same quantum of change.

We're looking for both the big ideas and the small, incremental changes. In lots of ways the small changes are easier because everyone can be involved. The power of small changes is potentially huge.

The business world is full of terms like 'competitiveness', 'strategic advantage' and so on. I think it's more useful to focus on 'attractiveness'. If we succeed in this the rest will take care of itself.

George Bernard Shaw (1856-1950).

Helen Keller (1880-1968).

Chuck Jones (1912-2002).

John W Gardner (1912-2002).

Work wisdom

People have to switch their psychology from figuring out the 15 ways why something can't work to 15 ways we can *make* it work. —*James Collins*

When I was young I observed that nine out of ten things I did were failures, so I did ten times more work. —*George Bernard Shaw*

Courage is not about eliminating risks. Courage is about going through the risk or going through the pain or going through the embarrassment or going through the unknown, and that's the stuff of heroes. —*Larry Wilson*

I long to accomplish great and noble tasks, but it is my chief duty to accomplish humble tasks as though they were great and noble. The world is moved along, not only by the mighty shoves of its heroes, but also by the aggregate of the tiny pushes of each honest worker. —*Helen Keller*

Anxiety is the handmaiden of creativity. —*Chuck Jones, animator (of Wile E Coyote fame)*

You put your pencil down here and now you've got the guts [to draw]. I know what I can do … At that moment you're one with the gods, because you realise that you have the tools, you're capable of doing it. There's no anxiety now. There was anxiety before. Anxiety is the springboard that leads to your ability to join up with the gods that can draw. —*Chuck Jones*

The society which scorns excellence in plumbing because plumbing is a humble activity, and tolerates shoddiness in philosophy because philosophy is an exalted activity, will have neither good plumbing nor good philosophy. Neither its pipes nor its theories will hold water. —*John W Gardner*

On my first day at school I was told I had to print the alphabet neatly in my work book. I drew a big chicken laying an egg. I got told off. It's funny 'cos I don't have many early memories but this one I can recall like it was only yesterday. —*Nikki Pickworth*

If you want to encourage creativity in the workplace you have to encourage people to take risks, that's what it's all about. You want to have a climate in the company where people feel comfortable. They're willing to throw out crazy ideas and nobody laughs, or everybody laughs, but so what, you just shrug it off. —*Yvon Chouinard, founder, Patagonia*

I believe you are your work. Don't trade the stuff of your life, time, for nothing more than dollars. That's a rotten bargain. —*Rita Mae Brown*

I am somehow less interested in the weight and convolutions of Einstein's brain than in the near certainty that people of equal talent have lived and died in cotton fields and sweatshops. —*Stephen J Gould*

Catch a man a fish, and you can sell it to him. Teach a man to fish, and you ruin a wonderful business opportunity. —*Karl Marx*

Don't trade the stuff of your life, time, for nothing more than dollars. That's a rotten bargain

A guide to shaping your creative career

1. What work would you choose if you had unlimited resources?
2. What are your core beliefs about work?
3. How would you *like* work to be?
4. How can you generate 'small starts' which are going to help your work prospects? Some examples:
   - Gain experience in fronting up to people and pushing the boundaries of your comfort zone.
   - Find a creative workplace and offer to work there for free.
   - Visit factories and suss them out for free materials. There are all sorts of ways in which you can get good resources without having any money.
   - Keep your eyes open for possible studio space. If you find something you like, find out who to ask and approach them.
   - Think of small-scale experiments which might enable you to make money from your creativity. For example, if you like the idea of designing greeting cards, try a few mock-ups and show them to your friends. If they respond warmly you might be on to something.

   What can you add to the list? Make it as big as possible – and test the ideas in action!
5. Think of your present abilities and make a list of ways you could earn money from them. Cut loose! Put the practicalities to one side and concentrate on possibilities.
6. What options do you have to raise money for your dreams? Small things count – $20 a week is more than $1000 for the year.
7. Identify obstacles to achieving your work goals. How can you overcome the obstacles?
8. Imagine writing your own obituary. What would you like to say about your work achievement? Maybe this is the ultimate in whole-life planning!
9. Check out the 'Help Yourself' section of the library (and explore the internet). There is an abundance of ideas but only you will be able to decide what to do in your particular circumstance.

Student feedback on 'work'

Always stand up for what you believe in. Don't sit on the fence or turn a blind eye because it will haunt you. Change things that can be changed to make a positive difference.

For me, job satisfaction is the ultimate. Work that includes my home and family life. When you wake in the morning you want to be there.

I haven't latched onto my ideal job yet. Freedom is important, enjoying life. My dad has his own business dealing in Aboriginal art. He goes for trips up to the Northern Territory and interacts with the artists of a remote community, photographs and writes about their lives and the stories behind their paintings. He is doing what he loves ...

A Wainuiomata man brought meaning into his life after being made redundant. Once or twice a week he cycled up and down the Wainui Hill clearing rubbish from the side of the road into plastic bags which the council then collected on their way over the hill.

I was on a night shift, packing and grading mussels. The most creative part was devising ways to get out of going to work. The whole time I kept telling myself "I have to get an education."

I come from a family who started with nothing. No money, no education. But they believed in themselves and each other. Each child in the family received support for what they were passionate about. They were not afraid of hard work or poverty and they followed their passion. Everyone in the family has pretty much shaped the life they chose – it works!

Why settle for a ten to twenty year wait for success – every moment is a success...

Make your life a work of art

▸ Zoe Crickett.

Creativity and community

In *Making Democracy Work* Robert Putnam argues that *social capital* is the key to successful communities. He says that financial success follows from social capital – not the other way around. Creativity is a key to social capital and therefore it is a good indicator of community well-being.

Our class agreement is the foundation of TLC's approach to creativity. All the items in the agreement are important, but in the context of community this one is the biggest:

> Work with commitment and trust, even where things don't make sense or feel uncomfortable. Be aware that frustration always plays a part in good learning.

Frustration always plays a part in good learning

Trust is a two-way process. To some extent we learn it from the trusting behaviour of others. If for any reason you were unable to trust members of your family (who are usually your first teachers) then it can be harder to develop trust of others and trust in yourself.

Self-trust requires that we pay attention to our hunches and learn how to connect with the information that comes through our senses. *Dis*trust on the other hand is like putting on a suit of armour – it may protect us but it also traps us.

So the nature of trust – and creativity too – leaves us with the dilemma of how to be vulnerable and reasonably safe at the same time.

Part of the answer is to build networks of trust which start small and grow larger. Each trusting transaction increases the network and each act of betrayal diminishes it. Once you get into a pattern of trust with people it is possible to take it further and further. The rewards of trust get bigger but the likelihood of betrayal remains similar to what it was at the beginning. Thus if a group navigates the early stage and keeps its integrity, there is a high chance that trust will be maintained no matter how big the temptations.

build networks of trust which start small and grow larger

◄ Armour can be attractive and distancing. It can be viewed as a metaphor for societies in which the protective barriers are high. It limits ordinary interaction although it enables the wearer to do battle more safely. Is today's business suit symbolic armour? (England's Mark Jenner is the man on the horse at a jousting tournament at Harcourt Park, Upper Hutt, New Zealand.)

Here's how nations get rich. It could be a choir or a bridge club or any voluntary group that gets together in a way that requires trust. Cricket is interesting because it is a very individual game, yet each member of the team is vital. It has built-in chaos factors which mirror what happens in society at large.

Trust steps outside the rat race and relates to principles rather than dominance. It accepts people as they are (provided they maintain their part of the 'deal').

At its best it incorporates forgiveness so that those who break the deal can return – preferably a little wiser and with their integrity restored.

The difference between a trust relationship and a dominance relationship is that trust is voluntary whereas dominance is imposed. Trust looks to the group and works on synergy. Dominance looks to the group and works on power. So all the trust organisations – sports clubs, amateur theatre groups and the like – discover something about synergy, which is to say that the whole is greater than the sum of its parts.

Dominance relationships sometimes do well, especially in crisis situations, but even the intense hierarchy of the military does better if there's a strong foundation of trust. Armies of conscripts are not as committed as armies of volunteers. Compulsory sport doesn't have the same zing as freely chosen sport. Art imposed by the state lacks the spirit of art which is driven by artists.

Nakedness demands trust and perhaps reflects higher social capital than knights in armour. It has its problems though!

The writer, left in the front row (Wellington, 1984)

When we look at our big environment there is a continuing struggle between dominance and trust, between control and creativity. Economic forces, for example, are mostly based on dominance because economic power is concentrated in the hands of such a small number of people. Creativity, in contrast, is available to everyone (including the dominators if they want to drop their armour for a while).

One of the reasons the big economy has gone haywire is that the step-by-step processes of trust have been eliminated. Those who have the financial power have chosen to minimize trust relationships with those who haven't.

In New Zealand – and perhaps throughout the Western world – economic change has swept aside whole communities of trust, for example, small towns dependent on a single industry, when that shuts down or goes overseas. Industries have moved across international borders without any regard for the communities where they started. They chase the greatest economic advantage.

Dominance and trust have probably lived side by side throughout the history of humanity. We have the option of fostering trust regardless of what others do. Perhaps it's a matter of thinking about another element of the class agreement:

5. Focus on what works. Ask for what you *want*. Use your energy constructively.

Like other forms of capital, social capital is productive, making possible the achievement of certain ends not attainable in its absence ... For example, a group whose members manifest trustworthiness and place extensive trust in one another will be able to accomplish much more than a comparable group lacking that trustworthiness and trust ... In a farming community ... where one farmer got his hay baled by another and where tools are extensively borrowed and lent. The social capital allows each farmer to get his work done with less physical capital in the form of tools and equipment. *—James Coleman, Foundations, quoted in Making Democracy Work*

Item 5 raises some questions about our relationship with the community.

- Do we have to relate to a money system that doesn't work?
- What do we want?
- Is 'opposition' the best use of our energy?

One option is to invest in trust and creativity. Make trust and creativity your 'weapons'.

Economic and political stupidity can't defeat your creativity unless you give them permission. Your inner power is greater than any external force. You can change the world through your own behaviour. Each act of trust, no matter how small, has an impact.

Mutual respect and co-operation contribute to the health and welfare of a community

There is another thing too. A television documentary called *The Great Leveller* showed that 'trust strategies' are good for your health. The Roseto Effect is named after a small town in America in which the incidence of heart attacks was half that in neighbouring towns – and seemed fully attributable to community spirit. Supportiveness, ritual, family and shared causes (even a shared enemy) appeared to be conducive to health.

The town was studied by Stewart Wolf, a physician, and John Bruhn, a sociologist, from 1935 to 1984. They found that mutual respect and co-operation contribute to the health and welfare of a community and its inhabitants, and that self-indulgence and lack of concern for others exert opposite influences. (See tinyurl.com/yc3nsh)

'Little business', like fairs and markets, enable people to engage in more complex ways than they could in a typical shopping mall. In many cases the stallholders have made the products, taken the financial risks and figured out promotion and packaging. In part it echoes the rural communities of earlier times. That doesn't mean a market is free of cheating, but if it's in a place like Eumundi (above) the locals tend to keep things honest. Nor does it mean there's a rustic approach to communication. You can get a sense of the organization on www.eumundimarkets.com.au.

The challenge is to put trust and creativity into action. The revelation is that small things make all the difference.

Confucius told his disciple Tsze-kung that three things are needed for government: weapons, food and trust. If a ruler can't hold on to all three, he should give up the weapons first and the food next. Trust should be guarded to the end: "Without trust we cannot stand". (Onora O'Neill, Reith Lectures, BBC, August 2002)

204

- In what ways do your relationships with other people require trust?
- What is the difference between trust and creativity?
- What is your community?
- Is community something that comes to you or something you make?
- How can you connect with community in a creative way?
- Ultimately all creativity somehow reaches out to people by whatever means it can. Publication, performance, display, usefulness ... How are you going to make this happen?

At right is a TLC exhibition – engaging with the community. The exhibitions are held every twelve weeks and attract thousands of visitors. Although there are financial outcomes (students sell work) the shows are more in the nature of a free performance. Students organise nearly everything and the experience is parallel to that of other voluntary social groups. In our case the visitors provide a crucial part of the 'creative spiral' by way of feedback. They talk about the art, puzzle over it and in some cases purchase it. The school community pays attention and the exhibitions evolve. Each show builds on what has happened before and produces a kind of dance which keeps growing. Darwin, if he was still around, might have found it just as intriguing as the evolution of animals.

Thoughts

It's tough to be creative about tackling the problems of life if you feel powerless, if you're angry at yourself and where life has put you. Creativity comes from the inner being of the person, and if that inner being lacks confidence and hope, even life's most basic acts, even that act of raising your own child, is without spirit. *—Dr Gloria Rodriguez*

One of the wonderful things that takes place within the folk tradition, particularly African tradition, is that people actually pray for what they want to take place within the human spirit and in society, through music and dance and rhythm ...

What better way to find the unity of people, the unity of community, by first going to battle with the things that hold us at bay inside ourselves. Within us, all the time, we are fighting the battles of our own thought, of our own contradictions. *—Abdel R Salaam*

I don't think art solves everything but it definitely becomes an alternative. What we have found is that the introduction of other cultures to other people, especially through their creative art forms, creates a better understanding of people and brings people together. *— James Parks Morton, Minister, Cathedral of St John the Divine, New York*

▲ Families can be communities too. Pictured are participants at the 2005 Ormond reunion in Mahia. About 800 were present. They are all connected directly or by marriage to JD Ormond and his wife Hannah whose eldest son George married Maraea Kiwi Te Ratahi Wharekete, a Maori princess and daughter of Chieftainess Rongomaiwahine. It's a great 'mixed' family to which the author is proud to belong.

▶ Checking out the Andy Goldsworthy sculpture at Gibbs' Farm, Kaukapakapa.

◀ A school can be a strong community and may contain robust subgroups. Pictured: TLC Advanced Diploma staff and students visiting the Gibbs Farm at Kaukapakapa.

Perspective

Everything depends on your perspective. If the Earth is flat and the sun revolves around the Earth, your perspective will be different from someone who sees our planet as a speck revolving around the sun in a giant universe. Perspective in art is a metaphor for perspective in life. What we see and experience is deeply entwined with the mental model through which we interpret our world. Maybe everyone constructs their own perspective and to some extent it serves as a unique filter.

Perspective in art is a metaphor for perspective in life

Our view of outer space comes via a wide array of tools that have little to do with everyday vision (radio waves, x-rays, magnetic waves, gravitational lenses and so on). Likewise 'inner space' is being mapped via electron microscopes, magnetic resonance imaging (MRI), ultrasound, electromyography, computed tomography (CT) and numerous other systems. Each technique is a way of seeing and each has its own perspective.

Contemporary art itself reflects many ways of seeing and there's not a lot of the formal 'vanishing point' perspective which was all the rage in the not-so-distant past. You're often left with the puzzle of figuring out an artist's personal perspective before you can engage fully with the work. It seems almost unbelievable that old fashioned 'visual perspective' became so dominant that it featured in a large majority of Renaissance paintings.

We've become so accustomed to the conventions of visual perspective that it's hard to imagine that it was revolutionary in its time. Before 1400 the main

Albrecht Dürer, *Draughtsman drawing a recumbent woman*, 1525.

part of the art-magician's bag of tricks

convention was symbolic, as indicated in the picture on page 452 from Koimesis, Church of St Clement, 1295. The painting enjoys a freedom which was later cramped by the discovery of mathematical perspective (and retrieved by the Cubists in the early 20th century).

New perspectives are emerging all the time because science is finding new ways to 'see', while poets and artists are offering new metaphors to describe our relationship with the universe.

Byzantine artists were more interested in stories than in visual realism but their descendants in the Renaissance found that the new methods gave extra power to the old tales.

The heart of perspective theory (in drawing) is that parallel lines converge to a 'vanishing point' on the horizon (which is at your viewing level). A wide-angle lens will show how vertical lines also head towards a vanishing point and things rapidly get complicated. For our purposes one-point and two-point perspective are sufficient – and they are still part of the art-magician's bag of tricks.

Illustration (dating from 1484) for Chaucer's *Canterbury Tales* — partly connecting with visual perspective and partly staying with the Byzantine approach.

The first diagram below shows a classical approach to creating a sense of distance. In the left illustration, the lines stay parallel. The middle illustration has an 'inside out' perspective and the final illustration has a skewed perspective. The distortions are important because we live on an almost-spherical planet which is usually portrayed by way of flat maps. Maps based on

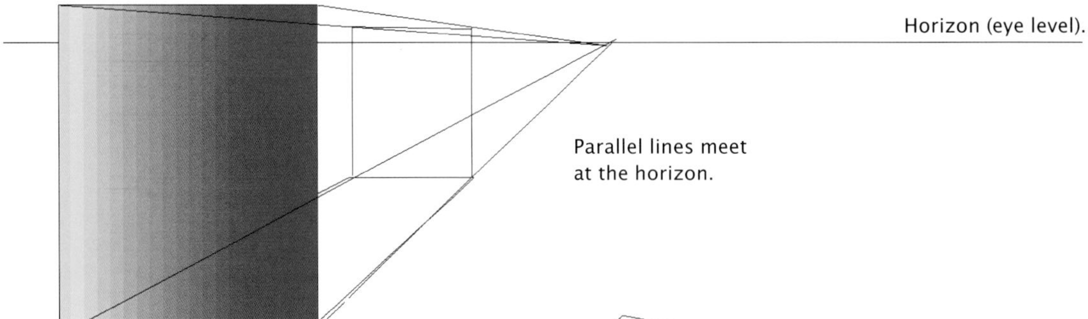

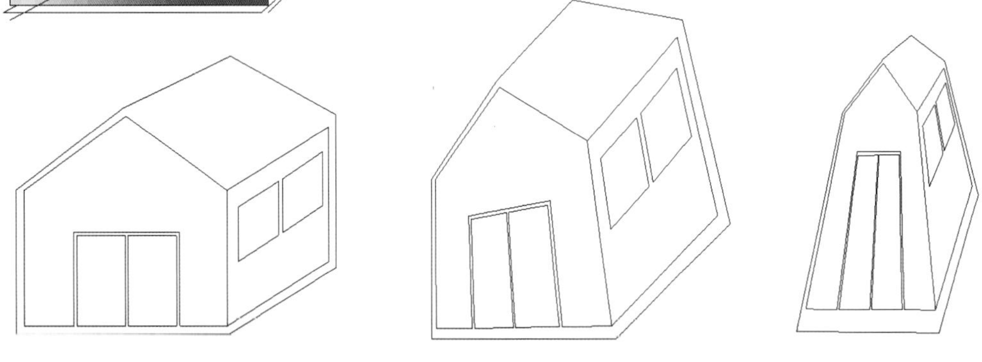

Strange things happen if you have false vanishing points or none.

William Hogarth's *Perspectival Absurdities* were intended to help people learn about perspective.

the Mercator Projection give a distorted perspective which makes Greenland look larger than Africa when it is approximately thirteen times smaller. (en.wikipedia.org/wiki/Mercator_projection)

Renaissance geometry still works because our subjective experience is that the Earth is flat. For artists that remains a workable lie.

Perspective: The relation of parts to one another and to the whole, in a mental view or prospect. — The Macquarie Dictionary

205 It's worth exploring perspective to understand how to make an illusionary reality. It's also interesting to consider the interplay between science and art. Renaissance artists immersed themselves in the theory of perspective and seem to have had few worries about incorporating technology. As a starter, draw a few cubes in different positions and give them a perspective using a vanishing point. Relate them to a single horizon.

206 Circles work in the same way as squares and rectangles. The next diagram illustrates how you can divide squares into smaller squares and add the circle to fit the same perspective. The key is to find the perspective mid-points and you can do this by drawing diagonals across the imaginary square. The intersection of the diagonals is the perspective centre point. Try different geometric shapes using vanishing points, e.g. circles, cylinders, spheres.

207 Find examples of perspective in photos and sketch them to get the feel of how it works.

208 Using a grid of lines drawn on clear acetate, try some perspective drawings of interiors, landscapes, buildings and so on. Use the grid as a guide for 'seeing' the perspective.

Remember that 'perspective' is really a convention. If we viewed the world through an insect eye, everything would be different. If we perceived infrared or ultraviolet light (as some creatures do) it would be different again. Time itself may turn out to have different perspectives, even though the idea of 'past, present and future' gives an overpowering shape to our view. Perhaps that's exactly the point

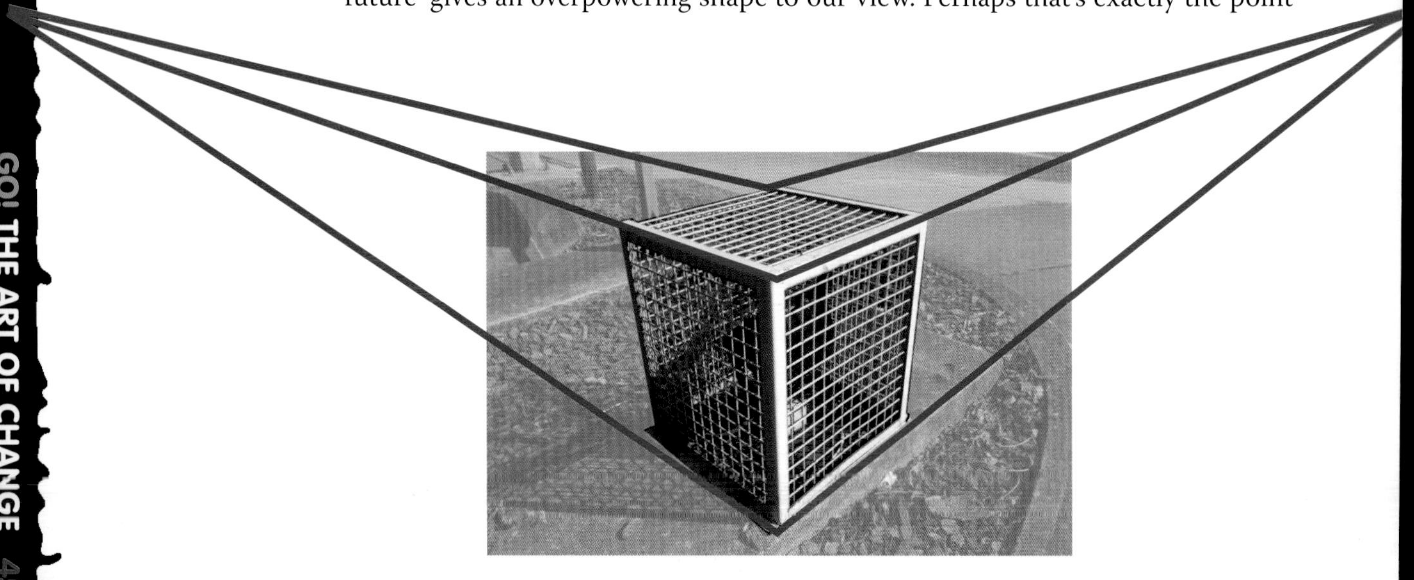

to ponder – whether the things we see are the basis of perspective, or whether perspective is the basis of the things we see. Photoshop contains quite a repertoire of tools to change 'perspective' at the press of a button.

And what is a bee's perspective?

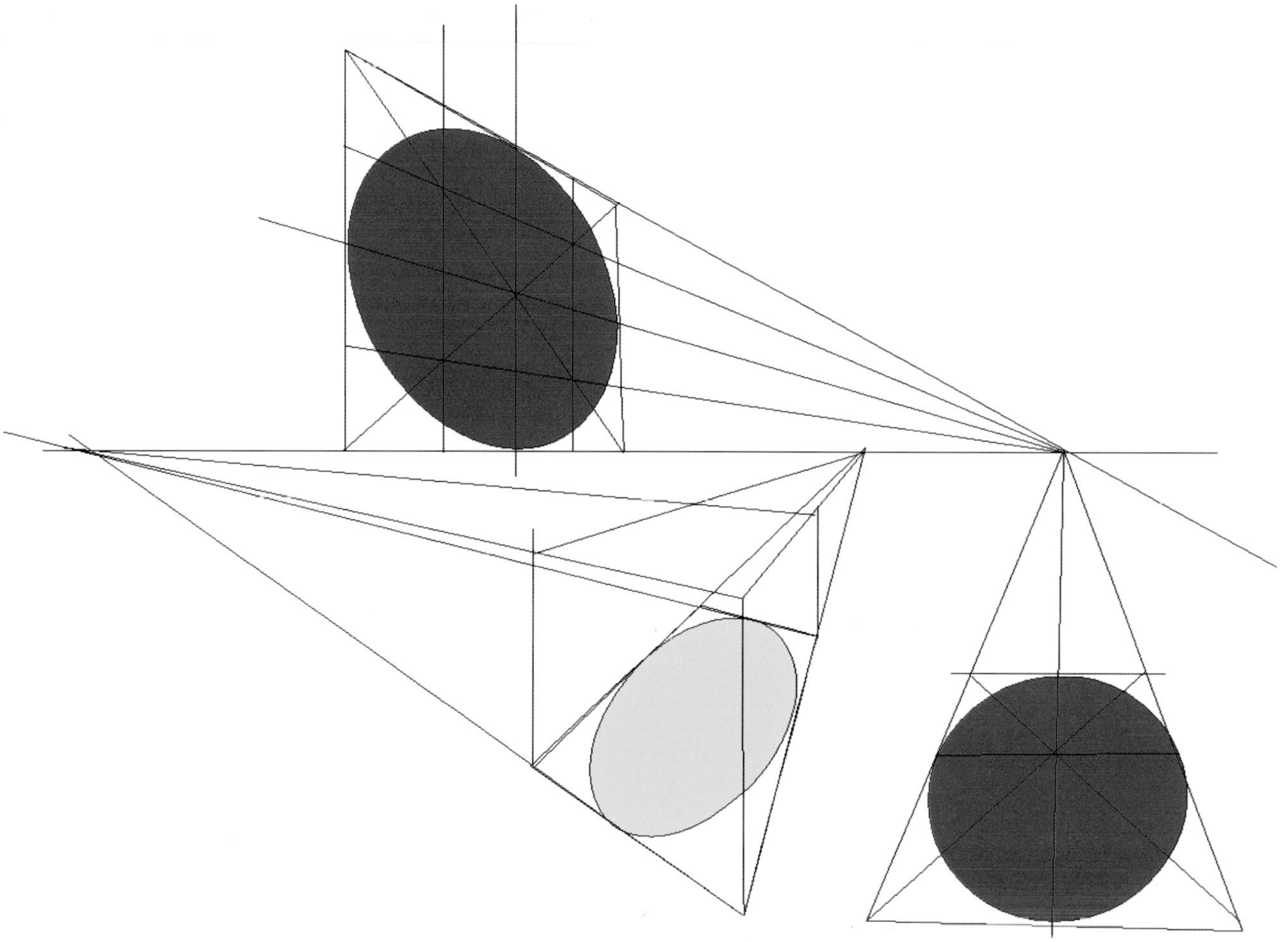

Drawing is no joke.
There is something very serious and mysterious about the fact that one can represent a living human being with line alone and create not only a likeness but, in addition, an image of how he really is.
That's the marvel!
—Picasso

In theory visual perspective can be reduced to geometry. The simplified diagrams you can make on a computer are close to the way a camera sees things. One difference is that the camera doesn't necessarily see vertical lines as parallel — they have their own 'vanishing point'.

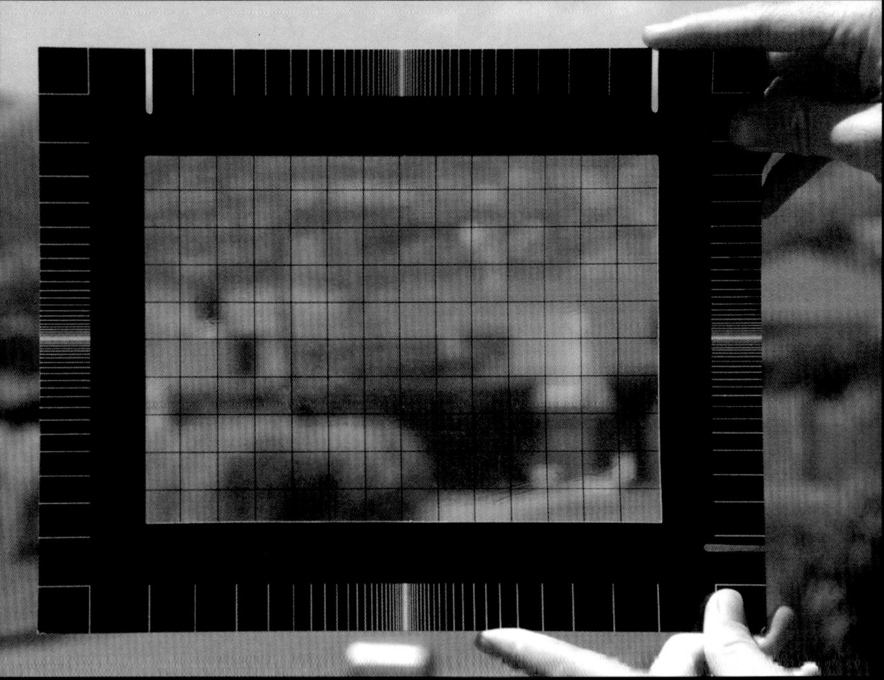

▲ One way to construct perspective directly from life is to use a grid such as the one illustrated. Mark a grid on your drawing material (it can be any size provided that the proportions are the same) and then copy the image frame-by-frame onto your drawing. It's slow and not entirely easy because you need to maintain exactly the same viewing point.

▶ Inconsistencies of perspective can do weird things (the three figures are identical and yet I still find it hard to believe). Sometimes you might do this deliberately if it's relevant to what you want to say.

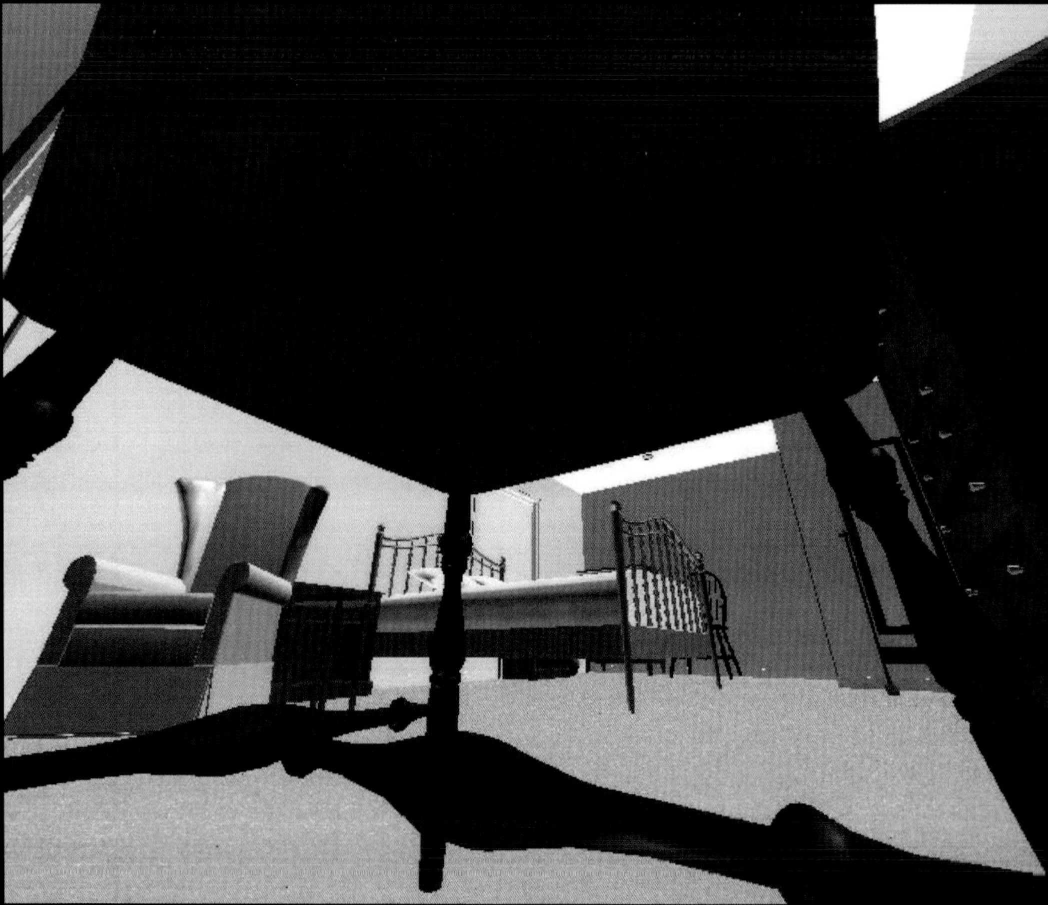

▲ Circles in perspective, Nambour.

▶ Cat's eye perspective of a room done on CAD (computer aided design) software by Don deMacedo. Shadows have perspective too. By extending the shadow lines you'd finally arrive at the light source. The wide-angle lens draws attention to the fact that perspective is happening in all directions.

▲ Our day-to-day experience of perspective is that distant things look smaller. We take it for granted, but it is a learned aspect of perception.

▷ The distant poppies have been copied into the foreground to illustrate the effect of perspective. In 'reality' the distant poppies are similar in size to the close ones, but in 'perspective' they shrink.

▷▷ Colour perspective. In general colours become cooler (more blue) as they become more distant.

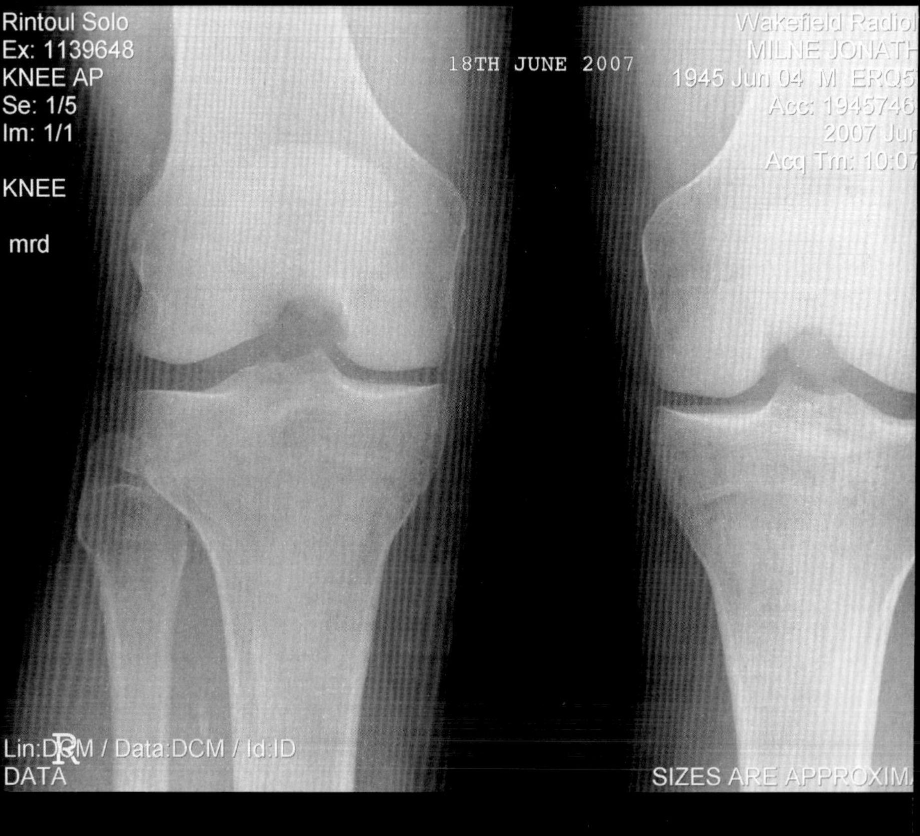

▲ Tones become softer (the darkest darks and the lightest lights usually belong to the foreground, although the sun can break the convention). The patch taken from the foreground illustrates the level of contrast.

▶ X-ray pictures are one of the more familiar ways of seeing our bodies from a different perspective.

▼ The **Find Edges** command produces a pen-like rendering in which the details are rich and surprising, a roiling mass of turbulent lines and shapes.

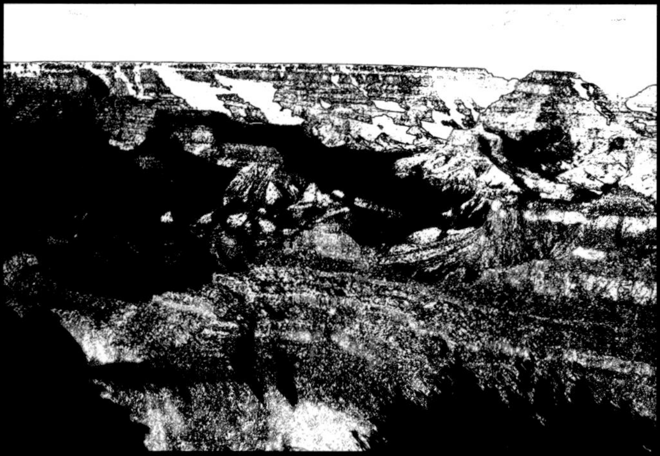

▼ And if you choose you can play with overlays and make worlds that seem completely disconnected from the canyon.

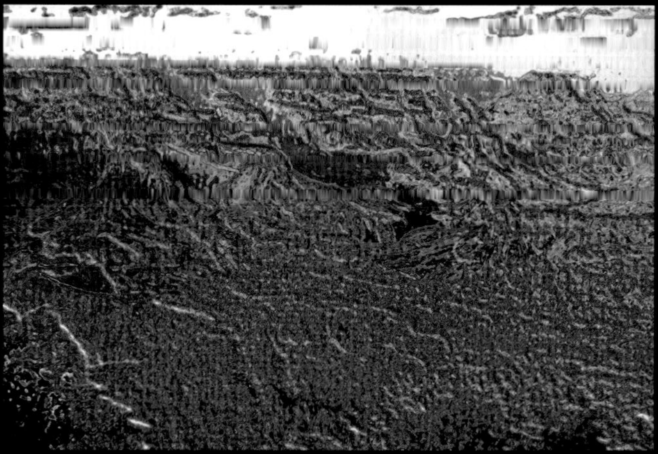

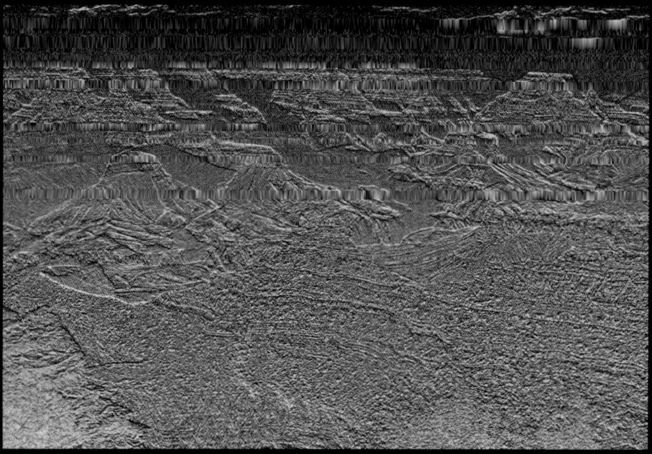

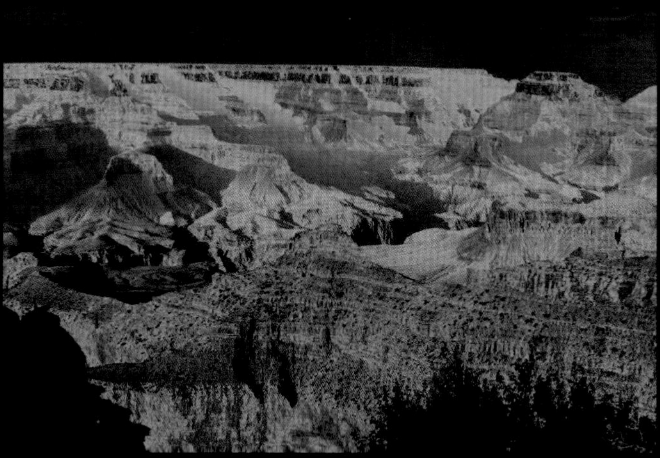

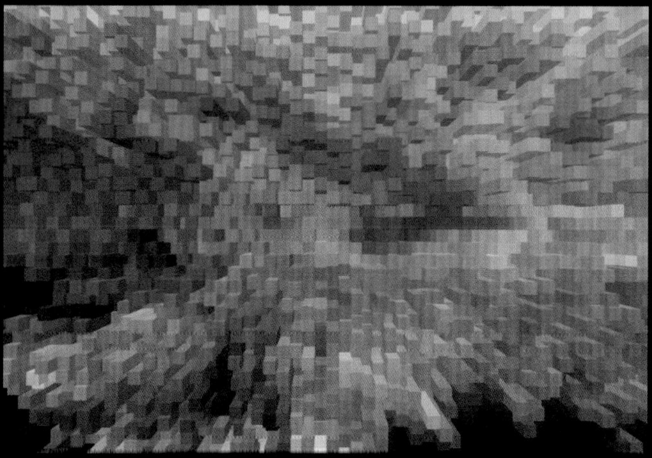

⩓ **Chrome**, like **Bas Relief**, creates a flattened reality.

▲ **Solarise** maintains the linear perspective but plays a disconcerting game with the colours.

⩓ **Bas Relief** flattens the image and turns in into something like the surface of a coin.

▲ **Extrude** superimposes a phoney perspective.

All of us are endowed
With an amazing creative ability
That transforms our humble daily activities
Into images of shadows and light,
Which are infused into the world and
Impressed on to other worldly beings.
All of us – the high and the low –
Are the continuous conductors
Of the Source of all life,
Touching one another with
The unending
Life of creation.
—*Lao Tzu*

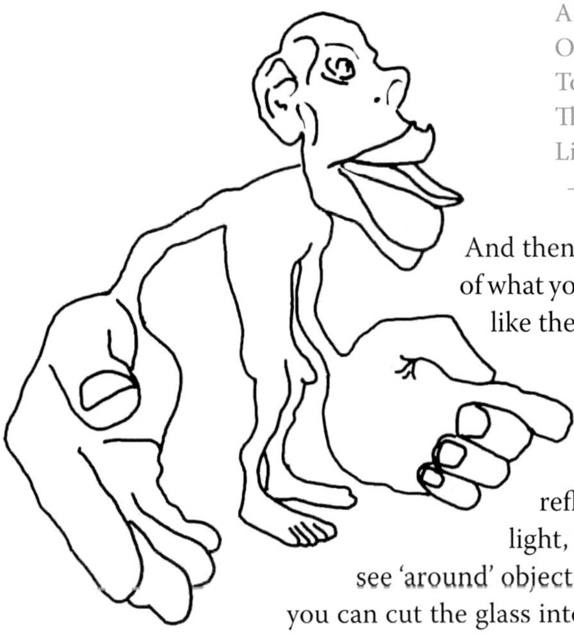

Drawing based on the sensory homunculus at the Natural History Museum in London.

And then there are other perspectives. Think of yourself in terms of what you feel rather than how you look. You might get something like the drawing at left:

Holograms could be the most challenging perspective of all. The classic hologram is an interference pattern, recorded photographically on glass. It is derived from reflected laser light. When the glass is illuminated by a laser light, the original image appears in three dimensions – you can see 'around' objects as far as the glass allows. What is more startling is that you can cut the glass into smaller pieces and the entire image is present on each piece. 1 + 1 = as-many-as-you-like. There are cosmologists who believe there is evidence for a holographic universe. www.crystalinks.com/holographic.html is a good place to look into the strangest mirror of all.

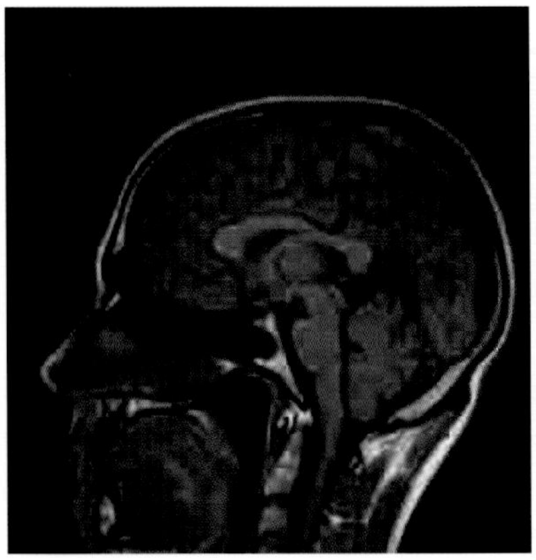

Magnetic resonance imaging has a different perspective (see en.wikipedia.org/wiki/MRI).

Visa hologram (on plastic rather than glass).

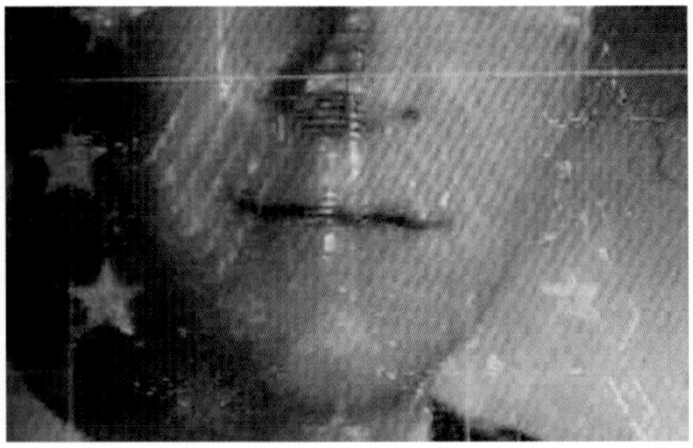

Another hologram. See en.wikipedia.org/wiki/Holography

▶ Our place in the universe gives another sort of perspective.

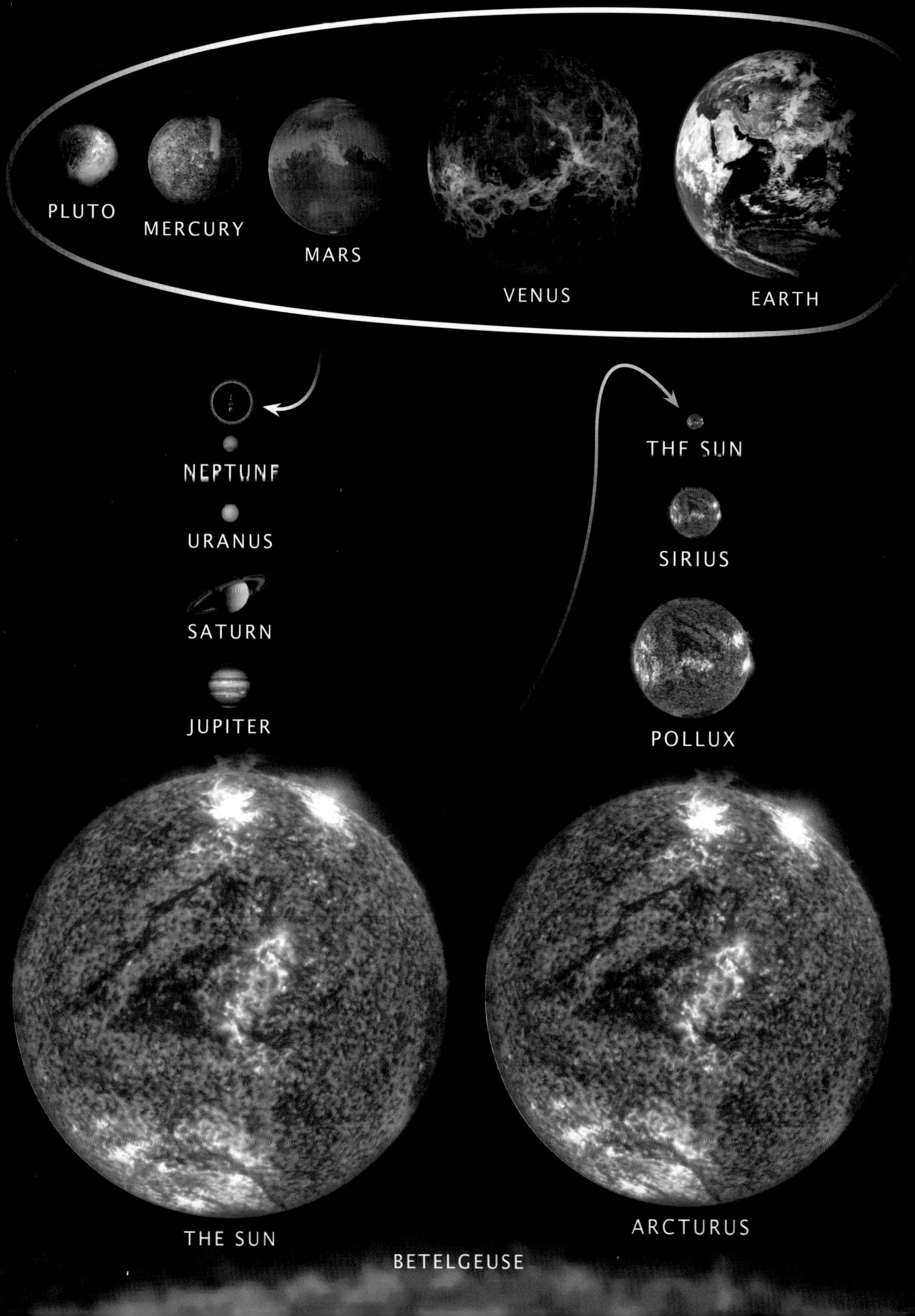
PLUTO
MERCURY
MARS
VENUS
EARTH
NEPTUNE
URANUS
SATURN
JUPITER
THE SUN
SIRIUS
POLLUX
THE SUN
ARCTURUS
BETELGEUSE

The hardest perspectives to see are those established by our shared ways of interpreting the world. The picture shows the TLC car park in the early days when the white lines weren't marked. Sarah Bullied used flour to make some pretend parking lines and drivers obediently followed the imagined rule.

It's hard to gauge the extent to which our perceptions are socially controlled. Most likely, every society has its own way of seeing the world. Perhaps, as Carlos Castaneda wrote in *The Art of Dreaming*, "[our ordinary world] which we believe to be unique and absolute, is only one in a cluster of consecutive worlds, arranged like the layers of an onion. [Juan Matus] asserted that even though we have been energetically conditioned to perceive solely our world, we still have the capability of entering into those other realms, which are as real, unique, absolute, and engulfing as our own world is."

Our sense of 'self' is an illustration of an imagined perspective. The fact is that about 90% of our genetic material belongs to other critters. Genetically the human body consists mostly of microbial hitchhikers (see www.newscientist.com/channel/health/mg19526171.300 the microbes-living-inside-us.html). Alan Watts' book *On the Taboo Against Knowing Who You Are* explores the notion that our 'self' is an illusion — and maybe the biggest shift we can make is to discover a perspective beyond the self.

The art of money

Creative people often insist that money isn't everything, and of course they're right. The reason I pay attention to money is that it enables me to pay the bills and do more of what I want to do. Money has been crucial to the development of The Learning Connexion and the institution as a whole has created new possibilities.

How can an artist make millions? The answer has more to do with courage than brains, inheritance or status.

Many artists are reluctant entrepreneurs, who view money as a necessary nuisance. This is a predictable consequence of intrinsic motivation – money is not a big deal for someone who is creating art for the sake of art. Not surprisingly, the non-materialist artists are intensely suspicious of those who make a fortune from their work.

Non-materialist artists are intensely suspicious of those who make a fortune from their work

Andy Warhol turned things inside-out when he said "Making money is art, and working is art and good business is the best art." (*The philosophy of Andy Warhol,* www.artelino.com/articles/andy warhol.asp). Andy is closer to the truth than the myth of the starving artist. Starvation is not conducive to creativity. Most of the artists we read about in the history books did quite well financially.

My own background made it easier to deal with money. My father was a contractor in the building trade and although he didn't talk to us about business, all his children developed a good tacit understanding of how business worked. The heart of it had very little to do with the details of tax returns and business plans.

Lani Morris, a New Zealand arts marketing expert, caught the essence of the artist's dilemma in the title of her seminar series 'Exposing a product to the risk of sale'. Lani said:

> Many artists are intrinsically motivated by their art rather than extrinsically motivated by money or fame or success. For many, an artist's lifestyle is a deeply driven thing and a lot of business programmes are not designed around that. Developing a body of work and pushing through into new areas of inquiry has a life of its own and is not the basis of a steady business plan.

> Most artists are also very right-hemisphere dominant. Business courses tend to be left-brain dominant, which can be meaningless and impenetrably boring to right-brain people. Artists are incredibly intelligent and skilled, and if you can teach the same business principles from a different perspective and in a different language, they go, 'Yippee!' and take off.
>
> *www.creativenz.govt.nz/files/resources/regions/hb5.pdf*

A fundamental need for artists is to maintain integrity while making sufficient money to do what they want to do. How does the non-material process of art connect with the materiality of money? One approach is to think of the money as a payment to enable you to make more art. In other words, it's not money for the art itself, it's for your own well-being and productivity.

Sometimes the art market goes crazy and artists receive huge sums which go beyond any conceivable personal need.

Roy Lichtenstein ended up getting $1million or more for just about any of the enlarged comic book images he had time to produce (and some of them went into tens of millions). It would have been incredibly hard for a money forger to have created wealth at the same rate! And Lichtenstein prices have continued to rise after his death.

At a more everyday level, Duncan Chatwin (a TLC student from a few years back), decided on an interesting pricing strategy. He phoned the *Holmes* TV show (part of national television in New Zealand) and said he wanted to raise US$1million for Amnesty International by selling a painting. Holmes thought it was newsworthy and gave Duncan a prime-time interview. Duncan in turn secured free space at the Queen's Wharf centre in Wellington and displayed a dozen of his paintings, along with the one designated for Amnesty. He put high prices on all of them. The show was viewed by about 15,000 people and only three of them were buyers, but Duncan made $180,000 – which isn't a bad début in the art world.

Critics figured that the prices were crazy because they wouldn't be sustainable, but they would probably have said the same when Andy Warhol went to Germany and did about 50 Polaroid photos of wealthy businessmen at US$50,000 apiece (an extra $25,000 for additional family members in the same picture). The photos were sent back to America and Andy's colleagues turned them into Warhol prints/paintings. In little more than a month Andy grossed about US$2.5million by being Andy. No doubt the images are now worth vastly more than the money paid.

In each case there's a pricing strategy. Lichtenstein helped to shape Pop art and then rode the wave for all it was worth. His pictures became collectors' items and the high prices steadily made the earlier works even more valuable. It's hard to say how much is 'art' and how much is a feeding frenzy of the super-rich. One of the critics said Roy was good at turning a sow's ear into a sow's ear, but despite the scepticism he made a heap of money and secured a place in art history.

despite the scepticism he made a heap of money and secured a place in art history

Warhol turned fame itself into an art. He made sure he was seen in all the right places and was so diligent at attending exhibitions that someone commented that he would go to the opening of an envelope. It paid handsomely (and contributed to the way we understand 'art').

Duncan poured great energy and passion into his paintings and then ensured that thousands of people saw them. He was prepared to take a huge number of rejections to get a single buyer – and it worked.

Despite seeming remote and unattainable, there's nothing stopping you from doing the same things. More typically, beginning artists do one of the following:

- *Price to sell.* Check out the selling price for similar work and offer yours in the same range.
- *Price according to what the work is worth for you personally.* If you treasure it, maybe opt for a really high price.
- Think of your whole career unfolding into the distant future and *price on the basis of what you'll be able to charge when you're famous* (sounds crazy but it can work).
- *The key ingredient is not technique – it's 'personality' and 'substance'.* If your art has something to say and is really distinctive, then it's in with a chance. If it looks like everyone else's art, then you'll be stuck with everyone else's prices. It's the same as any business start up – you're searching for a way to be relevant. In the case of an artist you probably have a much bigger desire to be true to yourself as well.

If you accidentally sell too low, count it as a learning experience. If you've done some good work which doesn't sell, try other ways to market it. Be endlessly patient – like Duncan you'll get a lot of rejections. And remember that prices are ideas rather than fixtures. If you've got Duncan's passion and staying power, the sky's the limit.

Money is just an abstract form of energy

Keep in mind that money itself is just an abstract form of energy. It's not an end in itself, it's a by-product. Many artists are totally indifferent to money and that's fine, but if you see yourself as a professional it's worth having a serious ponder about the way pricing can make things happen.

To establish your personal plan, look for 'right brain' business advisors and pay attention to people like you who have found ways to be commercially successful.

The interviews that follow are from a cross section of TLC graduates who are grappling with the issues in their own distinctive way.

Keep in mind that art is usually a slow path to financial security. Whereas an entrepreneur might expect results in a few months or years, an artist has to think in decades. If you've achieved the average wage at the end of your first ten years then you're doing well! Expect it to be tough and have faith that it will be great.

Other pathways

The great disaster of money-driven education is that it has moved aggressively to career-based results. In New Zealand there is an expectation that a school like The Learning Connexion will have a relationship with industry and will demonstrate career relevance.

Fortunately New Zealand has developed a comfortable acceptance of the 'creative industries' and we have been able to meet the requirements. The official word from the Department of Trade and Enterprise is worth reading (see www.nzte.govt.nz/section/11756.aspx) because it gives an indication of the economic significance of creativity:

Nobel prize winners practise poetry and other forms of creative writing and the visual arts at rates many times those of average scientists

> The creative industries sector is identified within the Growth and Innovation Framework as one of the keys to New Zealand's economic transformation. The sector was chosen both because of its potential for growth and its ability to enable innovation and improved productivity across other sectors within the economy. The creative industries sector currently contributes about $2.86 billion (3.1% total GDP), but the sector is growing at a faster rate than the economy as a whole, at a rate of 9%.
>
> Creative industries is a diverse sector, which includes screen production, television, music, design, fashion, textiles and digital content. New Zealand has already established competitive advantage in some niches within the sector, notably, screen production and post-production, and has a growing reputation across a number of other areas including fashion and design.
>
> In addition to our world class capability, the creative industries can leverage New Zealand's unique culture and as a knowledge based sector, it has the potential to generate wealth on a sustained basis and reposition New Zealand as a nation of new ideas and new thinking.

Michele and Robert Root-Bernstein

But the 'creative industries' are only a fraction of the story. The bigger picture is being pieced together by researchers such as Robert and Michele Root-Bernstein. The Root-Bernsteins made an ingenious study of scientists who had won Nobel prizes in chemistry. They said: "Particularly noteworthy is the fact that Nobel prize winners practise poetry and other forms of creative writing and the visual arts at rates many times those of average scientists ... We therefore feel confident in saying that the most creative scientists not only have the psychological profiles of artists, but more often than not *are* artists." (p.137, *Creativity: From Potential to Realization*, published by the American Psychological Association, 2004).

The Root-Bernsteins go on to say: "If scientists and artists really think the same way, then it should follow that they can also benefit from insights obtained in the complementary discipline." (p.141)

A vocationally-driven curriculum is likely to short-change the very careers it is trying to support

The implication is that a vocationally-driven curriculum is likely to short-change the very careers it is trying to support. From the TLC experience I suggest that the right sort of integration of art, science and other subjects will be especially beneficial for the individuals most likely to drive creative developments in their main field of work.

Historically the notion of a 'rounded education' had something going for it. What TLC is advocating is an integrated education which draws out creative processes in each subject area and encourages the interplay of different areas of knowledge.

TLC has taken art into unlikely places such as Georgia Tech, the School of Engineering at Cornell University and the Faculty of Science at Victoria University. Students' responses have ranged from exhilaration to puzzlement. The stumbling block (so far) has been the reluctance of administrators to try an experimental programme to test whether our claims are justified. Sooner or later we'll find willing collaborators and the evidence will gradually accumulate.

In practice our students aren't waiting for the research – they're coming to us from a wide variety of fields and they're getting involved. It has all the wonderful messiness of an educational earthquake and it's going to take a long time before we can deliver the sort of data which will persuade the sceptical academics.

The important point is that most of our students are not with us to become artists. They're doing things to enhance their lives. For many the goal is to give some scope to their 'right-mode' thinking and they believe that this will be good for them. It remains to be seen what will unfold when students leave the school although the early (and subjective) indications are highly positive.

The interviews which follow are therefore a little skewed because they focus entirely on people who have stayed with art. Nevertheless they are symbolic of the changes available to everyone who is prepared to embrace creativity.

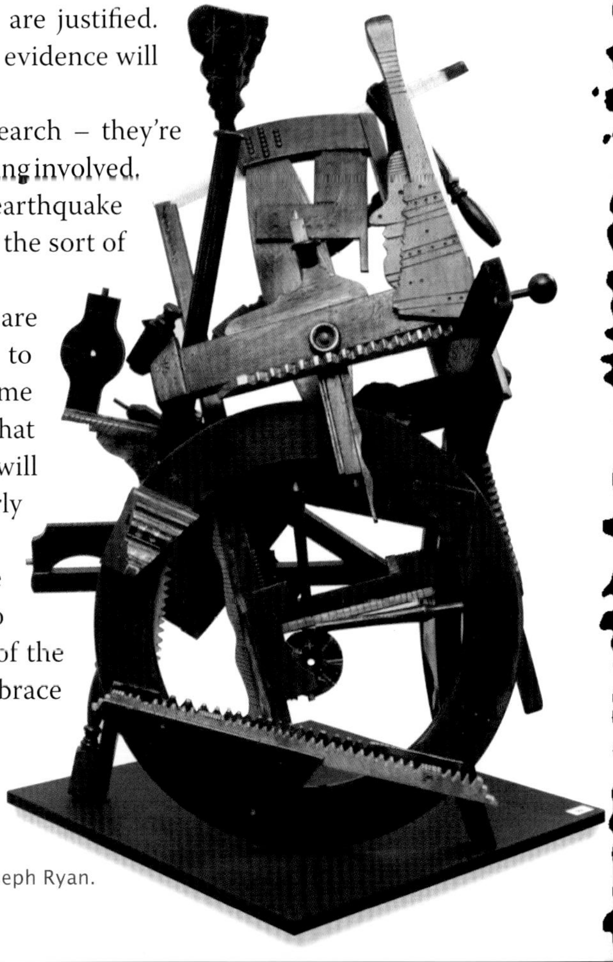

Artist: Joseph Ryan.

Sandro Kopp

If I have someone present it forces me to do something

Sandro Kopp (www.sandrokopp.com) was born in Germany; his mother is a New Zealander. He arrived at TLC in that curious phase when his career hadn't taken off. He was a young man who looked like a movie star and had an edgy mix of sensitivity and bravado.

Outwardly it looks like fame and fortune but on the inside there is relentless hard work and the money is monkish too. What steadily shines through is Sandro's personality and intelligence. He engages with people in an amazingly bold and courageous fashion. His big series of portraits involve single sittings that start in the early evening and may go through to the small (and larger) hours after midnight. It's the exposure of the total performer. There are no second takes – Sandro grapples with his perception of the sitter and makes a painting. He says:

Sandro Kopp brings Renaissance painting skills into the mysteries and uncertainty of the 21st century. He can immerse himself into the monkish routines of a painter and flick into the frenetic sociability of the movie industry (in which he has found some small parts, established a fan club and used his art fluency to good effect). Background: part of *The New You*.

> There are lots of different reasons why I like working from life. If I have someone present it forces me to do something. It keeps you painting until it's done! Drawing from life has that wonderful element that it's interactive and it's holding you up to the promise of making art.
>
> I do use photography in some of my work. Even on the face series I sometimes use my camera if the sitter needs a break and I work from the tiny condensed image. Sometimes that helps me to see things that I wouldn't usually see. In general I find that if you work from photography it's so easy to go all the way and make it look like a photo that's already two-dimensional. It's a much greater challenge to work from life. You've got to deal with depth and you've got the collection of moments as the sitter gets more and more tired or in some

cases more drunk. These can only be done at night, when I can control the light conditions, and this is the only factor that remains constant. I start at sunset and work as long as it takes. Usually it's about six hours, although the fastest was 2½ hours.

Overall, figurative painting is a language and it's ridiculous and immature to say that it doesn't exist anymore. People are doing it. People are speaking the language. There's something new to say with every person that speaks it. I'm doing it in my own vocabulary in my own style.

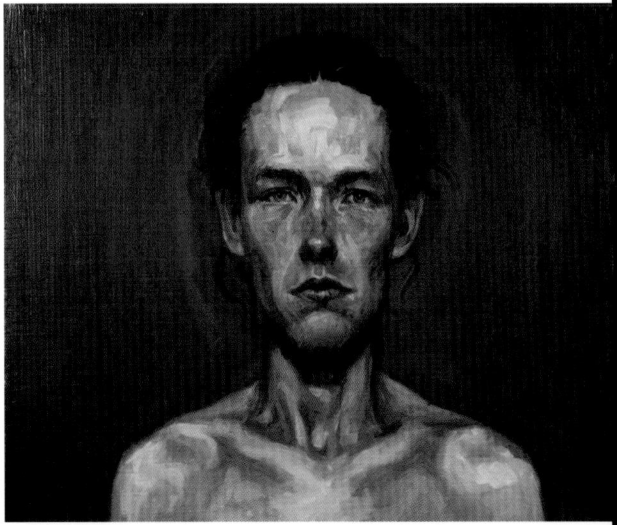

The New You — Jarl and *The New You — Carolyn*, part of Sandro Kopp's *The New You* set of paintings.

I used to contextualise myself a lot with the old masters, particularly early twentieth-century stuff like Klimt and Schiele. That was the angle I was coming from. I go to Europe once a year if I can and my prime objective is to see lots of art. I like to find art that feeds me, that touches me, that leads me back into my own life and my own work.

It's great that figurative painting has been pronounced dead. I'm doing this utterly old-fashioned and irrelevant thing and I can pretty much do what I want to. I've got free licence.

Last time I went to Europe the thing that got me off the most was the Saatchi Gallery in London which contains work that's been done in the last 25 years or so, and it's *great!* And it's great realising that I'm a contemporary artist despite what I'm doing. I think there was a huge attachment to conceptual and non-figurative art. There was a craving for something that was intelligent and different and the problem was that a lot of art became clever just for the sake of cleverness. There's so much incredibly clever art out there and it's got no flavour. There's nothing other than the cleverness and I think that's not enough.

I start at sunset and work as long as it takes

There's nothing wrong with conceptual art. I drink it in and I think about doing it myself but I know that it's not as satisfying. I think people are becoming more and more hungry for something that is aesthetically appealing and relates to them. That's where figurative art comes in because we're all people and by painting people there's something that echoes us whether it's highly abstracted or high realism. As soon as there's a figure it automatically gets the feeling of being related to one's self. Having a good look around at what is happening in the art market in Europe last year there's a whole school of young German painters, particularly based in Berlin and eastern Germany, who are doing fine figurative painting. A lot of landscapes, a lot of art incorporating architecture and a lot of art incorporating the figure. It's well painted and it's selling for loads and loads of money. I just thought *yes*, I've picked the right moment. It's become the hot item in New York and London as well as Germany. Figurative art is where it's at. Hopefully by the time it gets here I'll be in full roar and represented by a dealer gallery. People want art that feeds the senses and is lovingly and soulfully made – which escapes technique and is genuinely yummy. It's like a lovely meal that's well prepared and nourishes some need for something that's deep and relates to ourselves.

Sandro's wall of heads goes somewhere beyond traditional portraiture.

It's a material-bound, skill-limited, perception-filtered craft product. The works are completely bound by the choice of materials, canvas, oil paint and acrylic paint, linseed oil and that's about it. That has a whole story of its own because it immediately puts it in context with classical painting. Then it's limited by the degree of skill and my ability. What I try to do with these pictures is to paint what I see in one sitting. I'm not employing any effects, I'm not trying to give them any sort of meaning, I'm really trying to chase that edge of "how well can I put it down?"

People want art that feeds the senses and is lovingly and soulfully made – which escapes technique and is genuinely yummy.

You can *never* create a realistic painting because you're putting paint on canvas, it's a different reality. I've been working on them for one and a half years now and you can see that the earlier ones have a slightly different style and vocabulary than the later ones.

Maybe when someone else looks at them they'll be seeing a different person. The Freeman painting is very far from who Freeman is because the real person is blood and bones and breath and hair and he moves. This is just my craft product. It's technically relatively sound – I find that I'm slowly getting to a point where I'm confident painting faces. The pieces are all intensely personal because they are people who I know and relate to and who mean something to me. I'm not intending to sell them either, which is one of the reasons I'm finding it difficult to find somewhere to exhibit the set. I'd consider selling it for the right price to a public collection as a block – I'd never split these up. I entered one of them in the National Portrait Awards and I hated not having it here – there was this gap. Every piece that I do belongs to this series. The painting got honourably commended which meant I got a pat on the back rather than some money, but I was quite happy with that and I painted her again – so she's off to the Archibald Award in Australia.

You can never create a realistic painting because you're putting paint on canvas, it's a different reality.

I guess people always see narrative in figurative art. They'll say "You really captured her spirit. You really accentuated her wisdom or her sadness or whatever." But I didn't. That's the viewer's take on it. I'm just trying to paint what I see. The

question that the piece asks is "to what extent can you as the viewer experience another individual vicariously through this skill-bound, material-bound, perception-filtered craft product?" Ultimately it has nothing to do with the sitter. It's of them, completely, but at the same time it's not them. It's not mine either because it's filtered through my perceptions. The title is *The New You* because what you have here is this third entity that exists in this limbo space between myself and the sitter. We've spent the time facing each other, we've had this interaction, and this thing that has been created, which is not mine and not theirs, but exists nonetheless in the space between us. I love them. They're better then TV. I sit and I look at them for ages and I change around a couple of pieces and the whole setup changes. The implied hierarchy changes all the relationships.

Sandro Kopp's 14-figure painting.

I was going to do 12 when I started out. I'm now attracted to doing 45. I like odd numbers, like five high and nine across, because then you have a middle figure. Having a middle figure changes the whole dynamic. Five by nine is large enough so that if you're standing at a distance it would fill your peripheral vision. If I had 75 it would be quite good because then you could have 5x5 on three walls. You'd walk in and become completely subjected to all these people staring at you. I like the way people feel confronted by it.

One of Sandro's painting adventures was a kind of contest with Freeman White. They each set out to make a painting containing fourteen nudes. Sandro says:

It's not conceived for a private home and it was completely for my own and Freeman's benefit. It was very much a working piece there were figures that I took out and others that I put in. It changed tremendously over the 15 months that I spent painting it. It's not really a saleable piece but it's relevant to me and to what I'm doing. There's a lot of stuff I do like that – I know that ultimately it will strengthen my cred[ibility] but it doesn't put dinner on the table. At the moment the galleries believe that anything which involves nudes and portraits is pretty unpopular and they won't show anyone who doesn't have a history of selling.

I'm currently thinking of spending a few months putting together a nice body of landscapes that are true to myself and saleable. They do sell, but can I face prostituting myself by spending a lot of time on what is not in the heart of what interests me? I'm finding that difficult at the moment.

The notion of art being 'authentic' is complex.

There's a sense in my art of being connected to something greater than myself when I do it. In a way this is my form of worship but that's quite private and it's not something I make a big deal out of. It's something that happens, it's not what it's about.

The sublime and the mundane are side by side.

Ten years ahead I hope I have a space of my own. I've been doing a lot of film work over the past years and now I'm growing tired of the uncertainty of it and the superficiality of it. It's given me a lot of fun but what I want to do is paint. If I work on building a reputation, sooner or later a dealership will follow. I'll be living somewhere here on my own, with a garden, and some pigs and chickens maybe.

I'd like to have galleries taking my work in Auckland, America and Europe. The good thing is that the more you paint the better you get. You get faster but you keep pushing the goals higher. The quality of the work is rising. And even if this doesn't translate into money the good thing is that I'm doing what I enjoy. I'm not eating caviar every day but I can go snorkeling and get some crayfish. I'm living in my chosen home which is a beautiful spot on the planet and I'm supported by the government which isn't possible in many other places. Not many governments are as supportive to artists as the government

the more you paint

in New Zealand. I don't take it for granted. There are people who are pissed off that they are not getting more but beggars can't be choosers!

Did it make any difference getting a fairly full-on blast in a climactic part of *Lord of the Rings*?

For my art, no. But for the movie business, yes. I've been flown around the planet numerous times to attend conventions and sign autographs and be a glorified celebrity, which is ridiculous considering how little time I'm actually on screen. But it's great fun, good money and I've met some wonderful people. After meeting a lot of people who are considered to be famous I've found that *everyone* struggles to pay the bills, the only difference is that they have bigger bills.

I had a friend come and visit from Germany recently and she found me via TLC. After seeing all the information about me on the Web she thought I'd be living in a lap of luxury instead of being on the dole unable to buy new clothes. But that's the reality of it. I go over there and I get put up in nice hotels. It's helped me to realise the value of privacy. I'm really happy that I live here and I'm more or less anonymous. There are settings where you can't scratch your bum in public without wondering if someone is pointing a camera at you.

> *You're a lot better off listening to people first*

Like many artists Sandro has learned through teaching others.

When I first ran workshops I started out making plans and having very clear ideas about what I was trying to do. The more I've done it the more I realise that you're a lot better off listening to people first. Now I like to have a palette of options and I select according to what people need on the day. It makes it really difficult to write a brief for the class!

A lot of students want answers about life drawing and they want techniques explained. I can explain techniques and there are ways to make drawings more like what you are looking at, but if they stop there they'll miss out on their answer. For the most part I just try to get them to look and get excited about it. Maybe the core of my work is trying to transmit something of my enthusiasm.

I'm always looking at people's drawing. You see people who've been to classes and learnt practices which I despise, like breaking the body down into geometric elements. I try to get them to look at the organic forms in front of them. Just look at it and draw it.

I like the idea that you think about the way a line continues. How does the line continue around the part of the figure you can't see? The things I talk about include this, and finding the centre line. I talk about anatomy a lot. I talk about art history and try to give them a sense of what has been going on for the last 34,000 years or so. I draw attention to the amount of language that's available for inspiration.

As a postscript Sandro says: "I'm no longer on the dole and money has followed... I have found galleries in New Zealand and abroad..."

the better you get

Laura Muir

Laura Muir (www.lauramuir.co.nz) started her art career in her 50s. She was a psychotherapist with a successful business and a hankering to break out of her counselling role.

I never expected that it would turn into a professional thing

Somewhere, I can't remember when, I saw a TLC advertisement and I came along with a friend to nine sessions to learn to draw and paint. Later I started embroidery and then worries about my eyesight took me into machine embroidery and collage. Then I got to the point where there was no one to talk to about it and I approached [Jonathan Milne] directly. So that's when it really began for me because you suggested that I move on to paint. Up until then I'd only had those few sessions.

I never expected that it would turn into a professional thing but I was hugely curious about how to make art. I went overseas to find out what Venice was really like. It was exciting to find that what I could do was of interest to other people.

I'd got somewhere with the fabric but I also got to a point where I realised there was so much work in fabric that it would never get the returns. I've always felt that if it was good it should be paid for appropriately. I've lost three friends in the course of this because they don't really agree with that. I've had comments like this: "Oh so-and-so was here yesterday and she's a *real* artist."

The idea that you could actually learn to paint and draw is something that TLC taught me. Until then `, and a lot of my friends believed that too. Those three in particular haven't been able to cope with my transition. Once I indicated that I wanted to become professionally active they just faded away.

I think my excitement caused problems to them. One said to me that she thought I was obsessed. Seriously. I do have a lot of intense pleasure when I paint something and I know that it looks good and I know that someone's going to think so too and will buy it. The buying of it is extremely important. I hope it doesn't sound mercenary or go-getter because I'm very content with my place in life.

I had the idea that you were born with this ability

Laura's art grew from a near-vacuum. Her knowledge of art history was minimal, although she'd accumulated experience through photography. In some of her early explorations she adopted the style of painters that she liked.

You remember when I started and you showed me a picture by Seurat. I don't

recall why you showed me, but I thought I could do that and I went home and did it. I sold it down in Arrowtown where I was invited to be the guest artist – that was a laugh! Nothing else sold down there. So I knew what worked. I'd been looking at paintings for years and years. I wouldn't go to current exhibitions but I was always curious about those Impressionists. What did they see? Where was all that colour? Why don't we have colour in New Zealand like that? And when I went to Europe I found that they made it up!

The crossover to paint started when I used rollers to paint tissue paper and then put it into a collage. I didn't have to go to rock bottom and start up again. The transition through the paper collage was hugely helpful.

Remember I did the water print series and went to a gallery where they charged me a fortune for framing? At that stage I wasn't selling – I was an unknown. It was a disaster, although eventually all but two sold.

I also learned from TLC how to get through situations where things went wrong. I rang you up in a blue funk when a work had gone haywire and you asked what I thought I could do. I said I could stick some tissue paper on. So you said to do that and bring it in the following morning. You looked at it seriously. And that's another thing. Whatever I brought in you never jumped to conclusions. You always considered it and invited me to consider it. You can't imagine the degree of tension and worry there was at those times. Anyway you said it was very orange and it might help to try a little blue. Well I did, and I sold that work to someone I've become good friends with. She thinks it's the best nude she's ever seen. It's just part of a body and a lot of people don't realise it's a nude until they really look at it. And that's the other thing I knew I wanted with my paintings – I wanted something that would draw you in and you will live with it and keep finding new elements in it.

Laura has been hungry for technical knowledge and found that her TLC experience provided a foundation to do further work from books.

My first 'book mentor' was John Hammond – and that's helped me to learn lots more about painting. I learned a lot more about painting from John's book and I went to some of the places he's painted. Then I was ready to let that go. I now feel I have a style! I know how to build up a painting in layers. I had to overcome the thought that I wasn't born with a silver paintbrush – I realised that I could learn to paint.

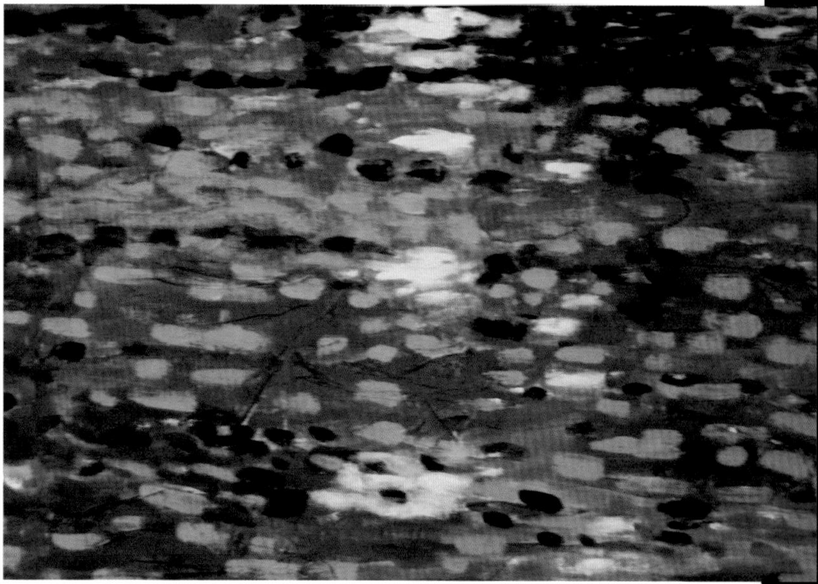

One of the big challenges for new artists is to reach potential buyers. Laura has approached 15 galleries and some have worked well. Many have been learning experiences.

I came upon the idea that if you get turned down by a gallery, use that as the point to take off and do something else immediately. Do something, whatever it is. And be aware that many of the gallery people are just retailers and they will use your work to make money but they're not interested in you.

The lows have caused me to make the effort to do something. They've been costly in terms of psychic energy but it's important to find a way through. I've seen people with talent who don't have the get-up-and-go to make things happen.

Success isn't free of worries.

Now I'm feeling as scared as hell that I won't be able to live up to Palette Gallery's ideas. I just have to calm down. It's been a very exciting week. I've got an exclusive contract with a dealer gallery. That to me was the pinnacle, I never thought I'd get there.

The money is improving. After a couple of modest years Laura is selling more work and getting much better prices.

One of the Auckland galleries told me that my work is under-priced, and that was encouraging too! I sent you the emails about asking for more than $1000 at van Helden and when I finally got the courage, it sold.

Since then she's broken the $4000 barrier. An injury provided some tough times.

I hurt my back – that was scary. My doctor was a huge support. We were doing the Accident Compensation stuff and I said I still can't sit or stand to paint but

Success isn't free of worries

I've been able to paint on my tummy, lying propped up with cushions. He was typing "Has been able to resume hobby ..." and I said "It's hardly a hobby, I sell paintings."

My family of origin was extremely dysfunctional and very critical and bitter, so the sort of support and friendliness and warmth I get from someone like my doctor is important.

The emotional ups and downs have been part of the journey.

It doesn't matter a fig what you've used if the final thing is a really good painting

I don't think you can make it easy really. Remember when I finished my course with you and I said I need to find a replacement mentor? A friend suggested someone and this person said to me, "Did you use photographs?" That's a thing I've learned from you – it doesn't matter a fig what you've used if the final thing is a really good painting. That stupid argument is still going on in the pages of art magazines and it's such a waste of time. I would never have got going if I hadn't been able to use photos. If I hadn't got going my enthusiasm would have faltered and died. I gave up the idea of getting a mentor and just got on with it.

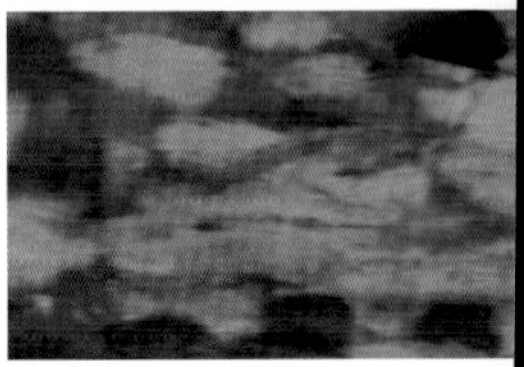

And Laura 'gets on with it' with a big sense of urgency.

I'll have to slow it down a bit or I'll just wear myself out. I'll just have to calm down. I have got time. I'm enjoying life, I have good health. I've lightened up considerably! It's a combination of course. Giving up being a psychotherapist. As a psychotherapist you can't be a person. My own reactions to things had to be put to one side and to some extent that encourages a lack of personality. It's very isolating. There's a lot more fun in my life now. The only thing that I find difficult is coming face to face with other artwork that I have nothing to say about.

Another part of professionalism is to put out an 'Artist's statement'. Laura anguished about what to say and it came out like this:

I am inspired by the natural and constructed world around me and the people in it. My paintings arise from a focused visualisation – seeing the whole, the parts, shapes, patterns, mass and line – and then organising all these relationships on the picture plane. Acrylics, oils and pastels, either on their own or sometimes combined, are my media of choice.

When the viewer engages and enjoys the complexity of marks and colour that is the finished painting my pleasure in its creation is further enhanced.

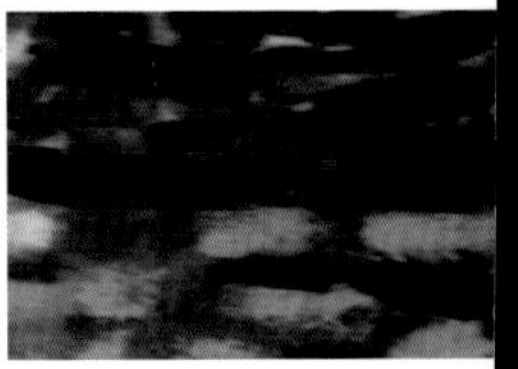

It's great to have the time, the energy and inclination to paint, and paint, and paint.

Perry Scott

I was born up in Rarotonga. My father was a doctor and he was running a hospital up there for a couple of years. My brother and I had a nanny who was a local woman. We sat around listening to all the songs being sung and all the social stuff of the day. I think it gets printed in you to some extent.

I grew up in a New Zealand culture that was mixed. My mother's second husband was Nga Puhi and we lived in a mixed farming community way up north. You get a bit of everything and that gets inflected into you – it's just there. I'm not very dogmatic about any aspect of it. I'm a little bit skeptical and analytical about it. But that's all right – this is a part of what we are and how we live. I feel connected to it.

I've always had the hankering for art since I was a kid. I used to draw and make things – I suppose everybody did. It was always there, right through high school. It wasn't available as part of the system when I went to high school in Tokoroa – they did have an art class but it wasn't available because I was doing

woodwork and metalwork. That was the way they shaped things in those days. On and off I've always been driven by personal curiosity.

In 1986 I did the craft design Maori certificate. It wasn't totally satisfying in terms of what I thought art was. I left that part way through. I am part-Maori and that was initially part of the attraction. But the course included a lot of politics and it didn't sit well with me, mainly because it was fairly simplistic and superficial. A lot of it was adversarial too so I moved away from it.

After that I did some traveling and a variety of different jobs. I maintained my interests, but poorly defined. I simply experimented and continued to be engaged in the process – mainly because I couldn't help myself – it was just a natural thing.

It was free of a lot of the things in art I found I didn't respond to – like a lot of the political narrative

I applied to go to Elam [the art school of Auckland University] and had been accepted – I thought I would go and finish my degree – and then I'd been scouting around and I questioned the value of doing another full four years. I heard about TLC's Masterclass through a friend. I was attracted by the materiality and process. It was free of a lot of the things in art I found I didn't respond to – like a lot of the political narrative. I decided to come and do the one year Masterclass as opposed to going to Elam.

The course was like an opening door and it's quite wide-ranging and free. I think it's essentially to do with the way materials are used – it's about the intrinsic properties that materials have. You aren't playing back into a historically created narrative. It's a very simple response and there's a great freedom in that if you're able to utilise it.

I think it's almost unavoidable that my work seems to say something more than the material. I try to leave out any obvious language. The material, if it speaks beyond itself, it's because we're creatures of language. To an extent that's an imposition of the viewer in response to the work. Material and process are the things that initially attract me but then there's the inevitability of people bringing their need to assert their familiarity with the work.

Perry Scott's serving of New Zealand clay.

One of Perry's works was an ice-cream scoop filled with what appeared to be ice-cream but was actually clay – part of the New Zealand land.

It does have something to do with the way I view the world. It has connotations of food and nourishment and that kind of thing. People can read into it but essentially it is just that. There's a bit of tomfoolery involved. It tricks your eye, so to speak. Then the material brings you back to where you can't be tricked. How people respond beyond that is their business.

In fact it was an ice-cream scoop of land, wasn't it?

◄ Detail of work in rubber by Perry Scott.

Yeah, in a way. But the context for it was almost surrealistic. It wasn't emphatically related to any particular point of view or politics or body of knowledge – it wasn't referential in any particular way. It was simply a material in an altered context.

The thing with humour is it's just the way I am. I think people take themselves far too seriously sometimes. It's often problematic, that view of life. They create narratives and meanings which inform their existence and they get tense and upset when the universe doesn't conform to their view of it. I think it's silly so I play on it. I try not to have malice – I just think that in the process something occurs and your sensibilities get tickled by it. That's a nice sort of content if there's going to be any content. It's a nice way to talk.

It's a double-edged thing – you can be whimsical and at the same time aware of the harder edge of things. I think there's a need to have a point of balance where somewhere in the middle there's a balanced way of trying to look at what you think reality is. You have to have some kind of flexibility to create a language that isn't necessarily based in conflict or dogma or any of those things that tend to close doors.

What is it like to work in an art world that is caught up in hierarchies and conflicts and fashions?

At a personal level you can live in a world that's as mysterious or as real as you want to make it

At times I find it difficult. My work hasn't been out there with a lot of exposure. You're operating in an area of mystery when you engage in materials and processes. You're pulled forward by mystery into an area that's forward of the edge where you might be. The art world is full of its own processes and methodologies and biases and education and preferences. That all gets expressed because it's just people. People often need the security of a framework. It gives them a sense that the meanings they attach to everything are significant and have been created historically. So there's a chronology, there's a history, there are accepted points of view, there are certain things that are taught and so on. If I'm sitting in the middle ground as an observer, looking at it all, I'm willing to engage with it but I can't be bothered playing the game that goes with it.

At a personal level you can live in a world that's as mysterious or as real as you want to make it. It depends how you operate. In the so-called real world there's a form to which people comply. Whether they are really able to justify the positions that are held is debatable. I feel disinclined to try and make it work with all of that. I think that's some kind of falsehood.

I'll make some moves with galleries but whether or not you get an invitation is something of a lottery. I heard a story the other day of a group of buyers who are influential. They have a reasonable amount of money and they have a hierarchy which establishes people in an order. One of their methods is to look at recent graduates, choose who they think are the up-and-coming ones and buy a piece of their work. A year later they'll put the work up for sale and buy it back themselves at an increased premium. Two years later they'll put it out for

sale and let someone else buy it at a much higher price. What they're doing is stimulating the market and establishing the reputation by the way they behave within it.

The work that I do doesn't fit neatly into the established patterns of familiarity. I can go out and create a show myself but I'm not hugely driven by it. I don't think my ego needs the adulation or the recognition. My primary interest is in doing the work, and quite often I get fairly uninterested in it when it's completed. I get excited in the process and for a short time afterwards. Then I can let it go very easily – it doesn't bother me at all.

It's just basic curiosity. It's true of most people who want to take an interest outside the mundane things we need to do to operate. I think everybody lives a life that is not well discerned by the wider community. Everybody has another way of living and I think you can be conscious of it and develop it and live in it more if you choose to. I think that's all it is, that curiosity. Being willing to be stimulated by it, and respond to it and use it and inquire about it.

The artist's role is to be in the business of being human and live the life you're living

If I had unlimited funds I like the idea of large scale. It's possible to look at the need for large scale as being an expression of ego but I did do some drawings and some plaster of Paris maquettes years ago which I would have liked to see in bronze, 18–22 feet high, and I like the idea of picking them up by helicopter and popping them out in the middle of nowhere. It wouldn't bother me if only one person bumped into them in 50 years, by accident. You could stand them in among tall trees. They were organic, tall slender forms. That kind of thing interests me. The big question ends up being 'Why?' It's a difficult one to answer. I think you'd do it and whether or not there is an answer is a moot point. It just is. That kind of thing quite appeals to me because I find that the gallery space and objects for people's environments have the language of people too much in them.

The artist's role is to be in the business of being human and live the life you're living. If the practice of your art happens to be what you're living then that's your ten-cents' worth going into the mix. I don't give it a huge importance – no more than someone who's building a deck down the road. If anything I tend to get a little annoyed by the kind of artificial importance and elevation that goes with it. The airs and graces that go with it are nonsensical. We live in a perpetual media frenzy and people go and do media studies so they know how to generate the frenzy more effectively. It's a bit nauseating because there's no real content there – it's just hype. I think we need some quiet contemplation. The space and time to think is important. It's a loss when everything is targeted to be absorbed in ten seconds. I don't know where art comes into that. It doesn't interest me to be able to be attractive in that kind of setting.

I've done the exercise a couple of times at exhibitions. One at Pataka (in Porirua). There were 35 pieces hanging on the wall and the average time people spent in the room was 27 seconds. What does that tell you? I think it goes back to the point that there's so much out there. The visual culture is just overwhelming, it's everywhere. Television, papers, your letterbox. It's coming

art is just the artist's dandruff

at you from all directions all the time. I think people get into the habit of just scanning.

I like Robert Franken's idea that art is just the artist's dandruff. I get uncomfortable with people being so horribly precious about it all.

But I do get anxious about the need to provide for myself as I get older. Knees and elbows and shoulders pack up and you know that the doctors are going to charge you twenty grand. And you need a place to live to keep the rain off your back. I don't want to be in a position where the conditions in which I live are dictated by circumstance. I want to dominate circumstance to the point where I have at least a basic amount of control. Sometimes the whole question about the practice of art comes up. I wonder about going fishing down in the southern ocean for a grand a week for a couple of years, and just get the financial things out of the way. My age is starting to come into the debate. I didn't worry about anything when I was 30. Now I'm 53. It's starting to creep up and I'm starting to spend more money getting my joints and things working better.

There's probably not a big target market for the odds and sods of rubber that I slap together. Yet at the same time you could find a benefactor come rocking through the door who decides you're the next flavour of the decade and buys everything you make. You just don't know.

There's a proliferation of artistic practice in the western world because wealth facilitates a kind of indulgence that you otherwise wouldn't have. The market is like a huge sponge soaking up a certain amount of this and a certain amount of that. To get a financial result an artist needs just two things – persistence and chance.

Susan Knaap

When Susan Knaap (www.susanknaap.com) started her course at TLC she was living in a caravan and things were fairly basic. She was feeling burnt out from work as a counselor in a hospital where part of her job was to talk to grieving parents of children who had died.

She came to an orientation week and felt cautious, partly because her art still seemed to her to be less than creative even though she had achieved several touches of success.

When I was a teenager my father was manager of a department store and I'd copy little pictures which he'd sell in the store. I think I got $40 each. I did the odd commission for friends. It was a bit of a buzz in that it helped me to buy my clothes but I got virtually no enjoyment out of doing the work itself because I was just copying. Then I got a new job and shelved it for about 15 years.

Initially I totally believed that the better you could copy something the better you were. But I felt quite constrained by painting things realistically. I could paint a piece of fruit but so what!

That was the first time I had a sense

Susan Knaap with her painting at the Florence Biennale.

The first big turning point came with a crazy mission to America.

I went over to Sacramento for a week in 1999 – I absolutely loved this artist over there, Susan Sarback, and went into huge debt to get there. That's what started me painting again. Then I came to TLC still doing that impressionist style and started what I'd call 'post-impressionism'. Even then I didn't know how to go forward because it wasn't feeling particularly fulfilling.

I remember doing a class and it was about finding what was important to you and putting it into your art. I always thought there was me and then there was my art and they were two separate things. Then I started thinking that if I actually did express who I was, what would it be? Interestingly it came out almost as a religious style. So I started doing crosses. I remember the tutors saying "You don't really want to be doing crosses because they're icons and everyone does them." I figured in a way it was like childhood stuff coming back. I'd been raised as a Catholic and I still love the whole ritual of religion even if I don't go to church. All those rich reds and golds and ambers started coming out. That was the first time I had a sense of art being about who I was.

of art being about who I was

That evolved over time. I gradually left form behind and went with things that were abstract but meant something to me. It moved into work that is a mix of chaos and order. A number of my works are called that because that's how it felt, that's how life felt. It was paint that was allowed to do its own thing and drip and behave like paint. There were often geometric shapes within it and that to me felt like the order.

When I did my first abstract class with Regina [Tuzzolino – TLC tutor] I was absolutely petrified of abstraction. I didn't know what it meant and I didn't think I could do it. It was like a completely foreign language to me. Having done it now I can't imagine why I found it so scary. She would talk a lot about "what is it you would like to express?" It was like a lot of journaling to get to a point where I thought "I'll see what happens with paint."

I dabbled with abstracted landscapes and I tried to look almost metaphorically at hills and sky. Then I realised that it was the sky more than anything that attracted me and the clouds particularly. I guess if I'm contemplating I look at clouds. I never tire of them because every moment there's something new and you can look at it as something quite spiritual. A lot of people like my cloud paintings because they think it's a nice cloud but there are others who see a spiritual element in it.

Susan Knaap with Prof. John T Spike, Director of 2005 Florence Biennale. The sculpture, *Grande Catalina* by Carole Feuerman, served as an eye-grabber outside Fortezza de Basso where the exhibition was held.

It's not religious. Some people thought that that was what I was doing with crosses but I saw a bigger picture than the cross. The way I paint now, the colours that I choose, *is* about spirituality. Now I'm totally expressing who I am so it's taken five years at TLC to get to that point.

I work from a sense that there's more to life than we see, that there's something at work beyond the obvious. My sense of spirituality is quite abstract so it probably works quite well – because for me there is no man in the clouds and I don't believe that any religion has captured the essence. I think they try and most of them have a kernel of truth. If I were to describe how I see God it would be more a sense of nature and life, the way that life works, and if you are connected to it things work out in the best way for you. We are all here as individuals working out what that means for ourselves.

My art is constantly about willingness to ditch the plan and go where the marks take me. Sometimes it's surprising and I look at it and think "That's not commercial" but strangely enough it is. The comments in the guest book at the exhibition indicate that the work is saying the same things to other people that it is saying to me.

You need to make money to keep painting but money has never been the object. To me you just have to paint. At the moment I'm taking my first break for a long time and it's feeling good because you almost run the well dry. You need to step back and get new inspiration. There'll be something in one of my latest paintings which says "Use an aspect of that and go from there."

There was definitely a phase when I was aware that a strong design, a piece of gold leaf and a bit of red would sell. You notice that at the exhibitions – where people are doing things because they know it will sell. But people get sick of that and the recipe goes flat. There must be one in every home by now, surely! People want something with a bit of substance. There was a woman who apparently sat in front of one of my paintings for an hour and a half just looking. She left a message saying "You've made this British tourist feel very humble" or something like that.

There are a couple of pieces in the exhibition and I wonder whether people are ready for them. There's one called *The Unveiling*, it's of a black circle, and then it's got red cloud formations over it. There were times I looked at it and hated it. I was about to paint over it and my brother walked in and said you can't paint over that. He said leave it for a while and see what happens. I put it in because I thought, why not?

One of the women who came for the exhibition opening said she had a son who worked in a bank in Dublin. He said that Susan Knaap is mentioned in bank circles as an up-and-coming artist. What they do is watch out for these people. It completely blew me away and made me laugh. How can you take that seriously when you're working on your tiny square on the mat in the living room, feeling faint from the fumes? When someone's talking about you in that way it seems utterly surreal. So I don't have any ambitions like that because I think the pressure would be too much. I'm too out on the fringe. I don't see my

work as being corporate. So I just see myself doing the same thing and the odd opportunity will come by.

At the time of our interview Susan was preparing her work for the Florence Biennale.

I've glued the canvases today. They're drying as we speak. There are going to be five strips of abstracted landscape, very vertical panels with clouds. I feel a sense of pressure doing this series but maybe I shouldn't. Maybe I should really go with it, let loose and see what happens. Once I start something will take over and it may be nothing like I planned.

Her approach to painting is a reflection of her life.

The nicest things that have happened have been nothing to do with me. If I ever try for something it never works out. The Florence Biennale came out of left field. I never had any thought of selling anything in the 'Going Solo' because I've seen people in it with good work who've sold very little. So again that was a lovely surprise. Nine sales happened in one hour.

I can't even describe the sense of excitement

My mum was there because it was her 70th birthday, so it was quite a day. I wasn't even going to the preview because I had no one to invite and the other artists had mailing lists of up to a hundred people. I thought it would be too embarrassing to turn up and have no one come so I told them weeks earlier that I wouldn't be there for the lunchtime preview. Two days before they said you *must* come because we want all our artists to be there. Don't worry, it's not going to be so bad.

So I arrived and I brought my mum and a couple of friends showed up. The hilarious thing was that it was other people's guests who came and bought my work. There was quite a group standing there and three of them bought various bits of work. That was a lovely feeling. I can't even describe the sense of excitement. When the second biggest painting sold, which I didn't even particularly like but there was just something about it, I let out quite an expletive at which stage this old woman turned around and seemed to be thinking "Who is this obscene person?" Then she saw my 'Artist' label on. But it was exciting. I don't think I'll ever forget that day.

this is not just a fine art school

Besides selling her art Susan has achieved outstanding ratings as a tutor. She says:

> I totally agree with your philosophy that this is not just a fine art school – it's actually teaching creative principles using art. I bring that out right from the start and people love it. One of the things that I do is to get everyone to go out for ten minutes and come back with six found objects. They come back with all sorts of things and you wonder where they've come from. I always check that it's not the stair banister.
>
> Then I ask them to get their acrylics and paint directly on them. For a moment they think, oh my god, can we do that? We're just used to painting on paper. I say no, just paint directly onto these things. Depending on what happens, if it's a leaf the paint kind of sits on top and fades away to not very much. If it's a piece of wood it has a lovely pastel effect. And plastic is amazing. Then I say get your gesso and paint the other half of whatever you've got. When that's dry paint the same colour. And that teaches them straight away what gesso is for. I had a guy say to me, we never learned this, we learned to put paint on paper, but I think none of us felt permission to try it on other things.
>
> What I do in that particular class is go right back to the basics. What is this thing? What is this paint medium? What do you do with it? I get them to spread it around with their fingers. I get them to try student acrylics and then artist acrylics and discover the differences. It's almost like taking them back to being a child when they were allowed to do things like that and giving them permission to do it.
>
> Once they get going it all changes. It's hard to get them out the door at five o'clock because they're engrossed with trying all sorts of things.
>
> All through the class people say "What happens if ... ?" And I say there's only one way to find out. That's very much about the philosophy here. If it fails you'll know why and you'll know what to do next time. I see my role as getting them to a point where they can do it all themselves.
>
> In my own work I do exactly the same thing – I try something. If it's hideous I'm likely to just throw paint at it and see what happens. Occasionally it looks fantastic! Often the paintings that I think are the worst turn out the best. I never doubt that something can be resolved. And I never feel that I'm not an artist just because a particular painting doesn't work. For me it's all part of a cycle.

Carl van den Berg

My father was involved in art from as young as I can remember. He was a master craftsman. He was in construction but he had incredible hand skills and in his spare time he made artwork. I was always around creativity. There are examples of his work here wooden carving, the marble carving on the window sill – pleasant reminders that although he's passed on he's still with me.

I was adopted so genetically I'm English but I was brought up by Dutch immigrants. My birth mother played music and painted landscapes. She had something going for her. She was of that era when it certainly wasn't encouraged. If anything it would have been discouraged. She was going to come here in February this year and spend time painting here – take it more seriously. Unfortunately she died of a heart attack before she got the opportunity. She was 57. My birth father was 44 and he died of a heart attack too. I suppose it's important to know about this stuff.

I think one man's recipe for success can be another man's recipe for disaster. I came up with the realisation that what was really important was to be completely 100% true to oneself. But who is that? Events influenced me to have the courage to say "I'm going to create art and see what evolves from that." I bought some pastels and started drawing. I've played around with painting as long as I can remember – at school, in my spare time – but I suppose it was just entertainment.

I'm going to create art and see what evolves from that

I had some real estate and there were changes in government policy that made it no longer tenable. I sold up. I went to Auckland and spent time with a

you don't know what's

dear friend who's been an artist all his life. We went to school together and we've known each other for 40 years. I started stretching canvasses and started painting in Auckland. That was in '98. From that point on art was all I did. Then I decided I would go to art school and because I lived in Island Bay and The Learning Connexion seemed like a place to start. I went along to one of the evenings and felt really comfortable about what was being said and enrolled in the foundation course. From then on I found great satisfaction.

Robert Franken [artist, TLC tutor] was a great encouragement in the process. Although it's not for everybody to embark on a project such as this it's not insurmountable if that's where your true nature lies. There are a lot of people who wouldn't embark on a creative lifestyle because you have to have a lot of faith. They simply aren't prepared to believe. When you least expect it and most need it, something unfolds. It's a journey which is continually evolving and unfolding but you have no control over it and the future is unknowable. But when you're in a day-to-day job you have the illusion of security because you always know more or less what you're going to be doing from week to week. In this situation it's quite different – I think it's more real.

Carl van den Berg's studio gallery in Levin, New Zealand.

I'd always had huge amounts of energy. People would be intimidated by it. Not intentionally on my part but it was kind of like the little energizer man. What really inspired me to set up my gallery was having been at The Learning Connexion and working in a space like Studio R. There was all this natural light, wooden floors and a really organic feeling about it. It's so wonderful to have space. I suppose it's a real luxury in today's times. I came in [to the Levin gallery] four times to have a visualisation about what could happen here. Many people dream about having a great studio space and life's too short to just dream about it. I wanted that and when I got here I went hammer and tongs to create a really pleasant environment in which to work. Originally it was Godfrey Bowen's shearing shed, then it was a tea room and then a health spa. Now it's my studio – what can I say – 220 square metres of space. The whole building is 315 square metres. Part of the visualisation was to create a studio space not only for myself but with the possibility that others could use it as well. I don't expect that to happen overnight – I'm hoping that the nature of the energy will permeate and bubble over and as more people realise what is here it may be utilised by others as well. I have no idea when that will happen or how. But you don't know what's going to happen in life anyway.

going to happen in life anyway

I have faith that the energy of creativity itself is very positive and I'm already getting feedback. Things are starting to simmer.

I came here thinking it would take six weeks, with all the bravado in the world. It took me three months to demolish what was in here. I recycled all the timber. It took me nine months to reline, rewire. I built all the doors and did all the painting. It took about a year. And then we had a flood and by the time we cleaned the mess up that was another four months. That was a little hiccup along the way. At the time it seemed quite something but we're back on track again.

People are starting to understand that creative energy is what makes things better

Some people thought I was mad. As it progressed I became less mad and people said "Wow, what a great space." I got a lot of wows.

I've been doing so much work on the building that I couldn't fill the space with a new exhibition of up-to-date artworks so the things on display are a reflection of my journey over the past few years.

People are starting to understand that creative energy is what makes things better. It enriches people and it enriches the society and the culture they live in. It's one of the truths about being human. People have a need to come to a realisation of that and to embrace it, and in doing so they come to an understanding that it makes their lives more whole. If people come to that realisation then we become more wholesome as a community and as a society and as a culture. There have been examples in history where certain regimes have tried to suppress that and the results have never been positive.

I think under the Labour government in New Zealand the climate has been rather good.

Painting by Carl van den Berg.

Others who I have known for a long time feel that they have left me behind in terms of the material aspect of life. New Zealand is a very wealthy country but it's often very difficult to realise the wealth of a nation when we're always wanting and desiring. Part of the unfolding of my life has been embracing the truth of creativity. My desires and wants have become less in a material sense. Years ago when I was at your school I set myself an exercise to paint in gouache and black and white, and part of that was to learn how to create great limitations and find endless possibilities. I can live off the smell of an oily rag. My needs in terms of daily living are minimal.

To create this particular situation I've put my whole life savings into it and the benefits are not necessarily defined in dollars. It's defined in terms of assisting people to become more whole in themselves.

A few people were a little disgruntled to find that their health spa was no longer here. I haven't had a lot of interaction with Levin because I was determined to get to this point. There was a huge amount of time just totally focused on this project. There were three and a half thousand nails to punch in this floor. Now there's a slow simmering of people who are curious, interested, supportive. There was a time when I thought "What am I doing?" There were other people saying "Good on him for giving it a go". There have been mixed responses but on the whole it's like a little snowball which is beginning to grow. People like what has happened so far but I tell them it's just creating a stage where things can happen. This is just the beginning of something that will unfold and evolve and hopefully will sustain my creativity and influence and encourage other people to embrace what I believe has enriched me.

Whether or not people get it, is up to them

I've had the door open for three weeks. People are suggesting endless things – getting signage, getting the kiln going. Goodness me, you've only got a certain amount of energy available to you. This isn't instant coffee, this is percolated coffee. This is a reflection on the immediacy of people's expectations in today's world. What I'm doing here takes time. The response has been pretty good. I've already sold two paintings, which I'm really pleased about. It's all about being positive, having a positive visualisation and not about self-punishment. It's about quietly embracing creativity and allowing the energy of creativity to work its own magic. If I try to be controlling over this it won't work. That's a lesson in itself.

I wander around in circles and meet myself in unexpected places. You either are or you aren't, I think. What drives me is always having ideas, wanting to express myself, wanting to say things but not necessarily wanting to write them down, and realising that in saying what it is that I want to say, we always speak in half truths. No matter how much we try to get our point across, it's always determined by whoever's reading it, their perception, and people perceive things differently. I've had artwork that I've given away and had returned and then someone else has gone and bought it. It's almost indefinable. I can't really explain it. It's something that I love doing. Whether or not people get it, is up to them. That's the nature of art.

Elizabeth Knapp

Elizabeth Knapp completed her TLC course and accepted an offer to run a gallery in Palmerston North. The deal was similar to a franchise – and although it was demanding it was also an opportunity.

The gallery has been open 2 ½ years. Many small businesses don't make it past the first year. I still feel like a kindergarten kid though. Yes, I'm more practised at speaking to people and greeting them and working in their presence. I often describe the feeling as rather like a fish having fallen out of the bowl, flapping around in full view.

It's very unpredictable, very fickle. I can go weeks, sometimes months without selling anything, and then for no apparent reason sell four or five paintings over a few days.

The deal I'm working with was wonderful when I was starting because I didn't know what the next step was going to be. I knew I was going to be painting, I knew I was going to be still learning but I probably wouldn't have had the courage to go so public. It wasn't something I enjoyed doing – I challenged myself to do it. When I take something on I like to give it my best shot. When I took it on I decided I would do it for four years and see how it goes. I'm past half way.

I need more marketing. Palmerston North is a difficult place to sell artwork. We just don't have the buying population that larger centres do, or tourist centres. I probably sell 70% of my work to people from outside the city. I'm just about ready for the step of sending work off to a gallery, perhaps in Auckland. I didn't want to do that too early. I hate being tied into things and I can't bear it when you send work off to a gallery and they say "Oh, can we have more of the same?"

Being here and working as I do gives me the maximum freedom. I don't have to please anyone except myself. I'm certainly keeping afloat. I've sold maybe $200,000 worth of work – but a lot of the money goes into materials and overheads. There's not a lot left over – and I've cut the overheads as much as possible. It will be very interesting to see how I go next year. I don't think people have a clue about the overheads and particularly people who are not aware of prices for original artwork in other centres. The odd person will come in and say it's very expensive – and I think I'm probably working for about 50 cents an hour! But it's building all the time and as the prices increase my overheads don't change.

One of the hazards of being so public is that organisations approach me to donate art to their fundraising campaigns. I have to be selective about who I donate work to. I do the hospice each year, along with other causes that promote me at the same time. I was delighted with the result for the Red Cross tsunami appeal. It was nerve-wracking – here I was, the new kid on the block among really well known artists in Wellington. Most probably they wouldn't have heard of me. All the proceeds went to the Red Cross – there was no reserve or anything like that.

Elizabeth Knapp painting in her studio gallery.

It was like an urge, since I was tiny, to be making something

You sort of quiver as the price takes off, around three or four hundred dollars. I was holding my wine glass in my hand, trying to remind myself not to snap the stem – because I've done that before in a moment of tension – and then the price went up to $600. I thought, I hope it reaches more than that. It ought to. Then all of a sudden it jumped to about $3000 and then to $4000. My chin must have been somewhere near my knees. So it was great. It was wonderful because it wasn't something manipulated by a gallery or someone external – it was simply the people squabbling over a piece of work which they wanted. And because they probably didn't know my name I knew they wanted the work because they loved it, and that's the best thing. It was an absolute buzz and although I could have done with the money it was the right thing to do. I have never sold a painting for that price. It's fabulous to be in a position where I can do what I love doing and someone else will get so much benefit out of it.

I have made things all my life. It was like an urge, since I was tiny, to be making something. Mud pies, whatever I could get my hands on. I used wood, stones, pumice. We didn't have a lot in the way of art materials – it was more inventing things. Projects like making sledges to travel along on the grass behind the tractor. I didn't really come to painting until about seven years ago when I came to TLC.

Prior to that my main thing had been making quilts at about 300 hours a pop. I knew there had to be a quicker way. I came down to Wellington because I wanted some space and I wanted to do something creative. Almost by accident I stumbled upon The Learning Connexion and once I'd spoken to Lydia I signed up on the spot. I think the underlying reason why I began it was that I always had this burning frustration that had to be explored in some way. I was a very 'silent' person and I felt that that was a voice for me.

It's been a huge self-development track and I feel great about it. It's changed my life considerably. I turned out to be a different sort of person from what I thought I was. I'm constantly coming at myself with a sense of surprise. I thought I had life sorted. When I began this stuff it was more like an explosion. Perhaps rather like people suddenly coming to writing in their thirties or forties – they have a lot of stuff to say, they have a lot of things that have never been expressed. That was the feeling for me. It felt extremely urgent. I was going to say I was very focused but more honestly I was totally obsessed.

I still have some very flat moments, as you do in life, and I've learnt to ease up in those times. Otherwise I create work that reflects the flatness. It's better to skip through to another medium or do something menial like making frames – which helps me to feel constructive and gives my head a rest.

When I started I had no business skills whatsoever and I'm one of the worst at record-keeping. I've had other people put me straight on that. I think it's a two-person job – you can't be an artist and be good at accounting and so on. Building on creativity I've totally lost my function for numbers! Electronic payments are fabulous because the customer gives you a card, the money goes straight into your account and you can forget it.

I felt like I had found my tribe

I'll be here for the next couple of years. After that I might be ready for a shift. A thing I love about Wellington is that they really celebrate people's individuality whereas this town is very conservative. It's pleasant in so many ways but I'd like to be in a centre where creativity is thriving. The biggest problem with Palmerston North is that it's flat. I believe that in a flat place people only think as far as the next object that is blocking their way. Whereas in a place with undulating terrain and something bigger than yourself, like the southern coast for example, that really inspires creativity because you're getting beyond yourself all the time.

The shock of working in public has had positive spin-offs.

At first I was terrified of people coming in the door, let alone watching me paint. The first three weeks were total agony for me. I was rather like a mouse and when someone stepped in the door I thought "What do I have to say, what do I have to say to them?" I had a little bit of practice after three weeks and it changed a lot and I was able to relax, but the whole first year was very difficult. Surprisingly there were distinct advantages too. I tend to get very intense about the piece that I'm working on and forget to stand back and really have a look at it. When I stopped to talk to people, even if it's only for a few minutes, it causes a mental shift and I can see in an instant what isn't working.

At first I was terrified of people coming in the door

The growth is a continuing reward for taking risks.

I came to TLC at a time when life was not going very well and I had been quite ill with depression. I thought about the feeling – that's what led me to it. When I'm doing art I have a sense of power and time just disappears on me. I thought yes, it's when I'm doing art. It's been a huge trip in self-development. I found it an incredibly nurturing place. I remember saying at one point that I had never felt so accepted and so loved in my life. I felt like I had found my tribe. I had always felt like the odd man out and yet around me were so many other people I could easily relate to. And with the support of the tutors it just turned into a party!

And now, yes, I teach, I have private students, I have TLC students. At the moment I have people coming off the street so fast I can't keep up with them. But I have to be careful to keep a balance because I want to paint, I want to do it myself. I don't want to get gobbled up in training other people. Although it's wonderful to be able to get them into their own creativity and watch their development.

But my own work is the priority. I have what I call my bread and butter lines and amazingly my dragonfly series has turned out to be like that. I never get bored with that because I use it as my play motif. It's constantly changing and growing, so although I know that my next dragonfly painting won't be on the wall for very long, I'm also enjoying it and it grows and challenges me. The other bread and butter line is my music paintings – people buy them constantly.

At present I'm working on my reconstruction series. This started through a painting I'd lost heart in. My life was changing a lot at that time and I wanted to cover up what I originally had with a new skin. It lets some of the underlying image come through and also creates something new from what had been. That gave birth to a whole new series and I began to play with the nature of the canvas just as much as the image. It's a symbol of growth.

Suzanne Tamaki with *Manu Wahine*, commission by the British Museum. Photo: Phil Reid, *Dominion Post*.

Suzanne Tamaki

The main thing was that my passion was fashion. I was into the frock and the accessories. It always had that Polynesian/Maori twist – it was very traditionally based and I was working with a lot of natural fibres. I couldn't afford to buy any materials so I went out into the bush and was collecting flax and leaves and flowers and learning how to weave and use traditional dyes.

When I was living in the city – that was in Auckland in 1991 – I realised there was no platform for Maori or Pacific Islanders to promote their work.

It was a subculture basically. We started doing our own shows and then we got hooked into the city council to do 'Style Pacifica'. It became bigger than us – we were doing these shows and helping to promote our friends and ourselves. I ended up taking on board a lot of other people to make it a complete show rather than a solo show because who wants to just come and see me? And who the hell am I anyway? Who's that Suzanne Tamaki – no one knows who she is – young upstart.

Because I had so many talented friends who were artists or performers or musicians it made sense if we collaborated and supported each other, because when you're in an urban environment and you're removed from your family you create your own family. You'll find with artists that they develop a very family-orientated space. What I loved about The Learning Connexion was the feeling that everybody was very close because they're so outside of the square that you are automatically drawn to each other to help and to understand each other's lifestyle.

It was never an overnight thing – the work kept developing and then it started being recognised as contributing to the arts community and the Polynesian community, and then people realised that what we were doing wasn't weird and freaky – it was actually the way that we as a people and our art are evolving. Then I started getting requests from museums and galleries and it was funny, they were mainly overseas. Like the Sydney Museum of Contemporary Art or the Festival of the Arts – they recognised what we were doing and asked us to go over there and perform. It wasn't until we went overseas that local people thought that what we were doing might be [illegible]. We kept saying, "If you want us you have to pay us." They'd be saying "Oh no, you have to do it for free." No no no no no – excuse me! We had to take it off-shore to be appreciated on our own shores.

I'm not sure how I fell into the role of tutor. I guess it was because of that communal lifestyle and sharing knowledge with all my artist friends, my sisters, and having children – maybe with children you're a natural teacher anyway. We took it out in the community and started running workshops. It was very easy. And then people picked me up, like The Learning Connexion and Whitireia,

▲ Suzanne Tamaki backstage with Melanie Hawea prior to a fashion show at Pataka in Porirua

▲ Melanie and costume ready for the show.

Aotearoa: Land of the Wrong White Crowd, a Suzanne Tamaki creation modeled by Kahui Tahau-Blackler and photographed by Greg Semu.

museums – to run weekend workshops. As you do more you obviously get a reputation but progress has been slow.

We set up Pacific Sisters in 1992. That's when I first started doing the promotional shows and really getting serious about my work. So we're looking at thirteen years – and three children later. As old as my boy. That's when I left mainstream. I was in advertising as a television producer and I was writing radio and television commercials. I left that job because I was pregnant and decided that I wanted to concentrate on being a mum, but of course that was really boring – who wants to be a mum! Okay – you can be a mum and have a life as well, but I didn't want to go back into the mainstream because they didn't actually support mothers in the workplace. So I stayed on the benefit, and it's lucky in New Zealand that you can be an artist and stay on the benefit and develop your work and your concepts and still pay the rent every week – and have time on your hands to create.

you can be a mum and have a life as well

It takes perseverance, tenacity, patience, tolerance, passion – if you don't have passion you won't last long. You have to be thick skinned because you're going to come against a lot of opposition. You have to believe in yourself and your work. I'm sure it would have been a shorter journey if I didn't have any children. Because of my children I'm split, I'm torn, I have to focus on my family and also create my works. You have to be multi-faceted because you have to do your creative side, then you need your administration side and then you need your marketing publicity side. And you need to be able to talk different talks. You talk with artists and then you talk with business people and then you talk with art institutions. You need to have almost different personalities – or is that just me! I like having different personalities.

You need a sense of humour so that you can laugh at yourself and laugh at things that go wrong. It's just life and life throws things in your way – you have to be able to cope with it. I think as artists we can become so isolated – you

need to also put yourself back out in the community. You need to be able to network and be self-motivated. You need to be able to get out and be inspired. That's me personally, anyway. I need the stimulation and the inspiration because otherwise I'd end up in a bit of a rut and it can be quite depressing and you feel you're the only one on the planet – as if you're a struggling artist working all alone. Oooh, poor me!

The shift from employment was awful! I didn't know what to do. Some weeks you'd owe a hundred dollars. It was depressing. But it pushes you to find new ways of coping and you develop new skills. I learnt how to cook! I learnt how to bake. I bake a great banana cake and fantastic muffins. If there's anything in the fridge I can turn it into a muffin. You don't really know what you're capable of until you get pushed into it.

I can't say that I'm poor because I've been overseas and I've seen poverty and at least I can say I've got a roof over my head. I've got a car. I'm rich! I've got no money but I've got a fantastic wardrobe. Thank god for designer friends and the green dollar – everyone does exchange, which is fantastic. I've got great artworks and if things get that rough I'll sell the art! I won't get precious about it. It's definitely a lifestyle change.

Maybe I'm poor in a money sense but I have a richness in that I have amazing friends, I have amazing networks and connections, I've seen some incredible shows and worked with incredible people, and my children have been exposed to this whole other lifestyle which if I was working a normal nine-to-five in an office they'd never see. My kids are incredibly creative and talented – and maybe that's the payoff. It's quite nice not to be rich, it keeps you humble and it keeps you honest. I'm much better off now and I've put my foot down. I value myself as an artist and I can put a price on it.

I had a conversation recently with someone who wanted me to do a show for them and I said that will be $1000 just to get me – never mind the other costs – you'll have to pay for accommodation and everything else. They said "Yep, that's fine." And I was cursing and thinking I should have asked for more. I was waiting for "I've got to consult the whanau and we've got to have a hui about it ..." It was quite funny. But it's about learning the value of your work, putting yourself out there and saying "I don't work for free. If you want me you have to pay for me." There are people who should know better – they're in art institutions and they're being paid for what they're doing. You have to be tough about it. I've lost a couple of jobs over it but that's fine – I'd rather not work. I don't need to do the hard yards anymore. What's the point of breaking your back?

I was cursing and thinking I should have asked for more

I remember when we were trying to get the money to go to Colombia. I was involved with the women's performance group called Magdalena. Magdalena is set up to support and nurture women artists in any field. They can help facilitate or arrange venues, they can give you all the paperwork, whatever you need. They were invited over to Colombia for this big international women's festival because we hosted it here in Paekakariki in 1999 and we met all these

Colombian women. So five of us spent a year fundraising. We got our airfares paid by Creative New Zealand but every month for a year we had a cabaret and had door sales and a raffle, mental stuff! We'd make a hundred dollars a month after we'd paid all the bills. Then I organized an art auction and we raised $3000 in one hit. That helped give us a little spending money over there.

One of the girls was our producer. Another was a documentary filmmaker so she filmed the whole thing. I did costumes. Rapai, she teaches kapahaka and Bridget does music. We went over and did these workshops with Colombian women. We wrote a piece as a group, they had their input and we had ours, and we based it on earth, wind, water and fire – and how the elements affect their stories and our stories. I took over a whole lot of wearable art costumes based on each element. There were about twenty of us. We taught them how to do a haka – a women's haka – and the poi – it was absolutely hilarious. And they taught us how to do these Colombian hanky dances. We had to wear these Colombian traditional outfits. I looked like a child's doll. All I needed was a big Afro and I would have looked like a big golliwog.

I'm this big Maori maiden, and no one has tattoos except bandits ...

We didn't realise that the Colombians' main diet is beans and rice. They're these tiny little people who are about five foot four and the men are about five foot six. I'm five foot eight. They're really little and I'm really big, I'm this big Maori maiden, and no one has tattoos except bandits, and I've got tattoos on my back and up my legs. I turned up at this show in a beautiful dress, very revealing because I had a tan by then, but all my tattoos in full glory. These two Colombian men were standing behind me talking fast and the interpreter said "Those men are talking about you. They think that you're a mountain woman who has come down to find herself a husband. Apparently they think you might throw them over your shoulder and go back to the mountains with one of them." I looked at them and said, "They'd be so lucky!" It was very different.

It was an amazing experience. That's when I was exposed to different levels of poverty. It was heart-breaking. I had to leave my baby Giovanni at home with his dad. Every day I'd wake up at the hotel at five o'clock in the morning and there were three women who had these little babies – well they might have been three or four years old but they were so small – and no nappies. They begged every day from five in the morning until the sun went down. These little babies would sit with their mothers in the sun. They don't have benefits over there. They can't just go on a benefit – they have to beg. So part of my thing about staying in a hotel was that our meals were part of the accommodation and I'd go down and get my breakfast and lunch and dinner and give it to these women. I thought God, I don't need it, and I had money – I'd just buy my food.

we don't want any beggars around our hotel and you're just encouraging them

I kept getting told by the hotel people not to feed the women – we don't want any beggars around our hotel and you're just encouraging them. I thought well you're not doing anything about it – so what do I do? Pretend that they're not there? I don't come from a culture that knows how to deal with beggars. I felt sorry for the kids. I saw a woman feed her baby and I thought that's all I want to do – I want to feed the baby. It was funny because I had all these condoms and I gave them to the women and said don't have any more babies. They didn't know what they were and I was trying to explain on the street how to use a condom. It was an education.

As for the future, it's good because now I can get funded to do things that I love. I love doing the shows, I love making the costumes. The costumes come first. And then I have to put them out there. I'm getting better at documenting the costumes. I think costumes have become more acceptable but the market has been flooded and there is a lot of crap out there. Every man and his dog wants a wearable art show now.

If I want to be taken seriously as a body-adornment artist my work has to be really good quality and I'm always doing something new and edgy which other people are going to imitate but that's the way that it is. I see it as a viable way to make money. I got the toi iho mark through Creative New Zealand which is the mark of authenticity and quality, which proves yes, I am a Maori. The mark works as a really good marketing tool. They set up expos and make connections with galleries, so I don't have to work so hard to go door-knocking to show my wares and go through all the blah blah of who I am and what I do. It got me into Te Papa. Last month they chose twelve artists and had this big opening. I sent my work in and they put it all in the front window. It was a little bit overwhelming but I was really flattered and every piece sold.

Two months before I had approached the buyer at Te Papa and she didn't think my stuff would sell. Now they call and say "Oh Suzanne, we need to replace all the stock." Which is great because now I've found an outlet where I can move things and make maybe an extra hundred a week. It's amazing what a difference that makes. But I'm also having to continually create this line and repeat it. I do that at night and during the day I can make all my other stuff which doesn't make any money but I really enjoy. I think it will get better.

As I've got older I've learnt to fine-tune and not to be so scattered with my energy. It's about time management and what I really want to do. The good thing about moving to Otaki is it removes me from the city and I don't have a whole lot of people turning up at my door and saying "Suzanne, we've got a show on Friday" – which is like, tomorrow – "and we need some costumes ... or we need you to perform or stage-manage – but we haven't got any money." I always feel like I have to do it. Maybe it's a Maori thing. It's always Maori ringing me up. "Oh come on Suzanne – we've done it for you, you need to do it for us." Just being able to remove myself from that. If they want me they at least have to pay my petrol or pay to have me. Then you really only get the serious offers. It's made me value my work and value myself, which is really good.

I can push people outside their boundaries and get them to do things that normally they wouldn't. Being quite confrontational in a way but getting people to step up a level. We need to be challenged. *I* like to be challenged. Otherwise you get too comfortable and you get in a rut and then you get bored. That's why you have platforms – step up and show us what you've got.

It's always Maori ringing me up

Sue Lund

Sue Lund was a student in the first year of TLC's Masterclass. She came to TLC after completing a BFA at the National Art School in Darlinghurst, Australia.

> Then I came back to New Zealand. I started delving into the abstract and didn't quite understand where I was going with it. I needed a bit more reassurance and that's when I joined the Masterclass and found that it's all okay.
>
> I'd had years and years of doing fifty thousand different jobs and it was purely that I liked painting. I hadn't really thought of the big picture – I just found something that I absolutely loved doing. I wanted to go there every single day and learn more and I suddenly felt really excited about it all. Nothing else had really grabbed me.
>
> I finished the degree around 2000. I was here a little while and then found TLC on the Web. I was wanting to do a Masters or something else and the Masterclass suited me fine.
>
> I've got a bit of a stubborn nature so there are aspects of my work where I'm going back to what I know. I wonder sometimes if I'm going back on my own track again. I've retained everything I've learnt through them but I'm still doing my own search.

At present what I'm purely exploring is colour. I'm going to tone down a lot of the colour and get right back to basics. I want to get the whole world into one picture but I'm going to tone them back, I think.

With the abstracts I just respond to colour. I put a colour down and then another colour goes into my head of what needs to be next to it. But then I end up getting so much colour that it becomes quite confusing. It might need a line over it, or a shape. You can't contain colour. It's like being out of control.

You can't contain colour. It's like being out of control

Sue has been captivated by the paint on her palette as much as the paint on the picture.

I'm peeling the paint off and what's underneath, I could never paint like that. I love it. It's much fresher than the work I'm doing!

At art school in Australia a huge amount of it was drawing. Research drawing and life drawing. We did about six to nine hours a week of life, which was just unbelievable. I'd get incredibly nervous before each one. It was really wicked. The school's known for its traditional drawings but at the end of our years there was probably more abstract work coming out. But I pretty much kept to traditional stuff. The brushes were getting bigger and the lines were getting

The first segment of Sue's giant painting project at TLC's Tuita campus.

a bit less but you could still see what it was. I feel I'm returning somewhat to figurative now – just to get a bit more control.

I'm doing landscapes and the plan is to do something that can make a bit of money on the side. There's a definite comfort level doing the landscapes because I know where I am. I'm quite addicted to the other stuff but it's not always comfortable.

There are certain colours that just ping for me so I go back to them time and time again. I wonder with the big canvasses whether I'm painting too big at the moment. I'm not always happy with the end result. They're never finished. I feel that they need to be simplified a little.

I haven't put the big ones out enough. I've had a couple of them around but they don't tend to sell. I probably need to have a show, I think. I did go in and see a dealer but it put me off. I might just have a show somewhere, put fliers around and do it that way. I didn't enjoy going in and talking to a dealer. I go around all the shows every week and the one I find the most friendly is Janne Land, but she's moved. To me she was primo because you could walk in and she'd acknowledge you.

I have applied for a grant so that I can get a website. I've done a business plan – it took months. I feel I'm still a really young painter. Give me ten years and I'll be really good. I think having a couple of shows will help me clarify what I'm doing. At the moment I keep painting for the floor. It's just going round and round and round.

At this stage Sue's abstract work was literally the floor – when it was dry, people walked on it. When the painting was completed it would be replaced by a new 'floor'.

The other students gave me quite a lot of support. I battled with whether I grasped entirely what the tutors were doing. I think I did. When I see my work up with the others I don't know if I was on a different track. I know in my own head what I want – I can learn all the rules in the world but I'll still stick to my own.

My aunty, Helen Stuart, was a painter. My family are very supportive – I'm really lucky in that respect. Everyone's always

A detail from Sue's Taita project.

said that I should do art. It wasn't until I was 30 that I found that was exactly what I wanted to do.

The best stuff I like reading is what other artists through the years think about and say

I had to totally meditate on the Masterclass readings before I could get into them. There was something good about them – but I also sieve a lot out. I look at a lot of books. The best stuff I like reading is what other artists through the years think about and say.

I suppose the biggest thing in what I'm painting is to find balance. All the colours are bouncing up and down and I try to flatten them out and make them all even. I think it's really important that I keep painting. I take it seriously and I know I'll do it forever.

To fully express my intentions, I write. It clarifies my mind and puts words in a fashion which makes sense to me. As I write I sometimes despair at what it is that this time I shall try to understand.

The paint has gone to a different place. I think resting, sheltering from a potential storm that may or may not be brewing.

I assume there is a simmer going on as the brusher and layer of paint is in a phase I know not.

I realise answers aren't everything and it's the journey that creates the inspiration, but I am at another crossroads, faced with more than one path to explore. If I take this one I may not see what the other offers. Then again I have my suspicions that they do all end up at a very similar place, the next junction of thought.

I assume focus is really the main battle.

I experience that as staying on a given route until the very end.

Only then will I see what it is that is to be seen.

If you have a couple of shows they come along and look ...

I've just done another one about opening a blind. I do find I feel quite blind. And my eyes, I need glasses. And it's just coming about the more I paint.

I've just applied for a studio in town and I'll have that one as my abstract and this one at home for my realist stuff. Then I'll work maybe five hours a day at the realistic stuff and spend the rest of my time on the abstract. I don't start my day until noon because then I can paint through the night until maybe five in the morning. I paint most days.

I'm not a marketer. I went about it all wrong the first time, I know that. I find it hard to talk about my paintings, to be honest. I know what I'm doing when I'm in it.

Gallery people will never listen to you if you're just emerging and they don't know who you are. They will never take you on straight away. But if you have a couple of shows they come along and look, and then they find you that way, that's what I've heard. Who knows, I don't know.

Freeman with his painting that won the 2006 Adam Portraiture Award. (Photo: *Dominion Post*)

Freeman White

Freeman White did a year at the Elam School of Art at Auckland University. He didn't like it.

> Art and creativity is such a personal journey and I think that in the early stages of my career I was really looking for myself. I got to a point where I believed I was on the right track, and that didn't really fit in with the university system. The greatest artists have always been great because of their direct expression and individuality and it's very difficult for a system, especially a university system, to cater for that individuality and to encourage students on their own individual paths. If a system can do that the results are so much more positive. At TLC it's certainly a lot more along those lines than the university system.
>
> My time here as a student was certainly a very positive experience and restored my confidence. Suddenly I could paint the paintings that I wanted to paint and I was still encouraged. The value in those paintings was seen. In the university system, as I experienced it, the idea seemed to be that you were a student and didn't yet have an identity, which I think is ridiculous. I just hated it. They were saying that everything you believe doesn't exist until you've been through the system.

The irony of these university systems is that they're trying to be contemporary but they're always lagging behind the artists who are the real originators. I'm not saying that what they're doing is wrong but I think they should be able to recognise that painting is a contemporary voice in art.

TLC's approach works really well when the student is self-motivated. You have to put in the time. The encouragement from The Learning Connexion was incredibly important for me in developing a sense of belonging and a sense that what I was doing could have a positive effect. That's what I was looking for – it's a huge thing.

Meeting a painter like Sandro Kopp made a massive difference. That was the start of a working friendship. I think everyone needs someone who is inspirational to work around. That feeling that you are not alone. Sandro and I meet together and we're interested in similar subject matter. We have totally different individual approaches but it's great to have someone who's so into painting and we kind of push each other. Sandro and I challenge each other and push each other a little further. It's really good to be in a situation where you don't get complacent.

As with other young artists, money is an issue.

It's been an interesting process. Over the last several years with a bit of part-time teaching, illustration, private commissions and one or two shows a year I make a sustainable living. But it took me five months to paint my last show and any average person in a job would probably end up with more money. The difference is that I get that money in one large sum. I've been on and off the dole as well – I was helped by the unemployment benefit. Now I've got some money and can go on holiday for three or four months overseas – to do something like that is exciting and inspirational. It's much more lifestyle-based than finance-based.

I don't see any reason why I shouldn't end up selling works for good prices, like $10,000 each, if I keep working hard. You've got to be careful where you show and how you show.

The gallery scene is very destructive. On opening night you get pats on the back but you have to spend so much time working in the studio by yourself to get those results. I'm lucky because Sandro Kopp and I do a lot of studio time together – maybe painting the same model – and that's what I'm really more passionate about – that time when you're working from life in the studio and you can't escape it. You've got a living, breathing person in front of you and you have to document what you see in a limited time. I love doing that but the irony is that those paintings don't seem to be what the galleries want.

I had a show in Germany last year which was really interesting. At the last minute I sold a painting which paid all my costs and the interesting thing was that the picture was a nude painted from life in the studio. It was part of a project where Sandro, myself and Matt de Goldie all did our paintings at the same time. That was the only painting that sold, a nude from life. The feedback I'm getting in New Zealand is that the galleries don't feel so comfortable with the nude as subject matter.

Painting has always been something that I can never escape. I'll continue to explore it for the rest of my life. The more I work on it now the more sustainable it seems to become. Ideally I'd like to be working in the studio exploring ideas and concepts about humanity without necessarily having to compromise to commercial demands. I'd like to be doing studio painting rather than commissions and illustrations – gradually building a reputation where I can live off my own artwork.

It's important to think ahead. When the work sells – and recently a lot of it has been selling – I'm fortunate that they've been recorded by my young brother who's a professional photographer. The photos are the only thing you have left and they're a vital record.

Painting has always been something that I can never escape

One of the tough things is that paintings may sell and the money disappear.

The first solo show I had was in a provincial gallery and I went overseas before it finished. Months later they sent me a cheque for $1000 and I was stoked but really they had ripped me off. They sold twelve paintings and I should have received around $3500. By the time I got back to New Zealand they had disbanded. But I got a call from a woman in Auckland who said that her daughter had bought three paintings from that show, more than eight years ago, and she had finally tracked me down. She now owns her own gallery and who knows what will develop from this?

Freeman has been staunchly figurative in his work. Sometimes there are dribbles and wild brush strokes but always there's something 'real'.

From a very early stage I painted animals and birds. I think it's attention to detail. I'm looking to paint something with quality. I put the hours in. But it really comes from the fact that my eyesight is quite bad and when I was young I had glasses. I can't really take for granted what I see. So that's the technical side of it.

These days we are living vicariously through technology and it's quite a valid time to be painting the human figure. It's

Painting by Freeman White.

a non-time-specific reference to humanity. Our concept of what it is like to be human has changed vastly in the last 2000 years yet our physicality hasn't changed much. I feel that painting the nude is terribly important. What I'm trying to show is a connection with the animalism of humanity.

How important is it to have the physical paint in front of you? What is the difference between having the real thing and a really classy reproduction?

I love paint, so the worst thing someone can say, and usually it's meant as a compliment, is "Wow, that looks just like a photograph!" But what about all the marks? The paint is incredibly important because I've spent the last 14 years of my life creating a dialogue with the medium. That's hours spent in the studio. The marks you lay down have a profound effect on the outcome. When I was young and had a crush on a girl I scraped a love heart into a tree with our initials on it. Years later the bark is all calloused around those marks and I thought wow, if I hadn't made those marks the whole pattern of growth of the tree would have been different. The marks that you lay down at the start shape what follows.

What I'm trying to show is a connection with the animalism of humanity

The process of painting is almost meditative and you lose track of time. Everything else is measured down to the millisecond and that's why time-based media are so apt, but in painting you almost capture time in the marks. A successful painting has an alchemic quality, the artist has somehow imbued the painting through the mark-making process with the energy of time.

To me it's about creating a dialogue with your medium. Paint has shapes and structures which will form through the way it dries, the way it interacts with different surfaces, its wetness and so on. This is the difference between a reproduction and an actual painting. A painter can't force paint to do something that it can't do. You're setting off reactions in paint and you go with it rather than forcing it to do anything. A painting almost paints itself – the reactions you set off are central to its personality. I've always been fascinated with the mix of the abstract qualities of paint and the refinement of detail.

The link between art and craft is a very interesting area to explore. Some of the contemporary art has tried to remove the art from craft. I think that craft is an incredibly important part of my art. The craft of painting takes a long time to learn and that's what gives me the foundation to take my work into the realm of fine art. I've been criticized by people who will say that there's so much craft in my art.

In painting you almost capture time in the marks

It's a battle that painters especially are facing these days – conceptualism is so hot. I look at it like a see-saw. If you've got too much concept and not enough physical actualisation it can be a bit stale.

Trueman's skills have since taken him to one of the pinnacles in New Zealand art. He won the Adam Portraiture Award and easily cracked the $10,000 barrier with the prize money.

He was surprised when his *Portrait of Hans,* a portrait of playwright Ryan McFadyen, won.

> I thought it had a good chance of being accepted into the show because of its painterly qualities, but I didn't really enter it to win. I think that James Holloway (the Scottish National Portrait Gallery director who judged the show) liked the painting as it was a real attempt at capturing the essence of the sitter while also using expressive paintwork and letting the medium speak.

James Holloway told Freeman he thought his painting was a little gem that sang out to him as the best painting in the show. *Portrait of Hans* has now become part of the permanent collection of the New Zealand Portrait Gallery.

> This win has basically reaffirmed that I'm moving in the right direction, not trying to paint in a style that is market-driven. All the successes and rejections I've had have only served to make me more resolute to continue on my own path as an artist. For me it has never been a choice, but something I have been drawn to and involved with to feel fulfilled as a human being.

Meanings

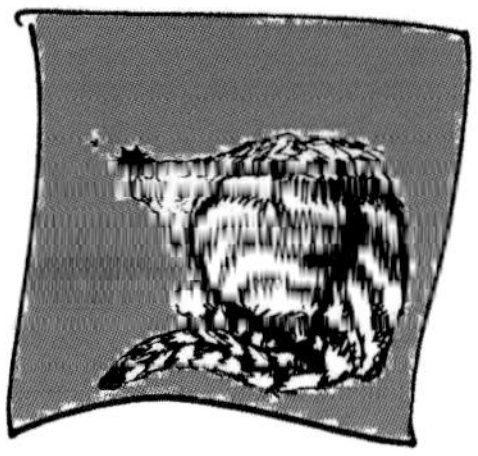

TLC students, staff and supporters are my heroes. Warts and all. We've built a community which celebrates individuality, supportiveness and the fundamental role of creativity at the centre of our humanity. The personal stories provide a glimpse of what this can mean.

- They are all works in progress
- Healthy obsession goes a long way
- Living cheaply makes a difference
- Personal satisfaction and meaning are essential
- Financial progress is erratic but broadly predictable
- We create our own luck
- Persistence is vital
- Skills are learned through practice
- Creativity comes from many different directions
- Success involves effective interactions with other people
- Big successes grow out of little successes
- You must have the resilience to get through setbacks (and to a large extent resilience can be learned)
- Laughter improves resilience
- Creative people find their own path (and conventional education and employment aren't always relevant)
- The drive comes from within

Another feature is that people who find ways to be creative are healthier. Stifled creativity is a sort of *dis-ease* which may be associated with depression and a host of other conditions. My own research (based on questionnaire responses from students) indicates an average 35% improvement in well-being when students study on the diploma programme. There is a considerable amount of research still to be done but the early findings are startling.

The results are consistent with research done by Pip Cotton as part of his doctorate with Massey University. After a series of in-depth interviews with TLC students he came up with the figures in the table over the page.

The big question is whether the benefits of the Diploma of Art and Creativity are transferable to other fields. Would a similar approach deliver the same value in science, business studies or medicine? I haven't time to be modest about this. The answer is yes.

While studying with TLC	No change from before	Only a little change	Agree change occurred	Strongly agree change occurred
I came to realise what I wanted to do next in life	11.4	6.7	35.2	46.3
A major personal problem was solved	12.1	9.4	44.6	33.6
I came to see myself as an artist	11.7	13.8	37.2	36.9
I learnt to appreciate art and artists more generally	11.4	6.7	35.2	46.5
Feelings about myself changed in positive ways	12.1	9.4	44.6	33.7
I came to realise art was a way to explore myself	12.1	8.4	38.6	40.6
My artwork helped me explore my relationship with New Zealand (Identity)	29.9	25.9	28.9	15.8
I came to recognise when my artworks were complete	12.8	18.1	47.0	21.8
I became more sensitive to environmental issues	40.3	21.8	24.8	12.8
I developed or regained confidence	13.1	8.4	44.3	33.9
I became more open to new ideas	11.4	9.4	41.3	37.6
I came to understand others' points of view better	21.8	15.1	39.9	22.8
I learnt to trust and act on my intuition	14.4	10.7	38.6	35.9

Completion Survey Personal Change Table (all years, all levels). 298 respondents. (Research: Pip Cotton). The figures indicate some of the benefits that could be expected from education built around creativity.

So what's stopping us? One of our tutors gave the answer when she said that it can take a long time to bring new tutors up to speed. That's it in a nutshell. It takes time to set the foundation but once you establish new habits, everything flows.

Although we've established a model at TLC we're still learning and we know how hard it can be to shift from old patterns, even among people who are keen to change. And institutions are even harder to shift because they're weighted with the inertia of history and the strait-jacket of conventions.

The New Zealand Government controversially moved in the right direction when it placed public and private providers on approximately the same footing and enabled some new approaches to grow. Thus TLC is completely independent and about 75% of our funding comes from the Government. We are hired by the Government to deliver our courses.

The funding created an important new option for students and we now have graduates who are seeding fresh thinking in all sorts of unlikely places.

We invite our students to explore their life situation, to figure out how to move forward and to pay attention to feedback. It's a mix of dialogue, techniques and action. Everything we do helps students to connect their own abilities and personalities with the world they live in. There's nothing radical here – no dogma, no coercion, no *laissez faire* grandstanding. Instead there's connectedness, awareness and relevance.

In the end our collective destiny is built from the creative actions of individuals.

Everyone can make a difference. New Zealand itself feels special because our politics and our people are fairly closely in tune. Humanity, in a subtle, endlessly complex way, wants to evolve. People understand that the weapons of war and the politics of greed put everything to pointless risk. The option is to develop tools of peace and a practical engagement with the ecology of planet Earth. The humble experience of working with materials and making art provides insights which are part of personal and global change.

More to read

This is a selection (in author order) of some of the material which influenced *GO!* There's no way to provide a comprehensive list because new books, videos and Web-based items are emerging all the time. Creativity is always a work in progress.

Alcorn, N. *To the Fullest Extent of his Powers* (Victoria University Press, Wellington, 1999). A biography of Dr CE Beeby, secretary for education in New Zealand for 20 years. Dr Beeby had a huge influence on education in New Zealand. TLC's older staff members were brought up in schools that had the Beeby style and we believe that he was on the right track before the majority of educators were aware that the track existed.

Ball, Philip. *Critical Mass: How one thing leads to another* (Arrow Books, 2004). Discover connectedness.

Bassett, Bruce W. *Isamu Noguchi*, videotape (Phaidon). A superb insight into Noguchi's approach to creativity. He's a fine role model (and everyone should find models that suit their own needs).

Bragg, Melvyn. *Andy Warhol*, BBC television documentary (Phaidon). Bragg is an outstanding interviewer and this is one of his best. Phaidon has many superb documentaries available and they bring us close to the strengths and foibles of some of the most notable artists of our time.

Campbell, Joseph. *A Joseph Campbell Companion*, material selected and edited by Diane K Osbon (HarperCollins, 1991). Campbell used the metaphors of mythology to deliver practical lessons in the art of living. Osbon has done a brilliant job of distilling the best.

Campbell, Joseph and Bill Moyers. *The Power of Myth* (First Anchor Books, 1991). Also available on DVD. Moyers, like Osbon, helps to make Campbell even more accessible. The book and DVD really go together.

Chuang Tzu (Zhuangzi). *The Way of Chuang Tzu*, interpreted by Thomas Merton. Chuang Tzu was a master teacher who lived from 370 to 301 BCE. He's holistic, creatively and richly funny. Merton, a Trappist monk, shares similar qualities.

Collings, Matthew. *This is Modern Art* (Seven Dials, 1999). A merry romp through contemporary art, free of pomposity – witty and engaging.

Crespelle, Jean Paul. *The Fauves* (New York Graphic Society, 1962). Available online at www.questia.com/library/book/the-fauves-by-jean-paul-crespelle.jsp Crespelle brings history alive. There are chapter headings like '1905: Scandal at the Salon d'Automne' which are too tempting to skip. The creative audacity of the artists shines through.

Cropley, Arthur J. *Creativity in Education and Learning* (Kogan Page, 2001). Cropley is an academic who pays attention to creativity in the classroom. His many books reward the patient reader.

Csikszentmihalyi, Mihaly. *Finding Flow* (Basic Books, 1997). Csikszentmihalyi is especially good at dealing with the enigmas of creativity (those qualities which seem, on the surface, to be contradictory).

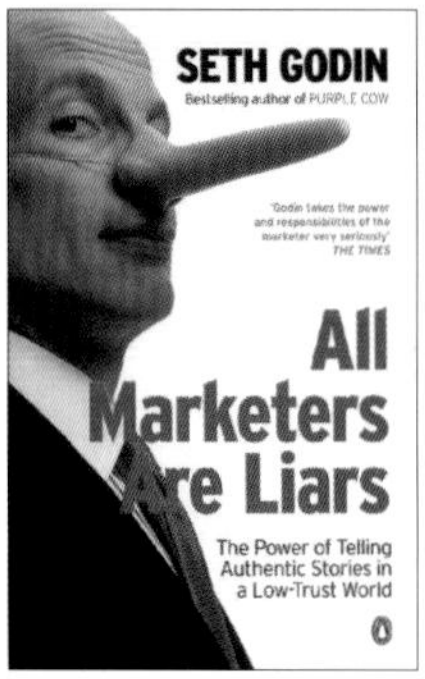

Edwards, Betty. *Drawing on the Artist Within* (Simon and Schuster, 1987). The chapter on analog drawing deserves a Nobel prize.

Edwards, Betty. *Drawing on the Right Side of the Brain* (Jeremy P Tarcher/Putnam, 2001). The best-selling 'how to draw' book of all time. It connects with earlier work (e.g. Kimon Nicolaides, *The Natural Way to Draw*) and sidesteps formulaic methods by going direct to perception. It deserves its fame.

Gallwey, Timothy. *The Inner Game of Tennis* (Random House, 1997). In the disguise of a book about tennis Gallwey is talking about body learning. He eloquently describes the disconnection between our cerebral brain (reading the instructions) and our body (doing the business). His tactics work.

Gladwell, Malcolm. *The Tipping Point* (Abacus, 2000). So often people give up within a whisker of the 'tipping point'. Beautifully written, upbeat and well-aligned with the science of change.

Godin, Seth. *All Marketers Are Liars* (Penguin, 2005). The subtitle is really what it's about: "The Power of Telling Authentic Stories in a Low-Trust World." You might think it is only for marketers, which it is, but who isn't a marketer? Artists, teachers, scientists, politicians and lovers are all marketing. Life is built on stories and beneath the packaging is a book on life.

Goerner, Sally. *After the Clockwork Universe – The Emerging Science and Culture of Integral Society* (Triangle Centre, 2007). Goerner is into global creativity and I liked this book so much I bought every available copy in New Zealand when it was first published.

Goleman, Daniel, Paul Kaufman and Michael Ray. *The Creative Spirit* (Plume, 1993). The American PBS documentary of the same name was a ground-breaker. It is especially successful in showing how creativity happens in very diverse fields. It gathers togethers an amazing group of creative people. It's better if you can source the documentary and use it in conjunction with the book.

Herrmann, Ned. *The Whole Brain Business Book* (McGraw-Hill Professional, 1996). Whether you go for the right brain/left brain theory is less important than the fact that we think in different ways. Herrmann unpacks the main styles and offers fresh insights to ideas which started with the Greeks. They have endured because they have value.

Huffington, Arianna Stassinopoulos. *Picasso, Creator and Destroyer* (Simon & Schuster, 1988). This is one of many books which remind us of the darker aspects of creativity. Picasso was incredibly gifted and incredibly difficult. Another book worth exploring is *Picasso – In His Words,* edited by Hiro Clark (Collins, 1993). It shows the richness of the artist's thinking as well as giving clues to his ruthlessness.

Hughes, Robert. *The Shock of the New* (BBC Books, 1991). Even though it grows less shocking it's still a wonderful journey through the art explosion of the 20th century. Hughes can be feisty and opinionated but it's his passion which raises the book above the boring caution of his competitors.

Kaupelis, Robert. *Experimental Drawing* (Watson-Guptill, 1992). Moves beyond the beginning elements of drawing into something divergent and exhilarating.

Langland, Tuck. *From Clay to Bronze* (Watson Guptill, 1999). If you want to dig into the technical aspects of virtually any area of art you'll find excellent allies in the library. *From Clay to Bronze* is outstanding (along with most things that have the Watson-Guptill imprint). It's likely you'll still need a guide, but the best books are really teachers in disguise.

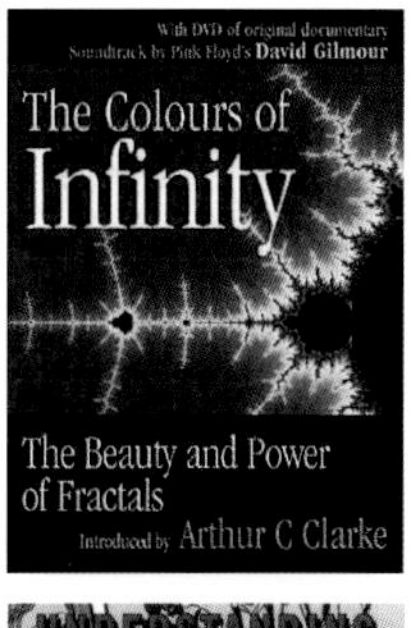

Lesmoir-Gordon, Nigel. *The Colours of Infinity: The Beauty and Power of Fractals* (includes DVD). The book is really a celebration of the classic documentary (on the DVD) and that's the point of buying it. It's like mathematics on LSD (complete with a Pink Floyd soundtrack) and it takes you to the heart of the creative process. If you're happy with lesser quality on the video you can access it free on video.google.com/videoplay?docid=-3034959314635185121

McCloud, Scott. *Understanding Comics* (Harper Perennial, 1994). Maybe this is one of the best books ever written on art history. Sure, it's all about comics but weren't the cave artists the first to get there? It's a long and spectacular tradition and McLeod takes the reader/viewer on a joyous graphic and philosophical ride. For up-to-the-minute treasures go to www.scottmccloud.com.

Neville, Bernie. *Educating Psyche* (Collins-Dove, 1989). It's listed among the thirty great books on education at www.great-ideas.org. The website says: "A major purpose of the book is to call attention to the neglected functions of play, spontaneity, intuition, imagination, nurturing, love, ecstasy, and transcendence – all of which are essential to a full and meaningful life."

New Scientist. A magazine rather than a book – see www.newscientist.com. Bedtime reading, often profound, sometimes hammy and superficial. A doorway to a wide range of creativity (good Web links and a huge archive if you subscribe). Boldly visual too – the graphics are zany and intelligent.

Nisker, Wes. *Crazy Wisdom* (Ten Speed Press, Millennium edition, 1998). With no-mind, blossoms invite the butterfly. With no-mind, the butterfly visits the blossoms. When the flower blooms, the butterfly comes. (Ryokan, 1758–1831).

Perry, Vicky. *Abstract Painting – Concepts and Techniques* (Watson-Guptill, 2005). Maybe abstraction is the art equivalent of quantum theory – hard to pin down but inescapable. Perry offers a window onto the mystery.

Pritzker, Steven and Mark Runco (eds). *Encyclopedia of Creativity* (Academic Press, 1999). A massive (1663 pages) two-volume set covering the field of creativity as it was at the end of the last century. A new edition is on the brew. An invaluable resource if you can afford the price tag.

Putnam, Robert. *Making Democracy Work* (Princeton University Press, 1994). Don't be put off by the subtitle: "Civic traditions in Modern Italy." Putnam makes a compelling argument about the basis of creative communities.

Richards, Ruth (ed). *Everyday Creativity and New Views of Human Nature: Psychological, Social and Spiritual Perspectives* (American Psychological Association, 2007). Contributors grapple with the most important themes of our time. Richards brings a subversive understanding that the secret of change lies in the apparent ordinariness of our own lives.

Root-Bernstein, Robert and Michèle. *Sparks of Genius: the 13 thinking tools of the world's most creative people* (Mariner Books, 1999). Links many of the attributes of 'art thinking' with creativity in any field. It is a prescription for revolutionary educational change. It's also an invitation to artists to rethink the value of what they do.

Runco, Mark A. *Creativity Theories and Themes: Research, Development, and Practice* (Academic Press, 2007). A current overview which has emerged from the field of psychology. Rigorously academic and a valuable contribution to the literature.

Stern, Arthur. *How to See Color and Paint It* (Watson-Guptill, 1988). Sometimes you find an author with the ability to convey explicit knowledge in a field where everyone else falls short. It lives up to its title and it's also a fine example of visual communication.

Sheldrake, Rupert. *The Sense of Being Stared At* (Three Rivers Press, 2003,). Sheldrake has built evidence around ordinary experiences. His research tests whether people know when they're being stared at. The results raise big questions about the way the world works. Perhaps the wildest ride is available in *The Evolutionary Mind: Conversations on Science, Imagination and Spirit.*

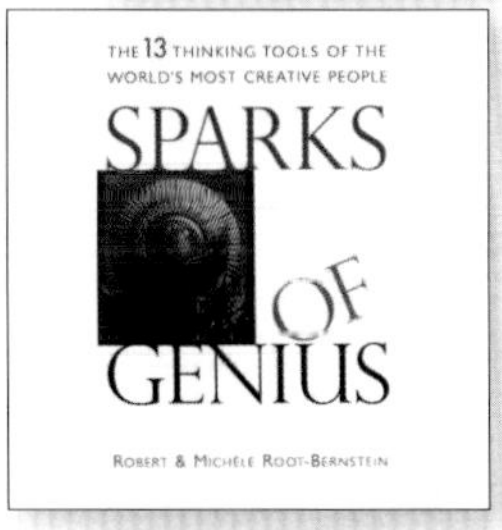

Stewart, Ian. *What Shape is a Snowflake?* (Weidenfeld and Nicolson, 2001). Art is arguably a subset of mathematics (the study of all possible patterns). Stewart is a fine writer with a knack of making patterns understandable in a way that has real appeal for artists. Rather than connecting with the horrors of the classroom, this particular book focuses on the magic of nature and does most of its talking in pictures rather than numbers.

Talbot, Michael. *The Holographic Universe* (Harper Collins, 1996). There's a children's song with the line 'Merrily, merrily merrily, life is but a dream.' It's a wild idea and Talbot presents a case that the universe, if not exactly a dream, could be very different from what it seems.

Von Oech, Roger. *A Whack on the Side of the Head: How you can be more creative* (Business Plus, 1998). Von Oech is one of the better 'creative recipe' writers. The recipes certainly help if you're stuck for ideas. The title relates to a faded tradition in which teachers, especially of the Zen variety, would do things to jolt students out of their complacency.

Watts, Alan. *The Book on the Taboo Against Knowing Who You Are* (Vintage, 1989). Watts merges ego with the universe. Originally published in 1966, it feels sparkling and new, all the more surprising because it connects with Vedanta which goes back more than 2200 years. Vedanta is a school of philosophy in India which is entirely focused on trying to understand the nature of reality. Watts comes about as close as anyone can to making sense of life, the universe and everything.

Wilde, Richard and Judith. *Visual Literacy* (Watson-Guptill, 1991; new edition 2000). How do we read visual images? The Wildes have compiled a set of assignments, presented almost entirely through images, which take you through the reading and creation of visual images.

Index

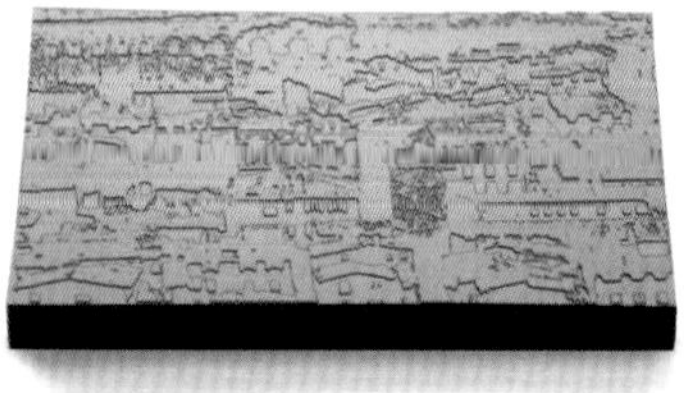

C

D

E

F

G

H

I

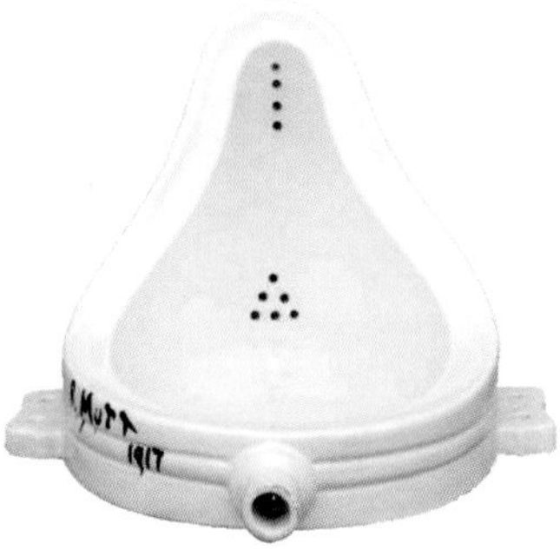

N

O

P

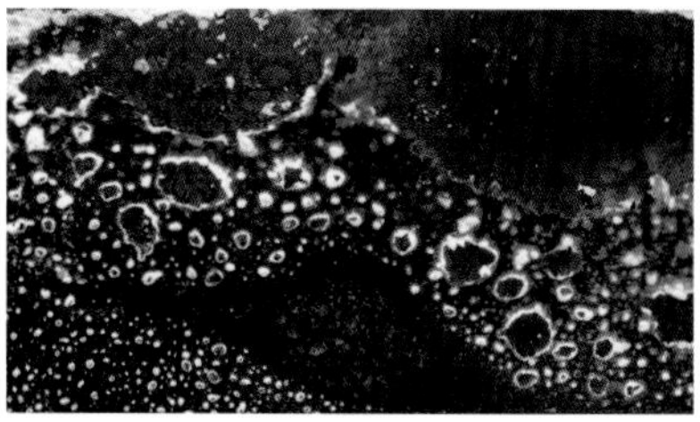

T

U

V

W

X

Y

Z